# Contract Law
# Casebook

*4th edition*

**Edited by P A Read**
LLB, DPA, Barrister

**HLT Publications**

HLT PUBLICATIONS
200 Greyhound Road, London W14 9RY

First published 1988
4th edition 1992

© The HLT Group Ltd 1992

ISBN 0 7510 0129 5

*British Library Cataloguing-in-Publication.*
A CIP Catalogue record for this book is
available from the British Library.

Printed and bound in Great Britain

*Acknowledgement*
The publishers and author would like to
thank the Incorporated Council of Law
Reporting for England and Wales for kind
permission to reproduce extracts from the
Weekly Law Reports.

# CONTENTS

# CONTENTS

# PREFACE

HLT Casebooks have been produced as companion volumes to the textbooks for certain Bar and LLB subjects. Their aim is to supplement and enhance a student's understanding and interpretation of a particular area of the law, and provide essential background reading.

Of the twenty-five new cases included in this latest edition of *Contract Law Casebook*, fifteen are decided at Court of Appeal level or above. There are included two Scottish cases (one a House of Lords' decision) and also a case from Singapore (Privy Council), and an Australian case which has a relevance to English contract law. There is also a new report on *Walford* v *Miles* ((1992) The Times 27 January) which finally reached the House of Lords.

The topics covered by these cases include mistake, misrepresentation, exclusion clauses and remedies. Probably the largest group however, is concerned with formation of a contract, its terms and construction. New cases are beginning to emerge on the 1989 Law of Property (Miscellaneous Provisions) Act (*Record* v *Bell* [1991] 1 WLR 853 and *Spiro* v *Glencrown Properties Ltd* [1991] 2 WLR 931). There are two unusual cases concerning guarantees (*Elpis Maritime* v *Marti Chartering* [1991] 3 All ER 758 and *In re a Debtor* (1991) The Times 25 November), and a number of cases on construction of terms (*GA Estates* v *Caviapen* (1991) The Times 22 October, *Richco International* v *Bunge* [1991] 2 Lloyd's Rep 93, and *Computer Systems Engineering* v *John Lelliott Ltd* (1991) The Times 21 February).

Cases reported on or before 1 May 1992 have been taken into consideration.

# TABLE OF CASES

# INTRODUCTION

**Addis v Gramophone Co Ltd** [1909] AC 488 House of Lords (Lord Loreburn LC, Lord James of Hereford, Lord Atkinson, Lord Collins, Lord Gorell and Lord Shaw)

Dismissed - measure of damages

*Facts*

The plaintiff was employed by the defendants as manager of their business in Calcutta, at a weekly salary, plus commission on the trade done. He could be dismissed on six months' notice. In October 1905, the defendants gave him six months' notice but, at the same time, appointed another to act as his successor and took steps to prevent the plaintiff from acting any longer as manager. The plaintiff claimed damages for breach of contract. The jury found for the plaintiff and awarded him £600 for wrongful dismissal and a further £340 in respect of excess commission, over and above what was earned by the plaintiff's successor in the six months between October 1905 and April 1906. The Court of Appeal held, by a majority, that there was no cause of action and entered judgment for the defendants.

*Held* (Lord Collins dissenting)

This decision would be reversed.

Lord Loreburn LC:

'To my mind, it signifies nothing in the present case whether the claim is to be treated as for wrongful dismissal or not. In any case, there was a breach of contract in not allowing the plaintiff to discharge his duties as manager and the damages are exactly the same in either view. They are, in my opinion, the salary to which the plaintiff was entitled for the six months between October 1905 and April 1906, together with the commission which the jury think he would have earned had he been allowed to manage the business himself. I cannot agree that the manner of dismissal affects these damages. Such considerations have never been allowed to influence damages in this kind of case.

If there be dismissal without notice, the employer must pay an indemnity; but that indemnity cannot include compensation either for the injured feelings of the servant, or for the loss he may sustain from the fact that his having been dismissed, of itself, makes it more difficult for him to obtain fresh employment. The cases relating to a refusal by a banker to honour cheques when he has funds in hand have, in my opinion, no bearing. That class of case has always been regarded as exceptional. And the rule as to damages in wrongful dismissal or, in breach of contract, to allow a man to continue in a stipulated service, has always been, I believe, what I have stated. It is too inveterate to be now altered, even if it were desirable to alter it.

Accordingly, I think that so much of the verdict of £600 as relates to that head of damages cannot be allowed to stand. As there is an additional dispute, how much of it does relate to that head of damages? The best course will be to disallow the £600 altogether and to state in the order that the plaintiff is entitled to be credited, in the account which is to be taken with salary, from October 1905 to April 1906.

As to the £340, I think there was evidence on which the jury were entitled to find that the plaintiff could have earned more commission if he had been allowed to remain as manager.

In the result, I respectfully advise your Lordships to order judgment for the plaintiff for £340 with a declaration that he is entitled to be credited, in the account now under investigation, with salary from October 1905 to April 1906 and with all commission on business actually done during that period which he would have been entitled to receive if he had been acting as manager.'

Lord Atkinson:

'The rights of the plaintiff, disembarrassed of the confusing methods by which they were sought to

1

be enforced, are, in my opinion, clear. He had been illegally dismissed from his employment. He could have been legally dismissed by the six months' notice which he in fact received, but the defendants did not wait for the expiry of that period. The damages the plaintiff sustained by this illegal dismissal were (1) the wages for the period of six months during which his formal notice would have been current; (2) the profits or commission which would, in all reasonable probability, have been earned by him during the six months had he continued in the employment; and possibly (3) damages in respect of the time which might reasonably elapse before he could find other employment. He has been awarded a sum possibly of some hundreds of pounds, not in respect of any of these heads of damage, but in respect of the harsh and humiliating way in which he was dismissed, including presumably the pain he experienced by reason, it is alleged, of the imputation upon him conveyed by the manner of his dismissal. This is the only circumstance which makes the case of general importance and this is the only point I think it necessary to deal with.

I have been unable to find any case decided in this country in which any countenance is given to the notion that a dismissed employee can recover in the shape of exemplary damages for illegal dismissal, in effect, damages for defamation, for it amounts to that, except the case of *Maw* v *Jones* (1890) 25 QBD 107 ... I have always understood that damages for breach of contract were in the nature of compensation not punishment and that the general rule of law applicable in such cases was that, in effect, stated by Cockburn CJ in *Engell* v *Fitch* (1868) LR 3 QB 314, 330 in these words:

"By the law of England, as a general rule, a vendor who, from whatever cause, fails to perform his contract, is bound [...] to place the purchaser, so far as money will do it, in the position he would have been in if the contract had been performed [...]"

In *Sikes* v *Wild* (1861) 1 B&S 587, 594, Lord Blackburn says:

"I do not see how the existence of misconduct can alter the rule of law by which damages for breach of contract are to be assessed. It may render the contract voidable on the ground of fraud, or give a cause of action for deceit, but surely it cannot alter the effect of the contract itself."

... in actions of tort motive, if it may be taken into account to aggregate damages as it undoubtedly may be, it may also be taken into account to mitigate them, as may also the conduct of the plaintiff himself who seeks redress. Is this rule to be applied to actions of breach of contract? There are few breaches of contract more common than those which arise where men omit or refuse to pay for what they have bought. Is the creditor or vendor who sues for one of such breaches to have the sum he recovers lessened if he should be shown to be harsh, grasping or pitiless, or even insulting in enforcing his demand, or lessened because the debtor has struggled to pay, has failed because of misfortune and has been suave, gracious and apologetic in his refusal? On the other hand, is that sum to be increased if it should be shown the debtor could have paid readily without any embarrassment, but refused with expressions of contempt and contumely, from a malicious desire to injure his creditor?'

*Commentary*

Distinguished in *Dunk* v *George Waller & Son Ltd* [1970] 2 WLR 1241. See also *Bliss* v *South East Thames Regional Health Authority* [1985] IRLR 308 and *O'Laoire* v *Jackel International Ltd* (1991) The Times 12 February.

**Albazero, The** [1976] 3 WLR 419 House of Lords (Lord Diplock, Viscount Dilhorne, Lord Simon of Glaisdale and Lord Fraser of Tullybelton)

Breach of contract - damages

*Facts*

The plaintiffs chartered a vessel from the defendant shipowners. Crude oil was to be shipped from Venezuela to Antwerp and the bill of lading named the plaintiffs as consignees. In the course of the voyage the vessel and her cargo became a total loss, but by then the cargo was vested in a third party.

Assuming that the loss arose from breaches by the defendants of the charterparty, were the plaintiffs entitled to recover substantial damages?

*Held*

They were not as the original contract contemplated that the plaintiffs would enter into separate contracts of carriage with whomsoever might become the owner of the goods.

**Anglia Television Ltd v Reed** [1971] 3 WLR 528 Court of Appeal (Lord Denning MR, Phillimore and Megaw LJJ)

Breach of contract - measure of damages

*Facts*

The plaintiffs were minded in 1968 to make a film of a play for television entitled 'The Man in the Wood' and they made many arrangements in advance. They arranged for a place where the play was to be filmed. They employed a director, a designer and a stage manager and so forth. They involved themselves in much expense. All this was done before they got the leading man. They required a strong actor capable of holding the play together. He was to be on the scene the whole time. They eventually found the man, the defendant, an American who has a very high reputation as an actor. By telephone conversation on 30 August 1968, it was agreed by Mr Reed, through his agent, that he would come to England and be available between 9 September and 11 October 1968 to rehearse and play in this film. He was to get a performance fee of £1,050, living expenses of £100 a week, his first class fares to and from the United States and so forth. It was all subject to the permit of the Ministry of Labour for him to come here. That was duly given on 2 September 1968 so the contract was concluded. But unfortunately, there was some muddle with the bookings: the defendant's agents had already booked him in America for some other play. So, on 3 September 1968 the agent said that the defendant would not come to England to perform in this play. He repudiated his contract. The plaintiffs tried hard to find a substitute but could not do so. So on 11 September they accepted his repudiation. They abandoned the proposed film and then sued Mr Reed for damages. He did not dispute his liability, but a question arose as to the damages, the plaintiffs claiming for the wasted expenditure - the director's fees, the designer's fees, the stage manager's and assistant manager's fees, and so on.

*Held*

They were entitled to succeed.

Lord Denning MR:

'It seems to me that a plaintiff in such a case as this has an election: he can either claim for loss of profits or for his wasted expenditure. But he must elect between them. He cannot claim both. If he has not suffered any loss of profits - or if he cannot prove what his profits would have been - he can claim in the alternative the expenditure which has been thrown away, that is, wasted by reason of the breach.

If the plaintiff claims the wasted expenditure, he is not limited to the expenditure incurred after the contract was concluded. He can claim also the expenditure incurred before the contract, provided that it was such as would reasonably be in the contemplation of the parties as likely to be wasted if the contract was broken. Applying that principle here, it is plain that when Mr Reed entered into his contract, he must have known perfectly well that much expenditure had already been incurred on director's fee and the like. He must have contemplated - or, at any rate, it is reasonably to be imputed to him - that if he broke his contract, all that expenditure would be wasted, whether or not it was incurred before or after the contract. He must pay damages for all the expenditure so wasted and thrown away.

It is true that if the defendant had never entered into the contract, he would not be liable and the expenditure would have been incurred by the plaintiff without redress: but the defendant, having made his contract and broken it, it does not lie in his mouth to say he is not liable when it was because of his breach that the expenditure has been wasted.'

*Commentary*

Applied: *Cullinane v British 'Rema' Manufacturing Co Ltd* [1953] 3 WLR 923. Applied in *C & P Haulage v Middleton* [1983] 1 WLR 1461.

**Balfour v Balfour** [1919] 2 KB 571 Court of Appeal (Warrington, Duke and Atkin LJJ)

Agreement - no intention that it be enforceable

*Facts*

After their marriage, the parties went to Ceylon where the husband was director of immigation. Fifteen years later they came home on leave. On medical advice, it was decided that the wife should remain in England, but she alleged that, as the husband was about to sail back to Ceylon, he had entered into an oral contract to make her an allowance of £30 a month until she rejoined him in Ceylon. At that time they had not agreed to live apart, although they subsequently did so when differences arose. The wife sought to recover money allegedly due to her under the oral agreement.

*Held*

Her action would fail as there was no contract in a legal sense.

Duke LJ:

'What is said on the part of the wife in the present case is that her arrangement with her husband that she should assent to that which was in his discretion to do or not was the consideration moving from her to her husband. The giving up of that which was not a right was not a consideration.'

Atkin LJ:

'It is quite common, and it is the natural and inevitable result of the relationship of husband and wife, that the two spouses should make agreements between themselves, agreements such as are in dispute in this action, agreements for allowances by which the husband agrees that he will pay to his wife a certain sum of money per week or per month or per year to cover either her own expenses or the necessary expenses of the household and of the children, and in which the wife promises either expressly or impliedly to apply the allowance for the purpose for which it is given. To my mind those agreements, or many of them, do not result in contracts at all, and they do not result in contracts even though there may be what as between other parties would constitute consideration for the agreement. The consideration, as we know, may consist either in some right, interest, profit, or benefit accruing to one party, or some forbearance, detriment, loss or responsibility given, suffered, or undertaken by the other. That is a well-known definition, and it constantly happens, I think, that such arrangements made between husband and wife are arrangements in which there are mutual promises, or in which there is consideration in form within the definition that I have mentioned. Nevertheless they are not contracts, and they are not contracts because the parties did not intend that they should be attended by legal consequences.'

*Commentary*

Distinguished in *Merritt v Merritt* [1970] 1 WLR 1211. See also *Gould v Gould* [1969] 3 WLR 490.

**Binions v Evans** [1972] 2 WLR 729 Court of Appeal (Lord Denning MR, Megaw and Stephenson LJJ)

Agreement to occupy cottage for life

*Facts*

A husband had worked for the landlords all his working life and he and his wife, the defendant, had lived in the landlords' cottage. After husband's death, the landlords agreed in writing that the defendant could occupy the cottage 'as tenant at will ... free of rent for the remainder of her life or until determined as hereinafter provided, 'ie, by four weeks' notice in writing. The landlords sold the cottage to the plaintiffs, subject to the defendant's tenancy, and for this reason they paid a reduced price. The plaintiffs gave the defendant notice to quit and subsequently sought an order for possession.

*Held*

Their claim would fail. Although the words 'tenant at will' had been used in the agreement, the rest of it was inconsistent with such a tenancy and the defendant could remain in the cottage for the rest of her days.

Lord Denning MR:

'In my opinion [the defendant], by virtue of the agreement, had an equitable interest in the cottage which the court would protect by granting an injunction against the landlords restraining them from turning her out. When the landlords sold the cottage to a purchaser 'subject to' her rights under the agreement, the purchaser took the cottage on a constructive trust to permit the widow to reside there during her life, or as long as she might desire. The courts will not allow the purchaser to go back on that trust.'

*Commentary*

Applied: *Errington v Errington* [1952] 1 KB 290. See also *Tanner v Tanner* [1975] 1 WLR 1346.

**Brooks Wharf & Bull Wharf Ltd v Goodman Brothers** [1937] 1 KB 534 Court of Appeal (Lord Wright MR, Romer LJ and Macnaghten J)

Theft from bonded warehouse - liability of importer for duty

*Facts*

The plaintiff bonded warehousemen agreed to warehouse the goods which the defendants had imported. The goods were stolen, but the plaintiffs still paid the customs duties and sued for the sum so paid. The defendants counterclaimed for the value of the goods, alleging negligence.

*Held*

The plaintiffs would succeed as the defendants, as importers, remained liable for the duty and there was no evidence of negligence on the plaintiffs' part.

**Currie v Misa**

See **Misa v Currie**

**Eastwood v Kenyon** (1840) 11 Ad & El 438 Court of Queen's Bench (Lord Denman CJ, Patteson, Williams and Coleridge JJ)

Consideration - voluntary pecuniary benefit

*Facts*

S, an infant, inherited a large estate. The plaintiff, S's guardian, spent money on improving the estate and on educating S. When she came of age, she promised to reimburse him. Later, she married the defendant who made a similar promise. The plaintiff sued the defendant on the promise.

*Held*

The claim would be dismissed as disclosing no cause of action. A pecuniary benefit, voluntarily conferred, is not a sufficient consideration to support a subsequent promise to reimburse. Further, the defendant's promise was not within s4 of the Statute of Frauds.

**Edwards v Skyways Ltd** [1964] 1 WLR 349 High Court (Megaw J)

Intention to create legal relations?

*Facts*

As it was necessary to make some of their pilots redundant, the defendants agreed that those concerned, including the plaintiff, would be given an ex gratia payment approximating to the defendants' contributions to their pension fund. Due to their financial difficulties, the defendants failed to make such a payment to the plaintiff: when he sued to recover the amount of the promised ex gratia payment, the defendants maintained that the agreement was not binding as there had been no intention to create legal relations and its terms were too vague.

*Held*

The plaintiff was entitled to succeed.

Megaw J:

'... the subject-matter of the agreement is business relations, not social or domestic matters. There was a meeting of minds - an intention to agree. There was, admittedly, consideration for the defendant company's promise. I accept the propositions of counsel for the plaintiff that in a case of this nature the onus is on the party who asserts that no legal effect was intended, and the onus is a heavy one ... the defendant company say, first ... that the mere use of the phrase "ex gratia" by itself, as a part of the promise to pay, shows that the parties contemplated that the promise, when accepted, should have no binding force in law. They say, secondly, that even if their first proposition is not correct as a general proposition, nevertheless here there was certain background knowledge, present in the minds of everyone, which gave unambiguous significance to "ex gratia" as excluding legal relationship.

As to the first proposition, the words "ex gratia" do not, in my judgment, carry a necessary, or even a probable, implication that the agreement is to be without legal effect. It is, I think, common experience amongst practitioners of the law that litigation or threatened litigation is frequently compromised on the terms that one party shall make to the other a payment described in express terms as "ex gratia" or "without admission of liability". The two phrases are, I think, synonymous ... No one would imagine that a settlement, so made, is unenforceable at law. The words "ex gratia" or "without admission of liability" are used simply to indicate ... that the party agreeing to pay does not admit any pre-existing liability on his part; but he is certainly not seeking to preclude the legal enforceability of the settlement itself by describing the contemplated payment as "ex gratia". So here, there are obvious reasons why the phrase might have been used by the defendant company in just such a way. They might have desired to avoid conceding that any such payment was due under the employers' contract of service. They might have wished - perhaps ironically in the event - to show, by using the phrase, their generosity in making a payment beyond what was required by the contract of service. I see nothing in the mere use of the words "ex gratia", unless in the circumstances some very special meaning has to be given to them, to warrant the conclusion that this promise, duly made and accepted, for valid consideration, was not intended by the parties to be enforceable in law.

The defendant company's second proposition seeks to show that in the circumstances here the words "ex gratia" had a special meaning ...

Thus, it is said, the phrase "ex gratia" was used, and was understood by all present to be used, deliberately and advisedly as a formula to achieve that there would be no binding legal obligation on the company to pay, and hence to save the recipient from a tax liability ... The question of tax liability, and the possible influence thereon of the use of the words "ex gratia", may indeed have been present in some degree, and as one element, in the minds of some of the persons ... That, however, is far from sufficient to establish that the parties - both of them - affirmatively intended not to enter into legal relations in respect of the defendant company's promise to pay.

6

Lastly, the defendant company say that, even if the agreement were otherwise in all respects a binding agreement, it is not enforceable because its terms are too vague. This is founded on the submission that the precise words used ... were "approximating to"; that these precise words are a part of the agreement; that they leave a discretion to the defendant company; that therefore there is no enforceable agreement, and they can refuse to pay anything ... I do not think that English law provides that in such circumstances the plaintiff would be entitled to nothing. At most "approximating to", if that were the contractual term, would on the evidence connote a rounding off of a few pounds downwards to a round figure.'

*Commentary*

Applied in *Kleinwort Benson Ltd* v *Malaysia Mining Corp Bhd* [1988] 1 WLR 799

**Esso Petroleum Ltd v Commissioners of Customs and Excise** [1976] 1 WLR 1 House of Lords (Lord Wilberforce, Viscount Dilhorne, Lord Simon of Glaisdale, Lord Fraser of Tullybelton and Lord Russell of Killowen)

Offer of World Cup coins

*Facts*

As a petrol sales promotion scheme, motorists were offered one coin bearing the likeness of a member of England's World Cup soccer team for every four gallons of petrol. Advertisements said, for example: 'One coin given with every four gallons of petrol.' The question arose as to whether, for tax purposes, the coins had been produced 'for general sale'.

*Held* (Lord Fraser of Tullybelton dissenting)

They had not.

Lord Simon of Glaisdale:

'Believing as I do that Esso envisaged a bargain of some sort between the garage proprietor and the motorist, I must try to analyse the transaction. The analysis that most appeals to me is ... a collateral contract of the sort described by Lord Moulton in *Heilbut, Symons & Co* v *Buckleton*:

" ... there may be a contract the consideration for which is the making of some other contract. 'If you will make such and such a contract I will give you one hundred pounds', is in every sense of the word a complete legal contract. It is collateral to the main contract ..."

So here. The law happily matches the reality. The garage proprietor is saying, "If you will buy four gallons of my petrol, I will give you one of these coins". None of the reasons which have caused the law to consider advertising or display material as an invitation to treat, rather than an offer, applies here. What the garage proprietor says by his placards is in fact and in law an offer of consideration to the motorist to enter into a contract of sale of petrol. Of course, not every motorist will notice the placard, but nor will every potential offeree of many offers be necessarily conscious that they have been made. However, the motorist who does notice the placard, and in reliance thereon drives in and orders the petrol, is in law doing two things at the same time. First, he is accepting the offer of a coin if he buys four gallons of petrol. Secondly, he is himself offering to buy four gallons of petrol: this offer is accepted by the filling of his tank ... Here the coins were not transferred for a money consideration. They were transferred in consideration of the motorist entering into a contract for the sale of petrol. The coins were therefore not produced for sale ... They are exempt from purchase tax.'

Viscount Dilhorne:

'True it is that Esso are engaged in business. True it is that they hope to promote the sale of their petrol, but it does not seem to me necessarily to follow or to be inferred that there was any intention on their part that their dealers should enter into legally binding contracts with regard to the coins; or any intention on the part of the dealers to enter into any such contract or any intention on the part of the purchaser of four gallons of petrol to do so.

If on the facts of this case the conclusion is reached that there was any such intention on the part of the customer, of the dealer and of Esso, it would seem to exclude the possibility of any dealer ever making a free gift to any of his customers, however negligible its value, to promote his sales.

If what was described as being a gift which would be given if something was purchased was something of value to the purchaser, then it could readily be inferred that there was a common intention to enter into legal relations. But here, whatever the cost of production, it is clear that the coins were of little intrinsic value.

I do not consider that the offer of a gift of a free coin is properly to be regarded as a business matter ... Nor do I think that such an offer can be comprehended within the "business relations" ... I see no reason to imply any intention to enter into contractual relations from the statements on the posters that a coin would be given if four gallons of petrol were bought.

Nor do I see any reason to impute to every motorist who went to a garage where the posters were displayed to buy four gallons of petrol any intention to enter into a legally binding contract for the supply to him of a coin. On the acceptance of his offer to purchase four gallons there was no doubt a legally binding contract for the supply to him of that quantity of petrol, but I see again no reason to conclude that because such an offer was made by him, it must be held that as the posters were displayed, his offer included an offer to take a coin. The gift of a coin might lead to a motorist returning to the garage to obtain another one, but I think the facts in this case negative any contractual intention on his part and on the part of the dealer as to the coin and suffice to rebut any presumption there may be to the contrary.

If, however, there was any contract relating to the coin or coins, the consideration for the entry into that contract was not the payment of any money but the entry into a contract to purchase four gallons or multiples of that quantity of petrol, in which case the contract relating to the coin or coins cannot be regarded as a contract of sale.

I therefore, while of opinion that there was no legally binding contract as to the coins and so that it has not been established that they were produced for sale, am also of opinion that if there was any such contract it was not one for sale.'

**Evans (J) & Son (Portsmouth) Ltd v Andrea Merzario Ltd** [1976] 1 WLR 1078 Court of Appeal (Lord Denning MR, Roskill and Geoffrey Lane LJJ)

Collateral contract - consideration

*Facts*

The plaintiffs had, from 1959-1967, used the defendants' services as forwarding agents for the import of machines from Italy to England. During that period, the plaintiffs' machines were stored below deck. In 1967, the defendants changed to containers, but orally assumed the plaintiffs that the latter's machines would be shipped below deck. On one voyage in 1968, they were not and, due to rough seas, several machines were lost overboard. The defendants sought to rely on their written standard terms which permitted them to carry cargo howsoever they wished and exempted them from liability in the case of loss.

*Held*

There was a collateral contract between the parties that the plaintiffs' machines would be carried below deck; the plaintiffs furnished consideration for the defendants' promise by entering into the main contract of carriage.

Lord Denning MR:

'The judge quoted largely from the well known case of *Heilbut, Symons & Co v Buckleton*, in which it was held that a person is not liable in damages for an innocent misrepresentation; and that the courts should be slow to hold that there was a collateral contract. I must say that much of what was said in that case is entirely out of date ... When a person gives a promise or an assurance to another, intending that he should act on it by entering into a contract, we hold that it is binding: *Dick Bentley Productions.*'

*Commentary*

Applied: *Bentley (Dick) Productions Ltd* v *Harold Smith (Motors) Ltd* [1965] 1 WLR 623

**Eves v Eves** [1975] 1 WLR 1338 Court of Appeal (Lord Denning MR, Browne LJ and Brightman J)

Unmarried couple - property in one name only

*Facts*

A married woman aged 19 began to live with the defendant, a married man: they intended to marry when they were free to do so. They found a house which was to be a home for themselves and their children, but the man said that as she was under 21, it should be conveyed into his name alone and the woman accepted this explanation. Although the man financed the purchase, the woman did a great deal of work to the house and she looked after the man and their two children. After the man had left to marry another woman, his former partner claimed a share in the property which had been their home.

*Held*

She was entitled to succeed and the appropriate share would be one-quarter of the equity.

Lord Denning MR:

'Although [the woman] did not make any financial contribution, it seems to me that this property was acquired and maintained by both their joint efforts with the intention that it should be used for their joint benefit until they were married and thereafter as long as the marriage continued. At any rate, [the man] cannot be heard to say to the contrary. He told her that it was to be their home for them and their children. He gained her confidence by telling her that he intended to put it in their joint names (just as married couples often do) but that it was not possible until she was 21. The judge described this as a "trick", and said that it "did not do him much credit as a man of honour". The man never intended to put it in joint names but always determined to have it in his own name. It seems to me that he should be judged by what he told her - by what he led her to believe - and not by his own intent which he kept to himself. ...

It seems to me that this conduct by [the man] amounted to a recognition by him that, in all fairness, she was entitled to a share in the house, equivalent in some way to a declaration of trust; not for a particular share, but for such share as was fair in view of all she had done and was doing for him and the children and would thereafter do. By so doing he gained her confidence. She trusted him. She did not make any financial contribution but she contributed in many other ways. She did much work in the house and garden. She looked after him and cared for the children ...

In view of his conduct, it would, I think, be most inequitable for him to deny her any share in the house. The law will impute or impose a constructive trust by which he was to hold it in trust for them both. But what should be the shares? I think one half would be too much. I suggest it should be one-quarter of the equity.'

**Foster v Robinson** [1951] 1 KB 149 Court of Appeal (Sir Raymond Evershed MR, Cohen and Singleton LJJ)

Surrender of tenancy by operation of law

*Facts*

A farmer owned a cottage which he let at a yearly rent to one of his employees, the defendant's father. Owing to age and infirmity, father ceased to work and the farmer agreed that he could continue to live in the cottage, rent free, for the rest of his life. Father's daughter had lived with him for a number of years and, on his death, she claimed the tenancy under the Rent Acts.

*Held*

The farmer was entitled to possession. His agreement with father had produced a surrender of the original tenancy by operation of law and daughter was estopped from asserting that it still existed.

Singleton LJ:

'The position of the father was altered by agreement between the parties; there was a complete change. The father became a licensee ... At his death he had had the advantage of the agreement and had paid no rent for three and a half years, and his daughter ... cannot be in a better position.'

**Gould v Gould** [1969] 3 WLR 490 Court of Appeal (Lord Denning MR, Edmund Davies and Megaw LJJ)

Husband's qualified promise

*Facts*

On leaving his wife, a husband orally agreed to pay her £15 a week 'as long as I can manage it'. He kept to this agreement for over a year, but then fell behind with the payments and five months later said he could not pay the full amount in future. The wife sued for the arrears.

*Held* (Lord Denning MR dissenting)

Her claim would fail as a legally binding agreement had not been within the contemplation of the parties.

Edmund Davies LJ:

'There can be no doubt that husband and wife can enter into a contract which binds them in law ... But it is on the spouse asserting that such a contract has been entered into to prove that assertion ... In the general run of cases the inclination would be against inferring that spouses intended to create a legal relationship ... The evidence establishing such an intention, needs, in my judgment, to be clear and convincing.

It is true that the facts of the present case differ from those of *Balfour* v *Balfour*, in that although the original agreement there relied on was entered into on the eve of the husband's leaving the wife to take up his governmental duties in Ceylon, at that time amity reigned between them; whereas here the arrangement sued on was made after the husband had left the wife. While I agree that in the present circumstances the probability that a legally-binding agreement was intended may be greater than in *Balfour* v *Balfour*, nevertheless the best key in my judgment to the parties' intention is the language they employed. The importance of this aspect of the case is not restricted simply to the question whether the agreement is bad for uncertainty, but extends to the initial question whether a legally binding agreement was ever intended within the parties' contemplation. According to the wife, the husband promised to pay her £15 a week "as long as he had it" and "as long as the business was OK". The husband's evidence was substantially to the same effect, namely,

" ... I suggested I would give her £15 each week; and she said for how long? and I said as long as I can manage it."

In my judgment those words import such uncertainty as to indicate strongly that legal relations were not contemplated.'

*Commentary*

Distinguished in *Merritt* v *Merritt* [1970] 1 WLR 1211. See also *Balfour* v *Balfour* [1919] 2 KB 571.

**Hardwick v Johnson** [1978] 1 WLR 683 Court of Appeal (Lord Denning MR, Roskill and Browne LJJ)

Family arrangement

*Facts*

When her son became engaged, mother said she would buy a house in which the couple could live and they could pay her rent. Mother bought a house; after their marriage, the couple lived in it, paying £7 a week, although it was not clear whether this was rent or contributions towards the purchase price. The couple became short of money and the weekly payments ceased: their marriage broke down and the son left home: mother sued for possession, even though her daughter-in-law had offered to make the weekly payments.

*Held*

Mother's claim could not succeed: a joint licence had been granted and daughter-in-law had not been in breach of it so it was not revocable as against her.

Lord Denning MR:

'So we have to consider once more the law about family arrangements. In the well-known case of *Balfour* v *Balfour* [1919] 2 KB 571, Atkin LJ said that family arrangements made between husband and wife "are not contracts because the parties did not intend that they should be attended by legal consequences". Similarly, family arrangements between parent and child are often not contracts which bind them, see *Jones* v *Padavatton* [1969] 1 WLR 328. Nevertheless these family arrangements do have legal consequences; and, time and time again, the courts are called on to determine what is the true legal relationship resulting from them ... The court has to look at all the circumstances and spell out the legal relationship. The court will pronounce in favour of a tenancy or a licence, a loan or a gift, or a trust, according to which of these legal relationships is most fitting in the situation which has arisen; and will find the terms of that relationship according to what reason and justice require ...

Of all these suggestions, I think the most fitting is a personal licence. The occupation of the house was clearly personal to this young couple. It was a personal privilege creating a licence such as we have often had: see *Errington* v *Errington and Woods* [1952] 1 KB 290. I do not think it could properly be called a contractual licence because it is difficult to say that this family arrangement was a contract. *Balfour* v *Balfour* is authority for saying there was no contract. I should have thought it was more in the nature of an equitable licence of which the court has to spell out the terms.'

*Commentary*

Although Roskill and Browne LJJ agreed as to the decision, they preferred to call it a contractual as opposed to an equitable licence.

**Hedley Byrne & Co v Heller & Partners** [1984] AC 465 House of Lords (Lord Reid, Lord Morris of Borth-y-Gest, Lord Hodson, Lord Delvin and Lord Pearce)

Negligence - duty of care in relation to information or advice

*Facts*

The appellants, an advertising agency, wished to make enquiries about the financial reliability of one of their customers, Easipower Ltd. Their bankers made enquiries of the respondents, Easipower's bankers. The respondents replied, first orally then in writing, stating that Easipower Ltd was financially sound, although this information was given 'without responsibility'. The appellants relied on this advice which proved to be inaccurate and they suffered considerable losses when Easipower went into liquidation.

*Held*

A duty of care in making statements may arise when the parties are in a 'special relationship'. But the appeal was dismissed because the respondents had excluded their responsibility.

Lord Hodson:

'... if in a sphere where a person is so placed that others could reasonably rely on his judgment or on his skill or on his ability to make careful enquiry, such person takes it on himself to give information or advice to, or allows his information or advice to be passed on to, another person who, as he knows or should know, will place reliance on it, then a duty of care will arise.'

Lord Pearce:

'The reason for some divergence between the law of negligence in word and that of negligence in act is clear. Negligence in word creates problems different from those of negligence in act. Words are more volatile than deeds. They travel fast and far afield. They are used without being expended and take effect in combination with innumerable facts and other words ... Damage by negligent acts to persons or property on the other hand is more visible and obvious, its limits are more easily defined ...'

Lord Devlin:

'It would be surprising if the sort of problem that is created by the facts of this case had never until recently arisen in English law. As a problem it is a by-product of the doctrine of consideration. If the respondents had made a nominal charge for the reference, the problem would not exist. If it were possible in English law to construct a contract without consideration, the problem would move at once out of the first and general phase into the particular; and the question would be, not whether on the facts of the case there was a special relationship, but whether on the facts of the case there was a contract.

The respondents in this case cannot deny that they were performing a service. Their sheet anchor is that they were performing it gratuitously and therefore no liability for its performance can arise. My Lords, in my opinion this is not the law. A promise given without consideration to perform a service cannot be enforced as a contract by the promisee; but if the service is in fact performed and done negligently, the promisee can recover in an action in tort. This is the foundation of the liability of a gratuitous bailee. In the famous case of *Coggs* v *Bernard*, where the defendant had charge of brandy belonging to the plaintiff and had spilt a quantity of it, there was a motion in arrest of judgment "for that it was not alleged in the declaration that the defendant was a common porter, nor averred that he had anything for his pains". The declaration was held to be good notwithstanding that there was not any consideration laid. Gould J said:

"The reason of the action is, the particular trust reposed in the defendant, to which he has concurred by his assumption, and in the executing which he has miscarried by his neglect."

This proposition is not limited to the law of bailment. In *Skelton* v *London & North Western Ry Co* Willes J applied it generally to the law of negligence. He said:

"Actionable negligence must consist in the breach of some duty ... if a person undertakes to perform a voluntary act, he is liable if he performs it improperly, but not if he neglects to perform it. Such is the result of the decision in the case of *Coggs* v *Bernard*."

Likewise in *Banbury* v *Bank of Montreal*, where the bank had advised a customer on his investments, Lord Finley LC said: "He is under no obligation to advise, but if he takes upon himself to do so, he will incur liability if he does so negligently." '

*Commentary*

Applied in *Cornish* v *Midland Bank plc* [1985] 3 All ER 513.

**Kleinwort Benson Ltd v Malaysia Mining Corp Bhd** [1989] 1 WLR 379 Court of Appeal (Fox, Ralph Gibson and Nicholls LJJ)

Letter of comfort - contractual effect?

*Facts*

The plaintiff bank negotiated with the defendants for the making of loan facility of up to £10m available to the defendants' wholly-owned subsidiary MMC Metals Ltd ('Metals'). The plaintiffs having sought from the defendants assurances as to the responsibility of the defendants for the repayment by Metals of any sums lent by the plaintiffs, the defendants provided a comfort letter containing the statement (in para 3): 'It is our policy to ensure that the business of [Metals] is at all times in a position to meet its liabilities to you under the ... arrangements.' Metals went into liquidation owing the whole amount of the facility and the plaintiffs sought payment from the defendants.

*Held*

Their action would fail as, on the facts, the letter gave rise to no more than a moral responsibility on the defendants' part to meet Metals' debt.

Ralph Gibson LJ:

'The concept of a comfort letter was, as counsel for the defendants acknowledged, not shown to have acquired any particular meaning at the time of the negotiations in this case with reference to the limits of any legal liability to be assumed under its terms by a parent company. ... The court would not, merely because the parties had referred to the document as a comfort letter, refuse to give effect to the meaning of the words used. But in this case it is clear ... that the concept of a comfort letter, to which the parties had resort when the defendants refused to assume joint and several liability or to give a guarantee, was known by both sides at least to extend to or to include a document under which the defendants would give comfort to the plaintiffs by assuming, not a legal liability to ensure repayment of the liabilities of its subsidiary, but a moral responsibility only. ... The comfort letter was drafted in terms which in para 3 do not express any contractual promise and which are consistent with being no more than a representation of fact. If they are treated as no more than a representation of fact, they are in that meaning consistent with the comfort letter containing no more than the assumption of moral responsibility by the defendants in respect of the debts of Metals. There is nothing in the evidence to show that, as a matter of commercial probability or common sense, the parties must have intended para 3 to be a contractual promise, which is not expressly stated, rather than a mere representation of fact which is so stated ...

For this purpose it seems to me that the onus of demonstrating that the affirmation appears on evidence to have been intended as a contractual promise must lie on the party asserting that it does, but I do not rest my conclusion on failure by the plaintiffs to discharge any onus. I think it is clear that the words of para 3 cannot be regarded as intended to contain a contractual promise as to the future policy of the defendants ... Most importantly [the] factual background explains, notwithstanding the commercial importance to the plaintiffs of security against failure by Metals to pay and the plaintiffs' reliance on the comfort letter, why the plaintiffs drafted and agreed to proceed on a comfort letter which, on its plain meaning, provided to the plaintiffs no legally enforceable security for the repayment of the liabilities of Metals. I therefore find it impossible to hold that by the words of para 3 the parties must be held to have intended that the plaintiffs be given that security.'

**Lewis v Averay** [1971] 3 WLR 603 Court of Appeal (Lord Denning MR, Phillimore and Megaw LJJ)

Contract - deception as to identity

*Facts*

The plaintiff advertised his motor car for sale in a local newspaper for £450. In reply, the rogue telephoned and asked to see the car. He came in the evening to Mr Lewis' flat. Mr Lewis showed him the car, which was parked outside. The rogue drove it and tested it. He said he liked it. They then went along to the flat of Mr Lewis' fiancee, Miss Kershaw (they have since married). He told them he was Richard Green and talked much about the film world. He led both of them to believe that he was the well known film actor, Richard Greene, who played Robin Hood in the 'Robin Hood' series. They talked about the car. He asked to see the log book. He was shown it and seemed satisfied. He said he would like to buy the car. They agreed a price of £450. The rogue wrote out a cheque and signed it 'R A Green'. He wanted to take the car at once. But Mr Lewis was not willing for him to have it until the cheque was cleared. To hold him off, Mr Lewis said that there were one or two small jobs he would like to do on the car before letting him have it and that would give time for the cheque to be cleared. The rogue said, 'Don't worry about those small jobs. I would like to take the car now'. Mr Lewis said: Have you anything to prove that you are Mr Richard Green?' The rogue thereupon brought out a special pass of admission to Pinewood Studios, which had an official stamp on it. It bore the name of Richard A Green and the address and also a photograph, which was plainly the photograph of this man, who was the rogue.

On seeing this pass, Mr Lewis was satisfied. He thought this man was really Mr Richard Greene, the film actor. By that time it was 11 o'clock at night. Mr Lewis took the cheque and let the rogue have the car, the log book and the Ministry of Transport test certificate. Each wrote and signed a receipt evidencing the transaction. Whilst the cheque was going through, the rogue sold the car to an innocent purchaser. He sold it to a young man called Mr Averay who was, at the time, under 21. He sold it for £200 and gave him a receipt in the name of Mr Lewis.

A fortnight later, Mr Averay wanted the workshop manual for the car. So his father, on his behalf, wrote to the name and address of the seller as given in the log book - that is, Mr Lewis. Then, of course, the whole story came to light. The rogue had cashed the cheque and disappeared. The police have tried to trace him, but without success.

Now Mr Lewis, the original owner of the car, sues young Mr Averay. Mr Lewis claims that the car is still his. He claims damages for conversion. The judge found in favour of Mr Lewis and awarded damages of £330 for conversion.

*Held*

The appeal would be allowed.

Lord Denning MR:

'The real question in the case is whether there was a contract of sale under which the property in the car passed from Mr Lewis to the rogue. If there was such a contract, then even though it was voidable for fraud, nevertheless Mr Averay would get a good title to the car. But if there was no contract of sale by Mr Lewis to the rogue - either because there was, on the face of it, no agreement between the parties, or because any apparent agreement was a nullity and void ab initio for mistake, then no property would pass from Mr Lewis to the rogue. Mr Averay would not get a good title because the rogue had no property to pass to him.

There is no doubt that Mr Lewis was mistaken as to the identity of the person who handed him the cheque. He thought that he was Richard Greene, a film actor of standing and worth; whereas, in fact he was a rogue whose identity is quite unknown. It was under the influence of that mistake that Mr Lewis let the rogue have the car. He would not have dreamed of letting him have it otherwise.

What is the effect of this mistake? There are two cases in our books which cannot, in my mind, be reconciled the one with the other. One of them is *Phillips* v *Brooks Ltd* [1919] 2 KB 243, where a jeweller had a ring for sale. The other is *Ingram* v *Little* [1960] 3 WLR 505, where two ladies had a car for sale. In each case the story is very similar to the present. A plausible rogue comes along. The rogue says he likes the ring, or the car, as the case may be. He asks the price. The sellers name it. The rogue says he is prepared to buy it at that price. He pulls out a cheque book. He writes, or prepares to write, a cheque for the price. The seller hesitates. He has never met this man before. He does not want to hand over the ring or the car not knowing whether the cheque will be met. The rogue notices the seller's hesitation. He is quick with his next move. He says to the jeweller in *Phillips* v *Brooks*: I am Sir George Bullough of 11 St James's Square'; or the ladies in *Ingram* v *Little*: 'I am P G M Hutchinson of Standstead House, Standstead Road, Caterham'; or to the post graduate student in the present case: 'I am Richard Greene, the film actor of the Robin Hood series'. Each seller checks up the information. The jeweller looks up the directory and finds there is a Sir George Bullough at 11 St James' Square. The ladies check up too. They look at the telephone directory and find there is a 'P G M Hutchinson of Standstead House, Standstead Road, Caterham'. The post graduate student checks up too. He examines the official pass of the Pinewood Studios and finds that it is a pass for 'Richard A Green' to the Pinewood Studios with this man's photograph on it. In each case the seller finds that this is sufficient confirmation of the man's identity. So he accepts the cheque signed by the rogue and lets him have the ring in the one case and the car and log book in the other two cases. The rogue goes off and sells the goods to a third person, who buys them in entire good faith and pays the price to the rogue. The rogue disappears. The original seller presents the cheque. It is dishonoured. Who is entitled to the goods? The original seller? Or the ultimate buyer?

It seems to me that the material facts in each case are quite indistinguishable the one from the other. In each case there was, to all outward appearance, a contract: but there was a mistake by the seller as to the identity of the buyer. This mistake was fundamental. In each case it led to the handing over of the goods. Without it, the seller would not have parted with them.

This case therefore, raises the question: What is the effect of a mistake by one party as to the identity of the other? It has sometimes been said that if a party makes a mistake as to the identity of the person with whom he is contracting, there is no contract, or if there is a contract, it is a nullity and void so that no property can pass under it.

For instance, in *Ingram* v *Little*, the majority of the court suggested that the difference between *Phillips* v *Brooks* and *Ingram* v *Little* was that in *Phillips* v *Brooks* the contract of sale was concluded (so as to pass the property to the rogue) before the rogue made the fraudulent misrepresentation ... whereas in *Ingram* v *Little*, the rogue made the fraudulent misrepresentation before the contract was concluded. My own view is that in each case, the property in the goods did not pass until the seller let the rogue have the goods.

Again it has been suggested that a mistake as to the identity of a person is one thing: and a mistake as to his attributes is another. A mistake as to identity, it is said, avoids a contract: whereas a mistake as to attributes does not. But this is a distinction without a difference. A man's very name is one of his attributes. It is also a key to his identity.

When two parties have come to a contract - or rather what appears, on the face of it, to be a contract - the fact that one party is mistaken as to the identity of the other does not mean that there is no contract or that the contract is a nullity and void from the beginning. It only means that the contract is voidable, that is, liable to be set aside at the instance of the mistaken person, so long as he does so before third parties have, in good faith, acquired rights under it.

Applied to the cases such as the present, this principle is in full accord with the presumption stated by Pearce LJ and also Devlin LJ in *Ingram* v *Little*. When a dealing is had between a seller like Mr Lewis and a person who is actually there present before him, then the presumption in law is that there is a contract, even though there is a fraudulent impersonation by the buyer representing himself as a different man than he is. There is a contract made with the very person there, who is present in person. It is liable, no doubt to be avoided for fraud, but it is still a good contract, under which title will pass unless and until it is avoided.

In this case, Mr Lewis made a contract of sale with the very man, the rogue, who came to the flat. I say that he 'made a contract' because, in this regard, we do not look into his intentions or into his mind to know what he was thinking, or into the mind of the rogue. We look to the outward appearances. On the face of the dealing, Mr Lewis made a contract under which he sold the car to the rogue, delivered the car and the log book to him and took a cheque in return. It was, of course, induced by fraud. The rogue made false representations as to his identity. But it was still a contract, though voidable for fraud. It was a contract under which this property passed to the rogue and, in due course, passed from the rogue to Mr Averay before the contract was voided.

Though I very much regret that either of these good and reliable gentlemen should suffer, in my judgment, it is Mr Lewis who should do so. I think the appeal should be allowed.'

*Commentary*

Followed: *Phillips* v *Brooks Ltd* [1919] 2 KB 243. Distinguished and doubted: *Ingram* v *Little* [1960] 3 WLR 505.

**Misa v Currie** (1876) 1 App Cas 554 House of Lords (Lord Chelmsford, Lord Hatherley and Lord O'Hagan)

Good consideration?

*Facts*

The appellant wine merchant purchased from Lizardi drafts on Cadiz. The day before the purchase money was payable, Lizardi deposited with his bankers, the respondents, to whom he was largely indebted, a document dated the following day requesting the appellant to pay the money to the respondents. Next day the appellant paid the amount by cheque: the respondents handed him Lizardi's request but on the same day Lizardi stopped payment and the appellant accordingly instructed his bankers not to honour the cheque and it was subsequently dishonoured, as were the drafts when they were presented. The respondents sued the appellant on the cheque.

*Held*

The respondents were entitled to succeed as, inter alia, there was good consideration between Lizardi and the appellant at the time the cheque was given.

*Commentary*

This decision affirmed the decision in *Currie* v *Misa* (1875) LR 10 Exch 153.

**Pettitt v Pettitt** [1970] AC 277 House of Lords (Lord Reid, Lord Morris of Borth-y-Gest, Lord Hodson, Lord Upjohn and Lord Diplock)

Cottage - beneficial interests

*Facts*

A wife paid for a cottage and it stood in her name. The husband carried out internal decorations, built a wardrobe, laid out the garden and constructed a wall. Subsequently they were divorced and the husband maintained that he was entitled to a beneficial interest in the cottage's proceeds of sale.

*Held*

This was not the case: he had merely done in his leisure time jobs which husbands normally do.

Lord Diplock:

'... many of the ordinary domestic arrangements between man and wife do not possess the legal characteristics of a contract. So long as they are executory they do not give rise to any chose in action for neither party intended that non-performance of their mutual promises should be the subject of sanctions in any court (see *Balfour* v *Balfour*). But this is relevant to non-performance only. If spouses do perform their mutual promises the fact that they could not have been compelled to do so while the promises were executory cannot deprive the acts done by them of all legal consequences on proprietary rights; for these are within the field of the law of property rather than of the law of contract. It would, in my view, be erroneous to extend the presumption accepted in *Balfour* v *Balfour* that mutual promises between man and wife in relation to their domestic arrangements are prima facie not intended by either to be legally enforceable to a presumption of a common intention of both spouses that *no* legal consequences should flow from acts done by them in performance of mutual promises with respect to the acquisition, improvement or addition to real or personal property - for this would be to intend what is impossible in law.'

**Rose & Frank Co v J R Crompton & Bros Ltd** [1925] AC 445 House of Lords (Earl of Birkenhead, Lord Atkinson, Lord Sumner, Lord Buckmaster and Lord Phillimore)

Contract - intention not to be legally enforceable

*Facts*

A contract between the parties relating to carbonising tissue paper concluded with a clause as follows:

'This arrangement is not entered into, nor is this memorandum written, as a formal or legal agreement, and shall not be subject to legal jurisdiction in the law courts either of the United States or England, but it is only a definite expression and record of the purpose and intention of the three parties concerned, to which they each honourably pledge themselves with the fullest confidence - based on past business with each other - that it will be carried through by each of the three parties with mutual loyalty and friendly co-operation.'

One of the parties to the agreement sued another for damages for breach of contract.

*Held*

The action could not succeed as the parties to the agreement had not intended it to be legally enforceable.

Lord Phillimore:

'It is true that when the tribunal has before it for construction an instrument which unquestionably creates a legal interest and the dispute is only to the quality and extent of that interest, then later repugnant clauses in the instrument cutting down that interest which the earlier part of it has given are to be rejected, but this doctrine does not apply when the question is whether it is intended to create any legal interest at all. Here, I think, the overriding clause in the document is that which provided that it is to be a contract of honour only and unenforceable at law.'

*Commentary*

Applied in *Kleinwort Benson Ltd* v *Malaysia Mining Corp Bhd* [1988] 1 WLR 799.

**Tanner v Tanner** [1975] 1 WLR 1346 Court of Appeal (Lord Denning MR, Browne LJ and Brightman J)

Mistress - rights to home purchased in man's name

*Facts*

The plaintiff, a married man, bought in his own name a house in part of which he installed his mistress, the defendant, and their twins. The defendant left a rent-controlled flat to live there and she makde no financial contribution to the purchase. However, she provided or bought furniture and she managed the rest of the house on the plaintiff's behalf. After the plaintiff had married someone else, he sought possession of the defendant's accommodation in his house.

*Held*

He was not entitled to such an order.

Lord Denning MR:

'It is impossible to suppose that in that situation she and the babies were bare licensees whom he could turn out at a moment's notice. He recognised this when he offered to pay her £4,000 to get her out. What then was their legal position? She herself said in evidence: "The house was supposed to be ours until the children left school." It seems to me that enables an inference to be drawn, namely that in all the circumstances it is to be implied that she had a licence - a contractual licence - to have accommodation in the house for herself and the children so long as they were of school age and the accommodation was reasonably required for her and the children. There was, it is true, no express contract to that effect, but the circumstances are such that the court should imply a contract by him - or, if need be, impose the equivalent of a contract by him - whereby they were entitled to have the use of the house as their home until the girls had finished school. It may be that if circumstances changed - so that the accommodation was not reasonably required - the licence might be determinable. But it was not determinable in the circumstances in which he sought to determine it, namely to turn her out with the children and to bring in his new wife with her family. It was a contractual licence of the kind which is specifically enforceable on her behalf, and which he can be restrained from breaking; and he could not sell the house over her head so as to get her out in that way. That appears from *Binions* v *Evans*.

If therefore the lady had sought an injunction restraining him from determining the licence, it should have been granted. The order for possession ought not to have been made.'

*Commentary*

See also *Binions* v *Evans* [1972] 2 WLR 729. Distinguished in *Horrocks* v *Forray* [1976] 1 WLR 230.

**Tsakiroglou & Co Ltd v Noblee and Thorl GmbH** [1961] 2 WLR 633 House of Lords (Viscount Simonds, Lord Reid, Lord Radcliffe, Lord Hodson and Lord Guest)

Frustration - alternative route

*Facts*

In October 1956 the plaintiff agreed to sell to buyers groundnuts for shipment from Port Sudan to Hamburg during November/December 1956. On 7 October 1956, the plaintiff booked cargo space in a vessel scheduled to call at Port Sudan at the relevant time. On 2 November 1956, the Suez Canal was closed. The seller failed to deliver and, when sued, pleaded frustration.

*Held*

The contract had not been frustrated as there was the alternative of a reasonable and practicable, though possibly more expensive, route via the Cape of Good Hope.

Reid JJ:

'It appears to me that the only possible way of reaching a conclusion that this contract was frustrated would be to concentrate on the altered nature of the voyage ... What the sellers had to do was simply to find a ship proceeding by what was a practicable and now a reasonable route - if perhaps not yet a usual route - to pay the freight and obtain a proper bill of lading and to furnish the necessary documents to the buyer ... That was their manner of performing their obligations ... I think that such changes in these matters as were made necessary, fell far short of justifying a finding of frustration.'

**Walford v Miles** (1992) The Times 27 January House of Lords (Lord Keith of Kinkel, Lord Ackner, Lord Goff of Chieveley, Lord Jauncey of Tullichettle and Lord Browne-Wilkinson)

Intention to create legal relations - comfort letters

*Facts*

The plaintiffs entered into negotiations with the defendants over the sale of the defendants' business, and reached the point of the plaintiffs agreeing to obtain a 'comfort letter' from the bank and not to withdraw from the negotiations. The defendants, in return, undertook to break off negotiations with a third party and deal only with the plaintiffs. In fact the defendants not only did not cease negotiations with the rival bidder, they eventually sold the business to that rival. The question arose as to whether this oral agreement was binding.

*Held*

Such an agreement would be too uncertain to be workable, as each party would be entitled to pursue their own interests.

Lord Ackner said a duty to negotiate in good faith was as unworkable in practice as it was inherently inconsistent with the position of a negotiating party. It was there that the uncertainty lay.

While negotiations were in existence, either party was entitled to withdraw from those negotiations at any time and for any reason. There could thus be no obligation to continue to negotiate until there was a 'proper reason' to withdraw. Accordingly a bare agreement to negotiate had no legal content.

**Wroth v Tyler** [1973] 2 WLR 405 High Court (Megarry J)

Contract of sale - wife's objection

*Facts*

The defendant entered into an agreement to sell his bungalow, with vacant possession, to the plaintiffs for £6,050. Completion was fixed for 31 October 1971. The day after the defendant entered into the agreement, his wife, who had not shown any opposition to the sale, but who was not enthusiastic about it, entered in the Land Charges Register a notice under s1 of the Matrimonial Homes Act 1967, without informing the defendant. The entry was revealed by a notice sent by the Land Registry to the defendant's building society, which notified the defendant's solicitors who, in turn, informed the defendant. The defendant tried to persuade his wife to remove the notice, but was unsuccessful. Consequently, he was unable to complete, but he offered to pay damages. The plaintiffs issued a writ in early 1972, seeking specific performance and damages in lieu or in addition. Judgment was given in December 1972.

*Held*

The plaintiffs were not entitled to an order for specific performance, with vacant possession or subject to the rights of occupation of the defendant's wife. However, they were entitled to damages for loss of bargain and here they would not be simply nominal. In the event, they were quantified as at the date of the judgment and they were assessed at £5,500.

Megarry J:

'The rule of common law is, that where a party sustains a loss by reason of a breach of contract, he is, so far as money can do it, to be placed in the same situation, with respect to damages, as if the contract had been performed.

... on principle, I would say that damages 'in substitution' for specific performance, must be a substitute, giving as nearly as may be what specific performance would have given ... the court has jurisdiction to award such damages as will put the plaintiff into as good a position as if the contract had been performed, even if to do so means awarding damages assessed by reference to a period subsequent to the date of the breach. This seems to me to be consonant with the nature of specific performance, which is a continuing remedy ... The conclusion that I have reached therefore, is that as matters stand, I ought to award damages to the plaintiffs of the order of £5,000 in substitution for decreeing specific performance ... This is a dismal prospect for the defendant but ... it is the plaintiffs who are wholly blameless.'

*Commentary*

Applied: *Hadley* v *Baxendale* (1854) 9 Exch 341 and *Bain* v *Fothergill* (1874) LR 7 HL 158. Applied in *Sharneyford Supplies Ltd* v *Edge* [1987] 2 WLR 363.

# 1   OFFER AND ACCEPTANCE

**Adams v Lindsell** (1818) 1 B & Ald 681 King's Bench (Lord Ellenborough)

Offer and acceptance - acceptance by post

*Facts*

On 2 September, the defendants wrote to the plaintiffs, offering a quantity of wool on certain conditions and requiring an answer 'in course of post'. The defendants misdirected the letter, which did not arrive until 5 September. The plaintiffs immediately sent a letter of acceptance which was delivered on 9 September. But on 8 September, a day after they could have expected to receive a reply if the initial letter had been properly addressed, the defendants had sold the wool to third parties.

*Held*

As soon as the letter of acceptance was posted on 5 September, it was effective, and a valid contract was concluded.

**Bigg v Boyd Gibbins Ltd** [1971] 1 WLR 913 Court of Appeal (Russell, Fenton, Atkinson and Cross LJJ)

Offer and acceptance - whether letter offer

*Facts*

The parties were negotiating for the sale and purchase of Shortgrove Hall and the plaintiffs wrote to the defendants 'For a quick sale I would accept £26,000'. In reply, the defendants wrote 'I accept your offer.' The plaintiffs alleged that this exchange constituted a contract and they sought specific performance.

*Held*

They would succeed.

Russell LJ:

'We were warned at an early stage in the argument, quite rightly, that agreement on price does not necessarily mean agreement for sale and purchase, and we were referred to the warning phrases used by Lord Greene MR in *Clifton* v *Palumbo*, where it was stated that "offer" does not always mean offer in the sense of an offer for actual sale, but might be related to a negotiation continuing, but with agreement on one term or one element of the contract which would or might subsequently be concluded. But bearing in mind those warnings, I am bound to say for myself the impression conveyed to my mind by these letters, and indeed the plain impression, is that the language used was intended to and did achieve the formation of an open contract.'

*Commentary*

Distinguished: *Clifton* v *Palumbo* [1944] 2 All ER 497 and *Harvey* v *Facey* [1893] AC 552.

**Blackpool & Fylde Aero Club Ltd v Blackpool Borough Council** [1990] 1 WLR 1195 Court of Appeal (Stocker, Bingham and Farquharson LJJ)

Tenders - failure to consider

*Facts*

The defendant local authority owned the local airport for which it granted concessions for the operation of scenic and pleasure flights. On the expiry date of the current concessions it invited the plaintiffs and seven other companies to tender for the new concession. The plaintiffs currently held the existing pleasure flight concession. The invitation to submit tenders was accompanied by a condition that no tender received after a certain date/time would be considered. The plaintiffs' tender was posted by hand in the town hall letterbox, before the expiry date, but unfortunately the box was not cleared regularly and the town clerk received the tender, which was higher than any of the others submitted, after the deadline. The local authority announced that they were not considering it because it was too late.

*Held*

Where invitations are issued to specified parties to submit tenders, and the submission procedure is clearly laid down, along with a fixed date for submission, then if an invitee complied with the submission procedure and submitted his tender within the deadline, he had not just a moral but a contractual right to be considered. Although an invitation to tender was normally no more than an offer to consider bids, circumstances could exist whereby it gave rise to binding contractual obligations. While the invitation did not specifically state this, a careful examination of what the parties said, and did, established a clear intention on the part of the defendants to be bound to examine, and give equal consideration to, all tenders submitted within the deadline. Since the plaintiffs had submitted on time, they were entitled to expect their tender to be considered in conjunction with all the other tenders. As it had not been so considered, they were entitled to damages for breach of contract.

Bingham LJ:

'It is of course true that the invitation to tender does not explicitly state that the council will consider timely and conforming tenders. That is why one is concerned with implication ... I readily accept that contracts are not to be lightly implied. Having examined what the parties said and did, the court must be able to conclude with confidence both that the parties intended to create contractual relations, and that the agreement was to the effect contended for.'

Stocker LJ:

'The format of the invitation to tender document itself suggests in my view that a legal obligation to consider a tender applied ... to any operator ... who complied with its terms and conditions ... I therefore agree that in all the circumstances of this case there was an intention to create binding legal obligations if and when a tender was submitted in accordance with the terms of the invitation to tender, and that a binding contractual obligation arose that the club's tender would be before the officer or committee by whom the decision was to be taken for consideration before a decision was made or any tender accepted. This would not preclude or inhibit the council from deciding not to accept any tender or to award the concession, provided the decision was bona fide and honest, to any tenderer. The obligation was that the club's tender would be before the deciding body for consideration before any award was made.'

**Bloxham's Case** (1864) 33 Beav 529 Rolls Court (Sir John Romilly MR)

Acceptance - need not be communicated

*Facts*

Mr Bloxham applied for 100 shares in a company, was told that he could have them and paid a deposit of £100, the secretary promising to return the cheque if the shares were not allotted. Mr Bloxham's name was entered in the register of allotment of shares, but he heard - and paid - no more.

*Held*

Nevertheless, Mr Bloxham was a shareholder.

**Bradbury v Morgan** (1862) 1 H & C 249 Court of Exchequer (Pollock CB, Bramwell and Channell BB)

Guarantee - death of guarantor

*Facts*

Leigh wrote to the plaintiffs requesting them to give credit to another man and guaranteeing payment up to £100. The plaintiffs complied and continued to do so after Leigh's death, of which they were not aware. Leigh's executors, the defendants, declined to pay the £100 owed by the other man.

*Held*

The plaintiffs were entitled to judgment.

Channell B:

'Whether the parties contemplated that the contract should extend beyond the life of the guarantor, is not the question ... the question is whether this is a case of mere authority or a contract. I am of opinion that it is a contract, and if so, it is not revoked by the death of the guarantor. A mere authority is determined by death, but in the case of a contract death does not in general operate as revocation, but only in exceptional cases, and this is not within them.'

**Branca v Cobarro** [1947] KB 854 Court of Appeal (Lord Greene MR, Tucker and Asquith LJJ)

Effect of 'provisional' agreement

*Facts*

A document signed by both parties made provision for the sale and purchase of a mushroom farm and concluded: 'This is a provisional agreement until a fully legalised agreement drawn up by a solicitor and embodying all the conditions herewith stated is signed.' Denning J decided that 'provisional' meant 'tentative' and therefore that the parties were not bound by the agreement contained in the document. The vendor, who was resisting the purchaser's claim for the return of his deposit, appealed.

*Held*

The appeal would be allowed.

Lord Greene MR:

'My reading of this document is that both parties were determined to hold themselves and one another bound. They realised the desirability of a formal document as many contracting parties do, but they were determined that there should be no escape for either of them in the interim period between the signing of this document and the signature of a formal agreement, and they have used words which are exactly apt to produce that result and do not, in my opinion, suggest that the fully legalised agreement is in any sense to be a condition to be fulfilled before the parties are bound, because, as I have said, the word "until" is certainly not the right word to import a condition or a stipulation as to the event referred to. In my judgment, if the parties never signed a fully legalised agreement, the event putting an end to the provisional operation of this agreement would never occur and this document would continue to bind the parties.'

**Brinkibon Ltd v Stahag Stahl und Stahlwarenhandelsgesellschaft mbH** [1982] 2 WLR 264 House of Lords (Lord Wilberforce, Lord Fraser of Tullybelton, Lord Russell of Killowen, Lord Bridge of Harwich and Lord Brandon of Oakbrook)

Offer and acceptance - acceptance by telex

*Facts*

Following negotiations relating to steel bars to be delivered from Egypt, an English company accepted, by telex sent from London to Vienna, the terms of sale offered by an Austrian company.

*Held*

The contract had been made in Austria and it followed that the English courts did not have jurisdiction in relation to it.

Lord Wilberforce:

'... with a general rule covering instantaneous communication inter praesentes, or at a distance, with an exception applying to non-instantaneous communication at a distance, how should communications by telex be categorised? In *Entores Ltd* v *Miles Far East Corp* the Court of Appeal classified them with instantaneous communications. Their ruling ... appears not to have caused either adverse comment, or any difficulty to businessmen. I would accept it as a general rule. Where the condition of simultaneity is met, and where it appears to be within the mutual intention of the parties that contractual exchanges should take place in this way, I think it a sound rule, but not necessarily a universal rule.

Since 1955 the use of telex communication has been greatly expanded, and there are many variants on it. The senders and recipients may not be the principals to the contemplated contract. They may be servants or agents with limited authority. The message may not reach, or be intended to reach, the designated recipient immediately: messages may be sent out of office hours, or at night, with the intention, or on the assumption, that they will be read at a later time. There may be some error or default at the recipient's end which prevents receipt at the time contemplated and believed in by the sender. The message may have been sent and/or received through machines operated by third persons. And many other variations may occur. No universal rule can cover all such cases; they must be resolved by reference to the intentions of the parties, by sound business practice and in some cases by a judgment where the risks should lie ...

The present case is, as *Entores Ltd* v *Miles Far East Corp* itself, the simple case of instantaneous communication between principals, and, in accordance with the general rule, involves that the contract (if any) was made when and where the acceptance was received. This was ... in Vienna.'

*Commentary*

Approved: *Entores Ltd* v *Miles Far East Corporation* [1955] 3 WLR 48.


**Brogden v Metropolitan Rail Co** (1877) 2 App Cas 666 House of Lords (Lord Cairns LC, Lord Hatherley, Lord Selborne, Lord Blackburn and Lord Gordon)

Contract - creation by conduct

*Facts*

Brogden had for years supplied the railway company with coal without a formal agreement. Wishing to regularise the situation, the company sent a draft form of agreement to Brogden, who inserted the name of an arbitrator in a space left blank for this purpose, signed it and returned it marked 'approved'. The company's agent put it in his desk and there it lay for two years with nothing further being done to complete its execution. Both parties acted thereafter on the strength of its terms, supplying and paying for coal in accordance with the terms of the draft agreement. After two years, a dispute arose and Brogden denied that any binding contract existed.

*Held*

A contract had been created by conduct and it came into existence either when the company ordered its first load of coal upon the terms of the draft, or at least when Brogden supplied it.

## Butler Machine Tool Co Ltd v Ex-Cello-O Corporation (England) Ltd [1979] 1 WLR 401 Court of Appeal (Lord Denning MR, Lawton and Bridge LJJ)

Offer and acceptance - counter - offer - battle of forms

*Facts*

In response to the appellants' enquiry, the respondents offered to sell them a machine tool, delivery in ten months' time, and the offer was stated to be subject to certain terms and conditions which 'shall prevail over any terms and conditions in the Buyer's order'. The respondents placed an order, subject to terms and conditions which were materially different to those of the appellants. At the foot of the respondents' form of order was a tear-off acknowledgment stating 'We accept your order on the terms and conditions stated thereon': this the appellants signed and returned accompanied by a letter stating that the order was being entered in accordance with the appellants' quotation. The original offer or quotation contained a price variation clause; the respondents' terms and conditions did not.

*Held*

There was a fixed price contract as the appellants had accepted what was, in effect, the respondents' counter-offer.

Lord Denning MR:

'... the judge thought that the sellers in their original quotation got their blow in first; especially by the provision that 'These terms and conditions shall prevail over any terms and conditions in the Buyer's order'. It was so emphatic that the price variation clause continued through all the subsequent dealings and that the buyer must be taken to have agreed to it. I can understand that point of view. But I think that the documents have to be considered as a whole. And, as a matter of construction, I think the acknowlegment ... is the decisive document. It makes it clear that the contract was on the buyers' terms and not on the sellers' terms: and the buyers' terms did not include a price variation clause.'

## Byrne & Co v Leon van Tienhoven & Co (1880) 5 CPD 344 Court of Common Pleas (Lindley J)

Offer by post - revocation

*Facts*

On 1 October, the defendants in Cardiff posted a letter to the plaintiffs in New York, offering to sell them 1,000 boxes of tin plates. On 8 October, the defendants posted a letter revoking the offer. On 11 October, the plaintiffs telegraphed their acceptance. On 15 October, the plaintiffs confirmed their acceptance by letter. On 20 October, the defendants' letter of revocation reached the plaintiffs.

*Held*

There was a contract as the revocation of the offer was inoperative until it was actually received on 20 October.

Lindley J:

'... the writer of the offer has expressly or impliedly assented to treat an answer to him by a letter duly posted as a sufficient acceptance or notification to himself, or, in other words, he has made the Post Office his agent to receive the acceptance and notification of it. But this principle appears to me to be inapplicable to the case of a withdrawal of an offer ... If the defendant's contentions were to prevail, no person who had received an offer by post and had accepted it, would know his position until he had waited such a time as to be quite sure that a letter withdrawing the offer had not been posted before his acceptance of it.'

*Commentary*

Applied in *Henthorn* v *Fraser* [1892] 2 Ch 27.

**Carlill v Carbolic Smoke Ball Co** [1893] 1 QB 256 Court of Appeal (Lindley, Bowen and A L Smith LJJ)

Offer to the world - acceptance

*Facts*

The defendants issued a newspaper advertisement in which they said they would pay £100 to any person who contracted influenza after using one of their smoke balls in a specified manner for a specified period. They also stated that they had deposited £1,000 with a named bank, to show their sincerity in the matter. The plaintiff, believing the accuracy of the advertisement, purchased one of the balls and used it as directed - but she caught 'flu nevertheless! She sued to recover the £100.

*Held*

He was entitled to succeed.

Lindley LJ:

'I will pass, before I proceed further, to some of the various contentions which were raised for the purpose of disposing of them. I will afterwards return to the serious question which arises. First, it was said no action will lie upon this advertisement because it is a policy of insurance. You have, however, only got to look at it, I think, to dismiss that contention. Then it was said that this is a wager or bet. Hawkins J examined that with his usual skill, and came to the conclusion that nobody ever thought of a bet, and that there is nothing whatever in common with a bet. I so entirely agree with him that I propose to pass that over as not worth serious attention.

Having got rid of the question of a policy, and having got rid of the question of a bet, let us see what we have left. The first observation I would make upon this is that we are not dealing with any inference of fact. We are dealing with an express promise to pay £100 in certain events. There can be no mistake about that at all. Read this how you will, and twist it about as you will, here is a distinct promise, expressed in language which is perfectly unmistakeable, that £100 reward will be paid by the Carbolic Smoke Ball Co to any person who contracts influenza after having used the ball three times daily, and so on. One must look a little further and see if this is intended to be a promise at all; whether it is a mere puff - a sort of thing which means nothing. Is that the meaning of it? My answer to that question is "No" and I base my answer upon this passage: "£1,000 is deposited with the Alliance Bank, Regent Street, showing our sincerity in the matter". What is that money deposited for? What is that passage put in for, except to negative the suggestion that this is a mere puff, and means nothing at all? The deposit is called in aid by the advertisers as proof of their sincerity in the matter. What do they mean? It is to show their intention to pay the £100 in the events which they have specified. I do not know who drew the advertisement, but he has distinctly in words expressed that promise. It is as plain as words can make it.

Then it is said that it is a promise that is not binding. In the first place it is said that it is not made with anybody in particular. The offer is to anybody who performs the conditions named in the advertisement. Anybody who does perform the conditions accepts the offer. I take it that if you look at this advertisement in point of law, it is an offer to pay £100 to anybody who will perform these conditions, and the performance of these conditions is the acceptance of the offer. That rests upon a string of authorities, the earliest of which is that celebrated advertisement case of *Williams* v *Carwardine*, which has been followed by a good many other cases concerning advertisements of rewards. But then it is said: "Supposing that the performance of the conditions is an acceptance of the offer, that acceptance ought to be notified". Unquestionably as a general proposition when an offer is made, you must have it not only accepted, but the acceptance notified. But is that so in cases of this kind? I apprehend that this is rather an exception to the rule, or, if not an exception, it is open to the observation that the notification of the acceptance need not precede the performance. This offer is a continuing offer. It was never revoked, and if notice of acceptance is required (Which I doubt very much, for I rather think the true view is that which is as expressed and explained by Lord Blackburn in *Brogden* v *Metropolitan Rail Co*), the person who makes the offer receives the notice of acceptance contemporaneously with his notice of the performance of the conditions. Anyhow, if notice is wanted, he gets it before his offer is revoked, which is all you want in principle. But I doubt very much whether the true view is not, in a case of this kind, that the person who makes the offer shows by his language and from the nature of the transaction that he does not expect and does not require notice of the acceptance apart from notice of the performance.

We have, therefore, all the elements which are necessary to form a binding contract enforceable in point of law subject to two observations. First of all, it is said that this advertisement is so vague that you cannot construe it as a promise; that the vagueness of the language, to which I will allude presently, shows that a legal promise was never intended nor contemplated. No doubt the language is vague and uncertain in some respects, and particularly in that the £100 is to be paid to any person who contracts influenza after having used the ball three times daily, and so on. It is said, "When are they to be used?" According to the language of the advertisement no time is fixed, and construing the offer most strongly against the person who has made it, one might infer that any time was meant, I doubt whether that was meant, and I doubt whether that would not be pushing too far the doctrine as to construing language most strongly against the person using it. I doubt whether business people, or reasonable people would understand that if you took a smoke ball and used it three times daily for the time specified - two weeks - you were to be guaranteed against influenza for the rest of your life. I do not think the advertisement means that, to do the defendants justice. I think it would be pushing their language a little too far. But if it does not mean that, what does it mean? It is for them to show what it does mean; and it strikes me that there are two reasonable constructions to be put on this advertisement, either of which will answer the purpose of the plaintiff. Possibily there are three.

It may mean that the promise of the reward is limited to persons catching the increasing influenza, or any colds, or diseases caused by taking colds, during the prevalence of the epidemic. That is one suggestion. That does not fascinate me, I confess. I prefer the other two. Another is, that you are warranted free from catching influenza, or cold, or other diseases caused by taking cold, while you are using this preparation. If this is the meaning, then the plaintiff was actually using the preparation when she got influenza. Another meaning - and the one which I rather think I should prefer myself - is becoming diseased within a reasonable time after having used the smoke ball. Then it is asked: "What is a reasonable time?" And one of my brothers suggested that that depended upon the reasonable view of the time taken by a germ in developing? I do not feel pressed by that. It strikes me that a reasonable time may be got at in a business sense, and in a sense to the satisfaction of a lawyer in this way. Find out what the preparation is. A chemist will tell you that. Find out from a skilled physician how long such a preparation could be reasonably expected to endure so as to protect a person from an epidemic or cold. In that way you will get a standard to be laid before a court by which it might exercise its judgment as to what a reasonable time would be. And it strikes me, I confess, that the true construction of this is that £100 will be paid to anybody who uses this smoke ball three times daily, for two weeks according to the printed directions, and who gets influenza, or a cold, or some other disease caused by taking cold, within a reasonable time after so using it. I think that that is the fair and proper business construction of it. If that is the true construction, it is enough for the plaintiff. Therefore, I say no more about the vagueness of the document.

I come now to the last point, which I think requires attention, ie, the question of the consideration. Counsel for the defendants has argued with great skill that this is a nudum pactum - that there is no consideration. We must apply to that argument the usual legal tests. Let us see whether there is no advantage to the defendants. Counsel says it is no advantage to them how much the ball is used. What is an advantage to them and what benefits them is the sale, and he has put the ingenious case that a lot of these balls might be stolen, and that it would be no advantage to them if the thief or other people used them. The answer to that I think is this. It is quite obvious that, in the view of the defendants, the advertisers, a use of the smoke balls by the public, if they can get the public to have confidence enough to use them, will react and produce a sale which is directly beneficial to them, the defendants. Therefore, it appears to me that out of this transaction emerges an advantage to them which is enough to constitute a consideration. But there is another view of it. What about the person who acts upon this and accepts the offer? Does not that person put himself to some inconvenience at the request of the defendants? Is it nothing to use this ball three times daily at the request of the defendants for two weeks according to the directions? Is that to go for nothing? It appears to me that that is a distinct inconvenience, if not a detriment, to any person who uses the smoke ball. When, therefore, you come to analyse this argument of want of consideration, it appears to me that there is ample consideration for the promise ...

It appears to me, therefore, that these defendants must perform their promise, and if they have been so unguarded and so unwary as to expose themselves to a great many actions, so much the worse for them. For once in a way the advertiser has reckoned too much on the gullibility of the public. It appears to me that it would be very little short of a scandal if we said that no action would lie on such a promise as this, acted upon as it has been.'

*Commentary*

Applied in *New Zealand Shipping Co Ltd* v *A M Satterthwaite & Co Ltd* [1974] 2 WLR 865.

**Chapelton v Barry Urban District Council** [1940] 1 KB 532 Court of Appeal (Slesser, MacKinnon and Goddard LJJ)

Hire of deck chair - conditions

*Facts*

Beside deck chairs stacked on a beach was a notice: 'Barry Urban District Council ... Hire of chairs, 2d per session of 3 hours ...' The plaintiff took two of the chairs and he received from the attendant two tickets which he put in his pocket without reading the statement printed on the back that 'The Council will not be liable for any accident or damage arising from hire of chair'. The canvas of the plaintiff's chair gave way and he suffered injury.

*Held*

He was entitled to damages.

MacKinnon LJ:

'If a man does an act which constitutes the making of a contract, such as taking a railway ticket, or depositing his bag in a cloakroom, he will be bound by the terms of the documents handed to him by the servant of the carriers or bailees, as the case may be. If, however, he merely pays money for something, and receives a receipt for it, or does something which may clearly only amount to that, he cannot be deemed to have entered into a contract in the terms of the words which his creditor has chosen to print on the back of the receipt, unless, of course, the creditor has taken reasonable steps to bring the terms of the proposed contract to the mind of the man. In this case there is no evidence at all upon which the county court judge could find that the defendants had taken any steps at all to bring the terms of their proposed contract to the mind of the plaintiff. In those circumstances, I am satisfied that the defendants could not rely upon the words on the back of the ticket issued to the plaintiff, and, having admittedly been negligent in regard to the condition of the chair, they had no defence to the plaintiff's cause of action.'

**Daulia Ltd v Four Millbank Nominees Ltd** [1978] 2 WLR 621 Court of Appeal (Buckley, Orr and Goff LJJ)

Oral offer to enter into written contract

*Facts*

The defendants wanted to sell certain properties and the plaintiffs were anxious to buy them. On 21 December the parties agreed terms and further agreed to exchange contracts the next day. When the plaintiffs attended the defendants' offices on 22 December to exchange the contracts, the defendants, who had in the meantime found another purchaser willing to pay a higher price, refused to complete the sale. The plaintiffs sued for breach of contract alleging that on 21 December, an agent of the defendants had promised them that if they attended at the defendants' offices the next morning and gave the defendants a signed and engrossed copy of the contract, together with a banker's draft for the deposit, the defendants would enter into a written contract with them for the sale of the properties.

*Held*

Assuming the facts to be as alleged, since the contract was for disposition of an interest in land and it was not in writing, it fell foul of s40(1) Law of Property Act 1925 and, accordingly, the plaintiffs' claim for damages for breach of contract would be struck out.

Goff LJ:

'Whilst I think the true view of a unilateral contract must, in general, be that the offeror is entitled to require full performance of the condition which he has imposed and, short of that, he is not bound; that must be subject to one important qualification, which stems from the fact that there must be an implied obligation on the part of the offeror not to prevent the condition becoming satisfied, which obligation, it seems to me, must arise as soon as the offeree starts to perform. Until then, the offeror can revoke the whole thing, but once the offeree has embarked on performance, it is too late for the offeror to revoke his offer.'

Buckley LJ:

'The defendants' offer to exchange contracts must have been subject to an implied obligation that the defendants would not render the performance by the plaintiffs of the acts necessary for acceptance impossible and I agree with Goff LJ that the defendants could not withdraw their offer once the plaintiffs had embarked on those acts.'

*Commentary*

For s40(1) of the Law of Property Act 1925, see now s2 of the Law of Property (Miscellaneous Provisions) Act 1989.

**Dickinson v Dodds** (1876) 2 Ch D 463 Court of Appeal (James, Mellish and Baggallay LJJ)

Offer - withdrawal

*Facts*

On 10 June, the defendant delivered to the plaintiff a written offer to sell a certain house 'to be left open until Friday 12 June, 9.00 am'. On Thursday 11 June, the defendant sold the house to a third party, Allan. That evening, the plaintiff was told of the sale by a fourth man. Before 9.00 am on 12 June, the plaintiff handed to the defendant a formal letter of acceptance.

*Held*

The defendant had validly withdrawn his offer and the plaintiff's purported acceptance was too late.

James LJ:

'It appears to me that there is neither principle nor authority for the proposition that there must be an express and actual withdrawal of the offer, or what is called a retraction. It must, to constitute a contract, appear that the two minds were at one, at the same moment of time, that is, that there was an offer continuing up to the time of the acceptance. If there was not such a continuing offer, then the acceptance comes to nothing. Of course it may well be that the one man is bound in some way or other to let the other man know that his mind with regard to the offer has been changed; but in this case, beyond all question, the plaintiff knew that Dodds was no longer minded to sell the property to him as plainly and clearly as if Dodds had told him in so many words, "I withdraw the offer." This is evident from the plaintiff's own statements in the bill ... It is to my mind quite clear that before there was any attempt at acceptance by the plaintiff, he was perfectly well aware that Dodds had changed his mind, and that he had in fact agreed to sell the property to Allan. It is impossible, therefore, to say there was ever that existence of the same mind between the two parties which is essential in point of law to the making of an agreement. I am of opinion, therefore, that the plaintiff has failed to prove that there was any binding contract between Dodds and himself.'

**Entores Ltd v Miles Far East Corporation** [1955] 3 WLR 48 Court of Appeal (Denning, Birkett and Parker LJJ)

Contract - place of acceptance

*Facts*

An English company in London was in communication with a Dutch company in Amsterdam by telex. The English company received an offer of goods from the Dutch company and made a counter offer which the Dutch company accepted - all by telex. For purposes of jurisdiction, where was the contract made?

*Held*

In London, where the English company received the acceptance.

Birkett LJ:

'I am of opinion that in the case of telex communications (which do not differ in principle from the cases where the parties negotiating a contract are actually in the presence of each other) there can be no binding contract until the offeror receives notice of the acceptance from the offeree. Counsel for the defendants submitted that the proper principle to be applied to a case like the present could be thus stated: "If A makes an offer to B, there is a concluded contract when B has done all that he can do to communicate his acceptance by approved methods." He further submitted that great difficulties would arise if telex communications were treated differently from acceptances by post or telegram.

In my opinion the cases governing the making of contracts by letters passing through the post have no application to the making of contracts by telex communications. The ordinary rule of law, to which the special considerations governing contracts by post are exceptions, is that the acceptance of an offer must be communicated to the offeror and the place where the contract is made is the place where the offeror receives the notification of the acceptance by the offeree. If a telex instrument in Amsterdam is used to send London the notification of the acceptance of an offer, the contract is complete when the telex instrument in London receives the notification of the acceptance (usually at the same moment that the message is being printed in Amsterdam) and the acceptance is then notified to the offeror, and the contract is made in London.'

*Commentary*

Approved in *Brinkibon Ltd* v *Stahag Stahl und Stahlwarenhandelsgesellschaft mbH* [1982] 2 WLR 264.

**Errington v Errington and Woods** [1952] 1 KB 290 Court of Appeal (Somervell, Denning and Hodson LJJ)

Offer - implied revocation

*Facts*

A father bought a house for his son and daughter-in-law to live in. The father put down £250 and borrowed £250 from a building society on the security of the house, repayable at 15s per week. He took the house in his own name and was responsible for the repayments. However, he told his daughter-in-law that the £250 was a present to them but left the couple to make the repayments. He told them that the house would be theirs when the mortgage was repaid and that he would transfer the house into their names. They duly paid the instalments, although they never contractually bound themselves to do so.

*Held*

In these circumstances, so long as the couple went on paying the instalments, the father's promise was irrevocable.

Denning LJ:

'The father's promise was a unilateral contract - a promise of the house in return for their act of paying the instalments. It could not be revoked by him once the couple entered on performance of the act, but it would cease to bind him if they left it incomplete and unperformed ...'

*Commentary*

Applied in *Binions* v *Evans* [1972] 2 WLR 729.

**Felthouse v Bindley** (1862) 11 CB (NS) 869 Court of Common Pleas (Willes, Byles and Keating JJ); affd (1863) 1 New Rep 401

Offer - 'If I hear no more ... '

*Facts*

The plaintiff offered to buy his nephew's horse by a letter, in which he said: 'If I hear no more about him, I shall consider the horse mine.' The nephew made no reply to the letter but told the defendant, an auctioneer, that he 'intended to reserve' the horse for his uncle. The defendant inadvertently sold the horse to a third party and the plaintiff sued him.

*Held*

Since there had been no acceptance of the plaintiff's offer, the plaintiff had no title to sue and the action must fail.

**Fisher v Bell** [1961] 1 QB 394 High Court (Lord Parker CJ, Ashworth and Elvers JJ)

Flick knife offered for sale?

*Facts*

A flick knife was displayed in a shop window and behind it was a ticket reading 'Ejector knife - 4s'. At that time it was an offence to, inter alia, offer for sale such a knife and the shopkeeper was acquitted of this offence. The prosecutor appealed.

*Held*

The appeal would be dismissed.

Lord Parker CJ:

'It is clear that, according to the ordinary law of contract, the display of an article with a price on it in a shop window is merely an invitation to treat. It is in no sense an offer for sale the acceptance of which constitutes a contract. That is clearly the general law of the country.'

*Commentary*

Applied in *Partridge* v *Crittenden* [1968] 1 WLR 1204

**Gibbons v Proctor** (1891) 64 LT 594 High Court (Day and Lawrence JJ)

Offer and acceptance - reward

*Facts*

The defendant ordered bandbills announcing a reward for anyone giving information to the superintendent of police leading to the arrest of a certain criminal. Before this order was placed, the plaintiff policeman gave this information to a fellow constable, but it reached the superintendent after the handbills had been printed and distributed.

*Held*

The plaintiff was entitled to the reward as the condition (communication to the superintendent) had been fulfilled after publication of the handbills: the handbills contained the defendant's offer of the reward.

**Harris v Nickerson** (1873) LR 8 QB 286 Queen's Bench (Blackburn, Quain and Archibald JJ)

Advertisement of sale a contract?

*Facts*

The defendant auctioneer advertised for sale by auction, inter alia, office furniture. The plaintiff travelled to the sale, intending to bid for the office furniture, but these lots were withdrawn from the sale. He sued to recover for two days' loss of time.

*Held*

His action could not succeed.

Quain J:

'To uphold the judge's decision [that the defendant was liable] it is necessary to go to the extent of saying that when an auctioneer issues an advertisement of the sale of goods, if he withdraws any part of them without notice, the persons attending may all maintain actions against him. In the present case, it is to be observed that the plaintiff bought some other lots; but it is said he had a commission to buy the furniture, either the whole or in part, and that therefore he has a right of action against the defendant. Such a proposition seems to be destitute of all authority; and it would be introducing an extremely inconvenient rule of law to say that an auctioneer is bound to give notice of withdrawal or to be held liable to everybody attending the sale. The case is certainly of the first impression. When a sale is advertised as without reserve, and a lot is put up and bid for, there is ground for saying, as was said in *Warlow* v *Harrison* (1859) 1 E & E 309, that a contract is entered into between the auctioneer and the highest bona fide bidder; but that has no application to the present case; here the lots were never put up and no offer was made by the plaintiff nor promise made by the defendant, except by his advertisement that certain goods would be sold. It is impossible to say that that is a contract with everybody attending the sale, and that the auctioneer is to be liable for their expenses if any single article is withdrawn. *Spencer* v *Hading* (1870) LR 5 CP 561 which was cited by the plaintiff's counsel, as far as it goes, is a direct authority against his proposition.'

### Hartog v Colin & Shields

See chapter 8 - Mistake.

### Harvela Investments Ltd v Royal Trust Co of Canada (CI) Ltd [1985] 3 WLR 276 House of Lords (Lord Fraser of Tullybelton, Lord Diplock, Lord Edmund Davies, Lord Bridge of Harwich and Lord Templeman)

Sale of shares - sealed bids

*Facts*

The vendors (the first defendants) invited the plaintiffs and the second defendants to submit, by sealed offer or confidential telex, a single offer for a parcel of shares by a stipulated date. The vendors bound themselves to accept the higher of the two bids and reserved no right to choose between unequal bids. The plaintiffs submitted a bid of C$2,175,000: the second defendants submitted a bid of 'C$2,100,000 or C$101,000 in excess of any other offer, whichever is the higher'. The vendors accepted the second defendants' bid as being a bid of C$2,276,000 and entered into a contract for the sale of the shares.

*Held*

The second defendants' referential bid was invalid as such bids are inconsistent with a sale by fixed bidding.

Lord Templeman:

'To constitute a fixed bidding sale all that was necessary was that the vendors should invite confidential offers and should undertake to accept the highest offer. Such was the form of the invitation. It follows that the invitation on its true construction created a fixed bidding sale and that [the second defendants were] not entitled to submit and the vendors were not entitled to accept a referential bid ... The task of the court is to construe the invitation and to ascertain whether the provisions of the invitation, read as a whole, create a fixed bidding sale or an auction sale. I am content to reach a conclusion which reeks of simplicity, which does not require a draftsman to indulge in prohibitions, but which obliges a vendor to specify and control any form of auction which he seeks to combine with confidential bidding. The invitation required [the second defendants] to name [their] price and required Harvela to name its price and bound the vendors to accept the higher price. The invitation was not difficult to understand and the result was bound to be certain and to accord with the presumed intentions of the vendors discernible from the express provisions of the invitation. Harvela named the price of $2,175,000; [the second defendants] failed to name any price except $2,100,000, which was less than the price named by Harvela. The vendors were bound to accept Harvela's offer.'

### Henthorn v Fraser [1892] 2 Ch 27 Court of Appeal (Lord Herschell, Lindley and Kay LJJ)

Offer - acceptance by post

*Facts*

The plaintiff, who lived in Birkenhead, was handed a note at the defendant's office in Liverpool, giving him an option to purchase certain property within fourteen days. The next day, the defendant posted a letter withdrawing the offer, which did not reach Birkenhead until 5.00 pm. Meanwhile, the plaintiff had posted a letter at 3.50 pm accepting the offer. That letter was delivered after the defendant's office was closed and was opened the following morning.

*Held*

A valid contract had been concluded at 3.50 pm.

**Lord Herschell:**

'Where the circumstances are such that it must have been within the contemplation of the parties that according to the ordinary usages of mankind, the post might be used as a means of communicating the acceptance of an offer, the acceptance is complete as soon as it is posted.'

*Commentary*

Applied: *Byrne & Co v Leon van Tienhoven & Co* (1880) 5 CPD 344 and *Stevenson v McClean* (1880) 5 QBD 346. Distinguished in *Holwell Securities Ltd v Hughes* [1974] 1 WLR 155.

**Holwell Securities Ltd v Hughes** [1974] 1 WLR 155 Court of Appeal (Russell, Buckley and Lawton LJJ)

Offer and aceptance - mode of acceptance prescribed

*Facts*

The plaintiffs were granted an option to purchase the defendant's freehold property and the agreement provided that the option was exercisable 'by notice in writing to the [defendant] at any time within six months from the date hereof ...' Within that time, the plaintiffs' solicitors wrote to the defendant giving notice of the exercise of the option. The letter was posted, properly addressed and prepaid, but it was never delivered.

*Held*

The option had not been validly exercised.

**Lawton LJ:**

'Now in this case, the "notice in writing" was to be one "to the Intending Vendor". It was to be an intimation to him that the grantee had exercised the option: he was the one who was to be fixed with the information contained in the writing. He never was, because the letter carrying the information went astray. The plaintiffs were unable to do what the agreement said they were to do, namely, fix the defendant with knowledge that they had decided to buy his property. If this construction of the option clause is correct, there is no room for the application of any rule of law relating to the acceptance of offers by posting letters since the option agreement stipulated what had to be done to exercise the option. On this ground alone I would dismiss the appeal.'

*Commentary*

Distinguished: *Henthorn v Fraser* [1892] 2 Ch 27 and *Bruner v Moore* [1904] 1 Ch 305.

**Household Fire Insurance Co v Grant** (1879) 4 Ex D 216 Court of Appeal (Thesiger, Baggallay and Bramwell LJJ)

Acceptance lost in post

*Facts*

The defendants applied for shares in a company, paid a deposit of 1/20th of their value and undertook to pay the rest within one year of the date of allotment. The letter of allotment was posted, but it never arrived. The company went into liquidation and the plaintiff liquidator sued for the balance due on the shares.

*Held* (Bramwell LJ dissenting)

He was entitled to succeed.

Thesiger LJ:

'There is no doubt that the implication of a complete, final, and absolutely binding contract being formed, as soon as the acceptance of an offer is posted, may in some cases lead to inconvenience and hardship. But such there must be at times in every view of the law. It is impossible in transactions which pass between parties at a distance, and have to be carried on through the medium of correspondence, to adjust conflicting rights between innocent parties, so as to make the consequences of mistake on the part of a mutual agent fall equally upon the shoulders of both. At the same time I am not prepared to admit that the implication in question will lead to any great or general inconvenience or hardship. An offerer, if he chooses, may always make the formation of the contract which he proposes dependent upon the actual communication to himself of the acceptance. If he trusts to the post he trusts to a means of communication which, as a rule, does not fail, and if no answer to his offer is received by him, and the matter is of importance to him, he can make inquiries of the person to whom his offer was addressed. On the other hand, if the contract is not finally concluded, except in the event of the acceptance actually reaching the offerer, the door would be opened to the perpetration of much fraud, and putting aside this consideration, considerable delay in commercial transactions, in which dispatch is, as a rule, of the greatest consequence, would be occasioned; for the acceptor would never be entirely safe in acting upon his acceptance until he had received notice that his letter of acceptance had reached its destination.

Upon balance of conveniences and inconveniences it seems to me ... more consistent with the acts and declarations of the parties in this case to consider the contract complete and absolutely binding on the transmission of the notice of allotment through the post, as the medium of communication that the parties themselves contemplated, instead of postponing its completion until the notice had been received by the defendant.'

## Hyde v Wrench (1840) 3 Beav 334 Rolls Court (Lord Langdale MR)

Offer - counter offer

*Facts*

On 6 June, the defendant offered to sell an estate to the plaintiff for £1,000. On 8 June, in reply, the plaintiff made an offer of £950 which was refused by the defendant on 17 June. Finally, on 29 June, the plaintiff wrote purporting to accept the original offer of £1,000.

*Held*

No contract existed. The counter offer of £950 destroyed the original offer of £1,000 which the plaintiff was incompetent to revive subsequently.

## McManus v Fortescue [1907] 2 KB 1 Court of Appeal (Sir Richard Henn Collins MR, Cozens-Hardy and Fletcher Moulton LJJ)

Auction sales subject to reserve

*Facts*

A corrugated iron building was put up for sale by auction with a reserve price of £200: the defendant auctioneer knocked it down to the plaintiff for £85.

*Held*

There was no binding contract of sale.

Sir Richard Henn Collins MR:

'The auction was subject to certain conditions of sale, and the material condition which we have to consider is condition (2), which says that each lot will be offered subject to a reserve price, and the vendors reserve the right of bidding up to such reserve price. It seems to me that at the root of the matter there lies this, that every bid at this auction was a conditional offer, subject to its being up to the reserve price. The fall of the hammer on such a bid was an acceptance by the auctioneer on behalf of the vendor of that offer. That conditional offer was not turned by such acceptance into an unconditional offer. The offer was conditional on the bid being up to the reserve price, and the acceptance by the auctioneer was therefore also conditional on the bid being up to the reserve price. There was or was not a contract of sale according to whether or not the bid had reached the reserve price.'

**New Zealand Shipping Co Ltd v A M Satterthwaite and Co Ltd** [1974] 2 WLR 865 Privy Council (Lord Wilberforce, Lord Hodson, Viscount Dilhorne, Lord Simon of Glaisdale and Lord Salmon)

Contract of carriage - exclusion clause

*Facts*

The consignor loaded goods on a ship for carriage to the plaintiff consignee in New Zealand. The carriage was subject to a bill of lading containing the following:

'it is hereby expressly agreed that no servant or agent of the carrier (including every independent contractor from time to time employed by the carrier) shall in any circumstances whatsoever be under any liability whatsoever to the shipper, consignee or owner of the goods or to any holder of the bill of lading for any loss or damage or delay of whatsoever kind arising or resulting directly or indirectly from any neglect or default on his part while acting in the course of or in connection with his employment and, without prejudice to the generality of the foregoing provisions in this clause, every exemption, limitation, condition and liberty herein contained and every right, exemption from liability, defence and immunity of whatsoever nature applicable to the carrier as to which the carrier is entitled hereunder shall also be available and shall extend to protect every such servant or agent of the carrier acting as aforesaid and for the purpose of all the foregoing provisions of this clause, the carrier is, or shall be, deemed to be acting as agent or trustee on behalf of and for the benefit of all persons who are or might be his servants or agents from time to time (including independent contractors as aforesaid) and all such persons shall to this extent be or deemed to be parties to the contract in or evidenced by this bill of lading.'

The cargo was damaged as a result of the negligence of the defendant stevedores, who had been employed by the carriers to unload the cargo. The plaintiffs, the holder of the bill of lading, sued for damage by negligence. The defendant pleaded the clause contained in the bill of lading.

*Held* (Viscount Dilhorne and Lord Simon of Glaisdale dissenting)

The defendant could rely on the clause and, accordingly, the action was dismissed.

Wilberforce LJ:

'The question in the appeal is whether the stevedore can take the benefit of the time limitation provision. The starting point in discussion on this question is provided by the House of Lords' decision in *Scruttons Ltd v Midland Silicones Ltd*. There is no need to question or even to qualify that case insofar as it affirms the general proposition that a contract between two parties cannot be sued on by a third party, even though the contract is expressed to be for his benefit. Nor is it necessary to disagree with anything which was said to the same effect in the Australian case of *Wilson v Darling Island Stevedoring & Lighterage Co Ltd*. Each of these cases was dealing with a simple case of a contract, the benefit of which was sought to be taken by a third person not a party to it and the emphatic pronouncements in the speeches and judgements were directed to this situation. But *Midland Silicones* left open the case where one of the parties contracts as agent for the third person; in particular, Lord Reid's speech spelt out, in four propositions, the prerequisites for the validity of such an agency contract. There is, of course, nothing unique to this case in the conception of agency contracts: well known and common instances exist in the field of hire purchase, of bankers' commercial credits and other transactions. Lord Reid said this:

"I can see a possibility of success of the agency argument if (first) the bill of lading makes it clear that the stevedore is intended to be protected by the provisions in it which limit liability, (secondly) the bill of lading makes it clear that the carrier, in addition to contracting for these provisions on his own behalf, is also contracting as agent for the stevedore that these provisions should apply to the stevedore, (thirdly) the carrier has authority from the stevedore to do that, or perhaps later ratification by the stevedore would suffice and (fourthly) that any difficulties about consideration moving from the stevedore were overcome. And then to affect the consignee, it would be necessary to show that the provisions of the Bills of Lading Act 1855 apply."

The question in this appeal is whether the contract satisfies these propositions. Clause I of the bill of lading, whatever the defects in its drafting, is clear in its relevant terms. The carrier, on his own account, stipulates for certain exemptions and immunities: among these is that conferred by article III(6) of the Hague Rules, which discharge the carrier from all liability for loss or damage unless suit is brought within one year after delivery.

In addition to these stipulations on his own account, the carrier, as agent for (inter alios) independent contractors, stipulates for the same exemptions.

Much was made of the fact that the carrier also contracts as agent for numerous other persons; the relevance of this argument is not apparent. It cannot be disputed that among such independent contractors, for whom, as agent, the carrier contracted, is the appellant company, which habitually acts as stevedore in New Zealand by arrangement with the carrier and which is, moreover, the parent company of the carrier. The carrier was, indisputably, authorised by the stevedore to contract as its agent for the purpose of clause I. All of this is quite straightforward and was accepted by all of the learned judges in New Zealand. The only question was, and is, the fourth question presented by Lord Reid, namely that of consideration.

It was on this point that the Court of Appeal differed from Beattie J, holding that it had not been shown that any consideration for the shipper's promise as to exemption moved from the promisee, ie the stevedore.

If the choice, and the antithesis, is between a gratuitous promise and a promise for consideration, as it must be in the absence of a tertium quid, there can be little doubt which, in commercial reality, this is. The whole contract is of a commercial character, involving service on one side, rates of payment on the other and qualifying stipulations as to both. The relations of all parties to each other are commercial relations, entered into for business reasons of ultimate profit. To describe one set of promises, in this context, as gratuitous or nudum pactum, seems paradoxical and is prima facie implausible. It is only the precise analysis of this complex of relations into the classic offer and acceptance with identifiable consideration, that seems to present difficulty, but this same difficulty exists in many situations of daily life, eg sales at auction; supermarket purchases; boarding an omnibus; purchasing a train ticket; tenders for the supply of goods; offers of reward; acceptance by post; warranties of authority by agents; manufacturers' guarantees; gratuitous bailments; bankers' commercial credits. These are all examples which show that English law, having committed itself to a rather technical and schematic doctrine of contract in application, takes a practical approach, often at the cost of forcing the facts to fit uneasily into the market slots of offer, acceptance and consideration.

In their Lordships' opinion, the present contract presents much less difficulty than many of those above referred to. It is one of carriage from Liverpool to Wellington. The carrier assumes an obligation to transport the goods and to discharge at the port of arrival. The goods are to be carried and discharged, so the transaction is inherently contractual. It is contemplated that a part of this contract, viz discharge, may be performed by independent contractors - viz the stevedore. By clause 1 of the bill of lading, the shipper agrees to exempt from liability, the carrier, his servants and independent contractors in respect of the performance of his contract of carriage. Thus, if the carriage, including the discharge, is wholly carried out by the carrier, he is exempt. If part is carried out by him and part by his servants, he and they are exempt. If part is carried out by him and part by an independent contractor, he and the independent contractor are exempt. The exemption is designed to cover the whole carriage, from loading to discharge, by whomsoever it is performed: the performance attracts the exemption or immunity in favour of whoever the performer turns out to be. There is possibly more than one way of analysing this business transaction into the necessary components; that which their Lordships would accept is to say that the bill of lading brought into existence a bargain initially unilateral, but capable of becoming mutual, between the shippers and the stevedore, made through the carrier as agent. This became a full contract when the stevedore performed services by discharging the goods. The performance of these services for the benefit of the shipper was the consideration for the agreement by the shipper that the stevedore should have the benefit of the exemptions and limitations contained in the bill of lading. The conception of a 'unilateral' contract of this kind was recognised in *Great Northern Railway Co* v *Witham* and is well established. This way of regarding the matter is very close to, if not identical to, that accepted by Beattie J in the Supreme Court; he analysed the transaction as one of an offer open to acceptance by action such as was found in *Carlill* v *Carbolic Smoke Ball Co*. But whether one describes the shippers' promise to exempt as an offer to be accepted by performance or as a promise in exchange for an act, seems, in the present context, to be a matter of semantics. The words of Bowen LJ in *Carlill* v *Carbolic Smoke Ball Co* ' ... why should not an offer be made to all the world which is to ripen into a contract with anybody who comes forward and performs the condition?' seems to bridge both conceptions: he certainly seems to draw no distinction between an offer which matures into a contract when accepted and a promise which matures into a contract after performance and, though in some special contexts (such as in connection with the right to withdraw) some further refinement might be needed, either analysis may be equally valid. On the main point in the appeal, their Lordships are in substantial agreement with Beattie J.

The following other points require mention

1    In their Lordships' opinion, consideration may quite well be provided by the stevedore, as suggested, even though (or if) it is already under an obligation to discharge to the carrier. (There is no direct evidence of the existence or nature of this obligation, but their Lordships are prepared to assume it). An agreement to do an act which the promisor is under an existing obligation to a third party to do, may quite well amount to valid consideration and does so in the present case; the promisee obtains the benefit of a direct obligation which he can enforce. This proposition is illustrated and supported by *Scotson* v *Pegg* which their Lordships consider to be good law.

2    The consignee is entitled to the benefit of, and is bound by, the stipulations in the bill of lading by his acceptance of it and request for delivery of the goods thereunder. This is shown by *Brandt* v *Liverpool, Brazil and River Plate Steam Navigation Co Ltd* and a line of earlier cases. The Bills of Lading Act 1855, section 1 (in New Zealand, the Mercantile Law Act 1908, section 13) gives partial statutory recognition to this clause, but where the statute does not apply, as it may well not do in this case, the previously established law remains effective.

3    The stevedore submitted, in the alternative, an argument that, quite apart from contract, exemptions from, or limitations of, liability in tort may be conferred by mere consent on the part of the party who may be injured. As their Lordships consider that the stevedore ought to succeed in contract, they prefer to express no opinion on this argument: to evaluate it requires elaborate discussion.

4    A clause very similar to the present was given effect by a United States District Court in *Carle and Montanari Inc* v *American Export Isbrandtsen Lines Inc*. The carrier in that case contracted, in an exemption clause, as agent for, inter alios, all stevedores and other independent contractors and although it is no doubt true that the law in the United States is more liberal than ours as regards third party contracts, their Lordships see no reason why the law of the Commonwealth should be more

restrictive and technical as regards agency contracts. Commercial consideration should have the same force on both sides of the Pacific.

In the opinion of their Lordships, to give the stevedore the benefit of the exemptions and limitations contained in the bill of lading, is to give effect to the clear intentions of a commercial document and can be given within existing principles. They see no reason to strain the law or the facts in order to defeat these intentions. It should not be overlooked that the effect of denying validity to the clause would be to encourage actions against servants, agents and independent contractors in order to get round exemptions (which are almost invariable and often compulsory) accepted by shippers against carriers, the existence and presumed efficacy, of which is reflected in the rates of freight. They see no attraction in this consequence.'

*Commentary*

Applied: *Great Northern Railway Co v Witham* (1873) LR 9 CP 16, *Carlill v Carbolic Smoke Ball Co* [1893] 1 QB 256 and *Scotson v Pegg* (1861) 6 H & N 295.

**Partridge v Crittenden** [1968] 1 WLR 1204 High Court (Lord Parker CJ, Ashworth and Blain JJ)

Brambling offered for sale?

*Facts*

It was an offence to offer for sale certain wild birds, including bramblings. Under the heading 'Classified Advertisements' in the periodical Cage and Aviary Birds, the appellant had advertised 'Quality Bramblefinch cocks, Bramblefinch hens, 25s each'.

*Held*

His conviction of this offence would be quashed.

Lord Parker CJ:

'I agree [that the conviction should be quashed] and with less reluctance than in *Fisher v Bell* [1961] 1 QB 394 ... I say "with less reluctance" because I think that when one is dealing with advertisements and circulars, unless they indeed come from manufacturers, there is business sense in their being construed as invitations to treat and not offers for sale. In a very different context Lord Herschell in *Grainger & Son v Gough (Surveyor of Taxes)* [1896] AC 325, said this in dealing with a price list:

"The transmission of such a price list does not amount to an offer to supply an unlimited quantity of the wine described at the price named, so that as soon as an order is given there is a binding contract to supply that quantity. If it were so, the merchant might find himself involved in any number of contractual obligations to supply wine of a particular description which he would be quite unable to carry out, his stock of wine of that description being necessarily limited."

It seems to me accordingly that not only is that the law, but common sense supports it.'

**Payne v Cave** (1789) 3 Term Rep 148 Court of King's Bench (Lord Kenyon CJ, Ashhurst, Buller and Grose JJ)

Auction sale - when contract concluded

*Facts*

Goods were put up for sale by auction and the defendant was the last bidder. Before the goods were knocked down to him, the defendant purported to withdraw his bid.

*Held*

He was entitled to do so. 'Every bidding is nothing more than an offer on one side which is not binding on either side till it is assented to. But according to what is now contended for [by the plaintiff], one party would be bound by the offer and the other not, which can never be allowed.'

*Commentary*

See now s57(2) of the Sale of Goods Act 1979

## Pharmaceutical Society of Great Britain v Boots Cash Chemists (Southern) Ltd
[1953] 1 QB 401 Court of Appeal (Somervell, Birkett and Romer LJJ)

Supermarket - when contract of sale concluded

*Facts*

Statute required that sales of certain poisons should be supervised by a registered pharmacist. A customer took one such poison off the shelf of a 'self-service' shop or supermarket and the transaction was supervised by a pharmacist at the cash desk.

*Held*

No offence had been committed because there had been no sale until the customer's money had been taken at the cash desk.

Somervell LJ:

'I agree entirely ... that in the case of the ordinary shop, although goods are displayed and it is intended that customers should go and choose what they want, the contract is not completed until the customer has indicated the article which he needs and the shopkeeper or someone on his behalf accepts that offer. Not till then is the contract completed, and, that being the normal position, I can see no reason for drawing any different inference from the arrangements which were made in the present case ...

I can see no reason for implying from this arrangement any position other than that ... it is a convenient method of enabling customers to see what there is for sale, to choose and, possibly, to put back and substitute, articles which they wish to have, and then go to the cashier and offer to buy what they have chosen. On that conclusion the case fails, because it is admitted that in those circumstances there was supervision in the sense required by the Act and at the appropriate moment of time.'

## Powell v Lee (1908) 99 LT 284 High Court (Channell and Sutton JJ)

Acceptance - communication

*Facts*

The defendants were the managers of a school. They had decided, by a narrow majority, to appoint the plaintiff headmaster. One of the majority, without authorisation, told the plaintiff that he had been selected as headmaster. Subsequently however, the managers of the school reversed their decision and appointed a third party. The plaintiff sued for breach of contract.

*Held*

His action would fail. For there to be a concluded contract, it was essential that there should be a communication made by the body of the persons (ie the managers) to the selected candidate.

Channell J:

> '... the managers ... did not authorise a communication to Mr Powell to the effect that he had been elected. To my mind, that implies that they reserved the power to consider the matter ... There must be notice of acceptance from the contracting party in some way and the mere fact that the managers did not authorise such a communication, which is the usual course adopted, implies that they meant to reserve the power to reconsider the decision at which they had arrived.'

**R v Clarke** (1927) 40 CLR 227 High Court of Australia (Isaacs ACJ, Higgins and Starke JJ)

Offer - information given for other reasons

*Facts*

A reward had been offered for information leading to the arrest and conviction of the murderer of two police officers. Clarke, who knew of the offer and was himself suspected of the crime, gave such information. He admitted that he had done so only to clear himself of the charge and at the time he gave the information, all thought of the reward had passed out of his mind.

*Held*

He was not entitled to the reward.

Higgins J:

> 'Clarke had seen the offer, indeed; but it was not present to his mind - he had forgotten it, and gave no consideration to it, in his intense excitement as to his own danger. There cannot be assent without knowledge of the offer; and ignorance of the offer is the same thing, whether it is due to never hearing of it or to forgetting it after hearing it.'

Isaacs ACJ:

> 'Instances easily suggest themselves where precisely the same act done with reference to an offer would be performance of the condition, but done with reference to a totally distinct object would not be such a performance. An offer of £100 to any person who should swim a hundred yards in the harbour on the first day of the year, would be met by voluntarily performing the feat with reference to the offer, but would not in my opinion be satisfied by a person who was accidentally or maliciously thrown overboard on that date and swam the distance simply to save his life, without any thought of the offer. The offeror might or might not feel morally impelled to give the sum in such a case, but would be under no contractual obligation to do so.'

**Routledge v Grant** (1828) 4 Bing 653

Revocation of offer

Best CJ:

> 'Here is a proposal [or offer] by the defendant to take property on certain terms; namely, that he should be let into possession in July. In that proposal he gives the plaintiff six weeks to consider; but if six weeks are given on one side to accept an offer, the other has six weeks to put an end to it. One party cannot be bound without the other. This was expressly decided in *Cooke* v *Oxley* (1790) 3 Term Rep 653 ... As the defendant repudiated the contract ... before the expiration of the six weeks, he had a right to say that the plaintiff should not enforce it afterwards.'

**Stevenson v McLean** (1880) 5 QBD 346 High Court (Lush J)

Offer - request for further information

*Facts*

The plaintiffs and the defendant had been negotiating about the sale of a quantity of iron belonging to the defendant. On Saturday, the defendant informed the plaintiff that he would sell 'for 40s net cash, open till Monday'. On Monday, the plaintiffs telegraphed, asking the defendant to telegraph back 'whether you would accept 40s for delivery over two months, or if not, longest limit you would give'. The defendant received the telegram and sold the iron to a third party. At 1.25 pm the defendant telegraphed that he had sold the iron. At 1.34 pm the plaintiffs, having received no reply to their telegram, telegraphed again accepting the offer. At 1.46 pm the defendant's telegram arrived. The plaintiffs sued for damages for breach of contract.

*Held*

Looking at the form of the telegram, the time it was sent and the state of the iron market, the first telegram sent by the plaintiffs was not a counter offer which destroyed the original offer, but a mere inquiry which should have been answered and not treated as a rejection of the offer.

*Commentary*

Applied in *Henthorn v Fraser* [1892] 2 Ch 27.

**Thompson v London Midland & Scottish Railway Co** [1930] 1 KB 41 Court of Appeal (Lord Hanworth MR, Lawrence and Sankey LJJ)

Railway ticket - conditions

*Facts*

The plaintiff's niece purchased a railway ticket for her; the ticket was stated to be issued subject to the company's general conditions. The plaintiff was illiterate and unable to read the ticket.

*Held*

The plaintiff was bound by the company's conditions and her illiteracy was of no effect: the defendants had done enough to bring their conditions to the notice of the class of persons to which the plaintiff belonged.

**Thornton v Shoe Lane Parking Ltd** [1971] 2 WLR 585 Court of Appeal (Lord Denning MR, Megaw LJ and Sir Gordon Willmer)

Automatic car park - notice

*Facts*

A notice displayed at the entrance to a car park stated 'All cars parked at owners risk'. The plaintiff approached the car park, took a ticket dispensed by an automatic machine and entered. The ticket stated that it was 'issued subject to the conditions of issue as displayed on the premises'. These conditions, displayed inside the car park, purported to exempt the defendants from liability for damage to cars, or any injury to the customer howsoever caused. When the plaintiff went to collect his car he was injured in an accident, partly caused by the defendants' negligence.

*Held*

The exemption clause was not a term of the contract and it did not, therefore, enable the defendants to escape liability.

Lord Denning MR:

'We have been referred to the ticket cases of former times from *Parker* v *South Eastern Ry Co* to *McCutcheon* v *David MacBrayne Ltd*. They were concerned with railways, steamships and cloakrooms, where booking clerks issued tickets to customers who took them away without reading them. In those cases, the issue of the ticket was regarded as an offer by the company. If the customer took it and retained it without obligation, his act was regarded as an acceptance of the offer: see *Watkins* v *Rymill* and *Thompson* v *London, Midland and Scottish Ry Co*. These cases were based on the theory that the customer, on being handed the ticket, could refuse it and decline to enter into a contract on those terms. He could ask for his money back. That theory was, of course, a fiction. No customer in a thousand ever read the conditions. If he had stopped to do so, he would have missed the train or the boat.

None of those cases has any application to a ticket which is issued by an automatic machine. The customer pays his money and gets a ticket. He cannot refuse it. He cannot get his money back. He may protest to the machine, even swear at it; but it will remain unmoved. He is committed beyond recall. He was committed at the very moment when he put his money into the machine. The contract was concluded at that time. It can be translated into offer and acceptance in this way. The offer is made when the proprietor of the machine holds it out as being ready to receive the money. The acceptance takes place when the customer puts his money into the slot. The terms of the offer are contained in the notice placed on or near the machine, stating what is offered for the money. The customer is bound by those terms as long as they are sufficiently brought to his notice beforehand, but not otherwise. He is not bound by the terms printed on the ticket if they differ from the notice, because the ticket comes too late. The contract has already been made: see *Olley* v *Marlborough Court Ltd*. The ticket is no more than a voucher or receipt for the money that has been paid (as in the deckchair case, *Chapelton* v *Barry Urban District Council*), on terms which have been offered and accepted before the ticket is issued. In the present case, the offer was contained in the notice at the entrance, giving the charges for garaging and saying, 'At owners' risk', ie at the risk of the owner so far as damage to the car was concerned. The offer was accepted when the plaintiff drove up to the entrance and, by the movement of his car, turned the light from red to green and the ticket was thrust at him. The contract was then concluded and it could not be altered by any words printed on the ticket itself. In particular, it could not be altered so as to exempt the company from liability for personal injury due to their negligence.

... the customer is bound by the exempting condition if he knows that the ticket is issued subject to it; or, if the company did what was reasonably sufficient to give him notice of it. Counsel for the defendants admitted here that the defendants did not do what was reasonably sufficient to give the plaintiff notice of the exempting condition. That admission was properly made. I do not pause to enquire whether the exempting condition is void for unreasonableness. All I say is that it is so wide and so destructive of rights that the court should not hold any man bound by it unless it is drawn to his attention in the most explicit way. It is an instance of what I had in mind in *J Spurling Ltd* v *Bradshaw*. In order to give sufficient notice, it would need to be printed in red ink with a red hand pointing to it, or something equally startling.

However, although reasonable notice of it was not given, counsel for the defendants said that this case came within the second question propounded by Mellish LJ, namely that the plaintiff 'knew or believed that the writing contained conditions'. There was no finding to that effect. The burden was on the defendants to prove it, and they did not do so. Certainly there was no evidence that the plaintiff knew of this exempting condition. He is not, therefore, bound by it ... the whole question is whether the exempting condition formed part of the contract. I do not think it did. The plaintiff did not know of the condition, and the defendants did not do what was reasonably sufficient to give him notice of it.'

**Upton-on-Severn Rural District Council v Powell**

See chapter 8 - Mistake

**Williams v Carwardine** (1833) 5 C & P 566 King's Bench (Denman CJ, Parke, Littledale and Patteson JJ)

Offer and acceptance - reward

*Facts*

The defendant offered a reward to anyone giving information leading to the conviction of a particular murderer. The plaintiff knew of the offer and, believing that she had not long to live, and in order to ease her conscience and in 'hopes of forgiveness hereafter', she gave the information. The jury found that the plaintiff was not induced by the offer of the reward, but by other motives.

*Held*

The plaintiff's motives were immaterial and she was entitled to the reward.

# 2  CONSIDERATION

**Ajayi, Emmanuel Ayodeji v R T Briscoe (Nigeria) Ltd** [1964] 1 WLR 1326 Privy Council (Lord Morris of Borth-y-Gest, Lord Hodson and Lord Guest)

Estoppel - hire purchase of lorries

*Facts*

The defendant hire-purchaser hired from the plaintiffs eleven lorries: the balance of the purchase price was to be paid by instalments ending on 30 January 1957, but the defendant failed to make the payments. On 12 July 1957 the defendant wrote to the plaintiffs to tell them that he had had to withdraw the lorries from service because of servicing difficulties, adding that he did not wish to forfeit the deposits which he had paid and that he would contribute for repairs carried out by the plaintiffs' servicing organisation. On 22 July the plaintiffs wrote to say that they were hoping to provide proper servicing facilities and that they were agreeable to the defendant 'withholding instalments ... as long as they [the lorries] are withdrawn from active service'. The defendant returned eight lorries for repair and the other three remained in his garage. When the plaintiffs sued for the instalments, the defendant pleaded equitable estoppel based on the letter of 22 July.

*Held*

He had failed to establish this defence.

Lord Hodson:

'The question remains whether the hire-purchaser has made good the defence. In their lordships' opinion he has not succeeded in so doing. The hire-purchaser did not alter his position by not putting forward counter proposals after receipt of the letter of July 22 1957. There is no evidence to support the contention that he did so by organising his business in a different way having regard to the fact that the lorries were out of service, and it cannot be inferred from the evidence given that such reorganisation was necessary. It can be said that the lorries were laid up and there is evidence to support the view that they were laid up after the receipt of the letter of July 22 1957. Nevertheless, in view of the evidence given by the owners' witness, not rejected by the trial judge (although contradicted by the hire-purchaser), it cannot be said to have been proved that the lorries were not made available for the hire-purchaser after they had been repaired.'

**Alan (W J) & Co Ltd v El Nasr Export & Import Co** [1972] 2 WLR 800 Court of Appeal (Lord Denning MR, Megaw and Stephenson LJJ)

Coffee - payment in different currency

*Facts*

A, sellers of coffee in Kenya, agreed by contract to sell coffee, to EN, the price to be 262s per cwt and payment to be made 'by confirmed irrevocable letter of credit to be opened at sight one month prior to shipment'. EN resold to sub-buyers who opened an irrevocable credit in sterling in favour of A. Credit up to £131,000 was secured in favour of A at a bank in Dar es Salaam. Although the credit was expressed in sterling and did not, in a number of details, conform with the contract between A and EN, A accepted and began to operate the credit. When the final shipment had been loaded, A prepared an invoice expressed in sterling for the balance of the money. Before A presented the invoice, sterling had been devalued. Subsequently, it appeared that the Kenyan pound would not be devalued. A claimed that Kenyan currency was the currency of the original transaction and claimed an additional payment from EN (in sterling) to make the price up to 262 Kenyan shillings at the current rate.

44

*Held*

A could not succeed as he had either irrevocably waived the right to payment in Kenyan currency or accepted a variation of the contract by accepting payment under a sterling letter of credit.

Lord Denning MR:

'Nevertheless, the one who waives his strict rights cannot afterwards insist on them. His strict rights are at any rate suspended so long as the waiver lasts. He may on occasion be able to revert to his strict legal rights for the future by giving reasonable notice in that behalf, or otherwise making it plain by his conduct that he will thereafter insist upon them: *Tool Metal Manufacturing Co Ltd* v *Tungsten Electrical Co Ltd*. But there are cases where no withdrawal is possible. It may be too late to withdraw; or it cannot be done without injustice to the other party. In that event, he is bound by his waiver. He will not be allowed to revert to his strict legal rights. He can only enforce them, subject to the waiver he has made ...

The judge rejected this doctrine (ie promissory estoppel) because, he said, "there is no evidence of the buyers having acted to their detriment". I know that it has been suggested in some quarters that there must be detriment. But I can find no support for it in the authorities cited by the judge. The nearest approach to it is the statement of Viscount Simonds in the *Tool Metal Case* [1955] 1 WLR 761, 764, that the other must have been led "to alter his position", which was adopted by Lord Hodson in *Ajayi* v *R T Briscoe (Nigeria) Ltd* . But that only means that he must have been led to act differently from what he otherwise would have done. And if you study the cases in which the doctrine has been applied, you will see that all that is required is that one should have "*acted* on the belief induced by the other party". That is how Lord Cohen put it in the *Tool Metal Case* and that is how I would put it myself ...'

*Commentary*

Applied: *Hughes* v *Metropolitan Railway Co* (1877) 2 App Cas 439.

**Argy Trading Development Co Ltd v Lapid Developments Ltd** [1977] 1 WLR 444 High Court (Croom-Johnson J)

Estoppel - fire insurance cover

*Facts*

Under the terms of a lease, the tenants were obliged to insure against loss or damage by fire. At the time the lease was granted, the landlords had the premises so covered: they told the tenants and charged them an appropriate proportion of the premium. This arrangement was continued for the following year but, after the landlords had been taken over, this policy was allowed to lapse. The tenants were not informed of the decision and some nine months later the premises were gutted by fire. The tenants sought damages against the landlord.

*Held*

Their action would be dismissed as there was no consideration for the landlords' alleged agreement to insure the premises. Further, the landlords were not estopped from denying that they were under a duty to insure.

Croom-Johnson J:

'Therefore, if there was no consideration given by the plaintiffs so as to support a contract on which they can sue, what is the effect of the estoppel alleged in the reply? The plaintiffs seek to say that by reason of representations express or implied made ... they acted to their detriment by not taking out their own insurance cover, and therefore the defendants are estopped from alleging there was no consideration. The representations referred to in the reply are first that the defendants would arrange and effect the insurance. That is a representation as to intention and not of an existing fact. Second, that the defendants had arranged to effect the insurance. That is representation of fact and was true at the time it was made. By itself it is not enough. Thereafter the plaintiffs go on to say that there were implied representations that they would continue the insurance or would not cancel the same without notice. Those again are representations of intention as to the future and not of existing fact. Estoppel at law will not be raised by those facts. The plaintiffs go further and rely on the form of equitable estoppel, promissory in effect, which was applied in *Central London Property Trust Ltd* v *High Trees House Ltd*. But there are restrictions on the use of that form of estoppel. In the first place, the representation must be intended to affect the legal relations of the parties. I do not think that that was so in this case. There was no intention to vary the lease. If there had been, then the plaintiffs would run into the difficulty of having to say, as they do ... but have not argued in this court, that there is an oral variation of an instrument under seal. Secondly, the promise may be used only as a shield and not as a sword. In *Combe* v *Combe* Birkett LJ said so in terms, and Asquith LJ stated that the promise could not found an action brought by the promisee where there was no consideration.

In the present case, if there was no contract such as the plaintiffs sue on because it turns out that there are no consideration [sic], then to estop the defendants from raising that in their defence would only be to try by a sidewind to make the promise give rise to the cause of action. This the plaintiffs cannot do.'

## Birmingham and District Land Co v London and North Western Rail Co (1888) 40 Ch D 268 Court of Appeal (Cotton, Lindley and Bowen LJJ)

Building scheme - further time

*Facts*

The plaintiffs entered into building agreements with B under which houses were to be erected within a specified time. Shortly afterwards, B said that building should be suspended as it was possible that the defendants would take a strip of the land, acting under statutory powers.

*Held*

B's discretion to suspend work raised an equity against him which would prevent him ejecting the plaintiffs until they had a reasonable time, after the expiration of the agreements, to erect the houses.

Cotton LJ:

'[The plaintiffs] founded an argument on the special form of the agreements, which were not agreements that the plaintiffs should for a certain number of years have the land to build upon, but agreements that they should for ten years from a past date in one case, and six years in the other case, have liberty to enter upon the land for the purpose of building houses, and it was urged that nothing took place which could have the effect of making a new agreement, or extending the old agreements. I quite agree that what passed did not make a new agreement, but, in my opinion, what took place between [B] and the plaintiffs would have prevented [B] from bringing ejectment or taking possession of the land as soon as the terms of years limited by the agreements respectively came to an end. It raised an equity against him which would prevent his so doing, and would oblige him, after notice given by him to the plaintiff company, to give them a reasonable time to complete the building operations which had been stopped by the action of his agent. *Hughes* v *Metropolitan Rail Co*, referred to by Lindley LJ during the argument, amply supports that proposition.'

*Commentary*

Followed: *Hughes* v *Metropolitan Rail Co* (1877) 2 App Cas 439.

**Brikom Investments Ltd v Carr** [1979] 2 WLR 737 Court of Appeal (Lord Denning MR, Roskill and Cumming-Bruce LJJ)

Estoppel - cost of repairs to flats' roofs

*Facts*

At a time when the roofs of blocks of flats were in need of repair, the plaintiff landlords offered their tenants 99 year leases, assuring them that they would repair the roofs at their (the plaintiffs') own expense. When granted, the leases provided that the plaintiffs could recover the repair costs from the tenants and they sought now to do so. One tenant (the first defendant) admitted that she would have bought her lease, even without the plaintiffs' assurance as to repairs. The second and third defendants were respectively an assignee and an assignee of an assignee of original purchasers of leases.

*Held*

The plaintiffs' claim had rightly been dismissed. They were estopped from claiming against the first defendant and also against the second and third defendants as their assurance, being an equity intended to be for the benefit of those from time to time holding the leases, extended also to assignees of the original tenants. It was mere speculation (and therefore irrelevant) that the first defendant would not have bought her lease without the plaintiffs' assurance as to roof repairs. The plaintiffs' claim also failed because they had waived their right to claim the cost of repairs from the tenants.

Lord Denning MR:

'Counsel for the landlords submitted that [the first defendant] could not rely on the principle in the *High Trees* case, because it was essential that she should have *acted* on the representation; and here she had not acted on it. On her own admission, he said, she would have gone on and taken the lease even if she had not been told about the roof. In all the cases, said counsel for the landlords, the courts had said that the party must have acted on the promise or representation in the sense that he must have altered his position on the faith of it, meaning that he must have been led to act differently from what he would otherwise have done: see *Alan & Co* v *El Nasr Export & Import Co*. This argument gives, I think, too limited a scope to the principle. The principle extends to all cases where one party makes a promise or representation, intending that it should be binding, intending that the other should rely on it, and on which that other does in fact rely, by acting on it, by altering his position on the faith of it, by going ahead with a transaction then under discussion, or by any other way of reliance. It is no answer for the maker to say: "You would have gone on with the transaction anyway". That must be mere speculation. No one can be sure what he would, or would not, have done in a hypothetical state of affairs which never took place ... Once it is shown that a representation was calculated to influence the judgment of a reasonable man, the presumption is that he was so influenced.'

Roskill LJ:

'... whichever is the right way of putting it, ever since *Hughes* v *Metropolitan Railway Co*, through a long line of cases of which there are many examples in the books, one finds that where parties have made a contract which provides one thing and where, by a subsequent course of dealing, the parties have worked that contract out in such a way that one party leads the other to believe that the strict rights under that contract will not be adhered to, the courts will not allow that party who has led the other to think the strict rights will not be adhered, suddenly to seek to enforce those strict rights against him. That seems to me to be precisely what the landlords are trying to do here. Having said ... "We will do these repairs at our expense", they then subsequently, as it would seem as a reprisal because of disapproval of opposition by these lessees in attempting to prevent the landlords getting planning permission to add another storey to these flats, belatedly tried to enforce against one of these lessees, and in the other two cases against assignees, the strict letter of the contract. I do not think that the common law or equity will allow them to take that step; and for my part, with profound respect to Lord Denning MR, I do not think it is necessary in order to reach that result to resort to the somewhat uncertain doctrine of promissory estoppel.'

## Carlill v Carbolic Smoke Ball Co

See chapter 1 - Offer and acceptance.

## Casey's Patents, Re, Stewart v Casey [1892] 1 Ch 104 Court of Appeal (Lindley, Bowen and Fry LJJ)

Consideration - past service

*Facts*

Stewart and Charlton, joint owners of certain patent rights, wrote to the defendant, Casey, saying that ' ... in consideration of your services as the practical manager in working both our patents ... we hereby agree to give you one third share of the patents ...' The patents were subsequently transferred to Casey. The plaintiffs now claimed their return.

*Held*

The action would be dismissed.

Bowen LJ:

'Even if it were true ... that a past service cannot support a future promise, you must look at the document and see if the promise cannot receive a proper effect in some other way. Now, the fact of a past service raises an implication that at the time it was rendered it was to be paid for and, if it was a service that was to be paid for, when you get in the subsequent document a promise to pay, that promise may be treated either as an admission which evidences, or as a positive bargain which fixes the amount of that reasonable remuneration on the faith of which the service was originally rendered'.

## Central London Property Trust Ltd v High Trees House Ltd [1947] KB 130 High Court (Denning J)

Promise without consideration - estoppel

*Facts*

By a lease of 1937, the plaintiffs leased a block of flats to the defendants for 99 years at a rent of £2,500 pa. With the advent of war and many vacancies in the flats, the plaintiffs agreed in 1940 to reduce the rent by 50%. No time limit was set for the reduction. By 1945 the flats were full again. The plaintiff company thereupon wrote to the defendants, asking for the full amount of rent plus arrears. Subsequently, the present action was instituted to test the legal position. The plaintiffs claimed the full rent for the last two quarters of 1945. The defendants pleaded, inter alia, that the agreement of 1940 related to the whole term of the lease; or, alternatively, that by failing to demand rent in excess of £1,250 before September 1945, the plaintiffs had waived their rights in respect of any rent in excess of that amount which had accrued before that date.

*Held*

The plaintiffs' claim would succeed although, as regards the earlier period, the promise to reduce the rent was binding even though it had been given without consideration.

Denning J:

'I find that the conditions prevailing at the time when the reduction in rent was made, had completely passed away by the early months of 1945. I am satisfied that the promise was understood by all parties only to apply under the conditions prevailing at the time when it was made, namely, when the flats were only partially let, and that it did not extend any further than that. When the flats became fully let, early in 1945, the reduction ceased to apply.

In those circumstances, under the law as I hold it, it seems to me that rent is payable at the full rate for the quarters ending September 29 and December 25, 1945.

If the case had been one of estoppel, it might be said that in any event the estoppel would cease when the conditions to which the representation applied came to an end, or it also might be said that it would only come to an end on notice. In either case it is only a way of ascertaining what is the scope of the representation. I prefer to apply the principle that a promise intended to be binding, intended to be acted on and in fact acted on, is binding so far as its terms properly apply. Here it was binding as covering the period down to the early part of 1945, and as from that time full rent is payable.'

*Commentary*

Distinguished: *Jorden* v *Money* (1854) 5 HL Cas 185. See also *Combe* v *Combe* [1951] 2 KB 215, *Brikom Investments Ltd* v *Carr* [1979] 2 WLR 737 and *Société Italo-Belge pour le Commerce et l'Industrie SA* v *Palm and Vegetable Oils (Malaysia) Sdn Bhd. The Post Chaser* [1982] 1 All ER 19.

**Chappell & Co Ltd v The Nestlé Co Ltd** [1959] 3 WLR 168 House of Lords (Viscount Simonds, Lord Reid, Lord Tucker, Lord Keith of Avonholm and Lord Somervell of Harrow)

Consideration - value

*Facts*

The plaintiffs (Chappell & Co Ltd) owned the copyright in a piece of music. The Hardy Co made records of the music, which they sold to the defendants (Nestlé Co Ltd) for 4d each. Nestlé advertised to the public that the records could be obtained from them for 1s 6d each, plus three wrappers from Nestlé's 6d chocolate bars. The wrappers, when received, were thrown away.

Section 8(1) of the Copyright Act 1956 permits a person to make a record of a piece of music for the purpose of its being sold retail if he gives notice to the owner of the copyright and pays him a royalty of six and a quarter per cent of 'the ordinary retail selling price'. The Hardy Co had given notice of their intention to manufacture the records, stating 1s 6d to be the ordinary retail selling price and offering to pay Chappell & Co royalties on this figure. Chappell & Co refused and sought an injunction restraining Nestlé & Co Ltd and the Hardy Co from infringing their copyright.

*Held* (Viscount Simonds and Lord Keith of Avonholm dissenting)

The wrappers were part of the consideration and the plaintiffs were therefore entitled to succeed.

Lord Reid:

'It seems to me clear that the main intention of the offer was to induce people interested in this kind of music to buy ... chocolate which otherwise would not have been bought ... The requirement that wrappers should be sent was of great importance to the Nestlé Co; there would have been no point in their simply offering records for 1s 6d each. It seems quite unrealistic to divorce the buying of the chocolate from the supplying of the records'.

Lord Somervell:

'I think they (the wrappers) are part of the consideration. They are so described in the offer ... This is not conclusive but, however described, they are, in my view in law, part of the consideration. It is said that when received the wrappers are of no value to Nestlés. This, I would have thought, irrelevant. A contracting party can stipulate for what consideration he chooses. A peppercorn does not cease to be good consideration if it is established that the promisee does not like pepper and will throw away the corn.'

## Collins v Godefroy (1831) 1 B & Ad 950 King's Bench (Lord Tenterden CJ)

Consideration - promisee subpoenaed

*Facts*

C had been subpoenaed by G to attend as a witness in an action. C subsequently brought an action against G, claiming a guinea a day as his fee for attendance. Assuming that G had expressly promised to pay the sum claimed as compensation for loss of time, was there was any consideration for the promise?

*Held*

There was not.

Lord Tenterden CJ:

'If it be a duty imposed by law upon a party regularly subpoenaed to attend from time to time to give his evidence, then a promise to give him any remuneration for loss of time incurred in such attendance is a promise without consideration.'

## Combe v Combe [1951] 2 KB 215 Court of Appeal (Asquith, Denning and Birkett LJJ)

Consideration - promise of maintenance

*Facts*

A divorced wife obtained a promise from her ex-husband to pay her £100 pa maintenance. The wife did not apply to the Divorce Court for maintenance - but not as a result of any request from her husband to this effect. The husband never made any of the payments and the wife sued for the arrears.

*Held*

She was not entitled to succeed as there had been no consideration for the husband's promise.

Denning LJ:

'the principle of the *High Trees* case ... does not create new causes of action where none existed before. It only prevents a party from insisting upon his strict legal rights when it would be unjust to allow him to enforce them, having regard to the dealings which have taken place between the parties ... The principle ... is that ... where one party has, by his words or conduct, made to the other a promise or assurance which was intended to affect the legal relations between them and to be acted on accordingly, then once the other party has taken him at his word and acted on it, the one who gave the promise or assurance cannot afterwards be allowed to revert to the previous legal relations as if no such promise or assurance has been made by him, but he must accept their legal relations subject to the qualification which he himself has so introduced, even though it is not supported in point of law by any consideration but only by his word.' ... seeing that the principle never stands alone as giving a cause of action in itself, it can never do away with the necessity of consideration when that is an essential part of the cause of action. The doctrine of consideration is too firmly fixed to be overthrown by a side-wind.'

Asquith LJ:

'What [the *High Trees*] case decides is that when a promise is given which (1) is intended to create legal relations: (2) is intended to be acted upon by the promisee; and (3) is in fact so acted upon, the promisor cannot bring an action against the promisee which involves the repudiation of his promise or is inconsistent with it. It does not, as I read it, decide that a promisee can sue on the promise.'

Birkett LJ:

'... we have had the great advantage of hearing Denning LJ deal with *Central London Property Trust Ltd* v *High Trees House Ltd* and *Robertson* v *Minister of Pensions* which formed such a prominent part of the judgment of the court below. I am bound to say that reading them for myself I think the description which was given by counsel for the husband in this court, namely, that the doctrine there enunciated was, so to speak, a doctrine which would enable a person to use it as a shield and not as a sword, is a very vivid way of stating what, I think, is the principle underlying both those cases.'

*Commentary*

See also *Argy Trading Development Co Ltd* v *Lapid Developments Ltd* [1977] 1 WLR 444.

**Crabb v Arun District Council** [1975] 3 WLR 847 Court of Appeal (Lord Denning MR, Lawton and Scarman LJJ)

Estoppel - right of way

*Facts*

The plaintiff explained to the defendants his plans for his land and these involved an access over their property. The defendants assured the plaintiff that his plans would be acceptable to them and, although no formal grant was made, the parties thereafter acted in the belief that he had been, or would be, granted such a right. Six months or so later the defendants erected gates, apparently taking account of the plaintiff's right of way, and after a similar period the plaintiff sold part of his land, again on that assumption. The defendants knew that the plaintiff intended to sell this part of his land. When the defendants denied the existence of the plaintiff's right of way, he sought the court's assistance.

*Held*

He was entitled to an injunction to enforce his rights.

Lord Denning MR:

'The basis of this proprietary estoppel - as indeed of promissory estoppel - is the interposition of equity. Equity comes in, true to form to mitigate the rigours of strict law. The early cases did not speak of it as "estoppel". They spoke of it as "raising an equity". If I may expand that, Lord Cairns said in *Hughes* v *Metropolitan Railway Co*: " ... it is the first principle upon which all Courts of Equity proceed ... " that it will prevent a person from insisting on his strict legal rights - whether arising under a contract, or on his title deeds, or by statute - when it would be inequitable for him to do so having regard to the dealings which have taken place between the parties. What then are the dealings which will preclude him from insisting on his strict legal rights? If he makes a binding contract that he will not insist on the strict legal position, a court of equity will hold him to his contract. Short of a binding contract, if he makes a promise that he will not insist on his strict legal rights - even though that promise may be unenforceable in point of law for want of consideration or want of writing - and if he makes the promise knowing or intending that the other will act on it, and he does act on it, then again a court of equity will not allow him to go back on that promise: see *Central London Property Trust* v *High Trees House, Charles Rickards* v *Oppenheim*. Short of an actual promise, if he, by his words or conduct, so behaves as to lead another to believe that he will not insist on his strict legal rights - knowing or intending that the other will act on that belief - and he does so act, that again will raise an equity in favour of the other, and it is for a court of equity to say in what way the equity may be satisfied. The cases show that this equity does not depend on agreement but on words or conduct ... In the circumstances it seems to me inequitable that the council should insist on their strict title as they did ...'

**D & C Builders Ltd v Rees** [1966] 2 WLR 288 Court of Appeal (Lord Denning MR, Danckwerts and Winn LJJ)

Debt - acceptance of smaller sum

*Facts*

The plaintiffs (D & C Builders) were a small firm who did work for the defendant, for which he owed them £482. After the amount had been outstanding for some time, the defendant's wife, acting for the defendant and knowing that the plaintiffs were in financial difficulties, offered them £300 in settlement. She said the plaintiffs could have £300 or nothing and rejected an offer to find the disputed £182 over a further twelve months. The plaintiffs reluctantly agreed, since without the £300 their firm would have gone bankrupt. The plaintiffs then sued for the balance.

*Held*

The plaintiffs' action was not barred: there had been no true accord and there was no equitable ground for rejecting their claim.

Lord Denning MR:

'... it is a daily occurrence that a merchant or tradesman, who is owed a sum of money, is asked to take less. The debtor says he is in difficulties ... The creditor ... accepts the proffered sum and forgives him the rest of the debt. The question arises: is the settlement binding on the creditor? The answer is that, in point of law, the creditor is not bound by the settlement. He can, the next day, sue the debtor for the balance and get judgment ...

This doctrine of the common law has come under heavy fire ... But a remedy has been found. The harshness of the common law has been relieved. Equity has stretched out a merciful hand to help the debtor. The courts have invoked the broad principle stated by Lord Cairns LC in *Hughes* v *Metropolitan Rail Co* ... This principle has been applied to cases where a creditor agrees to accept a lesser sum in discharge of a  greater ... In applying this principle, however, he must note the qualification. The creditor is barred from his legal rights only when it would be *inequitable* for him to insist on them. Where there has been a *true accord* under which the creditor voluntarily agrees to accept a lesser sum in satisfaction and the debtor *acts on* that accord by paying the lesser sum and the creditor accepts it, then it is inequitable for the creditor afterwards to insist on the balance. But he is not bound unless there has been truly an accord between them.

In the present case, on the facts as found by the judge, it seems to me that there was no true accord. The debtor's wife held the creditor to ransom. The creditor was in need of money to meet his own commitments, and she knew it. When the creditor asked for payment of the £480 due to him, she said to him in effect: "We cannot pay you the £480. But we will pay you £300 if you will accept it in settlement. If you do not accept it on those terms, you will get nothing. £300 is better than nothing." She had no right to say any such thing. She could properly have said: "We canot pay you more than £300. Please accept it on account." But she had no right to insist on his taking it in settlement. When she said: "We will pay you nothing unless you accept £300 in settlement", she was putting undue pressure on the creditor. She was making a threat to break the contract (by paying nothing) and she was doing it so as to compel the creditor to do what he was unwilling to do (to accept £300 in settlement): and she succeeded. He complied with her demand. That was ... a case of intimidation ... In these circumstances there was no true accord so as to found a defence of accord and satisfaction ... There is also no equity in the defendant to warrant any departure from the due course of law. No person can insist on a settlement procured by intimidation.'

**De La Bere v CA Pearson Ltd** [1908] 1 KB 280 Court of Appeal (Sir Gorell Barnes P, Vaughan Williams LJ and Bigham J)

Newspaper advice - consideration

*Facts*

Responding to an invitation in the defendants' newspaper, the plaintiff wrote: 'Kindly advise me how I can best invest £800 in two or three fairly safe securities ... Please also name a good stockbroker.' The defendants' city editor passed the letter to an outside broker who advised as to investment. The plaintiff sent the broker £1,400 and he misappropriated it. As the city editor could have discovered had he made inquiries, the broker was an undischarged bankrupt. The plaintiff claimed damages for breach of contract.

*Held*

His action would be successful.

Sir Gorell Barnes P:

'On the facts proved there was a contract, for good consideration, to take reasonable care to name a good stockbroker. The consideration was that the plaintiff, as a reader of *M A P* was asked to put forward his inquiries, with regard to financial matters, to the city editor, and the defendants agreed, if he did so, to answer the questions which he might put. Those being the facts, I think that there was a contract ...'

Vaughan Williams LJ:

'... I think that there was a contract between the plaintiff and the defendants. The defendants advertised offering to give advice with reference to investments. The plaintiff, accepting that offer, asked for advice and also asked for the name of "a good stockbroker". The questions and answers were, if the defendants chose, to be inserted in their paper as published. Such publication might obviously have a tendency to increase the sale of their paper. I think that this offer, when accepted, resulted in a contract for a good consideration.'

## Eastwood v Kenyon

See Introduction.

**Foakes v Beer** (1884) 9 App Cas 605 House of Lords (Earl of Selborne LC, Lord Blackburn, Lord Watson and Lord FitzGerald)

Judgment debt - payment of smaller sum

*Facts*

B had obtained judgment against F for £2,000. Sixteen months later, F asked for time to pay and B and F agreed in writing that if F paid £500 immediately and the balance by instalments, B would not to take 'any proceedings whatsoever' on the judgment. A judgment debt bears interest from the date of judgment, but the agreement did not mention interest. F finally paid the whole of the outstanding sum and B then claimed interest. B then applied to commence proceedings on the judgment and F pleaded the written agreement as a defence. B argued it was unsupported by consideration.

*Held*

Following the rule in *Pinnel's Case*, B was entitled to succeed.

The Earl of Selborne LC:

'If the question be (as, in the actual state of the law, I think it is) whether consideration is, or is not, given in a case of this kind, by the debtor who pays down part of the debt presently due from him for a promise by the creditor to relinquish, after further payments on account, the residue of the debt, I cannot say that I think consideration is given, in the sense in which I have always understood that word as used in our law.'

**Glasbrook Bros Ltd v Glamorgan County Council** [1925] AC 270 House of Lords (Viscount Cave LC, Viscount Finlay, Lord Shaw, Lord Carson and Lord Blanesburgh)

Consideration - duty to protect

*Facts*

During an industrial dispute, mine owners asked for additional police protection. The police decided that adequate protection could be given by keeping a mobile force on call. The mine owners wanted a permanent billet and agreed to pay for the facility at a specific rate. The appellants (Glasbrook Bros) claimed there was no consideration for the promise, since it was the duty of the council to supply police protection.

*Held* (Lord Carson and Lord Blanesburgh dissenting)

The council was entitled to recover the agreed sum.

Viscount Finlay:

'The colliery owners repudiated liability on the grounds that there was no consideration for the promise to pay for the police protection and that such an agreement was against public policy. The case was tried by Bailhache J, and he entered judgment for the plaintiffs, saying:

"There is an obligation on the police to afford efficient protection, but if an individual asks for special protection in a particular form, for the special protection so asked for in that particular form, the individual must pay."

This decision was affirmed by a majority on the appeal (Bankes and Scrutton LJJ, Atkin LJ dissenting). The colliery owners now appeal and ask that judgment should be entered for them.

It appears to me that there is nothing in the first point made for the colliery owners that there was no consideration for the promise. It is clear that there was abundant consideration. The police authorities thought that it would be best to give protection by means of a flying column of police, but the colliery owners wanted the "garrison" and promised to pay for it if it was sent.'

**Goldsworthy v Brickell** [1987] 2 WLR 133 Court of Appeal (Parker and Nourse LJJ and Sir John Megaw)

Equity - elderly farmer and neighbour

*Facts*

The plaintiff, aged 85, owned a large and valuable farm and the defendant, a neighbouring farmer, began to give him advice and practical assistance. Within a year, the defendant was effectively managing the plaintiff's farm and the plaintiff, in full possession of his faculties, granted the defendant a tenancy at £500 pa with an option to purchase at the 'prevailing value' on the plaintiff's death. A further agreement made the parties equal partners in the farm business. The plaintiff was reluctant to seek, and did not receive, independent advice in relation to either agreement. Two years later the partnership agreement was terminated by mutual consent and the defendant bought out the plaintiff's half interest and thereafter worked the farm for his own benefit, paying the plaintiff a rent of £3,000 pa when the market rent was about £12,500 pa. The plaintiff sought rescission of the tenancy agreement on the ground of undue influence.

*Held*

He was entitled to succeed and, in the circumstances, it was just and equitable that the tenancy agreement be set aside and the plaintiff granted possession of the farm.

Nourse LJ:

'If the defence of promissory estoppel is to succeed in this case the defendant must establish the following: firstly, a clear and unequivocal representation, either by words or conduct, that the plaintiff would not enforce his right to set the tenancy agreement aside; secondly, that the representation was made with the knowledge or intention that it would be acted on by the defendant in the manner in which it was acted on; thirdly, that the defendant, in reliance on the representation, acted to his detriment, or in some other way which would make it inequitable to allow the plaintiff to go back on his representation.

The first point to be made is that ... the defence does not in my view contain a properly pleaded defence of promissory estoppel. Secondly, perhaps as a consequence of that, the evidence at the trial did not establish either a clear and unequivocal representation by or on behalf of the plaintiff that he would not enforce his right to set the tenancy agreement aside or that the defendant, in reliance on any such representation, acted either to his detriment or at all. As to the first of those matters the judge said:

"If he thought about it, the defendant might reasonably have concluded that the plaintiff was choosing to treat the tenancy as valid, notwithstanding the discovery of terms dishonestly concealed (as I assume for the purposes of this argument) when he signed the document."

It cannot in my view have been enough that the defendant might reasonably have arrived at that conclusion. There could only have been a clear and unequivocal representation if he could not reasonably have arrived at any other conclusion. With regard to the second matter, the judge made no finding at all, and it was indeed accepted by counsel for the defendant that no evidence was given by or on behalf of the defendant to the effect that he had, in reliance on any material representation, acted to his detriment. Finally, I would add that it is very difficult to see how, on the evidence, the defendant did in fact act to his detriment or in some other material way. The payment of rent was no detriment, because that was no more than the price which he had to pay for his occupation of the land from day to day ...

I add only this. After it had been pointed out in argument that the assumption made below might not have been correct, counsel for the defendant took time to consider whether he should seek leave to advance the defence of acquiescence in this court. No such application was made. I therefore express no view on whether, if it had been made and granted, the defence would have prevailed, beyond saying that it must have been very well arguable that if all the circumstances of the present case had been looked at it would still have been just that the plaintiff should succeed.'

Parker LJ:

'I have ventured on a perhaps over-long consideration of Lord Scarman's speech in *National Westminster Bank plc* v *Morgan* because it appears to me to be important that no one should in future be led by it to suppose that the necessary ingredient of the presumption of undue influence is the existence of a relationship in which the will of one party is under the domination of the will of another.'

*Commentary*

Applied: *Tufton* v *Sperni* [1952] 2 TLR 516.


**Gore v Van der Lann** [1967] 2 WLR 358 Court of Appeal (Willmer, Harman and Salmon LJJ)

Injury to bus passenger - stay of proceedings

*Facts*

The plaintiff was an old age pensioner who applied for and received a free pass on the Liverpool Corporation's buses. The grant of the pass was subject to the following conditions:

'(4)  The pass is issued and accepted on the understanding that it merely constitutes and grants a licence to the holder to travel on the Liverpool Corporation's buses with and subject to the conditions that neither the Liverpool Corporation nor any of their servants or agents responsible for the driving, management, control or working of their bus system are to be liable to the holder or his or her representative for loss of life, injury or delay or other loss or damage to property however caused.'

The plaintiff was injured while boarding a bus and brought an action against the conductor, alleging the accident was due to his negligence.  The defendant relied on the condition in the free pass.  The Liverpool Corporation applied for an order to stay the action.

*Held*

The corporation was not entitled to a stay of proceedings.  The pass constituted a contract, not a licence, and accordingly, the exclusion of liability contained in the condition was void under Section 151 of the Road Traffic Act 1960.

Willmer LJ:

'On behalf of the plaintiff, it has been contended that the effect of the plaintiff's application and its acceptance by the Corporation, was to constitute "a contract for the conveyance of a passenger in a public service vehicle" which is rendered void by Section 151 of the Road Traffic Act 1960 ...  If this contention is well founded, it is obvious that, assuming negligence on the part of the defendant, it effectively demolishes any possible defence to the plaintiff's claim, not only by the defendant but also by the corporation itself ...

That is sufficient to dispose of the appeal; but I think it right to add that, even if I had thought that the issue of the free pass amounted to no more than the grant of a licence subject to conditions, I should still have arrived at the same conclusion so far as this application is concerned.  It is true that the condition accepted by the plaintiff when she accepted the offer of a free pass included a provision that the employees of the corporation were not to be liable to her for any injury or loss, but I cannot construe this provision as a promise by the plaintiff not to institute proceedings against an employee.  If the corporation desired such a promise from a holder of a free pass, they could have said so in clear and unambiguous terms.  In my judgment, the conditions are to be construed strictly against the corporation who put them forward.  It is not enough to say that a promise not to sue the employee is to be implied.  At the best for the corporation, the condition relied on its ambiguity, and any ambiguity must be resolved in favour of the plaintiff.'

**Harris v Sheffield United Football Club Ltd** [1987] 3 WLR 305 Court of Appeal (Kerr, Neill and Balcombe LJJ)

Police services - responsibility for cost

*Facts*

In order to maintain law and order, a substantial police presence was required inside the defendants' ground and this involved substantial payments of police overtime.  Their attendance, contended the police, amounted to 'special police services' for which, by statute, the defendants were obliged to pay.

*Held*

This was the case.

Neill LJ:

'The club has responsibilities which are owed not only to its employees and the spectators who attend but also to the football authorities to take all reasonable steps to ensure that the game takes place in conditions which do not occasion danger to any person or property.  The attendance of the police is necessary to assist the club in the fulfilment of this duty.  The matches take place regularly and usually at weekends during about eight months of the year. Though the holding of the matches is of some public importance because of the widespread support in the local community both for the game and the club, the club is not under any legal duty to hold the matches. The charges which the authority seek to make, and have made, relate solely to the officers on duty inside the ground and not to those in the street or other public places outside.

There is clear evidence that the chief constable would be unable to provide the necessary amount of protection for Bramall Lane and also to discharge his other responsibilities without making extensive use of officers who would otherwise have been off duty. Substantial sums by way of overtime have therefore to be paid.

The arrangements for the attendance of the officers are made to guard against the possibility, and for some matches the probability, of violence; the officers are not sent to deal with an existing emergency, nor can it be said that any outbreak of violence is immediately imminent.

In my judgment, looking at all these factors I am driven to the conclusion that the provision of police officers to attend regularly at Bramall Lane throughout the football season does constitute the provision of special police services. Nor in my opinion is it to the point that the club has stated that it does not expect the police to carry out any duties other than to maintain law and order.

The resources of the police are finite.

In my view, if the club wishes on a regular basis to make an exceptional claim on police services to deal with potential violence on its premises, then, however well intentional and public spirited it may be in assembling the crowd at Bramall Lane, the services which it receives are 'special police services' within the meaning of s15(1) of the [Police Act 1964].

The question then remains: are these services 'requested' by the club within the meaning of s15(1)? It was very strongly argued on behalf of the club that after 26 October 1983 the club made no relevant request for such services other than requests made on a 'without prejudice' basis.

In my view this part of the club's argument, unlike the argument on the meaning of 'special police services', lacks any real substance.

If the club is to hold matches at Bramall Lane it is necessary for police officers to attend inside the ground. Their presence is necessary to enable the club to meet its responsibilities to the players, the staff and the spectators as well as to comply with the rules imposed by the football authorities. It is not necessary to examine what steps could be taken, and by whom, to stop a match taking place if the club authorities declined to allow the police to attend. But there is no likelihood that the club authorities, who have acted with a great sense of responsibility throughout, would take such a course. It may be that the request for the police services can only be implied from all the circumstances and that it is made without enthusiasm.

But if the police attend in order to enable the match to take place then, in the circumstances existing in this case, I consider that a request is to be implied.'

**Hartley v Ponsonby** (1857) 7 E & B 872 Queen's Bench (Lord Campbell CJ, Erle, Coleridge and Crompton JJ)

Consideration - additional pay for dangerous voyage

*Facts*

The defendant had undertaken to pay the plaintiff more than he had originally promised if he would complete a sea voyage. The jury found, as facts, that it was unreasonable to put to sea with the number of seamen which remained of the original crew at the time the plaintiff was offered the increased sum to complete the voyage. The defendant pleaded that there was no consideration for the promise.

*Held*

The plaintiff was entitled to judgment on the basis that the jury's finding of fact meant that the remainder of the crew were no longer contractually bound to complete the voyage since it had become so dangerous. Accordingly they were free to strike a fresh bargain.

Erle J:

'I was deeply impressed, at the trial, with a sense of the extreme danger of sanctioning contracts for extra remuneration to sailors, made during the voyage for which they are under articles. And I think it the duty of the judge to impress upon the jury the peril of encouraging seamen to insist upon such extra remuneration when any emergency arises. But, on the other hand, it is clear there is a point of danger at which it is unreasonable for the captain to require his crew to proceed on the voyage. This is a question of degree, which cannot be defined by law, but must be left to the jury. I, therefore, explained fully to the jury what was meant by "unreasonable"; and I take it that the jury had this explanation in mind, when they found that it was in this case unreasonable to require the men to proceed. If that was so, the plaintiff and the others were free and in the same position as any other free seamen at Port Philip, and they might stipulate for any amount of remuneration; and, considering the circumstances, £40 may not have been an exorbitant sum. No doubt, therefore, the finding of the jury made the contract voluntary on both sides, and therefore binding.'

**Hirachand Punamchand v Temple** [1911] 2 KB 330 Court of Appeal (Vaughan Williams, Fletcher Moulton and Farwell LJJ)

Debt - payment of smaller sum by third party

*Facts*

Lt Temple was indebted to the plaintiffs as the maker of a promissory note. His father wrote the plaintiffs offering a smaller amount in full settlement of the debt: he enclosed a draft which the plaintiffs cashed. Could they then sue the son for the balance?

*Held*

They could not.

Vaughan Williams LJ:

'In my judgment, this draft having been sent to the plaintiffs by Sir Richard Temple, and retained and cashed by them, we ought to draw the conclusion that the plaintiffs, who kept and cashed the draft, agreed to accept it on the terms upon which it was sent ... Under these circumstances, assuming that there was no accord and satisfaction, what form of defence, if any, could be pleaded by the defendant? In my judgment it would be that the plaintiffs had ceased really to be holders of the negotiable instrument on which they sued. They had ceased to be such holders, because, in effect, in their hands the document had ceased to be a negotiable instrument quite as much as if there had been on the acceptance of the draft by the plaintiffs an erasure of the writing of the signature to the note ... But, alternatively, assuming that this was not so, and that the instrument did not cease to be a negotiable instrument, then, in my judgment, from the moment when the draft sent by Sir Richard Temple was cashed by the plaintiffs a trust was created as between Sir Richard Temple and the moneylenders in favour of the former, so that any money which the latter might receive upon the promissory note, if they did receive any, would be held by them in trust for him ...'

Fletcher Moulton LJ:

'I am of opinion that by that transaction between the plaintiffs and Sir Richard Temple the debt on the promissory note became extinct ... The effect of such an agreement between a creditor and a third party with regard to the debt is to render it impossible for the creditor afterwards to sue the debtor for it. The way in which this is worked out in law may be that it would be an abuse of the process of the court to allow the creditor under such circumstances to sue, or it may be, and I prefer that view, that there is an extinction of the debt: but whichever way it is put, it comes to the same thing, namely that, after acceptance by the creditor of a sum offered by a third party in settlement of the claim against the debtor, the creditor cannot maintain an action for the balance ... If a third person steps in and gives a consideration for the discharge of the debtor, it does not matter whether he does it in meal or in malt, or what proportion the amount given bears to the amount of the debt. Here the money was paid by a third person, and I have no doubt that, upon the acceptance of that money by the plaintiffs with full knowledge of the terms on which it was offered, the debt was absolutely extinguished.'

**Hughes v Metropolitan Rail Co** (1877) 2 App Cas 439 House of Lords (Lord Cairns LC, Lord O'Hagan, Lord Selborne, Lord Blackburn and Lord Gordon)

Landlord - implied undertaking

*Facts*

A landlord had given his tenant six months' notice to repair the premises. The lease would be forfeit if the tenant did not comply. The tenant agreed to do the necessary repairs but, at the same time, started negotiations for the sale of the lease to the landlord. The tenant had indicated that the repairs would not be effected while the negotiations were in progress. The negotiations lasted two months, but then broke down. The tenant had carried out no repairs to the premises. When six months from the original notice had expired, the landlord claimed the lease was forfeit.

*Held*

He was not entitled to forfeiture. The opening of negotiations amounted to a promise by the landlord not to rely on his strict legal rights and enforce the notice and, in reliance on the implied undertaking, the tenant had not carried out the repairs. The six months, therefore, were to run only from the breakdown of the negotiations.

Lord Cairns LC:

'It is the first principle upon which all courts of equity proceed, that if parties who have entered into definite and distinct terms involving certain legal results - certain penalties or legal forfeiture afterwards, by their own act or with their own consent, enter upon a course of negotiations which has the effect of leading one of the parties to suppose that the strict legal rights arising under the contract will not be enforced, or will be kept in suspense or held in abeyance, the person who otherwise might have enforced those rights will not be allowed to enforce them where it would be inequitable, having regard to the dealings which have thus taken place between the parties.'

*Commentary*

Followed in *Birmingham and District Land Co v London and North Western Rail Co* (1880) 40 Ch D 268. See also *Scandinavian Trading Tanker Co AB v Flota Petrolera Ecuatoriana. The Scaptrade* [1983] 2 WLR 248 and *Brikom Investments Ltd v Carr* [1979] 2 WLR 737, *Alan (WJ) & Co Ltd v El Nasr Export & Import Co* [1972] 2 WLR 800 and *Société Italo-Belge pour le Commerce et l'Industrie SA v Palm and Vegetable Oils (Malaysia) Sdn Bhd. The Post Chaser* [1982] 1 All ER 19.

**Jorden v Money** (1854) 5 HL Cas 185 House of Lords (Lord Cranworth LC, Lord Brougham and Lord St Leonards)

Estoppel - no representation as to existing fact

*Facts*

The appellants were entitled to the benefit of an annual income under a bond given by the respondent's late father and the respondent owed them £1,200. The appellants had said that they would not enforce the bond, out of consideration for the provision made for them by the respondents' father. In the light of this assurance, the respondent married, but the appellants now sought to recover the £1,200.

*Held* (Lord St Leonards dissenting)

They were entitled to do so: although there had been the intention never to proceed on the bond, the right to do so had never been abandoned.

Lord Cranworth LC:

'It appears to me ... that there is nothing within the meaning of the authorities or on principle to make this a representation by which Mr and Mrs Jorden are to be bound ... there has been nothing established which impeaches the right ... to enforce this bond. I do believe that [Mrs Jorden] often and often told this young man that she would ... never enforce this bond; I believe she said this over and over again, knowing that it would come to his ears, but that was all that was said either expressly or impliedly, and said with the qualification, "I will not give up my right to the bond; you must trust to my honour." That is the way in which I interpret what she has said from time to time, and, that being so, however discreditable or dishonourable it may be, having so spoken, to recede from it, it appears to me that that is a ground upon which your Lordships cannot safely act ...'

*Commentary*

Distinguished in *Central London Property Trust Ltd v High Trees House Ltd* [1947] KB 130.

**McArdle, Re** [1951] Ch 699 Court of Appeal (Sir Raymond Evershed MR, Jenkins and Hodson LJJ)

Consideration - past

*Facts*

A number of children were entitled to a house after their mother's death. During the mother's life, one of the children and his wife lived with her in the house and the wife made various improvements to the house. At a later date, all the children signed a document addressed to her, stating that 'in consideration' of these improvements, on the mother's death the wife would be entitled to £488 from the estate (being the amount spent on the improvements).

*Held*

This was a case of past consideration and the promise was merely gratuitous, since the work had already been done.

**New Zealand Shipping Co Ltd v A M Satterthwaite & Co Ltd**

See chapter 1 - Offer and acceptance.

**North Ocean Shipping Co Ltd v Hyundai Construction Co Ltd. The Atlantic Baron** [1979] 3 WLR 419 High Court (Mocatta J)

Consideration - extra payment

*Facts*

Shipbuilders forced the prospective owners of a ship they were building to pay them an additional sum of money (10 per cent) to complete the ship in circumstances where the additional sum was not payable under the original contract. The owners reluctantly paid the money - by increasing their letter of credit - in order to 'maintain amicable relations' with the builders.

*Held*

The agreement was binding and the extra money so paid could not be recovered.

Mocatta J:

'Counsel's argument for the owners that the agreement to pay the extra ten per cent was void for lack of consideration was based on the well-known principle that a promise by one party to fulfil his existing contractual duty towards his other contracting party is not good consideration; he relied on the well-known case of *Stilk* v *Myrick* for this submission. Accordingly there was no consideration for the owner's agreement to pay the further ten per cent, since the yard were already contractually bound to build the ship and it is common ground that the devaluation of the dollar had in no way lessened the yard's legal obligation to do this ... I remain unconvinced, however, that by merely securing an increase in the instalments to be paid of ten per cent the yard automatically became obliged to increase the return letter of credit pro tanto and were therefore doing no more than undertaking in this respect to fulfil their existing contractual duty. I think that here they were undertaking an additional obligation or rendering themselves liable to an increased detriment. I therefore conclude, though not without some doubt, that there was consideration for the new agreement ...

Having reached the conclusion that there was consideration for the agreement ... I must next consider whether even if that agreement, varying the terms of the original shipbuilding contract ... was made under a threat to break that original contract and the various increased instalments were made consequentially under the varied agreement, the increased sums can be recovered as money had and received. Counsel for the owners submitted that they could be, provided they were involuntary payments and not made, albeit perhaps with some grumbling, to close the transaction ...

I have come to the conclusion that the important points here are that (i) since there was no danger at this time in registering a protest, (ii) the final payments were made without any qualification, and (iii) were followed by a delay ... before the owners put forward their claim, the correct inference to draw, taking an objective view of the facts, is that the action and inaction of the owners can only be regarded as an affirmation of the variation ... of the terms of the original contract by the agreement to pay the additional ten per cent. In reaching this conclusion I have not, of course, overlooked the findings in the special case [that the owners never intended to affirm the agreement for extra payments] but I do not think that an intention on the part of the owners not to affirm the agreement for the extra payments, not indicated to the yard, can avail them in view of their overt acts. As was said in *Deacon* v *Transport Regulation Board* in considering whether a payment was made voluntarily or not: "No secret mental reservation of the doer is material. The question is - what would his conduct indicate to a reasonable man as his mental state." I think this test is equally applicable to the decision this court has to make whether a voidable contract has been affirmed or not and I have applied this test in reaching the conclusion I have just expressed.

I think I should add very shortly that having considered the many authorities cited, even if I had come to a different conclusion on the issue about consideration, I would have come to the same decision adverse to the owners on the question whether the payments were made voluntarily in the sense of being made to close the transaction.'

*Commentary*

Followed: *Stilk* v *Myrick* (1809) 2 Camp 317. See also: *Williams* v *Roffey Bros & Nicholls (Contractors) Ltd* [1990] 1 All ER 512

**Pao On v Lau Yiu Long** [1979] 3 WLR 435 Privy Council (Lord Wilberforce, Viscount Dilhorne, Lord Simon of Glaisdale, Lord Salmon and Lord Scarman)

Consideration - duress

*Facts*

The plaintiffs owned a private company ('Shing On') and the defendants were majority shareholders in Fu Chip, a public investment company. By a written agreement dated 27 February 1973, the plaintiffs contracted to sell Shing On's shares to Fu Chip, the price being an allotment of Fu Chip shares at a deemed value of $2.50 a share: the plaintiffs undertook that they would not sell 2.5 million of the shares allotted to them before the end of April 1974. By a subsiduary agreement of the same date, the defendants agreed to buy back, on or before 30 April 1974, 2.5 million Fu Chip shares at $2.50 a share. As it was generally expected that the Fu Chip shares would rise in value, the plaintiffs realised that they had made a bad bargain and they told the defendants that they would not complete the main agreement unless the subsiduary agreement was replaced by an agreement guaranteeing the price of the 2.5 million shares at $2.50 a share. Anxious to complete the main agreement, but knowing that they could claim specific performance of it, the defendants, wishing to avoid litigation, agreed. By 30 April 1974 Fu Chip's share price had fallen to 36 cents: the plaintiffs sought to enforce the guarantee. Before the Board, the questions for decision were: was there consideration for the contract of guarantee? If there was, was the defendant's consent vitiated by duress?

*Held*

The plaintiffs were entitled to succeed.

Lord Scarman:

'The Board agrees with the submission of counsel for the plaintiffs that the consideration expressly stated in the written guarantee is sufficient in law to support the Laus' promise of indemnity. An act done before the giving of a promise to make a payment or to confer some other benefit can sometimes be consideration for the promise. The act must have been done at the promisor's request, the parties must have understood that the act was to be remunerated either by a payment or the conferment of some other benefit, and payment, or the conferment of a benefit, must have been legally enforceable had it been promised in advance. All three features are present in this case. The promise given to Fu Chip under the main agreement not to sell the shares for a year was at Lau's request. The parties understood at the time of the main agreement that the restriction on selling must be compensated for by the benefit of a guarantee against a drop in price: and such a guarantee would be legally enforceable. The agreed cancellation of the subsiduary agreement left, as the parties knew, the Paos unprotected in a respect in which at the time of the main agreement all were agreed they should be protected.

Counsel's submission for the plaintiffs is based on *Lampleigh* v *Brathwait* (1615) Hob 105 ... The modern statement of the law is in the judgment of Bowen LJ in *Re Casey's Patents, Stewart* v *Casey* [1892] 1 Ch 104 ...

Counsel for the defendants does not dispute the existence of the rule but challenges its application to the facts of this case. He submits that it is not a necessary inference or implication from the terms of the written guarantee that any benefit or protection was to be given to the Paos for their acceptance of the restriction on selling their shares. Their Lordships agree that the mere existence or recital of a prior request is not sufficient in itself to convert what is prima facie past consideration into sufficient consideration in law to support a promise: as they have indicated, it is only the first of three necessary preconditions. As for the second of those preconditions, whether the act done at the request of the promisor raises an implication of promised remuneration or other return is simply one of the construction of the words of the contract in the circumstances of its making. Once it is recognised, as the Board considers it inevitably must be, that the expressed consideration includes a reference to the Paos' promise not to sell the shares before 30 April 1974, a promise to be performed in the future, though given in the past, it is not possible to treat the Laus' promise of indemnity as independent of the Paos' antecedent promise, given at Lau's request, not to sell. The promise of indemnity was given because at the time of the main agreement the parties intended that Lau should confer on the Paos the benefit of his protection against a falling price. When the subsidiary agreement was cancelled, all were well aware that the Paos were still to have the benefit of his protection as consideration for the restriction on selling. It matters not whether the indemnity thus given be regarded as the best evidence of the benefit intended to be conferred in return for the promise not to sell, or as the positive bargain which fixed the benefit on the faith of which the promise was given, though where, as here, the subject is a written contract, the better analysis is probably that of the "positive bargain". Their Lordships, therefore, accept the submission that the contract itself states a valid consideration for the promise of indemnity ...

There is no doubt, and it was not challenged, that extrinsic evidence is admissible to prove the real consideration where: (a) no consideration, or a nominal consideration, is expressed in the instrument, or (b) the expressed consideration is in general terms or ambiguously stated, or (c) a substantial consideration is stated, but an additional consideration exists. The additional consideration must not, however, be inconsistent with the terms of the written instrument. Extrinsic evidence is also admissible to prove the illegality of the consideration ...

The extrinsic evidence in this case shows that the consideration for the promise of indemnity, while it included the cancellation of the subsidiary agreement, was primarily the promise given by the Paos to the Laus, to perform their contract with Fu Chip, which included the undertaking not to sell 60% of the shares allotted to them before 30 April 1974. Thus the real consideration for the indemnity was the promise to perform, or the performance of, the Paos' pre-existing contractual obligations to Fu Chip. This promise was perfectly consistent with the consideration stated in the guarantee. Indeed, it reinforces it by imposing on the Paos an obligation now owed to the Laus to do what, at Lau's request, they had agreed with Fu Chip to do.

Their Lordships do not doubt that a promise to perform, or the performance of, a pre-existing contractual obligation to a third party can be valid consideration. In *New Zealand Shipping Co Ltd* v *AM Satterthwaite & Co Ltd* [1974] 2 WLR 865 the rule and the reason for the rule were stated ... Unless, therefore, the guarantee was void as having been made for an illegal consideration or voidable on the ground of economic duress, the extrinsic evidence establishes that it was supported by valid consideration.

Counsel for the defendants submits that the consideration is illegal as being against public policy. He submits that to secure a party's promise by a threat of repudiation of a pre-existing contractual obligation owed to another can be, and in the circumstances of this case was, an abuse of a dominant bargaining position and so contrary to public policy. This, he submits, is so even though economic duress cannot be proved.

This submission found favour with the majority in the Court of Appeal. Their Lordships, however, consider it misconceived. Reliance was placed on the old "seaman" cases of *Harris* v *Watson* (1791) Peake 72 and *Stilk* v *Myrick* (1809) 2 Camp 317 ...

Their Lordships' conclusion is that where businessmen are negotiating at arm's length it is unnecessary for the achievement of justice, and unhelpful in the development of the law, to invoke such a rule of public policy. It would also create unacceptable anomaly. It is unnecessary because justice requires that men, who have negotiated at arm's length, be held to their bargains unless it can be shown that their consent was vitiated by fraud, mistake or duress. If a promise is induced by coercion of a man's will, the doctrine of duress suffices to do justice. The party coerced, if he chooses and acts in time, can avoid the contract. If there is no coercion, there can be no reason for avoiding the contract where there is shown to be real consideration which is otherwise legal ... Accordingly, the submission that the additional consideration established by the extrinsic evidence is invalid on the ground of public policy is rejected.

Duress, whatever form it takes, is a coercion of the will so as to vitiate consent. Their Lordships agree with the observation of Kerr J in *The Siboen and The Sibotre* [1976] 1 Lloyd's Rep 293 that in a contractual situation commercial pressure is not enough. There must be present some factor "which could in law be regarded as a coercion of his will so as to vitiate his consent". This conception is in line with what was said in this Board's decision in *Barton* v *Armstrong* [1976] AC 104 by Lord Wilberforce and Lord Simon of Glaisdale ... In determining whether there was a coercion of will such that there was no true consent, it is material to enquire whether the person alleged to have been coerced did or did not protest; whether, at the time he was allegedly coerced into making the contract, he did or did not have an alternative course open to him such as an adequate legal remedy; whether he was independently advised; and whether after entering the contract he took steps to avoid it. All these matters are, as was recognised in *Maskell* v *Horner* [1915] 3 KB 106, relevant in determining whether he acted voluntarily or not.

In the present case there is unanimity amongst the judges below that there was no coercion of Lau's will. In the Court of Appeal the trial judge's finding ... that Lau considered the matter thoroughly, chose to avoid litigation, and formed the opinion that the risk in giving the guarantee was more apparent than real was upheld. In short, there was commercial pressure, but no coercion. Even if this Board was disposed, which it is not, to take a different view, it would not substitute its opinion for that of the judges below on this question of fact.

It is, therefore, unnecessary for the Board to embark on an enquiry into the question whether English law recognises a category of duress known as "economic duress". But, since the question has been fully argued in this appeal, their Lordships will indicate very briefly the view which they have formed. At common law money paid under economic compulsion could be recovered in an action for money had and received: see *Astley* v *Reynolds* (1731) 2 Stra 915. The compulsion had to be such that the party was deprived of "his freedom of exercising his will". It is doubtful, however, whether at common law any duress other than duress to the person sufficed to render a contract voidable; see Blackstone's Commentaries and *Skeate* v *Beale* (1841) 11 Ad & El 983 ... Recently two English judges have recognised that commercial pressure may constitute duress the pressure of which can render a contract voidable: see Kerr J in *The Siboen and The Sibotre* and Mocatta J in *North Ocean Shipping Co Ltd* v *Hyundai Construction Co Ltd* [1978] 3 All ER 1170. Both stressed that the pressure must be such that the victim's consent to the contract was not a voluntary act on his part. In their Lordship's view, there is nothing contrary to principle in recognising economic duress as a factor which may render a contract voidable, provided always that the basis of such recognition is that it must amount to a coercion of will, which vitiates consent. It must be shown that the payment made or the contract entered into was not a voluntary act.'

*Commentary*

*The Siboen and The Sibotre*: see *Occidental World Investment Corp* v *Skibs A/S Avanti* [1976] 1 Lloyd's Rep 293

**Pinnel's Case** (1602) 5 Co Rep 117 Court of Common Pleas

Payment of part

*Facts*

The plaintiff sued for £8 10s and the defendant pleaded that, before the date when the payment was due, he had paid the plaintiff £5 2s 2d which he (the plaintiff) had accepted in full satisfaction of the £8 10s.

*Held*

The plaintiff was entitled to judgment because of the defendant's 'insufficient pleading'. However, the whole court resolved that the payment and acceptance of parcel [part] before the day in satisfaction of the whole, would be a good satisfaction in regard of circumstance of time; for peradventure parcel of it before the day would be more beneficial to him than the whole at the day, and the value of the satisfaction is not material. So if I am bound in £20 to pay you £10 at Westminster and you request me to pay you £5 at the day at York, and you will accept it in full satisfaction of the whole £10 it is a good satisfaction for the whole for the expense to pay it at York, is sufficient satisfaction. The court also resolved that payment of a lesser sum on the day in satisfaction of a greater, cannot be any satisfaction for the whole, because it appears to the judges that by no possibility a lesser sum can be a satisfaction to the plaintiff for a greater sum; but the gift of a horse, hawk or robe, etc, in satisfaction is good, for it shall be intended that a horse, hawk or robe, etc, might be more beneficial to the plaintiff than the money, in respect of some circumstance, or otherwise the plaintiff would not have accepted of it in satisfaction. But when the whole sum is due, by no intendment the acceptance of parcel can be a satisfaction to the plaintiff.

*Commentary*

This decision was applied, amongst others, in *D& C Builders Ltd* v *Rees* [1966] 2 QB 617 and *Foakes* v *Beer* (1884) 9 App Cas 605.

**Rickards (Charles) Ltd v Oppenheim** [1950] 1 KB 616 Court of Appeal (Bucknill, Singleton and Denning LJJ)

Waiver - condition as to time

*Facts*

Wanting a new Rolls Royce, the defendant contracted with the plaintiffs to supply a chassis and to build a body on it within seven months, time being of the essence. As sub-contractors failed to complete the work within the stipulated time, the defendant waived the time condition by pressing for delivery on successive later dates. About three months after the original delivery date, the sub-contractor said the car would be ready in two weeks and, on the following day, the defendant gave the sub-contractor written notice that, unless he received the car within four weeks, he would be unable to accept delivery. The sub-contractors forwarded the notice to the plaintiffs after eight or nine days. The car was not delivered within the four weeks and, when it was, the defendant refused delivery.

*Held*

The defendant could rescind the contract. After waiving the initial stipulation as to time, he had been entitled to give reasonable notice again making time the essence and this he had done.

Denning LJ:

'If the defendant, as he did, led the plaintiffs to believe that he would not insist on the stipulation as to time, and that, if they carried out the work, he would accept it, and they did it, he could not afterwards set up the stipulation in regard to time against them. Whether it be called waiver or forbearance on his part, or an agreed variation or substituted performance, does not matter. It is a kind of estoppel. By his conduct he made a promise not to insist on his strict legal rights. That promise was intended to be binding, intended to be acted on, and was, in fact, acted on. He cannot afterwards go back on it. That, I think, ... was ... anticipated in *Bruner* v *Moore*. It is a particular application of the principle which I endeavoured to state in *Central London Property Trust Ltd* v *High Trees House Ltd*.

Therefore, if the matter stopped there, the plaintiffs could have said that, notwithstanding that more than seven months had elapsed, the defendant was bound to accept, but the matter does not stop there, because delivery was not given in compliance with the requests of the defendant. Time and time again the defendant pressed for delivery, time and time again he was assured that he would have early delivery, but he never got satisfaction, and eventually at the end of June he gave notice saying that, unless the car was delivered by 25 July, he would not accept it. The question thus arises whether he was entitled to give such a notice, making time of the essence ... In my judgment, he was entitled to give a reasonable notice making time of the essence of the matter. Adequate protection to the suppliers is given by the requirement that the notice should be reasonable.'

## Roscorla v Thomas (1842) 3 QB 234 Queen's Bench (Lord Denman CJ)

Consideration - past

*Facts*

In an action for breach of warranty as to the soundness of a horse, the declaration stated that in consideration that the plaintiff, at the request of the defendant, had bought of the defendant a horse for the sum of £30, the defendant promised that it was sound and free from vice. It was argued for the defendant that the precedent executed consideration was insufficient to support the subsequent promise.

*Held*

This was the case.

Lord Denman CJ:

'It may be taken as a general rule, subject to exceptions not applicable to this case, that the promise must be co-extensive with the consideration. In the present case, the only promise that would result from the consideration as stated and be co-extensive with it, would be to deliver the horse upon request.'

## Scandinavian Trading Tanker Co AB v Flota Petrolera Ecuatoriana. The Scaptrade [1983] 2 WLR 248 Court of Appeal (Sir John Donaldson MR, May and Robert Goff LJJ)

Estoppel - reliance on conduct

*Facts*

Under the terms of a charter, payments were to be made monthly in advance on the eighth day of each month; if the charterers defaulted, the owners could withdraw the vessel from hire. On some months, especially when the due date was a weekend, payments had been accepted up to three days late. Now, the charterers failed to pay an instalment due on Sunday 8 July 1979: it had not been paid by 12 July, so the owners withdrew the vessel. Were they prevented by equitable estoppel from doing so?

*Held*

They were not.

Robert Goff LJ:

'We turn therefore to the first of the two grounds of appeal, which relates to the effect of the owners having, before July 1979, accepted late payments of hire from the charterers. There was no dispute that, in this connection, the applicable principle was that of equitable estoppel. There was also no dispute that, in order to bring themselves within that principle, the charterers had to establish that two criteria had been fulfilled. First, they had to establish that the owners had represented unequivocally that they would not enforce their strict legal right, under the contract between the parties, to withdraw the vessel from the charterer's service in the event of a default in payment of an instalment of hire (see *Woodhouse AC Israel Cocoa Ltd SA v Nigerian Marketing Co Ltd* [1972] WLR 1090). Second, they had to establish that in the circumstances it would be inequitable to allow the owners to enforce their strict legal right, having regard to the dealings which had taken place between the parties (see *Hughes v Metropolitan Rly Co* (1877) 2 App Cas 439 at 448 per Lord Cairns LC). The first requirement may however be fulfilled if a reasonable man in the shoes of the charterers would have inferred from the owners' conduct that they were making such a representation (see *Bremer Handelsgesellschaft mbH v Vanden Avenne-Izegem PVBA* [1978] 2 Lloyd's Rep 109 at 126 per Lord Salmon). As to the second requirement, since the equitable estoppel is founded on a representation, it can only be unconscionable for the representor (here the owners) to enforce his strict legal right if the conduct of the representee (here the charterers) has been so influenced by the representation as to call for the intervention of equity. Whether or not the representee's conduct has been so influenced must depend on the evidence; but the court is entitled to infer from the evidence that his conduct has been so influenced ... In truth, although the totality of the evidence may provide some explanation why the charterers ... were surprised when the owners decided to exercise their right of withdrawal when they did, it falls far short of an unequivocal representation by the owners that they would not exercise that right ...

It is however also plain to us on the evidence that, in any event, the owners' conduct did not in any way influence the charterers' conduct in failing to pay the relevant hire instalment on time. In his judgment the judge stated that "there was scant evidence of any reliance by the charterers". We would go further, for, having been shown the relevant evidence, we are satisfied that the charterers' conduct in making the late payment in July 1979 was in no way influenced by the conduct of the owners. This is not even a case where the charterers were lulled into a state of false security by the owners' conduct, or where the owners' conduct, although not the sole cause, could be said to have conributed to the charterers' omission to pay in time. On the contrary, as appears from the evidence, the gentleman in the charterers' organisation immediately responsible for making the hire payment ... did not make the payment in time because he was instructed by his superior ... to hold his hand until it had become clearer whether the charter would continue for another year. In these circumstances, there can have been no causal connection at all between the owners' conduct and the charterers' omission to pay the July 1979 instalment of hire in time.'

*Commentary*

The House of Lords affirmed this decision [1983] 3 WLR 203.

## Scaptrade, The

See **Scandinavian Trading Tanker Co AB v Flota Petrolera Ecuatoriana.   The Scaptrade**

## Shadwell v Shadwell (1860) 9 CB (NS) 159 Common Bench (Erle CJ, Byles and Keating JJ)

Consideration - promisee contracted to marry

*Facts*

An uncle wrote to his nephew, the plaintiff, as follows: 'I am glad to hear of your intended marriage with Ellen Nicholl; and, as I promised to assist you at starting, I am happy to tell you that I will pay to you one hundred and fifty pounds yearly during my life ... ' It was argued, on a claim for arrears of the promised sum, that there was no consideration, since the nephew was already contractually bound to marry Ellen Nicholl.

*Held* (Byles J dissenting)

The plaintiff was entitled to succeed.

Erle CJ:

'... do these facts show that the promise was in consideration, either of the loss to be sustained by the plaintiff, or the benefit to be derived from the plaintiff to the uncle, at his, the uncle's, request? My answer is in the affirmative. First, do these facts show a loss sustained by the plaintiff at the uncle's request? When I answer this in the affirmative, I am aware that a man's marriage with the woman of his choice is in one sense a boon, and in that sense the reverse of a loss; yet, as between the plaintiff and the party promising an income to support the marriage, it may be a loss. The plaintiff may have made the most material changes in his position, and have induced the object of his affections to do the same, and have incurred pecuniary liabilities resulting in embarrassments, which would be in every sense a loss, if the income which had been promised should be withheld; and if the promise was made in order to induce the parties to marry, the promise so made would be, in legal effect, a request to marry. Secondly, do these facts show a benefit derived from the plaintiff to the uncle at his request? In answering again in the affirmative, I am at liberty to consider the relation in which the parties stood, and the interest in the *status* of the nephew which the uncle declares. The marriage primarily affects the parties thereto; but in the second degree it may be an object of interest with a near relative, and in that sense a benefit to him. This benefit is also derived from the plaintiff at the uncle's request, if the promise of the annuity was intended as an inducement to the marriage; and the averment that the plaintiff, relying on the promise, married, is an averment that the promise was one inducement to the marriage. This is a consideration averred in the declaration, and it appears to me to be expressed in the letter, construed with the surrounding circumstances. No case bearing a strong analogy to the present was cited; but the importance of enforcing promises which have been made to induce parties to marry has been often recognised ... the decision turns on a question of fact, whether the consideration for the promise is proved as pleaded. I think it is, and therefore my judgment ... is for the plaintiff.'

### Snelling v John G Snelling Ltd [1973] 1 QB 87 High Court (Ormrod J)

Agreement with third party - intended breach

*Facts*

The plaintiff and his brothers had financed the defendant company by way of loans. Requiring additional finance, the company's properties were mortgaged to a finance company and the brothers, directors of the defendant company, entered into an agreement between themselves that if one of them resigned voluntarily he would forfeit the amount of his loan. The plaintiff so resigned and sought repayment of his loan. In resisting the claim, could the defendant company rely on the agreement to which it was not a party?

*Held*

It could not do so directly, but as the other brothers (who were also defendants) had made out an unambiguous case, the plaintiff's claim would be dismissed and a declaration made that the defendant company was not obliged to repay his loan.

### Société Italo-Belge pour le Commerce et l'Industrie SA v Palm and Vegetable Oils (Malaysia) Sdn Bhd. The Post Chaser [1982] 1 All ER 19 High Court (Robert Goff J)

Sale of palm oil - time for declaration of ship

*Facts*

Sellers sold palm oil to buyers who in turn sold to sub-buyers. The contract provided: 'Declaration of ship be made to Buyers in writing as soon as possible after vessel's sailing'. The sellers gave the declaration after more than one month; the buyers did not protest or make any reservation, and at the buyers' request, the sellers handed over documents covering the sale to the sub-buyers. Two days later, though, the sub-buyers rejected the documents and the sellers did likewise later that day. The sellers were forced to sell the oil elsewhere at a lower price and they claimed the difference from the buyers by way of damages.

*Held*

Their claim should fail. Although time was here of the essence and the buyers had, by their request, waived their rights, the sellers had not been prejudiced by the buyers' representation that they would accept the documents and it was not therefore inequitable for the buyers to enforce their legal right to reject them.

Robert Goff J:

'... there next arises the question whether there was any sufficient reliance by the sellers on this representation to give rise to an equitable estoppel. Here there arose a difference between counsel for the sellers and counsel for the buyers as to the degree of reliance which is required. It is plain, however, from the speech of Lord Cairns LC in *Hughes* v *Metropolitan Rly Co* (1877) 2 App Cas 439 at 448, that the representor will not be allowed to enforce his rights "where it would be inequitable having regard to the dealings which have taken place between the parties". Accordingly there must be such action, or inaction, by the representee on the faith of the representation as will render it inequitable to permit the representor to enforce his strict legal rights ...

I approach the matter as follows. The fundamental principle is that stated by Lord Cairns LC, viz that the representor will not be allowed to enforce his rights "where it would be inequitable having regard to the dealings which have thus taken place between the parties". To establish such inequity, it is not necessary to show detriment; indeed, the representee may have benefited from the representation, and yet it may be inequitable, at least without reasonable notice, for the representor to enforce his legal rights. Take the facts of *Central London Property Trust Ltd* v *High Trees House Ltd* ... [1947] KB 130, the case in which Denning J breathed new life into the doctrine of equitable estoppel. The representation was by a lessor to the effect that he would be content to accept a reduced rent. In such a case, although the lessee has benefited from the reduction in rent, it may well be inequitable for the lessor to insist on his legal right to the unpaid rent, because the lessee has conducted his affairs on the basis that he would only have to pay rent at the lower rate; and a court might well think it right to conclude that only after reasonable notice could the lessor return to charging rent at the higher rate specified in the lease. Furthermore it would be open to the court, in any particular case, to infer from the circumstances of the case that the representee must have conducted his affairs in such a way that it would be inequitable for the representor to enforce his rights, or to do so without reasonable notice. But it does not follow that in every case in which the representee has acted, or failed to act, in reliance on the representation, it will be inequitable for the representor to enforce his rights for "the nature of the action, or inaction, may be insufficient to give rise to the inequity, in which event a necessary requirement stated by Lord Cairns LC for the application of the doctrine would not have been fulfilled.

This, in my judgment, is the principle which I have to apply in the present case. Here, all that happened was that the sellers ... presented the documents on the same day as the buyers made their representation; and within two days the documents were rejected. Now on these simple facts, although it is plain that the sellers did actively rely on the buyers' representation, and did conduct their affairs in reliance on it, by presenting the documents, I cannot see anything which would render it inequitable for the buyers thereafter to enforce their legal right to reject the documents. In particular, having regard to the very short time which elapsed between the date of the representation and the date of presentation of the documents on the one hand and the date of rejection on the other hand, I cannot see that, in the absence of any evidence that the sellers' position had been prejudiced by reason of their action in reliance on the representation, it is possible to infer that they suffered any such prejudice. In these circumstances, a necessary element for the application of the doctrine of equitable estoppel is lacking; and I decide this point in favour of the buyers.'

**Stilk v Myrick** (1809) 2 Camp 317 King's Bench (Lord Ellenborough)

Consideration - existing obligation

*Facts*

In the course of a sea voyage, two seamen deserted and the captain promised the remainder of the crew extra wages if they would work the ship back to London short-handed. The crew brought an action for the extra wages.

*Held*

The agreement was void for want of consideration.

Lord Ellenborough:

'Before they sailed from London they had undertaken to do all that they could under all the emergencies of the voyage ... the desertion of a part of the crew is to be considered an emergency of the voyage as much as their death ... those who remain are bound by the terms of their original contract to exert themselves to the utmost to bring the ship in safely to her destined port.'

*Commentary*

Followed in *North Ocean Shipping Co Ltd* v *Hyundai Construction Co Ltd. The Atlantic Baron* [1978] 1 WLR 328: refined and limited in *Williams* v *Roffey Bros & Nicholls (Contractors) Ltd* [1990] 1 All ER 512.

**Tanner v Tanner**

See Introduction.

**Thomas v Thomas** (1842) 11 LJ QB 104 Queen's Bench (Lord Denman CJ, Patteson and Coleridge JJ)

Consideration - sufficiency

*Facts*

A man having expressed - orally - the desire that his widow should have the use of a certain house, his executors agreed that she should have such use on payment of £1 a year towards the ground-rent and her undertaking to keep the house in good and tenantable repair. The executors contended that there was no consideration for their agreement.

*Held*

This was not the case.

Coleridge J:

'... we are not tied to look for the legal consideration for an instrument in any particular portion of it. It is usually found at the commencement; but if we find it in any other part we are bound to use it ... Here, in another part, we find an express agreement by the person to whom the premises are to be conveyed, to pay £1 a year for a particular purpose, namely, towards the ground-rent, payable in respect of the premises, and others thereto adjoining; and she enters also into a distinct agreement, that, as long as she is in possession, she will do repairs. That is a sufficient consideration ...'

**Tool Metal Manufacturing Co Ltd v Tungsten Electric Co Ltd** [1955] 1 WLR 761 House of Lords (Viscount Simonds, Lord Oaksey, Lord Tucker and Lord Cohen)

Temporary suspension - termination by counterclaim

*Facts*

In 1938 TMMC, who owned certain patents, formally agreed with TECO to give the latter a licence to manufacture products protected by the patents. The agreement was to last until 1947. In return TECO agreed to pay a royalty of 10 per cent and further promised to pay additional 'compensation' if they exceeded a certain quota. The agreement was terminable by six months' notice on either side. After the outbreak of war in 1939, the payment of compensation was suspended. In 1942, TMMC told TECO that they would prepare a new agreement and would not, in the meantime, claim compensation. No compensation was claimed during the war and TECO regulated their production accordingly. In 1944, negotiations over the new agreement broke down. In 1945, TECO sued TMMC for breach of the 1938 agreement alleging inter alia that it had been agreed that no compensation should be payable after 31 December 1939. TMMC denied the alleged agreement and maintained if there were such agreement, there was no consideration for it; and they counter-claimed, alleging that TECO were in breach of their contract since they had not paid compensation. They did not seek compensation for the period up to June 1945, but did seek compensation thereafter.

In the first action, the Court of Appeal (Somervell, Singleton and Cohen LJJ) decided that there had been no contract for the final termination of the payment of compensation, only a temporary arrangement pending a new agreement. However, on the principle in *Hughes* v *Metropolitan Rail Co*, this arrangement to suspend the payment of compensation was binding in equity on TMMC until terminated by proper notice, and the presentation of the draft new agreement in 1944 did not constitute such notice,

In the present action, TMMC claimed compensation as from 1 January 1947, treating the delivery of their counter-claim in the first action as a sufficient notice to determine the agreement to suspend payment of compensation. TECO pleaded, inter alia, that the delivery of the counter-claim was insufficient notice, since no time was specified in it for the termination of the arrangement.

*Held*

The delivery of the counter-claim was sufficient notice.

Lord Cohen:

'... it has never been decided that, in every case, notice should be given before a temporary concession ceases to operate. It might, for instance, cease automatically on the occurrence of a particular event. Still less has any case decided that, where notice is necessary, it must take a particular form.'

Romer LJ seems to have taken the view that the counterclaim could not be a notice, because you cannot terminate an agreement by repudiating it. The fallacy of this argument consists in treating the arrangement found to exist by the CA in the first action, as an agreement binding in law. It was not an agreement; it was a voluntary concession by TMMC which, for reasons of equity, the court held TMMC could not cease to allow without plain intimation to TECO of their intention to do so. The counter-claim seems to me a plain intimation of such change of intention, operating as from 1 June 1945 and for the future. Nonetheless, the intimation would fall short of what was required if it was the duty of TMMC to specify in the intimation the reasonable time which they would allow after receipt of the intimation to enable TECO to re-adjust their business to the altered conditions. I see no reason why equity should impose this burden on TMMC.'

**Ward v Byham** [1956] 1 WLR 496 Court of Appeal (Denning, Morris and Parker LJJ)

Consideration - performance of statutory duty

*Facts*

The parents of an illegitimate child separated and the father paid a neighbour £1 per week to look after the child. Subsequently, the mother wrote to the father to ask him to let her have the child and the £1 pw. The father was prepared to let her have the child and pay her the money if: (1) the mother could prove that the child would be well looked after and happy; and (2) the child was allowed to decide for herself whether or not she wished to live with her mother. The mother then looked after the child and the father paid the money until, seven months later, the mother married. The mother sued for breach of contract and the father pleaded want of consideration.

*Held*

The mother was entitled to succeed.

Denning LJ:

'I approach the case, therefore, on the footing that, in looking after the child, the mother is only doing what she is legally bound to do. Even so, I think that there was sufficient consideration to support the promise. I have always thought that a promise to perform an existing duty, or the performance of it, should be regarded as good consideration, because it is a benefit to the person to whom it is given. Take this very case. It is as much a benefit for the father to have the child looked after by the mother as by a neighbour. If he gets the benefit for which he stipulated, he ought to honour his promise, and he ought not to avoid it by saying that the mother was herself under a duty to maintain the child.

I regard the father's promise in this case as what is sometimes called a unilateral contract, a promise in return for an act, a promise by the father to pay £1 a week in return for the mother's looking after the child. Once the mother embarked on the task of looking after the child, there was a binding contract. So long as she looked after the child, she would be entitled to £1 a week.

*Commentary*

Distinguished in *Horrocks* v *Forray* [1976] 1 WLR 230.

**Williams v Roffey Bros & Nicholls (Contractors) Ltd** [1990] 1 All ER 512 Court of Appeal (Purchas, Glidewell and Russell LJJ)

Extra payment - consideration

*Facts*

The defendants contracted to refurbish a block of flats and sub-contracted the carpentry work to the plaintiff for £20,000: it was an implied term of the sub-contract that the plaintiff would receive interim payments according to the work completed. After the plaintiff had completed some of the work, and received interim payments of £16,200, he found himself in financial difficulty, partly because his price had been too low. Aware of these things, and facing a penalty if the main contract was not completed on time, the defendants agreed to pay the plaintiff an additional £575 per flat on completion to ensure that the plaintiff continued with the work and completed it on time.

*Held*

This agreement would be enforced. Although the plaintiff had not been required to undertake any work additional to his original contract, the advantages which the defendants hoped to obtain (avoidance of penalty and the need to engage another sub-contractor) were consideration for the extra payment.

Glidewell LJ:

'... following the view of the majority in *Ward* v *Byham* [1956] 1 WLR 496 and of the whole court in *Williams* v *Williams* [1957] 1 WLR 148 and that of the Privy Council in *Pao On* v *Lau Yiu* [1979] 3 WLR 435 the present state of the law on this subject can be expressed in the following proposition: (i) if A has entered into a contract with B to do work for, or to supply goods or services to, B in return for payment by B and (ii) at some stage before A has completely performed his obligations under the contract B has reason to doubt whether A will, or will be able to, complete his side of the bargain and (iii) B thereupon promises A an additional payment in return for A's promise to perform his contractual obligations on time and (iv) as a result of giving his promise B obtains in practice a benefit, or obviates a disbenefit, and (v) B's promise is not given as a result of economic duress or fraud on the part of A, then (vi) the benefit to B is capable of being consideration for B's promise, so that the promise will be legally binding.

As I have said, counsel for the defendants accepts that in the present case by promising to pay the extra ... the defendants secured benefits. There is no finding, and no suggestion, that in this case the promise was given as a result of fraud or duress.

If it be objected that the propositions above contravene the principle in *Stilks* v *Myrick* (1809) 2 Camp 317, I answer that in my view they do not: they refine and limit the application of that principle, but they leave the principle unscathed, eg where B secures no benefit by his promise. It is not in my view surprising that a principle enunciated in relation to the rigours of seafaring life during the Napoleonic wars should be subjected during the succeeding 180 years to a process of refinement and limitation in its application in the present day.

It is therefore my opinion that on his findings of fact in the present case, the judge was entitled to hold, as he did, that the defendants' promise to pay the extra ... was supported by valuable consideration, and thus constituted an enforceable agreement.

As a subsidiary argument, counsel for the defendants submits that on the facts of the present case the consideration, even if otherwise good, did not "move from the promisee". This submission is based on the principle illustrated in the decision in *Tweddle* v *Atkinson* (1861) 1 B & S 393.

My understanding of the meaning of the requirement that "consideration must move from the promisee" is that such consideration must be provided by the promisee, or arise out of his contractual relationship with the promisor. It is consideration provided by somebody else, not a party to the contract, which does not "move from the promisee". This was the situation in *Tweddle* v *Atkinson*, but it is, of course, not the situation in the present case. Here the benefits to the defendants arose out of their agreement ... with the plaintiff, the promisee. In this respect I would adopt the following passage from *Chitty on Contracts* (25th edn, 1983) para 173, and refer to the authorities there cited:

"The requirement that consideration must move from the promisee is most generally satisfied where some detriment is suffered by him: eg where he parts with money or goods, or renders services, in exchange for the promise. But the requirement may equally well be satisfied where the promisee confers a benefit on the promisor without in fact suffering any detriment." (Chitty's emphasis).

That is the situation in this case.'

**Woodhouse AC Israel Cocoa Ltd SA v Nigerian Produce Marketing Co Ltd** [1972] 2 WLR 1090 House of Lords (Lord Hailsham of St Marylebone LC, Viscount Dilhorne, Lord Pearson, Lord Cross of Chelsea and Lord Salmon)

Estoppel - representation as to payment

*Facts*

Nigerian sellers had for many years sold cocoa to an association to which the appellants belonged. Contracts were concluded on the association's standard form contract which provided, inter alia, for the settlement of all disputes by arbitration in London. Until 1963, the cocoa price was expressed in pounds sterling, but thereafter, at the seller's request, in Nigerian pounds and Lagos was substituted for London as the place of payment. In 1966 there were fears on the part of members of the association lest sterling were to be devalued. As a result of representations by the association, the sellers agreed in July 1967 that 'for transactions concluded from the 1st September 1967, payment may be made in pounds sterling in London or in £N in Lagos and that for transactions already concluded in £N, payment may be made in pounds sterling, provided the transfer charges are borne by the buyer concerned'. The appellants informed the sellers that they wished to avail themselves of this facility. On 29 August, the sellers wrote informing the association that circumstances beyond their control meant that they were forced to withdraw the option. On 30 September, however, the sellers wrote that 'payment can be made in sterling and in Lagos'. Subject to certain conditions, the association was told it was 'at liberty to make payment in sterling not only with contracts already entered into, but also with future contracts'. On the devaluation of the pound sterling, the buyers claimed they could discharge their contracts made before the date of devaluation by paying on delivery one pound sterling for every one Nigerian pound. The sellers disputed this.

*Held*

The representation of 30 September could not be construed in the way the buyers contended. It amounted to no more than a representation that the sellers would accept payment in Lagos of the sterling equivalent of the price calculated in Nigerian pounds. However, even if it could be said that the meaning of the letter was ambiguous and that the buyers could reasonably have understood it to contain a representation that the money on account could be treated as expressed in sterling, it could not give rise to an estoppel because, to do so, a representation must be clear and unequivocal and if a representation was not clear and unequivocal, it was irrelevant that the representee reasonably misconstrued it and acted on it.

Viscount Dilhorne:

'... it was said, and this was the appellants' main contention, that if the contracts were not varied so that payment might be made on the basis of one pound sterling for one Nigerian pound, at least the respondents had represented that it could and, as the appellants had relied on that representation to their detriment, the respondents were estopped from denying that payment could be so made. While I recognise that a party to a contract, while not agreeing to a variation of it, may nevertheless say that he will waive the performance by the other party of certain of its terms, and that if the other party relies on the waiver performance of the terms waived cannot be insisted on, in this case there was not a representation of the character alleged contained in or to be implied from the letter of 30th September. To found an estoppel, the representation must be clear and unequivocal. In my opinion, the letter of 30th September could not reasonably be understood to contain or to imply a clear and unequivocal representation of the nature alleged.'

*Commentary*

See also *Scandinavian Trading Tanker Co AB* v *Flota Petrolera Ecuatoriana. The Scaptrade* [1983] 2 WLR 248.

**Wyvern Developments Ltd, Re** [1974] 1 WLR 1097 High Court (Templeman J)

Estoppel - Official Receiver

*Facts*

Wyvern went into liquidation after Gresham Trust Ltd had obtained an order for specific performance against it in respect of the sale of certain land. As liquidator, the Official Receiver approved the sale of the land to Winter and the major shareholder in Wyvern now asked that this approval be modified or reversed on the ground that it was a sale at less than true value.

*Held*

No order would be made as the Official Receiver was contractually bound to do that which he had promised to do.

Templeman J:

'Gresham entered in the contract relying on the promise made by the Official Receiver and once they entered into that contract then, of course, they were barred from going to the court to enforce their lien; they had committed themselves and could do nothing but carry out that contract. Accordingly, in my judgment, the consideration for the promise of the Official Receiver was the promise by Gresham that instead of enforcing their lien by application to the court they would contract to sell their legal estate plus their right of lien; and in consideration of Gresham's promise, the Official Receiver agreed to concur by conveyancing the equitable interest of Wyvern, thus completing the title of Winter. That is sufficient to dispose of this application, because, in my judgment, the Official Receiver is contractually bound to do that which he promised to do and is anxious to do.

I should, however, mention the alternative submissions which were made. In the first place, counsel for the Official Receiver says that the approval by the Official Receiver ... of the contract created an estoppel and he prays in aid the principle of promissory estoppel exemplified in *Central London Property Trust Ltd* v *High Trees House Ltd* ... In my judgment ... estoppel applies where the promisor knows and intends that the promisee will irretrievably alter his position in reliance on the promise. The Official Receiver put into circulation a promise, on the strength of which both Gresham and Winter altered their legal relationships. They did so by entering into a contract which bound them both. Once that was done, the Official Receiver was estopped from denying that he was entitled and bound to perform his promise.'

# 3    CERTAINTY AND FORM OF CONTRACT

**Alpenstow Ltd v Regalian Properties plc** [1985] 1 WLR 721 High Court (Nourse J)

Sale of land - subject to contract

*Facts*

Following negotiations, the parties agreed in writing that, if planning consent was given, the plaintiffs would give the defendants notice of their willingness to sell at a stated price, within 28 days the defendants would inform them of their acceptance, subject to contract, and within seven days thereafter the plaintiffs would submit a draft contract. The agreement further provided for the approval and exchange of contracts within stated times. Planning permission was granted and the plaintiffs duly gave notice of willingness to sell, which the defendants accepted, but the plaintiffs then contended that there was not a binding contract.

*Held*

This was not the case.

Nourse J:

> '... the position is that the words "subject to contract" have a clear prima facie meaning, being in themselves merely conditional. But there might be a very strong and exceptional context which would induce the court not to give them that meaning in a particular case. The precise nature of the condition precedent to the coming into existence of a contract which these words import was spelled out by the Court of Appeal in *Eccles* v *Bryant* [1948] Ch 93. It is, as counsel for the owners submits, that there shall be an exchange of contracts in accordance with ordinary conveyancing practice. Before that either party can withdraw ...

> These particular and general considerations leave me in no doubt that the answer of counsel for [the defendants] is to be preferred to that of counsel for the [plaintiffs]. In my judgment this is a case where there is a very strong and exceptional context which must induce the court not to give the words 'subject to contract' their clear prima facie meaning, and I so hold. The fact that the agreements were professionally drawn is ultimately seen to be in favour of this view. You cannot credit the draftsman with an adherence to the conventional meaning of "subject to contract" without accusing him of lax and superfluous drafting. I think that he has shown himself to be worth more than that. Why write so much so well to so small effect?'

*Commentary*

Section 2 of the Law of Property (Miscellaneous Provisions) Act 1989 implemented, as from 27 September 1989, certain of the recommendations contained in the Law Commission's Report 'Transfer of Land: Formalities for Contracts for Sale etc of Land' dated June 1987. Paragraph 4.15 of that Report included remarks as follows:

> 'The vast majority of contracts for the sale or other disposition of land already involve writing. Where land is sold it is usual for each party to sign a document setting out all the terms of the contract, and for the parts to be exchanged. This practice can continue unaffected. Our recommendation will, however, prevent allegations that an oral contract was made at an earlier stage because it will be impossible to make an oral contract for the sale of land. This may have the beneficial effect of enabling negotiations to proceed more freely. It will still be possible to create contracts by correspondence, so it will still be desirable for the parties to use the formula "subject to contract" on letters which contain, or which refer to documents containing, the terms of the contract, if the letters are signed by a party to the contract. Use of the phrase, however, would not strictly still be necessary in letters written on behalf of the parties.'

**Bigg v Boyd Gibbins Ltd**

See chapter 1 - Offer and acceptance.


**British Bank for Foreign Trade Ltd v Novinex Ltd** [1949] 1 KB 263 Court of Appeal (Bucknill, Cohen and Singleton LJJ)

Contract - amount of commission

*Facts*

The defendants agreed to pay the plaintiffs 'an agreed commission' on certain business. The plaintiffs carried out their side of the bargain: were they entitled to any commission?

*Held*

In default of agreement, they should receive a reasonable commission, as assessed by the court.


**Campbell v Edwards** [1976] 1 WLR 403 Court of Appeal (Lord Denning MR and Geoffrey Lane LJ)

Price - surveyor's valuation

*Facts*

Wishing to assign the lease of her flat, in accordance with its terms the tenant first offered to surrender it to her landlord 'at a price fixed by a chartered surveyor to be agreed by the Landlord and the Tenant'. Surveyors were duly appointed and they said that the landlord should pay the tenant £10,000. The landlord asked two other firms to give a valuation: their figures were £3,500 and £1,250. The landlord sought, inter alia, a declaration that he was not bound by the original valuation: the claim was struck out: the landlord appealed.

*Held*

The appeal would be dismissed as, in the absence of fraud or collusion, the first valuation was binding on the parties by contract.

Lord Denning MR:

> 'It is simply the law of contract. If two persons agree that the price of property should be fixed by a valuer on whom they agree, and he gives that valuation honestly and in good faith, they are bound by it. Even if he has made a mistake they are still bound by it. The reason is because they have agreed to be bound by it. If there were fraud or collusion, of course, it would be different. Fraud or collusion unravels everything.

> It may be that, if a valuer gives a speaking valuation - if he gives his reasons or his calculations - and you can show on the face of them that they are wrong, it might be upset. But this not such a case. [The original valuers] simply gave the figure. Having given it honestly, it is binding on the parties. It is no good for either party to say that it is incorrect. But even if the valuation could be upset for mistake, there is no room for it in this case. The premises have been surrendered to the landlord. He has entered into occupation of them. Months have passed. There cannot be restitutio in integrum.'


**City and Westminster Properties (1934) Ltd v Mudd** [1958] 3 WLR 312 High Court (Harman J)

*Facts*

A lease granted by the plaintiffs to the defendant stipulated restricting the use of the premises to 'showrooms, workrooms and offices only'. The defendant was orally assured that he would be permitted to sleep there, but subsequently the plaintiffs brought an action for forfeiture for breach of covenant.

*Held*

The defendant was permitted to prove this collateral undertaking even though it contradicted the express terms of the lease.

## Couturier v Hastie

See chapter 8 - Mistake.

## Daulia Ltd v Four Millbank Nominees Ltd

See chapter 1 - Offer and acceptance.

## In re a Debtor (No 517 of 1991) (1991) The Times 25 November Chancery Division (Ferris J)

Oral agreement to vary a guarantee - whether valid - requirements of Statute of Frauds 1677

*Facts*

The debtor had guaranteed performance of a monetary debt by an associated company IHL, but claimed that he had agreed with a representative of the creditor company that monies advanced by him through another company to IHL should go in reduction or extinction of his liability under the guarantee.

That agreement was an oral one, not in writing as required by s4 of Statute of Frauds.

*Held*

The court found that an oral agreement varying the mode of performance of a guarantee could be relied upon by way of defence notwithstanding s4. That section merely had the effect of making any oral agreement unenforceable, thus it would be impossible to found a cause of action on it, but the agreement, whether verbal or written, could be relied on by way of defence.

## Eastwood v Kenyon

See Introduction.

## Elpis Maritime Co Ltd v Marti Chartering Co Inc (The Maria D) [1991] 3 All ER 758; [1991] TLR 369 House of Lords (Lord Keith, Lord Brandon, Lord Ackner, Lord Oliver and Lord Lowry)

Guarantees - Statute of Frauds 1677 - enforcement

*Facts*

The owners chartered their vessel, the Maria D, to the charterers for a voyage from Izmir, Turkey to Algeria for the carriage of a cargo of wheat. The contract was negotiated through brokers acting for both sides. Tramp Maritime acted for the owners and Marti Chartering for the charterers. During the course of the negotiations it was insisted that Marti should themselves provide a guarantee, initially only for demurrage, but later extended to include 5 per cent balance of freight. The written charterparty contract as finally drawn up consisted of several sheets. The first page was stamped and signed by Marti 'for and on behalf the charterers as brokers only'; other pages were signed or initialled, but with no indication that Marti were acting as brokers. The final page had stamp and signature for Marti below the heading 'Brokers'. The charterers signed separately.

The charterers failed to pay the $175,533 dollars due for demurrage and freight. Arbitration proceedings awarded the owners this full amount plus interest, but no part of the sum outstanding was paid by the charterers. The owners then brought an action against Marti as guarantors.

*Held*

The House of Lords found that s4 of Statute of Frauds 1677 prescribed two separate ways in which a contract of guarantee might be made enforceable: by a written agreement signed by the guarantor; or secondly by a note or memorandum of the agreement. In this case, though the note or memorandum must be in writing and signed by the party to be charged, the basic agreement to guarantee might be verbal.

It was not disputed that there was a verbal undertaking by Marti to guarantee the liabilities of the charterers in respect of freight balance and demurrage.

What was in question was whether clause 24 of the main charterparty contract constituted an 'adequate note or memorandum' for the purposes of s4. Clause 24 set out all the terms of the prior oral agreement of guarantee and was signed by Marti on the page containing the clause. The court considered that the question of whether Marti signed the page as brokers or on their own account to be irrelevant.

The charterparty, in whatever capacity Marti signed it, contained a sufficient note or memorandum to make the guarantee enforceable under the Statute of Frauds.

**Foley v Classique Coaches Ltd** [1934] 2 KB 1 Court of Appeal (Scrutton, Greer and Maugham LJJ)

Contract - no definite price

*Facts*

The defendants agreed in writing with the plaintiff to purchase land adjoining the plaintiff's petrol filling station, subject to the condition that the defendant would enter into a supplemental agreement to purchase petrol from the plaintiff for their motor coach business. The supplemental agreement provided that petrol would be so supplied 'at a price to be agreed by the parties in writing from time to time' and that the defendants would not purchase petrol elsewhere, as long as the plaintiff was able to supply it. The parties acted on the supplemental agreement for three years after the land was conveyed, but a dispute arose and the plaintiff sought, inter alia, a declaration that the petrol agreement was valid and binding.

*Held*

He was entitled to succeed as it was to be implied that the petrol would be supplied at a reasonable price. Further, the contract was not bad as being in restraint of trade.

Scrutton LJ:

' ... the parties obviously believed they had a contract, and they acted on that belief for three years. They had an arbitration clause which related to the subject-matter of the agreement as to the supply of petrol, and it seems to me that this arbitration clause applies to any failure to agree as to the price. As in the case of a tied house there is to be implied in this contract a term that the petrol shall be supplied at a reasonable price and shall be of reasonable quality. For these reasons I have come to the conclusion that ... there was an effective and enforceable contract, although no definite price had been agreed with regard to the petrol in the future.

It was said, secondly, on behalf of the defendants that the contract was bad, as being in restraint of trade. In my view, that contention is clearly untenable. The contract is a perfectly ordinary one to purchase petrol from a particular person, and as long as petrol of a reasonable price and quality is supplied there is no undue restraint of trade. It is suggested, however, that the injunction granted to restrain a breach ... of the agreement might have this result, and that if the defendants moved their coaching business, say to Edinburgh, they would still be required to purchase their petrol in London from the plaintiff. I think it is clear that the defendants' obligation to take their supplies of petrol from the plaintiff applies only to the business carried on by them on the land adjoining the respondent's petrol pumps, and has no application to a business carried on in Edinburgh or Aberdeen or any other place remote from London.'

*Commentary*

Applied: *Hillas & Co Ltd v Arcos Ltd* (1932) 147 LT 503. Distinguished: *May & Butcher Ltd v R* (1929) 151 LT 246n.

**Hillas & Co Ltd v Arcos Ltd** (1932) 147 LT 503 House of Lords (Lord Tomlin, Lord Warrington, Lord Thankerton, Lord Macmillan and Lord Wright)

Construction - 'fair specification'

*Facts*

The plaintiffs agreed to buy from the defendants '22,000 standards of softwood goods of fair specification over the season 1930' at 5 per cent below the official price.

*Held*

There was an enforceable contract.

Lord Tomlin:

'If the words "of fair specification" have no meaning which is certain or capable of being made certain, then ... there cannot have been a contract with regard to the 22,000 standards ... This may be the proper conclusion; but before it is reached it is, I think, necessary to exclude as impossible all reasonable meanings which would give certainty to the words. In my opinion, this cannot be done. The parties undoubtedly attributed to the words in connection with the 22,000 standards some meaning which was precise or capable of being made precise. ...

Reading the document ... as a whole, and having regard to the admissible evidence as to the course of the trade, I think that upon their true construction the words "of fair specification over the season, 1930", used in connection with the 22,000 standards, mean that the 22,000 standards are to be satisfied in goods distributed over kinds, qualities, and sizes in the fair proportions having regard to the output of the season 1930, and the classifications of that output in respect of kinds, qualities, and sizes. That is something which if the parties fail to agree can be ascertained just as much as the fair value of a property. ... Thus, there is a description of the goods which, if not immediately, yet ultimately, is capable of being rendered certain.'

**Kingswood Estate Co Ltd v Anderson** [1963] 2 QB 169 Court of Appeal (Willmer, Upjohn and Russell LJJ)

Oral agreement - part performance

*Facts*

A statutory tenant was willing to move to suitable alternative accommodation and, before she moved to the same, the landlords orally agreed that she and her invalid son were to be tenants in equity for their joint lives. The landlords now sought possession of the new accommodation and, by way of defence, the tenant relied on the oral agreement.

*Held*

The landlords' claim would be dismissed.

Willmer LJ:

'In these circumstances, it is plain that, if the tenant is to succeed, it must be on the basis that there was an agreement for a tenancy during the joint lives of the tenant and her son and the life of the survivor. As I have already said, this was the real case sought to be made on behalf of the tenant on the hearing of this appeal. Having regard to the fact that the tenant was sacrificing the security which she had ..., I entertain no doubt that there was good consideration to support such an agreement as is alleged on her behalf. On behalf of the landlords, however ... [inter alia] it is contended that, if there was such an oral agreement as is alleged, it would be unenforceable, because there was no memorandum in writing such as to satisfy s40 of the Law of Property Act 1925, and there was no sufficient evidence of part performance ... On the question of part performance, I do not think that there is any room for doubt. Where the question is whether there was an agreement for a tenancy, I cannot imagine any better evidence of part performance than the fact of the tenant going into actual occupation. It is said, however, that the act of the tenant in going into occupation was equivocal, in that it might be referable to any kind of tenancy agreement. I do not understand, however, that part performance must necessarily be referable to the agreement, and only the particular agreement, relied on. I cite from Anson's Law of Contract (21st Edn) (1959), p75, where the principle is stated, as I think correctly, in the following terms:

"The acts of performance relied upon must of themselves suggest the existence of a contract such as it is desired to prove, although they need not establish the exact terms of that contract."

As I understand it, if there is evidence of such part performance, that is sufficient to warrant the admission of oral evidence to prove what the exact terms of the contract were. I have no doubt that the evidence in the present case proved sufficient part performance within that principle. It follows that, notwithstanding the absence of any memorandum in writing, there was here sufficient proof of an agreement enforceable in equity ...'

*Commentary*

Section 40 of the Law of Property Act 1925 has been superseded by s2 of the Law of Property (Miscellaneous Provisions) Act 1925, with effect from 27 September 1989, and the doctrine of part performance cannot therefore apply to contracts for the sale, etc, of land made after that date.

**May & Butcher Ltd v R** [1934] 2 KB 17n House of Lords (Lord Buckmaster, Viscount Dunedin and Lord Warrington)

Sale of surplus tentage - no price agreed

*Facts*

A government department agreed, in consideration of the appellants agreeing to deposit £1,000 with them as security, to sell the whole of the old tentage which might become available up to 31 December 1921. The price or prices were to be agreed from time to time as the tentage became available and all disputes relating to the agreement were to be submitted to arbitration.

*Held*

As the price for the tentage had not been agreed, there was no binding or concluded contract, and there being a stipulation that the price should be agreed, it could not be implied that the price was to be a reasonable price.

Lord Warrington:

'... the decision of this case depends on the application of a well-known and elementary principle of the law of contracts, which is that, unless the essential terms of the contract are agreed on, there is no binding and enforceable obligation. In the present case, we have a document which purports to be an agreement for the sale by one party to the other party of certain specified goods at a price to be hereafter agreed on between them. If that price is thereafter agreed, then there is a binding contract within the principle to which I have alluded; each of the essential terms of the contract has then been agreed. If the parties fail to arrive at an agreement, then the price has not been ascertained in the way in which the parties stipulated that it should be ascertained, and there is, therefore, no binding agreement.

It is said that this case is to be treated on the same footing as if there had been no fixing of the price, as if the contract had been silent as to the price, and the law may then imply a reasonable price; but, in the present case, the facts preclude the application of any such principle. To do that would not be to imply something about which the parties have been silent, but it would be to insert in the contract a stipulation contrary to that for which they have bargained, to give them not as a result of their own agreement, but possibility a verdict by a jury, or some other means of ascertaining the stipulated price. To do that would be to contradict the express terms of the document which they have signed.

Then with regard to the application of the arbitration clause, the same considerations apply. In the first place, if I am right in the view I take that, in the events which have happened, there is no binding contract, then the arbitration clause is not binding, and there is no contract out of which, or in reference to which, any dispute can arise. But, more than that, to apply the arbitration clause would be, as in the attempted application of the doctrine as to reasonable price, to substitute the award of the arbitrator for that agreement between the parties, which was the term by which they had originally agreed to be bound.'

*Commentary*

Distinguished in *Foley* v *Classique Coaches Ltd* [1934] 2 KB 1.

**Nicolene Ltd v Simmonds** [1953] 1 QB 543 Court of Appeal (Singleton, Denning and Hodson LJJ)

Meaningless words

*Facts*

There was a contract for the sale of three thousand tons of steel reinforcing bars; the seller broke his contract, and when the buyer claimed damages the seller set up the defence that, owing to a sentence in one of the letters which were alleged to constitute the contract, there was no contract at all. The material words were: 'We are in agreement that the usual conditions of acceptance apply." There were no usual conditions of acceptance and so it was said that those words were meaningless, that there was nothing to which they could apply, and that, therefore, there was never any contract between the parties.

*Held*

This argument - and the meaningless words - would be rejected.

Denning LJ:

'In my opinion, a distinction must be drawn between a clause which is meaningless and a clause which is yet to be agreed. A clause which is meaningless can often be ignored, while still leaving the contract good, whereas a clause which has yet to be agreed may mean that there is no contract at all, because the parties have not agreed on all the essential terms. I take it to be clear law that, if one of the parties to a contract inserts into it an exempting condition in his own favour which the other side agrees and it afterwards appears that that condition is meaningless or is so ambiguous that no ascertainable meaning can be given to it, that does not render the whole contract a nullity. The only result is that the exempting condition is a nullity and must be rejected ...

In the case before the court there was nothing yet to be agreed. There was nothing left to further negotiation. The parties merely agreed that "the usual conditions of acceptance apply". That clause was so vague and uncertain as to be incapable of any precise meaning. It is clearly severable from the rest of the contract, and can be rejected without impairing the sense or reason ableness of the contract as a whole, and it should be so rejected. The contract should be held to be good and the clause should be ignored.'

**Record v Bell** [1991] 1 WLR 853 Chancery Division (Baker J)

Law of Property (Miscellaneous Provisions) Act 1989 s2

*Facts*

Solicitors for vendor and purchaser signed a contract for the sale of a house. On the day before exchange of contracts was due, the vendor's solicitor wrote to the purchaser's as to the question of Land Registry records recording vendor's title. Further communications including another letter and a telephone call followed. The purchaser's solicitor wrote a letter which was to be attached to the contract of sale 'to be a part of the contract'. Later, the queries as to title were resolved.

By the date for completion of the contract, the purchaser had not paid, the vendor sought specific performance. The purchaser sought leave to defend on the basis that the contract for sale of the house did not comply with s2 of the Law of Property (Miscellaneous Provisions) Act 1989.

*Held*

The court held, in granting specific performance of the contract for the sale of the house that although for that contract to comply with s2 of the LP(MP) Act 1989 (which provides that *either* the expressly agreed terms for a contract for sale of land should be set out specifically *or* where the contract referred to some other document in which terms were to be found, that other document should be clearly identified in the contract as signed by the parties) the terms contained in the letters exchanged between the parties' solicitors should be clearly referred to in each of the parts of the contract which were exchanged between the parties. This was clearly not the case.

However, the court found that the vendor's solicitor's letter constituted an offer of a warranty that the vendor would be shown in the Land Registry files as the owner and this offer and its acceptance by the purchaser (as demonstrated by his agreeing to exchange contracts) formed a collateral contract between the parties. This collateral contract was independent of the sale of land and as such outside the provisions of s2 of the Act, and as such could be specifically enforced.

Baker J:

'Section 2(1) [of 1989 Act] states that a contract for the sale or other disposition "can only be made in writing and only by incorporating all the terms which the parties have expressly agreed in one document." The "document' in that subsection must be the document which contains the contract for sale. Subsection (2) says "the terms may be incorporated in a document either by being set out in it or by reference to some other document." The former document was a direct reference to the document referred to in subs (1), and the purpose of subs (2) is to expand what is meant in subs (1) by incorporating the terms. There are two ways they could be incorporated. They could be set out at length in the contract for sale, or the contract for sale could refer to some other document in which these terms were to be found. The document referred to need not itself be signed, but it has to be identified in the document which is signed.

A letter of variation or a letter of additional terms, not itself a contract for sale, which is signed by both parties may be a variation of the original contract after it has been exchanged as, indeed, we have in this very case relating to the completion date. But it could not, as I see it, be part of the original contract without there being some reference to it contained in the contract for sale. The terms agreed before exchange have to be incorporated. I do not have to deal with the case of physical attachment of a paper containing an additional term without verbal reference to it in the main contract. On the facts before me, there was no reference in the contracts for sale to the supplementary term. It is true that Mr Offenbach's letter had been physically attached to the purchaser's part of the contract, but there was no similar attachment of the other party's letter to the other part of the contract. Under the Act of 1989 the terms have to be expressly incorporated in each of the contracts where there is more than one.'

**Scammell (G) & Nephew Ltd v Ouston** [1941] AC 251 House of Lords (Viscount Simon LC, Viscount Maughan, Lord Russell of Killowen and Lord Wright)

Expression too vague

*Facts*

Agreement was reached for the sale and purchase of a Commer van 'on the understanding that the balance of purchase price can be had on hire-purchase terms over a period of 2 years.' The vendor subsequently argued that no binding contract had been concluded.

*Held*

This was the case as the expression 'on hire-purchase terms' was too vague.

Lord Wright:

'In my opinion ... the correct view is that ... there never was a concluded contract between the parties. It is true that, when the appellants broke off the affair, they gave reasons for doing so which they could not justify, but, when they were sued for breach of contract, they were entitled to resist the claim on any good ground which was available, regardless of reasons which they had previously given ... There are, in my opinion, two grounds on which the court ought to hold that there never was a contract. The first is that the language used was so obscure and so incapable of any definite or precise meaning that the court is unable to attribute to the parties any particular contractual intention. The object of the court is to do justice between the parties, and the court will do its best, if satisfied that there was an ascertainable and determinate intention to contract, to give effect to that intention, looking at substance, and not mere form. It will not be deterred by mere difficulties of interpretation. Difficulty is not synonymous with ambiguity, so long as any definite meaning can be extracted. The test of intention, however, is to be found in the words used. If these words, considered however broadly and technically, and with due regard to all the just implications, fail to evince any definite meaning on which the court can safely act, the court has no choice but to say that there is no contract. Such a position is not often found, but I think that it is found in this case ... It is necessary requirement that an agreement, in order to be binding, must be sufficiently definite to enable the court to give it a practicable meaning. Its terms must be so definite, or capable of being made definite without further agreement of the parties, that the promises and performances to be rendered by each party are reasonably certain. In my opinion, that requirement was not satisfied in this case.

However, I think that the other reason, which is that the parties never in intention, nor even in appearance, reached an agreement, is a still sounder reason against enforcing the claim. In truth, in my opinion, their agreement was inchoate, and never got beyond negotiations. They did, indeed, accept the position that there should be some form of hire-purchase agreement, but they never went on to complete their agreement by settling between them what the terms of the hire--purchase agreement were to be. The furthest point they reached was an understanding or agreement to agree upon hire-purchase terms.'

**Spiro v Glencrown Properties Ltd** [1991] 2 WLR 931 Chancery Division (Hoffman J)

Whether option to purchase land is within Law of Property (Miscellaneous Provisions) Act 1989 s2

*Facts*

By a written agreement, the vendor of land granted an option to purchase land. The option could be exercised the same day and take-up of the option was to be signalled by notice in writing given by the purchaser to the vendor or his solicitor.

The option agreement was executed in two exchanged parts, each containing the agreed terms and each signed by the party or his solicitor and exchanged. The purchaser took up the option by written notice in the agreed manner, but failed to complete. The question arose as to whether the agreement was within s2 of the Law of Property (Miscellaneous Provisions) Act 1989.

*Held*

An option to buy land could be defined as a sale of land within the meaning of the Act. The relevant contract was the agreement creating the option which consisted of two exchanged parts, containing all relevant terms and duly signed by or on behalf of both parties. This duly complied with the requirements of s2 and the contract could not be set aside as unenforceable merely because the taking up of the option required some unilateral action on the part of the purchaser.

**Timmins v Moreland Street Property Co Ltd** [1957] 3 WLR 678 Court of Appeal (Jenkins, Romer and Sellers LJJ)

Note or memorandum - documents signed on same occasion

*Facts*

Having agreed orally to the sale and purchase of certain freehold property, the defendants gave the plaintiff a cheque and the plaintiff gave the defendants a receipt which acknowledged the receipt of the deposit but made no reference to the cheque.

*Held*

There was not an enforceable contract as there was not a sufficient memorandum or note signed by the party to be charged, the defendants, within s40 of the Law of Property Act 1925.

Jenkins LJ:

'... I am, on the whole, of opinion that where two documents relied on as a memorandum are signed and exchanged at one and the same meeting as part of the same transaction, so that they may fairly be said to have been to all intents and purposes contemporaneously signed, the document signed by the party to be charged should not be treated as incapable of referring to the other document merely because the latter, on a minute investigation of the order of events at the meeting, is found to have come second in the order of preparation and signing ...

I think it is still indispensably necessary, in order to justify the reading of documents together for this purpose, that there should be a document signed by the party to be charged which, while not containing in itself all the necessary ingredients of the required memorandum, does contain some reference, express or implied, to some other document or transaction ...

In the present case the only document signed by the defendant company is an ordinary cheque; that is to say, an order on the defendant company's bankers to pay a sum of money, the payees being a firm of solicitors. With the best will in the world, I find it quite impossible to spell out of this cheque any reference, express or implied, to any other document or to any transaction other than the order to pay a sum of money constituted by the cheque itself. The cheque, of course, gives no indication whatever of the purpose for which the payment was to be made, and I think it is clear that the mere fact that the payment must have been made for some purpose or for some consideration cannot reasonable be held to amount to a reference to some other document or transaction within the principle I have stated.'

*Commentary*

Section 40 of the Law of Property Act 1925 has been repealed by the Law of Property (Miscellaneous Provisions) Act 1989 and therefore now applies only to contracts entered into before 27 September 1989. For later contracts, see s2 of the 1989 Act.

**Andrews v Hopkinson** [1956] 3 WLR 732 High Court (McNair J)

Warranty - 'a good little bus'

*Facts*

The plaintiff was desirous of purchasing a second-hand car and the defendant, a car dealer, recommended a vehicle to him, saying 'It's a good little bus. I would stake my life on it'. The defendant sold the car to a finance company which let it on hire purchase to the plaintiff. A week later, the plaintiff was badly injured in an accident caused by the car having a serious steering defect. The plaintiff sued the defendant on the latter's oral undertaking, alleging it to be a collateral warranty.

*Held*

The plaintiff was entitled to damages; the consideration for the defendant's promise was the plaintiff's entering into the contract of hire purchase with the finance company.

*Commentary*

Applied: *Shanklin Pier Ltd* v *Detel Products Ltd* [1951] 2 KB 854.


**Bentley (Dick) Productions Ltd v Harold Smith (Motors) Ltd** [1965] 1 WLR 623 Court of Appeal (Lord Denning MR, Danckwerts and Salmon LJJ)

Sale of car - misrepresentation as to mileage

*Facts*

The defendants, car dealers, sold a Bentley to the plaintiffs and stated that the car had only done 20,000 miles since being fitted with a replacement engine and gear box. In truth, the mileage was nearer 100,000 and the car repeatedly broke down.

*Held*

The defendants were in breach of warranty and the plaintiffs were entitled to damages. Although the statement was made innocently, the defendants were in a position, as dealers, to check its accuracy and, having made the statement to induce the plaintiffs to enter into the contract, they would not be allowed to resile from it.

Lord Denning MR:

'The first point is whether this representation, namely that it had done 20,000 only since it had been fitted with a replacement engine and gear box, was an innocent misrepresentation (which does not give rise to damages), or whether it was a warranty. It was said by Holt CJ, and repeated in *Heilbut, Symons & Co* v *Buckleton* that: "An affirmation at the time of the sale is a warranty, provided it appear on evidence to be so intended". But that word "intended" has given rise to difficulties. I endeavoured to explain, in *Oscar Chess Ltd* v *Williams* that the question whether a warranty was intended depends on the conduct of the parties on their words and behaviour, rather than on their thoughts. If an intelligent bystander would reasonably infer that a warranty was intended, that will suffice. What conduct, then? What words and behaviour lead to the inference of a warranty?

Looking at the cases once more, as we have done so often, it seems to me that if a representation is made in the course of dealings for a contract for the very purpose of inducing the other party to act upon it, and actually inducing him to act upon it by entering into the contract, that is prima facie ground for inferring that it was intended as a warranty. It is not necessary to speak of it as being collateral.  Suffice it that it was intended to be acted upon and was, in fact, acted upon.  But the maker of the representations can rebut this inference if he can show that it really was an innocent misrepresentation, in that he was in fact innocent of fault in making it, and that it would not be reasonable in the circumstances for him to be bound by it ... in the present case it is very different. The inference is not rebutted.  Here we have a dealer, Smith, who was in a position to know, or at least to find out, the history of the car.  He could get it by writing to the makers.  He did not do so. Indeed, it was done later.  When the history of this car was examined, his statement turned out to be quite wrong.  He ought to have known better.  There was no reasonable foundation for it.'

*Commentary*

Applied in *Evans (J) & Son (Portsmouth) Ltd* v *Andrea Merzario Ltd* [1976] 1 WLR 1078. Distinguished: *Oscar Chess Ltd* v *Williams* [1957] 1 WLR 370.

**Bettini v Gye** (1876) 1 QBD 183 High Court (Blackburn, Quain and Archibald JJ)

Condition precedent?

*Facts*

The defendant director of the Royal Italian Opera in London engaged the plaintiff tenor for the period 30 March to 13 July 1875: it was a term of the agreement that the plaintiff would 'be in London without fail at least six days before the commencement of this engagement for ... rehearsals'.  Because of temporary illness, he said, he did not arrive until 28 March.  Was the defendant justified in refusing to proceed with the engagement?

*Held*

He was not as the stipulation in question was not a condition precedent.

Blackburn J:

'The answer ... depends on whether this part of the contract is a condition precedent to the defendant's liability or only an independent agreement, a breach of which will not justify a repudiation of the contract, but will only be a cause of action for a compensation in damages ... We think the answer ... depends on the true construction of the contract taken as a whole.  Parties may think some matter apparently of very little importance essential, and if they sufficiently express an intention to make the literal fulfilment of such a thing a condition precedent, it will be one, or they may think that the performance of some matter apparently of essential importance, and prima facie a condition, is not really vital, and may be compensated for in damages, and if they sufficiently express such an intention, it will not be a condition precedent ...

If the plaintiff's engagements had been only to sing in operas at the theatre it might very well be that previous attendance at rehearsals with the actors in company with whom he was to perform was essential.  If the engagement had only been for a few performances, or for a short time, it would afford a strong argument that attendance for the purpose of rehearsals during the six days immediately before the commencement of the engagement was a vital part of the agreement.  But we find on looking to the agreement that the plaintiff was to sing in theatres, halls, and drawing rooms, public and private, from Mar. 30 to July 13 1875, and that he was to sing in concerts as well as in operas ... As far as we can see the failure to attend at rehearsals during the six days immediately before Mar. 31, could only affect the theatrical performances, and, perhaps, the singing in duets or concerted pieces during the first week or fortnight of this engagement, which is to sing in theatres, halls, and drawing rooms, and concerts for fifteen weeks.  We think, therefore, that it does not go to the root of the matter so as to require us to consider it a condition precedent.  The defendant must, therefore, we think, seek redress by a cross claim for damages.'

**British Crane Hire Corporation Ltd v Ipswich Plant Hire Ltd** [1974] 2 WLR 856 Court of Appeal (Lord Denning MR, Megaw LJ and Sir Eric Sachs)

Incorporation of terms in contract - common understanding

*Facts*

Both the plaintiffs and the defendants were in the business of hiring out heavy earth-moving equipment. The defendants were carrying out drainage work and urgently needed a dragline crane. By telephone, they agreed to hire one from the plaintiffs and although the hiring rate was agreed, nothing was said about the conditions of hire. As was their custom, the plaintiffs sent their written standard terms to be signed by the defendants, but before the latter did so, due to the fault of neither party, the crane sank into marshy ground. The plaintiffs' standard terms contained an indemnity clause, making the defendants liable for any expense incurred in recovering the crane. The trial judge held that the plaintiffs' terms were incorporated into the contract and that the defendants were liable under the indemnity clause. He also found, as a fact, that there had been only two previous transactions between the parties.

*Held*

The contract was made on the plaintiffs' terms, not by the course of dealing, but on the common understanding of the parties.

Lord Denning MR:

'The judge found that the printed conditions were incorporated into the contract. The defendants appeal from that finding. The facts are these. The arrangements for the hire of the crane were all on the telephone. The plaintiffs agreed to let the defendants hire this crane. It was to be delivered on the Sunday. The hiring charges and transport charges were agreed. Nothing was said about conditions. There was nothing in writing. But soon after the crane was delivered, the plaintiffs, in accordance with their practice, forwarded a printed form to be signed by the hirer. It set out the order, the work to be done and the hiring fee, and that it was subject to the conditions set out on the back of the form. The defendants would ordinarily have sent the form back signed; but this time they did not do so. The accident happened before they signed it. So they never did so. But the plaintiffs say, nevertheless, from the previous course of dealing, the conditions on the form govern the relationship between the parties. They rely on condition 6:

"SITE CONDITIONS: The Hirer shall take all reasonable precautions to ensure that the Crane can safely be taken onto and kept upon or at the site and in particular to ensure that the ground is in a satisfactory condition to take the weight of the Crane and/or its load. The Hirer shall where necessary supply and lay timber or other suitable material for the crane to travel over and work upon and shall be responsible for the recovery of the Crane from soft ground".

Also on condition 8:

"... The Hirer shall be responsible for and indemnify the Owner against ... All ... expenses in connection with or arising out of the use of the plant ... "

In support of the course of dealing the plaintiffs relied on two previous transactions in which the defendants had hired cranes from the plaintiffs. One was 20 February 1969 and the other 6 October 1969. Each was on a printed form which set out the hiring of a crane, the price, the site, and so forth; and also setting out the conditions the same as those here. There were thus only two transactions, many months before, and they were not known to the defendants' manager who ordered this crane. In the circumstances, I doubt whether those two would be sufficient to show a course of dealing.'

**Bunge Corpn v Tradax SA** [1981] 1 WLR 711 House of Lords (Lord Wilberforce, Lord Fraser of Tullybelton, Lord Scarman, Lord Lowry and Lord Roskill)

Shipping contract - right to terminate

*Facts*

Under a contract for the sale and purchase of soya bean meal, it was agreed that a shipment was to be made in June. The buyers had to provide a vessel and to give at least 15 days' notice of its probable readiness. In the event, they gave such notice on 17 June and the sellers contended that the late notice was a breach of contract amounting to a repudiation.

*Held*

The sellers' view would be upheld and they were also entitled to damages.

Lord Scarman:

'I wish, however, to make a few observations on the topic of "innominate" terms in our contract law. In *Hong Kong Fir Shipping Co Ltd* v *Kawasaki Kisen Kaisha Ltd* the Court of Appeal rediscovered and reaffirmed that English law recognises contractual terms which, on a true construction of the contract of which they are part, are neither conditions nor warranties but are, to quote Lord Wilberforce's words in *Bremer Handelsgesellschaft mbH* v *Vanden Avenne-Izegem*, "intermediate". A condition is a term the failure to perform which entitles the other party to treat the contract as at an end. A warranty is a term breach of which sounds in damages but does not terminate, or entitle the other party to terminate, the contract. An innominate or intermediate term is one the effect of non-performance of which the parties expressly or (as is more usual) impliedly agree will depend on the nature and the consequences of breach. In the *Hong Kong Fir* case the term in question provided for the obligation of seaworthiness, breach of which it is well known may be trivial (eg one defective rivet) or very serious (eg a hole in the bottom of the ship). It is inconceivable that parties when including such a term in their contract could have contemplated or intended (unless they expressly say so) that one defective rivet would entitle the charterer to end the contract or that a hole in the bottom of the ship would not. I read the *Hong Kong Fir* case as being concerned as much with the construction of the contract as with the consequences and effect of breach. The first question is always, therefore, whether, on the true construction of a stipulation and the contract of which it is part, it is a condition, an innominate term, or only a warranty. If the stipulation is one which on the true construction of the contract the parties have not made a condition, and breach of which may be attended by trivial, minor or very grave consequences, it is innominate, and the court (or an arbitrator) will, in the event of dispute, have the task of deciding whether the breach that has arisen is such as the parties would have said, had they been asked at the time they made their contract, "It goes without saying that, if that happens, the contract is at an end" ... The seller needed sufficient notice to enable him to choose the loading port; the parties were agreed that the notice to be given him was 15 days; this was a mercantile contract in which the parties required to know where they stood not merely later with hindsight but at once as events occurred. Because it makes commercial sense to treat the clause in the context and circumstances of this contract as a condition to be performed before the seller takes his steps to comply with bargain, I would hold it to be not an innominate term but a condition.'

**Cehave NV v Bremer Handelsgesellschaft mbH** [1975] 3 WLR 447 Court of Appeal (Lord Denning MR, Roskill and Ormrod LJJ)

Cattle food - shipment 'in good condition'

*Facts*

A German company agreed to sell a Dutch company a quantity of pellets to be used in cattle food at a price of approximately £100,000. The contract provided 'shipment to be made in good condition'. Upon arrival, it was discovered that part of the cargo in one hold of the ship had been severely damaged by overheating and the buyers purported to reject the whole cargo. Because the sellers refused to return the purchase price, the pellets were sold by order of a Dutch Court and subsequently repurchased at a substantially reduced price by the buyers because of a fall in the market price. The buyers used the cargo in almost the same manner and quantity to make cattle food as they would have done with sound pellets. The arbitrator and Commercial Court judge held the 'shipment in good condition' clause to be a condition of the contract.

### Held

The clause was not a condition but an intermediate stipulation: the Sale of Goods Act did not require a rigid division of terms in contracts for the sale of goods into 'conditions' and 'warranties' only.

Lord Denning MR:

'1    *The general law apart from the sale of goods*

For the last 300 or 400 years, the courts have had to grapple with this problem: in what circumstances can a party, who is in breach himself of a stipulation of the contract, call on the other side to perform his part or sue him for non-performance? At one time the solution was thought to depend on the nature of the stipulation itself and not on the extent of the breach or its consequences. Under the old form of pleading, a plaintiff had to aver and prove that he had performed all conditions precedent or that he was ready and willing to perform them. The question, therefore, was whether the stipulation (which he had broken) was a condition precedent or not, or, in the terminology of the 18th century, whether it was an *independent* covenant (the breach of which did not debar him from suing the other side), or a *dependent* covenant (the breach of which did debar the plaintiff, because the performance by the other was *dependent* on the plaintiff performing his).

This distinction was well stated by Serjeant Williams in his notes to *Pordage* v *Cole*:

"... Where there are several covenants, promises, or agreements, which are independent of each other, one party may bring an action against the other for a breach of his covenant etc, without averring a performance of the covenants, etc on his, the plaintiff's part, and it is no excuse for the defendants to allege in his plea a breach of the covenants, etc on the part of the plaintiff ... But where the covenants etc are *dependent*, it is necessary for the plaintiff to aver and prove a performance of the covenants etc on his part, to entitle himself to an action for the breach of the covenants on the part of the defendant ..."

Although that division was treated as exhaustive, nevertheless, when the courts came to apply it, they had regard to the extent of the breach. This was done by Lord Mansfield in 1777 in the great case of *Boone* v *Eyre*, of which there was no satisfactory record until Lord Kenyon, in 1796, produced a manuscript note of it: see *Campbell* v *Jones* and *Glazewood* v *Woodrow*. It is summarised in the notes to *Cutter* v *Powell*. The plaintiff conveyed to the defendant a plantation in the West Indies, together with the stock of negroes on it, in consideration of £500 down and an annuity of £100 a year, and covenanted that he had a good title to the plantation and was lawfully possessed of the negroes. Some time later, the defendant discovered that the plaintiff had no title to the negroes and stopped paying the annuity. The court held that the defendant was liable to pay the annuity. He could not escape simply because the plaintiff had not "a title to a few negroes". His remedy was to bring a cross-action for damages. It would be different "if the plaintiff had no title to the plantation itself", for then the plaintiff could not have recovered the annuity. In the language of those times, if the breach went to the whole consideration, the covenant was considered to be a condition precedent and the defendant could plead the breach in bar of the action, but if the breach went "only to a part, where a breach may be paid for in damages, there the defendant has a remedy on his covenant, and shall not plead it as a condition precedent". In short, if the breach went to the root of the matter, the stipulation was to be considered a condition precedent; but if the breach did not go to the root, the stipulation was considered to be an independent covenant which could be compensated for in damages: see *Davidson* v *Gwynne* per Lord Ellenborough, *Ellen* v *Topp* and *Graves* v *Legg*.

Apart from those cases of "breach going to the root", the courts at the same time were developing the doctrine of "anticipatory breach". When one party, before the day when he is obliged to perform his part, declares in advance that he will not perform it when the day comes, or by his conduct evinces an intention not to perform it, the other may elect to treat his declaration or conduct as a breach going to the root of the matter and to treat himself as discharged from further performance: see *Hochster* v *De La Tour*. By his prior declaration or conduct, the guilty party is said to repudiate the contract. The word "repudiation" should be confined to those cases of an *anticipatory* breach, but it is also used in connection with cases of an *actual* breach going to the root of the contract: see *Heyman* v *Darwins Ltd* per Lord Wright. All of them were gathered together by Lord Blackburn in his famous speech in *Mersey Steel and Iron Co* v *Naylor Benzon & Co*:

"The rule of law, as I have always understood it, is that where there is a contract in which there are two parties, each side having to do something (it is so laid down in the notes to *Pordage* v *Cole*), if you see that the failure to perform one part of it goes to the root of the contract, goes to the foundation of the whole, it is a good defence to say, 'I am not going on to perform my part of it when that which is the root of the whole and the substantial consideration for my performance is defeated by your misconduct' ... I repeatedly asked Mr Cohen whether or not he could find any authority which justified him in saying that every breach of contract ... must be considered to go to the root of the contract, and he produced no such authority. There are many cases in which the breach may do so: it depends upon the construction of the contract."

Those last words are clearly a reference to a "condition" strictly so called, in which any breach entitled the other to be discharged from further performance. But the earlier words are quite general. They refer to all terms other than conditions strictly so called.

## 2    The Sale of Goods Act 1893

Such was the state of the law when the Sale of Goods Act 1893 was passed on 20 February 1894. I have studied the then current edition of Benjamin on Sale and the little books which Judge Chalmers wrote before and after the Act, and the proceedings in Parliament. These show that until the year 1893, there was much confusion in the use of the words "condition" and "warranty" But that confusion was removed by the Act itself and by the judgment of Bowen LJ in *Bentsen* v *Taylor & Sons & Co*. Thenceforth those words were used by lawyers as terms of art. The difference between them was this: if the promisor broke a *condition* in any respect, however slight, it gave the other party a right to be quit of his obligations and to sue for damages, unless he, by his conduct, waived the condition, in which case he was bound to perform his future obligations but could sue for the damage he had suffered. If the promisor broke a *warranty* in any respect, however serious, the other party was not quit of his future obligations. He had to perform them. His only remedy was to sue for damages: see *The Mihalis Angelos*. *Wickman Machine Tool Sales Ltd* v *L Schuler AG*.

Now that division was not exhaustive. It left out of account the vast majority of stipulations which were neither "conditions" nor "warranties", strictly so called, but were intermediate stipulations, the effect of which depended on the breach. The cases about these stipulations were legion. They stretched continuously from *Boone* v *Eyre* in 1777 to *Mersey Steel* v *Naylor* in 1884. I cannot believe that Parliament, in 1893, intended to give the go-by to all these cases, or to say that they did not apply to the sale of goods. Those cases expressed the rules of the common law. They were preserved by Section 61(2) of the 1893 Act which said:

"The rules of the common law, including the law merchant, save in so far as they are inconsistent with the express provisions of this Act ... shall continue to apply to contracts for the sale of goods."

There was nothing in the Act inconsistent with those cases. So they continued to apply.

In 1962, in *Hong Kong Fir Shipping Co Ltd* v *Kawasaki Kisen Kaisha Ltd* the Court of Appeal drew attention to this vast body of case law. They showed that, besides conditions and warranties, strictly so called, there are many stipulations of which the effect depends on this: if the breach goes to the root of the contract, the other party is entitled to treat himself as discharged: but if it does not go to the root, he is not. In my opinion, the principle embodied in these cases applies to contracts for the sale of goods just as to all other contracts.

The task of the court can be stated simply in the way in which Upjohn LJ stated it. First, see whether the stipulation, on its true construction, is a condition strictly so called, that is a stipulation such that, for any breach of it, the other party is entitled to treat himself as discharged. Second, if it is not such a condition, then look to the extent of the actual breach which has taken place. If it is such as to go to the root of the contract, the other party is entitled to treat himself as discharged; but otherwise not. To this may be added an anticipatory breach. If the one party, before the day on which he is due to perform his part, shows by his words or conduct that he will not perform it in a vital respect when the day comes, the other party is entitled to treat himself as discharged.

"Shipped in good condition"

This brings me back to the particular stipulation in this case: "shipped in good condition". Was this a condition strictly so called, so that any breach of it entitled the buyer to reject the goods? Or was it an intermediate stipulation so that the buyer cannot reject unless the breach is so serious as to go to the root of the contract?

If there was any previous authority holding it to be a *condition* strictly so called, we should abide by it, just as we did with the clause "expected ready to load": see *Finnish Government (Ministry of Food)* v *H Ford & Co Ltd* and *The Mihalis Angelos*. But there is no such authority with the clause "shipped in good condition". I regard this clause as comparable to a clause as to quality, such as "fair and average quality". If a small portion of the goods sold was a little below that standard, it would be met by commercial men by an allowance off the price. The buyer would have no rights to reject the whole lot unless the divergence was serious and substantial: see *Biggin & Co Ltd* v *Permanite Ltd* by Devlin J and *Ashington Piggeries Ltd* v *Christopher Hill Ltd* by Lord Diplock. That is shown in this very case by clause 5 in Form 100 of the Cattle Food Trade Association which contains percentages of contamination, below which there is a price allowance and above which there is a right in the buyer to reject. Likewise with the clause "shipped in good condition"; if a small portion of the whole cargo was not in good condition and arrived a little unsound, it should be met by a price allowance. The buyers should not have a right to reject the whole cargo unless it was serious and substantial. This is borne out by the difficulty which often arises (as in this case) on a cif contract as to whether the damage was done before shipment or took place after shipment; for in the latter case, the buyer would have no claim against the seller but would be left to his claim against the insurers. So, as a matter of good sense, the buyer should be bound to accept the goods and not reject them unless there is a serious and substantial breach, fairly attributable to the seller.

In my opinion, therefore, the term "shipped in good condition" was not a condition strictly so called; nor was it a warranty strictly so called. It was one of those intermediate stipulations which gives no right to reject unless the breach goes to the root of the contract.

On the facts stated by the Board of Appeal, I do not think the buyers were entitled to reject these instalments of the contract. The board only said that "not all the goods in hold Number 1 were shipped in good condition". That does not say how many were bad. In any case, their condition cannot have been very bad, seeing that all of them were, in fact, used for the intended purpose. The breach did not go to the root of the contract. The buyer is entitled to damages, but not to rejection.'

## City and Westminster Properties (1934) Ltd v Mudd

See chapter 3 - Certainty and form of contract.

**De Lassalle v Guildford** [1901] 2 KB 215 Court of Appeal (Sir A L Smith MR, Henn Collins and Romer LJJ)

Collateral warranty

*Facts*

The plaintiff said he would not take up the lease of a house unless the defendant owner assured him that the drains were in good order. The defendant gave that assurance: the plaintiff took up the lease (which was silent as to the condition of the drains): the drains turned out not to have been in good order.

*Held*

The plaintiff was entitled to damages for breach of the collateral warranty as to the condition of the drains.

Sir A L Smith MR:

'In the present case, did the defendant assume to assert a fact, or merely to state an opinion or judgment upon a matter of which he had no special knowledge and upon which the plaintiff ... might be expected also to have an opinion. What is it the defendant asserts? I paraphrase the evidence: "You need have no certificate of a sanitary inspector; it is quite unnecessary; the drains are in perfect condition, I give you my word upon the subject. Will that satisfy you? If so, hand me over the counterpart." What more deliberate and emphatic assertion of a fact could well be made during the course of the dealing which led up to the counterpart lease being handed over to the defendant? That the question asked and the answer given were seriously intended ... to be the basis of the contractual relation between the parties, I cannot doubt. There is the evidence that the plaintiff would not take the lease unless the drains were guaranteed, and surely the statements made by the defendant were not made on the assumption that they were to be of no avail to the plaintiff except they were made fraudulently. In my judgment, everything necessary to establish a warranty has in this case been proved.

The next question is: Was the warranty collateral to the lease so that it might be given in evidence and given effect to? It appears to me in this case clear that the lease did not cover the whole ground, and that it did not contain the whole of the contract between the parties. The lease is entirely silent about the drains ... There is nothing in the lease as to the then condition of the drains - i e, at the time of the taking of the lease, which was the vital point in hand. Then why is not the warranty collateral to anything which is to be found in the lease? The present contract or warranty by the defendant was entirely independent of what was to happen during the tenancy. It was what induced the tenancy, and in no way affected the terms of the tenancy during the three years which was all the lease dealt with. The warranty in no way contradicts the lease, and without the warranty the lease never would have been executed.'

**Esso Petroleum Co Ltd v Mardon** [1976] 2 WLR 583 Court of Appeal (Lord Denning MR, Ormrod and Shaw LJJ)

Lease of petrol station - estimate of sales

*Facts*

The plaintiffs acquired a busy main street site for a petrol station on the basis of calculations showing an estimated annual consumption of 200,000 gallons from the third year. The planning authority insisted on access only from side streets: this falsified the calculations but, through lack of care, the plaintiffs failed to revise their original estimate. During negotiations for a tenancy, the plaintiffs' representative, a person of 40 years' experience, told the defendant in good faith that throughput had been estimated at 200,000 gallons in the third year. This the defendant doubted, but in the light of the representative's greater expertise he took the tenancy. It turned out that the site was capable only of an annual throughput of some 70,000 gallons and, although he took a new tenancy at a reduced rent, the defendant lost heavily. In response to the plaintiffs' claim for possession and petrol supplied, the defendant claimed damages for breach of warranty and negligent misrepresentation.

*Held*

He was entitled to succeed and the measure of damages was the loss he had suffered by having been induced to enter into a disastrous contract. By taking a new tenancy, he had acted reasonably in attempting to mitigate his losses.

Lord Denning MR:

'Counsel for Esso retaliated, however, by citing *Bisset* v *Wilkinson* where the Privy Council said that a statement by a New Zealand farmer that an area of land "would carry 2,000 sheep" was only an expression of opinion. He submitted that the forecast here of 200,000 gallons was an expression of opinion and not a statement of fact; and that it could not be interpreted as a warranty or promise.

Now, I would quite agree with counsel for Esso that it was not a warranty - in this sense - that it did not *guarantee* that the throughput *would be* 200,000 gallons. But, nevertheless, it was a forecast made by a party, Esso, who had special knowledge and skill. It was the yardstick ... by which they measured the worth of a filling station. They knew the facts. They knew the traffic in the town. They knew the throughput of comparable stations. They had much experience and expertise at their disposal. They were in a much better position than Mr Mardon to make a forecast. It seems to me that if such a person makes a forecast - intending that the other should act on it and he does act on it - it can well be interpreted as a warranty that the forecast is sound and reliable in this sense that they made it with reasonable care and skill. It is just as if Esso said to Mr Mardon. "Our forecast of throughput is 200,000 gallons. You can rely on it as being a sound forecast of what the service station should do. The rent is calculated on that footing." If the forecast turned out to be an unsound forecast, such as no person of skill or expierence should have made, there is a breach of warranty ... It is very different from the New Zealand case where the land had never been used as sheep farm and both parties were equally able to form an opinion as to its carrying capacity.

In the present case it seems to me that there was a warranty that the forecast was sound, that is that Esso had made it with reasonable care and skill. That warranty was broken. Most negligently Esso made a "fatal error" in the forecast they stated to Mr Mardon, and on which he took the tenancy. For this they are liable in damages ...

It seems to me that *Hedley Byrne*, properly understood, covers this particular proposition: if a man, who has or professes to have special knowledge or skill, makes a representation by virtue thereof to another - be it advice, information or opinion - with the intention of inducing him to enter into a contract with him, he is under a duty to use reasonable care to see that the representation is correct, and that the advice, information or opinion is reliable. If he negligently gives unsound advice or misleading information or expresses an erroneous opinion, and thereby induces the other side into a contract with him, he is liable in damages ...

Applying this principle, it is plain that Esso professed to have - and did in fact have - special knowledge or skill in estimating the throughput of a filling station. They made the representation - they forecast a throughput of 200,000 gallons - intending to induce Mr Mardon to enter into a tenancy on the faith of it. They made it negligently. It was a "fatal error". And thereby induced Mr Mardon to enter into a contract of tenancy that was disastrous to him. For this mispresentation they are liable in damages.'

**Evans (J) & Son (Portsmouth) Ltd v Andrea Merzario Ltd**
See Introduction.

**Eyre v Measday** [1986] 1 All ER 488 Court of Appeal (Slade, Purchas LJJ and Sir Ronaleyn Cumming-Bruce)

Sterilisation - collateral warranty

*Facts*

The plaintiff consulted the defendant gynaecologist in order to have a sterilisation operation. The defendant, in explaining the procedure involved, informed the plaintiff that it was a permanent procedure and that the operation was irreversible. He did not advise the plaintiff that there was a small risk of her becoming pregnant after the operation. The plaintiff (and her husband) believed that the operation would render her absolutely sterile. After the operation, however, the plaintiff became pregnant and gave birth to a child.

The plaintiff brought an action against the defendant alleging that, in informing her that the operation was irreversible but failing to inform her of the small risk that the operation would be unsuccessful, the defendant had been in breach of a contractual term, or an express or implied collateral warranty, that the operation would render her absolutely sterile.

*Held*

The defendant's contractual undertaking was to perform a particular operation rather than to render the plaintiff absolutely sterile. When a medical practitioner contracts to carry out a particular operation, the court would imply a term into the contract that the operation would be performed with reasonable skill and care. But the court would be reluctant to imply a term or collateral warranty that the expected result would actually be achieved. On the present facts, applying the doctrine of *The Moorcock* (1889) 14 PD 64, no intelligent lay bystander could have drawn the inference that the defendant was intending to give such a warranty.

**Federal Commerce and Navigation Ltd v Molena Alpha Inc. The Nanfri, The Benfri, The Lorfri** [1978] 3 WLR 991 House of Lords (Lord Wilberforce, Viscount Dilhorne, Lord Fraser of Tullybelton, Lord Russell of Killowen and Lord Scarman)

Charterparties - right to terminate

*Facts*

Under three identical charterparties, the charterers were entitled to make deductions from the hire in certain events, including slow steaming, and to give instructions to the masters of the vessels relating to certain matters. A dispute arose as to slow steaming deductions and the owners threatened to withdraw the charterers' ability to give instructions to the masters, knowing that this would place them in serious difficulties. The charterers alleged that the owners' conduct amounted to a repudiation of the charterparties.

*Held*

It did as it went to the root of the contracts.

Lord Fraser of Tullybelton:

'Treating the [relevant clause] then as an innominate or intermediate term, I proceed to consider whether the threatened breach of it here was so fundamental as to amount to repudiation of the contract. The test of repudiation has been formulated in various ways by different judges. I shall adopt the formulation by Buckley LJ in *Decro-Wall International SA* v *Practitioners in Marketing Ltd* as follows:

" ... will the consequences of the breach be such that it would be unfair to the injured party to hold him to the contract and leave him to his remedy in damages as and when a breach or breaches may occur? If this would be so, then a repudiation has taken place."

Judged by that test I have no doubt that the breach here was repudiatory. The whole purpose of the contract from the charterers' point of view was that they should have the use of the ship for carrying on their trade ... but if the owner's threat had been carried out it would have been ruinous to that trade. I need not repeat the umpire's findings as to the consequences in full but I attach particular importance to his finding ...

"The Charterers were likely to be blacklisted as grain carriers by Continental Grain, which is one of the world's largest shippers of grain. In consequence the Charterers' reputation would be very seriously damaged and they would probably have been unable to obtain business for the vessels from other major shippers of grain."

Such damage to their reputation might well have been lasting and not limited to the duration of actual interruption of the trade. In face of that finding, I am, with all respect to Kerr J, unable to agree with his view that the owners were only creating a "temporary impasse". It was said that the breach was not repudiatory because the owners were merely reacting against the charterers' unilateral deductions from the hire, and particularly against their revival of a stale claim for deductions. This is really a plea in mitigation but it does not affect the result. If the owners' reaction involved committing a breach that went to the root of the contract, they cannot in my opinion escape the legal consequences by pleading that they had been provoked. I would therefore hold that the breach was repudiatory.'

**Ferguson v John Dawson & Partners (Contractors) Ltd** [1976] 1 WLR 1213 Court of Appeal (Megaw, Lawton and Browne LJJ)

Contract of services or for services?

*Facts*

The defendant building contractors orally engaged the plaintiff as a general labourer, 'purely working as a lump labour force'. Both parties regarded the plaintiff as a 'self-employed labour only sub-contractor'. The plaintiff was injured in the course of his work and the defendants were liable if he had been working for them under a contract of service as opposed to a contract for services.

*Held* (Lawton LJ dissenting)

The plaintiff's action would succeed.

Megaw LJ:

'I reject the defendants' contention that on legal analysis there were no contractual terms governing the relationship between the plaintiff and the defendants other than a term "self-employed labour only sub-contractor". There were such other contractual terms. For this purpose it does not matter whether they were originally incorporated by implication when the plaintiff was taken on by Mr Murray [the defendants' site agent], or were added thereafter by the acceptance of the parties by conduct. What the relevant terms were was sufficiently proved by the evidence of Mr Murray himself, the defendants' site agent, in cross-examination. His evidence, except in minor respects, is not, as the defendants suggest, merely evidence of what was done in performance of the contract. It is evidence of what the contractual rights and obligations were throughout the plaintiff's work for the defendants. True, it is not expressed in the questions and answers as being agreed terms of a contract. But I have no doubt that Mr Murray understood, and everyone understood, that what he was being asked about was the relationship between the parties - the rights and obligations of the defendants and the workman, including the plaintiff, which were understood and accepted to exist, that is, on legal analysis, the contractual terms.

*James Miller & Partners Ltd* v *Whitworth Street Estates (Manchester) Ltd* and *L Schuler AG* v *Wickman Machine Tool Sales Ltd,* House of Lords authorities relied on by the defendants, are not relevant. They hold that, subject to certain exceptions, you may not look at what has been done in pursuance of a contract in order to construe that contract. There are a number of other reasons, also, why I think those decisions are not relevant here. But the main reason is that we are not here concerned with construing a contract, but with evidence as to what the terms of a contract were - the implication of terms ...

Mr Murray accepted that he was responsible for "hiring and firing". In other words, as between the defendants and the workmen, including the plaintiff, he, Mr Murray, could dismiss them. There would be no question of his being able to determine a contract between the defendants and a sub-contractor. He could move men from site to site, if he was so minded; and, in support of the existence of that contractual right on behalf of the defendants, he gave instances of having done so. If tools were required for the work, it was for the defendants to provide them. Again, as confirmation of that contractual obligation, Mr Murray gave evidence of instances where the plaintiff had required tools for the work which he had been required to do, and the defendants had provided them. It was for Mr Murray to tell the workmen, including the plaintiff, what particular work they were to do: "I tell him what to take and what to do". The centurian in St Matthew's gospel says to the man under him "Do this, and he doeth it". The man under him is a servant, not an independent contractor. All these things are in relation to the contractual relationships existing. "I tell him what to do" and he does it on Mr Murray"s instructions because, when legal analysis has to be applied, it is a term of the contract that the plaintiff shall carry out the defendants' instructions what to do when they tell him to do it. The men, including the plaintiff, were employed on an hourly basis. The money paid to them would be correctly described as a "wage".

In my judgment, on the tests laid down in the authorities, all of this indicates beyond doubt that the reality of the relationship was employer and employee: a contract of service ...

My own view would have been that a declaration by the parties, even if it be incorporated in the contract, that the workman is to be, or is to be deemed to be, self-employed, an independent contractor, ought to be wholly disregarded - not merely treated as not being conclusive - if the remainder of the contractual terms, governing the realities of the relationship, show the relationship of employer and employee ... I find difficulty in accepting that the parties, by a mere expression of intention as to what the legal relationship should be, can in any way influence the conclusion of law as to what the relationship is. I think that it would be contrary to the public interest if that were so: for it would mean that the parties, by their own whim, by the use of a verbal formula, unrelated to the reality of the relationship, could influence the decision on whom the responsibility for the safety of workmen, as imposed by statutory regulations, should rest.'

**G A Estates v Caviapen Trustees Ltd** (1991) The Times 22 October Court of Session (Lord Coulsfield)

Construction of contracts

*Facts*

In this Scottish case, the plaintiffs, in a sale of land, warranted to the defendants that the land was fit for the purpose of constructing a particular development. The defendants, when they discovered that the land was not suitable for the purpose stated, refused to pay. The plaintiffs sought payment relying on the contra proferentem rule, contending the warranty had been drafted specifically in favour of the defendants and should, if ambiguous, be construed in the manner least favourable to them. The defendants, counterclaiming, argued that the clause was not conceived as a favour to them and was not intended to benefit one party more than another. The contra proferentem rule had no relevance.

*Held*

In order for the contra proferentem rule to be justified, the argument that the warranty was a special feature and was never normally included in contracts for sale of land was to be rejected. No special rule of construction (such as contra proferentem) applied here.

## Greaves & Co (Contractors) Ltd v Baynham Meikle and Partners

See chapter 18 - Sale of goods, consumer credit and supply of goods and services.


## Harvela Investments Ltd v Royal Trust Co of Canada (CI) Ltd

See chapter 1 - Offer and acceptance.


## Heilbut, Symons & Co v Buckleton [1913] AC 30 House of Lords (Viscount Haldane LC, Lord Atkinson and Lord Moulton)

Purchase of shares - warranty

*Facts*

The respondent enquired of the appellants, rubber merchants in London, 'I understand you are bringing out a rubber company' and was told, 'We are'. He asked 'if it was alright' (ie financially sound) and was told, 'We are bringing it out.' The company was not a rubber company properly so called and the respondent lost a considerable amount of money when the value of the shares in the company, which he had purchased, fell heavily. He claimed damages for breach of contract, for breach of warranty that the company was a rubber company.

*Held*

There was no breach of contract. The appellants' statements were not intended to be a contractual undertaking; nor had either party so regarded them.

Lord Moulton:

'There is no controversy between the parties as to certain points of fact and of law. It is not contested that the only company referred to was the Filisola Rubber and Produce Estates Limited, or that the reply of Mr Johnston to the plaintiff's question over the telephone was a representation by the defendants that the company was a "rubber company", whatever may be the meaning of that phrase; nor is there any controversy as to the legal nature of that which the plaintiff must establish. He must show a warranty, ie a contract collateral to the main contract to take the shares, whereby the defendants, in consideration of the plaintiff taking the shares, promised that the company itself was a rubber company. The question in issue is whether there was any evidence that such a contract was made between the parties.

It is evident, both on principle and on authority, that there may be a contract, the consideration for which is the making of some other contract. "If you will make such and such a contract, I will give you one hundred pounds", is, in every sense of the word, a complete legal contract. It is collateral in the main contract, but each has an independent existence and they do not differ in respect of their possession to the full character and status of a contract. But such collateral contracts must, from their very nature, be rare. The effect of a collateral contract, such as that which I have instanced, would be to increase the consideration of the main contract by 100l and the more natural and usual way of carrying this out, would be by so modifying the main contract, and not by executing a concurrent and collateral contract. Such collateral contracts, the sole effect of which is to vary or add to the terms of the principal contract, are therefore viewed with suspicion by the law. They must be proved strictly. Not only the terms of such contracts, but the existence of an animus contrahendi on the part of all the parties to them, must be clearly shown. Any laxity on these points would enable parties to escape from the full performance of the obligations of contracts unquestionably entered into by them and, more especially, would have the effect of lessening the authority of written contracts by making it possible to vary them by suggesting the existence of verbal collateral agreements relating to the same subject matter.

There is, in the present case, an entire absence of any evidence to support the existence of such a collateral contract. The statement of Mr Johnston, in answer to the plaintiff's question, was beyond controversy, a mere statement of fact, for it was in reply to a question for information and nothing more. No doubt it was a representation as to fact and, indeed, it was the actual representation upon which the main case of the plaintiff rested. It was this representation which he alleged to have been false and fraudulent and which, he alleged, induced him to enter into the contracts and take the shares. There is no suggestion throughout the whole of his evidence that he regarded it as anything but a representation. Neither the plaintiff, nor the defendants, were asked any question, or gave any evidence, tending to show the existence of any animus contrahendi, other than as regards the main contracts. The whole case for the existence of a collateral contract therefore rests on the mere fact that the statement was made as to the character of the company, and if this is to be treated as evidence sufficient to establish the existence of a collateral contract of the kind alleged, the same result must follow with regard to any other statement relating to the subject matter of a contract made by a contracting party prior to its execution. This would negate entirely the firmly established rule that an innocent representation gives no right to damages. It would amount to saying that the making of any representation prior to a contract relating to its subject matter is sufficient to establish the existence of a collateral contract that the statement is true and therefore to give a right to damages if such should not be the case.

In the history of English law we find many attempts to make persons responsible in damages by reason of innocent misrepresentations and, at times, it has seemed as though the attempts would succeed. On the Chancery side of the Court, the decisions favouring this view usually took the form of extending the scope of the action for deceit. There was a tendency to recognise the existence of what was sometimes called "legal fraud", ie that the making of an innocent statement of fact without reasonable grounds, or of one which was inconsistent with information which the person had received or had the means of obtaining, entailed the same legal consequences as making it fraudulently. Such a doctrine would make a man liable for forgetfulness or mistake or even for honestly interpreting the facts known to him or drawing conclusions from them in a way which the Court did not think to be legally warranted. The high-water mark of these decisions is to be found in the judgment pronounced by the Court of Appeal in the case of *Peek* v *Derry*, when they laid down that where a defendant has made a mis-statement of fact and the Court is of the opinion that he had no reasonable grounds for believing that it was true, he may be made liable in an action of deceit if it has materially tended to induce the plaintiff to do an act by which he has incurred damage. But on appeal to your Lordships' House, this decision was unanimously reversed and it was definitely laid down that, in order to establish a cause of action sounding in damages for misrepresentation, the statement must be fraudulent or what is equivalent thereto, must be made recklessly, not caring whether it be true or not. The opinions pronounced in your Lordships' House in that case, show that both in substance and in form the decision was, and was intended to be, a reaffirmation of the old common law doctrine that actual fraud was essential to an action for deceit and it finally settled the law that an innocent misrepresentation gives no right of action sounding in damages.

On the Common Law side of the Court, the attempts to make a person liable for an innocent misrepresentation have usually taken the form of attempts to extend the doctrine of warranty beyond its just limits and to find that a warranty existed in cases where there was nothing more than an innocent misrepresentation. The present case is, in my opinion, an instance of this. But in respect of the question of the existence of a warranty, the Courts have had the advantage of an admirable enunciation of the true principle of law which was made in very early days by Holt CJ with respect to the contract of sale. He says: "An affirmative at the time of the sale is a warranty, provided it appears on evidence to be so intended." So far as decisions are concerned, this has, on the whole, been consistently followed in the courts of Common Law. But, from time to time, there have been dicta inconsistent with it which have, unfortunately, found their way into text books and have given rise to confusion and uncertainty in this branch of the law. For example, one often sees quoted the dictum of Bayley J in *Cave* v *Coleman*, where, in respect of a representation made verbally during the sale of a horse, he says that "being made in the course of dealing, and before the bargain was completed, it amounted to a warranty" - a proposition that is far too sweeping and cannot be supported. A still more serious deviation from the correct principle is to be found in a passage in the judgment of the Court of Appeal in *De Lassalle* v *Guildford* which was cited to us in the argument in the present case. In discussing the question whether a representation amounts to a warranty or not, the judgment says:

"In determining whether it was so intended, a decisive test is whether the vendor assumes to assert a fact of which the buyer is ignorant, or merely states an opinion or judgment upon a matter of which the vendor has no special knowledge, and on which the buyer may be expected also to have an opinion and to exercise his judgment."

With all deference to the authority of the Court that decided that case, the proposition which it thus formulates cannot be supported. It is clear that the Court did not intend to depart from the law laid down by Holt CJ and cited above, for, in the same judgment, that dictum is referred to and accepted as a correct statement to the law. It is therefore evident that the use of the phrase "decisive test" cannot be defended. Otherwise it would be the duty of a judge to direct a jury that if a vendor states a fact of which the buyer is ignorant, they must, as a matter of law, find the existence of a warranty, whether or not the totality of the evidence shows that the parties intended the affirmation to form part of the contract; and this would be inconsistent with the law as laid down by Holt CJ. It may well be that the features thus referred to in the judgment of the Court of Appeal in that case, may be criteria of value in guiding a jury in coming to a decision whether or not a warranty was intended; but they cannot be said to furnish decisive tests, because it cannot be said, as a matter of law, that the presence or absence of those features is conclusive of the intention of the parties. The intention of the parties can only be deduced from the totality of the evidence and no secondary principles of such a kind can be universally true.

It is, my Lords, of the greatest importance, in my opinion, that this House should maintain, in its full integrity, the principle that a peson is not liable in damages for an innocent misrepresentation, no matter in what way or under what form the attack is made. In the present case, the statement was made in answer to an enquiry for information. There is nothing which can, by any possibility, be taken as evidence of an intention on the part of either or both of the parties that there should be a contractual liability in respect of the accuracy of the statement. It is a representation as to a specific thing and nothing more. The judge, therfore, ought not to have left the question of warranty to the jury and if, as a matter of prudence, he did so in order to obtain their opinion in case of appeal, he ought then to have entered judgment for the defendants, notwithstanding the verdict.'

## Hong Kong Fir Shipping Co Ltd v Kawasaki Kisan Kaisha Ltd [1962] 2 WLR 474 Court of Appeal (Sellers, Upjohn and Diplock LJJ)

Charter - vessel breakdowns

*Facts*

The defendants chartered the vessel 'Hong Kong Fir' from the plaintiffs for 24 months; the charter party provided 'she being fitted in every way for ordinary cargo service'. It transpired that the engine room staff were incompetent and the vessel spent less than nine weeks of the first seven months of the charter at sea because of breakdowns and consequent repairs required to make her seaworthy. The defendants repudiated the charter party and claimed that the term as to seaworthiness was a condition of the contract, any breach of which entitled them so to do.

*Held*

The term was neither a condition nor a warranty and in determining whether the defendants could terminate the contract, it was necessary to look at the consequences of the breach to see if they deprived the innocent party of substantially the whole benefit he should have received under the contract. On the facts, this was not the case, because the charter party still had a substantial time to run.

Diplock LJ:

'No doubt there are many simple contractual undertakings, sometimes express but more often, because of their very simplicity ("It goes without saying"), to be implied, of which it can be predicted that every breach of such an undertaking must give rise to an event which will deprive the party not in default of substantialy the whole benefit which it was intended that he should obtain from the contract. And such a stipulation, unless the parties have agreed that breach of it shall not entitle the non-defaulting party to treat the contract as repudiated, is a "condition". So too, there may be other simple contractual undertakings of which it can be predicted that *no* breach can give rise to an event which will deprive the party not in default of substantially the whole benefit which it was intended that he should obtain from the contract; and such a stipulation, unless the parties have agreed that breach of it shall entitle the non-defaulting party to treat the contract as repudiated, is a "warranty".

There are, however, many contractual undertakings, of a more complex character which cannot be categorised as being "conditions" or "warranties" if the late nineteenth-century meaning adopted in the Sale of Goods Act 1893 and used by Bowen LJ in *Bentsen* v *Taylor Sons & Co* be given to those terms. Of such undertakings, all that can be predicted is that some breaches will, and others will not, give rise to an event which will deprive the party not in default of substantially the whole benefit which it was intended that he should obtain from the contract; and the legal consequences of a breach of such an undertaking, unless provided for expressly in the contract, depend upon the nature of the event to which the breach gives rise and do not follow automatically from a prior classification of the undertaking as a "condition" or a "warranty". For instance, to take Bramwell B's example in *Jackson* v *Union Marine Insurance Co Ltd* itself, breach of an undertaking by a shipowner to sail with all possible dispatch to a named port, does not necessarily relieve the charterer of further performance of his obligation under the charter party, but if the breach is so prolonged that the contemplated voyage is frustrated, it does have this effect.

In 1874, when the doctrine of frustration was being foaled by "impossibility of performance" out of "condition precedent", it is not surprising that the explanation given by Bramwell B should give full credit to the dam by suggesting that, in addition to the express warranty to sail with all possible dispatch, there was an implied *condition precedent* that the ship should arrive at the named port in time for the voyage contemplated. In *Jackson* v *Union Marine Insurance Co Ltd* there was no breach of the express warranty; but if there had been, to engraft the implied condition upon the express warranty would have been merely a more complicated way of saying that a breach of a shipowner's undertaking to sail with all possible dispatch may, but will not necessarily, give rise to an event which will deprive the charterer of substantially the whole benefit which it was intended that he should obtain from the charter. Now that the doctrine of frustration has matured and flourished for nearly a century, and the old technicalities of pleading "conditions precedent" are more than a century out of date, it does not clarify but, on the contrary, obscures the modern principle of law where such an event *has* occurred as a result of a breach of an express stipulation in a contract, to continue to add the now unnecessary colophon "Therefore it was an implied *condition* of the contract that a particular 'kind of breach' of an express *warranty* should not occur". The common law evolves not merely by breeding new principles but also, when they are fully grown, by burying their progenitors.

As my brethren have already pointed out, the shipowner's undertaking to tender a seaworthy ship has, as a result of numerous decisions as to what can amount to "unseaworthiness", become one of the most complex of contractual undertakings. It embraces obligations with respect to every part of the hull and machinery, stores and equipment, and the crew itself. It can be broken by the presence of trivial defects easily and rapidly remediable, as well as by defects which must inevitably result in a total loss of the vessel.

Consequently, the problem in this case is, in my view, neither solved nor soluble by debating whether the shipowner's express or implied undertaking to tender a seaworthy ship is a "condition" or a "warranty". It is like so many other contractual terms; an undertaking, one breach of which may give rise to an event which relieves the charterer of further performance of his undertakings if he so elects, and another breach of which may not give rise to such an event but entitle him only to monetary compensation in the form of damages. It is, with all deference to Mr Ashton Roskill's skilful argument, by no means surprising that among the many hundreds of previous cases about the shipowner's undertaking to deliver a seaworthy ship, there is none where it was found profitable to discuss in the judgments the question whether that undertaking is a "condition" or a "warranty"; for the true answer, as I have already indicated, is that it is neither, but one of that large class of contractual undertakings, one breach of which may have the same effect as that ascribed to a breach of "condition" under the Sale of Goods Act 1893 and a different breach of which may have only the same effect as that ascribed to a breach of "warranty" under that Act. The cases referred to by Sellers LJ illustrate this and I would only add that in the dictum which he cites from *Kish* v *Taylor* it seems to me, from the sentence which immediately follows it, as from the actual decision in the case, and the whole tenor of Lord Atkinson's speech itself, that the word "will" was intended to be "may".'

*Commentary*

Applied in *Decro-Wall International SA* v *Practitioners in Marketing Ltd* [1971] 1 WLR 361.

**Liverpool City Council v Irwin** [1976] 2 WLR 562 House of Lords (Lord Wilberforce, Lord Cross of Chelsea, Lord Salmon, Lord Edmund-Davies and Lord Fraser of Tullybelton)

Landlord and tenant - covenant implied?

*Facts*

The council owned a tower block containing some 70 dwelling units, access to which was by a common staircase and two lifts. Mr and Mrs Irwin were tenants of one unit: their tenancy agreement imposed certain obligations on them, but none on the council. Over the years the condition of the block deteriorated; there were defects in the stairs and lifts and internal rubbish chutes became blocked. The Irwins alleged, inter alia, a breach on the part of the council of its implied covenant for their quiet enjoyment of the property.

*Held*

Such a covenant was to be implied but, on the facts, the council had not been in breach of it.

Lord Wilberforce:

'The court here is simply concerned to establish what the contract is, the parties not having themselves fully stated the terms. In this sense the court is searching for what must be implied.

What then should this contract be held to be? There must first be implied a letting, ie a grant of the right of exclusive possession to the tenants. With this there must, I would suppose, be implied a covenant for quiet enjoyment, as a necessary incident of the letting. The difficulty begins when we consider the common parts ...

There can be no doubt that there must be implied (i) an easement for the tenants and their licensees to use the stairs, (ii) a right in the nature of an easement to use the lifts and (iii) an easement to use the rubbish chutes.

But are these easements to be accompanied by any obligation on the landlord, and what obligation?

My Lords, ... it is necessary to define what test is to be applied, and I do not find this difficult. In my opinion such obligation should be read into the contract as the nature of the contract iself implicitly requires, no more, no less; a test in other words of necessity. The relationship accepted by the corporation is that of landlord and tenant; the tenant accepts obligations accordingly, in relation, inter alia, to the stairs, the lifts and the chutes. All these are not just facilities, or conveniences provided at discretion; they are essentials of the tenancy without which life in the dwellings, as a tenant, is not possible. To leave the landlord free of contractual obligation as regards these matters, and subject only to administrative or political pressure, is, in my opinion, totally inconsistent with the nature of this relationship. The subject matter of the lease (high-rise blocks) and the relationship created by the tenancy demands, of its nature, some contractual obligation on the landlord ...

It remains to define the standard. My Lords, if, as I think, the test of the existence of the term is necessity the standard must surely not exceed what is necessary having regard to the circumstances. To imply an absolute obligation to repair would go beyond what is a necessary legal incident and would indeed be unreasonable. An obligation to take reasonable care to keep in reasonable repair and usability is what fits the requirements of the case. Such a definition involves - and I think rightly - recognition that the tenants themselves have their responsibilities. What it is reasonable to expect of a landlord has a clear relation to what a reasonable set of tenants should do for themselves ...

I would hold therefore that the corporation's obligatioin is as I have described. And in agreement, I believe, with your Lordships, I would hold that it has not been shown in this case that there was any breach of that obligation.'

### Lombard North Central plc v Butterworth

See chapter 14 - Remedies for breach of contract - damages.

### London Export Corpn Ltd v Jubilee Coffee Roasting Co Ltd [1958] 1 WLR 661 Court of Appeal (Jenkins, Parker and Pearce LJJ)

Incorporation of custom

*Facts*

An association's rules provided, inter alia, that an umpire who had made an award at an arbitration should not be a member of the board of appeal hearing an appeal from his decision. After hearing the parties, the board asked the umpire to join them while they deliberated on their decision: such attendance was customary in the trade.

*Held*

The board's ultimate decision had been rightly set aside.

Jenkins LJ:

'It appears to me, when all have been looked at, that the relevant principle or law cannot be stated with any greater precision than this: That an alleged custom can be incorporated into a contract only if there is nothing in the express or necessarily implied terms of the contract to prevent such inclusion and, further, that a custom will only be imported into a contract where it can be so imported consistently with the tenor of the document as a whole.'

### Luxor (Eastbourne) Ltd v Cooper [1941] AC 108 House of Lords (Viscount Simon LC, Lord Thankerton, Lord Russell of Killowen, Lord Wright and Lord Romer)

Estate agent's commission - implied term?

*Facts*

Wishing to dispose of two cinemas, the appellants agreed to pay the respondent commission on completion of the sales. Although the respondent introduced a willing and able purchaser, the appellants decided that they would not proceed with the transactions. The respondent claimed as damages for breach of contract the amount that he would have received by way of commission.

*Held*

He was not entitled to succeed.

Viscount Simon LC:

'I find it impossible to formulate with adequate precision the tests which should determine whether or not a "just excuse" exists for disregarding the alleged implied term, and this leads me to consider whether there really is any such implied term at all. The matter may be tested in this way. If such an implied term must be assumed, then this amounts to saying that, when the owner gives the agent the opportunity of earning commission on the express terms thus stated, the agent might have added: "From the moment that I produce a duly qualified offeror, you must give up all freedom of choice, and carry through the bargain, if you reasonably can, with my nominee." The vendor must reply: "Of course. That necessarily follows." However, I am by no means satisfied that the vendor would acquiesce in regarding the matter in this light. I doubt whether the agent is bound, generally speaking, to exercise any standard of diligence in looking for a possible purchaser. He is commonly described as "employed", but he is not "employed" in the sense in which a man is employed to paint a picture or to build a house, with the liability to pay damages for delay or want of skill. The owner is offering to the agent a reward if the agent's activity helps to bring about an actual sale, but that is no reason why the owner should not remain free to sell his property through other channels. The agent necessarily incurs certain risks, eg the risk that his nominee cannot find the purchase price, or will not consent to terms reasonably proposed to be inserted in the contract of sale. I think that, upon the true construction of the express contract in this case, the agent also takes the risk of the owner not being willing to conclude the bargain with the agent's nominee. This last risk is ordinarily a slight one, for the owner's reason for approaching the agent is that he wants to sell.

If it really were the common intention of owner and agent that the owner should be bound in the manner suggested, there would be no difficulty in so providing by an express term of the contract, but, in the absence of such an express term, I am unable to regard the suggested implied term as "necessary".'

### Malcolm v Chancellor, Masters and Scholars of the University of Oxford (1990) The Times 23 March High Court (Mr Gavin Lightman QC)

Terms of contract incomplete

*Facts*

The plaintiff had received from the defendant publishers an 'absolute commitment' to publish his book but they subsequently declined to do so. The plaintiff sought specific performance or damages for breach of contract.

*Held*

His action would be dismissed. With considerable regret, his Lordship came to the conclusion that no completed contract could be spelt out of what had passed between the parties: for example, how many copies were to be printed, in hardback or paperback or both, at what price and yielding what royalty? Too much was missing. In any case, his Lordship would not have regarded specific performance as a proper or practicable remedy in a case like the present, where close co-operation between author and publisher was clearly essential. Had he been able to find a binding contract to publish, his Lordship would have been minded to award substantial damages.

### Maredelanto Compania Naviera SA v Bergbau-Handel Gmbh. The Mihalis Angelos.
See **Mihalis Angelos, The**

**Mihalis Angelos, The** [1970] 3 WLR 601 Court of Appeal (Lord Denning MR, Edmund-Davies and Megaw LJJ)

Charter - breach of condition

*Facts*

On 25 May 1965 the owners of the 'Mihalis Angelos' let the vessel to charterers for the voyage from Haiphong, Vietnam, to Hamburg, the vessel being 'expected ready to load under the charter about 1 July 1965'. At the time the charter was made, she was on her way to Hong Kong to discharge and to be surveyed, and she only completed discharging on 23 July. It was found as a fact that the owners had no reasonable grounds for believing her to be ready to load about 1 July.

*Held*

Law and practice had established that an 'expected ready to load' clause was a condition, any breach of which gave the charterer the right to terminate the contract.

Lord Denning MR:

'The contest resolved itself simply into this: was the "expected ready to load" clause a condition, such that for breach of it the charterers could throw up the charter? Or was it a mere warranty, such as to give rise to damages if it was broken but not a right to cancel, seeing that cancellation was expressly dealt with in the cancelling clause? Sir Frederick Pollock divided the terms of the contract into two categories, conditions and warranties. The difference between them was this: if the promisor broke a *condition* in *any* respect, however slight, it gave the other party a right to be quit of his future obligations and to sue for damages, unless he, by his conduct, waived the condition, in which case he was bound to perform his future obligations but could sue for the damage he suffered. If the promisor broke a *warranty* in *any* respect, however serious, the other party was not quit of his future obligations. He had to perform them. His only remedy was to sue for damages.

This division was adopted by Sir MacKenzie Chalmers when he drafted the Sale of Goods Act and by Parliament when it passed it. It was stated by Fletcher Moulton LJ, in his celebrated dissenting judgment in *Wallis, Son & Wells* v *Pratt & Haynes*, which was adopted in its entirety by the House of Lords. It would be a mistake, however, to look on that division as exhaustive. There are many terms of many contracts which cannot be fitted into either category. In such cases, the courts, for nigh on 200 years, have not asked themselves: was the term a condition or a warranty? But rather was the breach such as to go to the root of the contract? If it was, then the other party is entitled, at his election, to treat himself as discharged from any further performance. That is made clear by the judgment of Lord Mansfield in *Boone* v *Eyre* and by the speech of Lord Blackburn in *Mersey Steel and Iron Co* v *Naylor, Benzon & Co* and the notes to *Cutter* v *Powell*. *Hong Kong Fir Shipping Co Ltd* v *Kawasaki Kisen Kaisha Ltd* is a useful reminder of this large category.

Although this large category exists, there is still remaining a considerable body of law by which certain stipulations have been classified as "conditions" so that any failure to perform, however slight, entitles the other to treat himself as discharged. Thus a statement in a charter party on 19 October 1860 that the ship is "now in the port of Amsterdam" was held to be a "condition". On that date she was just outside Amsterdam and could not get in owing to strong gales; but she got in a day or two later when the gales abated. The Court of Exchequer Chamber held that the charterer was entitled to call off the charter; see *Behn* v *Burness*, overruling the Court of Exchequer.

The question in this case is whether the statement by the owner, "expected ready to load under this charter about 1 July 1965" is likewise a "condition". The meaning of such a clause is settled by a decision of this court. It is an assurance by the owner that he honestly expects that the vessel will be ready to load on that date and that his expectation is based on reasonable grounds: see *Samuel Sanday & Co* v *Keighley, Maxted & Co*. The clause with that meaning has been held in this court to be a "condition", which, if not fulfilled, entitled the other party to treat himself as discharged; see *Finnish Government (Ministry of Food)* v *H V Ford & Co Ltd*. Those were sale of goods cases; but I think that the clause should receive the same interpretation in charter party cases. It seems to me that if the owner of a ship, or his agent, states in a charter that she is "expected ready to load about 1 July 1965", he is making a representation as to his own state of mind, ie of what he himself expects; and what is more, he puts it in the contract as a term of it, binding himself to its truth. If he or his agent breaks that term by making the statement without any honest belief in the truth, or without any reasonable grounds for it, he must take the consequences. It is, at lowest, a misrepresentation, which entitles the other party to rescind and, at highest, a breach of contract, which goes to the root of the matter. The charterer who is misled by the statement is entitled, on discovering its falsity, to throw up the charter. It may therefore properly be described as a "condition". I am confirmed in this view by the illustration given by Scrutton LJ himself in all the editions of his work on charter parties:

"A ship was chartered 'expected to be at X about the 15 December ... shall with all convenient speed sail to X'. The ship was in fact then on such a voyage that she could not complete it and be at X by 15 December. *Submitted*, that the charterer was entitled to throw up the charter."

I do not regard *Associated Portland Cement Manufacturers [1900] Ltd* v *Houlder Brothers & Co Ltd* as any authority to the contrary. The facts are too shortly reported for any guidance to be got from it.

I hold, therefore, that on 17 July 1965 the charterers were entitled to cancel the contract on the ground that the owners had broken the "expected ready to load" clause.'

Megaw LJ:

'In my judgment, such a term ought to be regarded as being a condition of the contract, in the old sense of the word "condition": that is, that when it has been broken, the other party can, if he wishes, by intimation to the party in breach, elect to be released from performance of his further obligations under the contract; and he can validly do so without having to establish that, on the facts of the particular case, the breach has produced serious consequences which can be treated as "going to the root of the contract" or as being "fundamental", or whatever other metaphor may be thought appropriate for a frustration case.'

*Commentary*

Applied in *Decro-Wall International SA* v *Practitioners in Marketing Ltd* [1971] 1 WLR 361.


**Miller (James) and Partners Ltd v Whitworth Street Estates (Manchester) Ltd** [1970] 2 WLR 728 House of Lords (Lord Reid, Lord Hodson, Lord Guest, Viscount Dilhorne and Lord Wilberforce)

Construction - conduct subsequent to execution of contract

*Facts*

A building contract, between English owners and Scottish contractors, in respect of premises in Scotland made provision for arbitration. Although it was held that English law was the proper law of the contract, arbitration had proceeded according to Scots law. Could the English courts require the arbiter to state a case?

*Held*

They could not because the parties had, on the facts, accepted that the arbitration was subject to Scots law.

Lord Hodson:

'I cannot assent to the view ... that as a matter of construction the contract can be construed not only in its surrounding circumstances but also by reference to the subsequent conduct of the parties.

I am satisfied, however, that, whether the proper law of the contract is English or Scottish, the arbitration being admittedly a matter of procedure as opposed to being a matter of substantive law is on principle and authority to be governed by the lex fori, in this case Scottish law. Furthermore, the parties have, in my judgment, plainly submitted to the Scottish arbitration on the footing that Scottish procedure was to govern.'

**Moorcock, The** (1889) 14 PD 64 Court of Appeal (Lord Esher MR, Bowen and Fry LJJ)

Contract - implied term as to use of wharf

*Facts*

By agreement between the parties, the plaintiffs' vessel proceeded to the defendants' wharf to discharge and load a cargo. Both parties knew that when the tide ebbed a vessel at the wharf would be grounded. When the plaintiffs' ship was moored there, she took ground and, owing to inequalities in the river bed, sustained damage. Although the defendants had no legal control over the river bed, they could ascertain its state but they had not done so.

*Held*

The defendants were liable in respect of the damage suffered by the plaintiffs' vessel.

Lord Esher MR:

'Whether they can see the actual bottom of the river or not at low water is not, to my mind, the least material. Supposing at low water there were two feet of water always over the mud; it makes no difference that they cannot see the bottom. They can feel for the bottom by sounding, or in some similar way, and find out its condition with as much accuracy, may, with a great deal more accuracy, than if they could see it with their own eyes. When it is so easy to do this, and when, in order to earn money, business requires a ship to be brought alongside their wharf, in my opinion honesty of business requires, and we are bound to imply it, that the defendants have undertaken to see that the bottom of the river is reasonably fit for the purpose, or that they ought, at all events, take reasonable care to find out whether the bottom of the river is reasonably fit for the purpose for which they agree that their jetty should be used, and then if not, either procure it to be made reasonably fit for the purpose, or inform the persons with whom they have contracted that it is not so. That, I think, is the least that can be implied as the defendants' duty, and that is what I understand the learned judge has implied. He then goes on to say that, as a matter of fact, they did not take such reasonable measures in this case. I mayself have not the least doubt in making this implication as part of the contract. I, therefore, have no doubt that the defendants broke the contract, and they are, therefore, liable to the plaintiffs for the injury which the vessel sustained.'

*Commentary*

See also *Associated Japanese Bank (International) Ltd* v *Crédit du Nord SA* [1988] 1 WLR 255.

**Neilson v Stewart** 1991 SLT 523 House of Lords (Lord Keith, Lord Brandon, Lord Ackner, Lord Oliver, Lord Jauncey)

Formation - uncertainty - severance

*Facts*

A sale of shares was agreed between seller and purchaser. The agreement included a loan repayment which was to be deferred for one year 'after which time repayment shall be negotiated to our mutual satisfaction'. The purchaser failed to complete the agreement and subsequently argued that the phrase in question rendered the whole agreement unenforceable by reason of uncertainty. The seller's argument was that there were two severable agreements, one for the sale of shares, which was enforceable, and one for the arrangements of the loan, which was not enforceable.

*Held*

The House of Lords held that in fact both parts of the agreement were enforceable. The parties did not apparently intend the loan to be fixed as to time and manner of payment, all loans were repayable on demand and it was not essential that interest should be payable. Any apparent ambiguities could thus be resolved. The seller's action for damages for breach of contract by the buyer was successful.

*Commentary*

As a Scottish case this was of general interest, but not necessarily a binding precedent for English contractual law. As now confirmed by the House of Lords, it is, of course, of more far-reaching significance

**Oscar Chess Ltd v Williams** [1957] 1 WLR 370 Court of Appeal (Denning, Hodson and Morris LJJ)

Age of car - condition or representation?

*Facts*

In May 1955, the defendant acquired a new car from the plaintiffs, who were motor car dealers and who took the defendant's Morris in part exchange. The defendant said it was a 1948 model, as per the registration document, and the plaintiffs made him an allowance of £290. The registration book had been altered by an unknown third party and the car was, in reality, a 1939 model worth £175. The County Court judge held that it was a condition of the contract that the car was a 1948 model.

*Held* (Morris LJ dissenting)

The defendant's statement as to the age of the car was a mere representation, not a term of the contract. He had no special knowledge as to its age and the plaintiffs knew that he was relying on the date in the registration book. Therefore the defendant was not liable.

Denning LJ:

'I entirely agree with the judge that both parties assumed that the Morris was a 1948 model and that this assumption was fundamental to the contract. But this does not prove that the representation was a term of the contract. The assumption was based by both of them on the date given in the registration book as the date of first registration. They both believed it was a 1948 model when it was only a 1939 one. They were both mistaken and their mistake was of fundamental importance.

The effect of such a mistake is this: It does not make the contract a nullity from the beginning, but it does, in some circumstances, enable the contract to be set aside in equity. If the buyer had come promptly, he might have succeeded in getting the whole transaction set aside in equity on the ground of this mistake: see *Solle* v *Butcher*; but he did not do so and it is too late for him to do it: see *Leaf* v *International Galleries*. His only remedy is in damages and, to recover these, he must prove a warranty.

In saying that he must prove a warranty, I used the word "warranty" in its ordinary English meaning to denote a binding promise. Everyone knows what a man means when he says "I guarantee it" or "I warrant it" or "I give you my word on it". He means that he binds himself to it. That is the meaning it has borne in English Law for 300 years, from the leading case of *Chandelor* v *Lopus* (1603) Cro Jac 4 onwards. During the last fifty years, however, some lawyers have come to use the word "warranty" in another sense. They use it to denote a subsidiary term in contract, as distinct from a vital term, which they call a "condition". In so doing, they depart from the ordinary meaning, not only of the word "warranty" but also of the word "condition". There is no harm in their doing this, so long as they confine this technical use to its proper sphere, namely to distinguish between a vital term, the breach of which gives the right to treat the contract as at an end, and a subsidiary term which does not. But the trouble comes when one person uses the word "warranty" in its ordinary meaning and another uses it in its technical meaning. When Holt CJ in *Crosse* v *Gardner* (1689) Carth 90 (as glossed by Buller J in *Pasley* v *Freeman* (1789) 3 Term Rep 51, 57) and *Medina* v *Stoughton* (1700) 1 Salk 210 made his famous ruling that an affirmation at the time of a sale is a warranty, provided it appears on evidence to be so intended, he used the word "warranty" in its ordinary English meaning of a binding promise: and when Lord Haldane LC and Lord Moulton in 1913 in *Heilbut, Symons & Co* v *Buckleton* adopted his ruling, they used it likewise in its ordinary meaning. These different uses of the word seem to have been the source of confusion in the present case. The judge did not ask himself, "Was the representation (that it was a 1948 Morris) intended to be a warranty?" He asked himself "Was it fundamental to the contract?" He answered it by saying that it was fundamental; and therefore it was a condition and not a warranty. By concentrating on whether it was fundamental, he seems to me to have missed the crucial point in the case, which is whether it was a term of the contract at all. The crucial question is: was it a binding promise or only an innocent misrepresentation? The technical distinction between a "condition" and a "warranty" is quite immaterial in this case, because it is far too late for the buyer to reject the car. He can, at best, only claim damages. The material distinction here is between a statement which is a term of the contract and a statement which is only an innocent misrepresentation. This distinction is best expressed by the ruling of Lord Holt: Was it intended as a warranty or not? Using the word "warranty" there in its ordinary English meaning: because it gives the exact shade of meaning that is required. It is something to which a man must be taken to bind himself.

In applying Lord Holt's test, however, some misunderstanding has arisen by the use of the word "intended". It is sometimes supposed that the tribunal must look into the minds of the parties to see what they themselves intended. That is a mistake. Lord Moulton made it quite clear that "the intention of the parties can only be deduced from the totality of the evidence". The question whether a warranty was intended depends on the conduct of the parties, on their words and behaviour, rather than on their thoughts. If an intelligent bystander would reasonably infer that a warranty was intended, that will suffice. And this, when the facts are not in dispute, is a question of law. That is shown by *Heilbut, Symons & Co* v *Buckleton* itself, where the House of Lords upset the finding by a jury of a warranty.

It is instructive to take some recent instances to show how the courts have approached this question. When the seller states a fact which is or should be within his own knowledge and of which the buyer is ignorant, intending that the buyer should act on it and he does so, it is easy to infer a warranty: see *Couchman* v *Hill*, where the farmer stated that the heifer was served, and *Harling* v *Eddy*, where he stated that there was nothing wrong with her. So also, if he makes a promise about something which is or should be within his own control: see *Birch* v *Paramount Estates Ltd* [1958] 167 EG 396, decided on 2 October 1956, in this court, where the seller stated that the house would be as good as the show house. But if the seller, when he states a fact, makes it clear that he has no knowledge of his own, but has got his information elsewhere and is merely passing it on, it is not so easy to imply a warranty. Such a case was *Routledge* v *McKay* [1954] 1 WLR 615, 636, where the seller "stated that it was a 1942 model and pointed to the corroboration found in the book", and it was held that there was no warranty.

Turning now to the present case; much depends on the precise words that were used. If the seller says "I believe it is a 1948 Morris, here is the registration book to prove it", there is clearly no warranty. It is a statement of belief, not a contractual promise. But if the seller says "I guarantee that is a 1948 Morris. This is borne out by the registration book, but you need not rely solely on that. I give you my own guarantee that it is ", there is clearly a warranty. The seller is making himself contractually responsible, even though the registration book is wrong.

In this case, much reliance was placed by the judge on the fact that the buyer looked up *Glass's Guide* and paid £290 on the footing that it was a 1948 model: but that fact seems to me to be neutral. Both sides believed the car to have been made in 1948 and, in that belief, the buyer paid £290. That belief can be just as firmly based on the buyer's own inspection of the log book as on a contractual warranty by the seller.

Once that fact is put on one side, I ask myself: What is the proper inference from the known facts? It must have been obvious to both that the seller had himself no personal knowledge of the year when the car was made. He only became owner after a great number of changes. He must have been relying on the registration book. It is unlikely that such a person would warrant the year of manufacture. The most he could do would be to state his belief and then produce the registration book in verification of it. In these circumstances, the intelligent bystander would, I suggest, say that the seller did not intend to bind himself so as to warrant that it was a 1948 model. If the seller was asked to pledge himself to it, he would at once have said "I cannot do that. I have only the log book to go by, the same as you."

The judge seems to have thought that there was a difference between written contracts and oral contracts. He thought that the reason why the buyer failed in *Heilbut, Symons & Co* v *Buckleton* and *Routledge* v *McKay* was because the sales were afterwards recorded in writing and the written contracts contained no reference to the representation. I agree that that was an important factor in those cases. If an oral representation is afterwards recorded in writing, it is good evidence that it was intended as a warranty. If it is not put into writing, it is evidence against a warranty being intended. But it is by no means decisive. There have been many cases where the courts have found an oral warranty collateral to a written contract, such as *Birch* v *Paramount Estates*. But when the purchase is not recorded in writing at all, it must not be supposed that every representation made in the course of the dealing is to be treated as a warranty. The question then is still: Was it intended as a warranty? In the leading case of *Chandelor* v *Lopus* in 1603 a man, by word of mouth, sold a precious stone for £100 affirming it to be a bezar stone, whereas it was not. The declaration averred that the seller affirmed it to be a bezar stone, but did not aver that he warranted it to be so. The declaration was held to be ill because "the bare affirmation that it was a bezar stone, without warranting it to be so, is no cause of action". That has been the law from that day to this and it was emphatically reaffirmed by the House of Lords in *Heilbut, Symons & Co* v *Buckleton*.

One final word: It seems to me clear that the motor dealers who bought the car relied on the year stated in the log book. If they had wished to make sure of it, they could have checked it then and there by taking the engine number and chassis number and writing to the makers. They did not do so at the time, but only eight months later. They are experts and, not having made that check at the time, I do not think they should now be allowed to recover against the innocent seller, who produced to them all the evidence he had, namely the registration book. I agree that it is hard on the dealers to have paid more than the car is worth: but it would be equally hard on the seller to make him pay the difference. He would never have bought the Hillman at all unless he had got the allowance of £290 from the Morris. The best course in all these cases would be to "shunt" the difference down the train of innocent sellers until one reaches the rogue who perpetrated the fraud: but he can rarely be traced or, if he can, he rarely has the money to pay the damages. So one is left to decide between a number of innocent people who is to bear the loss. That can only be done by applying the law about representations and warranties as we know it: and that is what I have tried to do. If the rogue can be traced, he can be sued by whomsoever has suffered the loss: but if he cannot be traced, the loss must lie where it falls. It should not be inflicted on innocent sellers, who sold the car many months, perhaps many years, before and have forgotten all about it and have conducted their affairs on the basis that the transaction was concluded. Such a seller would not be able to recollect, after all this length of time, the exact words he used, such as whether he said "I believe it is a 1948 model", or "I warrant it is a 1948 model". The right course is to let the buyer set aside the transaction if he finds out the mistake quickly and comes promptly, before other interests have irretrievably intervened; otherwise the loss must lie where it falls: and that is, I think, the course prescribed by law. I would allow this appeal accordingly.'

*Commentary*

Applied: *Routledge* v *McKay* [1954] 1 WLR 615. Distinguished in *Bentley (Dick) Productions Ltd* v *Harold Smith (Motors) Ltd* [1965] 1 WLR 623.

**Prenn v Simmonds** [1971] 1 WLR 1381 House of Lords (Lord Reid, Lord Donovan, Lord Wilberforce, Lord Pearson and Lord Diplock)

Contract - construction

*Facts*

Following detailed negotiations, agreement was reached for the sale and purchase of shares if 'profits' reached a certain level. Did this refer to profits of the group or just of the holding company?

*Held*

In the light of the aim of the agreement and commercial good sense, the reference to 'profits' was to the consolidated profits of the group.

Lord Wilberforce:

'There were prolonged negotiations between solicitors, with exchanges of draft clauses, ultimately emerging in ... the agreement. The reason for not admitting evidence of these exchanges is not a technical one or even mainly one of convenience ... It is simply that such evidence is unhelpful. By the nature of things, where negotiations are difficult, the parties' positions, with each passing letter, are changing and until the final agreement, although converging, still divergent. It is only the final document which records a consensus. If the previous documents use different expressions, how does construction of those expressions, itself a doubtful process, help on the construction of the contractual words? If the same expressions are used, nothing is gained by looking back; indeed, something may be lost since the relevant surrounding circumstances may be different. And at this stage there is no consensus of the parties to appeal to. It may be said that previous documents may be looked at to explain the aims of the parties. In a limited sense this is true; the commercial, or business object, of the transaction, objectively ascertained, may be a surrounding fact ... And if it can be shown that one interpretation completely frustrates that object, to the extent of rendering the contract futile, that may be a strong argument for an alternative interpretation, if that can reasonably be found. But beyond that it may be difficult to go; it may be a matter of degree, or of judgment, how far one interpretation, or another, gives effect to a common intention; the parties, indeed, may be pursuing that intention with differing emphasis, and hoping to achieve it to an extent which may differ, and in different ways. The words used may, and often do, represent a formula which means different things to each side, yet may be accepted because that is the only way to get "agreement" and in the hope that disputes will not arise. The only course then can be to try to ascertain the "natural" meaning. Far more, and indeed totally, dangerous it is to admit evidence of one party's objective - even if this is known to the other party. However strongly pursued this may be, the other party may only be willing to give it partial recognition, and in a world of give and take, men often have to be satisfied with less than they want. So, again, it would be a matter of speculation how far the common intention was that the particular objective should be realised ... In my opinion, then, evidence of negotiations, or of the parties' intentions ... ought not to be received, and evidence should be restricted to evidence of the factual background known to the parties at or before the date of the contract, including evidence of the "genesis" and objectively the "aim" of the transaction.'

**Reardon Smith Line Ltd v Hansen-Tangen** [1976] 1 WLR 989 House of Lords (Lord Wilberforce, Viscount Dilhorne, Lord Simon of Glaisdale, Lord Kilbrandon and Lord Russell of Killowen)

Charter - words of identification or contractual description?

*Facts*

In order to perform a charter, a steamship company nominated a vessel 'to be built by Osaka Shipbuilding Co Ltd and known as Hull No 354 until named'. Osaka was unable to build the ship in its own yard and so subcontracted the work to Oshima, a newly created company in which it held 50 per

111

cent of the shares. Osaka provided a large part of Oshima's work force and managerial staff. In Osaka's books the ship was numbered 354; in Oshima's 004. Although the vessel when built complied fully with the physical specifications in the charter and was fit for the contemplated service, delivery was refused.

*Held*

The charterers were not entitled to refuse delivery.

Lord Wilberforce:

'The appellants sought, necessarily, to give to the ... provision in the ... charter contractual effect. They argued that these words formed part of the "description" of the future goods contracted to be provided, that, by analogy with contracts for the sale of goods, any departure from the description entitled the other party to reject, that there were departures in that the vessel was not built by Osaka and was not Hull No 354. I shall attempt to deal with each of these contentions.

In the first place, I am not prepared to accept that authorities as to "description" in sale of goods cases are to be extended, or applied, to such a contract as we have here. Some of these cases either in themselves (*Re Moore & Co and Landauer & Co*) or as they have been interpreted (eg *Behn* v *Burness*) I find to be excessively technical and due for fresh examination in this House. Even if a strict and technical view must be taken as regards the description of unascertained future goods (eg commodities) as to which each detail of the description must be assumed to be vital, it may be, and in my opinion is, right to treat other contracts of sale of goods in a similar manner to other contracts generally, so as to ask whether a particular item in a description constitutes a substantial ingredient of the "identity" of the thing sold, and only if it does to treat it as a condition ... It is one thing to say of given words that their purpose is to state (identify) an essential part of the description of the goods. It is another to say that they provide one party with a specific indication (identification) of the goods so that he can find them and if he wishes sub-dispose of them. The appellants wish to say of words which "identify" the goods in the second sense, that they describe them in the first. I have already given reasons why I can only read the words in the second sense. The difference is vital. If the words are read in the first sense, then, unless I am right in the legal argument above, each element in them has to be given contractual force. The vessel must, as a matter of contract, and as an essential term, be built by Osaka and must bear their yard number 354; if not, the description is not complied with and the vessel tendered is not that contracted for. If in the second sense, the only question is whether the words provide a means of identifying the vessel. If they fairly do this, they have fulfilled their function ...

So the question becomes simply whether, as a matter of fact, it can fairly be said that - as a means of identification - the vessel was ... "built by Osaka Shipping Co Ltd and known as Hull No 354, until named". To answer this, regard may be had to the actual arrangements for building the vessel and numbering it before named. My Lords, I have no doubt ... that an affirmative answer must be given. I shall not set out the evidence which clearly makes this good. The fact is that the vessel always was Osaka Hull No 354 - though also Oshima No 004 - and equally it can fairly be said to have been "built" by Osaka as the company which planned, organised and directed the building and contractually engaged ... to build it, though also it could be said to have been built by Oshima. For the purpose of the identificatory clause, the words used are quite sufficient to cover the facts. No other vessel could be referred to: the reference fits the vessel in question.

There are other facts not to be overlooked. (1) So long as the charterers could identify the nominated vessel they had not the slightest interest in whatever contracting or sub-contracting arrangements were made in the course of the building ... (2) In making the arrangements they did for building the vessel, Osaka acted in a perfectly straightforward and open manner. They cannot be said to be substituting one vessel for another; they have not provided any ground on which the charterers can claim that their bargain has not been fulfilled. The contracts all down the chain were closely and appropriately knitted into what Osaka did. (3) If the market had risen instead of falling, it would have been quite impossible for Osaka ... to refuse to tender the vessel in accordance with the charters on the ground that it did not correspond with that contracted for. No more on a falling market is there, in my opinion, any ground on which the charterers can reject the vessel. In the end I find this a simple and clear case.'

*Commentary*

See also *Staffordshire Area Health Authority* v *South Staffordshire Waterworks Co* [1978] 1 WLR 1387.

**Reigate v Union Manufacturing Co (Ramsbottom) Ltd** [1918] 1 KB 592 Court of Appeal (Pickford, Bankes and Scrutton LJJ)

Agency - right of principal to terminate

*Facts*

The defendants appointed the plaintiff sole agent for the sale of certain goods for an initial period of seven years. During that period the defendants became insolvent, went into voluntary liquidation and ceased to carry on business. The plaintiff claimed damages for breach of contract.

*Held*

He was entitled to succeed.

Scrutton LJ:

'I think these principles have been clearly established. Before you consider what has been decided in other cases, the first thing is to see what the parties have agreed to in the case under consideration; and, secondly, before troubling about seeing what you are to imply into the contract, the first thing is to see what the parties have expressed in the contract; and, when you have understood what the parties have expressed in the words there used, you are not to add implications because you think it would have been a reasonable thing to have put in the contract, or because you think you would have insisted on such a term being in the contract. You must only imply a term if it is necessary in the business sense to give efficacy to the contract - that is, if it is such a term that you can be confident that if at the time the contract was being negotiated someone had said to the parties: "What will happen in such a case?" they would have both replied, "Of course, so and so. We did not trouble to say that: it is too clear"' Unless you can come to some such conclusion as that, we ought not to imply a term which the parties themselves have not expressed when they have expressed other terms ... As I understand, it is suggested that the contract is only to remain in force so long as the company carry on their business. Is that a necessary implication? Supposing that the parties had been asked this: "You have not said so, but I suppose if the company ceases to carry on business this contract is at an end," would they both have said, "Yes, of course"? I should be very much surprised if they would. I expect they would immediately have found that they disagreed as to what the position was; and, unless I am satisfied that it is a necessary implication which must have been in the minds of both of them, I have no business to imply a term which they themselves have not expressed, particularly when I find they have thought sufficiently about the matter to express the conditions on which the agreement was to be determined - first, the obvious one that it was to be determined if the agent died; secondly, they assumed it might be determined after seven years if a particular notice was given. For these reasons I find an express condition that the contract is to continue for seven years, subject to the company refusing orders that they had reasonable ground to refuse, and no ground for implying a term that the seven years shall be subject to the implied condition that the company is carrying on business.'

### Richco International Ltd v Bunge and Co Ltd [1991] 2 Lloyd's Rep 93 QBD (Phillips J)

Construction of terms - contracts in a string

*Facts*

Several contracts were negotiated in string. Among the clauses were conditions as to ports of shipment and loading arrangements. The charterers sought to interpret clauses differently in certain aspects of the contract.

*Held*

Where contracts are in a string, exactly the same meaning must be given to clauses in contracts throughout the chain. The same weighting should also be given to the importance (or lack of it) of similar clauses.

### Rickards (Charles) Ltd v Oppenheim

See chapter 2 - Consideration.

### Sagar v H Ridehalgh & Son Ltd [1931] 1 Ch 310 Court of Appeal (Lord Hanworth MR, Lawrence and Romer LJJ)

Wages - deduction for bad work

*Facts*

The plaintiff weaver was employed by the defendants and trade union wage rates were incorporated in the contract of employment. For more than thirty years, the defendants had made reasonable deductions for bad work and most other mills did the same. For bad work the defendants deducted one shilling from the plaintiff's pay.

*Held*

They were entitled to do so.

Lawrence LJ:

'The employers based their contention on two alternative grounds, either that the established practice of making reasonable deductions for bad work in the defendants' mill was incorporated into the plaintiff's contract of service by reason of his having agreed to be employed upon the same terms as the other weavers in that mill or else that the general usage of making reasonable deductions for bad work prevailing in the cotton weaving trade of Lancashire was so well known and understood that every weaver engaging in that trade must be taken to have entered upon his employment on the footing of that usage.

As regards the first of these grounds. It is clearly established by the evidence ... that the practice of making reasonable deductions for bad work has continuously prevailed at the defendants' mill for upwards of thirty years, and that during the whole of that time all weavers employed by the defendants have been treated alike in that respect. The practice was, therefore, firmly established at the defendants' mills when the plaintiff entered upon his employment there. Further, I think that it is clear that the plaintiff accepted employment in the defendant's mill on the same terms as the other weavers employed at that mill. I draw this inference not only from the statement of claim (as explained by the particulars) and from the plaintiff's own evidence, but also from the fact that this action is avowedly brought to test the legality of the practice prevailing at the defendants' mill and not to determine whether this particular plaintiff was employed upon some special terms which would make that practice inapplicable to his contract of service. Although I entirely agree with the learned judge in finding it difficult to believe that the plaintiff did not know of the existence of the practice at the mill, I think that it is immaterial whether he knew of it or not, as I am satisfied that he accepted his employment in the same terms as to deductions for bad work as the other weavers at the mill.

In the result I have come to the conclusion that the practice of making reasonable deductions for bad work prevailing at the defendants' mill was incorporated in the plaintff's contract of service. Further, I am of opinion that the second ground is also established by the evidence, namely, that the practice in the defendants' mill is in accordance with the general usage of making reasonable deductions for bad work prevailing in the weaving trade of Lancashire, which usage in the absence of any stipulation to the contrary would be incorporated into every contract of service as a weaver in a Lancashire cotton mill without special mention.'

**Schawel v Reade** [1913] 2 Ir Rep 81 House of Lords (Lord Moulton, Lord Atkinson and Lord Macnaghten)

Sale of horse - warranty

*Facts*

The plaintiff, who required a stallion for stud purposes, went to the defendant's stables to look for a horse. While he was inspecting a horse the defendant said: 'You need not look for anything: the horse is perfectly sound. If there was anything the matter with the horse, I would tell you.' The plaintiff thereupon terminated his examination and a few days later a price was agreed upon. Three weeks later the plaintiff bought the horse. It was totally unfit for stud purposes. The judge left the following question to the jury: 'Did the defendant at the time of the sale represent to the plaintiff in order that the plaintiff might purchase the horse that the horse was fit for stud purposes and did the plaintiff act upon that representation in the purchase of the horse?' The issue before the House of Lords was whether the jury's affirmative answer amounted to a finding of a warranty.

*Held*

It did.

Lord Moulton:

'It would be impossible, in my mind, to have a clearer example of an express warranty where the word "warranty" was not used. The essence of such warranty is that it becomes plain by the words and action of the parties that it is intended that in the purchase the responsibility of the soundness shall rest upon the vendor; and how in the world could a vendor more clearly indicate that he is prepared and intends to take upon himself the responsibility of the soundness than by saying: "You need not look at that horse, because it is perfectly sound," and sees that the purchaser thereupon desists from his immediate independent examination?'

**Schuler (L) AG v Wickman Machine Tool Sales Ltd** [1973] 2 WLR 683 House of Lords (Lord Reid, Lord Morris of Borth-y-Gest, Lord Wilberforce, Lord Simon of Glaisdale and Lord Kilbrandon)

Breach of 'condition' - right to terminate

*Facts*

The respondents were the exclusive selling agents in the UK for the appellants' presses. The agency agreement provided:

'It shall be a condition of this agreement that (the respondent) shall send its representative to visit (the six largest UK motor manufacturers) at least once every week.'

115

The respondents committed some minor breaches of this term and the appellants terminated the agreement, claiming that by reason of the term being a condition, they were entitled so to do.

*Held* (Lord Wilberforce dissenting)

The parties could not have intended that the appellants should have the right to terminate the agreement if the respondents failed to make one of the obliged number of visits which, in total, amounted to nearly 1,500. A provision elsewhere in the agreement gave the appellants the right to determine the agreement if the respondents committed a 'material' breach: this indicated that the parties had not intended to use the word 'condition' in its technical sense.

Lord Reid:

'Schuler maintain that the word "condition" has now acquired a precise legal meaning; that particularly since the enactment of the Sale of Goods Act 1893, its recognised meaning in English law is a term of a contract any breach of which by one party gives to the other party an immediate right to rescind the whole contract. Undoubtedly the word is frequently used in that sense. There may, indeed be some presumption that in a formal legal document it has that meaning. But it is frequently used with a less stringent meaning. One is familiar with printed "conditions of sale" incorporated into a contract, and with the words "for conditions see back" printed on a ticket. This simply means that the "conditions" are terms of the contract.

In the ordinary use of the English language "condition" has many meanings, some of which have nothing to do with agreements. In connection with an agreement, it may mean a pre-condition: something which must happen or be done before the agreement can take effect. Or it may mean some state of affairs which must continue to exist if the agreement is to remain in force. The legal meaning on which Schuler rely is, I think, one which would not occur to a layman; a condition in that sense is not something which has an automatic effect. It is a term, the breach of which by one party gives to the other an option either to terminate the contract or to let the contract proceed and, if he so desires, sue for damages for the breach.

Sometimes a breach of a term gives that option to the aggrieved party because it is of a fundamental character going to the root of the contract, sometimes it gives that option because the parties have chosen to stipulate that it shall have that effect. Blackburn J said in *Bettini v Gye*:

"Parties may think some matter, apparently of very little importance, essential; and if they sufficiently express an intention to make the literal fulfilment of such a thing a condition precedent, it will be one."

In the present case it is not contended that Wickman's failure to make visits amounted, in themselves, to fundamental breaches. What is contended is that the terms of clause 7 "sufficiently express an intention" to make any breach, however small, of the obligation to make visits a condition, so that any breach shall entitle Schuler to rescind the whole contract if they so desire.

Schuler maintain that the use of the word "condition" is, in itself, enough to establish this intention. No doubt some words used by lawyers do have a rigid inflexible meaning. But we must remember that we are seeking to discover intention as disclosed by the contract as a whole. Use of the word "condition" is an indication - even a strong indication - of such an intention, but it is by no means conclusive. The fact that a particular construction leads to a very unreasonable result must be a relevant consideration. The more unreasonable the result, the more unlikely it is that the parties can have intended it and if they do intend it, the more necessary it is that they shall make that intention abundantly clear.

Clause 7(b) requires that over a long period, each of the six firms shall be visited every week by one or other of two named representatives. It makes no provision for Wickman being entitled to substitute others, even on the death or retirement of one of the named representatives. Even if one could imply some rights to do this, it makes no provision for both representatives being ill during a particular week. And it makes no provision for the possibility that one or other of the firms may tell

Wickman that they cannot receive Wickman's representative during a particular week. So if the parties gave any thought to the matter at all, they must have realised the probability that in a few cases out of the 1,400 required visits, a visit as stipulated would be impossible. But if Schuler's contention is right, failure to make even one visit entitles them to terminate the contract, however blameless Wickman might be. This is so unreasonable that it must make me search for some other possible meaning of the contract. If none can be found, then Wickman must suffer the consequences. But only if that is the only possible interpretation.

If I have to construe clause 7 standing by itself, then I do find difficulty in reaching any other interpretation. But if clause 7 must be read with clause 11, the difficulty disappears. The word "conditions" would make any breach of clause 7(b), however excusable, a material breach. That would then entitle Schuler to give notice under clause 11(a)(i), requiring the breach to be remedied. There would be no point in giving such a notice if Wickman were clearly not in fault, but if it were given, Wickman would have no difficulty in showing that the breach had been remedied. If Wickman were at fault, then on receiving such a notice, they would have to amend their system so that they could show that the breach had been remedied. If they did not do that within the period of the notice, then Schuler would be entitled to rescind.

In my view, that is a possible and reasonable construction of the contract and I would therefore adopt it. The contract is so obscure that I can have no confidence that this is its true meaning, but for the reasons which I have given, I think that it is the preferable construction. It follows that Schuler were not entitled to rescind the contract as they purported to do. So I would dismiss this appeal.'

### Shanklin Pier Ltd v Detel Products Ltd [1951] 2 KB 854 High Court (McNair J)

Warranty - third party caused to enter into contract

*Facts*

The defendants were manufacturers of paint and they assured the plaintiffs that their paint was suitable for piers and would last seven years. In consequence, the plaintiffs stipulated in their contract with a firm of painters that the defendants' paint be used. It proved unsatisfactory and lasted only three months.

*Held*

The defendants were liable on a collateral warranty.

McNair J:

'... I am satisfied that, if a direct contract of purchase and sale of the (paint) had then been made between the plaintiffs and the defendants, the correct conclusion on the facts would have been that the defendants gave to the plaintiffs the warranties substantially in the form alleged in the statement of claim ...'

*Commentary*

Applied in *Andrews* v *Hopkinson* [1956] 3 WLR 732.

### Shell UK Ltd v Lostock Garage Ltd [1976] 1 WLR 1187 Court of Appeal (Lord Denning MR, Ormrod and Bridge LJJ)

Agreement for supply of petrol - implied term?

*Facts*

The defendants operated a garage and they entered into a solus agreement with the plaintiffs for the supply of petrol. After 20 years, there was a petrol price 'war': the plaintiffs introduced a support scheme of subsidies which they applied to two other of their garages in the neighbourhood, but not to the defendants. Erroneously believing that the tie to the plaintiffs had ended, the defendants obtained petrol from Mansfield at a lower cost. The plaintiffs threatened Mansfield with proceedings for inducing a breach of contract, so they (Mansfield) ceased supplying the defendants and they (the defendants) resumed taking supplies from the plaintiffs. In proceedings for damages and an injunction, the defendants argued that the solus agreement was subject to an implied term that the plaintiffs would not abnormally discriminate against the defendants so as to render their (the defendants') sales uneconomic.

*Held* (Bridge LJ dissenting)

This was not the case.

Lord Denning MR:

'*Implied terms*

It was submitted by counsel for Lostock that there was to be implied in the solus agreement a term that Shell, as the supplier, should not abnormally discriminate against the buyer and/or should supply petrol to the buyer on terms which did not abnormally discriminate against him. He said that Shell had broken that implied term by giving support to the two Shell garages and refusing it to Lostock; that, on that ground, Shell were in breach of the solus agreement; and that Lostock were entitled to terminate it.

This submission makes it necessary once again to consider the law as to implied terms. I ventured with some trepidation to suggest that terms implied by law could be brought within one comprehensive category, in which the courts could imply a term such as was just and reasonable in the circumstances: see *Greaves & Co (Contractors) Lrt* v *Baynham Meikle & Partner; Liverpool City Council* v *Irwin*. But, as I feared, the House of Lords have rejected it as quite unacceptable. As I read the speeches, there are two broad categories of implied terms.

(i)    *The first category*

The first category comprehends all those relationships which are of common occurrence, such as the relationship of seller and buyer, owner and hirer, master and servant, landlord and tenant, carrier by land or by sea, contractor for building works, and so forth. In all those relationships the courts have imposed obligations on one party or the other, saying they are implied terms. These obligations are not founded on the intention of the parties, actual or presumed, but on more general considerations: see *Luxor (Eastbourne) Ltd* v *Cooper* per Lord Wright; *Lister* v *Romford Ice and Cold Storage Co* per Viscount Simonds and Lord Tucker (both of whom give interesting illustrations); *Liverpool City Council* v *Irwin* per Lord Cross of Chelsea and Lord Edmund-Davies. In such relationships the problem is not solved by asking: what did the parties intend? or, would they have unhesitatingly agreed to it, if asked? It is to be solved by asking; has the law already defined the obligation or the extent of it? If so, let it be followed. If not, look to see what would be reasonable in the general run of such cases (see per Lord Cross of Chelsea) and then say what the obligation shall be. The House in *Liverpool City Council* v *Irwin* went through that very process. They examined the existing law of landlord and tenant, in particular that relating to easements, to see if it contained the solution to the problem; and, having found that it did not, they imposed an obligation on the landlord to use reasonable care. In these relationships the parties can exclude or modify the obligation by express words, but unless they do so, the obligation is a legal incident of the relationship which is attached by the law itself and not by reason of any implied term.

Likewise, in the general law of contract, the legal effect of frustration does not depend on an implied term. It does not depend on the presumed intention of the parties, nor on what they would have answered, if asked, but simply on what the court iself declares to amount to a frustration: see *Davis Contractors* v *Fareham Urban District Council* per Lord Radcliffe.

(ii)   *The second category*

The second category comprehends those cases which are not within the first category. These are cases, not of common occurrence, in which from the particular circumstances a term is to be implied.

In these cases the implication is based on an intention imputed to the parties from their actual circumstances: see *Luxor (Eastbourne) Ltd* v *Cooper* per Lord Wright. Such an imputation is only to be made when it is necessary to imply a term to give efficacy to the contract and make it a workable agreement in such manner as the parties would clearly have done if they had applied their mind to the contingency which has arisen. These are the "officous bystander" type of case: see *Lister* v *Romford Ice & Cold Storage Co* per Lord Tucker. In such cases a term is not to be implied on the ground that it would be reasonable, but only when it is necessary and can be formulated with a sufficient degree of precision. This was the test applied by the majority of this court in *Liverpool City Council* v *Irwin*; and they were emphatically upheld by the House on this point; see per Lord Cross of Chelsea and Lord Edmund Davies.

There is this point to be noted about *Liverpool City Council* v *Irwin*. In this court the argument was only about an implication in the second category. In the House of Lords that argument was not pursued. It was only the first category.

Into which of the two categories does the present case come? I am tempted to say that a solus agreement between supplier and buyer is of such common occurrence nowadays that it could be put into the first category; so that the law could imply a term based on general considerations. But I do not think this would be found acceptable. Nor do I think the case can be brought within the second category. If Shell had been asked at the beginning: "Will you agree not to discriminate abnormally against the buyer?" I think they would have declined. It might be a reasonable term, but it is not a necessary term. Nor can it be formulated with sufficient precision. On this point I agree with Kerr J. It should be noticed that in *Esso Petroleum Co Ltd* v *Harper's Garage (Stourport) Ltd* Mocatta J also refused to make such an implication and there was no appeal from his decision.

In the circumstances, I do not think any term can be implied ...

"He who comes to equity"

There is another way of reaching the same result. As I have already said, I do not think there was any implied term that Shell would not abnormally discriminate against Lostock. So there was no breach of contract by Shell. Nevertheless, there was conduct by Shell which was unfair to Lostock. It was not done by Shell deliberately so as to injure Lostock. It was done to avoid the impact of the Price Code; so as not to break the code in the overall conduct of their business. But, whatever the reason, the fact is that Shell insisted on maintaining the tie in circumstances where it was unfair and unreasonable for them to do so. To my mind this frees the garage from the tie during the time when the support scheme was operated by Shell to the prejudice of the garage. At any rate no court would grant Shell an injunction against the garage. It is well settled that "he who comes to equity must do equity". I need only refer to such cases as *Stickney* v *Keeble*; *Measures Brothers Ltd* v *Measures*; and *Chappell* v *Times Newspapers Ltd*. So long as Shell were operating the support scheme to the prejudice of Lostock, a court of equity would not grant Shell any equitable relief by way of injunction or otherwise. And a court of law would not grant Shell any damages because they could prove no loss, and in any case they were themselves the cause of any loss. If Shell had continued the support scheme for any substantial length of time - so that it struck at the root of the consideration for the tie - Lostock might have been relieved altogether from the tie. But, as the support scheme was short-lived, Lostock were only relieved of the tie during its continuance.'

**Shirlaw v Southern Foundries (1926) Ltd**

See **Southern Foundries (1926) Ltd v Shirlaw.**

**Southern Foundries (1926) Ltd v Shirlaw** [1940] AC 701 House of Lords (Viscount Maugham, Lord Atkin, Lord Wright, Lord Romer and Lord Porter)

Contract appointing managing director - act of third party

*Facts*

The respondent was appointed the appellants' managing director for a period of ten years. At that time, the appellants' articles provided that the power to remove the managing director was 'subject to the provisions of any contract between him and the company'. Three years later FF Ltd acquired financial control of the appellants: new articles were adopted giving FF Ltd the power to remove any of the appellants' directors: they removed the respondent. Was there a term to the effect that the appellants would not remove the respondent from office?

*Held* (Viscount Maugham and Lord Romer dissenting)

There was and he was entitled to damages for breach of it.

Lord Wright:

'As I follow the appellant company's case, it is that a contract between A and B can, apart from any express or implied condition in the contract, be dissolved at the will of C, a stranger to the contract, without the consent of B, one of the contracting parties. It is contended that this is so because, by an arrangement between A and C, A has vested this power in C. No authority is cited to justify such a proposition. A contract is a consensual agreement between A and B, between whom the rights and liabilities exist. I do not understand on what principle B can be ejected from his contractual rights by the stranger C, with whom he has no privity. The appellants promised that the respondent should hold the office of managing director for ten years, subject to the express or implied conditions. The appellants now have to justify his removal while the contract period was running. No doubt there might be cases in which, apart from the contract provisions, the appellants could resist a claim for damage. There might, for instance, be a change in the law, or there might be a requisition by the government of the works and undertaking of the appellant company which might in certain events frustrate and dissolve the contract irrespective of the will of the parties. Even in such cases, however, it has been held that the requisition must not be self-induced ... Apart from government interference, or the like, the contract can only rightfully be dissolved by the will of the parties who entered into it. That will may be evinced by the conditions, express or implied, which were originally agreed to, and by action in accordance with them, or by a subsequent agreement to rescind the contract. Nothing of the sort, however, can be shown by the appellants. They have to justify the determination of the contract, or the case will be one of breach or repudiation. If their only justification is the action of Federated, that, in my opinion, is no defence. The alteration of the articles did not constitute a breach of contract by the appellant company as against the respondent, but his removal the following year did, and entitled him to damages. In my opinion, the appellant company fail in their defence, and the appeal should be dismissed.'

*Commentary*

See also *Associated Japanese Bank International Ltd* v *Crédit du Nord SA* (1988) NLJ Law Reports 109.


**Thake v Maurice** [1986] 2 WLR 337 Court of Appeal (Kerr, Neill and Nourse LJJ)

Vasectomy - failure to warn

*Facts*

A differently constituted Court of Appeal had, shortly after the hearing of *Eyre* v *Measday*, to consider an appeal on similar facts. Here a man had undergone a vasectomy; his wife, nevertheless, fell pregnant. There were, however, a number of differences between the facts in the two cases. Firstly, there were differences in the consent forms signed by the plaintiffs in the two cases. Secondly, it was felt, particularly by Slade LJ in the former case, that different considerations may apply to sterilisation operations on men and women. The third, and most important difference, was that here it was common ground that there was a need for warning to be given that the operation might not have the desired result and no such warning had been given.

*Held* (Kerr LJ dissenting)

Whilst the defendant had not been in breach of contract, nevertheless, on the particular facts, on the claim in negligence, the failure by the defendant to give his usual warning amounted to a breach of the duty of care which he owed to the plaintiff.

In his dissenting judgment, Kerr LJ found that, in the unusual circumstances of the case, the revival of the plaintiff's fertility also gave rise to a breach of contract on the part of the defendant.

**Wells (Merstham) Ltd v Buckland Sand and Silica Co Ltd** [1964] 2 WLR 453 High Court (Edmund Davies J)

Warranty - third party purchasing sand

*Facts*

The defendants warranted to the plaintiffs that their 'B W Sand' conformed to a certain analysis. Such sand would be suitable for chrysanthemum growing and the defendants knew that this was why the plaintiffs wanted it. To save costs, the plaintiffs placed their order through a third party, but they (the third party) did not tell the defendants that the sand was for re-sale to the plaintiffs. The sand delivered to the plaintiffs did not conform to the warranty: the plaintiffs chrysanthemums suffered disastrously.

*Held*

The plaintiffs were entitled to damages for breach of warranty and it was irrelevant that the order had been placed through a third party.

Edmund Davies J:

'Fundamental to the conception of a collateral contract is "an intention on the part of either or both parties that there should be a contractual liability in respect of the accuracy of the statement" But in this connexion it is well to bear in mind the cautionary words of Denning LJ in *Oscar Chess Ltd* v *Williams* that,

"It is sometimes supposed that the tribunal must look into the minds of the parties to see what they themselves intended. That is a mistake ... The question whether a warranty was intended depends on the conduct of the parties, on their words and behaviour, rather than on their thoughts. If an intelligent bystander would reasonably infer that a warranty was intended, that will suffice. And this, when the facts are not in dispute, is a question of law."

Approaching in this way the facts as I have found them, in my judgment a warranty was here intended and expressed that the constituents of B W sand were (and would be found to be) as set out in the analysis supplied, and on the basis of that warranty the plaintiffs entered into contracts to buy such sand ...

Then does it make any difference that, the warranty having been given to the plaintiffs, all the purchases other than the first were made by the plaintiffs from a third party? ... it would be absurd in the circumstances of the case to regard that warranty as being impliedly restricted to orders placed directly by the plaintiffs with the defendants.

As between A (a potential seller of goods) and B (a potential buyer), two ingredients, and two only, are in my judgment required in order to bring about a collateral contract containing a warranty: (1) a promise or assertion by A as to the nature, quality or quantity of the goods which B may reasonably regard as being made animo contrahendi, and (2) acquisition by B of the goods in reliance on that

121

promise or assertion ... A warranty may be enforceable notwithstanding that no specific main contract is discussed at the time when it is given, though obviously an animus contrahendi (and, therefore, a warranty) would be unlikely to be inferred unless the circumstances show that it was within the present contemplation of the parties that a contract based on the promise would shortly be entered into. Furthermore, the operation of the warranty must have a limitation in point of time which is reasonable in all the circumstances.'

# 5  MISREPRESENTATION

**Armstrong v Jackson** [1917] 2 KB 822 High Court (McCardie J)

Broker selling own shares to client - rescission

*Facts*

The plaintiff instructed the defendant broker to purchase some shares for him and the defendant sent a contract note purporting to show that these instructions had been carried out. The plaintiff did not take up the shares immediately but eventually, on the defendant's advice, he did so, duly paying the defendant for them. Some years later (the value of the shares having fallen) it appeared that the contract note was fictitious and that the shares in question had previously been owned by the defendant.

*Held*

The plaintiff was entitled to have the whole transaction set aside.

McCardie J:

'... in the present case, the plaintiff is prima facie entitled to a decree setting aside the transaction in question. But counsel for the defendant vigorously contended that no such decree can be made here. In the first place, it was argued that, inasmuch as the contract between the parties was executed no rescission can be granted unless fraud can be proved against the defendant ... The position of principal and agent gives rise to particular and onerous duties on the part of the agent, and the high standard of conduct required from him springs from the fiduciary relationship between his employers and himself. His position is confidential, and readily lends itself to abuse. Hence, a strict and salutary rule is required to meet the specific situation. The rules of English law, as they now exist, spring from the original strictness of the requirements of equity when the fiduciary relationship exists. These requirements are superadded to the common law obligations of diligence and skill ... It is, I think, immaterial that the plaintiff in the present case took a transfer of the shares and became the registered holder thereof. Such facts do not impair his right to rescission. So to hold would impair, gravely and injuriously, the powers of the court ... If, however, a finding against the defendant of personal deceit be essential to the plaintiff's claim for rescission, then I regret to say that I feel no doubt that such a case has been established.'

**Bell v Lever Brothers Ltd** [1932] AC 161 House of Lords (Lord Hailsham, Lord Blanesburgh, Lord Warrington, Lord Atkin and Lord Thankerton)

Mistake - belief that contract not otherwise terminable

*Facts*

Levers owned 99.5 per cent of the issued share capital of the Niger Company Ltd, which had, inter alia, an extensive cocoa business. The Niger Company was making heavy losses, which were being met by Levers. Levers approached Bell with an invitation to assist in the reorganisation and management of Niger. Bell was, at that time, joint manager of a London bank. Under his engagement with the bank he was entitled on retirement, after a few further years' service, to substantial pension rights. These would be forfeited if he were to leave the bank to take up other work, so some substituted provision was essential to him. The conditions of his employment were, in due course, embodied in letters passing between Levers and Bell. Levers were to take out and pay all premiums upon an endowment policy on his life, maturing at sixty or previous death, for an amount of approximately £16,000. The policy was to belong to Mr Bell and the premiums were to be paid by Levers, notwithstanding the termination of his engagement, unless it was terminated by Bell. In consideration for this, Bell was to leave the employment of the bank in order to undertake his new employment. He was to be appointed chairman of Niger for five years at an annual salary, during which time he was to devote the whole of his time and attention, during business hours, 'to the business' of Levers. Later, his service agreement was renewed. In fact, he was exclusively employed in the business of Niger. Levers were bound to maintain Bell in his office in Niger for the prescribed term at the prescribed remuneration. But as between Bell and Niger, the terms of service were to be found in the Articles of the company: there was no contract to serve Levers in a post from which Levers could dismiss Bell. Levers could stop payment, or cease to maintain Bell in his office. If Bell failed to discharge his duties, but that was all, Niger's powers were not dependent on any breach of duty. The financial position of Niger was successfully transformed and, after a while, remuneration was paid by Niger direct. In 1925 and 1926, agreements were entered into between Niger and three other cocoa companies acting as a 'pool' and fixing a buying price and a selling price. Each company was required to notify the others of purchases and sales of cocoa. Clauses in the agreements associated the directors of each company in the obligations undertaken. Bell was fully conversant with the agreements, but he did not know about the 'directors' clause. In late 1927, Bell traded in cocoa on his own behalf. None of these transactions caused any damage to Niger or to Levers. Nor was any confidential information used. The transactions did, however, involve a breach of the directors' clause. By 1929, Niger's position had so improved that it was considering an amalgamation with its main competitor. Bell was a guiding light during the negotiations. By the scheme, the assets of both companies were, for the most part, to be transferred to a new company, each of the old companies receiving shares in the new. Niger would therefore become a mere holding company.

Bell's employment by Niger had therefore to end and terms of settlement were agreed, compensation to be £30,000 and the continuation of the policy. Bell's exceptional services were also acknowledged expressly in the settlement. Later, Bell became aware of the directors' clause and thereupon informed Levers of the private transactions. Levers considered the transactions to have been highly improper and issued this writ. In the writ, they claimed that the transactions constituted misconduct so as to entitle Levers to terminate the service agreement; alternatively, that the settlement agreement was obtained by false and fraudulent concealment of the transactions; further, the agreement was made and money paid thereunder was paid under a mistake of fact. Various amendments were made to the claim and Niger was added as co-plaintiff.

The jury at the trial rejected the allegations of fraud. They found that there had been breaches of duty to the plaintiffs, entitling Levers to put an end to the service contract and entitling Niger to remove Bell from his position. They found that Levers had not known about the transactions when they entered the settlement agreements and would not have entered them had they known, also that Bell did not have the transactions in mind when he was negotiating the settlement.

*Held*

The plaintiffs were not entitled to avoid the agreement as the mistake was not sufficiently fundamental in character.

Lord Warrington:

'The final question ... is only relevant to the issue of whether there was a mutual mistake ... I will assume for the present that .... the learned judge was entitled to deal with the matter of the footing of mutual mistake ... The learned judge thus describes the mistake involved in this case as sufficient to justify a court in saying that there was no true consent - namely:

"Some mistake or misapprehension as to some facts ... which, by the common intention of the parties, whether expressed or more generally implied, constitute the underlying assumption, without which the parties would not have made the contract they did."

That a mistake of this nature, common to both parties, is, if proved, sufficient to render a contract void is, I think, established law. This principle, however, is confined to cases in which "the mistake is as to the substance of the whole consideration, going, as it were, to the root of the matter" (*Kennedy v Panama etc Mail Co* (1867) LR 2 QB 580, 588 ...) ... [In] the present case [it] is, in my opinion, clear that each party believed that the remunerative offices, compensation for the loss of which was the subject of the negotiations, were offices which could not be determined except by the consent of the holder thereof and further believed that the other party was under the same belief and was treating on that footing. The real question, therefore, is whether the erroneous assumption on the part of both parties to the agreements that the service contracts were indeterminable except by agreement, was of such a fundamental character as to constitute an underlying assumption without which the parties would not have made the contract they in fact made, or whether it was only a common error as to a material element, but one not going to the root of the matter and not affecting the substance of the consideration.'

Lord Atkin:

'Mistake as to quality of the thing contracted for raises more difficult questions. In such a case, a mistake will not affect assent unless it is the mistake of both parties and is as to the existence of some quality which makes the thing without the quality essentially different from the thing as it was believed to be ...'

*Commentary*

Distinguished in *Grist* v *Bailey* [1966] 3 WLR 618. Aplied in *Magee* v *Pennine Insurance Co Ltd* [1969] 2 WLR 1278. See also *Associated Japanese Bank (International) Ltd* v *Crédit du Nord SA* [1988] 1 WLR 255.

**Bissett v Wilkinson** [1927] AC 177 Privy Council (Viscount Dunedin, Lord Atkinson, Lord Phillimore, Lord Carson and Lord Merrivale)

Expression of opinion - number of sheep land would carry

*Facts*

A vendor admitted that he had told prospective purchasers that certain land in New Zealand 'would carry 2,000 sheep' and that they bought the land in this belief. It turned out that the land did not have this capacity and, inter alia, the purchasers claimed rescission of the agreement.

*Held*

Their claim would fail.

Lord Merrivale:

'In an action for rescission, as in an action for specific performance of an executory contract, when misrepresentation is the alleged ground of relief of the party who repudiates the contract, it is, of course, essential to ascertain whether that which is relied on is a representation of a specific fact, or a statement of opinion, since an erroneous opinon stated by the party affirming the contract, though it may have been relied on and have induced the contract on the part of the party who seeks rescission, gives no title to relief unless fraud is established ...

In the present case, as in those cited, the material facts of the transaction, the knowledge of the parties respectively, and their relative positions, the words of representation used, and the actual condition of the subject-matter spoken of, are relevant to the two inquiries necessary to be made. What was the meaning of the representation? Was it true? ...

As was said by Sim J [the trial judge]:

"In ordinary circumstances, any statement made by an owner who has been occupying his own farm as to its carrying capacity would be regarded as a statement of fact ... This, however, is not such a case. The purchasers knew all about Hogan's block and knew also what sheep the farm was carrying when they inspected it. In these circumstances ... the purchasers were not justified in regarding anything said by the vendor as to the carrying capacity as being anything more than an expression of his opinion on the subject."

In this view of the matter their Lordships concur.

Whether the vendor honestly and in fact held the opinion which he stated remained to be considered. This involved examination of the history and condition of the property. If a reasonable man with the vendor's knowledge could not have come to the conclusion he stated, the description of that conclusion as an opinion would not necessarily protect him against rescission for misrepresentation, but what was actually the capacity in competent hands of the land the purchasers purchased had never been, and never was, practically ascertained ...

It is of dominant importance that Sim J negatived the purchasers' charge of fraud.

After attending to the close and very careful examination of the evidence which was made by learned counsel for each of the parties, their Lordships entirely concur in the view which was expressed by the learned judge who heard the case. The purchasers failed to prove that the farm, if properly managed, was not capable of carrying 2,000 sheep.'

## Brikom Investments Ltd v Seaford [1981] 1 WLR 863 Court of Appeal (Ormrod and Griffiths LJJ)

Landlord and tenant - implied covenant to repair

*Facts*

The plaintiff let a flat to the defendant for a term of seven years. Under s32 of the Housing Act 1961, where a lease was for 'a term of less than seven years' the landlord was impliedly liable for certain internal repairs. A fair rent was assessed and registered on the basis that the plaintiffs were liable for those repairs and in correspondence they accepted that liability. When they failed to carry out some of such repairs, the defendant carried them out himself and deducted the cost from his rent. The plaintiffs claimed, inter alia, arrears of rent on the basis of the full registered rent.

*Held*

They were not entitled to succeed.

Ormrod LJ:

'In our judgment it would clearly be inequitable to hold that the tenant was liable for the full amount of the arrears of a rent which reflects, in part, that the landlords were liable for the repairs, and at the same time that the tenant was liable for the cost of such repairs.

This is the classic situation which the doctrine of estoppel was designed to meet. Counsel for the tenant put his case in alternative ways. Either the landlords, by demanding a rent fixed on the basis of the rent officer's allocation of liability for repairs, represented that they accepted liability accordingly, or the landlords, by not taking steps to have the registered rent changed so as to reflect the true position and suing for the enhanced rent, had made their election and could not be heard, in these proceedings, to assert a claim inconsistent with the position they had adopted.

Counsel for the landlords, however, contended that the representation was a representation of law and not of fact, and therefore could not give rise to an estoppel, and that the tenant was seeking to use the estoppel as a sword, that is to recover the cost of the repairs, and not, in the classic phrase, as a shield. He relied on two cases ... in neither of which had the party alleging estoppel acted to his detriment, nor had the other party gained any advantage from the representation.

These dichotomies are dangerously neat and apt to mislead. Representations of fact shade into representations of law, and swords, with a little ingenuity, can be beaten into shields, or shields into swords. In this case the shield may have quite a sharp edge but it is nonetheless a shield and the representation was essentially one of fact, ie that the landlords accepted liability for the s32 repairs to the tenant's flat in return for the enhanced rent. We would hold that so long as the enhanced rent is claimed the landlords cannot put the burden of the s32 repairs on the tenant. But they can take immediate action to have the fair rent corrected so as to reflect the true position in regard to repairs, and will then be entitled to the benefit of the tenant's covenant. The tenant, therefore, succeeds on this point.'

**Brown v Raphael** [1958] Ch 636 Court of Appeal (Lord Evershed MR, Romer and Ormerod LJJ)

Implied representation

*Facts*

Auction particulars of the reversion in a trust fund stated that the annuitant was 'believed to have no aggregate estate': this belief was held honestly but mistakenly and the eventual purchaser sought, inter alia, rescission of the contract. The name of the vendor's solicitors appeared at the foot of the auction particulars.

*Held*

The purchaser was entitled to succeed as it was impliedly represented that there were reasonable grounds for the material belief.

Lord Evershed MR:

'In order that the plaintiff may succeed ... it is necessary that three things should be established: (i) he must show that the language relied on imports or contains a representation of some material fact; (ii) he must show that the representation is untrue; and (iii) he must show that, in entering into the contract, he was induced so to do in reliance on it. The learned judge concluded all those three matters in the plaintiff's favour ... in my judgment there is no ground shown for this court to disturb the learned judge's conclusions. ...

The first point is, to my mind, the most significant and perhaps the most difficult: Is there here a representation of a material fact? ...

I am ... entirely of the same opinion as was the learned judge, namely, that this is a case in which there was not merely the representation that the defendant entertained the belief, but also, inescapably, the further representation that he, being competently advised, had reasonable grounds for supporting that belief. The learned judge put the matter thus in his judgment. He first observed that, if the purchaser was not entitled to suppose that the vendor was in possession of facts which enabled him to express an opinion which was based on reasonable grounds, that would, he thought (and I agree with him) make business dealings, certainly in this class of business, almost impossible. He said:

"It must be remembered that in this case the purchaser going to the auction had no means whatever of finding out anything about the annuitant's means. When the contract was signed, the purchaser did not even know the name of the annuitant. On the other hand, the vendor must be expected to be in possession of facts unavailable to the purchaser and the purchaser is entitled to suppose that he is in possession of facts which enable him to express an opinion which is based on reasonable grounds. As I have already said, if that is not so, business relationships become quite impossible. It may be different where the facts on which the opinion is expressed are equally available to both parties. Then the opinion may be no more than an expression of opinion, but, where the opinion is expressed on facts assumed to be available to the vendor, which certainly are not available to the purchaser, and that opinion is expressed to induce the contract, in my judgment the purchaser is entitled to expect that the opinion is expressed on reasonable grounds."

The learned judge, using that general language in relation to this case, was reflecting the language of Bowen LJ in *Smith v Land & House Property Corpn* (1884) 28 Ch D 7. I, therefore, am satisfied that the relevant language int he present case involved the representation that there were reasonable grounds for the belief, and certainly that was a representation of a most material fact.'

## Clarke v Dickson (1858) EB & B 148 Court of Queen's Bench (Crompton J)

Misrepresentation - restitution impossible

*Facts*

In 1850 the plaintiff was induced to take shares in a company by the defendants' misrepresentation. Four years later, when the company was in bad circumstances, with the plaintiff's assent it was registered as a company with limited liability. Subsequently it was wound up and the plaintiff then discovered the falsity of the representations. He sued to recover the money he had paid for the shares.

*Held*

His action would fail.

Crompton J:

'When once it is settled that a contract induced by fraud is not void, but voidable at the option of the party defrauded, it seems to me to follow that, when that party exercises his option to rescind the contract, he must be in a state to rescind; that is, he must be in such a situation as to be able to put the parties into their original state before the contract. Now here I will assume ... that the plaintiff bought his shares from the defendants and not from the company, and that he might at one time have had a right to restore the shares to the defendants if he could, and demand the price from them. But then what did he buy? Shares in a partnership with others. He cannot return those; he has become bound to those others. Still stronger, he has changed their nature: what he now has and offers to restore are shares in a quasi corporation now in process of being wound up ... The plaintiff must rescind *in toto* or not at all; he cannot both keep the shares and recover the whole price. That is founded on the plainest principles of justice. If he cannot return the article he must keep it, and sue for his real damage in an action on the deceit. Take the case I put in the argument, of a butcher buying live cattle, killing them, and even selling the meat to his customers. If the rule of law were as the plaintiff contends, that butcher might, upon discovering a fraud on the part of the grazier who sold him the cattle, rescind the contract and get back the whole price: but how could that be consistently with justice? The true doctrine is, that a party can never repudiate a contract after, by his own act, it has become out of his power to restore the parties to their original condition.'

## Derry v Peek (1889) 14 App Cas 337 House of Lords (Lord Halsbury LC, Lord Watson, Lord Bramwell, Lord FitzGerald and Lord Herschell).

Misrepresentation - belief in truth in an action for deceit

*Facts*

A special Act incorporating a tramway company provided that the carriages might be moved by animal power and, with the consent of the Board of Trade, by steam power. The directors issued a prospectus containing a statement that by this special Act the company had the right to use steam instead of horses. The plaintiff bought shares on the strength of this statment. The Board of Trade later refused to consent to the use of steam and the company was wound up. The plaintiff brought an action for deceit.

*Held*

1. In an action for deceit, it is not enough to establish misrepresentation alone; something more must be proved to cast liability on the defendant.

2. There is an essential difference between the case where the defendant honestly believes in the truth of a statement although he is careless, and where he is careless with no such honest belief.

3. A mere statement by the defendant that he believed something to be true is not conclusive proof that it was so. Fraud is established where it is proved that a false statement is made:

a) knowingly;

b) without belief in its truth;

c) recklessly, careless as to whether it be true or false. There must, to prevent fraud, always be an honest belief in its truth.

If fraud is proved, the motive of the person making the statement is irrelevant. It matters not that there was no intention to cheat or injure the person to whom the statement was made.

4. The defendants were not fraudulent in this case. They made a careless statement but they honestly believed in its truth.


**Doyle v Olby (Ironmongers) Ltd** [1969] 2 WLR 673 Court of Appeal (Lord Denning MR, Winn and Sachs LJ)

Fraudulent misrepresentations - measure of damages

*Facts*

After buying an ironmonger's business, things turned out to be very different from what the vendors had led the plaintiff to believe. He was awarded damages for fraudulent misrepresentations and the appeal concerned, inter alia, the measure of damages.

*Held*

The defendants were bound to make reparation for all the actual damage directly flowing from the fraudulent inducements.

Lord Denning MR:

'On principle the distinction seems to be this: in contract, the defendant has made a promise and broken it. The object of damages is to put the plaintiff in as good a position, as far as money can do it, as if the promise has been performed. In fraud, the defendant has been guilty of a deliberate wrong by inducing the plaintiff to act to his detriment. The object of damages is to compensate the plaintiff for all the loss he has suffered, so far, again, as money can do it. In contract, the damages are limited to what may reasonably be supposed to have been in the contemplation of the parties. In fraud, they are not so limited. The defendant is bound to make reparation for all the actual damage directly flowing from the fraudulent inducement. The person who has been defrauded is entitled to say: "I would not have entered into this bargain at all but for your representation. Owing to your fraud, I have not only lost all the money I paid you, but what is more, I have been put to a large amount of extra expense as well and suffered this or that extra damages." All such damages can be recovered: and it does not lie in the mouth of the fraudulent person to say that they could not reasonably have been foreseen. For instance, in this very case the plaintiff has not only lost money which he paid for the business, which he would never have done if there had been no fraud; he put all that money in and lost it; but also has been put to expense and loss in trying to run a business which has turned out to be a disaster for him. He is entitled to damages for all his loss subject, of course, to giving credit for any benefit that he has received. There is nothing to be taken off in mitigation: for there is nothing more that he could have done to reduce his loss. He did all that he could reasonably be expected to do.'

*Commentary*

See also *Naughton* v *O'Callaghan* [1990] 3 All ER 191, Chapter 14, below and *East* v *Maurer* following.

**East v Maurer** [1991] 2 All ER 733 Court of Appeal (Mustill, Butler-Sloss, and Beldam LJJ)

Fraudent misrepresentation - assessment of damages

*Facts*

In 1979, the defendant who owned two hair salons agreed to sell one to the plaintiffs. The plaintiffs were induced to buy, in part by a representation from the defendant to the effect that he hoped in future to work abroad, and that he did not intend to work in the second salon, save in emergencies. In fact, the defendant who had built up a considerable reputation in the area, continued to work regularly at the second salon and many of his clients followed him. The result of this was that the plaintiffs saw a steady fall-off in business and never made a profit. They were finally forced to sell it in 1989, for considerably less than they paid. The plaintiffs sued for breach of contract and fraudulent misrepresentation. The court at first instance found that the defendant's representations were false. The defendant appealed on the basis that damages awarded were assessed on the wrong basis.

*Held*

The Court of Appeal held that the proper approach was to assess the profit the plaintiff might have made had the defendant not made the representation(s).

'Reparation for all actual damage' as indicated by Lord Denning in *Doyle* v *Olby* (above) would include loss of profits. The assessment of profits was however to be on a tortious basis. The effect of such an approach may well result in the amount of damages awarded being reduced (as they were here, by one third).

*Commentary*

See also *Royscott Trust* v *Rogerson* [1991] 3 WLR 57 (below).

**Edgington v Fitzmaurice** (1885) 29 Ch D 459 Court of Appeal (Cotton, Bowen and Fry LJJ)

Prospectus - representation as to object of loan

*Facts*

The plaintiff, who was a shareholder of the Army and Navy Provision Market (Limited), ('the company'), received a circular issued by the directors inviting subscriptions for debenture bonds to the amount of £25,000 with interest. The circular stated that the company had bought a lease of a valuable property and that the company had spent various sums of money on it. The debentures were being issued to raise money for alterations of and additions to the property and to transport fish from the coast for sale in London. The circular was challenged as being misleading in certain respects. It was alleged that it was framed in such a way as to lead to the belief that the debentures would be a charge on the property of the company, that the prospectus omitted any reference to a second mortgage, that the whole balance of the mortgage which was referred to might be called in within four years and that the real object of the issue was to pay off pressing liabilities of the company, not to complete the alterations, etc. The plaintiff, who had taken debentures, claimed repayment of the sum he had advanced with interest on the ground that it had been obtained from him by fraudulent mis-statements; alternatively, for damages for failure to so charge the property. The defendants, who were the directors and certain officers of the company, claimed that the temporary nature of the second mortgage meant that it was not necessary to mention it, that they were not aware that the first mortgage could be called in as alleged, that the secretary and manager had no authority to represent that the debenture holders would have any charge and that they believed that the money would be used as set out in the circular and, indeed, some of it had been so expended.

*Held*

The mis-statement as to the objects of the loan was a material misrepresentation of intention involving a mis-statement of fact upon which the plaintiff had acted to his detriment. It followed that the directors were liable to an action for deceit, even though the plaintiff was also influenced by his belief that he was entitled to a charge on the company's property.

Bowen LJ:

'There must be a mis-statement of an existing fact: but the state of a man's mind is as much a fact as the state of his digestion. It is true that it is very difficult to prove what the state of a man's mind at a particular time is, but if it can be ascertained, it is as much a fact as anything else. A misrepresentation as to the state of a man's mind is, therefore, a mis-statement of fact.'

**Erlanger v New Sombrero Phosphate Co** (1878) 3 App Cas 1218 House of Lords (Lord Cairns LC, Lord Hatherley, Lord Penzance, Lord O'Hagan, Lord Selbourne, Lord Blackburn and Lord Gordon)

Rescission - promoters' breach of duty

*Facts*

The respondents sought the rescission of a contract for the purchase of a small island in the West Indies on the ground that all the circumstances attending the transaction had not been disclosed by the vendors, a syndicate of which the appellants were members. The syndicate had formed a company - the respondents - and had sold the island to it, but they had not appointed competent officials to enable the company to form an independent judgment as to the propriety of the purchase.

*Held*

The contract had rightly been set aside.

Lord Penzance:

'... I think it is clear that the company having, in the first instance, a right to relieve itself from this contract, which the promoters have unfairly fastened upon it, it is for the vendors to show affirmatively that the company has forfeited that right. The actual lapse of time before commencing the suit was not very great. Delay, as it seems to me, has two aspects. Lapse of time may so change the condition of the thing sold, or bring about such a state of things, that justice cannot be done by rescinding the contract subject to any amount of allowances or compensations. This is one aspect of delay, and it is in many cases particularly applicable to property of a mining character. But delay must also imply acquiescence, and in this aspect it equally bars the respondent company's right, for such a contract as is now under consideration is only voidable, and not void ... And so dealing with the facts of the present case, I find myself unable to conclude affirmatively that it has been made out by the argument that either the character of the property, or the way in which the company had dealt with it, did in point of fact preclude the possibility of justice being worked out on the basis of the contract being rescinded ... The substantial question, therefore, is whether there was such delay as fairly imports acquiescence ... On the whole I am unable to satisfy myself, either that it is not practicable to do justice on the basis of the contract being rescinded, or that the company has by any laches or delay laid itself fairly open to the imputation of having acquiesced in the contract which they now seek to set aside.'

**Esso Petroluem Co Ltd v Mardon**

See chapter 4 - Contents of contracts.

**Gran Gelato Ltd v Richcliff (Group) Ltd** [1992] 1 All ER 865 Chancery Division (Nicholls V-C)

Solicitors' negligence - misrepresentation - damages

*Facts*

In 1984 the defendant granted to the plaintiffs an underlease of basement and ground floor shop premises for a term of almost 10 years. The underlease was carved out of two headleases. Unknown to either the plaintiffs or their solicitors both headleases contained 'break' clauses giving the main lessor the right to terminate the lease prematurely. In the course of the preliminary negotiations the plaintiffs' solicitors sent 'inquiries before lease' (enquiring about the existence of these or similar clauses) to the defendant's solicitors. They answered that such clauses did 'not to the lessor's knowledge' exist. Three years later the head lessor exercised the break clause and terminated the head lease - the plaintiffs' underlease was of course terminated also, though it still had about 4 and a half years to run.

*Held*

The defendant's solicitors' response to the inquiries before lease was a misrepresentation. Under normal conveyancing rules, the solicitor acting for the seller did not in general owe the buyer a duty of care when answering questions, because the buyer has a remedy against the seller for misrepresentation. Here the defendants had clearly intended that the plaintiff would act on the accuracy of the answers provided. The onus was therefore on the vendors to establish that their solicitors had acted in some way outside the norm to create a special duty of care towards the plaintiff, since they were unable to do this the plaintiff's claim against the vendor's solicitors would fail. Regardless of any element of contributory negligency on the part of their own solicitors, however, they would have a right of action against the vendors.

## Hedley Byrne & Co v Heller and Partners

See Introduction.

## Howard Marine & Dredging Co Ltd v A Ogden & Sons (Excavations) Ltd [1978] 2 WLR 515 Court of Appeal (Lord Denning MR, Bridge and Shaw LJJ)

Misrepresentation as to capacity of barges

*Facts*

In 1974, the Northumbrian Water Authority was planning to construct a large sewage works and it invited contractors to tender for the excavation works. The defendants were invited to tender. They were experienced excavators but, in this particular case, the material was to be dumped at sea, and this they knew nothing about. Furthermore, they would be obliged to hire barges to carry the material. The defendants invited, inter alia, the plaintiffs to tender for the hire of the barges and the plaintiffs, who owned some barges which were potentially suitable, sent their manager to the site to look at the material to be carried. He formed the view that the barges would be suitable and offered them to the defendants for £1,800 per week, stating that they would carry 850 cubic metres of material each. He said nothing about the weight each would carry. The defendants asked him about this and he gave an explanation which the defendants did not properly understand, so that they retained the impression that 850 cubic metres could be carried. In fact, the capacity did also depend upon the density of the material. The defendants, using the plaintiffs' tender, tendered for and won the Authority contract. The price of barge hire was later reduced to £1,724 per week. Howards asked Ogdens to confirm the order for the barges and, at this time, the manager was asked about the capacity in tonnes and he stated it to be 1,600. This was wrong, but he had innocently relied on a mistaken entry in the Lloyd's Register for the two barges. Eventually a firm order was given for £1,500 per week and the barges put to work. Later, Ogdens discovered that the payload was only 1,055 tonnes and they refused to pay more than £2,000 hire. Howards withdrew the barges and Ogdens hired others to complete the work. Howards issued a writ for the outstanding hire and Ogdens counter claimed for misrepresentation.

*Held* (Lord Denning dissenting)

The defendants were entitled to succeed on their counterclaim by virtue of s2(1) of the Misrepresentation Act 1967.

Bridge LJ:

'...It does not appear to me that Howards ever intended to bind themselves by ... a collateral warranty ... The first question then is whether Howards would be liable in damages in respect of (the) misrepresentation if it had been made fraudulently ... An affirmative answer to that question is inescapable ... Howards must be liable unless they proved that (the Manager) had reasonable ground to believe what he said ... the onus passes to the representor ... In the course of negotiations leading to a contract, the 1967 Act imposes an absolute obligation not to state facts which the representor cannot prove he had a reasonable ground to believe ... the question remains whether his evidence, however benevolently viewed, is sufficient to show that he had an objectively reasonable ground to disregard the figure in the ship's documents and to prefer the Lloyd's Register figure. I think it is not ... I would accordingly allow the appeal.'

Shaw LJ:

'... It must have been apparent to everyone concerned ... that the profitability of Ogden's contract ... must depend on the payload of the barges. So the question, though swamped by a number of others, must, or should have stood out by its content, as relating to a matter of substance and importance. It called for an answer ... which could be relied on ... What was asked for was a specific fact. Ogdens had not themselves ... such ready and facile means (of ascertaining what the fact was) as was available to (the manager) ... I would venture to hold that Ogdens have a cause of action in negligence at common law ... '

**JEB Fasteners Ltd v Marks Bloom & Co** [1983] 1 All ER 583 Court of Appeal (Stephenson and Donaldson LJJ and Sir Sebag Shaw)

Misrepresentation - negligent information or advice

*Facts*

The defendants, a firm of accountants, prepared accounts for a company which was not a party to the proceedings. The accounts were prepared in a negligent manner. The figure entered as representing the company's stock was described as 'valued at lower of cost and net realisable value' whereas the figure was in fact based on the company's own valuation of the stock's net realisable value. As a result of this error a small net profit was shown for the year when in fact a substantial loss had been incurred. The defendants know that the company was experiencing financial difficulties and was seeking financial assistance from various sources, one of which was the plaintiffs. The accounts were shown to the plaintiffs and they decided to take the company over, largely because they would thereby secure the services of the company's two directors who had considerable experience in the plaintiffs' trade. Despite having the opportunity to do so, the defendants never informed the plaintiffs of their error. The takeover did not produce successful results and the plaintiffs sought damages for negligence.

*Held*

The judge had rightly dismissed the plaintiffs' action as the defendants had not caused their loss. There was ample evidence to support the judge's conclusion.

**Laurence v Lexcourt Holdings Ltd** [1978] 1 WLR 1128 High Court (Brian Dillon QC)

Misrepresentation - planning permission

*Facts*

The plaintiffs claimed specific performance of an agreement for a lease. The premises were unoccupied at the time when the freehold was bought by the plaintiffs in 1970. They comprised a pair of shops with living accommodation above. The plaintiffs used the ground floor and part of the first as offices, having had planning permission to do so. The rest of the first and second floors were not covered by the permission and were unoccupied until the defendants took possession after the agreement for the lease had been made. The defendants were an accounting company. Before the agreement for the lease was made, nothing at all was said about the restricted planning permission. The plaintiff had forgotten about it. The defendants were in a great hurry to get possession and they failed to make the usual enquiries. Afterwards, enquiries were made and the terms of the permission were discovered. They also revealed that the property was affected by a new road plan. Proposals had existed for some time and were known to both parties, but they did not attach any importance to them as they did not believe that they would come to fruition. The parties agreed that the plaintiffs would apply for planning permission for office user of the remaining part of the first floor and of the second floor. Application was made, but permission granted for a limited period of three years. The lease was for fifteen years. The defendants and plaintiffs could not agree on alternative leasehold arrangements and the defendants gave up possession and ceased paying rent. The defendants claimed to rescind on the ground of, inter alia, misrepresentation.

*Held*

The defendants were entitled to rescission.

Brian Dillon QC:

' ... where there has been a misrepresentation it is well settled that it is no defence to the person who has made the misrepresentation to say, "Oh well, the party who was misled could have checked and found out the facts for himself and he really has only himself to blame that he relied on me and did not make the enquiries that he might have made ...". I think the defendants are entitled to succeed on the ground of misrepresentation because it is not right, in my view, to describe property as offices and offer them for a 15 year letting as offices when the only planning permission as offices which is available is for ... two years ...'

I turn to the alternative submissions of the defendants on the ground of mistake. I find as a fact that there was a common mistake between the parties in that when the agreement of February 1974 was made, both (parties) believed that there was planning permission available without restriction for the use of the first and second floors of no 50 as offices. The law on the question of common mistake and relief in equity was stated by Denning LJ in a well known passage in *Solle* v *Butcher*, where he said:

"A contract is also liable in equity to be set aside if the parties were under a common misapprehension either as to facts or as to their relative and respective rights, provided that the misapprehension was fundamental and that the party seeking to set it aside was not himself at fault."

There are, therefore, the two requirements to be considered. Was the misapprehension fundamental and were the defendants who are seeking to set the agreement aside, themselves at fault?

The question of fault was considered by Goff J in *Grist* v *Bailey* [1967] Ch 532. He said:

"There remains one other point and that is the condition laid down by Denning LJ that the party seeking to take advantage of the mistake must not be at fault. Denning LJ did not develop that at all and it is not, I think, with respect, absolutely clear what it comprehends. Clearly there must be some degree of blameworthiness beyond the mere fault of having made a mistake; but the question is how much, or in what way? Each case must depend on its own facts ..."

In the present case, there is no doubt that the defendants were imprudent in proceeding without making the usual searches and enquiries, but they did not owe any duty of care to the plaintiffs to make those searches and their mistake did not bring about Mr Laurence's mistake. In a sense, if they had searched and obtained the information and mentioned to Mr Laurence what they had discovered, Mr Laurence's memory would have been jogged and he would then not have made a mistake, but I do not think that makes the defendants responsible for Mr Laurences' mistake or forgetfulness. It seems to me that whatever Denning LJ did have in mind in his qualification in *Solle* v *Butcher* does not cover the failure to search on the part of the defendants in this case and I do not think, therefore, that they were disentitled from relying on the mistake because they failed to search. Was the mistake, then, a fundamental mistake? *Solle* v *Butcher* and *Grist* v *Bailey* were both cases in which the mistake concerned whether a tenancy of the premises was a protected tenancy under the Rent Acts and I think they show that a mistake of that nature is a fundamental mistake, whether it be the case that the premises are being sold on the footing that they are subject to a protected tenancy when, in truth, because the tenant has died, they are not so subject, or whether it be the case that the premises are being sold on the basis that they are subject to a tenancy which is not protected when, in truth, it is protected for some of the rather technical reasons that arise under the Rent Acts. I do not see any real difference in point of importance between the Rent Acts and the Planning Acts, which are both major acts affecting land. I think it is fundamental to people who are taking land for a term as long as 15 years with a view to their use as offices, that planning permission should be available for more than a mere two or three years and I think, therefore, that this mistake, which was common to both parties, was a fundamental mistake which entitles the defendants to avoid the agreement. I do not see that it matters that the mistake was as to the legal suitability of the land for a particular use, rather than as to its physical description. Whether the case be put on mistake or misrepresentation, I think the absence of the planning permission was fundamental ...'

**Leaf v International Galleries** [1950] 2 KB 86 Court of Appeal (Sir Raymond Evershed MR, Denning and Jenkins LJJ)

Misrepresentation - right to rescind

*Facts*

The plaintiff bought from the defendants an oil painting of Salisbury Cathedral which was represented to him as a painting by Constable, a representation which was held to be one of the terms of the contract. Five years later he discovered that it was not a Constable and he sought rescission of the contract on the ground of innocent misrepresentation.

*Held*

He could not succeed.

Denning LJ:

'The question is whether the buyer is entitled to rescind the contract on that account. I emphasise that this a claim to rescind only. There is no claim in this action for damages for breach of condition or breach of warranty. The claim is simply one for rescission ... The only question is whether the buyer is entitled to rescind. The way in which the case is put by counsel for the buyer is this. He says this was an innocent misrepresentation and that in equity he is entitled to claim rescission even of an executed contract of sale on that account. He points out that the judge has found that it is quite possible to restore the parties to the same position that they were in originally, by the buyer simply handing back the picture to the sellers in return for the repayment of the purchase price.

In my opinion, this case is to be decided according to the well known principles applicable to the sale of goods. This was a contract for the sale of goods. There was a mistake about the quality of the subject-matter, because both parties believed the picture to be a Constable, and that mistake was in one sense essential or fundamental. Such a mistake, however, does not avoid the contract. There was no mistake about the subject-matter of the sale. It was a specific picture of "Salisbury Cathedral". The parties were agreed in the same terms on the same subject-matter, and that is sufficient to make a contract: see *Solle* v *Butcher*. There was a term in the contract as to the quality

135

of the subject-matter, namely, as to the person by whom the picture was painted - that it was by Constable. That term of the contract was either a condition or a warranty. If it was a condition, the buyer could reject the picture for breach of the condition at any time before he accepted it or was to be deemed to have accepted it, whereas, if it was only a warranty, he could not reject it but was confined to a claim for damages.

I think it right to assume in the buyer's favour that this term was a condition, and that, if he had come in proper time, he could have rejected the picture, but the right to reject for breach of condition has always been limited by the rule that once the buyer has accepted, or is deemed to have accepted, the goods in performance of the contract, he cannot therefore reject, but is relegated to his claim for damages ... In this case this buyer took the picture into his house, and five years passed before he intimated any rejection. That, I need hardly say, is much more than a reasonable time. It is far too late for him at the end of five years to reject this picture for breach of any condition. His remedy after that length of time is for damages only, a claim which he has not brought before the court.'

*Commentary*

Distinguished in *Peco Arts Inc* v *Hazlitt Gallery Ltd* [1983] 1 WLR 1315.

**Long v Lloyd** [1958] 1 WLR 753 Court of Appeal (Jenkins, Parker and Pearce LJJ)

Misrepresentation - right to rescind

*Facts*

The defendant haulage contractor advertised for sale a lorry as being in 'exceptional condition' and he told the plaintiff, a prospective purchaser, that it did 11 miles to the gallon and that he had told him, after a trial run, all that was wrong with the vehicle. The plaintiff purchased the lorry and, two days later, on a short run, further faults developed and the plaintiff noticed that it did only about 5 miles to the gallon. That evening he reported these things to the defendant and the plaintiff accepted the defendant's offer to pay for some of the repairs. The next day the lorry set out on a longer journey - to Middlesbrough - and it broke down: the following day the plaintiff wrote to the defendant asking for the return of his money. The lorry had not been in a roadworthy condition, but the defendant's representations concerning it had been honestly made.

*Held*

The plaintiff was not entitled to rescission of the contract as he had finally accepted the lorry before he had purported to rescind.

Pearce LJ:

'On the following day the plaintiff, knowing all that he did about the condition and performance of the lorry, despatched it, driven by his brother, on a business trip to Middlesbrough. That step, at all events, appears to us to have amounted, in all the circumstances of the case, to a final acceptance of the lorry by the plaintiff for better or for worse, and to have conclusively extinguished any right of rescission remaining to the plaintiff after completion of the sale. Accordingly, even if the plaintiff should be held ... to have had a right to rescission which survived the completion of the contract, we think that on the facts of this case he lost any such right before his purported exercise of it.'

**Museprime Properties Ltd v Adhill Properties Ltd** [1990] 36 EG 114 High Court (Scott J)

Misrepresentation - rescission

*Facts*

In a sale by auction of three properties the particulars wrongly represented the rents from the properties as being open to negotiation. The statements in the auction particulars and made later by the auctioneer himself misrepresented the position with regard to rent reviews. In fact on two of the three properties rent reviews had been triggered and new rents agreed. The plaintiff company successfully bid for the three properties - commercial and residential premises in Finchley - and discovered the true situation. They commenced an action for rescission. The defendant company countered with the defence that the misrepresentations were not such as to induce any reasonable person to enter into a contract.

*Held*

The plaintiffs had established, and indeed the defendants conceded, that misrepresentation had occurred and any material misrepresentation is a ground for rescission. The judge referred, with approval, to the view of Goff and Jones: *Law of Restitution* (3rd edn (1986) p168) as follows:

'In our view any misrepresentation which induces a person to enter into a contract should be a ground for rescission of that contract. If the misrepresentation would have induced a reasonable person to enter into the contract, then the court will ... presume that the representee was so induced, and the onus will be on the representor to show that the representee did not rely on the misrepresentation either wholly or in part. If, however, the misrepresentation would not have induced a reasonable person to contract, the onus will be on the misrepresentee to show that the misrepresentation induced him to act as he did. But these considerations go to the question of the onus of proof. To disguise them under the cloak of "materiality" is misleading and unnecessary.'

Here the plaintiffs had established their claim to rescission of the contract on the ground of material misrepresentation because the inaccurate statements had induced them to buy the properties. They would therefore be awarded the return of their deposit, damages in respect of lost conveyancing expenses and interest.

**Peyman v Lanjani** [1985] 2 WLR 154 Court of Appeal (Stephenson, May and Slade LJJ)

Breach of contract - election to affirm or rescind

*Facts*

In October 1978 the defendant agreed to take an assignment of the lease of a restaurant. The assignment required the landlord's consent and the defendant arranged for his agent to impersonate him at an interview with the landlord's agent, believing that he would give a better impression. Consent was given and the lease duly assigned. In February, the defendant agreed, through his agent, to sell the lease to the plaintiff, taking the plaintiff's house in part exchange. Contracts were exchanged, subject to the landlord's consent and the defendant's agent again impersonated him in seeking to obtain it. After learning of the original impersonation, and before the landlord's consent had been given, the plaintiff paid £10,000 under the agreement and took possession as a licensee. After consulting a new solicitor, and still before the landlord had given his consent, the plaintiff purported to rescind the contract.

*Held*

He was entitled to do so.

May LJ:

'... the doctrine of election comes into play when at a particular stage of a relationship or transaction between two parties the conduct of one is held as a matter of law to entitled the other to a choice between two mutually inconsistent courses of action. We are concerned with the choice which arose as a result of Mr Lanjani's breach of contract resulting from his inability to provide a good title to his leasehold interest in the restaurant. A similar choice arises in law when a party to a contract becomes entitled to rescind it by reason of the discovery of fraud on the part of the other party. Other instances arise when a landlord becomes entitled to forfeit a lease because of his tenant's breach of covenant ... For the purposes of this judgment I will confine myself to the case where a party to a contract becomes entitled either to rescind it or to affirm it as the result of some conduct on the part of the other party to it, but in my opinion the same principles apply where as a result of the application of the relevant law to the material facts such a choice becomes available.

The next feature of the doctrine of election in these cases which in my opinion is important is that when the person entitled to make the choice does so one way or the other, and this has been communicated to the other party to the contract, then the choice becomes irrevocable even though, if and when the first person seeks to change his mind, the second cannot show that he has altered his position in any way.

This being so, I do not think that a party to a contract can realistically or sensibly be held to have made this irrevocable choice between rescission and affirmation unless he has actual knowledge not only of the facts of the serious breach of the contract by the other party which is the precondition of his right to choose, but also of the fact that in the circumstances which exist he does have that right to make that choice which the law gives him. To hold otherwise ... would in my opinion not only be unjust, it would be contrary to the principles of law which one can extract from the decided cases.'

### Phillips v Brooks Ltd [1919] 2 KB 243 High Court (Horridge J)

Contract induced by fraud - property passed?

*Facts*

North entered the shop of the plaintiff jeweller and selected an emerald ring. When writing a cheque (which he signed 'George Bullough') he said: 'You see who I am; I am Sir George Bullough' and he gave the plaintiff an address in St James' Square. The plaintiff had heard of Sir George Bullough as a man of means and a directory told him that Sir George lived at the address North had given. The plaintiff allowed North to take the ring (as it was, he said, his wife's birthday tomorrow), but the cheque was returned marked 'No account' and North was subsequently convicted of obtaining the ring by false pretences. Meanwhile, though, he had pledged the ring with the defendant pawnbrokers and the plaintiff now sought its return.

*Held*

His action would fail.

Horridge J:

'I think the seller intended to contract with the person present, and there was no error as to the person with whom he contracted, although the plaintiff would not have made the contract if there had not been a fraudulent misrepresentation ... In this case there was a passing of the property and the purchaser had a good title, and there must be judgment for the defendants, with costs.'

*Commentary*

Followed in *Lewis* v *Averay* [1971] 3 WLR 603 and *Dennant* v *Skinner* [1948] 2 KB 164. Distinguished in *Ingram* v *Little* [1960] 3 WLR 504.

### Redgrave v Hurd (1881) 20 Ch D 1 Court of Appeal (Sir George Jessel MR, Baggallay and Lush LJJ)

Misrepresentation - opportunity to discover

*Facts*

A solicitor, the plaintiff, was contemplating retirement and he advertised for a partner who would also purchase his house. The defendant responded and, amongst other things, agreed to purchase the plaintiff's house. However, he refused to complete the purchase as he alleged that he had discovered that the practice, of which he was now a partner, was 'utterly worthless' and that representations made in

138

regard thereto by the plaintiff were false. The plaintiff sought specific performance, the defendant rescission.

*Held*

The defendant was entitled to succeed.

Lush LJ:

'In one part of the judgment of the learned judge in the court below he appears to hold that, where a false representation has been made and papers are handed to the party to whom it is made, from which, if he chose, he might detect the falsehood, and he does not do so, he is in the same position as if he had done so. I entirely differ from that view, and think what my learned borther said is the correct view of the law - that where a false representation has been made, it lies on the party who makes it to show that, although he made the false representation, the defendant - the other party - did not rely on it. The onus probandi is on him to show that the other party waived it, and relied on his own knowledge. Nothing of that kind appears here.'

**Resolute Maritime Inc v Nippon Kaiji Kyokai. The Skopas**
See **Skopas, The**

**Royscott Trust v Rogerson** [1991] 3 WLR 57 Court of Appeal (Balcombe and Ralph Gibson LJJ)

Measure of damages - innocent misrepresentation

*Facts*

A car dealer agreed to sell a car on HP to a customer for a cash price of £7,600, of which the customer was to pay a deposit of £1,200. These amounts were mistakenly stated as £8,000 and £1,600 respectively to the finance company and all future transactions were based on these figures.

The customer paid part of the sum due to the finance company, but in 1987 he dishonestly sold the car; and later ceased to make any payments. The amount unpaid by that time was, the finance company claimed, £3,625. They based this figure on the difference between the amount repaid to them by the customer and the amount £6,400 which they had advanced to the car dealer. The figures supplied to the finance company, however, had been mistakenly set too high, and the finance company sued the car dealer for innocent misrepresentation and claimed damages under s2(1) of the Misrepresentation Act (MA) 1967.

*Held*

The measure of damages recoverable under s2(1) of the MA 1967 was a tortious rather than contractual one. The finance company was entitled to recover damages in respect of all losses occurring as a natural consequence, including unforeseeable losses, subject to the normal rules on remoteness. It was in any event a foreseeable event that a customer buying a car on HP might dishonestly sell the car. The act by the customer was not a novus actus, the chain of causation was unbroken.

The car dealers were liable for innocent misrepresentation and the finance company could claim the £3,625 plus interest.

**Sharneyford Supplies Ltd v Edge** [1987] 2 WLR 363 Court of Appeal (Kerr, Parker and Balcombe LJJ)

Breach of contract - amount of damages

*Facts*

The defendant agreed to sell a maggot farm to the plaintiff with vacant possession. However the tenants on the land had security of tenure and it was impossible therefore to convey good title to the plaintiff. The plaintiff claimed against the tenant for breach of contract and sought damages under two heads:

a) cost of investigating title and other expenses in the sum of £472.05; and

b) loss of profits from December 1979 to June 1982, that being the date when the plaintiff found other premises at which to carry on the business of breeding maggots. The loss of profits amounted to £131,544 with interest.

Mervyn Davies J followed strictly the rule in *Bain* v *Fothergill* and thus in essence all the plaintiff received for the defendant's negligent misrepresentation was the expenses. The plaintiff appealed.

*Held*

The appeal would be allowed as the defendant had failed to satisfy the requirement engrafted on the rule in *Bain* v *Fothergill*, ie that the vendor must show that he did all that he reasonably could to perform the contract by removing any defect in title which he agreed to transfer.

Balcombe LJ:

'The question then arises: did Mr Edge establish that he had done all that he reasonably could to mitigate the effect of his breach of contract by trying to remove this defect on his title? The judge held that he had ... He summarised in numbered paragraphs what Mr Edge had done ... Of these numbered paragraphs, paras (i) to (v) inclusive dealt with events up to and including the exchange of contracts. I fail to see how these can have any relevance to the question at issue. Of the events subsequent to the date of contract, the only steps which it could be said that Mr Edge (or his solicitor, whose acts or omissions for this purpose must be attributed to Mr Edge) took to try and remove the defect on his title were the telephone conversation with Mr Hill between 14 and 19 November 1979 and the letters of 6 and 29 February 1980. The one striking omission is that at no time did Mr Edge give to Messrs Meek and Holt notice to determine their tenancy, either at common law or under s25 of the Landlord and Tenant Act 1954. In the absence of such notices having been given, I find it impossible to say that Mr Edge had done all that he reasonably could to try and remove the defect on his title and acquire vacant possession of the farm. Counsel for the third party submitted that such notices would have been to no avail, since under s25 of the 1954 Act a notice of not less than six months is necessary, and any such notice would necessarily have expired long after the date fixed for completion; further, there was no likelihood that Mr Edge could have successfully resisted an application by Messrs Meek and Holt for a new tenancy. However, it is by no means certain that Messrs Meek and Holt, if served with formal notice to determine their tenancy, and thereby realising the seriousness with which Mr Edge treated the matter, would have sought to resist giving up possession. It is significant that neither Mr Meek nor Mr Holt was called to give evidence at the trial and, as has already been said, the burden of proof to establish that he had taken all reasonable steps rested on Mr Edge. But in any event that argument is similar to that which was rejected in both *Day* v *Singleton* and *Malhotra* v *Choudhury*: that it matters not that the attempt to clear the title might have failed: it must at least have been tried. It follows that I am unable to accept the judge's conclusion that Mr Edge had, by himself or his solicitor, done what he reasonably could to try to acquire vacant possession of the farm ... I also disagree with his conclusion that there was no bad faith on the part of Mr Edge ... if one adopts the definition of "bad faith" in this context given by Stephenson LJ in *Malhotra* v *Choudhury* ... On this ground alone I would allow this appeal.

However, it was argued before us, as it was before the judge, that Mr Edge's obligation to use his best endeavours to clear the defect on his title extended to an obligation on his part to pay the £12,000 to buy out Messrs Meek and Holt, if that was a reasonable sum in all the circumstances. It is not clear from his judgment whether the judge accepted this submission as a matter of principle. He said that he had "taken account" of the suggestion that the £12,000 offer ought to have been pursued, at any rate in the sense that there should have been negotiations to reduce that figure. However, he then went on to say that, in view of the intimation that the figure was not negotiable, he did not think that Mr Edge was obliged to take that course ...

If a vendor is liable to use his best endeavours to clear any defect from his title, I can see the logic of the argument that those endeavours could include, in an appropriate case, the payment of a sum of money to a third party. However, logic has played little part in the development of this particular branch of the law, and to apply it strictly in this instance would only serve to demonstrate the illogicality of some of the earlier distinctions. The particular difficulty I find in following this argument to its logical conclusion is that the rule in *Bain* v *Fothergill* would then cease to exist, since there would be few cases in which a defect in title could not be removed if the sum offered were large enough. While I accept that it would be no bad thing if the rule were to cease to exist, I cannot believe that this is a valid way of removing it. Further, the practical problems would be great. How would the court determine, in any given case, whether the sum which an incumbrancer might require to surrender the incumbrance which constituted a defect on the title was reasonable? In a case, such as *JW Cafés Ltd* v *Brownlow Trust Ltd* ..., when the defect consists of restrictive covenants affecting the title, how far would the vendor have to go in trying to procure the removal of these restrictive covenants, and at what price? To extend the principle of *Day* v *Singleton* [1899] 2 Ch 320 to this extent, logical though it might otherwise appear, could be productive of endless litigation. Although there is no authority directly in point, I am fortified in my view by a passage in the leading textbook, *Williams on Vendor and Purchaser* (4th edn, 1936) p 1020:

"And where his [the vendor's] title is imperfect, he is of course not liable to pay substantial damages if he declines to buy in any outstanding estate or incumbrance. Such an act as this would depend on others' consent, and does not lie entirely within his own power."

It was also argued before us that the continued acceptance by Mr Edge of the supply of maggots from Messrs Meek and Holt, and the 1982 negotiations for the grant of a new lease to them, in some way amounted to a failure by Mr Edge to use his best endeavours to clear the defect in his title. I am unable to follow this argument. While there appears to have been no evidence to justify the judge's finding ... that the maggots were being produced and had to be used (impliedly by Mr Edge and no one else), so long as the tenancy had not been determined there was no reason why Mr Edge should not accept the rent payable under it; his failure was to take the necessary steps to terminate the tenancy. Similarly, the 1982 negotiations were not of themselves of any significance; the most that can be said about them is that they were inconsistent with any attempt by Mr Edge to recover vacant possession from Messrs Meek and Holt.

The notice of appeal also included as a ground of appeal that the judge ought to have followed the decision of Graham J in *Watts* v *Spence* ... Counsel for the plaintiff very wisely did not attempt to argue this ground before us. In the circumstances I need only say that, like the judge, I find the criticism of *Watts* v *Spence* in *McGregor on Damages* (14th edn, 1980) pp 1000-1002, paras 1486-1489 entirely convincing.

In the circumstances I would allow this appeal and substitute for the second declaration made by the judge on the preliminary issues a declaration that the quantum of damages recoverable by the plaintiff for breach of contract be assessed in accordance with the general law but so that the plaintiff may also recover such further damages (if any) in tort for innocent misrepresentation as the court shall determine.'

*Commentary*

Applied: *Bain* v *Fothergill* (1874) LR 7 HL 158 and *Wroth* v *Tyler* [1973] 2 WLR 405.

The rule in *Bain* v *Fothergill* was abolished by s3 of the Law of Property (Miscellaneous Provisions) Act 1989 as from 27 September 1989.

**Skopas, The** [1983] 1 WLR 857 High Court (Mustill J)

Agent's liability

*Facts*

In an action arising out of the sale and purchase of the vessel The Skopas, there arose this preliminary question of law: If an agent, acting in his express or ostensible authority, makes a statement which is untrue in circumstances where he did not have reasonable ground to believe that it was true, can he be held liable under the Misrepresentation Act 1967?

*Held*

He could not.

Mustill J:

'It may ... be objected that ... there is ... room to read s2(1) [of the 1967 Act] as creating an additional liability in the agent. I do not agree. The 1967 Act is concerned with representations made in the particular context of a contract, and it seems to me that it was aimed at the position of the parties to the contract. It was therefore natural that there should be created under subss(1) and (2) rights which are prima facie absolute, and independent of any general duty of care, a concept which plays no part in the law of contract. The purpose of the 1967 Act was to fill a gap which existed, or was believed to exist, in the remedies of one contracting party for an innocent representation by the other. But there was no such gap in the case of the agent; he was already subject to the ordinary liabilities in fraudulent negligence, the doctrine of *Hedley Byrne & Co Ltd* v *Heller & Partners Ltd* [1964] AC 465 having been recognised before the 1967 Act was passed. What purpose would there be in creating an entirely new absolute liability, independent of proof that the representee fell within the scope of a duty of care, simply because the representor happened to be an agent, concerned in the making of a contract, but not himself a party to it? I can see none; and, since, as I have suggested, the words of s2(1) must be read as extending to the principal, I consider that their operation should be confined to him alone ...'

**Smith v Hughes** (1871) LR 6 QB 597 Court of Queen's Bench (Sir Alexander Cockburn CJ, Blackburn and Hannen JJ)

Sale of oats - buyer's mistaken belief

*Facts*

A trainer of racehorses bought some oats. He thought, he said, that he had purchased old oats; in fact they were new so he refused to pay for them and the county court decided that right was on his side.

*Held*

There must be a new trial.

Blackburn J:

'... on the sale of a specific article, unless there be a warranty making it part of the bargain that it possesses some particular quality, the purchaser must take the article he has bought, though it does not possess that quality. And I agree that, even if the vendor was aware that the purchaser thought that the article possessed that quality, and would not have entered into the contract unless he had so thought, still the purchaser is bound, unless the vendor was guilty of some fraud or deceit upon him. A mere abstinence from disabusing the purchaser of that impression is not fraud or deceit, for, whatever may be the case in a court of morals, there is no legal obligation on the vendor to inform the purchaser that he is under a mistake which has not been induced by the act of the vendor.'

**Sybron Corp v Rochem Ltd** [1983] 3 WLR 713 Court of Appeal (Stephenson, Fox and Kerr LJJ)

Mistake - fraud discovered after pension awarded

*Facts*

Having opted for early retirement, the appellant manager was awarded a discretionary pension by the respondent employers. It was subsequently discovered that the appellant had been a party, with other employees subordinate to him, to fraudulent misconduct. The respondents sought, in effect, to have the pension arrangements set aside.

*Held*

There were entitled to succeed as the pension arrangements had been made under a mistake of fact induced by the appellant's breach of duty.

Kerr LJ:

'Since mistake induced by misrepresentation has not been pleaded, although I think that, in the circumstances of this case, it might well have been, the issue is whether or not [the appellant] was in breach of a duty to his employers which induced the mistake on their part. As to this, it seems to me that there can only be one answer. [The appellant] was throughout in fraudulent breach of a clear duty owed to his employers to put an end to the activities of ... the ... conspirators, who were engaged in seeking to destroy the employers' business for their own purposes, and this continuing breach of his duty induced the mistake. His duty was to report the activities of the conspirators in any event, and to dismiss them forthwith in so far as it lay within his powers to do so. Covering up and deliberately concealing their activities, which is what he was doing throughout, was the clearest possible breach of duty for a person in his position, and equally clearly it induced the mistake in question. All that *Bell* v *Lever Bros Ltd* [1932] AC 161 decides in this regard, at most, is that [the appellant] was under no duty to disclose his own misconduct. I say "at most" because I am far from convinced that *Bell* v *Lever Bros Ltd* applies, even to this extent, to cases where the concealment is fraudulent, as here, since the absence of fraud was stressed throughout the appellate proceedings in that case, including the speeches of Lord Atkin and Lord Thankerton ... with which Lord Blanesburgh agreed. On no view, however, can *Bell* v *Lever Bros Ltd* be invoked by [the appellant] to a greater extent than this. The fact that compliance by [the appellant] with his duties in this regard would in this case inevitably have revealed his own fraudulent complicity is irrelevant ...

I therefore do not accept that it makes any difference that the pension arrangements as such were not directly induced by misrepresentation or breach of duty on the part of [the appellant]. What matters is that when these arrangements were concluded and acted on by his employers, he was in clear breach of his duty to his employers, and indeed in fraudulent breach, and that these breaches induced the mistake on their part, which caused them not to exercise their rights under ... the scheme.'

**With v O'Flanagan** [1936] Ch 575 Court of Appeal (Lord Wright MR, Romer LJ and Clauson J)

Continuing representation - sale of medical practice

*Facts*

Desiring to sell his medical practice, the defendant truthfully told the plaintiff that it brought in £2,000 pa and that he had a panel of 1,480 persons. During the four months of negotiations before the contract of sale was signed the defendant was ill: takings dwindled to practically nothing and the number of panel patients fell to 1,260. These facts were not disclosed to the plaintiff, but he discovered them immediately after completion and he sought rescission of the contract.

*Held*

He was entitled to succeed.

Romer LJ:

'The only principle invoked by the [plaintiff] in this case is as follows. If A, with a view to inducing B to enter into a contract makes a representation as to a material fact, then if at a later date and before the contract is actually entered into, owing to a change of circumstances, the representation then made would to the knowledge of A be untrue and B subsequently enters into the contract in ignorance of that change of circumstances and relying upon that representation, A cannot hold B to the bargain. There is ample authority for that statement and, indeed, I doubt myself whether any authority is necessary, it being, it seems to me, so obviously consistent with the plainest principles of equity.'

# 6   EXCLUSION CLAUSES

**Ailsa Craig Fishing Co Ltd v Malvern Fishing Co Ltd** [1983] 1 WLR 964 House of Lords (Lord Wilberforce, Lord Elwyn-Jones, Lord Salmon, Lord Fraser of Tullybelton and Lord Lowry)

Exception clause - loss of fishing boat

*Facts*

The appellants' fishing boat sank in Aberdeen harbour and was a complete loss. The judge found that the loss had been caused by negligence on breach of contract on the part of the respondent security company, but the respondents sought to rely on the clause that limited their liability to £1,000 or £10,000, according to the circumstances. The appellants contended, inter alia, that the clause could not apply because there had been a total failure by the respondents to perform the contract.

*Held*

This contention would be rejected.

Lord Fraser of Tullybelton:

'The question whether Securicor's liability has been limited falls to be answered by construing the terms of the contract in accordance with the ordinary principles applicable to contracts of this kind. The argument for limitation depends on certain special conditions attached to the contract prepared on behalf of Securicor and put forward in their interest. There is no doubt that such conditions must be construed strictly against the proferens, in this case Securicor, and that in order to be effective they must be "most clearly and unambiguously expressed" ... It has sometimes apparently been regarded ... as a proposition of law, that a condition excluding liability can never have any application where there has been a total breach of contract, but I respectfully agree with the Lord President (Lord Emslie) who said in his opinion in the present case that that was a misunderstanding ...

There are later authorities which lay down very strict principles to be applied when considering the effect of clauses of exclusion or of indemnity ... In my opinion these principles are not applicable in their full rigour when considering the effect of conditions merely limiting liability. Such conditions will of course be read contra proferentem and must be clearly expressed but there is no reason why they should be judged by the specially exacting standards which are applied to exclusion and indemnity clauses.'

*Commentary*

Applied in *Mitchell (George) (Chesterhall) Ltd v Finney Lock Seeds Ltd* [1983] 3 WLR 163.


**British Crane Hire Corporation Ltd v Ipswich Plant Hire Ltd**

See chapter 4 - Contents of contracts.


**Chapelton v Barry Urban District Council**

See chapter 1 - Offer and acceptance.


**Computer and Systems Engineering plc v John Lelliott Ltd** (1991) The Times 21 February Court of Appeal (Purchas, Taylor and Beldam LJJ)

Standard form contracts - exclusion clauses - strict interpretation

*Facts*

A standard form contract excluded liability for 'flooding or burst pipes'. Damage was caused to the plaintiff's property by a fractured sprinkler pipe. The question was whether the subcontractor's negligence was within the exclusion clause.

*Held*

The damage caused was not within the meaning of the exclusion clause, which would be interpreted strictly, and the plaintiff could claim.

**Curtis v Chemical Cleaning & Dyeing Co Ltd** [1951] 1 KB 805 Court of Appeal (Somervell, Singleton and Denning LJJ)

Damage to wedding dress - exclusion clause

*Facts*

The plaintiff took a white satin wedding dress to the defendants to be cleaned. On being asked to sign a 'receipt' which stated, inter alia, that articles were 'accepted on condition that the company is not liable for any damage howsoever arising', she asked why her signature was required: she was told it was because the defendants did not accept liability for damages to beads and sequins. When the dress was returned to the plaintiff, there was a stain on it: her action for damages was successful and the defendants appealed.

*Held*

The appeal would be dismissed.

Denning LJ:

'If the party affected signs a written document, knowing it to be a contract which governs the relations between him and the other party, his signature is irrefragable evidence of his assent to the whole contract, including the exempting clauses, unless the signature is shown to be obtained by fraud or misrepresentation: see *L'Estrange* v *Graucob* [1934] 2 KB 394. What is a sufficient misrepresentation for this purpose? ...

In my opinion, any behaviour by words or conduct is sufficient to be a misrepresentation if it is such as to mislead the other party about the existence or extent of the exemption. If it conveys a false impression, that is enough. If the false impression is created knowingly, it is a fraudulent misrepresentation; if it is created unwittingly, it is an innocent misrepresentation ... by failing to draw attention to the width of the exemption clause, the assistant created the false impression that the exemption related to the beads and sequins only, and that it did not extend to the material of which the dress was made. It was done perfectly innocently, but, nevertheless, a false impression was created ... it was a sufficient misrepresentation to disentitle the cleaners from relying on the exemption, except in regard to the beads and sequins ... In my opinion, when a condition, purporting to exempt a person from his common law liabilities, is obtained by an innocent misrepresentation, the party who has made that misrepresentation is disentitled to rely on the exemption. Whether one calls that a rule of law or one of equity does not matter in these days.'

**Dillon v Baltic Shipping Co (The Mikhail Lermontov)** [1991] 2 Lloyd's Rep 155 NSW Court of Appeal Australia

Exclusion clauses - ticket terms and conditions part of contract?

*Facts*

The plaintiff and her daughter booked a cruise on the 'Mikhail Lermontov' by paying a deposit. One week later they received a document headed 'Booking Form CTC Cruises'. This form contained, inter alia, the clause:

'Contract of Carriage for travel as set out ... will be made only at the time of issuing the tickets and will be subject to conditions and regulations printed on the tickets ...'

Having paid the balance, the plaintiff received tickets containing terms and conditions, limiting the shipping line's liability for personal injury and death. Just over a week into the cruise, the liner struck a rock and sank. The plaintiff suffered personal injury and nervous shock.

The plaintiff claimed damages for personal injuries, loss of property and loss of the enjoyment of the holiday. The defendants argued that limitation clauses, referred to on the ticket, formed part of the conditions of the contract and that they were entitled to rely on them.

*Held*

The statement in the initial brochure (supplied on receipt of the deposit) was insufficient to draw the attention of the customer to the fact that limitation clauses were contained in the ticket terms and conditions. The issue of a ticket with terms and conditions printed in full occurred after payment of the balance and a firm contract of carriage was already in existence. At the time the contract of carriage came into force, the plaintiff had not had a reasonable opportunity to see and agree to conditions and terms referred to, and which the defendants sought to impose on all the passengers when tickets were delivered, which was about a month or more later.

Exclusion or limitation clauses thus referred to, on the ticket, could not be said to be incorporated into the contract and could not be relied upon.

**Flamar Interocean Ltd v Denmac Ltd (The Flamar Pride and Flamar Progress)** [1990] 1 Lloyd's Rep 434 High Court (Potter J)

Exclusion clause - UCTA 1977 - reasonableness

*Facts*

The owners of the two vessels claimed damages for breach of contract against the defendants, the technical managers of the vessels. The contract(s) in question was a ship's management contract for each vessel, pertaining to pre-delivery inspection of the vessels, maintenance inspections, insurance and so on. The question arose as to whether the technical managers (the defendants) could rely on an exclusion clause in the contract.

*Held*

Under s2(2) of the Unfair Contract Terms Act 1977 a person could not exclude or restrict his liability for negligence, save insofar as the clause might satisfy the test of reasonableness. It was incontestable that there had been negligence, in (inter alia): (a) failure to require adequate and thorough pre-delivery tests to be carried out; (b) failure to engage someone with experience of refrigerated vessels; and (c) failure to provide liability insurance cover. The clauses in question did not satisfy the test of reasonableness as laid out in s11(1) of the 1977 Act, providing that the term shall be fair and reasonable having regard to the circumstances 'which were, or ought reasonably to have been, known to or in the contemplation of the parties when the contract was made'. The exclusion clause could not be relied on by the defendants.

**George Mitchell (Chesterhall) Ltd v Finney Lock Seeds Ltd** [1983] 3 WLR 163 House of Lords (Lord Diplock, Lord Scarman, Lord Roskill, Lord Bridge of Harwich and Lord Brightman)

Clause limiting liability - fundamental breach

*Facts*

The plaintiffs orally ordered 30 lbs of late cabbage seed from the defendant. An invoice was presented on which conditions were printed and which the plaintiff knew were there. One of these conditions sought to limit the defendant's liability for defective seed to the price paid for that seed. Owing to the defendant's negligence, the seed was of the wrong type and was commercially useless. The price of the seed was £192; and the loss suffered by the plaintiff exceeded £61,000.

*Held*

1) On their true construction, the conditions limited the liability of the defendants to a refund of the price paid. *Photo Productions*; *Ailsa Craig Fishing* applied.

   Lord Bridge:

   'The *Photo Productions* case gave the final quietus to the doctrine that a "fundamental breach" of contract deprived the party in breach of the benefit of clauses in the contract excluding or limiting his liability.'

2) But that in all the circumstances, including the fact of the clear recognition in the seed trade that reliance on the conditions would not be fair or reasonable and that the defendants could insure against crop failure without materially increasing the price of seeds, it would not be fair or reasonable to allow reliance on the conditions, which were accordingly unenforceable.

## Harris v Wyre Forest District Council

See **Smith v Eric S Bush** below.

## Hollier v Rambler Motors (AMC) Ltd [1972] 2 WLR 401 Court of Appeal (Salmon and Stamp LJJ and Latey J)

Exemption clause - previous dealings

*Facts*

The plaintiff sent his motor car to the defendants' garage for repairs. There had been three or four previous such transactions over a period of five years and, on at least two occasions, the plaintiff had signed an invoice containing an exemption clause in favour of the defendants, but on this occasion did not. The car was damaged by fire caused by the defendants' negligence.

*Held*

There was not sufficient previous course of dealing between the parties to impart the exemption clause into the present oral contract.

Salmon LJ:

   'I am bound to say that ... I do not know of any other case in which it had been decided, or even argued, that a term could be implied into an oral contract on the strength of a course of dealing (if it can be so called) which consisted, at the most, of three or four transactions over a period of five years.'

*Commentary*

Applied: *McCutcheon v David MacBrayne Ltd* [1964] 1 WLR 125. Distinguished: *Kendall (Henry) & Sons v William Lillico & Sons Ltd* [1968] 3 WLR 110.

**L'Estrange v Graucob (F) Ltd** [1934] 2 KB 394 Court of Appeal (Scrutton and Maughan LJJ)

Exemption clause - sale of automatic machine

*Facts*

The plaintiff purchased an automatic machine from the defendants by a contract contained in the defendants' written 'Sale Agreement' which she signed. The machine proved faulty and the defendants sought to rely on an exemption clause in the agreement.

*Held*

Having signed the agreement, the plaintiff was bound by it.

Scrutton LJ:

'In this case the plaintiff has signed a document headed "Sales Agreement" which she admits had to do with an intended purchase and which contained a clause excluding all conditions and warranties. That being so, the plaintiff, having put her signature to the document, and not having been induced to do so by any fraud or misrepresentation, cannot be heard to say that she is not bound by the terms of the document because she did not read them.'

**Levison v Patent Steam Carpet Cleaning Co Ltd** [1977] 3 WLR 90 Court of Appeal (Lord Denning MR, Orr LJ and Sir David Cairns)

Exemption clause - fundamental breach

*Facts*

By telephone, the plaintiffs asked the defendants to collect their Chinese carpet worth £900 for cleaning. When the defendants' van driver called, he asked for the owner's signature on one of their order forms: one of the plaintiffs obliged, without reading the terms and conditions set out in small print above his signature. One of those conditions provided that the carpet's maximum value was deemed to be £40; another that all merchandise was 'expressly accepted at the owner's risk'. The carpet was never returned and, eventually, the defendants said that it had been stolen. The plaintiffs sued successfully to recover the carpet's full value: the defendants appealed.

*Held*

The appeal would be dismissed: there had been a fundamental breach of contract against which the defendants' exemption clauses did not afford them protection.

Orr LJ:

'On the first of the major issues in this appeal I agree with both Lord Denning MR and Sir David Cairns that the only contract between the parties was a written contract ... incorporating the printed terms and conditions; and like Sir David Cairns I should have reached the same conclusion in the absence of any previous dealing between the parties.

As to the second major issue, whether the effect of ... the contract is to exclude liability of the defendants, for fundamental breach, I am content, following the decision of this court in *Alderslade* v *Hendon Laundry Ltd* [1945] KB 189 and the observations made in the House of Lords in *Suisse Atlantique Société d' Armament Maritime SA* v *NV Rotterdamsche Kolen Centrale* [1966] 2 WLR 944, to hold that it has no such effect because the words "All merchandise is expressly accepted at the owner's risk" are in my judgment, in the context of this contract, insufficiently clear or strong to be so construed, and having reached this conclusion I do not find it necessary to consider the factor of relative bargaining power.

On the final and crucial issue as to the burden of proof I agree that as a matter both of justice and of common sense the burden ought to rest on the bailee who, if the goods have been lost while in his possession, is both more likely to know the facts and in a better position to ascertain them than the bailor, and I would on this issue follow the decision of McNair J in *Woolmer* v *Delmer Price Ltd* [1955] 1 QB 291, and the view expressed by Denning LJ in *J Spurling Ltd* v *Bradshaw* [1956] 1 WLR 461.'

### McCutcheon v David MacBrayne Ltd [1964] 1 WLR 125 House of Lords (Lord Reid, Lord Hodson, Lord Guest, Lord Devlin and Lord Pearce)

Oral contract - previous transactions

*Facts*

At the appellant's request, his brother-in-law took his car to the respondents' office in Islay where he was quoted the freight for shipping to the mainland. Brother-in-law paid and was given a receipted invoice which he did not read. On the voyage, the ship sank, as a result of the respondents' negligent navigation, and the car was lost. The appellant claimed damages for negligence and the respondents relied on an exclusion clause exhibited in their office and on the ship: on the invoice was a statement, too, that goods were carried subject to the conditions specified on the respondents' notices. It was the respondents' usual practice to ask consignors to sign a risk note, but due to an oversight brother-in-law was not asked to sign one on this occasion. Both the appellant and brother-in-law had shipped goods through the respondents before: sometimes risk notes had been signed and, although the appellant knew that conditions of some kind existed, neither of them had ever read them. The respondents contended that, by reason of the previous dealings, the conditions were imported into the contract of carriage.

*Held*

This was not the case.

Lord Reid:

'The respondents contend that, by reason of the knowledge thus gained by the appellant and his agent in these previous transactions, the appellant is bound by their conditions. But this case differs essentially from the ticket cases. There, the carrier in making the contract hands over a document containing or referring to conditions which he intends to be part of the contract. So if the consignor or passenger, when accepting the document, knows or ought as a reasonable man to know that this is the carrier's intention, he can hardly deny that the conditions are part of the contract, or claim, in the absence of special circumstances, to be in a better position than he would be if he had read the document. But here, in making the contract neither party referred to, or indeed had in mind, any additional terms, and the contract was complete and full effective without any additional terms. If it could be said that when making the contract [brother-in-law] knew that the respondents always required a risk note to be signed and knew that the purser was simply forgetting to put it before him for signature, then it might be said that neither he nor his principal could take advantage of the error of the other party of which he was aware. But counsel frankly admitted that he could not put his case as high as that. The only other ground on which it would seem possible to import these conditions is that based on a course of dealing. If two parties have made a series of similar contracts each containing certain conditions, and then they make another without expressly referring to those conditions it may be that those conditions ought to be implied. If the officious bystander had asked them whether they had intended to leave out the conditions this time, both must, as honest men, have said "of course not". But again the facts here will not support that ground. According to [brother-in-law], there had been no consistent course of dealing; sometimes he was asked to sign and sometimes not. And, moreover, he did not know what the conditions were. This time he was offered an oral contract without any reference to conditions, and he accepted the offer in good faith.

The respondents also rely on the appellant's previous knowledge. I doubt whether it is possible to spell out a course of dealing in his case. In all but one of the previous cases he had been acting on behalf of his employer in sending a different kind of goods and he did not know that the respondents always sought to insist on excluding liability for their own negligence. So it cannot be said that, when he asked his agent to make a contract for him, he knew that this or, indeed, any other special term would be included in it. He left his agent a free hand to contract, and I see nothing to prevent him from taking advantage of the contract which his agent in fact made.

"The judicial task is not to discover the actual intentions of each party: it is to decide what each was reasonably entitled to conclude from the attitude of the other." [Law of Contract by William M Gloag].

In this case I do not think that either party was reasonably bound or entitled to conclude from the attitude of the other as known to him that these conditions were intended by the other party to be part of this contract. I would therefore allow the appeal ...'

*Commentary*

Distinguished: *Parker* v *South Eastern Railway Co* (1877) 2 CPD 416. Applied in *Hollier* v *Rambler Motors (AMC) Ltd* [1972] 2 WLR 401.


**Micklefield v SAC Technology Ltd** [1990] 1 WLR 1002 High Court (John Mowbray QC)

Option lost if wrongfully dismissed?

*Facts*

The plaintiff director was entitled to subscribe for shares in the company under a share option scheme. The scheme provided that if he 'ceases to be employed [by the company] for any reason whatsoever, any option granted to him shall ... lapse and not be exercisable'. Further, the scheme provided that if he ceases to be so employed 'he shall not be entitled, and by applying for an option ... shall be deemed irrevocably to have waived any entitlement by way of compensation for loss of office or otherwise howsoever to any sum or other benefit to compensate him for the loss of any rights under the scheme'. The plaintiff gave notice of his intention to exercise the option; eight days later (and eight days before, in accordance with the terms of the scheme, he would have purchased the shares) his employment was terminated and he was given six months' salary in lieu of notice. Assuming (as the plaintiff contended) that he had been wrongfully dismissed, was he entitled to damages for loss of the option?

*Held*

He was not so entitled.

John Mowbray QC:

'... the principle that a man cannot be permitted to take advantage of his own wrong (that is, in this context, from a breach by him of the contract), is subject to an exception. I refer to the speech of Lord Jauncey, with which all the rest of their Lordships agreed, in *Alghussein Establishment* v *Eton College* [1988] 1 WLR 587 at 595 where he said:

"For my part, I have no doubt that the weight of authority favours the view that, in general, the principle is embodied in a rule of construction rather than in an absolute rule of law."

If that is correct, and the rule is only one of construction, then it can be excluded by a sufficiently clear contrary provision in the contract ... It follows that, so long as ... the scheme is sufficiently clear, it will exclude the principle.

In my judgment, ... the scheme is clear and decisive enough to exclude the principle as well as to operate as an exemption clause. It expressly applies if an option holder ceases to be an executive for any reason. That, on its terms, includes the case of his being wrongly dismissed. If the clause stopped there, one might perhaps doubt whether it was meant to apply to a wrongful dismissal. As I see it, the rest of the clause, though, makes it clear that it can only apply in the case of a wrongful dismissal. It goes on with a waiver of any entitlement by way of compensation for loss of office. Such an entitlement could only arise in a case of wrongful dismissal and the word "waiver" makes it clear that it is some right of the plaintiff's that is being removed from him. Counsel for the plaintiff said it would be necessary to refer openly to a wrongful dismissal, but I do not take that view. I think this is a clause which is intended and clearly sufficient to enable the company to escape part of its liability.'

His Lordship also decided that s3 of the Unfair Contract Terms Act 1977 did not apply to share option schemes: see ibid, Schedule 1, para 1(e).

*Commentary*

*Alghussein Establishment* v *Eton College* [1988] 1 WLR 587: see Chapter 15, below.


**Olley v Marlborough Court Ltd** [1949] 1 KB 532 Court of Appeal (Bucknill, Singleton and Denning LJJ)

Hotel - notice in bedroom

*Facts*

The plaintiffs arrived at a hotel, booked in at reception and paid in advance. They went up to their room where a notice purported to exempt the proprietors for articles lost or stolen unless handed to the manageress for safe custody. During their stay some clothing was stolen from their room.

*Held*

The contract had been concluded when the plaintiffs booked and paid for their room and the defendants could not unilaterally vary the contract to include as a term the notice in the bedroom, which the plaintiffs only saw at a later stage.

Denning LJ:

'The only other point in the case is whether the hotel company are protected by the notice which they put in the bedrooms, "The proprietors will not hold themselves responsible for articles lost or stolen, unless handed to the manageress for safe custody". The first question is whether that notice formed part of the contract. Now people who rely on a contract to exempt themselves from their common law liability, must prove that contract strictly. Not only must the terms of the contract be clearly proved, but also the intention to create legal relations - the intention to be legally bound - must also be clearly proved. The best way of proving it is by a written document, signed by the party to be bound. Another way is by handing him, before or at the time of the contract, a written notice specifying its terms and making it clear to him that the contract is on those terms. A prominent public notice which is plain for him to see when he makes the contract, or an express oral stipulation would, no doubt, have the same effect. But nothing short of one of these three ways will suffice. It has been held that mere notices put on receipts for money do not make a contract. (See *Chapelton* v *Barry Urban District Council* ). So also, in my opinion, notices put up in bedrooms do not of themselves make a contract. As a rule, the guest does not see them until after he has been accepted as a guest. The hotel company no doubt hopes that the guest will be bound by them, but the hope is vain unless they clearly show that he agreed to be bound by them, which is rarely the case.'


**Parker v South Eastern Railway Co** (1877) 2 CPD 416 Court of Appeal (Mellish, Baggallay and Bramwell LJJ)

Clause on back of ticket - effect

*Facts*

The plaintiff deposited a bag in a cloakroom of a railway station owned by the defendants. He was given a ticket which stated on its face, 'see back'. On the back was a clause limiting the defendants' liability to £10. The plaintiff's bag, worth £24 10s, was lost.

*Held*

The plaintiff was bound by the clause, even though he had not read it; the defendants had done all that was reasonably necessary to bring the clause to his attention.

Mellish LJ:

'The question then is, whether the plaintiff was bound by the conditions contained in the ticket. In an ordinary case, where an action is brought on a written agreement which is signed by the defendant, the agreement is proved by proving his signature and, in the absence of fraud, it is wholly immaterial that he has not read the agreement and does not know its contents. The parties may, however, reduce their agreement into writing, so that the writing constitutes the sole evidence of the agreement, without signing it; but in that case, there must be evidence independently of the agreement itself to prove that the defendant has assented to it. In that case also, if it is proved that the defendant has assented to the writing constituting the agreement between the parties, it is, in the absence of fraud, immaterial that the defendant had not read the agreement and did not know its contents. Now if, in the course of making a contract, one party delivers to another a paper containing writing and the party receiving the papers knows that the papers contain conditions which the party delivering it intends to constitute the contract, I have no doubt that the party receiving the paper does, by receiving and keeping it, assent to the conditions contained in it, although he does not read them and does not know what they are. I hold, therefore, that the case of *Harris v Great Western Railway* was rightly decided, because in that case, the plaintiff admitted, on cross examination, that she believed there were some conditions on the ticket. On the other hand, the case of *Henderson v Stevenson* LR 2 Sc & Div 470, is a conclusive authority that if the person receiving the ticket does not know that there is any writing upon the back of the ticket, he is not bound by a condition printed on the back. The facts in the cases before us differ from those in both *Henderson v Stevenson* and *Harris v Great Western Railway* because, in both the cases which have been argued before us, though the plaintiffs admitted that they knew there was writing on the back of the ticket, they swore not only that they did not read it, but that they did not know or believe that the writing contained conditions, and we are to consider whether, under those circumstances, we can lay down, as a matter of law, either that the plaintiff is bound or that he is not bound by the conditions contained in the ticket, or whether his being bound depends on some question of fact to be determined by the jury and, if so, whether, in the present case, the right question was left to the jury.

Now I am of the opinion that we cannot lay down, as a matter of law, either that the plaintiff was bound or that he was not bound by the conditions printed on the ticket, from the mere fact that he knew there was writing on the ticket but did not know that the writing contained conditions. I think there may be cases in which a paper containing writing is delivered by one party to another in the course of a business transaction, where it would be quite reasonable that the party receiving it should assume that the writing contained in it no condition and should put it in his pocket unread. For instance, if a person driving through a turnpike gate received a ticket upon paying the toll, he might reasonably assume that the object of the ticket was that by producing it, he might be free from paying toll at some other turnpike gate and might put it in his pocket unread. On the other hand, if a person who ships goods to be carried on a voyage by sea receives a bill of lading signed by the master, he would plainly be bound by it, although afterwards, in an action against the shipowners for the loss of the goods, he might swear that he had never read the bill of lading and that he did not know that it contained the terms of the contract of carriage and that the shipowner was protected by the exception contained in it. Now the reason why the person receiving the bill of lading would be bound, seems to me to be that in the great majority of cases, persons shipping goods do know that the bill of lading contains the terms of the contract of carriage; and the shipowner, or the master delivering the bill of lading, is entitled to assume that the person shipping goods has that knowledge. It is, however, quite possible to suppose that a person who is neither a man of business nor a lawyer might, on some particular occasion, ship goods without the least knowledge of what a bill of lading was, but in my opinion, such a person must bear the consequences of his own exceptional ignorance, it being plainly impossible that business could be carried on if every person who delivers a bill of lading had to stop to explain what a bill of lading was.

Now the question we have to consider is whether the railway company was entitled to assume that a person depositing luggage and receiving a ticket in such a way that he could see that some writing was printed on it, would understand that the writing contained the conditions of contract; this seems to me, to depend upon whether people in general would, in fact, and naturally, draw that inference. The railway company, as it seems to me, must be entitled to make some assumptions respecting the person who deposits luggage with them: I think they are entitled to assume that he can read and that he understands the English language and that he pays such attention to what he is about as may be reasonably expected from a person in such a transaction as that of depositing luggage in a cloakroom. The railway company must, however, take mankind as they find them and if what they do is sufficient to inform people in general that the ticket contains conditions, I think that a particular plaintiff ought not to be in a better position than other persons on account of his exceptional ignorance or stupidity or carelessness. But if what the railway company do is not sufficient to convey to the minds of people in general that the ticket contains conditions, then they have received goods on deposit without obtaining the consent of the persons depositing them to the conditions limiting their liability. I am of the opinion, therefore, that the proper direction to leave to the jury in these cases is, that if the person receiving the ticket did not see or know that there was any writing on the ticket, he is not bound by the conditions; that if he knew there was writing and knew or believed that the writing contained conditions, then he is bound by the conditions; that if he knew there was writing on the ticket, but did not know or believe that the writing contained conditions, nevertheless he would be bound if the delivering of the ticket to him was in such a manner that he could see there was writing upon it was, in the opinion of the jury, reasonable notice that the writing contained conditions.

I have, lastly, to consider whether the direction of the learned judge was correct, namely, "Was the plaintiff, under the circumstances, under any obligation in the exercise of reasonable and proper caution, to read, or to make himself aware, of the condition?" I think that this direction was not strictly accurate and was calculated to mislead the jury. The plaintiff was certainly under no obligation to read the ticket, but was entitled to leave it unread if he pleased; and the question does not appear to me to direct the attention of the jury to the real question, namely whether the railway company did what was reasonably sufficient to give the plaintiff notice of the condition.

On the whole, I am of the opinion that there ought to be a new trial.'

*Commentary*

Distinguished in *McCutcheon* v *David MacBrayne Ltd* [1964] 1 WLR 125.


## Phillips Products v Hyland

See *Thompson* v *T Lohan (Plant Hire) Ltd* below.


**Photo Production Ltd v Securicor Transport Ltd** [1980] 2 WLR 283 House of Lords (Lord Wilberforce, Lord Diplock, Lord Salmon, Lord Keith and Lord Scarman)

Exception clause - fundamental breach

*Facts*

The plaintiffs employed the defendants to provide security services at their factory, including night patrols. While on such a patrol, an employee of the defendants deliberately lit a small fire, which got out of control and completely destroyed the factory and its contents, of value £615,000. The defendants in their defence, relied on an exemption clause; the Court of Appeal followed and applied *Harbutt's Plasticine* and found for the plaintiffs.

*Held*

There was no rule of law preventing the defendants from relying on the clause and, on its true construction, it exempted them from liability.

Lord Wilberforce:

'There are further provisions limiting, to stated amounts, the liability of Securicor, on which it relies in the alternative if held not to be totally exempt.

It is first necessary to decide on the correct approach to a case such as this, where it is sought to invoke an exception or limitation clause in the contract. The approach of Lord Denning MR in the Court of Appeal was to consider first whether the breach was "fundamental". If so, he said, the court itself deprives the party of the benefit of an exemption or limitation clause. Shaw and Waller LJJ subsequently followed him in this argument.

Lord Denning MR, in this, was following the earlier decision of the Court of Appeal and, in particular, his own judgment in *Harbutt's Plasticine Ltd* v *Wayne Tank and Pump Co Ltd*. In that case, Lord Denning distinguished two cases: (a) the case where, as the result of a breach of contract, the innocent party has, and exercises, the right to bring the contract to an end; and (b) the case where the breach automatically brings the contract to an end without the innocent party having to make an election whether to terminate the contract or to continue it. In the first case, Lord Denning MR, purportedly applying this House's decision in *Suisse Atlantique Societe d'Armement Maritime SA* v *NV Rotterdamsche Kolen Centrale* but, in effect, two citations from two of their Lordships' speeches, extracted a rule of law that the "termination" of the contract brings it and, with it, the exclusion clause, to an end. The *Suisse Atlantique Case* in his view -

"affirms the long line of cases in this court that when one party has been guilty of a fundamental breach of the contract ... and the other side accepts it, so that the contract comes to an end ... then the guilty party cannot rely on an exception or limitation clause to escape from his liability for the breach."

See (*Harbutt's Case*). He then applied the same principle to the second case.

My Lords, whatever the intrinsic merit of this doctrine, as to which I shall have something to say later, it is clear to me that so far from following this House's decision in the *Suisse Atlantique Case*, it is directly opposed to it and that the whole purpose and tenor of the *Suisse Atlantique Case* was to repudiate it. The lengthy and perhaps, I may say, sometimes indigestible speeches of their Lordships, are correctly summarised in the headnote -

"(3) That the question whether an exception clause was applicable where there was a fundamental breach of contract was one of the true constructions of the contract."

That there was any rule of law by which exception clauses are eliminated, or deprived of effect, regardless of their terms, was clearly not the view of Viscount Dilhorne, Lord Hodson or myself. The passages invoked for the contrary view of a rule of law consists only of short extracts from two of the speeches, on any view, a minority. But the case of the doctrine does not even go so far as that. Lord Reid, in my respectful opinion, and I recognise that I may not be the best judge of this matter, in his speech read as a whole, cannot be claimed as a supporter of a rule of law. Indeed, he expressly disagreed with Lord Denning MR's observations in two previous cases (*Karsales (Harrow) Ltd* v *Wallis* and *UGS Finance Ltd* v *National Mortgage Bank of Greece*) in which he had put forward the 'rule of law' doctrine. In order to show how close the disapproved doctrine is to that sought to be revived in *Harbutt's Case*, I shall quote one passage from the *Karsales Case*:

"Notwithstanding earlier cases which might suggest the contrary, it is now settled that exempting clauses of this kind, no matter how widely they are expressed, only avail the party when he is carrying out his contract in its essential respects. He is not allowed to use them as a cover for misconduct or indifference or to enable him to turn a blind eye to his obligations. They do not avail him when he is guilty of a breach which goes to the root of the contract."

Lord Reid comments as to this that he could not deduce from the authorities cited in the *Karsales Case* that the proposition stated in the judgment could be regarded as in any way "settled law". His conclusion is stated thus: "In my view, no such rule of law ought to be adopted", adding that there is room for legislative reform.

My Lords, in the light of this, the passage from the *Suisse Atlantique Case* cited by Lord Denning MR, has to be considered. For convenience, I restate it:

"If fundamental breach is established, the next question is what effect, if any, that has on the applicability of other terms of the contract. This question has often arisen with regard to clauses excluding liability, in whole or in part, of the party in breach. I do not think that there is generally much difficulty where the innocent party has elected to treat the breach as a repudiation, bring the contract to an end and sue for damages. Then the whole contract has ceased to exist, including the exclusion clause, and I do not see how that clause can then be used to exclude an action for loss which will be suffered by the innocent party after it has ceased to exist, such as loss of the profit which would have accrued if the contract had run in full term."

It is with the utmost reluctance that, not forgetting the "beams" that may exist elsewhere, I have to detect here a note of ambiguity, or perhaps even of inconsistency. What is referred to is "loss which will be suffered by the innocent party after (the contract) has ceased to exist" and I venture to think that all that is being said, rather elliptically, relates only to what is to happen in the future and is not a proposition as to the immediate consequences caused by the breach; if it were, that would be inconsistent with the full and reasoned discussion which follows.

It is only because of Lord Reid's great authority in the law that I have found it necessary to embark on what, in the end, may be superfluous analysis. For I am convinced that, with the possible exception of Lord Upjohn, whose critical passage, when read in full, is somewhat ambiguous, their Lordships, fairly read, can only be taken to have rejected those suggestions for a rule of law which had appeared in the Court of Appeal and to have firmly stated the question is one of construction, not merely of course of the exclusion clause alone, but of the whole contract.

Much has been written about the *Suisse Atlantique Case*. Each speech has been subjected to various degrees of analysis and criticism, much of it constructive. Speaking for myself, I am conscious of imperfections of terminology, though sometimes in good company. But I do not think that I should be conducing to the clarity of the law by adding to what was already too ample a discussion, a further analysis which, in turn, would have to be interpreted. I have no second thoughts as to the main proposition that the question whether, and to what extent, an exclusion clause is to be applied to a fundamental breach, of a breach of a fundamental term, or, indeed, to any breach of contract, is a matter of construction of the contract. Many difficult questions arise and will continue to arise in the infinitely varied situations in which contracts come to be breached: by repudiatory breaches, accepted or not, anticipatory breaches, by breaches of conditions or of various terms and whether by negligent or deliberate action, or otherwise. But there are ample resources in the normal rules of contract law for dealing with these, without the super-imposition of a judicially invented rule of law. I am content to leave the matter there with some supplementary observations.

1     The doctrine of "fundamental breach", in spite of its imperfections and doubtful parentage, has served a useful purpose. There were a large number of problems, productive of injustice, in which it was worse than unsatisfactory to leave exception clauses to operate. Lord Reid referred to these in the *Suisse Atlantique Case*, pointing out at the same time that the doctrine of fundamental breach was a dubious specific. But since then, Parliament has taken a hand: it has passed the Unfair Contract Terms Act 1977. This Act applies to consumer contracts and those based on standard terms and enables exception clauses to be applied with regard to what is just and reasonable. It is significant that Parliament refrained from legislating over the whole field of contract. After this Act, in

commercial matters generally, when the parties are not of unequal bargaining power and when risk are normally borne by insurance, not only is the case for judicial intervention undemonstrated, but there is everything to be said, and this seems to have been Parliament's intention, for leaving the parties free to apportion the risks as they think fit and for respecting their decisions.

At the stage of negotiation as to the consequences of a breach, there is everything to be said for allowing the parties to estimate their respective claims according to the contractual provisions they have themselves made, rather than for facing them with a legal complex so uncertain as the doctrine of fundamental breach must be. What, for example, would have been the position of Photo Productions' factory if, instead of being destroyed, it had been damaged, slightly or moderately or severely? At what point does the doctrine (with logical justification I have not understood) decide, ex post facto, that the breach was (factually) fundamental before going on to ask whether, legally, it is to be regarded as fundamental? How is the date of "termination" to be fixed? Is it the date of the incident causing the damage, or the date of the innocent party's election, or some other date? All these difficulties arise from the doctrine and are left unsolved by it.

At the judicial stage there is still more to be said for leaving cases to be decided straightforwardly on what the parties have bargained for, rather than on analysis which becomes progressively more refined, of decisions in other cases on normal principles of contractual law with minimal citation of authority. I am sure that most commercial judges have wished to be able to do the same (cf *Angelia, (The) Trade and Transport Inc* v *Iino Kaiun Kaisha Ltd* per Kerr J). In my opinion they can and should.

2    *Harbutt's Plasticine Ltd* v *Wayne Tank and Pump Co Ltd* must clearly be overruled. It would be enough to put that on its radical inconsistency with the *Suisse Atlantique Case*. But even if the matter were res integra, I would find the decision to be based on unsatisfactory reasoning as to the "termination" of the contract and the effect of "termination" on the plaintiffs' claim for damage. I have, indeed, been unable to understand how the doctrine can be reconciled with the well accepted principle of law stated by the highest modern authority that when, in the context of a breach of contract, one speaks of "termination", what is meant is no more than that the innocent party or, in some cases, both parties, are excused from further performance. Damages in such cases are then claimed under the contract, so what reason in principle can there be for disregarding what the contract itself says about damages, whether it "liquidates", them, or limits them, or excludes them? These difficulties arise in part from uncertain or inconsistent terminology. A vast number of expressions are used to describe situations where a breach has been committed by one party, of such a character as to entitle the other party to refuse further performance; discharge, rescission, termination, the contract is at an end, or dead, or displaced; clauses cannot survive, or simply go. I have come to think that some of these difficulties can be avoided; in particular the use of "rescission", even if distinguished from rescission ab initio as an equivalent for discharge, though justifiable in some contexts (see *Johnson* v *Agnew*) may lead to confusion in others. To plead for complete uniformity may be to cry for the moon. But what can and ought to be avoided is to make use of these confusions in order to produce a concealed and unreasoned legal innovation: to pass, for example, from saying that a party, victim of a breach of contract, is entitled to refuse further performance, to saying that he may treat the contract as at an end, or as rescinded, and to draw from this the proposition, which is not analytical but one of policy, that all or (arbitrarily) some of the clauses of the contract lose, automatically, their force, regardless of intention.

If this process is discontinued, the way is free to use such words as "discharge" or "termination" consistently with principles as stated by modern authority which *Harbutt's Case* disregards. I venture, with apology, to relate the classic passages. In *Heyman* v *Darwins Ltd* Lord Porter said:

"To say that the contract is rescinded or has come to an end or has ceased to exist may, in individual cases, convey the truth with sufficient accuracy, but the fuller expression that the injured party is thereby absolved from future performance of his obligations under the contract, is a more exact description of the position. Strictly speaking, to say that upon acceptance of the renunciation of a

157

contract the contract is rescinded, is incorrect. In such a case the injured party may accept the renunciation as a breach going to the root of the whole of the consideration. By that acceptance he is discharged from further performance and may bring an action for damages, but the contract itself is not rescinded."

Similarly Lord Macmillan: see also *Boston Deep Sea Fishing and Ice Co Ltd* v *Ansell* per Bowen LJ. In *Moschi* v *Lep Air Services Ltd* my noble and learned friend, Lord Diplock drew a distinction (relevant for that case) between primary obligations under a contract, which on "rescission" generally comes to an end, and secondary obligations which may then arise. Among the latter, he included an obligation to pay compensation, ie damages. And he stated in terms that this latter obligation "is just as much an obligation arising from the contract as are the primary obligations that it replaces". My noble and learned friend has developed this line of thought in an enlightening manner in his opinion, which I have now had the benefit of reading.

These passages, I believe to state correctly the modern law of contract in the relevant respects; they demonstrate that the whole foundation of *Harbutt's Case* is unsound. A fortiori, in addition to *Harbutt's Case* there must be overruled *Wathes (Western) Ltd* v *Austins (Menswear) Ltd*, which sought to apply the doctrine of fundamental breach to a case where, by election of the innocent party, the contract had not been terminated, an impossible acrobatic, yet necessarily engendered by the doctrine. Similarly, *Charterhouse Credit Co Ltd* v *Tolly* must be overruled, though the result might have been reached on construction of the contract.

3     I must add to this, by way of exception to the decision not to "gloss" the *Suisse Atlantique*, a brief observation on the deviation cases, since some reliance has been placed on them, particularly on the decision of this House in *Hain Steamship Co Ltd* v *Tate & Lyle Ltd* (so earlier than the *Suisse Atlantique*) in the support of the *Harbutt* doctrine. I suggested in the *Suisse Atlantique* that these cases can be regarded as proceeding on normal principles applicable to the law of contract generally, viz that it is a matter of the parties' intentions whether and to what extent clauses in shipping contracts can be applied after a deviation, ie a departure from the contractually agreed voyage or adventure. It may be preferable that they should be considered as a body of authority sui generis, with special rules derived from historical and commercial reasons. What, on either view, they cannot do is to lay down different rules as to contracts generally from those later stated by this House in *Heyman* v *Darwins Ltd*. The ingenious use by Donaldson J in *Kenyon, Son & Craven Ltd* v *Baxter Hoare & Co Ltd* of the doctrine of deviation in order to reconcile the *Suisse Atlantique* case with *Harbutt's Case*, itself based in part on the use of the doctrine of deviation, illustrates the contortions which that case has made necessary and would be unnecessary if it vanished as an authority.

4     It is not necessary to review fully the numerous cases in which the doctrine of fundamental breach has been applied or discussed. Many of these have now been superseded by the Unfair Contract Terms Act 1977. Others, as decisions, may be justified as depending on the contract (cf *Levison* v *Patent Steam Carpet Cleaning Co Ltd*) in the light of well-known principles such as that stated in *Alderslade* v *Hendon Laundry Ltd*.

In this situation, the present case has to be decided. As a preliminary, the nature of the contract has to be understood. Securicor undertook to provide a service of periodical visits for a very modest charge, which works out at 26p per visit. It did not agree to provide equipment. It would have no knowledge of the value of Photo Productions' factory; that, and the efficacy of their fire precautions, would be known to Photo Productions. In these circumstances, nobody could consider it unreasonable that as between these two equal parties, the risk assumed by Securicor should be a modest one and that Photo Productions should carry the substantial risk of damage or destruction.

The duty of Securicor was, as stated, to provide a service. There must be implied an obligation to use care in selecting their patrolmen, to take care of the keys and, I would think, to operate the service with due and proper regard to the safety and security of the premises. The breach of duty committed by Securicor lay in a failure to discharge this latter obligation. Alternatively, it could be put on a vicarious responsibility for the wrongful act of Musgrove, viz starting a fire on the premises; Securicor would be responsible for this on the principle stated in *Morris* v *C W Martin & Sons Ltd*. This being the breach, does condition 1 apply? It is drafted in strong terms: "Under no circumstances, any injurious act or default by any employee". These words have to be approached with the aid of the cardinal rules of construction that they must be read contra proferentem and that in order to escape from the consequences of one's own wrongdoing, or that of one's servants, clear words are necessary. I think that these words are clear. Photo Productions in fact relied on them for an argument, that since they exempted from negligence, they must be taken as not exempting from the consequence of deliberate acts. But this is a perversion of the rule that if a clause can cover something other than negligence, it will not be applied to negligence. Whether, in addition to negligence, it covers other, eg deliberate acts, remains a matter of construction, requiring, of course, clear words. I am of the opinion that it does and, being free to construe and apply the clause, I must hold that liability is excluded. On this part of the case I agree with the judge and adopt his reasons for judgment. I would allow the appeal.'

*Commentary*

Applied: *Suisse Atlantique Société d'Armement Maritime SA* v *NV Rotterdamsche Kolen Centrale* [1966] 2 WLR 944. Overruled: *Harbutt's Plasticine Ltd* v *Wayne Tank and Pump Co Ltd* [1970] 2 WLR 198. Applied in *Mitchell (George) (Chesterhall) Ltd* v *Finney Lock Seeds Ltd* [1983] 3 WLR 163 and *Aforos Shipping Co SA* v *Pagnan. The Aforos* [1983] 1 WLR 195.

## R & B Customs Brokers Co Ltd v United Dominions Trust Ltd [1987] 1 WLR 659n
Court of Appeal (Dillon and Neill LJJ)

Exclusion clause - 'dealing as consumer'

*Facts*

The plaintiffs bought from the defendant finance company a Colt Shogun ('the car'), the car having been supplied by the third party motor dealer who took the plaintiffs' Volvo in part exchange. The plaintiffs took the car on 21 September but, for some unknown reason, the defendants did not sign the conditional sale agreement ('the agreement') until 3 November and this was accepted to be the date of the contracts between the dealer and the defendants and the defendants and the plaintiffs respectively. Between these dates, the plaintiffs discovered that the car's roof leaked and the dealer took it in for repair on 5 November. The leak was not cured then or subsequently and in the following February the plaintiffs rejected the car and claimed their money back. The car was the second or third vehicle which the plaintiffs had acquired on credit terms and the agreement provided, inter alia, that any implied conditions as to the condition or quality of the car or its fitness for any particular purpose in relation to business transactions were excluded.

*Held*

Unless excluded by the agreement's express terms, the sale was subject to an implied condition as to fitness under s14(3) of the Sale of Goods Act 1979. On the facts, this was a consumer transaction (as opposed to a business transaction) and the implied condition was not excluded. It followed that the plaintiffs were entitled to judgment.

Dillon LJ:

'... I have no doubt that the requisite degree of regularity is not made out on the facts. [The plaintiff's] evidence that the car was the second or third vehicle acquired on credit terms was in my judgment and in the context of this case not enough. Accordingly, I agree with the judge that, in entering into the conditional sale agreement with the defendants, the company was "dealing as consumer". The defendants' [agreement] is thus inapplicable and the defendants are not absolved from liability under s14(3).'

**Rutter v Palmer** [1922] 2 KB 87 Court of Appeal (Bankes, Scrutton and Atkin LJJ)

Exclusion clause - sale of car

*Facts*

The plaintiff placed his car with the defendant dealer for sale on commission and the deposit note stated that 'customers' cars are driven by your staff at customers' sole risk'. While showing the car to a prospective purchaser, one of the defendant's drivers negligently caused the vehicle to collide with a lamp post.

*Held*

The defendant was effectively exempt from liability.

Scrutton LJ:

'The contract here is a contract by a garage proprietor to sell a car on commission. In order to bring about a purchase, a trial of the car may be necessary, and this involves the driving of the car by one of the servants of the garage proprietor. What is the liability of the latter in these circumstances? He is only liable for his own negligence, and for that of his servants. If an accident happens without any negligence on his part or on the part of his servants, he would not be liable; but if there has been negligence on his or his servants' part, which has caused the accident, he would be liable. That being so, this clause has been introduced into the contract, which he makes with his customer: "Customers' cars are driven by your staff at customers' sole risk". It seems to me that two obvious limitations must be put upon the meaning of these words. In the first place, "staff" must mean "staff of qualified drivers" - it does not include a typist or a charwoman - and, secondly, "driven" does not include joy-riding, but must mean driven for the purpose of the bailment, that is to say, for the purpose of selling the car. The clause cannot mean that the garage proprietor is to be exempt from liability if an accident happens while it is being taken out by a member of his clerical staff for pleasure. Thus limited, the clause, which is regularly inserted in all contracts by garage proprietors to sell customers' cars on commission and for that purpose to take them out for a trial run, can only have one meaning, and that is that the owner of the car must effect his own insurance against accidents due to the negligence of the garage proprietor's servants - that is to say, accidents for which without the clause the garage proprietor would be liable.

It was contended on behalf of the plaintiff that the clause was ambiguous and must, therefore, be construed strictly against the party relying upon it ... I can find no ambiguity in this clause.'

**Smith v Eric S Bush, Harris v Wyre Forest District Council** [1989] 2 WLR 790 House of Lords (Lord Keith of Kinkel, Lord Brandon of Oakbrook, Lord Templeman, Lord Griffiths and Lord Jauncey of Tullichettle)

Surveyor's report - disclaimer of liability

*Facts*

The cases were heard together: their facts were similar and they involved the same points of law. In *Smith* the plaintiff applied to the Abbey National Building Society to enable her to buy a terraced house in Norwich for £17,500. She paid an inspection fee and signed an application form which stated that a copy of the survey report and mortgage valuation obtained by the society would be given to her. The form also contained a disclaimer to the effect that neither the society nor its surveyor warranted that the report and valuation would be accurate and that the report and valuation would be supplied without any acceptance of responsibility. The society instructed the defendant surveyors: in due course the plaintiff received a copy of their report and it contained a disclaimer in similar terms. On the strength of the report, the plaintiff completed the purchase, but the defendants had failed to notice that chimney breasts had been removed and 18 months later the house flues collapsed, causing substantial damage. The plaintiff sued for negligence and the defendants, inter alia, relied on the disclaimer which the plaintiff admitted she had read.

*Held*

The plaintiff was entitled to succeed.  The defendants had owed her a duty of care, they had been in breach of that duty and in view of the Unfair Contract Terms Act 1977, they could not rely on the disclaimer.

Lord Templeman:

'It was submitted ... that the valuation ... obtained by the Abbey National was essential to enable them to fulfil their statutory duty imposed by the Building Societies Act 1962.  But in *Candler* v *Crane Christmas & Co* [1951] 1 All ER 426 the draft accounts were prepared for the company, which was compelled by statute to produce accounts.

In the present appeals ... the contractual duty of a valuer to value a house for the Abbey National did not prevent the valuer coming under a tortious duty to Mrs Smith, who was furnished with a report of the valuer and relied on the report.

In general, I am of the opinion that in the absence of a disclaimer of liability the valuer who values a house for the purpose of a mortgage, knowing that the mortgagee will rely and the mortgagor will probably rely on the valuation, knowing that the purchaser mortgagor has in effect paid for the valuation, is under a duty to exercise reasonable skill and care and that duty is owed to both parties to the mortgage for which the valuation is made.  Indeed, in both the appeals now under consideration the existence of such a dual duty is tacitly accepted and acknowledged because notices excluding liability for breach of the duty owed to the purchaser were drafted by the mortgagee and imposed on the purchaser.  In these circumstances it is necessary to consider the second question which arises in these appeals, namely whether the disclaimers of liability are notices which fall within the Unfair Contract Terms Act 1977 ...

Section 11(3) of the 1977 Act provides that, in considering whether it is fair and reasonable to allow reliance on a notice which excludes liability in tort, account must be taken of "all the circumstances obtaining when the liability arose or (but for the notice) would have arisen".  Section 13(1) of the Act prevents the exclusion of any right or remedy and (to that extent) s2 also prevents the exclusion of liability "by reference to ... notices which exclude ... the relevant obligation or duty".  ...  In my opinion both these provisions support the view that the 1977 Act requires that all exclusion notices which would in common law provide a defence to an action for negligence must satisfy the requirement of reasonableness.

The answer to the second question involved in these appeals is that the disclaimer of liability made by ... the Abbey National on behalf of the appellant surveyors in *Smith*'s case constitute notices which fall within the 1977 Act and must satisfy the requirement of reasonableness.

The third question is whether in relation to each exclusion clause it is, in the words of s11(3) of the 1977 Act:

"fair and reasonable to allow reliance on it, having regard to all the circumstances obtaining when the liability arose or (but for the notice) would have arisen." ...

Counsel for the surveyors ... urged on behalf of his clients in this appeal, and on behalf of valuers generally, that it is fair and reasonable for a valuer to rely on an exclusion clause, particularly an exclusion clause which is set forth so plainly in building society literature.  The principal reasons urged by counsel for the surveyors are as follows.  (1) The exclusion clause is clear and understandable and reiterated and is forcefully drawn to the attention of the purchaser.  (2) The purchaser's solicitors should reinforce the warning and should urge the purchaser to appreciate that he cannot rely on a mortgage valuation and should obtain and pay for his own survey.  (3) If valuers cannot disclaim liability they will be faced by more claims from purchasers, some of which will be unmeritorious but difficult and expensive to resist.  (4) A valuer will become more cautious, take more time and produce more gloomy reports, which will make house transactions more difficult. (5) If a duty of care cannot be disclaimed the cost of negligence insurance for valuers and therefore the cost of valuation fees to the public will be increased.

Counsel for the surveyors also submitted that there was no contract between a valuer and a purchaser and that, so far as the purchaser was concerned, the valuation was "gratuitous", and the valuer should not be forced to accept a liability he was unwilling to undertake. My Lords, all these submissions are, in my view, inconsistent with the ambit and thrust of the 1977 Act ...

It is open to Parliament to provide that members of all professions or members of one profession providing services in the normal course of the exercise of their profession for reward shall be entitled to exclude or limit their liability for failure to exercise reasonable skill and care. In the absence of any such provision valuers are not, in my opinion, entitled to rely on a general exclusion of the common law duty of care owed to purchasers of houses by valuers to exercise reasonable skill and care in valuing houses for mortgage purposes.'

Lord Griffiths:

'It must ... be remembered that this is a decision in respect of a dwelling house of modest value in which it is widely recognised by surveyors that purchasers are in fact relying on their care and skill. It will obviously be of general application in broadly similar circumstances. But I expressly reserve my position in respect of valuations of quite different types of property for mortgage purposes, such as industrial property, large blocks of flats or very expensive houses. In such cases it may well be that the general expectation of the behaviour of the purchaser is quite different. With very large sums of money at stake prudence would seem to demand that the purchaser obtain his own structural survey to guide him in his purchase and, in such circumstances with very much larger sums of money at stake, it may be reasonable for the surveyors valuing on behalf of those who are providing the finance either to exclude or limit their liability to the purchaser.'

**Smith v South Wales Switchgear Ltd** [1978] 1 WLR 165 House of Lords (Lord Wilberforce, Viscount Dilhorne, Lord Salmon, Lord Fraser of Tullybelton and Lord Keith of Kinkel

Conditions - indemnity

*Facts*

The respondents engaged the appellants to overhaul the electrical equipment in their factory, which contract was stated to be subject to the respondents' General Conditions. These conditions contained a clause purporting to make the appellants liable to indemnify the respondents against 'Any liability, loss, claim or proceedings whatsoever ... (i) in respect of personal injury to, or death of, any person whosoever ... (ii) in respect of any injury or damage whatsoever to any property, real or personal, arising out of or in the course of ... the execution of (the) order'. An employee of the appellants was seriously injured, due to the negligence of the respondents, who claimed against the appellant to be indemnified against his claim for damages.

*Held*

The clause did not, in its true construction, apply to the respondents' negligence.

Lord Fraser of Tullybelton:

'I come now to the question of construction. The indemnity clause is as follows:

"23 In the event of this order involving the carrying out of work by the Supplier and its sub-contractors on land and/or premises of the Purchaser, the Supplier will keep the Purchaser indemnified against: (a) all losses and costs incurred by reason of the Supplier's breach of any statute, bye-law or regulation. (b) Any liability, loss, claim or proceedings whatsoever under Statute or Common Law (i) in respect of personal injury to, or death of, any person whomsoever, (ii) in respect of any injury or damage whatsoever to any property, real or personal, arising out of or in the course of or caused by the execution of this order. The Supplier will insure against and cause all sub-contractors to insure against their liability hereunder, and will produce to the Purchaser on demand the policies of insurance with current renewal receipts therefor."

The principles which are applicable to clauses which purport to exempt one party to a contract from liability, were stated by Lord Greene MR in *Alderslade* v *Hendon Laundry Ltd* and were quoted with approval by Lord Morton of Henryton in the Privy Council in *Canada Steamship Lines Ltd* v *R* where he summarised them as follows:

"(i) If the clause contains language which expressly exempts the person in whose favour it is made (hereafter called 'the proferens') from the consequences of the negligence of his own servants, effect must be given to that provision ... (ii) if there is no express reference to negligence, the court must consider whether the words used are wide enough, in their ordinary meaning, to cover negligence on the part of the servants of the proferens. If a doubt arises at this point, it must be resolved against the proferens ... (iii) if the words used are wide enough for the above purpose, the court must then consider whether 'the head of damage may be based on some ground other than that of negligence', to quote again Lord Greene MR in the *Alderslade Case*. The 'other ground' must not be so fanciful or remote that the proferens cannot be supposed to have desired protection against it, but subject to this qualification, which is, no doubt, to be implied from Lord Greene's words, the existence of a possible head of damage other than that of negligence is fatal to the proferens even if the words used are, prima facie, wide enough to cover negligence on the part of his servants."

These rules were stated in relation to clauses of exemption, but they are, in my opinion, equally applicable to a clause of indemnity which in many cases, including *Canada Steamship Lines Ltd* v *R* is merely the obverse of the exemption. The statement has been accepted as authoritative in the law of Scotland: see *North of Scotland Hydro-Electric Board* v *D & R Taylor*, which was concerned with a clause of indemnity and it was accepted by both parties, rightly in my opinion, as being applicable to the present appeal.

The argument based on the first of Lord Morton of Henryton's tests can be disposed of quickly. Counsel for the respondents argued that paragraph (b) in the present indemnity clause contained language which "expressly" entitled the respondents to indemnity against the consequence of their own negligence and that the first test was satisfied. The argument was that the words "any liability, loss, claim or proceedings whatsoever", amounted to an express reference to such negligence because they covered any liability however caused. The argument was supported by reference to the opinions of Buckley and Orr LJJ in *Gillespie Brothers & Co Ltd* v *Roy Bowles Transport Ltd*, where great emphasis was placed on the word "whatsoever" occurring in an indemnity clause as showing that the indemnity was intended to apply to all claims and demands however caused, including claims for negligence. I agree with the decision in that case and with the statement by Buckley LJ that the clause was one "which cannot sensibly be construed as subject to an implied qualification", but I am unable to agree with Buckley LJ's conclusion that the clause contained "an agreement in express terms" to indemnify the proferens. I do not see how a clause can "expressly" exempt or indemnify the proferens against his negligence unless it contains the word "negligence" or some synonym for it and I think that is what Lord Morton of Henryton must have intended, as appears from the opening words of his second test ("If there is no express reference to negligence"). On this point I agree with the opinion of the Lord Justice Clerk (Lord Wheatley) in the present case and of Lord Maxwell in *Clark* v *Sir William Arrol & Co Ltd*. The word "whatsoever" occurs in paragraph (b) of clause 23 here, but, in my opinion, it is no more than a word of emphasis and it cannot be read as equivalent to an express reference to negligence. To hold that it could, would be to invest it with the same sort of magic property as the word "allenarly" used to have in relation to an alimentary literent in Scotland and there is no justification for that. In the present case. I am clearly of the opinion that there is no express provision that the respondents are to be indemnified against the results of their own negligence and that the Second Division were right in so holding.

I pass then to consider the second test. The words "Any liability ... whatsoever under ... Common Law ... in respect of personal injury" which occur near the beginning of clause 23(b), if read in isolation, are of course wide enough to cover liability arising from negligence of the respondents or their servants. But they cannot properly be read in isolation from their context in clause 23 and in the general conditions. I have reached the opinion that clause 23(b), read as a whole, does not apply to liability arising from negligence by the respondents or their servants. The general conditions are evidently intended to apply to many contracts where the respondents are "the Purchaser" and some other party is the supplier of goods or service to them. But clause 23 applies only "in the event of (the particular contract) involving the carrying out of work by the supplier *and* its sub-contractors on" the respondents' premises. (Counsel for the appellants accepted, rightly in my opinion, that the word "and" which I have italicised, must be read as if it were, or included, "or". Otherwise, in a case such as the present, where no sub-contractors were involved, the clause would not apply at all. That seems absurd.) The clause is thus looking to cases where the employees of the supplier will be working on the respondents' premises and it very naturally provides for an indemnity against the consequences of negligence by those employees while working there. But the employees of the respondents would not require to do any work in carrying out the contract and it seems unlikely that the parties intended that the respondents were to be indemnified by the appellants against liability as occupiers of the factory, especially as the indemnity is against claims in respect of injury to any person whomsoever and is not limited to servants of the suppliers or sub-contractors. Moreover, the indemnity is, in the final words of paragraph (b), in respect of injuries etc, "arising out of or in the course of or caused by the execution of this order" and the only parties who will be concerned in "execution" of the order are the appellants and any sub-contractors. "In the course of" must convey some connection with execution of the order beyond the merely temporal; and thus they appropriately apply to activities of the party who is carrying out work under the order.

The scope of the indemnity is defined in paragraphs (a) and (b) of clause 23. It was accepted by both parties in argument that paragraph (a) is concerned only with breaches of criminal law. That appears rather less clearly in the March 1970 version ("all losses and costs incurred by reason of the Suppliers' breach of any statute, bye-law or regulation") than in the original version ("all fines, penalties and loss incurred ...") but I think it is clear enough. Paragraph (b) is evidently concerned with civil liability. In contrast with paragraph (a) it is not expressly limited to liabilities incurred by reason of the acts or omissions of the supplier. So far as it goes, that contrast is in favour of the respondents, but it is not, in my opinion, enough to overcome the other indications that I have mentioned, which point in favour of the appellants.

Some further support for the appellants' argument is to be derived from the final part of clause 23 dealing with insurance. No doubt these provisions are obscure and the reference to sub-contractors insuring against "their liability hereunder" (which I read as meaning "under this clause") is inept, as no liability was imposed on sub-contractors under the clause, nor could it have been, as no sub-contractors were parties to the contract. But it evidently contemplates both suppliers and sub-contractors, if any, having liabilities under paragraph (b) of the clause; these must, I think, be separate liabilities arising from the respective acts or omissions. Otherwise the effect of the insurance provisions would be to require double (or multiple) insurance by suppliers and (apparently all) sub-contractors against liability arising from acts or omissions of any part, including the respondents; it seems to me most unlikely that that can have been intended.

For these reasons, the construction of clause 23 goes, in my opinion, further than raising a doubt to be resolved against the respondents as the proferens under the second test and leads to a positive conclusion adverse to them. That is enough for the decision of the appeal, but if it were necessary to go on to consider the third test, I would hold that the head of damage under liability at common law for personal injury, may be based on some ground other than the respondents' own negligence. The possibility of common law liability falling on the respondents, as occupiers of the premises, through the fault of the suppliers' servants, is, in my opinion, not fanciful or remote. Nor is the possibility of claims for nuisance or for breach of contract caused by defective work by the suppliers. No doubt the respondents would have a right of relief against the supplier in most, if not all, of these cases, but that is not a sufficient answer, as they might well prefer to rely on the protection of an express right of indemnity rather than on their right to raise an action of relief with all its inevitable hazards. See *North of Scotland Hydro Electric Board* v *D & R Taylor* per the Lord Justice Clerk (Thomson) and Lord Patrick.'

**Spurling (J) Ltd v Bradshaw** [1956] 1 WLR 461 Court of Appeal (Denning, Morris and Parker LJJ)

Exemption clause - loss howsoever caused

*Facts*

The defendant bought eight barrels of orange juice and sent them to the plaintiff warehousemen to be stored. The plaintiffs sent a 'landing account' acknowledging receipt and stating: 'The company's conditions as printed on the back hereof cover the goods ...' Those conditions included: 'We will not in any circumstances ... be liable for any loss ... howsoever ... occasioned ... even when such loss ... may have been occasioned by the negligence ... of ourselves or our servants or agents ...' On the same day the plaintiffs sent an invoice for storage fees and there appeared on the invoice: 'All goods are handled ... in accordance with the conditions as over and warehoused at owner's risk ...': there were no conditions 'as over'. When eventually released by the plaintiffs, the juice was in bad condition. At the trial, the defendant conceded that he had received many landing accounts from the plaintiffs in respect of other goods but he said that he had never read the conditions on the back of them.

*Held*

The conditions formed part of the contract as the defendant had sufficient notice of them and the plaintiffs were protected by the exempting clause.

Denning LJ:

'Another thing to remember about these exempting clauses is that in the ordinary way the burden is on the bailee to bring himself within the exception. A bailor, by pleading and presenting his case properly, can always put the burden of proof on the bailee. In the case of non-delivery, for instance, all he need plead is the contract and a failure to deliver on demand. That puts on the bailee the burden of proving either loss without his fault (which would be a complete answer at common law) or, if the the loss was due to his fault, that it was a fault from which he is excluded by the exempting clause ... I do not think that the Court of Appeal in *Alderslade* v *Hendon Laundry Ltd* ... had the burden of proof in mind at all. Likewise, with goods that are returned by the bailee in a damaged condition, the burden is on him to show that the damage was done without his fault: or that, if fault there was, it was excused by the exempting clause. Nothing else will suffice. Where, however, the only charge made in the pleadings - or the only reasonable inference on the facts - is that the damage was due to negligence and nothing more, then the bailee can rely on the exempting clause without more ado. That was, I think, the case here. As I read the pleadings, and the way in which the case was put to the judge, the defendant was complaining of negligence and nothing more. The clause therefore avails to exempt the plaintiffs provided that it was part of the contract.

This brings me to the question whether this clause was part of the contract. Counsel for the defendant urged us to hold that the plaintiffs did not do what was reasonably sufficient to give notice of the conditions within *Parker* v *South Eastern Ry Co*. I agree that the more unreasonable a clause is, the greater the notice which must be given of it. Some clauses which I have seen would need to be printed in red ink on the face of the document with a red hand pointing to it before the notice could be held to be sufficient. The clause in this case, however, in my judgment, does not call for such exceptional treatment, especially when it is construed, as it should be, subject to the proviso that it only applies when the warehouseman is carrying out his contract and not when he is deviating from it or breaking it in a radical respect. So construed, the judge was, I think, entitled to find that

165

sufficient notice was given. It is to be noticed that the landing account on its face told the defendant that the goods would be insured if he gave instructions; otherwise they were not insured. The invoice, on its face, told him they were warehoused "at owner's risk". The printed conditions, when read subject to the proviso which I have mentioned, added little or nothing to those explicit statements taken together. Next it was said that the landing account and invoice were issued after the goods had been received and could not therefore be part of the contract of bailment: but the defendant admitted that he had received many landing accounts before. True he had not troubled to read them. On receiving this account, he took no objection to it, left the goods there, and went on paying the warehouse rent for months afterwards. It seems to me that by the course of business and conduct of the parties, these conditions were part of the contract.

In these circumstances, the plaintiffs were entitled to rely on this exempting condition.'

**Suisse Atlantique Société d'Armement Maritime SA v NV Rotterdamsche Kolen Centrale** [1966] 2 WLR 944 House of Lords (Viscount Dilhorne, Lord Reid, Lord Hodson, Lord Upjohn and Lord Wilberforce)

Exception clause - fundamental breach

*Facts* - they appear in the following judgment:

Lord Upjohn:

'My Lords, in this appeal, your Lordships are concerned with the rights and obligations of the contracting parties to a consecutive voyage charter party dated December 21 1956 made between the appellants, owners of this ship, and the respondents, the charterers. It provided for the carriage of coal for two years' consecutive voyages, terminating in March 1959, between Hampton Road, Baltimore to Philadelphia on one side of the Atlantic and one safe port, Belgium, Holland or Germany, on the other side, returning in ballast to the USA for a further cargo. Clause 3 of the charter party provided for loading at an agreed rate with a widely drawn provision excluding from loading time (or lay days as they are usually called) time lost from a variety of events and causes immaterial to the matters in issue before your Lordships. The clause provided: "If longer detained, charterer to pay $1,000 US currency per running day (or pro rata for part thereof) demurrage." There was a similar provision for demurrage if the time for the agreed rate of discharge was exceeded.

Whether because of the fall in freight rates after the re-opening of the Suez Canal in April of 1957 or for some other reason, the ship greatly exceeded the permitted lay time in port and your Lordships were told that at one time the owners sailed the ship away, treating the contract as repudiated by the charterers and accepting that repudiation. This led to an arbitration between the parties, not yet determined and without prejudice to that arbitration, the parties, on October 8 1957, agreed to perform the charter party for the remainder of the stipulated term. Thereafter, save for the first voyage, the ship always greatly exceeded the lay days in port, both loading and unloading and, in fact, during the term of the charter party the ship performed only eight voyages. The charterers do not dispute their liability to pay demurrage for these lost days, which amounts to the substantial sum of approximately $150,000. The owners, however, allege that but for the days lost in port, the ship could have performed some six to nine additional profitable voyages during that time and upon that footing they claim large additional damages for loss of profit which the ship could have earned by reason of these additional voyages.

This dispute was referred to arbitration and has reached this House upon a consultative case by the arbitrators.

When the matter first came before your Lordships, it was opened, as in the courts below, upon the footing that though the delays (beyond the lay days) in port were considerable, such delays did not amount to repudiatory conduct on the part of the charterers.

It is not in doubt that every time the charterers exceeded the lay days in port they committed a breach of contract; a breach, however, for which the parties have agreed damages at the rate of $1,000 a day. But the owners argue that as this is not a single voyage charter but one contract for the performance of a number of consecutive voyages, damages are not to be determined solely by the length of the detention of the ship in excess of the lay days in port, as it was admitted that they would have been in a single voyage charter, but that there was a further obligation upon the charterers to load and discharge within the lay time provided by the charter party so that the ship might perform such a number of consecutive voyages, each of a duration not exceeding the sea passage plus the permitted lay times in port, as provided to be capable of performance within the term of the charter. In other words, in a consecutive voyage charter there is a larger obligation upon the charterers to load and discharge the cargo within the lay days so that the owners may benefit from the profitable employment of their ship contemplated by the charter party for the period of the charter. This obligation was said to arise either as a matter of construction of the charter party regarded as a whole, or from an implied term that the charterers would co-operate or concur in doing all things necessary to enable the owners to perform the maximum possible amount of freight which could, in the ordinary course of events, be performed or earned during the term of the charter.

My Lords, the charter party, in my opinion, does not bear this construction. It is clear that the charterers have broken no express clause of the charter party, except the provision for detention in the port of loading or discharge in excess of the lay days. The voyages have been in fact consecutive and I, for my part, can find nothing in the contract which imposed upon the charterers as a matter of construction or as a matter of necessary implication, an obligation to undertake any additional requirement of loading within the lay days for breach of which they will be liable in damages beyond the rate of demurrage specified in the contract for exceeding those days. As both Mocatta J and the Court of Appeal held, there was only one breach by the charter party, namely a breach of the obligation to load and discharge at an agreed rate and the detention of the ship in a port beyond that date was a breach of contract for which the parties had agreed damages ...

At the conclusion of his main argument, counsel for the owners endeavoured to take a new point not raised in the courts below, namely that the charterers had committed a fundamental breach of the contract which amounted to a repudiation and, upon that footing, it was urged that the owners were entitled to general damages for lack of profitability and were not confined to demurrage.

Your Lordships, in the special circumstances of this case, permitted this appeal to be reargued de nova after supplemental cases have been lodged by each side. The owner's basic argument on this new case is that after the first voyage, there were such delays beyond the lay days each time that the ship entered port for loading or discharge, that the delays, each admittedly a breach of the charter party, amounted cumulatively to a repudiation of the contract which entitled the respondents, at their option, to accept and to treat the contract as at an end and sail away. This appeal comes before your Lordships on a consultative case by the arbitrators and the relevant facts have not yet been found on this point, so for the purposes of this point, it is necessary to make the double assumption in favour of the owners, first that it is open to the arbitrators on the facts to find that there has been a breach of contract by the charterers which goes to its root and entitled the owners to treat the contract as at an end and secondly, that in fact they will so find ... for the purpose solely of dealing with the argument, I am prepared to make the assumptions desired by the owners.

But what seems to be quite clear, making these assumptions, is that there has been no acceptance by the owners of the repudiation which brought the contract to an end. On the contrary, it seems to me clear that, by their conduct, the owners expressly affirmed the contract. The relevant facts were known at all material times to them, for they must have been currently aware of the excessive delays in port; they had already sailed away once - I say nothing about that for it is still sub judice - but it was for the owners, knowing of the delays, to make up their minds whether to sail away again. They did not do so and with full knowledge of the facts, elected to treat the contract as on foot until the expiry of the charter party by effluxion of time. It is this feature which gives rise to the whole difficulty in this interesting case. For it is common ground that had the owners accepted the assumed repudiation and sailed away, thereby terminating the contract, none of its terms survived and damages for breach of contract would have been at large, including damages for loss of profitable employment of the ship for the term of the charter party.

In general it cannot be disputed that where a party, having an option to treat a contract at an end nevertheless affirms it, that contract and all its terms must remain in full force and effect for the benefit of both parties during the remainder of the period of performance, for it is not possible even for the innocent party to make a new contract between the parties without the concurrence of the other ... Now it is, in my opinion, quite clear that as a matter of construction of the charter party, the demurrage clause both as to loading and discharging is expressed without limitation of time and therefore applies throughout the term of the contract ... Therefore, to succeed in this appeal, the owner must displace the demurrage clause. He seeks to do in reliance on the well known doctrine that in certain circumstances a party to a contract cannot rely on an exception or limitation clause inserted solely for his benefit. But before examining this doctrine, the first question which logically must be asked is, surely, whether this demurrage clause is a clause of exception or limitation. Whatever the ultimate ambit of the doctrine may be found to be, it is, in my opinion, confined to clauses which are truly inserted for the purpose only of protecting one contracting party from the legal consequences of other express terms of the contract, or from terms which would otherwise be implied by law, or from the terms of the contract regarded as a whole; just as one party may waive a clause which is inserted solely for his benefit ... so per contra there are occasions when a party cannot be permitted to rely on such a clause. But if the clause is inserted for the benefit of both, I know of no authority - and none has been cited - which entitles one party unilaterally to disregard its provisions. In my opinion, the demurrage with which we are concerned is a clause providing for agreed damages and is different from a clause excluding or limiting liability for damages by breach of contract by one party. An agreed damages clause is for the benefit of both; the party establishing breach by the other need prove no damage in fact; the other must pay that, no less but no more. But where liability for damages is limited by a clause, then the person seeking to claim damages must prove them at least up to the limit laid down by the clause; the other party, whatever may be the damage in fact, can refuse to pay more if he can rely on the clause. As Greer J said in relation to a demurrage clause in *Aktieselskabet Reidar* v *Arcos Ltd* [1926] 2 KB 83, 86: "this clause was put in for my benefit as well as yours; it measures the damages I have to pay ... " Counsel for the owners sought to say that the agreed damages of $1,000 a day were much too low to be an estimate of damage and that it might be open to the arbitrators to hold that in truth this was in the nature of a penalty clause or a limitation clause, limiting liability. I do not think it is open now to the owners to make this submission. It is quite clear on the authorities that the parties need not agree on a true estimate of damage. They are perfectly entitled to agree on a low rate. See *Cellulose Acetate Silk Co Ltd* v *Widnes Foundry (1926) Ltd* [1933] AC 20.

Accordingly, in my opinion, the demurrage clause is a clause which, the contract being affirmed, remains an agreed damages clause for the benefit of both parties and it is not a clause of exception or limitation inserted for the benefit of one party only to which the doctrine under consideration can properly be applied. That is sufficient to dispose of this appeal.

But in view of the arguments that have been addressed to your Lordships, I think it is right that I should express my views thereon upon the footing that the demurrage clause in this case is, indeed, a clause of exception or limitation of liability inserted solely for the benefit of the charterer and that it is therefore a clause to which, in certain circumstances, the doctrine relied upon by the appellants applies. That the doctrine exists is not in doubt, but it is necessary to examine the authorities to understand the principle upon which it is based.

There was much discussion during the argument upon the phrases "fundamental breach" and "breach of a fundamental term" and I think it is true that in some of the cases these terms have been used interchangeably; but in fact they are quite different. I believe that all your Lordships are agreed and, indeed, it has not seriously been disputed before us that there is no magic in the words "fundamental breach"; this expression is no more than a convenient shorthand expression for saying that a particular breach or breaches of contract by one party is or are such as to go to the root of the contract, which entitles the other party to treat such breach or breaches as a repudiation of the whole contract. Whether such breach or breaches do constitute a fundamental breach depends on the construction of the contract and on all the facts and circumstances of the case. The innocent party may accept that breach or those breaches as a repudiation and treat the whole contract as at an end and sue for damages generally, or he may, at his option, prefer to affirm the contract and treat it as continuing on foot, in which case he can sue only for damages for breach or breaches of the particular stipulations in the contract which has or have been broken.

But the expression "fundamental term" has a different meaning.

A fundamental term of a contract is a stipulation which the parties have agreed either expressly or by necessary implication, or which the general law regards as a condition which goes to the root of the contract, so that any breach of that term may at once, and without further reference to the facts and circumstances, be regarded by the innocent party as a fundamental breach and this is conferred on him by the alternative remedies at his option that I have just mentioned ...

... the law is now quite clearly established that unless the parties otherwise agree, the usual and customary course on any voyage described in a charter party is a fundamental term and therefore *any* breach of it (however, for practical purposes, irrelevant) is a fundamental breach ...

... the necessary result, in my opinion, is that the principle upon which one party to a contract cannot rely on the clause of exception or limitation of liability inserted for his sole protection, is not because they are regarded as subject to any special rule of law applicable to such clauses as being in general opposed to the policy of the law for some other reason but ... it is the consequence of the application of the ordinary rules applicable to all contracts that if there is a fundamental breach accepted by the innocent party, the contract is at an end; the guilty party cannot rely on any special terms in the contract. If not so accepted, the clauses of exception or limitation remain in force like all the other clauses of the contract ...

... as, in my opinion, the owners have expressly affirmed the contract, they cannot escape the consequences of the demurrage clause unless, as a matter of construction of that clause, they can show that it has no application to the events of this clause; this they cannot do for the reasons I have already given. Accordingly upon the footing that the demurrage clause is a clause of exclusion or limitation, this does not avail the owners in this case.

But, my Lords, again having regard to the arguments addressed to your Lordships, I think I ought to make one or two observations upon the question of construction of exclusion or limitation clauses.

It cannot be doubted that even while the contract continues in force (that is, there has been no fundamental breach, but only some lesser breach), exclusion clauses are strictly construed. Why this should be so is largely a matter of history and I think probably stems from the fact that in so many cases exception clauses are to be found in rather small print, sometimes on the back of the main terms of the contract and that the doctrine of "contra proferentes" has been applied. But whatever the reason, that they are strictly construed against the contracting party seeking protection, even during the currency of the contract, cannot be doubted ...

But where there is a breach of a fundamental term, the law has taken an even firmer line, for there is a strong, though rebuttable, presumption that in inserting a clause of exclusion or limitation in their contract, the parties are not contemplating breaches of fundamental terms and such clauses do not apply to relieve a party from the consequences of such a breach even where the contract continues in force. This result has been achieved by a robust use of a well known canon of construction that wide words which, taken in isolation, would bear one meaning must be so construed as to give business efficacy to the contract and the presumed intention of the parties upon the footing that both parties are intending to carry out the contract fundamentally ...

My Lords, in view of the introduction in the questions posed by the arbitrator of the impact of a presumed wilful default, for my part, I think it is only necessary to say that it seems to me as a matter of general principle that wilful default in connection with the matter we are now considering is relevant and relevant only to one matter, that is to say whether, in fact, the owners can establish a fundamental breach. In cases such as this, where there has been no breach of any fundamental term, the question as to whether there has been a fundamental breach must be a question of fact and degree in all the circumstances of the case, but one of the elements in reaching a conclusion upon that matter is necessarily the question as to whether there has been a wilful breach, for as a practical matter it cannot be doubted that it is easier to find as a fact, for such it primarily is, that the charterers are evincing an intention no longer to be bound by the terms of the contract and are therefore guilty of repudiatory conduct if it can be established that the breaches have been wilful and not innocent. I say no more than that. My Lords, I would dismiss this appeal.'

*Commentary*

Applied in *Photo Productions Ltd* v *Securicor Transport Ltd* [1980] 2 WLR 283.

**Thompson v T Lohan (Plant Hire) Ltd** [1987] 1 WLR 649 Court of Appeal (Fox, Dillon and Woolf LJJ)

Exclusion clause - unfair term?

*Facts*

The second defendants (hirers) hired an excavator with a driver from the first defendants. Clause 8 of the contract of hire provided that the driver then became the agent of the hirer who was totally responsible for all their acts. Whilst performing his duties negligently the driver killed the plaintiff's husband, who was an employee of the first defendants. The plaintiff recovered damages against the first defendants [the driver's employers]. The first defendants sought to recoup the money they had paid out from the second defendants. The second defendants argued that Clause 8 of the contract was contrary to s2(1) of the Unfair Contract Terms Act 1977 and thus invalid.

*Held*

This argument could not succeed.

Fox LJ:

'I come now to the final question, which concerns the operation of s2(1) of the Unfair Contract Terms Act 1977. Section 2 provides:

"(1) A person cannot by reference to any contract term or to a notice given to persons generally or to particular persons exclude or restrict his liability for death or personal injury resulting from negligence. (2) In the case of other loss or damage, a person cannot so exclude or restrict his liability for negligence except in so far as the term or notice satisfies the requirement of reasonableness."

I should also refer to s4(1):

"A person dealing as consumer cannot by reference to any contract term be made to idemnify another person (whether a party to the contract or not) in respect of liability that may be incurred by the other for negligence or breach of contract, except in so far as the contract term satisfies the requirement of reasonableness."

It is said on behalf of the third party that, assuming clause 8 to be otherwise valid and effective according to its tenor (as I have found), it operates to exclude or restrict a liability for death or personal injury resulting from negligence; and that therefore it offends in this case the provisions of s2(1) of the Act and is struck down.

We were referred to the decision of this court in *Phillips Product Ltd* v *Hyland (Note)* [1987] 1 WLR 659. The case is concerned with the construction of the Act of 1977. So far as material the facts were these. In 1980 Phillips, who were steel stockholders, were carrying out extensions to their factory. They arranged with a builder, Mr Pritchard, that he should do the building work but they themselves were to be responsible for buying materials and arranging for the provision of plant, so far as necessary. However, they gave Mr Pritchard permission to place an order with the defendants, Hamstead (Plant Hire) Co Ltd, for the hiring of a JCB excavator. Mr Pritchard made arrangements on the telephone for the hire of a JCB excavator with a driver. The first defendant, Mr Hyland, arrived at Phillip's premises with a JCB machine, of which he was the driver.

Kenneth Jones J found Mr Hyland had made it perfectly plain to Mr Pritchard that he would brook no interference in the way in which he operated the JCB. However, during the course of his operating the JCB excavator, Mr Hyland collided with a part of Phillips's building, doing a good deal of damage to it. In consequence, Phillips issued a writ against Mr Hyland and Hamstead, and claimed damages against both defendants. It was conceded on behalf of the defendants that Mr Hyland had driven the JCB excavator without reasonable care and that the cost of making good the damage was £3,000. Accordingly, the judge gave judgment for Phillips against him in that sum.

At the trial the argument centred on the liability or otherwise of Hamstead in tort. It was conceded on their behalf that, apart from any special terms in the contract of hire, they were liable for the negligence of Mr Hyland as their employee so as to entitle Phillips to judgment against them for such sum as was awarded against Mr Hyland. However, it was contended on behalf of Hamstead that clause 8 of the terms of hire which, for all practical purposes are the same as clause 8 in the general terms and conditions in the present appeal, gave a complete defence to the claim. In giving the judgment of the Court of Appeal, Slade LJ said, post, p 665(g)-(h).

"Certainly there is nothing which leads to the conclusion that a plant owner who uses the general conditions is not excluding his liability for negligence in the relevant sense by reference to the contract term clause 8. We are unable to accept that in the ordinary sensible meaning of words in the context of s2 and the Act as a whole, the provisions of clause 8 do not fall within the scope of s2(2). A transfer of liability from A to B necessarily and inevitably involves the exclusion of liability so far as A is concerned."

It was held that, in the circumstances, of that case, clause 8 could not operate, having regard to the provisions of s2(2), to give an indemnity as claimed.

Mr Samuels, for the third party, says that is the same in this case, and that the words from the judgment of Slade LJ to which I have referred exactly cover the position here. It is said that there is a transfer of liability from Lohan to the third party, and that that is exactly what s2(1) of the Act of 1977 is effective to prevent. In my view the comparison of this case with the *Phillips* case is not justified. It seems to me that the *Phillips* case was a quite different case, and the Court of Appeal was not addressing its mind to the problem which we have to determine in the present case.

In the *Phillips* case there was a tortfeasor, Hamstead, who were vicariously liable to Phillips for the damage done by their servant, Hyland. Thus Hamstead were liable to Phillips for negligence, but were seeking to exclude that liability by relying upon clause 8. If that reliance had been successful, the result in the *Phillips* case would be that the victim would be left with no remedy by virtue of the operation of clause 8. Prima facie the victim was entitled to damages for negligence against Hamstead, because Hamstead were vicariously liable in negligence for the acts of their own servant. So one starts from that point. There was a plain liability of Hamstead to Phillips. That was, as Slade LJ said, a case of a plant owner excluding his liability for negligence in the relevant sense by reference to the contract term, clause 8. I should mention that the *Phillips* case turned upon s2(2) of the Act, but that is of no consequence in the present case.

If one then turns to the present case, the sharp distinction between it and the *Phillips* case is this, that whereas in the *Phillips* case there was a liability in negligence of Hamstead to Phillips (and that was sought to be excluded), in the present case there is no exclusion or restriction of the liability sought to be achieved by reliance upon the provisions of clause 8. The plaintiff has her judgment against Lohan and can enforce it. The plaintiff is not prejudiced in any way by the operation sought

171

to be established of clause 8. All that has happened is that Lohan and the third party have agreed between themselves who is to bear the consequences of Mr Hill's negligent acts. I can see nothing in s2(1) of the Act of 1977 to prevent that. In my opinion, s2(1) is concerned with protecting the victim of negligence and, of course, those who claim under him. It is not concerned with arrangements made by the wrongdoer with other persons as to the sharing or bearing of the burden of compensating the victim. In such a case it seems to me there is no exclusion or restriction of the liability at all. The liability has been established by Hodgson J. It is not in dispute and is now unalterable. The circumstance that the defendants have between themselves chosen to bear the liability in a particular way does not affect that liability; it does not exclude it, and it does not restrict it. The liability to the plaintiff is the only relevant liability in the case, as it seems to me, and that liability is still in existence and will continue until discharge by payment to the plaintiff. Nothing is excluded in relation to the liability, and the liability is not restricted in any way whatever. The liability of Lohan to the plaintiff remains intact. The liability of Hamstead to Phillips was sought to be excluded.

In those circumstances it seems to me that, looking at the language of s2(1), this case does not fall within its prohibition. I reach that conclusion on the language of s2 itself, and without reference to s4, to which I have referred and on which Mr Judge, for Lohan, relied. I do not find it necessary to consider it further, having regard to the conclusion which I have reached upon the language of s2 itself.

For the reasons which I have given, it seems to me that the judge came to the correct conclusion in this case, and I would therefore dismiss this appeal.'

## Thompson v London, Midland and Scottish Railway Co

See chapter 1 - Offer and acceptance.

## Thornton v Shoe Lane Parking Ltd

See chapter 1 - Offer and acceptance.

## Tudor Grange Holdings Ltd v Citibank NA [1991] 4 All ER 1; [1991] TLR 217 Chancery Division (Brown-Wilkinson VC)

Contractual exclusion clauses - previous settlements

*Facts*

At a hearing in chambers the defendant bank and others applied to have an action by the plaintiff company struck out. Judgment was given in open court.

By a deed of release, dated March 1989, the plaintiffs purported to release Citibank and its associates from 'all claims, demands and causes of action prior to the date hereof'.

The question arose as to whether this release was, under s10 of Unfair Contract Terms Act 1977, reasonable. The argument lay that it was not, and since it failed to satisfy the test of reasonableness it could not be binding.

*Held*

Section 10 was held not to be intended to cover the present situation; it did not cover settlements and compromises on events that had already occurred. In the view of the court the Act was aimed solely at exemption clauses, clauses modifying future liability - it was not concerned with retrospective claims or settlements. The claim by the plaintiffs was accordingly struck out and the release which they had agreed remained binding on them.

# 7 INCAPACITY

**Ashbury Railway Carriage & Iron Co v Riche** (1875) LR 7 HL 653 House of Lords (Lord Cairns LC, Lord Chelmsford, Lord Hatherley, Lord O'Hagan and Lord Selborne)

Company - contract ultra vires

*Facts*

The company's objects set out in its Memorandum of Association enabled it to manufacture, sell and hire railway plant, fittings and rolling stock. The company contracted to finance the construction of a railway, but repudiated and was sued.

*Held*

The contract was ultra vires and the company was not liable thereon because it was outside the scope of the objects clause.

Lord Cairns LC:

' ... the question is as to the competency and power of the company to make the contract. Now I am clearly of the opinion that this contract was entirely, as I have said, beyond the objects of the memorandum of the association. If so, it was thereby placed beyond the powers of the company to make the contract. If so, it is not a question whether the contract ever was ratified or was not ratified. It was a contract void at its beginning, it was void because the company could not make the contract.'

*Commentary*

As to the present ultra vires rule, see ss35, 35A and 35B of the Companies Act 1985 as substituted by s108 of the Companies Act 1989 from a date yet to be fixed.


**Chaplin v Leslie Frewin (Publishers) Ltd** [1966] 2 WLR 40 Court of Appeal (Lord Denning MR, Danckwerts and Winn LJJ)

Minor - publication of memoirs

*Facts*

An infant contracted to give the defendant publishing company rights to publish his memoirs.

*Held*

This was a contract which could bind the infant if it were substantially for his benefit which (Lord Denning MR dissenting) on the facts it was.


**Clements v London and North Western Railway Co** [1894] 2 QB 482 (Lord Esher, Kay and A L Smith LJJ)

Minor - insurance scheme

*Facts*

An infant, on entering the service of the defendant railway company, agreed to join the company's insurance scheme, thereby giving up any claim for personal injury he may have had under the relevant statute, the Employers' Liability Act 1880. The scheme was, in some ways, more favourable than his entitlements under the Act, but in other ways less beneficial.

*Held*

As the contract was, on the whole, beneficial to the infant, he was bound by it.

*Commentary*

Applied in *Roberts* v *Gray* [1913] 1 KB 520.

**Cowern v Nield** [1912] 2 KB 419 High Court (Phillimore and Bray JJ)

Minor - trading contract

*Facts*

The defendant minor set up business dealing in hay and clover and the plaintiff agreed to buy some from him.

*Held*

The contract could not be enforced.

Bray J:

'The learned county court judge found that this contract was for the infant's benefit, and having found that fact he ruled, as a matter of law, that the action was maintainable against the infant. In my opinion he was wrong in so holding. It is true that there are certain contracts which, if it is proved that they are for the benefit of the infant, can be enforced against the infant ... Now, whatever the exceptions to the rule that an infant cannot make a binding contract may be, I am satisfied that there is no exception applicable to an ordinary trading contract. It was suggested to us that a man had got to learn a trade, and the question was asked why he should not begin to learn it when he was an infant. If that were so, every infant might trade, and would be responsible for every contract made for his benefit. There is no case in the books in which an infant has been held liable upon such a contract.'

**De Francesco v Barnum** (1890) 45 Ch D 430 High Court (Fry LJ)

Minor - dancing apprenticeship

*Facts*

By deed a minor was apprenticed to the plaintiff for seven years to be instructed in stage dancing. Under the deed, inter alia, the minor would not marry during that time and her services would be entirely at the plaintiff's disposal: no provision was made for remuneration, except during an engagement, or for clothes, lodging or food, except when working abroad. The deed also provided that the plaintiff could terminate the apprenticeship at any time. The minor accepted an engagement in breach of the deed and the plaintiff sought, inter alia, an injunction.

*Held*

His action would fail.

Fry LJ:

'I approach this subject with the observation that it appears to me the question is: Is the contract for the benefit of the infant? Not, Is any one particular stipulation for the benefit of the infant? Because it is obvious that the contract of apprenticeship or the contract of labour must, like any other contract, contain some stipulations for the benefit of the one contracting party, and some for the benefit of the other. It is not because you can lay your hand on a particular stipulation which you may say is against the infant's benefit that therefore the whole contract is not for the benefit of the infant. The court must look at the whole contract, having regard to the circumstances of the case, and determine subject to any principles of law which may be ascertained by the cases, whether the contract is or is not beneficial. That appears to me to be in substance a question of fact ... We have, ... to put it shortly, the contract under which the infant is placed, I might almost say, absolutely at the disposal of the teacher. The child may be required to undertake any engagements at any theatre in England, or any theatre in the United Kingdom, or anywhere else in the world. The child is to receive no remuneration, no maintenance except when employed, there is no correlative obligation on Signor de Francesco to find employment for the child, there is power in him to put an end to a child's chances who is under his care at any time during the term or any part of the term.

Those are stipulations of an extraordinary and an unusual character which throw, or appear to throw, an inordinate power into the hands of the master without any correlative obligation on his part. I cannot, therefore, say that on the face of this instrument it appears to be one which the court ought to hold for the benefit of the infant ... It may be that evidence could be tendered which would show me that no other form of contract is available, that the same contract prevails in every school, and that no person can hope to enter the profession of a ballet dancer except by an apprenticeship in these terms. That may be so. But no evidence of the sort has been tendered before me. I have undoubtedly this in favour of upholding it, that the school of the plaintiff is said ... to be a very excellent school, and for anything I know it may be the best in London, and I have already said Signor de Francesco is a person who is well able to and does protect the interests of the girls who are under his care on their tours and so on. At the same time this, it seems to me, does place in his hands an inordinate power which, except under the pressure of some evidence which has not been given, I cannot help being of opinion is not for the infant's benefit.

I hold, therefore, this instrument is one by which the [infant is] not bound ...'

## Denmark Productions Ltd v Boscobel Productions Ltd [1968] 3 WLR 841 Court of Appeal (Harman, Salmon and Winn LJJ)

Minors - enforceability of agreement

*Facts*

When they were just under twenty-one, the four members of the pop group 'The Kinks', who up to that time had not been particularly successful, entered into a management agreement.

*Held*

The trial judge rejected the contention that the agreement was unenforceable because of their infancy and they did not appeal against that aspect of his decision.

## Doyle v White City Stadium Ltd (1935) 1 KB 110 Court of Appeal (Lord Hanworth MR, Romer and Slesser LJJ)

Minor - boxing contract

*Facts*

An infant professional boxer made a contract to fight for £3,000, win, lose or draw. Under the terms of the contract, the fight was subject to the rules of the British Boxing Board of Control. The rules contained a provision that a boxer who was disqualified forfeited his prize money. The infant was disqualified for hitting below the belt and sued for his £3,000.

*Held*

The rules were, on the whole, for the infant's benefit (they encouraged clean fighting) and, accordingly, he was bound by them. His claim for the £3,000 must fail.

Slessor LJ:

'But in substance, two arguments have been used in this case to support the view that ... the plaintiff is entitled himself to have it paid over to him by the promoters. The first of those arguments rests upon the fact that he is an infant. It is said that any contract or alleged contract he has entered into under these rules is not binding on him on account of his infancy. If that contention is right, it is an answer to the defendant's claim to keep the money ... It is an argument which ... does not find favour with me. It depends really on two separate considerations - first whether this agreement is of the order of agreement under which an infant can properly bind himself and, secondly, if it does come within that order, whether this particular agreement can be stated to be so for the benefit of the infant as to be binding on him.

I would like to associate myself with what has been said by Kay LJ in *Clements* v *London and North Western Railway Co* to the effect that it is doubtful whether there is a general principle, that if an agreement be for the benefit of the infant it shall bind him ... I am not prepared here to say that there is any general principle that all agreements for the benefit of an infant will necessarily bind him ... In all those circumstances, I think that without laying down any general principles and looking at the facts of this case ... the learned judge was right when he said that he could find in *Clements* v *London and North Western Railway Co* ample authority for saying that this contract was so associated with the Class of contract of service which an infant may make so as to be binding on him, that it was binding upon him.

There remains the question, was it for his benefit? ... there are many dicta to the effect that where a contract imposes a penalty or a forfeiture that is not good as against the infant. But I, on the other hand, have been impressed with the consideration which has been pointed out in several cases that an infant cannot make a contract of service without having in it some incidents which may not, in themselves, be directly beneficial to him, but may be beneficial to the master. In *Wood* v *Fenwick* (1842) 10 M&W 195, the headnote says:

"A contract of hiring and services for wages, is a contract beneficial to and binding upon an infant, though it contain clauses for referring disputes to arbitration and for the imposition of forfeitures in case of neglect of duty, to be deducted from the wages."

In contracts of apprenticeship, which are admittedly contracts binding upon an infant, the right of the master to proceed, not only financially but, in the old days, corporeally against the infant, have not made the contract of apprenticeship invalid as against the infant. Therefore I agree that this contract is for the benefit of the infant and is one binding on him.'

**Edwards v Carter** [1893] AC 360 House of Lords (Lord Herschell LC, Lord Watson, Lord Halsbury, Lord Macnaghten, Lord Morris and Lord Shand)

Minor - covenant in marriage settlement

*Facts*

An infant covenanted by a marriage settlement dated 16 October 1883, to settle after acquired property. The infant attained majority in November 1883 and, in 1887, became entitled under the will of his father to a large sum of money which, in accordance with the marriage settlement, he should have settled on trustees. In July 1888 he repudiated the marriage settlement. The trustees of the settlement commenced proceedings to enforce the covenant.

*Held*

The law gives an infant the privilege of repudiating obligations undertaken during minority within a reasonable time after coming of age. If the infant chooses to be inactive, his opportunity is lost. In the present case, four a half years would not be regarded as a reasonable time. The covenant in the settlement was therefore binding.

Lord Herschell LC:

'It is said in considering whether a reasonable time has elapsed, you must take into account the fact
that he did not know what were the terms of settlement and that it contained the particular covenant
... it seems to me that in measuring a reasonable time, whether in point of fact he had not acquainted
himself with the nature of the obligation which he had undertaken, is wholly immaterial; the time
must be measured in precisely the same way, whether he had so made himself acquainted or not.'

## Fawcett v Smethurst (1914) 84 LJKB 473 High Court (Atkin J)

Minor - hire of motor car

*Facts*

The infant defendant hired a motor car from the plaintiff for the purpose of driving it six miles to fetch
his bag. The defendant drove the six miles to where his bag was and then, upon meeting a friend, drove
him to a place some twenty miles further on. Without the infant defendant being in anyway negligent
in the driving of the car, it was damaged beyond repair. The plaintiff sued for the value of the car.

*Held*

The defendant was not liable in tort since the taking of the car for a longer journey than that
contemplated by the contract, did not render him a trespasser and he was not liable in contract because
the mere hiring of the car did not render him liable for damage not caused by any want of skill or care on
his part. Although the hiring of the car might be a necessary, it would not be so if an onerous term
(that the car should be at the hirer's sole risk) formed part of the contract of hiring.

Atkin J:

'In *Burnard* v *Haggis* (1863) the defendant who was a Cambridge undergraduate and an infant, hired a
horse for the purpose of going for a ride, expressly stating that he did not want a horse for jumping.
The defendant lent the horse to a friend who used it for jumping, with the result that it fell and was
injured. The court held that the defendant was liable on the ground that the act resulting in the injury
to the horse, was one which was quite outside the contract and could not be said to be an abuse of the
contract. In *Jennings* v *Rundall* on the other hand, where the defendant, an infant, had hired a horse
to be ridden for a short journey and took it for a much longer journey, with the result that it was
injured, the court held the defendant not liable upon the ground that the action was founded in contract
and that the plaintiff could not turn what was in substance a claim in contract, to one in tort ... In
my opinion, the claim in the present case is in substance a claim in contract and must be dealt with
on that footing.

That being so, before the plaintiff can succeed I must be satisfied that the contract was made in the
terms which he alleges and, further, that the contract was in fact one for a necessary. Upon the
evidence I am not satisfied that was a term of the contract .... He (the defendant) was to be
responsible for all risks to which the car might be exposed. In my opinion (it) ... might be a
contract for a necessary. I do not think, however, that it follows that such a contract would be one
for a necessary if it contained an onerous term, such as the plaintiff alleges was embodied in the
contract before us. The effect of the contract alleged by the plaintiff would be to impose upon the
defendant an absolute responsibility in respect of this car ... a contract containing such a term would
not be a reasonable one ... and I do not think that such a contract would be one for a necessary.'

## Flight v Bolland (1828) 4 Russ 298 Rolls Court (Sir John Leach MR)

Minor - specific performance of contract

*Facts*

The plaintiff infant sought specific performance of a contract: could his action be sustained?

*Held*

It could not.

Sir John Leach MR:

'No case of a bill filed by an infant for the specific performance of a contract made by him has been found in the books. It is not disputed that it is a general principle of courts of equity to interpose only where the remedy is mutual. The plaintiff's counsel principally rely upon a supposed analogy afforded by cases under the Statute of Frauds where the plaintiff may obtain a decree for specific performance of a contract signed by the defendant although not signed by the plaintiff. It must be admitted that such now is the settled rule of the court, although seriously questioned by Lord Redesdale upon the ground of want of mutuality. But these cases are supported, first, because the Statute of Frauds only requires the agreement to be signed by the party to be charged, and next, it is said that the plaintiff, by the act of filing the bill, has made the remedy mutual. Neither of these reasons apply to the case of an infant. The act of filing the bill by his next friend cannot bind him, and my opinion, therefore is, that the bill must be dismissed with costs, to be paid by the next friend.'

**Leslie (R) Ltd v Sheill** [1914] 3 KB 607 Court of Appeal (Lord Sumner, Kennedy LJ and AT Lawrence J)

Minor - fraudulent misrepresentation

*Facts*

The plaintiffs, registered moneylenders, were induced to make two loans of £200 each by the fraudulent misrepresentations of the defendant that he was of full age. The plaintiffs sued to recover the £400.

*Held*

Their action could not succeed.

Lord Sumner:

'In the present case there is clearly no accounting. There is no fidicuary relation. The money was paid over in order to be used as the defendant's own, and he has so used and, I suppose, spent it. There is no question of tracing it, no possibility of restoring the very thing got by the fraud, nothing but a compulsion through a personal judgment to pay an equivalent sum out of his present or future resources, in a word nothing but a judgment in debt to repay the loan. I think this would be nothing but enforcing a void contract. So far as I can find the Court of Chancery never would have enforced any liability under circumstances like the present any more than a court of law would have done ...'

*Commentary*

For the court's power to order restitution in the case of contracts entered into after 9 June 1987, see s3 of the Minors' Contracts Act 1987.

**Nash v Inman** [1908] 2 KB 1 Court of Appeal (Sir Herbert Cozens-Hardy MR, Fletcher Moulton and Buckley LJJ)

Minor - fancy waistcoats

*Facts*

A tailor commenced proceedings to recover £122.19s.6d for clothes, including eleven fancy waistcoats, supplied to an infant Cambridge undergraduate.

*Held*

That the action must fail, as the evidence showed that the infant already had sufficient clothing suitable to his position.

Fletcher Moulton LJ:

'An infant, like a lunatic, is incapable of making a contract of purchase in the strict sense of the words; but if a man satisfies the needs of the infant or lunatic by supplying to him necessaries, the law will imply an obligation to repay him for the services so rendered and will enforce that obligation ... That the articles were necessaries had to be alleged and proved by the plaintiff as part of his case and the sum he recovered was based on a quantum meruit. If he claimed anything beyond this he failed and it did not help him that he could prove that the prices were agreed prices. All this is ... confirmed by the provision of section 2 of the Sale of Goods Act 1893 - an Act which was intended to codify the existing law. That section expressly provides that the consequence of necessaries sold and delivered to an infant is that he must pay a reasonable price therefor ...'

**Roberts v Gray** [1913] 1 KB 520 Court of Appeal (Cozens-Hardy MR, Farwell and Hamilton LJJ)

Minor - billiards instruction

*Facts*

The infant defendant made a contract with the plaintiff, a leading professional billiards player. Pursuant to the contract, the plaintiff and the defendant agreed to accompany each other on a world billiards tour. The plaintiff was to pay for the defendant's travelling expenses and, in course of the tour, teach the defendant the art and profession of a billiards player. The plaintiff incurred expenses in making preparations for the tour and the defendant repudiated the contract before the tour began. The plaintiff sued for breach of contract.

*Held*

The contract was one for necessaries and the plaintiff was entitled to recover damages for the breach.

Hamilton LJ:

'I am unable to appreciate why a contract, which is in itself binding because it is a contract for necessaries not qualified by unreasonable terms, can cease to be binding merely because it is executory ... If the contract is binding at all, it must be binding for all such remedies as are appropriate to the breach of it.'

*Commentary*

Applied: *Clements* v *London and North Western Railway Co* [1894] 2 QB 482.

**Steinberg v Scala (Leeds) Ltd** [1923] 2 Ch 452 Court of Appeal (Lord Sterndale MR, Warrington and Younger LJJ)

Minor - purchase of shares

*Facts*

The plaintiff, in infant, paid £50 on applying for shares in the defendant company and another £200 for calls on the shares allotted to her. Unable to meet further calls, she rescinded the contract and sought, inter alia, the return of her £250.

*Held*

Although she had been entitled to repudiate the contract, she could not recover the £250 as there had not been a total failure of consideration.

Lord Sterndale MR:

'... I think the argument for the plaintiff has rather proceeded on the assumption that the question whether she can rescind and the question whether she can recover her money are the same questions. They are two quite different questions ... although the contract may be rescinded the money paid cannot be recovered unless there has been an entire failure of the consideration for which the money has been paid. Therefore, it seems to me, that is the question to which we have to address ourselves: Has there been here a total failure of the consideration for which the money was paid?

The plaintiff ... has had the shares allotted to her, and there is evidence that the shares were of some value, that they had been dealt in at from 9s to 10s a share. Her shares were only half-paid up and, therefore, if she had attempted to sell them she would only have got half of that money, but that is quite a tangible and substantial sum.

In those circumstances is it possible to say that there is a total failure of consideration? ... The argument for the plaintiff is to this effect: That it is necessary, in order to show that the consideration has not entirely failed, to show that the plaintiff has not only had something which was worth value in the market and for which she could have got value, but that she has, in fact, received that value. It was admitted that if she had sold the shares and received the £125 which would have been receivable according to one of the prices mentioned in evidence, she could not have recovered the money, but it is said that as she did not in fact do that, and had only an opportunity of receiving that benefit, there has been a total failure of consideration. I cannot see that. If she has something which has money's worth, then she has received some consideration; received the very thing for which she paid her money, and the fact that, although it has money's worth, she has not turned that money's worth into money does not seem to me to prevent it being some valuable consideration for the money which she has paid.'

# 8   MISTAKE

**Amalgamated Investment and Property Co Ltd v John Walker & Sons Ltd** [1977] 1 WLR 164 Court of Appeal (Buckley, Lawton LJJ and Sir John Pennycuick)

Contract - mistake - frustration

*Facts*

Having ceased to use a purpose-built bonded warehouse and bottling factory for those purposes, the defendants advertised the premises for sale as suitable for occupation or redevelopment. The plaintiffs agreed, subject to contract, to buy the property for £1,710,000. In their enquiries before contract the plaintiffs asked whether the property was designated as a building of special architectural or historic interest: on 14 August the defendants replied in the negative although, unknown to the parties, an official of the Department of the Environment had included the building in a list of buildings which it was proposed should be so designated. Contracts were exchanged on 25 September and the following day the department wrote to the defendants to inform them that the designation was about to be given legal effect, a step which was taken the next day. The plaintiffs sought rescission of the contract on the ground of common mistake or a declaration that it was void or voidable. At the trial, the judge found that the property's value without redevelopment potential was probably £1.5m less than the contract price.

*Held*

The plaintiffs could not succeed: on the facts, there had been no common mistake and performance of the contract would not be radically different.

Buckley LJ:

'For the application of the doctrine of mutual mistake as a ground for setting the contract aside, it is of course necessary to show that the mistake existed at the date of the contract; and so counsel for the plaintiffs relies in that respect not on the signing of the list by the officer who alone was authorised to sign it on behalf of the Secretary of State, but on the decision of [the official] to include the property in the list. That decision, although in fact it led to the signature of the list in the form in which it was eventually signed, was merely an administrative step in the carrying out of the operations of the branch of the Ministry ... It seems to me that it is no more justifiable to point to that date as being the crucial date than it is to point to other earlier dates or later dates. The crucial date, in my judgment, is the date when the list was signed. It was then that the building became a listed building, and it was only then that the expectations of the parties (who no doubt both expected that this property would be capable of being developed, subject always of course to obtaining planning permission, without it being necessary to obtain listed building permission) were disappointed ... In my judgment, there was no mutual mistake as to the circumstances surrounding the contract at the time when the contract was entered into. The only mistake that there was one which related to the expectation of the parties. They expected that the building would be subject only to ordinary town planning consent procedures, and that expectation has been disappointed. But at the date when the contract was entered into I cannot see that there is any ground for saying that the parties were then subject to some mutual mistake of fact relating to the circumstances surrounding the contract ...

I now turn to the alternative argument which has been presented to us in support of this appeal, which is on frustration. Counsel for the plaintiffs has relied on what was said in the speeches in the House of Lords in *Davis Contractors Ltd* v *Fareham Urban District Council* [1956] 3 WLR 37, and it may perhaps be useful if I refer to what was said by Lord Radcliffe:

"So, perhaps, it would be simpler to say at the outset that frustration occurs whenever the law recognises that, without default of either party, a contractual obligation has become incapable of being performed because the circumstances in which performance is called for would render it a thing radically different from that which was undertaken by the contract."

... Then, a little later on, after referring to *Denny, Mott and Dickson Ltd* v *James B Fraser & Co Ltd* [1944] AC 265, Lord Radcliffe said:

"It is for that reason that special importance is necessarily attached to the occurrence of any unexpected event that, as it were, changes the fact of things. But, even so, it is not hardship or inconvenience or material loss itself which calls the principle of frustration into play. There must be as well such a change in the significance of the obligation that the thing undertaken would, if performed, be a different thing from that contracted for."

Now, the obligation undertaken to be performed in this case by the defendants was to sell this property for the contract price, and of course, to show a good title and so forth. The defendants did not warrant in any way that planning permission could be obtained for the development of the property. No doubt both parties considered that the property was property which could advantageously be developed and was property for which planning permission would probably be satisfactorily obtained. But there was no stipulation in the contract relating to anything of that kind; nor as I say, was there any warranty on the part of the defendants. I am prepared to assume for the purposes of this judgment that the law relating to frustration of contract is capable of being applied in the case of a contract for sale of land ... But, making that assumption I have reached the conclusion that there are not here the necessary factual bases for holding that this contract has been frustrated. It seems to me that the risk of property being listed as property of architectural or historical interest is a risk which inheres in all ownership of buildings. In many cases it may be an extremely remote risk. In many cases it may be a marginal risk. In some cases it may be a substantial risk. But it is a risk, I think, which attaches to all buildings and it is a risk that every owner and every purchaser of property must recognise that he is subject to. The purchasers in the present case bought knowing that they would have to obtain planning permission in order to develop the property. The effect of listing ... makes the obtaining of planning permission, it may be, more difficult, and it may also make it a longer and more complicated process. But still, in essence, the position is that the would-be developer has to obtain the appropriate planning permissions, one form of permission being the "listed building permission" ... It is a risk which I think the purchaser must carry, and any loss that may result from the maturing of that risk is a loss which must lie where it falls. Moreover, the plaintiffs have not yet established that they will be unable to obtain all the necessary planning permissions, including "listed building permission". So it has not yet, I think, been established that the listing of this building has had the drastic effect which the figures ... suggest that it may have had. It may well turn out to be the case that "listed building permission" will be obtainable here and the purchasers will be able to carry into effect the development which they desire.'

## Associated Japanese Bank (International) Ltd v Credit du Nord SA [1989] 1 WLR 255

High Court (Steyn J)

Guarantee - mistake as to subject matter

*Facts*

Under a sale and leaseback transaction the plaintiffs (AJB) purchased four machines from a Mr Bennett and then leased them back to him. As a condition of the transaction, the defendants (CDN) guaranteed Bennett's obligations and at all material times both parties believed that the machines existed and were in Bennett's possession. After Bennett defaulted in payments under the lease it was discovered that the machines did not exist and that Bennett had perpetrated a fraud. When the plaintiffs sued on the guarantee, the defendants contended that it was void ab intio for common mistake.

*Held*

The plaintiffs' claim would be dismissed.

Steyn J:

'It might be useful if I now summarised what appears to me to be a satisfactory way of approaching this subject. Logically, before one can turn to the rules as to mistake, whether at common law or in equity, one must first determine whether the contract itself, by express or implied condition precedent or otherwise, provides who bears the risk of the relevant mistake. It is at this hurdle that many pleas of mistake will either fail or prove to have been unnecessary. Only if the contract is silent on the point is there scope for invoking mistake. That brings me to the relationship between common law mistake and mistake in equity. Where common law mistake has been pleaded, the court must first consider this plea. If the contract is held to be void, no question of mistake in equity arises. But, if the contract is held to be valid, a plea of mistake in equity may still have to be considered: see *Grist* v *Bailey* [1966] 2 All ER 875 ... Turning now to the approach to common law mistake, it seems to me that the following propositions are valid although not necessarily all entitled to be dignified as propositions of law.

The first imperative must be that the law ought to uphold rather than destroy apparent contracts. Second, the common law rules as to a mistake regarding the quality of the subject matter, like the common law rules regarding commercial frustration, are designed to cope with the impact of unexpected and wholly exceptional circumstances on apparent contracts. Third, such a mistake in order to attract legal consequences must substantially be shared by both parties, and must relate to facts as they existed at the time the contract was made. Fourth, and this is the point established by *Bell* v *Lever Bros Ltd* [1932] AC 161, the mistake must render the subject matter of the contract essentially and radically different from the subject matter which the parties believed to exist ... Fifth, there is a requirement which was not specifically discussed in *Bell* v *Lever Bros Ltd*. What happens if the party who is seeking to rely on the mistake had no reasonable grounds for his belief? An extreme example is that of the man who makes a contract with minimal knowledge of the facts to which the mistake relates but is content that it is a good speculative risk. In my judgment a party cannot be allowed to rely on a common mistake where the mistake consists of a belief which is entertained by him without any reasonable grounds for such relief: cf *McRae* v *Commonwealth Disposals Commission* (1951) 84 CLR 377 at 408. That is not because principles such as estoppel or negligence require it, but simply because policy and good sense dictate that the positive rules regarding common mistake should be so qualified ... a recognition of this qualification is consistent with the approach in equity where fault on the part of the party adversely affected by the mistake will generally preclude the granting of equitable relief: see *Solle* v *Butcher* [1949] 2 All ER 1107 at 1120.

*Applying the law to the facts*

It is clear, of course, that in this case both parties, the creditor and the guarantor, acted on the assumption that the lease related to existing machines. If they had been informed that the machines might not exist, neither AJB nor CDN would for one moment have contemplated entering into the transaction. That, by itself, I accept, is not enough to sustain the plea of common law mistake. I am also satisfied that CDN had reasonable grounds for believing that the machines existed. That belief was based on CDN's discussions with Mr Bennett, information supplied by ... a respectable firm of lease brokers, and the confidence created by the fact that AJB were the lessors.

The real question is whether the subject matter *of the guarantee* (as opposed to the sale and lease) was essentially different from what it was reasonably believed to be. The real security of the guarantor was the machines. The existence of the machines, being profit-earning chattels, made it more likely that the debtor would be able to service the debt. More importantly, if the debtor defaulted and the creditor repossessed the machines, the creditor had to give credit for 97.5 per cent of the value of the machines. If the creditor sued the guarantor first, and the guarantor paid, the guarantor was entitled to be subrogated to the creditor's rights in respect of recovery against the debtor ... No doubt the guarantor relied to some extent on the creditworthiness of Mr Bennett. But I find that the prime security to which the guarantor looked was the existence of the four machines as described to both parties. For both parties the guarantee of obligations under a lease with non-existent machines was essentially different from a guarantee of a lease with four machines which both parties at the time of the contract believed to exist. The guarantee is an accessory contract. The non-existence of the subject matter of the principal contract is therefore of fundamental importance. Indeed the analogy of the classic res extincta cases, so much discussed in the authorities, is fairly close. In my judgment, the stringent test of common law mistake is satisfied; the guarantee is void ab initio ...

*Equitable mistake*

Having concluded that the guarantee is void ab initio at common law, it is strictly unnecessary to examine the question of equitable mistake. Equity will give relief against common mistake in cases where the common law will not, and it provides more flexible remedies, including the power to set aside the contract on terms. It is not necessary to repeat my findings of fact save to record again the fundamental nature of the common mistake, and that CDN was not at fault in any way. If I had not decided in favour of CDN on construction and common law mistake, I would have held that the guarantee must be set aside on equitable principles.'

**Avon Finance Co Ltd v Bridger** [1985] 2 All ER 281 Court of Appeal (Lord Denning MR, Brandon and Brightman LJJ)

Non est factum - reasonable care

*Facts*

The defendants, an elderly couple, had purchased a house. Part of the purchase price was made up of a mortgage to a building society. The defendants' son had obtained a loan from the plaintiff finance company and, as security for the loan, had undertaken to obtain the execution by the defendants of a legal charge on their property. The son procured the defendants' signatures to the legal charge by telling them that the documents they were signing were in connection with the mortgage to the building society. When the son defaulted in his payments to the plaintiffs, they sought recovery of the loan by bringing an action for possession of their property against the defendants.

*Held*

The defendants were not entitled to rely on the defence of non est factum. This doctrine was of limited application and could only be relied on if a defendant had exercised reasonable care in the transaction and it was not possible, in the circumstances of this case, to find that the defendants had exercised the appropriate reasonable care. It was further held, however, that the transaction was voidable in equity on the grounds of undue influence.

*Commentary*

It should be noted that this decision was made in October 1979. Applied: *Saunders* v *Anglia Building Society* [1970] 3 WLR 1078. Distinguished: *Lloyds Bank Ltd* v *Bundy* [1974] 3 WLR 501. Distinguished in *Coldunell Ltd* v *Gallon* [1986] 2 WLR 466.

**Barrow Lane and Ballard Ltd v Phillip Phillips & Co Ltd** [1929] 1 KB 574 High Court (Wright J)

Goods perished - contract void?

*Facts*

The plaintiffs bought 700 bags of Chinese ground-nuts and resold them to the defendants without removing them from the warehouse. At the time of the resale, neither party knew that someone had 'made away' with 109 of the bags.

*Held*

By virtue of s6 of the Sale of Goods Act 1893, the contract of resale was void.

Wright J:

'It has now been ascertained and agreed that at the date of the contract on 11 October 1927, there were not 700 bags in the parcel but only 591 bags, 109 having by that time been fraudulently abstracted or irregularly delivered ... Now if the whole 700 bags had remained in the wharf ... and if the fraudulent abstraction had been subsequent to that date and the parcel had been intact on that date, there could be no question, I think, that the property must have passed ... from the plaintiffs to the defendants. But that in fact was not so. When the contract of 11 October was made there was not in existence any parcel such as is described in the contract. There was a parcel of 591 bags, but there was not a parcel of 700 bags. If, on the other hand, the whole 700 bags had been stolen on 11 October 1927, without the knowledge of either party, or if it had been destroyed by fire - if for any such reason it did not exist as a parcel at all on 11 October, there can be no doubt that s6 of the Sale of Goods Act 1893, would have applied ... There is no contract in other words, because the intention of both parties is completely frustrated; they are contracting about something which has no existence in fact and the law then says that, the contract having reference to specific goods and those specific goods not existing, there is nothing on which the contract can operate, and the rule has been established for many years that the seller is not treated as warranting the existence of those specific goods, but the case is one of failure of intention and mistake.

This case raises a further problem which so far as I know, and so far as learned counsel have been able to ascertain, has never come before the court before. The problem is this: Where there is a contract for the sale of specific goods, such as the parcel of goods in this case, and some of the parcel, but not all of the parcel, has ceased to exist at all times relevant to the contract, because they have been stolen and taken away and cannot be followed or discovered anywhere, what then is the position? Does the case come within s6 of the Sale of Goods Act so that it would be the same as if the whole parcel had ceased to exist? In my judgment it does. The contract here was for a parcel of 700 bags. A contract for a parcel of 700 bags is something different from a contract for 591 bags and, in my judgment, the position is no different from what it would have been if the whole 700 bags had ceased to exist. The result is that the parties are contracting about something which, without the knowledge or fault of either party, at the date of the contract does not exist, and to compel the buyer under those circumstances to take 591 bags would be to compel him to take something which he had not contracted to take, and would in my judgment to unjust.'

## Bell v Lever Brothers Ltd

See chapter 5 - Misrepresentation.

## Boulton v Jones (1857) 27 LJ Ex 117 Court of Exchequer (Pollock CB, Martin, Bramwell and Channell BB)

Mistake - intention to deal with particular person

*Facts*

The defendant sent to the shop of Brocklehurst a written order for certain goods. Unknown to the defendant, Brocklehurst had that day assigned his business to the plaintiff. The order had been addressed to Brocklehurst (against whom the defendant had a set-off), but the goods were sent by the plaintiff. The defendant did not become aware of the change of ownership until after the goods had been consumed.

*Held*

The plaintiff was not entitled to sue and deprive the defendant of his set-off.

Pollock CB:

'The point raised was this, whether the order in writing did not impart, on the part of the buyer, the defendant, an intention to deal exclusively with Brocklehurst; the person who had succeeded him, the plaintiff, having executed the order without any notice to the defendant of the change, until he received the invoice, subsequently to his consumption of the goods. The decision of the jury did not dispose of that point, and it was the point reserved. Now the rule of law is clear, that if you propose to make a contract with A, then B cannot substitute himself for A without your consent and to your disadvantage, securing to himself all the benefit of the contract. The case being, that if B sued, the defendant would have the benefit of a set-off, of which he is deprived by A's suing. If B sued, the defendant could plead his set-off; as B does not sue, but another party, with whom the defendant did not contract, all that he can do is to deny that he ever was indebted to the plaintiff.'

## Citibank NA v Brown Shipley & Co Ltd; Midland Bank v Brown Shipley & Co Ltd
[1991] 2 All ER 690 Queen's Bench Division (Waller J)

Mistaken identity induced by fraud - passing of title

*Facts*

In several separate transactions involving different banks a person claiming to be a signatory of a company's account at one bank (the issuing bank) telephoned another bank (the receiving bank) with a request to buy substantial amounts of foreign currency, payment to be made by a bankers' draft issued by the issuing bank. The caller then telephoned the issuing bank, instructing them to prepare this bankers' draft to be drawn on the company's account. This the issuing company did; they handed the draft over to a messenger who purported to be from the company, in exchange for a letter that purported to confirm the telephoned instructions, with forged signatures. The draft was then paid to the receiving bank, who after checking that the draft was genuinely issued by the issuing bank and had been issued in the ordinary course of business, paid the cash to the fraudster. In due course the receiving bank presented the draft to and were paid by the issuing bank. When the fraud was finally discovered the issuing bank brought an action against the receiving bank to recover the value of the draft on the basis that title in the draft had never passed to the receiving bank, as it could not derive good title from the fraudster, and the banks did not have a contract between them.

*Held*

It was irrelevant that the delivery of the bankers' draft from the issuing bank to the receiving bank with the authority of the issuing bank established a voidable contract between the two banks.

The fact that the issuing bank had mistakenly dealt with a fraudster instead of the company with whom they thought they were dealing did not affect the formation of the contract between the two banks; admittedly the fraudster, because of mistaken identity had no title, but he was merely a 'conduit'. Title did not have to pass from the fraudster to the receiving bank.

Of the two innocent parties, the issuing bank must bear the loss.

## Couturier v Hastie (1856) 9 Ex 102 Court of Exchequer Chamber (Coleridge, Maule, Cresswell, Wightman, Williams, Talfourd and Compton JJ)

Mistake - right to repudiate contract

*Facts*

The contract was for the purchase of a quantity of Indian corn 'when shipped' on the 'Kezia Page' from

Salonica to a safe port in the United Kingdom. The ship left Salonica, but because of the weather, had to put into Tunis Bay, where the cargo was found to have fermented and had to be sold.

*Held*

The contract could be repudiated.

Coleridge J:

'... For the plaintiffs it was contended that the parties plainly contracted for the sale and purchase of goods ... that a vendor of goods undertakes that they exist and that they are capable of being transferred ... and that as the goods in question had been sold and delivered to other parties before the contract in question was made, there was nothing on which it could operate ...

On the other hand, it was argued that this was not a mere contract for the sale of an ascertained cargo, but that the purchaser bought the adventure and took upon himself all risks from the shipment of the cargo ... it appears to us that the contract in question was for the sale of a cargo supposed to exist and to be capable of transfer and that inasmuch as it had been sold and delivered to others by the captain before the contract in question was made, the plaintiffs cannot recover in this action ...'

*Commentary*

See also *McRae* v *Commonwealth Disposals Commission* (1950) 84 CLR 377.

**Cundy v Lindsay** (1878) 3 App Cas 459 House of Lords (Lord Cairns LC, Lord Hatherley, Lord Penzance and Lord Gordon)

Sale of goods induced by fraud

*Facts*

Alfred Blenkarn hired a room at a corner house in Wood Street, Cheapside. The entrance was in Little Love Lane, but he described the premises as '37 Wood Street, Cheapside'. The respondents were linen manufacturers in Belfast. Blenkarn wrote to the plaintiffs concerning a purchase from them of their goods, describing his premises as comprising a warehouse and signing himself 'Blenkiron and Co'. Blenkiron and Co carried on business at number 132 Wood Street and were a highly respectable firm. The respondents, who knew of the firm but did not know their address, sent the goods to 'Blenkiron and Co' at 37 Wood Street. Blenkarn sold the goods to, inter alia, Messrs Cundy who were bona fide purchasers and who resold them in the course of their trade. Payment not being made, Blenkarn's fraud was discovered and criminal proceedings taken against him. Messrs Lindsay then sued Messrs Cundy for unlawful conversion.

*Held*

They were entitled to succeed.

Lord Cairns LC:

'... by the law of our country, the purchaser of a chattel takes the chattel, as a general rule, subject to what may turn out to be certain infirmities in the title. If he purchases the chattel in market overt, he obtains a title which is good against all the world, but if he does not ... and if it turns out that the chattel has been found by the person who professed to sell it, the purchaser will not obtain a title good against the real owner. If it turns out that the chattel has been stolen ... the purchaser will not obtain a title. If it turns out that the chattel has come into the hands of the person who professed to sell it by a de facto contract, that is to say, a contract which has purported to pass the property to him from the owner of the property, there the purchaser will obtain a good title, even although afterwards it would appear that there were circumstances connected with that contract which would enable the original owner of those goods to reduce it and set it aside, because these circumstances so enabling the original owner of the goods, or of the chattel, to reduce the contract and set it aside, will not be allowed to interfere with a title for valuable consideration obtained by some third party during the interval while the contract remains unreduced ... Blenkarn ... was acting here just in the same way as if he had forged the signature Blenkiron and Co ... and as if when, in return, the goods were forwarded and letters were sent accompanying them, he had intercepted the goods and intercepted the letters and had taken possession of the goods ... how is it possible to imagine that in that stage of things any contract could have arisen between the respondents and Blenkarn? Of him they knew nothing and of him they never thought ... as, between him and them, there was no consensus of mind which could lead to any agreement or contract whatever ... My Lords, that being so, it is idle to talk of the property passing. The property remained ... the property of the respondents ...'

Lord Hatherley:

'I have come to the same conclusion ... There was no real contract whatever with Blenkarn; no goods had been delivered to anybody except for the purposes of transferring the property to Blenkiron ... there was no sale at all; there was ... a false representation ... from beginning to end the respondents believed that they were dealing with Blenkiron and Co ... Blenkarn cannot ... have ... made a good title to a purchaser ...'

Lord Penzance:

'... I am not aware, my Lords, that there is any decided case in which a sale and delivery intended to be made to one man, has been held to be a sale and delivery so as to pass the property to another, against the intent and will of the vendor ... In the present case, Blenkarn pretended that he was ... Blenkiron & Co with whom, alone, the vendors meant to deal. No contract was ever intended with him and the contract which was intended failed for want of another party to it ... the respondents were never brought personally into contact with Blenkarn; all their letters ... were addressed to Blenkiron and Co ... and finally the goods in dispute were ... sent to Blenkiron and Co, though at a wrong address.'

## Dennant v Skinner [1948] 2 KB 164 High Court (Hallett J)

Sale by auction - purchaser's identity

*Facts*

At an auction sale, the plaintiff auctioneer sold a Commer van: the purchaser told him that his name was King, son of the owner of the well-known firm King's Motors of Oxford. Five more vehicles were knocked down to the man, including a Standard car. The plaintiff eventually accepted a cheque in payment for all of the vehicles and the man signed a form which stated that 'ownership of the vehicles will not pass to me' until the cheque had been cleared. The man was allowed to remove the vehicles: his cheque was dishonoured and it turned out that he had no connection with King's Motors. The plaintiff sued an eventual purchaser for the return of the Standard or its value.

*Held*

His action would fail.

Hallett J:

'Two sentences from the plaintiff's evidence seem to me to be crucial. He said:

"When I took the cheque from King I believed him to be King's of Oxford. If I had not so believed him I should not have accepted the cheque."

That seems to be really important on the question of the effect the verbal representation had on the plaintiff's mind. There is no evidence, it seems to me, that the plaintiff was induced to sell the car to King in the belief that King was connected in the manner which he had described with this highly reputable firm. That seems to have been entirely immaterial from the point of view of selling the car. The Commer van had been sold before King's identity was mentioned at all, and the mention of his identity was only made in the ordinary way, as I interpret the evidence, for the purpose of the plaintiff's completing the auctioneer's memorandum. The effect which the misrepresentation had on the plaintiff's mind was to induce him to accept the cheque instead of requiring cash to be paid before the vehicle was delivered ... I am of the opinion, on the evidence, that there was no mistake as to the contracting parties at the time the contract of sale was made and so no mistake affecting the plaintiff's assent to the sale and the passing of the property ... The [form] contemplates that the ownership of the vehicle has not passed to the bidder, but as I have already said, in my judgment, it had passed on the fall of the hammer, and, if subsequently the bidder executed the document acknowledging that the ownership of the vehicle would not pass to him, that could not have any effect on what had already taken place. Accordingly, the only way it seems to me in which this document could be used to satisfy the plaintiff's argument is to find that it had the effect of divesting the property from King and re-vesting it in the plaintiff, the seller. I do not think that such a view of the document is sound. In my view, the property had passed on the falling of the hammer. The right to possession had passed when the plaintiff, persuaded and misled by King's lies, parted with his seller's lien, and there was nothing left on which he could found a claim in detinue against some third person, in this case the defendant, who was thus put in possession of the vehicle.'

*Commentary*

Applied: *Phillips* v *Brooks Ltd* [1919] 2 KB 243

**Foster v Mackinnon** (1869) LR 4 CP 704 Common Pleas (Bovill CJ, Byles, Keating and Montague Smith JJ)

Mistake as to nature of document signed

*Facts*

The defendant, an elderly gentleman, signed a bill of exchange on being told that it was a guarantee similar to one which he had previously signed. He had only been shown the back of the paper.

*Held*

There should be a new trial.

Byles J:

'It seems plain, on principle and on authority, that if a blind man, or a man who cannot read, or who, for some reason (not implying negligence) forbears to read, has a written contract falsely read over to him, the reader misreading it to such a degree that the written contract is of a nature altogether different from the contract pretended to be read from the paper which the blind or illiterate man afterwards signs; then, at least if there be no negligence, the signature obtained is of no force. And it is invalid not merely on the ground of fraud, where fraud exists, but on the ground that the mind of the signer did not accompany the signature; in other words, he never intended to sign and therefore, in contemplation of law, never did sign the contract to which his name is appended. In the present case, ... he was deceived, not merely as to the legal effect, but as to the actual contents of the instrument.'

*Commentary*

Approved in *Saunders* v *Anglia Building Society* [1970] 3 WLR 1078.

**Gallie v Lee**

See **Saunders v Anglia Building Society**

**Grist v Bailey** [1966] 3 WLR 618 High Court (Goff J)

Mistake - rescission of sale agreement of house

*Facts*

The parties agreed to the sale and purchase for £850 of a freehold house 'subject to the existing tenancy thereof', the defendant vendor mistakenly believing that the occupier was a statutory tenant. Indeed, the court found that the mistake was common to both parties. The plaintiff purchaser sought specific performance and the defendant counterclaimed for rescission.

*Held*

The defendant would succeed on offering a fresh contract to sell the property to the plaintiff at a proper vacant possession price.

Goff J:

'Such being the state of the evidence, in my judgment there was a common mistake - namely, that there was still subsisting a protected tenancy ... and it is to be remembered that the language ... of the agreement is "subject to the existing tenancy thereof". In my view, this was nonetheless a common mistake, though the parties may have differed in their belief as to who the tenant was ... although that may have a bearing on materiality.

Then, was it fundamental? In view of ... evidence to which I have referred, and the evidence of ... a surveyor called on behalf of the defendant, that in his opinion the vacant possession value ... was £2,250, in my judgment it must have been if [the occupier] had no rights under the Rents Acts ...

There remains one other point, and that is the condition laid down by Denning LJ [in *Solle* v *Butcher*] that the party seeking to take advantage of the mistake must not be at fault. Denning LJ did not develop that at all, and it is not, I think with respect, absolutely clear what it comprehends. Clearly, there must be some degree of blameworthiness beyond the mere fault of having made a mistake; but the question is, how much or in what way? Each case must depend on its own facts, and I do not consider that the defendant or her agents were at fault so as to disentitle them to relief ...

The result, in my judgment, is that the defendant is entitled to relief in equity, and I do not feel that this is a case for simply refusing specific performance. Accordingly, the action fails, and on the counterclaim I order rescission. It is clear that this being equitable relief may be granted unconditionally or on terms, and counsel on behalf of the defendant, has offered to submit to a condition that the relief I have ordered should be on condition that the defendant is to enter into a fresh contract at a proper vacant possession price, and if required by the plaintiff, I will impose that term.'

*Commentary*

Distinguished: *Bell* v *Lever Bros Ltd* [1932] AC 161.

**Hadley v Baxendale**

See chapter 14 - Remedies for breach of contract - damages.

**Hartog v Colin & Shields** [1939] 3 All ER 566 High Court (Singleton J)

Mistake - price per pound or per piece?

*Facts*

The plaintiff alleged that the defendants had agreed to sell him 3,000 Argentine hare skins and had failed to deliver them. He claimed loss of profit or, alternatively, the difference between the contract price and the market price at the time of the breach.

The defendants pleaded that their offer was, by mistake, wrongly expressed. They alleged that they had intended to offer the goods sold at certain prices per piece and not at those prices per pound, as their offer was expressed. They further alleged that the plaintiff was well aware of this mistake on their part and thus they denied that any binding contract had been entered into.

*Held*

There was no binding contract.

Singleton J:

'... Counsel for the defendants took upon himself the onus of satisfying me that the plaintiff knew that there was a mistake and sought to take advantage of that mistake. In other words, realising that there was a mistake, the plaintiff did that which James LJ in *Tamplin* v *James* (1880) Ch D 215 at page 221 described as "snapping up the offer". It is important, I think, to realise that in all the ... negotiations ... and discussions ... the prices ... had been discussed per piece ... and never at a price per pound ... I am satisfied from the evidence given to me, that the plaintiff must have realised and did in fact know, that a mistake had occurred ... I am satisfied that it was a mistake on the part of the defendants or their servants which caused the offer to go forward in that way and I am satisfied that anyone with any knowledge of the trade must have realised that there was a mistake ... The offer was wrongly expressed and the defendants, by their evidence and by the correspondence, have satisfied me that the plaintiff could not reasonably have supposed that that offer contained the offerer's real intention ... there must be judgment for the defendants.'

**Ingram v Little** [1960] 3 WLR 504 Court of Appeal (Sellers, Pearce and Devlin LJJ)

Contract - identity of party to it

*Facts*

The three plaintiffs advertised their motor car for sale in a local newspaper. A swindler answered their advertisement, calling himself Hutchinson and giving as his weekend address a local hotel. One of the plaintiffs later telephoned him at the hotel, asking for him by that name. He called at the plaintiffs' house and viewed the car, then he went for a drive in it with one of the plaintiffs, during which he told her that he came from Surrey and that his home was at Caterham. After the drive they returned to the house and agreed on a price for the car, £717, but when the plaintiffs realised that he proposed to pay the £717 by cheque, they refused and said that they wanted cash. The rogue then tried to persuade her that he was respectable, saying he was a P G M Hutchinson and giving her a Caterham address. He said that he was a businessman. One of the plaintiffs left the room and went out to the local post office, where, by checking in the appropriate telephone directory, she ascertained that a P G M Hutchinson did live at the address given by the rogue. She informed the other plaintiffs and, believing that the rogue was P G M Hutchinson, they accepted the cheque. The rogue put the address on the back of it. The rogue was not P G M Hutchinson of the Caterham address at all and the cheque was dishonoured. Subsequently, the car was sold by one Hardy to Little for £780. The rogue disappeared and was never traced. The defendant later sold the car on to a dealer. The plaintiffs sued the defendant for the return of the car or, alternatively, for damages for its conversion. It was found as facts that the rogue and Hardy were one and the same person and that the defendant was a bona fide purchaser for value without notice.

*Held* (Devlin LJ dissenting)

The plaintiffs' mistake as to the identity of the person with whom they were dealing prevented the formation of a contract with the rogue so he could pass no title in the car to the defendant.

Sellers LJ:

'Where two parties are negotiating together and there is no question of one or the other purporting to act as agent for another and an agreement is reached, the normal and obvious conclusion would no doubt be that they are the contracting parties ...

The mere presence of an individual cannot, however, be conclusive that an apparent bargain he may make is made with him. If he were disguised in appearance and dressed to represent someone else and the other party, deceived by the disguise, dealt with him on the basis that he was that person and would not have contracted had he known the truth, then it seems clear there would be no contract established. If words are substituted for outward disguise so as to depict a different person from the one physically present, in what circumstances would the result be different? ... Personal knowledge of the person fraudulently represented cannot, I think, be an essential feature. It might be a very strong factor, but the qualities of a person not personally known might be no less strong ...

... If less had been said by the rogue and if nothing had been done by (the plaintiffs) to confirm his statements ... the result might have been different ... and it might have been held that an offer in such circumstances was to the party present, whatever his true identity would be ... The question in each case should be solved, in my opinion, by applying the test which Slade J applied: "How ought the promisee to have interpreted the promise?" in order to find whether a contract has been entered into.'

Pearce LJ:

'... the often quoted passage from Pothier is misleading. For it seems to substitute for the objective English test "How ought the promisee to have interpreted the promise?", the entirely different subjective test, "What did the promisor intend when he made the promise?" and, if taken literally, it seems to involve "an inquisition into the feelings" and into the motives of the promisor.

... The judge approached the matter on an objective basis. He pointed out, however, that he would have reached the same result by approaching the matter on the subjective test suggested by Pothier. In cases such as this, the cheat is fully aware of the offeror's actual state of mind ... he has himself deliberately and fraudulently induced it.

... The mere fact that the offeror is dealing with a person bearing an alias or false attributes, does not create a mistake which will prevent the formation of the contract ... for in such a case, there is no other identity for which the identity of the offeree is mistaken.

... An apparent contract made orally inter praesentes raises particular difficulties. The offer is apparently addressed to the physical person present ... yet clearly, though difficult, it is not impossible to rebut the prima facie presumption that the offer can be accepted by the person to whom it is physically addressed ... if a shopkeeper sells goods in a normal cash transaction to a man who misrepresents himself as being some well known figure, the transaction will normally be valid. For the shopkeeper was ready to sell goods for cash to the world at large ... Thus the nature of the proposed contract must have a strong bearing on the question of whether the intention of the offeror (as understood by the offeree) was to make his offer to some other particular identity rather than to the physical person to whom it was orally offered ... I do not find [*Phillips* v *Brooks Ltd*] easy to evaluate, because the facts are far from clear. It appears from the report that the name of Sir George Bullough was not mentioned until after the deal had apparently been concluded and the cheque in payment of the goods had been, or was being, written out ... Each case must be decided on its own facts ...'

*Commentary*

Distinguished: *Phillips* v *Brooks Ltd* [1919] 2 KB 243. Distinguished and doubted in *Lewis* v *Averay* [1971] 3 WLR 603.

**King's Norton Metal Co Ltd v Edridge, Merrett and Co Ltd** (1897) 14 TLR 98 Court of Appeal (A L Smith, Rigby and Collins LJJ)

Sale of goods induced by fraud

*Facts*

The plaintiffs were metal manufacturers at King's Norton and the defendants were metal merchants at Birmingham. The plaintiffs received a letter purporting to come from one Hallam and Co in Sheffield. At the head of the paper was a representation of a large factory with a number of chimneys and, in one corner, was a statement that Hallam had depots and agencies at Belfast, Lille and Ghent. The letter contained a request for a quotation of prices for brass rivet wire. The plaintiffs quoted prices and Hallam and Co then ordered some goods which were never paid for. It turned out that one Wallis had adopted the name of Hallam and Co and had fraudulently obtained the goods by these means. Wallis then sold the goods to the defendants, who bought them bona fide and without notice. The plaintiffs brought this action to recover damages for conversion.

The judge dismissed the claim upon the ground that the property in the goods had passed to Wallis, who sold them to the defendant before the plaintiffs had disaffirmed the contract.

*Held*

This decision had been correct.

AL Smith LJ:

'... if a person induced by false pretences contracted with a rogue to sell goods to him and the goods were delivered, the rogue could, until the contract was disaffirmed, give a good title to the goods to a bona fide purchaser for value ... The question was, with whom, upon this evidence, which was all one way, did the plaintiffs contract to sell the goods? Clearly with the writer of the letters ... there was a contract by the plaintiffs with the person who wrote the letters ...'

**Lake v Simmons** [1927] AC 487 House of Lords (Viscount Haldane, Viscount Sumner, Lord Atkinson, Lord Wrenbury and Lord Blanesburgh)

Goods obtained by trick - no consensus ad idem

*Facts*

The appellant jeweller insured his goods with the respondents but the cover did not apply to 'loss by theft or dishonesty committed by any ... customer ... in respect of goods entrusted to him by the assured.' Esmé, a practised and previously convicted criminal, was living at Stonelands, a well-known residence, with Mr Van der Borgh as his wife, which she was not. Having previously dealt with Esmé as Mrs Van der Borgh of Stonelands in relation to relatively small items, the appellant allowed her to take away two valuable necklets for, she said, her husband's inspection. However, Esmé disposed of them and retained the proceeds and she was subsequently convicted of theft. The appellant claimed under the policy.

*Held*

He was entitled to succeed as, when he permitted Esmé to take the necklets, there had been no consensus ad idem between them and it followed that the goods had not been 'entrusted' to her.

Viscount Haldane:

'Esmé Ellison was a mere intermediary, little more than a porter, so far as any contract was concerned, a person entrusted with the possession for purposes which seem to fall short of all those specified in the exception. She certainly got no property. Having regard to the circumstances that in contemplation of law she stole the necklets from the appellant, it is only in a qualified sense that she got even the possession. No doubt, she got possession physically, but there was no mutual assent

193

to any contract which would give her even the qualified proprietary right to hold it as a bailee proper. The appellant thought that he was dealing with a different person, the wife of Van der Borgh, and it was on that footing alone that he parted with the goods. He never intended to contract with the woman in question. It was by a deliberate fraud and trick that she got possession. There was not the agreement of her mind with that of the seller that was required in order to establish any contractual right at all. The latter was entirely deceived as to the identity of the person with whom he was transacting. It was only on the footing and in the belief that she was Mrs Van der Borgh that he was willing to deal with her at all. In circumstances such as these, I think that there was no such consensus ad idem as, for example Lord Cairns, in his judgment in *Cundy* v *Lindsay* declared to be requisite for the constitution of a contract. No doubt physically the woman entered the shop and pretended to bargain in a particular capacity, but only on the footing of being a different person from what she really was. There was never any contract which could afterwards become voidable by reason of a false representation made in obtaining it, because there was no contract at all, nothing excepting the result of a trick practised on the jeweller.'

## Laurence v Lexcourt Holdings Ltd

See chapter 5 - Misrepresentation.

## Leaf v International Galleries

See chapter 5 - Misrepresentation.

## Lewis v Averay

See Introduction.

## McRae v Commonwealth Disposals Commission (1951) 84 CLR 377 High Court of Australia (Dixon, Fullagar and McTiernan JJ)

Contract - purchase of non-existent tanker

*Facts*

The defendants invited tenders for an oil tanker, loaded with oil, lying on Jourmand Reef off Papua. The plaintiff's tender was accepted and he incurred considerable expense in going to retrieve the vessel and its contents. There was no ship to be found where the vessel was supposed to be - and no place known as Jourmand Reef. The plaintiff claimed, inter alia, damages for breach of contract.

*Held*

He was entitled to succeed.

Dixon and Fullagar JJ:

'The position ... may be summed up as follows: It was not decided in *Courturier* v *Hastie* that the contract in that case was void. The question whether it was void or not did not arise. If it had arisen, as in an action by the purchaser for damages, it would have turned on the ulterior question whether the contract was subject to an implied condition precedent. Whatever might then have been held on the facts of *Courturier* v *Hastie*, it is impossible in this case to imply any such term. The terms of the contract and the surrounding circumstances clearly exclude any such implication. The buyers relied upon, and acted upon, the assertion of the seller that there was a tanker in existence. It is not a case in which the parties can be seen to have proceeded on the basis of a common assumption of fact so as to justify the conclusion that the correctness of the assumption was intended by both parties to be a condition precedent to the creation of contractual obligation. The officers of the Commission made an assumption, but the plaintiffs did not make an assumption in the same sense. They knew nothing except what the Commission had told them. If they had been asked, they would certainly not have said: "Of course, if there is no tanker, there is no contract." They would have said: "We shall have to go and take possession of the tanker. We simply accept the Commission's assurance that there is a tanker and the Commission's promise to give us that tanker." The only proper construction of the contract is that it included a promise by the Commission that there was a tanker in the position specified. The Commission contracted that there was a tanker there ... If, on the other hand, the case of *Couturier* v *Hastie* and this case ought to be treated as cases raising a question of "mistake", then the Commission cannot in this case rely on any mistake as avoiding the contract, because any mistake was induced by the serious fault of their own servants, who asserted the existence of a tanker recklessly and without any reasonable ground. There *was* a contract, and the Commission contracted that a tanker existed in the position specified. Since there was no such tanker, there has been a breach of contract, and the plaintiffs are entitled to damages for that breach.

Before proceeding to consider the measure of damages one other matter should be briefly mentioned. The contract was made in Melbourne, and it would seem that its proper law is Victorian law. Section 11 of the Victorian Goods Act 1928, corresponds to s6 of the English Sale of Goods Act 1893, and provides that "where there is a contract for the sale of specified goods, and the goods without the knowledge of the seller have perished at the time when the contract is made the contract is void". This has been generally supposed to represent the legislature's view of the effect of *Couturier* v *Hastie*. Whether it correctly represents the effect of the decision in that case or not, it seems clear that the section has no application to the facts of the present case. Here the goods never existed and the seller ought to have known that they did not exist.'

**Magee v Pennine Insurance Co Ltd** [1969] 2 WLR 1278 Court of Appeal (Lord Denning MR, Winn and Fenton Atkinson LJJ)

Mistake - agreement to compromise

*Facts*

When the plaintiff bought a car, the man at the garage filled in an insurance proposal form stating - incorrectly - that the plaintiff held a driving licence. The plaintiff signed the form, but the trial judge found that he had not been fraudulent in so doing. The policy was renewed each year and, four years after the contract of insurance had first been made, the insured car was accidentally damaged and the plaintiff made a claim. By letter, the defendant insurance company offered £385 in settlement and this offer the plaintiff orally accepted. The defendants then discovered the mis-statements in the proposal and refused to pay the £385.

*Held* (Winn LJ dissenting)

Although the acceptance of the defendants' offer constituted a contract of compromise binding at law, in view of the parties' common and fundamental mistake (that the policy was good and binding) the contract was voidable in equity and would be set aside.

Lord Denning MR:

'Accepting that the agreement to pay £385 was an agreement of compromise, is it vitiated by mistake? The insurance company was clearly under a mistake. It thought that the policy was good and binding. It did not know, at the time of that letter, that there had been misrepresentations in the proposal form. If the plaintiff knew of its mistake - if he knew that the policy was bad - he certainly could not take advantage of the agreement to pay £385. He would be "snapping at an offer which he knew was made under a mistake"; and no man is allowed to get away with that. But I prefer to assume that the plaintiff was innocent. I think we should take it that both parties were under a common mistake. Both parties thought that the policy was good and binding. The letter ... was written on the assumption that the policy was good whereas it was in truth voidable.

What is the effect in law of this common mistake? Counsel for the plaintiff said that the agreement to pay £385 was good, despite this common mistake. He relied much on *Bell v Lever Brothers Ltd* and its similarity to the present case. He submitted that, inasmuch as the mistake there did not vitiate that contract, the mistake here should not vitiate this one. I do not propose today to go through the speeches in that case. They have given enough trouble to commentators already. I would say simply this: A common mistake, even on a most fundamental matter, does not make a contract void at law; but it makes it voidable in equity. I analysed the cases in *Solle v Butcher*, and I would repeat what I said there:

"A contract is also liable in equity to be set aside if the parties were under a common misapprehension either as to facts or as to their relative and respective rights, provided that the misapprehension was fundamental and that the party seeking to set it aside was not himself at fault."

Applying that principle here, it is clear that, when the insurance company and the plaintiff made this agreement to pay £385, they were both under a common mistake which was fundamental to the whole agreement. Both thought that the plaintiff was entitled to claim under the policy of insurance, whereas he was not so entitled. That common mistake does not make the agreement to pay £385 a nullity, but it makes it liable to be set aside in equity.

This brings me to a question which has caused me much difficulty. Is this a case in which we ought to set the agreement aside in equity? I have hesitated on this point, but I cannot shut my eyes to the fact that the plaintiff had no valid claim on the insurance policy; and, if he had no claim on the policy, it is not equitable that he should have a good claim on the agreement to pay £385, [holding the] insurance company to an agreement which it would not have dreamt of making if it had not been under a mistake. I would, therefore, allow the appeal and give judgment for the insurance company.'

*Commentary*

Applied: *Bell v Lever Brothers Ltd* [1932] AC 161.

### Peco Arts Inc v Hazlitt Gallery Ltd [1983] 1 WLR 1315 High Court (Webster J)

Mistake - drawing reproduction

*Facts*

The plaintiff bought from the defendants, a well-known and reputable art gallery, a drawing which both parties thought to be an original. It was an express term of the contract that it was an original inscribed by the artist, but eleven years later the plaintiff discovered that it was a reproduction. He sought, inter alia, recovery of the purchase price plus interest.

*Held*

He was entitled to succeed and his action was not time-barred as, on the facts, he could not with reasonable diligence have discovered the mistake at an earlier date.

*Commentary*

Distinguished: *Leaf v International Galleries* [1950] 2 KB 86.

### Phillips v Brooks Ltd

See chapter 5 - Misrepresentation.

### Raffles v Wichelhaus (1864) 2 H & C 906 Exchequer (Pollock CB, Martin and Pigott BB)

Mistake - different ships

*Facts*

The plaintiff agreed to sell to the defendants a number of bales of cotton, to arrive ex 'Peerless' from Bombay. It later appeared that the defendants were referring to a ship which sailed in October, but the plaintiff meant another and different ship, albeit of the same name, which sailed in December. It was argued that from the moment it appeared that there were two ships called 'Peerless' sailing from Bombay, there was no consensus ad idem and therefore no binding contract.

*Held*

This argument was sound: the defendant meant one ship and the plaintiff another.

**Riverlate Properties Ltd v Paul** [1974] 3 WLR 564 Court of Appeal (Russell, Stamp and Lawton LJJ)

Mistake of lessor in drafting lease

*Facts*

It was a prospective lessee's understanding that she was not to be responsible for the exterior of the premises or for structural repairs, but the prospective lessor intended that she should contribute to their costs. Due to a mistake in drafting on the part of the lessor, the lease as executed provided that it was solely responsible for these things.

*Held*

The lessor was not entitled to rescission, with or without an option to the lessee to accept rectification to cure the mistake.

Russell LJ:

'Is the plaintiff entitled to rescission of the lease on the mere ground that it made a serious mistake in the drafting of the lease which it put forward and subsequently executed, when (a) the defendant did not share the mistake, (b) the defendant did not know that the document did not give effect to the plaintiff's intention, and (c) the mistake of the plaintiff was in no way attributable to anything said or done by the defendant? What is there in principle, or in authority binding on this court, which requires a person who has acquired a leasehold interest on terms on which he intended to obtain it, and who thought when he obtained it that the lessor intended him to obtain it on those terms, either to lose the leasehold interest, or, if he wish to keep it, to submit to keep it only on the terms which the lessor meant to impose but did not? In point of principle, we cannot find that this should be so. If reference be made to principles of equity, it operates on conscience. If conscience is clear at the time of the transaction, why should equity disrupt the transaction? If a man may be said to have been fortunate in obtaining a property at a bargain price, or on terms that make it a good bargain, because the other party unknown to him has made a miscalculation or other mistake, some high-minded men might consider it appropriate that he should agree to a fresh bargain to cure the misclaculation or mistake, abandoning his good fortune. But if equity were to enforce the views of those high-minded men, we have no doubt that it would run counter to the attitudes of much the greater part of ordinary mankind (not least the world of commerce), and would be venturing on the field of moral philosophy in which it would soon be in difficulties ...

*Solle* v *Butcher* (in this court) was a case of common mistake: the order made was analogous to those made in *Garrard* v *Frankel* and *Paget* v *Marshall*, in that the defendant was given an option, those cases being referred to by Denning LJ in that respect. But the details of those cases and their rationes decidendi did not fall for consideration, and insofar as they may be said to support the view that rescission may be grounded on mere unilateral mistake they are not to be regarded as having been approved ...

Consequently, since the defendant neither directly nor through her solicitor ... knew of the plaintiff's mistake, and was not guilty of anything approaching sharp practice in relation thereto, it is a case of mere unilateral mistake which cannot entitle the plaintiff to rescission of the lease either with or without the option to the defendant to accept rectification to cure the plaintiff's mistake.'

### Commentary

Distinguished: *Garrard* v *Frankel* (1862) 30 Beav 445.

### Rose (Frederick E) (London) Ltd v Pim (Wm H) Junior & Co Ltd [1953] 2 QB 450

Court of Appeal (Singleton, Denning and Morris LJJ)

Mutual mistake as to meaning

### Facts

The plaintiffs, who were merchants, received from their Middle East house an order for 'Moroccan horsebeans described here as feveroles.' The plaintiffs asked the defendants what feveroles were and the defendants assured them that they were just horsebeans. The plaintiffs thereupon contracted orally with the defendants for a quantity of horsebeans. The oral agreement was later reduced to writing in the same terms. It turned out that feveroles were something quite different from horsebeans and the plaintiffs sought rectification of the document to read feveroles.

### Held

Rectification would be refused as the written contract was a fair reflection of the oral agreement made between the parties.

Denning LJ:

'The buyers now, after accepting the goods, seek to rectify the contract. Instead of it being a contract for "horsebeans" simpliciter, they seek to make it a contract for "horsebeans described in Egypt as feveroles". The judge has granted their request. He has found that there was a "mutual and fundamental mistake" and that the defendants and the plaintiffs, through their respective market clerks, "intended to deal in horsebeans of the feverole type"; and he has held that, because that was their intention - their "continuing common intention" - the court could rectify their contract to give effect to it. In this I think he was wrong. Rectification is concerned with contracts and documents, not with intentions. In order to get rectification it is necessary to show that the parties were in complete agreement on the terms of their contract, but by an error wrote them down wrongly; and in this regard, in order to ascertain the terms of their contract, you do not look into the inner minds of parties - into their intentions - any more than you do in the formation of any other contract. You look at their outward acts, that is, at what they said or wrote to one another in coming to their agreement, and then compare it with the document which they have signed. If you can predicate with certainty what their document was, and that it is, by a common mistake, wrongly expressed in the document, then you rectify the document; but nothing less will suffice. It is not necessary that all the formalities of the contract should have been executed so as to make it enforceable at law (see *Shipley Urban District Council* v *Bradford Corporation* [1936] Ch 375); but formalities apart, there must have been a concluded contract. There is a passage in *Crane* v *Hegeman-Harris Co Inc* [1939] 1 All ER 662, 664 which suggests that a continuing common intention alone will suffice, but I am clearly of opinion that a continuing common intention is not sufficient unless it has found expression in outward agreement. There could be no certainty at all in business transactions if a party who had entered into a firm contract could afterwards turn round and claim to have it rectified on the ground that the parties intended something different. he is allowed to prove, if he can, that they agreed something different (see *Lovell & Christmas* v *Wall* per Lord Cozens-Hardy MR and per Buckley LJ (1911) 104 LT 85, 88, 93) but not that they intended something different.

The present case is a good illustration of the distinction. The parties no doubt intended that the goods should satisfy the inquiry of the Egyptian buyers, namely, "horsebeans described in Egypt as feveroles". They assumed that they would do so, but they made no contract to that effect. Their agreement as outwardly expressed, both orally and in writing, was for "horsebeans". That is all that the defendants ever committed themselves to supply; and all that they should be bound to. There was, no doubt, an erroneous assumption underlying the contract - an assumption for which it might have been set aside on the grounds of misrepresentation or mistake - but that is very different from an erroneous expression of the contract, such as to give rise to rectification.'

**Saunders v Anglia Building Society** [1970] 3 WLR 1078 House of Lords (Lord Reid, Lord Hodson, Viscount Dilhorne, Lord Wilberforce and Lord Pearson)

Mistake - plea of non est factum

*Facts*

The plaintiff, executrix of Mrs Gallie, a widow aged 84, ran a boarding house in Essex with the assistance of her nephew. Her nephew had possession of the deeds of the house and she was quite content that he should use them to raise money if he so wished, so long as she could stay in the house for the rest of her life. Lee, a friend of the nephew, was a man heavily in debt. Lee had a document of sale drawn up in respect of the house and took it to Mrs Gallie for her to sign. The nephew acted as witness. When she asked what the document was, she was told by Lee that it was a deed of gift in favour of the nephew. Lee paid Mrs Gallie nothing, but raised a loan for himself on the strength of the document. When he defaulted on one of the mortgages, the building society sought to recover possession and the plaintiff raised the defence of non est factum.

*Held*

The building society would succeed.

Lord Reid:

'The existing law seems to me to be in a state of some confusion. I do not think that it is possible to reconcile all the decisions, let alone all the reasons given for them. In view of some general observations made in the Court of Appeal I think that it is desirable to try to extract from the authorities the principles on which most of them are based. When we are trying to do that my experience has been that there are dangers in there being only one speech in this House. Then statements in it have often tended to be treated as definitions and it is not the function of a court or of this House to frame definitions; some latitude should be left for future developments. The true ratio of a decision generally appears more clearly from a comparison of two or more statements in different words which are intended to supplement each other.

The plea of non est factum obviously applies when the person sought to be held liable did not in fact sign the document. But at least since the sixteenth century it has also been held to apply in certain cases so as to enable a person who in fact signed a document to say that it is not his deed. Obviously any such extension must be kept within narrow limits if it is not to shake the confidence of those who habitually and rightly rely on signatures when there is no obvious reason to doubt their validity. Originally this extension appears to have been made in favour of those who were unable to read owing to blindness or illiteracy and who therefore had to trust someone to tell them what they were signing. I think that it must also apply in favour of those who are permanently or temporarily unable through no fault of their own to have without explanation any real understanding of the purport of a particular document, whether that be from defective education, illness or innate incapacity.

But that does not excuse them from taking such precautions as they reasonably can. The matter generally arises where an innocent third party has relied on a signed document in ignorance of the circumstances in which it was signed, and where he will suffer loss if the maker of the document is allowed to have it declared a nullity. So there must be a heavy burden of proof on the person who seeks to invoke this remedy. He must prove all the circumstances necessary to justify its being granted to him, and that necessarily involves his proving that he took all reasonable precautions in the circumstances. I do not say that the remedy can never be available to a man of full capacity. But that could only be in very exceptional circumstances; certainly not where his reason for not scrutinising the document before signing it was that he was too busy or too lazy. In general I do not think that he can be heard to say that he signed in reliance on someone he trusted. But, particularly when he was led to believe that the document which he signed was not one which affected his legal rights, there may be cases where this plea can properly be applied in favour of a man of full capacity.

The plea cannot be available to anyone who was content to sign without taking the trouble to try to find out at least the general effect of the document. Many people do frequently sign documents put before them for signature by their solicitor or other trusted advisers without making any enquiry as to their purpose or effect. But the essence of the plea non est factum is that the person signing believed that the document he signed had one character or one effect whereas in fact its character or effect was quite different. He could not have such a belief unless he had taken steps or been given information which gave him some grounds for his belief. The amount of information he must have and the sufficiency of the particularity of his belief must depend on the circumstances of each case. Further the plea cannot be available to a person whose mistake was really a mistake as to the legal effect of the document, whether that was is own mistake or that of his adviser. That has always been the law and in this branch of the law at least I see no reason for any change.

We find in many of the authorities statements that a man's deed is not his deed if his mind does not go with his pen. But that is far too wide. It would cover cases where the man had taken no precautions at all, and there was no ground for his belief that he was signing something different from that which in fact he signed. I think that it is the wrong approach to start from that wide statement and then whittle it down by excluding cases where the remedy will not be granted. It is for the person who seeks the remedy to show that he should have it.

Finally, there is the question to what extent or in what way must there be a difference between that which in fact he signed and that which he believed he was signing. In an endeavour to keep the plea within bounds there have been many attempts to lay down a dividing line. But any dividing line suggested has been difficult to apply in practice and has sometimes led to unreasonable results. In particular I do not think that the modern division between the character and the contents of a document is at all satisfactory. Some of the older authorities suggest a more flexible test so that one can take all factors into consideration. There was a period when here as elsewhere in the law hard and fast dividing lines were sought, but I think that experience has shown that often they do not produce certainty but do produce unreasonable results.

I think that in the older authorities difference in practical result was more important than difference in legal character. If a man thinks that he is signing a document which will cost him £10 and the actual document would cost him £1,000 it could not be right to deny him this remedy simply because the legal character of the two was the same. It is true that we must then deal with questions of degree but that is a familiar task for the courts and I would not expect it to give rise to a flood of litigation.

There must I think be a radical difference between what he signed and what he thought he was signing - or one could use the words "fundamental" or "serious" or "very substantial". But what amounts to a radical difference will depend on all the circumstances. If he thinks he is giving property to A whereas the document gives it to B the difference may often be of vital importance, but in the circumstances of the present case I do not think that it is. I think that it must be left to the courts to determine in each case in light of all the facts whether there was or was not a sufficiently great difference. The plea non est factum is in sense illogical when applied to a case where the man in fact signed the deed. But it is none the worse for that if applied in a reasonable way.'

*Commentary*

Approved: *Foster* v *Mackinnon* (1869) LR 4 CP 704. Overruled: *Carlisle and Cumberland Banking Co* v *Bragg* [1911] 1 KB 489. Applied in *Avon Finance Co Ltd* v *Bridges* [1985] 2 All ER 281.

### Scriven Bros & Co v Hindley & Co [1913] 3 KB 564 High Court (A T Lawrence J)

Mistake as to subject-matter of contract

*Facts*

An auctioneer offered for sale the plaintiffs' hemp and tow, samples of which had been on view. The tow was knocked down to the defendants who thought they had been bidding for hemp, a more valuable commodity.

*Held*

There was no binding contract of sale as the parties had never been ad idem.

### Smith v Hughes

See chapter 5 - Misrepresentation.

### Solle v Butcher [1950] 1 KB 671 Court of Appeal (Bucknill, Denning and Jenkins LJJ)

Mistake - lease could be set aside?

*Facts*

The plaintiff, who was a partner in a firm of estate agents, introduced the defendant to the representative of the head lessor of a block of flats. In 1938 one of the flats was let to one Taylor for three years, at an annual rent of £140. He also had the right to the use of a garage. During the war, the flats suffered considerable damage and became unoccupied. In 1947, the defendant took a long lease of the house comprising the block, with a view to renovating and letting them. The plaintiff and the defendant had conversations about the rents to be charged, but both believed that the rent of £140 in 1938 was not a standard rent under the Rent Acts. In the course of renovating the house, the flat which had been let to Taylor was altered in size and, in 1947, it was let by the defendants to the plaintiff for seven years at £250 p a. The garage was expressly included. Relations between the parties deteriorated and the plaintiff sued the defendant in the county court, alleging that the standard rent was £140. The defendant claimed that he had granted the lease to the plaintiff on his oral assurance that the rent was in no way controlled by any letting of the flat before it suffered war damage. He also counter claimed that the lease had been entered into under a common mistake of fact and asked for rescission.

*Held* (Jenkins LJ dissenting)

There had been a mistake of fact and the lease could be set aside in equity.

Bucknill LJ:

'It seems to me that in all essential respects, this flat was the same as the flat which was let to Taylor in 1937 ... It seems to me that on the particular facts of this case, the demise of the garage had no material effect upon the identity of the flat ... I do not agree with the view taken by the judge that the parties never addressed their minds to the issue of identity. It seems to me that the reason why they thought that the Rent Restriction Acts did not apply was ... that they made a mistake and thought the work done made such a substantial alteration as to make it, in effect, a different flat ... was the mistake a question of fact or a question of law? In my opinion it was a question of fact and the principle applies to this case which was laid down by Lord Westbury in his speech in *Cooper* v *Phibbs* (1867) LR 2 HL 149, 170 where he said:

"If parties contract under a mutual mistake and misapprehension as to their relative and respective rights, the result is that the agreement is liable to be set aside as having proceeded upon a common mistake."

In my opinion therefore, there was a common mistake of fact on a matter of fundamental importance, namely as to the identity of the flat within the dwelling house previously let at a standard rent of £140 a year and that the principle laid down in *Cooper* v *Phibbs* applies.'

Denning LJ:

'... I think that the structural alterations and improvements were not such as to destroy the identity of the original flat. The landlord was entitled, therefore, to increase the rent by 8% of their cost, but was not able, on this account, to charge a new rent unrestricted by the Acts ... the addition of the garage does not change the identity of the flat ... It is quite plain that the parties were under a mistake ... mistake is of two kinds: first, mistake which renders a contract void ... and, secondly, mistake which renders the contract ... voidable ... such as the kind of mistake which was dealt with by the courts of equity ...

Applying these principles, it is clear that here there was a contract. The parties agreed in the same terms on the same subject matter. It is true that the landlord was under a mistake which was, to him, fundamental ... but whether it was his own mistake or a mistake common to both him and the tenant, it is not a ground for saying that the lease was, from the beginning, of a nullity...

The court ... had power to set aside the contract whenever it was of the opinion that it was unconscious for the other party to avail himself of the legal advantage which he had obtained ... a contract will be set aside if the mistake of one party has been induced by a material misrepresentation of the other, even though it was not fraudulent or fundamental; or if one party, knowing that the other is mistaken about the terms of an offer, or the identity of the person by whom it is made, lets him remain under his delusion and concludes a contract on the mistaken terms instead of pointing out the mistake ... a contract is also liable in equity to be set aside if the parties were under a common misapprehension either as to facts or as to their relative and respective rights, provided that the misapprehension was fundamental and that the party seeking to set it aside was not himself at fault ... Applying that principle to this case, the facts are that the plaintiff ... formed the view that the building was not controlled. He told the valuation officer so ... He read to the defendant an opinion of counsel relating to the matter and told him that in his opinion he could charge £250 and that there was no previous control ... The plaintiff not only let the four other flats ... but also took one himself ... Now he turns round and says ... that he wants to take advantage of the mistake to get the flat at £140 a year ... On the defendant's evidence ... I should have thought that there was a good deal to be said for the view that the lease was induced by an innocent material misrepresentation by the plaintiff. It seems to me that the plaintiff was not merely expressing an opinion on the law: he was making an unambiguous statement as to private rights; and a misrepresentation is equivalent to a misrepresentation of fact for this purpose ... But it is unnecessary to come to a firm conclusion on this point because ... there was clearly ... a common misapprehension which was fundamental and in no way due to any fault of the defendant; and *Cooper* v *Phibbs* affords ample authority for saying that, by reason of the common misapprehension, this lease can be set aside on such terms as the court thinks fit ... In the ordinary way, of course, rescission is only granted when the parties can be restored to substantially the same position as that in which they were before the contract was made, but as Lord Blackburn said in *Erlanger* v *New Sombrero Phosphate Co* (1878) 3 App Cas 1218, 1278-9: "The practice has always been for a court of equity to give this relief whenever, by the exercise of its powers, it can do what is practically just, though it cannot restore the parties precisely to the state they were in before the contract" ... What terms, then, should be imposed here? I think the court ... should impose terms which will enable the tenant to choose either to stay on at the proper rent or to go out ...'

**Upton-on-Severn Rural District Council v Powell** [1942] 1 All ER 220 Court of Appeal
(Lord Greene MR, Luxmoore and Goddard LJJ)

Fire brigade - implied promise to pay for its services

*Facts*

When a fire broke out on the defendant's farm in the Upton police district, he telephoned the Upton police and asked for the fire brigade. The police informed the Upton brigade and it duly responded. At the time the brigade was called all concerned were under the impression that the farm was in the Upton fire district; in fact, it was in the Pershore fire district. The defendant was entitled to the Pershore fire service without charge; if Upton fire brigade went out of its district it was entitled to make a charge. Upton fire brigade, the plaintiffs, sued to recover an appropriate charge.

*Held*

The plaintiffs were entitled to succeed.

Lord Greene MR:

'What the defendant wanted was somebody to put out his fire, and put it out as quickly as possible, and in ringing up the Upton police he must have intended that the inspector at Upton would get the Upton fire brigade; that is the brigade which he would naturally ask for when he rang up Upton. Even apart from that, it seems to me quite sufficient if the Upton inspector reasonably so construed the request made to him, and, indeed, I do not see what other construction the inspector could have put upon that request. It follows, therefore, that on any view the appellant must be treated as having asked for the Upton fire brigade. That request having been made to the Upton fire brigade by a person who was asking for its services, does it prevent there being a contractual relationship merely because the Upton fire brigade, which responds to that request and renders the services, thinks, at the time it starts out and for a considerable time afterwards, that the farm in question is in its area, as the officer in charge appears to have thought? In my opinion, that can make no difference. The real truth of the matter is that the appellant wanted the services of Upton; he asked for the service of Upton - that is the request that he made - and Upton, in response to that request, provided those services. He cannot afterwards turn round and say: "Although I wanted Upton, although I did not concern myself when I asked for Upton as to whether I was entitled to get free services, or whether I would have to pay for them, nevertheless, when it turns out that Upton can demand payment, I am not going to pay them, because Upton were under the erroneous impression that they were rendering gratuitous services in their own area." That, it seems to me, would be quite wrong on principle.'

# 9    DURESS AND UNDUE INFLUENCE

**Allcard v Skinner** (1887) 36 Ch D 145 Court of Appeal (Cotton, Lindley and Bowen LJJ)

Undue influence - gift to sisterhood

*Facts*

In 1867 an unmarried woman aged 27 sought a clergyman as a confessor. The following year she became an associate of the sisterhood of which he was spiritual director and in 1871 she was admitted a full member, taking vows of poverty, chastity and obedience. Without independent advice, she made gifts of money and stock to the mother superior on behalf of the sisterhood. She left the sisterhood in 1879 and in 1884 claimed the return of the stock. Proceedings to recover the stock were commenced in 1885.

*Held*

Although the plaintiff's gifts were voidable, (Cotton LJ dissenting) she was disentitled to recover because of her conduct and the delay.

Lindley LJ:

'... I believe that in this case there was in fact no unfair or undue influence brought to bear upon the plaintiff other than such as inevitably resulted from the training she had received, the promise she had made, the vows she had taken, and the rules to which she had submitted herself. But her gifts were in fact made under a pressure which, while it lasted, the plaintiff could not resist, and were not, in my opinion, past recall when the pressure was removed. When the plaintiff emancipated herself from the spell by which she was bound she was entitled to invoke the aid of the court in order to obtain the restitution from the defendant of so much of the plaintiff's property as had not been spent in accordance with the wishes of the plaintiff but remained in the hands of the defendant. The plaintiff now demands no more.

I proceed to consider the second point which arises in this case, viz, whether it is too late for the plaintiff to invoke the assistance of the court. More than six years had elapsed between the time when the plaintiff left the sisterhood and the commencement of the present action. The action is not one of those to which the Statute of Limitations in terms applies, nor is that statute pleaded. But this action very closely resembles an action for money had and received, laches and acquiescence are relied upon as a defence, and the question is whether this defence ought to prevail. In my opinion, it ought ...

It is not, however, necessary to decide whether this delay alone would be a sufficient defence to the action. The case by no means rests on mere lapse of time. There is far more than inactivity and delay on the part of the plaintiff. There is conduct amounting to confirmation of her gift. Gifts liable to be set aside by the court on the ground of undue influence have always been treated as voidable, and not void ... such gifts are voidable on equitable grounds only. A gift intended when made to be absolute and irrevocable, but liable to be set aside by a court of justice, not on the ground of change of mind on the part of the donor, but on grounds of public policy based upon the fact that the donor was not sufficiently free relatively to the donee - such a gift is very different from a loan which the borrower knows he is under an obligation to repay, and is also different from a gift expressly made revocable, and never intended to be absolute and unconditional. A gift made in terms absolute and unconditional naturally leads the donee to regard it as his own, and the longer he is left under this impression the more difficult it is justly to deprive him of what he has naturally so regarded.

So long as the relation between the donor and the donee which invalidates the gifts lasts, so long is it necessary to hold that lapse of time affords no sufficient ground for refusing relief to the donor. But this necessity ceases when the relation itself comes to an end; and if the donor desires to have his gift declared invalid and set aside, he ought, in my opinion, to seek relief within a reasonable time after the removal of the influence under which the gift was made. If he does not, the inference is strong, and if the lapse of time is long the inference becomes inevitable and conclusive - that the donor is content not to call the gift in question or, in other words, that he elects not to avoid it, or, what is the same thing in effect, that he ratifies and confirms it ... In this particular case the plaintiff considered, when she left the sisterhood, what course she should take, and she determined to do nothing, but to leave matters as they were. She insisted on having back her will, but she never asked for her money until the end of five years or so after she left the sisterhood. In this state of things I can only come to the conclusion that she deliberately chose not to attempt to avoid her gifts but to acquiesce in them, or, if the expression be preferred, to ratify or confirm them. I regard this as a question of fact, and upon the evidence I can come to no other conclusion than that which I have mentioned. Moreover, by demanding her will and not her money, she made her resolution known to the defendant.'

## Atlas Express Ltd v Kafco (Importers and Distributors) Ltd [1989] 3 WLR 389 High Court (Tucker J)

Duress - commercial pressure

*Facts*

The plaintiffs, a national road carrier, contracted with the defendants a small company, to deliver cartons of basketware to branches of Woolworth throughout the United Kingdom. Before entering into the contract, the plaintiffs' manager had inspected the cartons and estimated that each load would contain a minimum of 400 and possibly as many as 600 cartons: on that basis he agreed a charge of £1.10 per carton. In fact, the first load contained only 200 cartons, so the manager said they would not take any more unless the defendants agreed to pay a minimum of £440 per load. As they were heavily dependent on their Woolworth contract and could not at that time find an alternative carrier, the defendants agreed to the new terms but later refused to pay at the new rate.

*Held*

The defendants were not bound by the new terms: economic duress had vitiated the new agreement and, in any case, there was no consideration for it.

Tucker J:

'The issue which I have to determine is whether the defendants are bound by the [new] agreement signed on their behalf ... The defendants contend that they are not bound, for two reasons: first, because the agreement was signed under duress; second, because there was no consideration for it.

The first question raises an interesting point of law, ie whether economic duress is a concept known to English law.

Economic duress must be distinguished from commercial pressure, which on any view is not sufficient to vitiate consent. The borderline between the two may in some cases be indistinct. But ... authors ... appear to recognise that in appropriate cases economic duress may afford a defence, and in my judgment it does. It is clear to me that in a number of English cases judges have acknowledged the existence of this concept.

Thus, in *D & C Builders Ltd* v *Rees* [1965] 3 All ER 837 at 841 Lord Denning MR said: "No person can insist on a settlement procured by intimidation." And in *Occidental Worldwide Investment Corp* v *Skibs A/S Avanti, The Siboen and the Sibotre* [1976] 1 Lloyd's Rep 293 at 336 Kerr J appeared to accept that economic duress could operate in appropriate circumstances. A similar conclusion was reached by Mocatta J in *North Ocean Shipping Co Ltd* v *Hyundai Construction Co Ltd, The Atlantic Baron* [1978] 3 All ER 1170 at 1182.

In particular, there are passages in the judgment of Lord Scarman in *Pao On* v *Lau Yiu* [1979] 3 All ER 65 at 78-79 which clearly indicate recognition of the concept ...

A further case, which was not cited to me was *B & S Contracts and Design Ltd* v *Victor Green Publications Ltd* [1984] ICR 419 at 423, where Eveleigh LJ referred to the speech of Lord Diplock in another uncited case, *Universe Tankships Inc of Monrovia* v *International Transport Workers' Federation* [1982] 2 All ER 67 at 75-76:

"The rationale is that his apparent consent was induced by pressure exercised on him by that other party which the law does not regard as legitimate, with the consequence that the consent is treated in law as revocable unless approbated either expressly or by implication after the illegitimate pressure has ceased to operate on his mind."

In commenting on this Eveleigh LJ said of the word "legitimate" ([1984] ICR 419 at 423):

"For the purpose of this case it is sufficient to say that if the claimant has been influenced against his will to pay money under the threat of unlawful damage to his economic interest he will be entitled to claim that money back ..."

Reverting to the case before me, I find that the defendants' apparent consent to the agreement was induced by pressure which was illegitimate and I find that it was not approbated. In my judgment that pressure can properly be described as economic duress, which is a concept recognised by English law, and which in the circumstances of the present case vitiates the defendants' apparent consent to the agreement.

In any event, I find that there was no consideration for the new agreement. The plaintiffs were already obliged to deliver the defendants' goods at the rates agreed under the terms of the original agreement. There was no consideration for the increased minimum charge of £440 per trailer.'

### Avon Finance Co Ltd v Bridger

See chapter 8 - Mistake.

### Backhouse v Backhouse [1978] 1 WLR 243 High Court (Balcombe J)

Unequal bargaining power - husband and wife

*Facts*

Following the breakdown of their marriage, a husband was anxious to have the matrimonial home transferred into his sole name. He did not advise the wife to take independent legal advice and she received no consideration for the transfer except release from her liability under the mortgage of the property.

*Held*

Financial arrangements between the parties would be made on the basis that the transfer to the husband had not taken place.

Balcombe J:

'Counsel for the husband says that the wife was not poor or ignorant. She was certainly not wealthy ... She was not in my view "ignorant" in the sense that, as I said, she was an intelligent woman, but she certainly was given no value for her transfer, merely the release from her liability on the mortgage, and she received no independent advice. As for this last, I accept that no one can make a person go to solicitors if they do not wish to do so, but this wife was never even invited to do so before she signed away what was her only substantial capital asset ... When a marriage has broken down, both parties are liable to be in an emotional state. The party remaining in the matrimonial home, as the husband did in this case, has an advantage. The wife is no doubt in circumstances of great emotional strain. It seems to me that she should at least be encouraged to take independent advice so that she may know whether or not it is right for her, whatever the circumstances of the breakdown of the marriage may be, to transfer away what is her only substantial capital asset. It is possible that this is something which may come under the general heading which Lord Denning MR referred to in *Lloyds Bank Ltd* v *Bundy* as "inequality of bargaining power" where he summarised the various categories in which transactions can be set aside: duress, unconscionable transactions and so on, and suggested that through all these instances runs a single thread, that they rest on inequality of bargaining power. If that be right then it seems to me that this transaction is an example of something which is done where the parties did not have equal bargaining power and should not be at any rate encouraged by the courts. I consider too that counsel for the wife had a valid point when she said that by analogy with s34 of the Matrimonial Causes Act 1973, which precludes parties from contracting out of their right to apply to the court for an order containing financial arrangements, the court should not look with favour on assignments of proprietary interests in the matrimonial home made without the benefit of legal advice.

As it happens I do not have before me the issue whether the transfer should be set aside. In the end it may make very little difference, having regard to the very wide powers that are given to the court to produce a just result under ss23, 24 and 25 of the 1973 Act. I propose to approach the problem in this case on the basis that the transfer in question had not been made.'

**Bank of Baroda v Shah** [1988] 3 All ER 24 Court of Appeal (Dillon, Neill and Stocker LJJ)

Undue influence - bank's position

*Facts*

By way of a legal charge, the defendant husband and wife charged their property with the payment to the plaintiffs of all moneys at any time owed to the bank by Seasonworth Ltd ('Seasonworth'). The defendants entered into the charge as a result of misrepresentation and undue influence exerted by the wife's brother, one of two directors of Seasonworth whose solicitors (Shah & Burke) acted for the defendants in connection with the charge although they (the defendants) had not instructed them to do so. Seasonworth defaulted in its obligations to the bank: the bank sought possession of the defendants' property.

*Held*

An order for possession would be made.

Dillon LJ:

'Specifically, the defendants assert that, whatever the bank may have supposed: (i) they did not in fact have any solicitors, independent or not, to act for them or advise them; (ii) Shah & Burke were in fact only acting for Seasonworth and Jayantilal Shah [the wife's brother]; and (iii) accordingly, when Singh & Ruparell [the bank's solicitors] sent the legal charge ... to Shah & Burke for execution, that was tantamount to sending it to Jayantilal Shah himself to get it executed by the defendants for the bank, and if so was a direct parallel to the situation in *Avon Finance Co Ltd* v *Bridger* [1985] 2 All ER 281 given the bank's knowledge of Jayantilal Shah's influence or possible influence over the defendants ...

It is impossible, in the light of *Coldunell Ltd* v *Gallon* [1986] 1 All ER 429 for this court to hold that there was an obligation in law on the bank or its solicitors to ensure that the defendants had entirely independent legal advice before the defendants executed the legal charge ... If therefore solicitors were acting for the defendants, who were also the solicitors acting for Seasonworth, that was not a situation which Singh & Ruparell were able to challenge or were required to challenge. They were entitled to assume that Shah & Burke would act honestly and would give proper advice to the defendants, if Shah & Burke were, as they represented, acting for the defendants ... Beyond that, however I do not see how Singh & Ruparell could have asked Shah & Burke for proof that Shah &

Burke were indeed authorised by the defendants to act for the defendants; that was something that Singh & Ruparell had to take on trust, and when the legal charge executed by the defendants was returned to them by Shah & Burke they were entitled to treat the return of it as confirmation that Shah & Burke had indeed been acting as solicitors for the defendants.

Against that background it is plain, in my judgment, that Singh & Ruparell never intended for a moment to leave it to Jayantilal Shah or Seasonworth to get the legal charge executed by the defendants. They left that to Shah & Burke in the capacity of solicitors for the defendants which Shah & Burke had represented themselves as holding and which Singh & Ruparell believed them to hold. The fact that, unknown to Singh & Ruparell, Shah & Burke had no authority from the defendants does not lead to the conclusion that Singh & Ruparell are to be treated as having entrusted the task of getting the legal charge executed by the defendants to Shah & Burke in the capacity which they actually did hold, namely as agents for Jayantilal Shah and solicitors for Seasonworth.

Accordingly in my judgment the defendants fail to bring this case within the *Turnbull* v *Duval* [1902] AC 429 and *Chaplin* v *Brammall* [1908] 1 KB 233 line of authorities.

In reaching the opposite conclusion the judge relied in particular on my judgment in *Kingsnorth Trust Ltd* v *Bell* [1986] 1 All ER 423. But the facts of that case are, in my judgment, significantly different from the facts of the present case, in that in that case there had been no suggestion at all that the husband's solicitors, Messrs Burnetts, had ever been instructed to act for the wife, before the lender's solicitors, Messrs Trump & Partners, asked Messrs Burnetts to get the mortgage executed by the wife.'

### Bank of Credit and Commerce International SA v Aboody [1989] 2 WLR 759 Court of Appeal (Slade, Balcombe and Woolf LJJ)

Undue influence - husband and wife

*Facts*

A husband and wife owned a family company (Eratex Ltd) and the company's liabilities to its bank were secured, inter alia, by charges of the wife's house. The bank sought to enforce the securities and the wife pleaded actual undue influence by the husband. Although the judge found that such influence had been established, he refused to set aside the charges as it had not been proved that they were manifestly disadvantageous to the wife. The wife appealed.

*Held*

The appeal would be dismissed as the judge's conclusion that there had been no manifest disadvantage was correct and, further, it was probable that the wife would have entered into the charges even in the absence of undue influence.

Slade LJ:

'We now turn to consider the point of law which constitutes the first ground of appeal, namely that a party who proves that a transaction was induced by the actual exercise of undue influence is entitled to have it set aside without also proving that the transaction was manifestly disadvantageous to him or her.

Ever since the judgments of this court in *Allcard* v *Skinner* (1887) 36 Ch D 145 a clear distinction has been drawn between (1) those cases in which the court will uphold a plea of undue influence only if it is satisfied that such influence has been affirmatively proved on the evidence (commonly referred to as cases of "actual undue influence" and, in argument before us, as "class 1" cases); (2) those cases (commonly referred to as cases of "presumed undue influence," and, in argument before us, as "class 2" cases) in which the relationship between the parties will lead the court to presume that undue influence has been exerted unless evidence is adduced proving the contrary, eg by showing that the complaining party has had independent advice.

There are well established categories of relationship, such as a religious superior and inferior and doctor and patient where the relationship as such will give rise to the presumption (frequently referred to in argument before us as "class 2A" cases). The relationship of husband and wife does not as such give rise to the presumption: see *National Westminster Bank plc* v *Morgan* [1985] AC 686, 703B, and *Bank of Montreal* v *Stuart* [1911] AC 120. Nor does the normal relationship of banker and customer as such give rise to it. Nevertheless, on particular facts (frequently referred to in argument as "class 2B" cases) relationships not falling within the class 2A category may be shown to have become such as to justify the court in applying the same presumption.

"the presumption of undue influence, like other presumptions, is a tool of the lawyer's trade whose function it is to enable him to arrive at a just result by bridging a gap in the evidence at a point where, in the nature of the case, evidence is difficult or impossible to come by:" see *In re The Estate of Brocklehurst, decd* [1978] Ch 14, 43, per Bridge LJ.

In the majority of reported cases on undue influence successful plaintiffs appear to have succeeded in reliance on the presumption. If on the facts both pleas are open to him, a plaintiff in such a case may well be advised to rely on actual and presumed undue influence cumulatively or in the alternative.

In the present case, however, no doubt after carefully considered advice, no attempt has been made to plead or submit that Mrs Aboody is entitled to the benefit of any presumption. Her case throughout has been pleaded and argued on the footing that it is a class 1 case, so that the onus falls on her to establish undue influence - an onus which, subject to the question of manifest disadvantage, the judge considered that she had discharged ...

...we must reject the first ground of appeal. In our judgment, and in the light of *National Westminster Bank plc* v *Morgan* [1985] AC 686, even a party who affirmatively proves that a transaction was induced by the exercise of undue influence is not entitled to have it set aside in reliance on the doctrine of undue influence without proving that the transaction was manifestly disadvantageous to him or her.

Since Mrs Aboody's claim in the present case is based exclusively on undue influence, it thus becomes necessary to consider whether, contrary to the judge's view, she has shown that all or any of the six transactions were manifestly disadvantageous to her ... Eratex Ltd was the family business and the sole or principal means of support of Mr and Mrs Aboody. Eratex Ltd might still have collapsed with or without the facilities covered by the six transactions. But at least these facilities gave it some hope of survival. The judge found that ... it had "more than an equal chance of surviving," and that, [later], it had "at least a reasonably good chance of surviving." If it had survived, the potential benefits to Mrs Aboody would have been substantial.

In the end, we can see no sufficient grounds for disagreeing with his conclusion that on balance a manifest disadvantage has not been shown by Mrs Aboody in respect of any of the six transactions ...

... in our judgment ... the jurisdiction exercised by the court in such cases is not essentially of a punitive nature; its purpose is to do justice to the complainant in suitable circumstances giving him or her relief from a disadvantageous transaction. We think that, at least in ordinary circumstances, it would not be appropriate for the court to exercise this jurisdiction in a case where the evidence establishes that on balance of probabilities the complainant would have entered into the transaction in any event. In the present case there is the additional factor that the transactions under attack are relied on not by Mr Aboody himself but by the bank, which was not personally responsible for exerting the undue influence. Even if Mrs Aboody had succeeded on all the other issues in this case, we are therefore disposed to think that it would not have been right to grant her equitable relief as against the bank, our decision being based not merely on narrow considerations of causation.'

**Barton v Armstrong** [1975] 2 WLR 1050 Privy Council (Lord Wilberforce, Lord Simon of Glaisdale, Lord Cross of Chelsea, Lord Kilbrandon and Sir Garfield Barwick)

Duress - reason for contracting

*Facts*

Armstrong and Barton had struggled for control of a public company and Barton had executed a deed (and certain ancillary deeds) in the course of various negotiations. Barton alleged that these deeds had been executed by him under duress exerted by Armstrong and were therefore void. It was found as a fact that Armstrong had uttered threats to kill Barton, but the Court of Appeal of the Supreme Court of New South Wales found that Barton had not discharged the onus of showing that, but for the threats, he would not have executed the deeds.

*Held* (Lord Wilberforce and Lord Simon of Glaisdale dissenting)

The deeds were void as Armstrong had failed to establish that his threats had contributed nothing to Barton's decision to sign them.

Lord Cross of Chelsea:

'Their Lordships turn now to consider the question of law ... It is hardly surprising that there is no direct authority on the point, for if A threatens B with death if he does not execute some document and B, who takes A's threats seriously, executes the document it can be only in the most unusual circumstances that there can be any doubt whether the threats operated to induce him to execute the document. But this is a most unusual case and the findings of fact made below do undoubtedly raise the question whether it was necessary for Barton in order to obtain relief to establish that he would not have executed the deed in question but for the threats ...

Had Armstrong made a fraudulent misrepresentation to Barton for the purpose of inducing him to execute the [deeds] the answer to the problem which has arisen would have been clear. If it were established that Barton did not allow the representation to affect his judgment then he could not make it a ground for relief even though the representation was designed and known by Barton to be designed to affect his judgment. If on the other hand Barton relief on the misrepresentation Armstrong could not have defeated his claim to relief by showing that there were other more weighty causes which contributed to his decision to execute the deed, for in this field the court does not allow an examination into the relative importance of contributory causes. "Once make out that there has been anything like deception, and no contract resting in any degree on that foundation can stand" (per Lord Cranworth LJ in *Reynell* v *Sprye* (1852) 1 De GM & G 660 ... Their Lordships think that the same rule should apply in cases of duress and that if Armstrong's threats were "a" reason for Barton's executing the deed he is entitled to relief even though he might well have entered into the contract if Armstrong had uttered no threats to induce him to do so.'

**Coldunell Ltd v Gallon** [1986] 2 WLR 466 Court of Appeal (Oliver and

Purchas LJJ)

Undue influence - son and parents

*Facts*

A son had exercised undue influence over his parents in obtaining their signatures to a transaction which was manifestly to their disadvantage. The plaintiffs had not appointed the son as their agent; his intervention in the transaction had been unauthorised. The son's unilateral assumption of the conduct of the transaction did not constitute him the plaintiff's agent.

*Held*

In consequence - distinguishing *Avon Finance* and *Kingsnorth Trust* - the plaintiffs were not tainted by the son's undue influence and the parents were not entitled to equitable relief by way of avoiding the transaction.

*Commentary*

Followed in *Bank of Baroda* v *Shah* [1988] 3 All ER 24.

**Cornish v Midland Bank plc** [1985] 3 All ER 513 Court of Appeal (Kerr, Croom-Johnson and Glidewell LJJ)

Undue influence - banker and customer

*Facts*

The plaintiff, a customer of the defendant bank, signed a second mortgage in favour of the bank without appreciating, and without being informed by the bank, that it was so worded as to secure not only a loan of £2,000 for house renovations, but also unlimited further advances made to her husband.

*Held*

Although the plaintiff was entitled to damages as the defendants had been in breach of their duty to her, the mortgage itself would not be set aside.

Croom-Johnson LJ:

'... between the trial by Taylor J and the hearing of this appeal the judgment in *National Westminster Bank plc* v *Morgan* has been reversed in the House of Lords (see ... [1985] 2 WLR 588). Lord Scarman, who made the principal speech, stated that to raise the presumption of undue influence it was necessary to show that the transaction had itself been wrongful in that it amounted to one in which an unfair advantage had been taken of another person. He considered the facts and held that there was no evidence that the bank had taken advantage of Mrs Morgan. The transaction had not been disadvantageous to her or gone beyond the normal business relationship of banker and customer.

Lord Scarman said ... [1985] 2 WLR 588 at 600:

"It was, as one would expect, conceded by counsel for the wife that the relationship between banker and customer is not one which ordinarily gives rise to a presumption of undue influence; and that in the ordinary course of banking business a banker can explain the nature of the proposed transaction without laying himself open to a charge of undue influence."

Faced with that fresh authority, counsel for the present plaintiff has properly conceded that the judge's decision on undue influence cannot stand. In this case the only relationship between the plaintiff and the bank was that of banker and customer. No unfair advantage was taken of her. The transaction of taking a second mortgage of the farm was not disadvantageous to her. That part of this appeal which submits that the mortgage should not be set aside must be allowed.'

*Commentary*

Followed: *National Westminster Bank plc* v *Morgan* [1985] 2 WLR 588. Applied: *Hedley Byrne & Co Ltd* v *Heller & Partners Ltd* [1963] 3 WLR 101.

**Cresswell v Potter** [1978] 1 WLR 255n High Court (Megarry J)

Unconscionable bargain - matrimonial home

*Facts*

The matrimonial home had been conveyed to a husband and wife as joint tenants at law and in equity. After the marriage had broken down the wife was handed a document to execute by an enquiry agent who acted on behalf of the husband and his solicitor. This document was described as a conveyance. By it, in return for an indemnity against the liabilities under a mortgage of the property but for no other consideration, the wife released and conveyed to the husband all her interest in the matrimonial home. She believed, according to her evidence, that she was signing a document that would make it possible to sell the property without affecting her rights in it. The enquiry agent, for his part, could remember very little about the execution of the document. Megarry J considered the three requirements laid down in *Fry v Lane*; poverty and ignorance of the plaintiff; sale at an undervalue, and lack of independent advice.

*Held*

These three requirements - or their modern equivalents - were here satisfied so the conveyance would be set aside.

**Dimskal Shipping Co SA v International Transport Workers' Federation (The Evia Luck)** [1991] 4 All ER 871; [1990] 1 Lloyd's Rep 319 House of Lords (Lord Keith, Lord Templeman, Lord Ackner, Lord Goff and Lord Lowry)

Economic duress - threat to black ship - improper pressure?

*Facts*

The Evia Luck was a ship owned by the plaintiffs, a Panamanian registered company whose vessels sailed under the Panamanian flag of convenience. The International Transport Workers Federation (ITF) had been conducting a long campaign against flags of convenience. While the ship was in harbour in Sweden, it was boarded by agents of ITF, who informed the master, and the owners, that the ship would be blacked and loading would not be continued until the company entered into certain agreements with ITF. These included payment of back pay to the Greek and Filipino crew, new contracts of employment at higher wages and guarantees for future payments. At first the owners would not agree and the ship was in fact blacked. Yielding to pressure, the company agreed to sign the various agreements, which were expressly declared to be governed by English law. The company incurred losses of some £100,000 or more, due to delays in loading and sailing, and having to pay back-pay to the crew.

They sought a declaration that the agreements were void on the grounds of duress and claimed restitution of all sums paid under such void agreements.

*Held*

The House of Lords in discussing what constituted economic duress, said the fact that ITF's conduct was quite legal in Sweden was irrelevant. In stipulating that the agreements were to be governed by English law, the defendants had to accept English law as the proper law of contract. Under English law a contract obtained by duress was voidable, and improper economic pressure (blacking the ship) constituted one form of duress. The owners were thus entitled to avoid the agreements they entered into because of pressure from ITF.

**Fry v Lane** (1888) 40 Ch D 312 High Court (Kay J)

Undue influence - sale by 'poor, ignorant men'

*Facts*

Two men had sold their reversionary interests in certain property, according to them at a greatly undervalued price, and they sought to have the transactions set aside.

*Held*

They should succeed.

Kay J:

'On the evidence before me, I cannot hesitate to conclude that the price of £170 in J B Fry's case and £270 in George Fry's case, were both considerably below the real value ... Both J B Fry and his brother George were poor, ignorant men, to whom the temptation of the immediate possession of £100 would be very great. Neither of them in the transaction of the sale of his share was, in the words of Sir John Leach, "on equal terms" with the purchaser. Neither had independent advice. The solicitor who acted for both parties in each transaction seems, from the Law List, to have been admitted in March 1877. In October 1878, the time of completing the sale of J B Fry's share, he had not been more than a year and a half on the roll. His inexperience probably in some degree accounts for his allowing himself to be put in the position of solicitor for both parties in such a case. I think that in each transaction he must have been considering the purchaser's interest too much properly to guard that of the vendors. Nothing could be more obvious than to test the value by obtaining an offer from one or more of the leading offices in London which deal in purchases of this kind ...

I regret that I must, on the evidence, come to the conclusion that, though there was a semblance of bargaining by the solicitor in each case, he did not properly protect the vendors, but gave a great advantage to the purchasers who had been former clients, and for whom he was then acting. The circumstances illustrate the wisdom and necessity of the rule that a poor, ignorant man selling an interest of this kind should have independent advice, and that a purchase from him at an undervalue should be set aside if he has not. The most experienced solicitor acting for both sides, if he allows a sale at an undervalue, can hardly have duly performed his duty to the vendor. To act for both sides in such a case and permit a sale at an undervalue is a position in which no careful practitioner would allow himself to be placed.'

*Commentary*

Applied in *Cresswell* v *Potter* [1978] 1 WLR 255n

## Goldsworthy v Brickell

See chapter 2 - Consideration.

## Kings North Trust Ltd v Bell [1986] 1 WLR 119 Court of Appeal (Sir John Donaldson MR, Dillon LJ and Mustill J)

Undue influence - husband and wife

*Facts*

The defendant executed a mortgage deed in favour of the plaintiffs, induced so to do by a fraudulent misrepresentation made by her husband as to the purpose of the loan. The Court of Appeal observed that there is no presumption in law that a transaction between husband and wife for the husband's benefit was procured by undue influence (see *Bank of Montreal* v *Stuart* [1911] AC 120). In the instant case, however, it was established that the execution of the document by the defendant was procured by undue influence on the part of the husband and that she had not had independent advice. The plaintiffs argued that they were not bound by the fraudulent misrepresentation made by the husband.

*Held*

They were under the law of agency, a creditor who instructed a husband as agent to obtain the signing of a document by his wife, was liable for any fraudulent misrepresentation made by the husband to obtain his wife's signature, irrespective of how personally innocent the creditor was.

It was observed, per curiam, that in circumstances such as these, the creditor ought, for his own protection, to insist that the person liable to be influenced had independent advice.

*Commentary*

Distinguished in *Coldunell Ltd* v *Gallon* [1986] 2 WLR 466 and *Midland Bank plc* v *Perry* (1987) The Times 28 May.  See also *Midland Bank plc* v *Shephard* [1988] 3 All ER 17.


**Levison  v  Patent  Steam  Carpet  Cleaning  Co  Ltd**

See chapter 6 - Exclusion clauses.


**Lloyds Bank Ltd v Bundy** [1974] 3 WLR 501 Court of Appeal (Lord Denning MR, Cairns LJ and Sir Eric Sachs)

Undue influence - banker and customer

*Facts*

The defendant was an elderly farmer who was not well versed in business affairs:  his farmhouse was his only asset.  Both he and his son banked with the plaintiffs, as did the son's company.  The defendant charged his houses to the bank to secure the company's overdraft and subsequently signed a further guarantee and charge.  An assistant manager of the plaintiff bank, with the son, later told the defendant that they would only continue to support the company if he increased the guarantee and charge: he did so, the assistant manager appreciating that the defendant relied on him implicitly to advise him about the transaction 'as bank manager'.

*Held*

The guarantee and charge would be set aside.

Lord Denning MR:

'Gathering all together, I would suggest that through all these instances there runs a single thread. They rest on "inequality of bargaining power".  By virtue of it, the English law gives relief to one who, without independent advice, enters into a contract on terms which are very unfair or transfers property for a consideration which is grossly inadequate, when his bargaining power is grievously impaired by reason of his own needs or desires, or by his own ignorance or infirmity, coupled with undue influences or pressures brought to bear on him by or for the benefit of the other.  When I use the word "undue" I do not mean to suggest that the principle depends on proof of any wrongdoing. The one who stipulates for an unfair advantage may be moved solely by his own self-interest, unconscious of the distress he is bringing to the other.  I have also avoided any reference to the will of the one being "dominated" or "overcome" by the other.  One who is in extreme need may knowingly consent to a most improvident bargain, solely to relieve the straits in which he finds himself.  Again, I do not mean to suggest that every transaction is saved by independent advice.  But the absence of it may be fatal.  With these explanations, I hope this principle will be found to reconcile the cases.  Applying it to the present case, I would notice these points.

(1)    The consideration moving from the bank was grossly inadequate.  The son's company was in serious difficulty ... The bank considered that their existing security was insufficient.  In order to get further security, they asked the father to charge the house - his sole asset - to the uttermost ... That was for the benefit of the bank.  But not at all for the benefit of the father, or indeed for the company. The bank did not promise to continue the overdraft or to increase it.  On the contrary, they required the overdraft to be reduced.  All that the company gained was a short respite from impending doom.

(2)    The relationship between the bank and the father was one of trust and confidence.  The bank knew that the father relied on them implicitly to advise him about the transaction.  The father trusted the bank.  This gave the bank much influence on the father.  Yet the bank failed in that trust.  They allowed the father to charge the house to his ruin.

(3)   The relationship between the father and the son was one where the father's natural affection had much influence on him.

(4)   He would naturally desire to accede to his son's request. He trusted his son. There was a conflict of interest between the bank and the father. Yet the bank did not realise it. Nor did they suggest that the father should get independent advice. If the father had gone to his solicitor - or to any man of business - there is no doubt that any one of them would say: "You must not enter into this transaction. You are giving up your house, your sole remaining asset, for no benefit to you. The company is in such a parlous state that you must not do it."

These considerations seem to me to bring this case within the principles I have stated. But, in case that principle is wrong, I would also say that the case falls within the category of undue influence of the second class stated by Cotton LJ in *Allcard* v *Skinner*. I have no doubt that the assistant bank manager acted in the utmost good faith and was straightforward and genuine. Indeed the father said so. But beyond doubt he was acting in the interests of the bank - to get further security for a bad debt. There was such a relationship of trust and confidence between them that the bank ought not to have swept up his sole remaining asset into their hands - for nothing - without his having independent advice. I would therefore allow this appeal.'

*Commentary*

Distinguished in *Avon Finance Co Ltd* v *Bridger* [1985] 2 All ER 281.

See also *Backhouse* v *Backhouse* [1978] 1 WLR 243 and *Alec Lobb (Garages) Ltd* v *Total Oil GB Ltd* [1985] 1 WLR 173.

**Lobb (Alec) (Garages) Ltd v Total Oil GB Ltd** [1985] 1 WLR 173 Court of Appeal (Waller, Dunn and Dillon LJJ)

Solus agreement - unconscionable bargain?

*Facts*

In 1969, the plaintiff's garage business was in financial straits. In return for financial support from the defendants, they granted to the defendants a 51 year lease of their premises at a full market rent, then took for themselves a sub-lease (a 'leaseback') at a low rent for 21 years. In addition, they agreed to buy all their petrol from the defendants for a period of at least seven, and possibly as much as 21, years. In 1979, the plaintiffs sued to have the lease set aside and the exclusive purchase agreement declared voidable as being in unreasonable restraint of trade.

*Held*

The exclusive sale agreement was valid and the lease would not be set aside.

Dillon LJ:

'Inequality of bargaining power must anyhow be a relative concept. It is seldom in any negotiation that the bargaining powers of the parties are absolutely equal. Any individual wanting to borrow money from a bank, building society or other financial institution in order to pay his liabilities or buy some property he urgently wants to acquire will have virtually no bargaining power; he will have to take or leave the terms offered to him. So, with house property in a seller's market, the purchaser will not have equal bargaining power with the vendor. But Lord Denning MR did not envisage that any contract entered into in such circumstances would, without more, be reviewed by the courts by the objective criterion of what was reasonable: see *Lloyds Bank Ltd* v *Bundy*. The courts would only interfere in exceptional cases where as a matter of common fairness it was not right that the strong should be allowed to push the weak to the wall. The concepts of unconscionable conduct and of the exercise by the stronger of coercive power are thus brought in, and in the present case they are negatived by the deputy judge's findings.

Even if, contrary to my view just expressed, the company and Mr and Mrs Lobb had initially in 1969 a valid claim in equity to have the lease and lease-back set aside as a result of the inequality of bargaining power, that claim was, in my judgment, barred by laches well before the issue of the writ in this action.'

Dunn LJ:

'In *Harper's* case the House of Lords was careful not to find that a 21-year tie was unreasonable in all circumstances. Each case depended on its own facts, and all their Lordships emphasised that it was ultimately public policy which prohibited the enforcement of covenants in restraint of trade (see [1967] 1 All ER 699 esp at 723-724, [1968] AC 269 esp at 323-324 per Lord Pearce). In *Amoco Australia Pty Ltd* v *Rocco Bros Motor Engineering Co Pty Ltd* [1975] 1 All ER 968 at 978, [1975] AC 561 at 579 Lord Cross, giving the advice of the Board, emphasised that the adequacy of the consideration received by the covenantor for the benefits which he obtained from the agreement, was relevant to the question of the reasonableness of a restraint imposed by the agreement. In *Foley* v *Classique Coaches Ltd* [1934] 2 KB 1, [1934] All ER Rep 88 the fact that the petrol was to be purchased by the covenantor at a reasonable price was held to be relevant to the question of the reasonableness of the covenant.

The special circumstances relied on by counsel for Total as justifying the covenants in restraint of trade may be summarised as follows. Total had paid the market price for a 51-year lease, which was for all practical purposes equivalent to a freehold. The company was insolvent, and the sum of £35,000 was designed to enable it to pay its debts, and to save the Lobbs from personal bankruptcy. Fifty-one years was the shortest term which would justify a payment sufficient to discharge the debts of the company. Without such a sum there was no realistic prospect that the company would be able to continue in business for any length of time. The company was independently advised with regard to the transaction by its solicitors and accountants, and insisted on proceeding contrary to their advice. By reason of the underlease, Mr and Mrs Lobb were able to continue to trade and to pass on the business to their sons. In July 1969, by reason of the terms of certain mortgages the company was already bound to buy all its petrol from Total for a number of years. Hence the company's freedom to trade was already restricted, and the further restrictions imposed by the underlease were illusory. The term of 21 years was the maximum term Total was prepared to grant, although Mr Lobb would have preferred a longer underlease.

In my judgment the transaction in question amounted to a rescue operation for the benefit of the company and the Lobbs which Total was reluctant to undertake, but which it undertook in order to preserve the site as an outlet for its petrol. The break clauses in the underlease enabled the company to cease to trade if the rescue operation should fail. The transaction was of advantage to the plaintiffs since it enabled the company to continue to trade from the site, which it did for another ten years, and was of advantage to Total since it preserved an outlet.

In *Harper's* case none of these circumstances existed. There was a loan to the dealer of £7,000 secured by a mortgage, and there was no special reason for a tie as long as 21 years. In the instant case Total paid a fair price for the 51-year lease and the covenants in restraint of trade only lasted for 21 years. There was ample consideration for the grant of the lease, and the underlease was necessary if the Lobbs were to continue trading from the site. In my judgment public policy does not require that such arrangements should be unenforceable. On the contrary, it seems to me that public policy should encourage a transaction which enabled trading by the plaintiff to continue, and preserved an outlet for the defendant's products. I would hold that in the special circumstances of this case Total has established that the covenants in restraint of trade were reasonable.'

*Commentary*

Applied: *Esso Petroleum Co Ltd* v *Harper's Garage (Stourport) Ltd* [1967] 2 WLR 871. Distinguished: *Lloyds Bank Ltd* v *Bundy* [1974] 3 WLR 501.

**Midland Bank plc v Perry** (1987) The Times 28 May Court of Appeal (Fox, Lloyd and Stocker LJJ)

Undue influence - husband and wife

*Facts*

Induced by her husband's undue influence, a wife signed a charge over the matrimonial home as security for moneys due to a bank. It was found that the bank manager had been negligent in failing to ensure that the wife understood the nature of the charge.

*Held*

Nevertheless, the charge would not be set aside: the husband had not been the bank's agent in obtaining his wife's signature and there was no evidence of bad faith on the bank's part. There is no presumption that a wife has been influenced by her husband.

*Commentary*

Distinguished: *Kingsnorth Trust Ltd v Bell* [1986] 1 WLR 119.

**Midland Bank plc v Shephard** [1988] 3 All ER 17 Court of Appeal (Neill and Balcombe LJJ)

Husband and wife - presumption of undue influence?

*Facts*

The husband's account with the plaintiffs was overdrawn so he arranged to transfer the overdraft to a new joint account with his wife: the mandate, which they both signed, provided, inter alia, that 'any loan or overdraft [was] our joint and several responsibility'. Needing a loan for business purposes, the husband arranged a £10,000 overdraft on the joint account: although the wife knew of her husband's intention to borrow the money, she was not told that it would be a liability on the joint account. The husband became bankrupt; the plaintiffs sued the wife.

*Held*

They were entitled to succeed as there was no evidence that the husband had induced the wife to sign the mandate by means of fraudulent misrepresentation or by some fraudulent concealment or that he had induced the wife to sign by exercising undue influence over her.

Neill LJ:

'... counsel for the defendant confined himself to submitting that she had an arguable defence based upon the undue influence of Mr Shephard. The submission was developed on the following lines. (a) There was no direct communication between the bank and the defendant before the joint account was opened. (b) The defendant was never told that by signing the mandate she would immediately become personally liable for the existing overdraft transferred from Mr Shephard's previous account, nor was it explained to her that she might become personally liable for a future overdraft on the joint account. (c) Mr Shephard acted as the agent for the bank in obtaining the defendant's signature to the mandate. (d) Mr Shephard misled the defendant by failing to inform her of her actual and potential liability. (e) Mr Shephard abused the trust which his wife had in him. (f) Though fraud had not hitherto been alleged, the conduct of Mr Shephard amounted to fraudulent misrepresentation or fraudulent concealment. (g) There was no evidence that the defendant herself had any business knowledge or experience.

In support of these submissions counsel for the defendant referred to several authorities, including *Turnbull & Co v Duval* [1902] AC 429 and *Kingsnorth Trust Ltd v Bell* [1986] 1 All ER 423. In addition we were referred by counsel for the bank to the decision of the House of Lords in *National Westminster Bank plc v Morgan* [1985] 1 All ER 821. From these authorities the following relevant propositions can be extracted.

217

(1) The confidential relationship between husband and wife does not give rise by itself to a presumption of undue influence ...

(2) Even if the relationship between the parties gives rise to a presumption of undue influence, the transaction will not be set aside unless it was to the manifest disadvantage of the person influenced ...

(3) The court should examine the facts to see whether the relevant transaction had been, or should be presumed to have been, procured by undue influence, and if so whether the transaction was so disadvantageous to the person seeking to set it aside as to be unfair.

(4) The court will not enforce a transaction at the suit of a creditor if it can be shown that the creditor entrusted the task of obtaining the alleged debtor's signature to the relevant document to someone who was, to the knowledge of the creditor, in a position to influence the debtor and who procured the signature of the debtor by means of undue influence or by means of fraudulent misrepresentation ...

I come now to apply these propositions and the authorities to the facts of the present case. In order to establish a defence of undue influence it would be necessary for the defendant to prove (a) that she was induced or must be presumed to have been induced to sign the mandate by the undue influence of Mr Shephard, or by his fraudulent misrepresentations or fraudulent concealment of material facts; (b) that the contract into which she was induced to enter was manifestly disadvantageous to her; and (c) that in the circumstances the acts of Mr Shephard are to be attributed to the bank.

I propose to deal first with point (b). It was strongly argued by counsel for the bank that the contract was for the opening of a joint account from which the defendant was intended to and did obtain a substantial benefit herself ... In my judgment it can properly be argued that the signing of the mandate was potentially disadvantageous to the defendant and therefore I would not myself reject the defence of undue influence on the ground that this element of the defence was not even arguable.

As to the other elements of the defence, however, I take a different view. In the first place I consider that there is no basis whatever for the suggestion that Mr Shephard induced the defendant to sign the mandate by means of any fraudulent misrepresentation, or by some fraudulent concealment. This suggestion was put forward at a comparatively late stage of the argument before us, but it is not supported by any of the evidence, nor can I find in any of the three affidavits sworn by the defendant any hint that the defendant was charging her husband with fraud. It may also be noticed that Mr Shephard has sworn two affidavits in support of the defendant's case and, we were told, they are living together as man and wife.

Secondly, I cannot see in the evidence any support for the proposition that Mr Shephard induced the defendant to sign the mandate by exercising some dominating influence over her. The facts of this case are far removed from those which were examined by the Court of Appeal in *Kingsnorth Trust Ltd v Bell* or those considered in the earlier case of *Avon Finance Co Ltd v Bridger* [1985] 2 All ER 281 where elderly parents were induced to sign a legal charge at the behest of their son and by means of his deception. In the present case the defendant signed the standard joint account mandate which was required to be signed by every customer who wished to operate a joint account. The document was in no way unusual and I can see no evidence whatever that the defendant was pressed or unduly influenced to sign it.

Finally I should deal with the suggestion that the bank are disentitled to enforce the mandate because they sent or gave the document to Mr Shephard and did not themselves obtain the defendant's signature. The defence must fail in any event in the absence of any proof that the defendant was unduly influenced to sign the mandate, but even if Mr Shephard had exercised some dominating influence over her, there is no evidence to show that the bank knew that he would or might bring such influence to bear, or that they used Mr Shephard in order that he should exert pressure on his wife (compare the judgment of Brightman LJ in *Avon Finance Co Ltd v Bridger*). As I said earlier, this was an ordinary document, which was signed as a matter of routine when a joint account was opened. It will be remembered that in her first affidavit ... the defendant said that she was made a party to the account in order to pay the household expenses when her husband was abroad on business.

In my judgment the evidence in this case does not disclose even a shadowy defence of undue influence.'

**National Westminster Bank plc v Morgan** [1985] 2 WLR 588 House of Lords (Lord Scarman, Lord Keith of Kinkel, Lord Roskill, Lord Bridge of Harwich and Lord Brandon of Oakbrook)

Undue influence - banker and customer

*Facts*

Mrs Morgan and her husband owned a house. It was mortgaged to the building society, who threatened to seek possession for unpaid debts. The defendant bank offered to 'refinance' the couple and to relieve the pressure put on them by the society. This was to be done by way of a loan, secured by a further mortgage, this time in favour of the bank. Mr Morgan readily agreed, but when the bank manager visited Mrs Morgan to obtain her signature to the mortgage deed, she wanted reassurance that the loan to be made would not be used by her husband for the purpose of his business, but would go to pay off the society. The manager reassured her and she signed the deed. The loan was not repaid and the bank, in turn, sued for possession of the house. Mrs Morgan argued that the bank manager exercised undue influence over her and that a special relationship existed between her and the bank which required it to ensure that she receive independent legal advice before entering into a further mortgage. She also sought to rely upon the remarks of Lord Denning in *Lloyd's Bank* v *Bundy*.

*Held*

The bank was entitled to possession.

Lord Scarman:

'... the relationships which may develop a dominating influence of one over another are infinitely various. There is no substitute in this branch of the law for a "meticulous examination of the facts."

A meticulous examination of the facts of the present case reveals that [the bank] never "crossed the line". Nor was the transaction unfair to the wife. The bank was, therefore, under no duty to ensure that she had independent advice. It was an ordinary banking transaction whereby the wife sought to save her home; and she obtained an honest and truthful explanation of the bank's intention which, notwithstanding the terms of the mortgage deed which in the circumstances the trial judge was right to dismiss as "essentially theoretical", was correct; for no one has suggested that ... the bank sought to make the wife liable, or to make her home the security, for any debt of her husband other than the loan and interest necessary to save the house from being taken away from them in discharge of their indebtedness to the building society.

For these reasons, I would allow the appeal. In doing so, I would wish to give a warning. There is no precisely defined law setting limits to the equitable jurisdiction of a court to relieve against undue influence. This is the world of doctrine, not of neat and tidy rules. The courts of equity have developed a body of learning enabling relief to be granted where the law has to treat the transaction as unimpeachable unless it can be held to have been procured by undue influence. It is the unimpeachability at law of a disadvantageous transaction which is the starting point from which the court advances to consider whether the transaction is the product merely of one's own folly or of the undue influence exercised by another. A court in the exercise of this equitable jurisdiction is a court of conscience. Definition is a poor instrument when used to determine whether a transaction is or is not unconscionable: this is a question which depends on the particular facts of the case.'

## Commentary

Followed in *Cornish* v *Midland Bank plc* [1985] 3 All ER 513. See also *Midland Bank plc* v *Shephard* [1988] 3 All ER 17 and *Bank of Credit and Commerce International SA* v *Aboody* [1989] 2 WLR 759.


# North Ocean Shipping Co Ltd v Hyundai Construction Co Ltd. The Atlantic Baron

See chapter 2 - Consideration.


# Occidental World Investment Corp v Skibs A/S Avanti. The Sibeon and The Sibotre

[1976] 1 Lloyd's Rep 293 High Court (Kerr J)

Charterparty - hire reduced under duress?

## Facts

T was the defendants' manager and he agreed to let the two ships out under time charterparties to the chartering subsidiary of the plaintiff company. During the period of the hire, the plaintiffs' general financial position was deteriorating and they resolved to seek a reduction in the rates of hire. A meeting was arranged with T and he was given the impression that (i) the subsidiary was a company with no substantial assets which had suffered enormous losses; (ii) they were dependent on their parent company's support for their survival; and (iii) the parent company was willing to let them go into liquidation if the rates were not reduced. In fact, these statements were untrue, but T agreed a reduction in rates. The defendants contended, inter alia, that they were not bound by this agreement as it had been entered into under duress.

## Held

Although T had acted under great pressure, there was nothing which could in law be regarded as a coercion of his will which would vitiate his consent. Accordingly, the plea of duress failed.

Kerr J:

'... [Counsel] submitted that ... a contract can only be set aside for duress to the person but not in any other case of duress. He said that in every case in which a party enters into a contract otherwise than under duress to the person, any payment or forbearance pursuant to such contract is regarded as voluntary, whatever may have been the nature or degree of compulsion, short of violence to the person, which may have caused him to enter into the contract ... I do not think that English law is as limited as submitted by [Counsel] ... For instance, if I should be compelled to sign a lease or some other contract for a nominal but legally sufficient consideration under an imminent threat of having my house burnt down or a valuable picture slashed, though without any threat of physical violence, I do not think that the law would uphold the agreement. I think that a plea of coercion or compulsion would be available in such cases. The latter is the term used in a line of Australian cases of strong persuasive authority to which I was referred ... The true question is ultimately whether or not the agreement in question is to be regarded as having been concluded voluntarily...'


# Pao On v Lau Yiu Long

See chapter 2 - Consideration.


# Schroeder (A) Music Publishing Co Ltd v Macaulay [1974] 1 WLR 1308 House of Lords
(Lord Reid, Viscount Dilhorne, Lord Diplock, Lord Simon of Glaisdale and Lord Kilbrandon)

Music publishers - agreement in restraint of trade?

*Facts*

The respondent, an unknown songwriter, entered an agreement with the appellants to given them copyright of all compositions for a 5 year period. The agreement was terminable by the employers on one month's notice but not by the respondent. The publishers were under no obligation to publish any of the songs. The respondent sought a declaration that the contract was contrary to public policy.

*Held*

He was entitled to succeed.

Lord Reid:

'... The public interest requires in the interests both of the public and of the individual that everyone should be free so far as practicable to earn a livelihood and to give to the public the fruits of his particular abilities. The main question to be considered is whether and how far the operation of the terms of this agreement is likely to conflict with this objective. The respondent is bound to assign to the appellants during a long period the fruits of his musical talent. But what are the appellants bound to do with those fruits? Under the contract nothing. If they do use the songs which the respondent composes they must pay in terms of the contract. But they need not do so. As has been said they may put them in a drawer and leave them there ...

It was argued that there must be read into this agreement an obligation on the publisher to act in good faith. I take that to mean that he would be in breach of contract if by reason of some oblique or malicious motive he refrained from publishing work which he would otherwise have published. I very much doubt this but even if it were so it would make little difference. Such a case would seldom occur and then would be difficult to prove.

I agree with the appellants' argument to this extent. I do not think that a publisher could reasonably be expected to enter into any positive commitment to publish future work by an unknown composer. Possibly there might be some general undertaking to use his best endeavours to promote the composer's work. But that would probably have to be in such general terms as to be of little use to the composer.

But if no satisfactory positive undertaking by the publisher can be devised, it appears to me to be an unreasonable restraint to tie the composer for this period of years so that his work will be sterilised and he can earn nothing from his abilities as a composer if the publisher chooses not to publish. If there had been in clause 9 any provision entitling the composer to terminate the agreement in such an event the case might have had a very different appearance. But as the agreement stands not only is the composer tied but he cannot recover the copyright of work which the publisher refuses to publish.'

Lord Diplock:

Standard forms of contracts are of two kinds. The first, of very ancient origin, are those which set out the terms on which mercantile transactions of common occurrence are to be carried out. Examples are bills of lading, charterparties, policies of insurance, contracts of sale in the commodity markets. The standard clauses in these contracts have been settled over the years by negotiation by representatives of the commercial interests involved and have been widely adopted because experience has shown that they facilitate the conduct of trade. Contracts of these kinds affect not only the actual parties to them but also others who may have a commercial interest in the transactions to which they relate, as buyers or sellers, charterers or shipowners, insurers or bankers. If fairness or reasonableness were relevant to their enforceability the fact that they are widely used by parties whose bargaining power is fairly matched would raise a strong presumption that their terms are fair and reasonable.

The same presumption, however, does not apply to the other kind of standard form of contract. This is of comparatively modern origin. It is the result of the concentration of particular kinds of business in relatively few hands. The ticket cases in the 19th century provide what are probably the first examples. The terms of this kind of standard form of contract have not been the subject of negotiation between the parties to it, or approved by any organisation representing the interests of the weaker party. They have been dictated by that party whose bargaining power, either exercised alone or in conjunction with other providing similar goods or services, enables him to say: "If you want these goods or services at all, these are the only terms on which they are obtainable. Take it or leave it."

To be in a position to adopt this attitude towards a party desirous of entering into a contract to obtain goods or services provides a classic instance of superior bargaining power. It is not without significance that on the evidence in the present case, music publishers in negotiating with song-writers whose success has been already established do not insist on adhering to a contract in the standard form they offered to the respondent. The fact that the appellants' bargaining power vis-à-vis the respondent was strong enough to enable them to adopt this take-it-or-leave it attitude raises no presumption that they used it to drive an unconscionable bargain with him, but in the field of restraint of trade it calls for vigilance on the part of the court to see that they did not.'

**Universe Tankships Inc of Monrovia v International Transport Workers' Federation** [1982] 2 WLR 803 House of Lords (Lord Diplock, Lord Cross of Chelsea, Lord Russell of Killowen, Lord Scarman and Lord Brandon of Oakbrook)

Ship 'blacked' - economic duress?

*Facts*

A ship was 'blacked' until union demands as to pay and conditions were satisfied. In order to have the blacking lifted, the ship owners, inter alia, made a contribution to the union's welfare fund.

*Held* (Lord Scarman and Lord Brandon dissenting)

This contribution was recoverable by the owners as money had and received for their use.

Lord Diplock:

'It is ... in my view crucial to the decision of the instant appeal to identify the rationale of this development of the common law. It is not that the party seeking to avoid the contract which he has entered into with another party, or to recover money that he has paid to another party in response to a demand, did not know the nature or the precise terms of the contract at the time when he entered into it or did not understand the purpose for which the payment was demanded. The rationale is that his apparent consent was induced by pressure exercised on him by that other party which the law does not regard as legitimate, with the consequence that the consent is treated in law as revocable unless approbated either expressly or by implication after the illegitimate pressure has ceased to operate on his mind. It is a rationale similar to that which underlies the avoidability of contracts entered into and the recovery of money exacted under colour of office, or under undue influence or in consequence of threats of physical duress.

Commercial pressure, in some degree, exists wherever one party to a commercial transaction is in a stronger bargaining position than the other party. It is not, however, in my view, necessary, nor would it be appropriate in the instant appeal, to enter into the general question of the kinds of circumstances, if any, in which commercial pressure, even though it amounts to a coercion of the will of a party in the weaker bargaining position, may be treated as legitimate and, accordingly, as not giving rise to any legal right of redress. In the instant appeal the economic duress complained of was exercised in the field of industrial relations to which very special considerations apply ...

The use of economic duress to induce another person to part with property or money is not a tort per se; the form that the duress takes may, or may not, be tortious. The remedy to which economic duress gives rise is not an action for damages but an action for restitution of property or money exacted under such duress and the avoidance of any contract that had been induced by it; but where the particular form taken by the economic duress used is itself a tort, the restitutional remedy for money had and received by the defendant to the plaintiff's use is one which the plaintiff is entitled to pursue as an alternative remedy to an action for damages in tort.'

### Vantage Navigation Corp v Suhail and Saud Bahwan Building Materials LLC. The Alev [1989] 1 Lloyd's Rep 138 High Court (Hobhouse J)

Duress - unlawful threat

*Facts*

On 5 August 1983 the plaintiffs chartered the vessel 'Aleu' for a voyage from South America to the Arabian Gulf carrying a cargo of steel. The defendants had property in the cargo. The hirers were financially unsound and though they made some of the instalment payments they then defaulted and the plaintiffs received no more payments from them. As the plaintiffs were obliged by the terms of the bills of lading to carry the cargo to its destination this would involve them in considerable costs. They therefore entered into negotiations with the defendants which resulted in an agreement whereby the defendants agreed, inter alia, to pay port costs and other expenses and not to detain or arrest the vessel while in port at Mina Qaboos. This agreement was secured in part by threats made by the plaintiffs toward the defendants, including a statement that unless the defendants paid what the plaintiffs wanted they would not get their cargo. When the ship was in port and had commenced unloading the defendants ignored the agreement and arrested the ship. They pleaded duress to any breach of contract and claimed damages.

*Held*

On the evidence, the agreement clearly fell within the principles of economic duress. During their negotiations with the defendants the plaintiffs did make an illegal threat to withhold the cargo and they were fully aware that, since they were legally obliged to carry the cargo, even if at a loss of profit to themselves, such a threat would be unlawful. The defendant's right to rely on duress was therefore established and the contract was voidable on the ground of duress.

### Woodstead Finance Ltd v Petrou (1986) 136 NLJ 188 Court of Appeal (Sir Nicolas Browne-Wilkinson V-C, Mustill and Nourse LJJ)

Undue influence - charge over wife's property

*Facts*

The husband obtained a loan of £25,000 for six months at an interest rate equivalent to 42% per annum. This loan from the plaintiff company was secured by a charge over the defendant wife's property and by her guarantee. The wife had been told to take independent advice before executing the documents, but did not do so. Did the transaction constitute a manifest and unfair disadvantage to the defendant?

*Held*

It did not. Following *National Westminster Bank* v *Morgan* [1985] 2 WLR 588, Sir Nicholas Browne-Wilkinson V-C said:

> 'unless it can be demonstrated that the grant of the legal charge by the wife to the plaintiff company ... constituted a manifest and unfair disadvantage to her, any defence based on undue influence cannot succeed.'

Whilst the terms of the loan appeared harsh, the uncontradicted evidence was that such terms were normal for short term loans, having regard to the circumstances of the loan and the husband's appalling record of payments. There was, in consequence, no evidence of manifest disadvantage to the wife.

# 10   PRIVITY OF CONTRACT

**Andrews v Hopkinson**

See chapter 4 - Contents of contracts.

**Beswick v Beswick** [1967] 3 WLR 932 House of Lords (Lord Reid, Lord Hodson, Lord Guest, Lord Pearce and Lord Upjohn)

Contract - enforcement by stranger to it

*Facts*

Peter Beswick was a coal merchant. In 1962 he contracted with John Beswick, his nephew, to sell the business in consideration of: (1) that for the rest of Peter's life, John would pay him £6.10s per week; (2) that if Peter's wife survived him, John would pay her £5 a week. John took over the business and paid the agreed sum to Peter until he died in November 1963. He made one payment of £5 to Peter's widow and then ceased payments. The widow commenced proceedings, claiming arrears and specific performance and brought the action both as administratrix of the deceased husband's estate and in her own capacity.

*Held*

The widow was entitled, as administratrix, to an order for specific performance, but the effect of ss56(1) and 205(1)(xx) of the Law of Property Act 1925 was not to confer upon a third party any right to sue upon a contract.

Lord Hodson:

'The surviving issues in this case are two: first, whether the Court of Appeal were justified in making an order for specific performance by directing that the appellant do pay to the respondent, during the remainder of her life, an annuity, in accordance with the agreement; second, whether or not the common law rule that a contract such as this one, which purports to confer a benefit on a stranger to the contract, cannot be enforced by the stranger, has been to all intents and purposes (with few exceptions) destroyed by the operation of Section 56(1) of the Law of Property Act 1925 - I will deal with this section first. It provides:

"A person may take an immediate or other interest in land or other property, or the benefit of any condition, right of entry, covenant or agreement over or respecting land or other property, although he may not be named as a party to the conveyance or other instrument."

The definition of Section 205 provides:

"(1)   In this Act, unless the context otherwise requires, the following expressions have the meanings hereby assigned to them respectively, that is to say ... (xx) Property includes any thing in action and any interest in real or personal property ..."

One cannot deny that the view of Lord Denning MR, expressed so forcibly, not for the first time in his judgment in this case, reinforced by the opinion of Danckwerts LJ in this case, is of great weight, notwithstanding that it runs counter to the opinion of all the other judges who have been faced by the task of interpreting this remarkable section ...

Apart from the definition section (Section 205) I doubt whether many would have been disposed to the view that the general law, which declares who can sue on a contract, had received the mortal blow which Section 56 is said to have inflicted on it ... But for the saving words "unless the context otherwise requires", I should have felt grave difficulty in resisting the argument that Parliament, even if it acted per incuriam, had somehow allowed to be slipped into consolidating legislation, which had nothing to do with the general law of contract, an extraordinary provision which had such a drastic effect ... I am unable to believe that such an enormous change in the law has been made by Section 56 as to establish that an agreement by A with B to pay money to C gives C a right to sue on the contract.

Like my noble and learned friend, Lord Reid ... I am of the opinion that Section 56 ... does not have the revolutionary effect claimed for it, appearing as it does in a consolidation act. I think, as he does, that the context does otherwise require a limited meaning to be given to the word "property" in the section.

Although, therefore, the appellant would succeed if the respondent relied only on Section 56 of the Act of 1925, I see no answer to the respondent's claim for specific performance and no possible objection to the order made by the Court of Appeal on the facts of this case.'

## Binions v Evans

See Introduction.

## British Motor Trade Association v Salvadori [1949] Ch 556 High Court (Roxburgh J)

Breach of contract - procurement

*Facts*

The plaintiffs sought to protect the motor trade and the public by ensuring that list prices of cars were neither cut nor inflated. To this end, purchasers of new cars covenanted with the plaintiffs and the supplier that they would not re-sell for one year. The defendant dealers, through agents, brought cars, signed the covenant and then re-sold at much more than list prices.

*Held*

Each defendant was guilty of procuring breaches of contract and the plaintiffs were entitled to damages and injunctions.

Roxburgh J:

'... in my judgment, any active step taken by a defendant, having knowledge of the covenant, by which he facilitates a breach of that covenant is enough. If this be so, a defendant, by agreeing to buy, paying for, and taking delivery of a motor car known by him to be offered to him in breach of covenant, takes active steps by which he facilitates a breach of covenant, and it is not seriously contended that in any of the cases with which I am concerned the defendant did not know of the existence of the covenant or thought that the covenantor had obtained a release. The plaintiffs, will succeed even if I have construed the word "interference" too broadly, because, if a further element of inducement must be present, that further element can be found.'

## Dunlop Pneumatic Tyre Co Ltd v Selfridge & Co Ltd [1915] AC 847 House of Lords (Viscount Haldane LC, Lord Dunedin, Lord Atkinson, Lord Parker of Waddington, Lord Sumner and Lord Parmoor)

Contract - right of third party to sue

*Facts*

The plaintiffs sold some of their tyres to a company, on condition that the company would not re-sell the tyres below certain prices, and that if a sale took place to a trade customer, the company would extract a similar undertaking from the trade customer. The company sold the tyres to the defendant, which undertook to observe the condition as to price. The defendant sold tyres to their own customers below the specified price, an act clearly in breach of its agreement with the company. The action was not brought by the company, but by the plaintiff, Dunlop, who sought damages and an injunction to restrain any further breaches.

*Held*

The plaintiff was not a party to the contract and the action, accordingly, would be dismissed with judgment for the defendant.

Viscount Haldane LC:

'My Lords, in the law of England, certain principles are fundamental. One is that only a person who is a party to the contract can sue on it. Our law knows nothing of a jus quaesitum tertio arising by way of contract. Such a right may be conferred by way of property, as, for example, under a trust, but it cannot be conferred on a stranger to a contract as a right to enforce the contract in personam. A second principle is that if a person with whom a contract not under seal has been made is to be able to enforce it, consideration must have been given by him to the promisor or to some other person at the promisor's request ... A third proposition is that a principal not named in the contract may sue upon it if the promisee really contracted as his agent. But again, in order to entitle him so to sue, he must have given consideration, either personally or through the promisee, acting as his agent in giving it ...

The case for the appellants is that they permitted and enabled Messrs Dew (the company), with the knowledge and by the desire of the respondents, to sell to the latter on the terms of the contract ... But it appears to me that even if this is so, the answer is conclusive. Messrs Dew sold to the respondents goods which they had a title to obtain from the appellants independently of this contract. The consideration by way of discount under the contract ... was to come wholly out of Messrs Dew's pocket and neither directly nor indirectly out of that of the appellants. If the appellants enabled them to sell ... the respondents on the terms they did, this was not done as any part of the terms of the contract sued on.

No doubt it was provided as part of these terms that the appellants should acquire certain rights, but these rights appear on the face of the contract as jura quaesta tertio, which the appellants could not enforce. Moreover, even if this difficulty can be got over by regarding the appellants as the principals of Messrs Dew in stipulating for the rights in question, the only consideration disclosed by the contract is one given by Messrs Dew, not as their agents, but as principals acting on their own account ...

Two contracts - one by a man on his own account as principal, and another by the same man as agent - may be validly comprised in the same piece of paper. But they must be two contracts and not one, as here. I do not think that a man can treat one and the same contract, as made by him, in two capacities. He cannot be regarded as contracting for himself and for another uso flatu.

(The) contract has been reduced to writing and it is in the writing that we must look for the whole of the terms made between the parties. These terms cannot, in my opinion, consistently with the settled principles of English law, be construed as giving to the appellants any enforceable rights as against the respondents.'

Lord Dunedin:

'My Lords, I am content to adopt from a work of Sir Frederick Pollock, to which I have often been under obligation, the following words as to consideration:

"An act of forbearance of one party, or the promise thereof, is the price for which the promise of the other is bought and the promise thus given for value is enforceable." (*Pollock on Contracts, 8th Edn p 175*)

Now the agreement sued on is an agreement which, on the face of it, is an agreement between Dew and Selfridge. But, speaking for myself, I should have no difficulty in the circumstances of the case in holding it proved that the agreement was truly made by Dew as agent for Dunlop or, in other words, that Dunlop was the undisclosed principal and, as such, can sue on the agreement. Nevertheless, in order to enforce it, he must show consideration as above defined, moving from Dunlop to Selfridge.

In the circumstances, how can he do so? What then did Dunlop do, or forbear to do, in a question with Selfridge? The answer must be nothing ... To my mind, this ends the case.'

### Flavell, Re, Murray v Flavell (1883) 25 Ch D 89 Court of Appeal (Cotton and Lindley LJJ)

Deceased partner - widow entitled to annuity?

*Facts*

The defendant was a widow and executrix of the estate of T W Flavell deceased. The deceased was a solicitor who carried on business in partnership. A clause of the partnership agreement provided that the continuing partner pay an annuity to the widow of the retiring or deceased partner. By his will, the deceased devised all his real and personal estate to his wife. He did not, however, direct how the annuity payable under the partnership agreement was to be applied. The question arose whether the annuity payable formed part of the deceased's assets or whether the widow was beneficially entitled to it.

*Held*

The widow was entitled to the annuity.

Lindley LJ:

'... What kind of a document are we dealing with? It is not a voluntary or fraudulent deed, but a bargain between two partners that if one dies the survivor is to carry on the business, and pay an annuity to be applied for the benefit of the widow. What is the matter with it? It is not fraudulent; it is not a legacy; it is not revocable. It is said to be a voluntary settlement; but if it is, that does not matter if it cannot be impeached. I do not, however, think that it was a voluntary settlement; it was a contract for value. Then it is said that the annuity formed part of the testator's assets, and cannot be diverted from his creditors. The answer is, that it is no part of his assets at all. Unless this contract can be impeached on the ground of fraud, I cannot see why it should not be supported.'

### Gore v Van der Lann

See chapter 2 - Consideration.

### Jackson v Horizon Holidays Ltd [1975] 3 WLR 1468 Court of Appeal (Lord Denning MR, Orr and James LJJ)

Contract for benefit of third parties

*Facts*

The plaintiff entered into a contract for a holiday for himself, his wife and two children. The holiday failed to comply with the description given by the defendant and the plaintiff sued, claiming damages.

*Held*

The plaintiff was entitled to damages not only for himself, but also for his wife and children.

Lord Denning MR:

'We have had an interesting discussion as to the legal position when one person makes a contract for the benefit of a party. In this case, it was a husband making a contract for the benefit of himself, his wife and children ...

It would equally be a mistake to say that in any of these instances there was a trust. The transaction bears no resemblance to a trust. There was no trust fund and no trust property. No, the real truth is that, in each instance, the father ... was making a contract himself for the benefit of the whole party. In short, a contract by one for the benefit of third persons.

What is the position when such a contract is broken? At present, the law says that the only one who can sue is the one who made the contract. None of the rest of the party can sue, even though the contract was made for their benefit. But when that one does sue, what damages can he recover? Is he limited to his own loss? Or can he recover for the others? ... He can, of course, recover his own damages, but can he not recover for the others? I think he can. The case comes within the principle stated by Lush LJ in *Lloyds* v *Harper*:

"I consider it to be an established rule of law that where a contract is made with A for the benefit of B, A can sue on the contract for the benefit of B and recover all that B could have recovered if the contract had been made with B himself."

It has been suggested that Lush LJ was thinking of a contract in which A was trustee for B. But I do not think so. He was a common lawyer speaking of the common law. His words were quoted with considerable approval by Lord Pearce in *Beswick* v *Beswick*. I have myself often quoted them. I think they should be accepted as correct, at any rate so long as the law forbids the third person themselves to sue for damages. It is the only way a just result can be achieved.'

*Commentary*

But see *Woodar Investment Developments Ltd* v *Wimpey Construction UK Ltd* [1980] 1 WLR 277.

**Les Affréteurs Réunis Société Anonyme v Leopold Walford (London) Ltd** [1919] AC 801 House of Lords (Lord Birkenhead LC, Viscount Finlay, Lord Atkinson and Lord Wrenbury)

Contract - rights of third party

*Facts*

The respondents acted as brokers in effecting a time charter of the appellants' ship. Under the charterparty, a commission of three per cent was payable to the respondents, although they were not a party to that agreement. The ship was requisitioned by the French Government and, by way of defence, it was pleaded that there was a custom of the trade that commission was payable only in respect of hire duly earned.

*Held*

The respondents were entitled to their commission.

Lord Wrenbury:

'We have here to do with a contract between two parties reserving a benefit to a third. The two parties are the shipowners and the charterers, the third party is the broker of one of them, who is to be remunerated in respect of a contract which is being made for the hire of a ship. The particular form of contract in question is of course prepared by, or is under the eyes of, the broker who is negotiating the matter. It is sent to the principals for signature, and they sign it, and there is contained in it a clause which reserves a benefit to the broker. Under those circumstances an action is brought by the broker against the shipowner for the commission which is expressed to be payable to him under the contract between the shipowner and the charterer - a contract to which he himself, I agree, was not a party. By agreement between the parties the record is to be treated as if the charterer were joined as a plaintiff in the action. The case is one in which an action can be brought on behalf of a person to whom a benefit is reserved, although he is not a party to it ... Under those circumstanes the shipowners, the defendants in the action, defend the action and in effect are here saying: "It is perfectly true that we attached our signature to this document; it is perfectly true that it contains ... this stipulation in favour of a third party; but that means nothing at all - that is not the bargain at all to which we were parties. The matter is governed by a certain custom."

My Lords, I feel myself in great difficulty in understanding a contention of that sort. It is said that in this particular business there exists a custom (and I will take it for the moment that the custom is proved) that in time charterparties broker's commission is payable out of hire earned and is not payable unless hire is earned. In this contract, however there is a stipulation that the commission shall be on the estimated gross amount of hire on signing the charter ship lost or not lost. I find myself quite unable to understand how it can be set up that into a contract expressed in those terms there can be introduced a custom to an exactly contrary effect. Directly it is conceded that the broker, although not a party to the contract, can sue on the contract, inasmuch as he can sue by the charterer as trustee for him, it appears to me that the case really is over.'

**Lord Strathcona Steamship Co Ltd v Dominion Coal Co Ltd** [1926] AC 108 Privy Council (Viscount Haldane, Lord Shaw, Lord Wrenbury, Lord Carson and Lord Blanesburgh)

Charter of ship - violation

*Facts/Held*

The facts and decision appear sufficiently from the extract of the judgment by Lord Shaw.

Lord Shaw:

'There are three questions which arise in the appeal - these are ... Second, whether any rights of the Dominion Coal Company, as charterers of the vessel, existed as against the appellants, the Lord Strathcona Steamship Company, as owners thereof, there having been no direct privity of contract between those parties ...

Upon the point of privity of contract and the nature of the right of remedy still open to the charterers of the vessel, the following facts and dates have to be kept in view. The writ was issued by the respondents on 31 July 1920. It was directed against the appellants as present owners and against the Lord Curzon Steamship Company as parties to the charter party ... A declaration was claimed by the respondents under the charter party, under which the appellants could be called upon, as in an action of specific performance, to perform the obligations under the charter in the same sense and degree as the original owners, the Lord Curzon Steamship Company. It will be necessary to see whether, under the principles of English jurisprudence, this demand can be justified as stated, or whether, under the other claims made in the writ, English equity is able to afford to the charterers against the present owners, the appellants, any remedy for the wrong arising to them by the threatened loss of their rights under the charter party.

The charter party is dated 20 April 1914, corrected to 24 July 1914. The ship has been built in England for the Lord Curzon Steamship Co under plans provided by the Dominion Coal Company and it was agreed that, when complete, she should be chartered to the respondents and this was done by the charter party mentioned. Then occurred a series of transmissions of title to the ship (to Lord Strathcona Company 22 June 1920).

So far as the knowledge of the existence of the charter party was concerned, their Lordships are clearly of the opinion that all these successive owners were well aware of it and this knowledge was, by notice, passed very clearly and properly on from each owner to the successor ... In the opinion of the Board, the appellants thoroughly understood that the charter party and its responsibilities and obligations thereunder were to be respected. This is not a mere case of notice of the existence of a covenant affecting the use of the property sold, but it is the case of the acceptance of their property expressly sub conditione.

The position of the law, accordingly, is that the appellants are possessed of a ship with regard to which a long running charter party is current, the existence of which was fully disclosed, together indeed, with an obligation which the appellants appear to have accepted to respect and carry out that charter party. The proposal of the appellants and the arguments submitted by them is to the effect that they are not bound to respect and carry forward this charter party, either in law or in equity, but that, on the contrary, they can, in defiance of its terms of which they had knowledge, use the vessel at their will in any other way. It is, accordingly, when the true facts are shown, a very simple case raising the question of whether an obligation affecting the user of the subject of sale, namely a ship, can be ignored by the purchaser so as to enable that purchaser who has bought a ship notified not to be a free ship but under charter, to wipe out the condition of purchase and use the ship as a free ship ...

Their Lordships think that the judgment of Knight Bruce LJ (in *De Mattos* v *Gibson* (1858) 4 De G&J 276 at 282) plainly applies to the present case:

"Reason and justice seem to prescribe that, at least as a general rule, where a man by gift or purchase acquires property from another with knowledge of a previous contract, lawfully and for valuable consideration made by him with a third person, to use and employ the property for a particular purpose in a specified manner, the acquirer shall not, to the material damage of the third person, in opposition to the contract and inconsistently with it, use and employ the property in a manner not allowable to the giver or seller."

A principle, not without analogy, had previously been laid down in reference to the user of land ...

The general character of the principle on which a Court of Equity acts was explained in *Tulk* v *Moxhay* (1848) 2 Ph 774. The plaintiff there was the owner in fee of Leicester Square and several houses forming the Square. He sold the property to one Elms in fee and the deed of conveyance contained a covenant obliging Elms, his heirs and assigns, to "keep and maintain the said piece of ground and Square Garden ... in its then form ... in an open state, uncovered with any buildings". Elm sold to others and the property came into the hands of the defendant, who admitted that he had purchased with notice of the covenant. The defendant,"having manifested an intention to alter the character of the Square Garden, and asserted a right if he thought fit to build upon it", the plaintiff who still remained owner of several houses in the Square, filed a bill for an injunction. All this is familiar knowledge, but it appears to have been sometimes forgotten what was the nature of the argument of the defendant. He contended that the covenant did not run with the land so as to be binding upon him as a purchaser ...

The remedy is a remedy in equity by way of injunction against acts inconsistent with the covenant, with notice of which the land was acquired ... a remedy in equity by injunction against the violation of restrictive covenants ...

But, *Tulk* v *Moxhay* is important for a further and vital consideration - namely that it analyses the true situation of a purchaser who, having bought upon the terms of the restriction upon free contract existing, thereafter, when vested in the lands, attempts to divest himself of the condition under which he had bought:

"It is said that the covenant, being one which does not run with the land, this Court cannot enforce it; but the question is not whether the covenant runs with the land, but whether a party shall be permitted to use the land in a manner inconsistent with the contract entered into by his vendor and with notice of which he purchased ... "

In the opinion of the Board, these views, much expressive of the justice and good faith of the situation, are still part of English equity jurisprudence ...

A perusal of the numerous decisions on this branch of the law shows that much difficulty has been caused by the attempt to extend these principles to cases to which they could not, by the nature of the case, have been meant to apply. It has been forgotten that - to put the point very simply - the person seeking to enforce such a restriction must, of course, have and continue to have, an interest in the subject matter of the contract. For instance, in the case of land, he must continue to hold the land in whose favour the restrictive covenant was meant to apply. That was clearly the state of matters in the case of *Tulk* v *Moxhay* applicable to the possession of real estate in Leicester Square. It was also clearly the case in *De Mattos* v *Gibson* (1858) 4 De G&J 276, in which the person seeking to enforce the injunction had an interest in the use of the ship. In short, in regard to the user of land or of any chattel, an interest must remain in the subject matter of the covenant before a right can be conceded to an injunction against the violation by another of the covenant in question ... for the present is, as has been seen, a case as to the user of a ship, with regard to the subject matter of which, namely the vessel, the respondent has, and will have during the continuance of the period covered by the charter party, a plain interest so long as she is fit to go to to sea. Again, to adopt the language of Knight Bruce LJ in the *De Mattos* v *Gibson Case* (at p 283):

"Why should it (the Court) not prevent the commission or continuance of a breach of such a contract when its subject, being valuable, as for instance a trading ship or some costly machine, the original owner and possessor, or a person claiming under him, with notice and standing in his right, having the physical control of the chattel, is diverting it from the agreed object, that object being of importance to the other? A system of laws in which such a power does not exist must surely be very defective. I repeat that, in my opinion, the power does exist here."

If a man acquires from another rights in a ship which is already under charter, with notice of rights which required the ship to be used for a particular purpose and not inconsistently with it, then he appears to be plainly in a position of a constructive trustee, with obligations which a Court of Equity will not permit him to violate ... the injunction granted (in this case) was correct.'

*Commentary*

Not followed in *Port Line Ltd* v *Ben Line Steamers Ltd* [1958] 2 WLR 551.

**Lumley v Gye** (1853) 2 E & B 216 Court of Queen's Bench (Coleridge, Erle, Wightman and Crompton JJ)

Contract to perform - procurement to breach

*Facts*

The plaintiff theatre manager claimed damages from the defendant for causing her to break a contract by which she had undertaken to perform at the plaintiff's theatre for a specified time.

*Held* (Coleridge J dissenting)

The plaintiff's action would succeed.

Crompton J:

'Whatever may have been the origin or foundation of the law as to enticing of servants, and whether it be, as contended by the plaintiff, an instance and branch of a wider rule, or, as contended by the defendant, an anomaly and an exception from the general rule of law on such subjects, it must now be considered clear law that a person who wrongfully and maliciously, or, which is the same thing, with notice, interrupts the relation subsisting between master and servant by procuring the servant to depart from the master's service, or by harbouring and keeping him as servant after he has quitted it and during the time stipulated for as the period of service, whereby the master is injured, commits a wrongful act for which he is responsible at law. I think that the rule applies wherever the wrongful interruption operates to prevent the service during the time for which the parties have contracted that the service shall continue, and I think that the relation of master and servant subsists, sufficiently for the purpose of such action, during the time for which there is in existence a binding contract of hiring and service between the parties. I think that it is a fanciful and technical and unjust distinction to say that the not having actually entered into the service, or that the service is not actually continuing, can make any difference. The wrong and injury are surely the same whether the wrongdoer entices away the gardener, who has hired himself for a year, the night before he is to go to his work, or after he has planted the first cabbage on the first morning of his service. I should be sorry to support a distinction so unjust, and so repugnant to common sense, unless bound to do so by some rule or authority of law plainly showing that such distinction exists.'

**Port Jackson Stevedoring Pty Ltd v Salmon & Spraggon (Australia) Pty Ltd. The New York Star** [1981] 1 WLR 138 Privy Council (Lord Wilberforce, Lord Diplock, Lord Fraser of Tullybelton, Lord Scarman and Lord Roskill)

Bill of lading - rights of stranger to contract

*Facts*

The respondent company was consignee of a shipment of razor blades from Canada to Australia and the appellant company commonly acted as stevedore for the carrier at the port of discharge - Sydney. Clauses 17 of the bill of lading barred any action not brought within one year of the delivery of the goods or the date when they should have been delivered. As a result of the stevedore's negligence, the goods were stolen from the wharf in Sydney and the respondents sued - after more than a year. Could the stevedore rely on cl 17?

*Held*

The stevedore could claim exemption from liability under that clause.

Lord Wilberforce:

'First, as to the Board's decision in *Satterthwaite's* case. This was a decision, in principle, that the Himalaya clause is capable of conferring on a third person falling within the description "servant or agent of the Carrier (including every independent contractor from time to time employed by the Carrier)" defences and immunities conferred by the bill of lading on the carrier as if such persons were parties to the contract contained in or evidenced by the bill of lading. But the decision was not merely a decision on this principle, for it was made clear that in fact stevedores employed by the carrier may come within it, and moreover that they normally and typically will do so. It may indeed be said that the significance of *Satterthwaite's case* lay not so much in the establishment of any new legal principle as in the finding that, in the normal situation involving the employment of stevedores by carriers, accepted principles enable and require the stevedore to enjoy the benefit of contractual provisions in the bill of lading. In the words of Mason and Jacobs JJ in the High Court:

"When the circumstances described by Lord Reid (sc in *Scruttons Ltd v Midland Silicones Ltd*) exist, the stevedore will on the generally accepted principles of the law of contract be entitled to his personal contractual immunity. The importance of [*Satterthwaite's* case] is the manner in which on the bare facts of the case their Lordships were able to discern a contract between the shipper and the stevedore, and, we would add, to do so in a manner which limited the approach to those commercial contexts in which immunity of the stevedore was clearly intended in form and almost certainly known by both the shipper and the stevedore to be intended."

Although, in each case, there will be room for evidence as to the precise relationship of carrier and stevedore, and as to the practice at the relevant port, the decision does not support, and their Lordships would not encourage, a search for fine distinctions which would diminish the general applicability, in the light of established commercial practice, of the principle.'

**Port Line Ltd v Ben Line Steamers Ltd** [1958] 2 WLR 551 High Court (Diplock J)

Charterparty - whether binding on purchaser

*Facts*

The facts and decision appear sufficiently from the extract of judgment of Diplock J.

Diplock J:

'The only issue which I have to determine is as to the respective rights of the plaintiffs and the defendants to the compensation or requisition hire which the defendants have received from the Crown in respect of the vessel ...

The plaintiffs contend: (1) that throughout the relevant period they had a valid and subsisting contract with Silver Line Ltd; (2) that by virtue of that contract, they were entitled, as against the defendants, on the principle laid down in *Strathcona (Lord) Steamship Co Ltd* v *Dominion Coal Ltd* [1926] AC 108, to have the vessel used for the carriage of their goods ... The defendants challenge these contentions ... they say ... the *Strathcona* was wrongly decided; even if rightly decided, it applies only where the subsequent purchaser has express notice of the terms of a subsisting charter party; in any event, it lays down no principle which entitles the plaintiffs to have the vessel used for the carriage of their goods and it imposes no obligation on the defendants to account as constructive trustees ... (Diplock J then considered the point of frustration of the contract).

... In the result, I hold that at all material times there was a valid and subsisting contract between Silver Line and the plaintiffs, for breach of which (if there was any breach during the period of requisition) the plaintiffs could recover damages from Silver Line. But that is a claim with which I am not concerned. What is said, however, is that by virtue of that contract, the plaintiffs were entitled as against the defendants, Ben Line, to have the vessel used for the carriage of their goods.

The plaintiffs' charter party with Silver Line ... gave (the plaintiffs) no right of property in, or to possession of, the vessel. It was one by which Silver Line agreed with the plaintiffs that for 30 months from 9 March 1955, they would render services by their servants and crew to carry the goods which were put on the vessel by the plaintiffs ... By parting with their property in the vessel on 8 February 1956 and retaining a right to possession and use which terminated on its requisition, Silver Line put it out of their power to continue to perform their contractual services after the vessel was requisitioned. It is true that during the period of requisition (which is the only period with which I am concerned) Silver Line could not have performed their contractual services to the plaintiffs anyway ... This, however, is a matter between Silver Line and the plaintiffs, with which I am not called upon to deal except in so far (if at all) as it may be relevant to the determination of the plaintiffs' rights against the defendants. There was no privity of contract between the plaintiffs and the defendants. On what ground, therefore, can they assert against the defendants all or any of the contractual rights they would have had against Silver Line by virtue of the existence of such contractual rights?

It is contended that the plaintiffs' rights against the defendants stem from the principle laid down by Knight Bruce LJ in *De Mattos* v *Gibson* in 1858, as approved by the Privy Council in the *Lord Strathcona Case*. The principle laid down by Knight Bruce LJ in *De Mattos* v *Gibson* ... was in the following oft quoted terms:

"Reason and justice seem to prescribe that, at least, as a general rule, where a man by gift or purchase acquires property from another with knowledge of a previous contract, lawfully and for valuable consideration made by him with a third person, to use and employ the property for a particular purpose in a specified manner, the acquirer shall not to the material damage of the third person, in opposition to the contract and inconsistently with it, use and employ the property in a manner not allowable to the giver or seller."

... The broad principle as laid down by Knight Bruce LJ applies to all species of property - real property, chattels and choses in action alike ... in the *Strathcona Case* which, being a decision of the Privy Council, is not binding upon me ...

It may be relevant to note that in the *Strathcona Case*, the buyers of the vessel subject to the time charter in favour of the plaintiffs, had express notice of the terms of the charter and had covenanted with the sellers to perform and accept all responsibilities under it. It was, as the board said, not a mere case of notice of the existence of a covenant affecting the use of the property sold, but a case of acceptance of the property expressly sub conditione. The initial emphasis on this, and the reference at a later stage to the possibility that a shipowner might declare himself a trustee of his obligations under a charter party so as to bind his assignee, might suggest, as a possible ratio decidendi, that the *Strathcona Case* was one where either the purchaser used expressions which amounted to a declaration of trust in favour of the charterers, or the vendor himself accepted the benefit of the covenant as trustee for the charterers. But an examination of the Board's opinion as a whole, seems to indicate that they accepted the full doctrine of Knight Bruce LJ as respects chattels, namely, that mere notice does not give rise to the equity, the only qualification that the Board imposed being that "an interest must remain" (sc in the person seeking the remedy) "in the subject matter of the covenant before a right can be conceded to an injunction against the violation by another of the covenant in question". The only remedy which the Board in terms recognised, is a remedy by injunction against the use of the ship by the purchaser inconsistent with the charter party, but they said, in a passage on which Mr Roskill for the plaintiffs strongly relies, that the purchaser "appears to be plainly in the position of a constructive trustee with obligations which a court of equity will not permit him to violate."

These passages pose several problems: (1) If, as the Board states, the ship is the "subject matter" of the covenant of which the violation by another is to be restrained, it is difficult to see in what sense a charterer, under a gross time charter, has an interest in that subject matter ... (2) whether the reference to the subsequent purchase with notice as being also "plainly" in the position of a constructive trustee imparts that equity provides other remedies against him by his cestui que trust ... is nowhere discussed in the *Strathcona* ... (3) the Board in the *Strathcona Case*, beyond saying that that case was not one of "mere notice", did not discuss what kind of notice to the purchaser of the charterer's rights give rise to the equity, namely, whether at the time of his acquisition of his interest in the vessel, he must have actual knowledge of the charterer's rights against the seller, the violation of which it is sought to restrain, or whether "constructive notice" will suffice ...

The *Strathcona Case*, although decided over 30 years ago, has never been followed in the English courts and has never come up for direct consideration ... The difficulty I have found in ascertaining its ratio decidendi, the impossibility which I find of reconciling the actual decision with well established principles of law, the unsolved and, to me, insoluble problems which that decision raises, combine to satisfy me that it was wrongly decided. I do not propose to follow it ...

If I am wrong in my view that the case was wrongly decided, I am certainly averse from extending it one iota beyond that which, as I understand it, it purported to decide. In particular, I do not think that it purported to decide (1) that anything short of actual knowledge by the subsequent purchaser at the time of the purchase of the charterer's rights, the violation of which it is sought to restrain, is sufficient to give rise to the equity; (2) that the charterer has any remedy against the subsequent purchaser with notice, except a right to restrain the use of the vessel by such purchaser in a manner inconsistent with the terms of the charter; (3) that the charterer has any positive right against the subsequent purchaser to have the vessel used in accordance with the terms of his charter ...

As is obvious from what I have already said, in my view this claim fails: (1) Because *Strathcona* was wrongly decided; (2) because even if it were rightly decided, the defendants do not come within its principles, as they had no actual knowledge at the time of their purchase, of the plaintiffs' rights under their charter ...'

*Commentary*

Not followed: *Lord Strathcona Steamship Co Ltd* v *Dominion Coal Co Ltd* [1926] AC 108.

**Schebsman, Re** [1944] Ch 83 Court of Appeal (Lord Greene MR, Luxmoore and du Parcq LJJ)

Lump sum payable to former employee - part of his estate?

*Facts*

Schebsman was employed by a Swiss Company and its English subsidiary. He ceased employment in March 1940 and by a contract dated 20 September 1940 made between Schebsman, the Swiss Company, and the English subsidiary, it was agreed that the English company would pay him a lump sum immediately and a further sum by instalments over a period of 6 years. It was further agreed that if he should die within the 6 year period, sums would be paid to his wife and if she should die, then to his daughter. Schebsman was declared bankrupt in March 1942 and died in May of the same year. His trustee in bankruptcy claimed that the sums payable to the widow and/or the daughter formed part of his estate.

*Held*

Schebsman was not a trustee for the payments to be made to the wife or daughter and the payments did not form part of his estate.

Du Parcq LJ:

'It is, in my opinion, convenient to approach the problems raised in this appeal by first considering the position of the parties at common law. It is clear that Mrs Schebsman, who was not a party to the agreement, acquired no rights under it and has never been in a position to maintain an action upon it ... Nor, I think, is it disputed and it may be said to be self-evident, that the English company's agreement to pay these moneys into the hands of Mrs Schebsman was a valid agreement, a breach of which would be regarded by the courts as an "unlawful act" and a "legal wrong" ... I may now express my own agreement with a proposition submitted by counsel for the appellant. He said that the duty to pay into the hands of a nominated person is discharged when the money has been paid to that person, and that the party bound to make a payment has no control over its destination. As a general proposition that is true and can hardly be questioned ... But the proposition, accurate as it is, may be misleading unless it is considered together with another proposition which I take to be equally unexceptional and which I will now state.

It is open to parties to agree that, for a consideration supplied by one of them, the other will make payments to a third person for the use and benefit of that third person and not for the use and benefit of the contracting party who provides the consideration. Whether or not such an agreement has been made in a given case is clearly a question of construction, but assuming that the parties have manifested their intention so to agree, it cannot, I think, be doubted that the common law would regard such an agreement as valid and as enforceable (in the sense of giving a cause of action for damages for its breach to the other party to the contract) and would regard the breach of it as an unlawful act.

I have said that the question whether a contract imposes a liability on one of the parties to confer a benefit on a third party, not privy to the contract, is always one of construction. From the point of view of the common law, with which alone I am now dealing, I have no doubt that the general rules of construction laid down by Blackburn J in *Burges* v *Wickham* (1863) 3 B&S 669 must be applied.

According to the general law of England, the written record of a contract must not be varied or added to by verbal evidence of what was the intention of the parties.

I now turn to the agreement in the present case in order to seek, in the document itself, the answer to the question whether the parties intended that, after the death of the debtor the company should be under an obligation to make payments to Mrs Schebsman for her own benefit and to the debtor's personal representatives under a corresponding obligation to accept payment to Mrs Schebsman for her own benefit as a fulfilment of the contract. It seems to me to be plain upon the face of the contract that this was the intention of the parties ...

I may now summarise the position at common law as follows: (i) it is the right, as well as the duty, of the company to make the prescribed payments to Mrs Schebsman and to no other person; (ii) Mrs Schebsman may dispose of the sums so received as she pleases ... (iii) if anyone standing in the shoes of the debtor were to intercept the sums payable to Mrs Schebsman and refuse to account to her for them, he would be guilty of a breach of the debtor's contract with the company; (iv) the obligation undertaken by the company cannot be varied at the will of the other party to the contract, but may be varied consensually at any time, although the debtor is no longer living, as it could have been in his lifetime.

It now remains to consider the question whether and, if so, to what extent, the principles of equity affect the position of the parties.

It was argued by counsel for the appellant that one effect of the agreement ... was that a trust was thereby created and that the debtor constituted himself trustee for Mrs Schebsman of the benefit of the covenant under which payments were to be made to her. Uthwatt J rejected this contention and the argument has not satisfied me that he was wrong. It is true that, by the use possibly of unguarded language, a person may create a trust ... but unless an intention to create a trust is clearly to be collected from the language used and the circumstances of the case, I think that the court ought not to be astute to discover indications of such an intention. I have little doubt that in the present case, both parties intended to keep alive their common law right to vary consensually the terms of the obligation undertaken by the company and, if circumstances had changed in the debtor's lifetime, injustice might have been done by holding that a trust had been created and that those terms were, accordingly, unalterable ...'

**Scruttons Ltd v Midland Silicones Ltd** [1962] 2 WLR 186 House of Lords (Viscount Simonds, Lord Reid, Lord Keith of Avonholm, Lord Denning and Lord Morris of Borth-y-Gest)

Bill of lading - clause limiting liability

*Facts*

The plaintiffs bought a drum of chemicals, which was shipped by consignors in New York on a vessel owned by the United States Line. The bill of lading contained a clause limiting the liability of the shipowners. The defendants were stevedores who had contracted with the US Lines to act for them in London. Under the contract between the defendants and the US Lines, the defendants were to have the benefit of the clause in the bill of lading (the defendants were not parties to the bill of lading). The plaintiffs were not aware of the existence of the contract between the defendants and the US Lines. As a result of the defendants' negligence, the drum was damaged. The plaintiffs sued the defendants in negligence and the defendants pleaded the clause limiting liability in the bill of lading.

*Held*

The defendants were not protected by the clause and the plaintiffs were entitled to recover the full extent of the damage.

Viscount Simonds:

'The question is whether the appellants ... who admittedly, by their negligence, caused damage to certain cargo consigned to the respondents under a Bill of Lading, can take advantage of a provision for limitation of liability contained in that document. In judgments, with which I entirely agree and to which but for the importance of the case, I should think it necessary to add nothing, the learned judge (Diplock J) and the Court of Appeal have unanimously answered the question in the negative

... Then, to avert the consequences which would appear to follow from the fact that the stevedores were not a party to the contract conferring immunity on the carriers, it was argued that the carriers contracted as agents for the stevedores. They did not expressly do so; if, then, there was an agency, it was the case of an agent acting for an undisclosed principal. I am met at once by the difficulty that there is no ground whatever for saying that the carriers were contracting as agents for this firm of stevedores or any other stevedores whom they might employ.

Next, it was argued that there was an implied contract between the cargo owners, the respondents and the stevedores, that the latter should have the benefit of the immunity clause in the bill of lading. This argument presents, if possible, greater difficulties ... In the present case, the cargo owners had a contract with the carriers which knew nothing of the relations between the carrier and the stevedores. It was no business of theirs. They were concerned only to have the job done which the carriers had contracted to do. There is no conceivable reason why an implication should be made that they had entered into any contractual relation with the stevedores.

But, my Lords, all these contentions were but a prelude to one which, had your Lordships accepted it, would have been the foundation of a dramatic decision of this House. It was argued, if I understood the argument, that if A contracts with B to do something for the benefit of C, then C, though not a party to the contract, can sue A to enforce it. This is independent of whether C is A's undisclosed principal or a beneficiary under a trust of which A is trustee. It is sufficient that C is an "interested person". My Lords, if this is the law of England, then, subject always to the question of consideration, no doubt, if the carrier purports to contract for the benefit of the stevedores, the latter can enforce that contract. Whether that premise is satisfied in this case is another matter ...

Learned counsel for the respondents met it, as they had successfully done in the courts below, by asserting a principle which is, I suppose, as well established as any in our law, a "fundamental" principle, as Viscount Haldane LC called it in *Dunlop Pneumatic Tyre Co Ltd* v *Selfridge & Co Ltd*; an "elementary" principle, as it has been called times without number, that only a person who is a party to a contract can sue on it ... If the principle of jus quaesitum tertio is to be introduced into our law, it must be done by Parliament after a due consideration of its merits and demerits. I should not be prepared to give it my support without a greater knowledge than I at present possess of its operation in other systems of law.

I come, finally, to the case which is said to require us to decide in favour of the appellant. The *Elder Dempster Case* [1924] All ER Rep 135 ... When, therefore, it is urged that the *Elder Dempster Case* decided that, even if there is no general exception to what I have called the fundamental rule that a person not a party to a contract cannot sue to enforce it, there is at least a special exception in the case of a contract for carriage of goods by sea, an exception which is to be available to every person, servant or agent of the contracting party or independent contractor, then I demand that that particular exception should be plainly deductible from the speeches that were delivered ... The question then is whether there is to be extracted from *Elder Dempster* a decision that there is in a contract for carriage of goods by sea, a particular exception to the fundamental rule in favour of all persons, including stevedores and other independent contractors. The question must clearly, in my opinion, be answered in the negative ...'

Lord Reid:

'Although I may regret it, I find it impossible to deny the existence of the general rule that a stranger to a contract cannot, in a question with either of the contracting parties, take advantage of provisions of the contract, even where it is clear from the contract that some provision in it was intended to benefit him. That rule appears to have been crystallised a century ago in *Tweddle* v *Atkinson* and finally established in this house in *Dunlop* v *Selfridge*. There are, it is true, certain well established exceptions to that rule - though I am not sure that they are really exceptions and do not arise from other principles. But none of these in any way touches the present case.

The actual words used by Lord Haldane in the *Dunlop Case* were made the basis of an argument that, although a stranger to a contract may not be able to sue for any benefit under it, he can rely on the contract as a defence if one of the parties to it sues him in breach of his contractual obligations - that he can use the contract as a shield, though not as a sword. I can find no justification for that. If the other contracting party can prevent the breach of contract well and good, but if he cannot, I do not see how the stranger can. As was said in *Tweddle* v *Atkinson*, the stranger cannot "take advantage" from the contract ...

So this case depends on the proper interpretation of the *Elder Dempster Case*. What was decided there is clear enough. The ship was under time charter; the bill of lading made by the shippers and the charterers provided for exemption from liability in the event which happened, and this exemption was held to ensure to the benefit of the shipowners who were not parties to the bill of lading, but whose servant, the master, caused damage to the shipper's goods by his negligence. The decision is binding on us, but I agree that the decision by itself will not avail the present appellants because the facts of this case are very different from those in the *Elder Dempster Case*.

It can hardly be denied that the ratio decidendi of the *Elder Dempster* decision is very obscure ... I do not think that it is my duty to pursue the unrewarding task of seeking to extract a ratio decidendi from what was said in this House in *Elder Dempster*. Nor is it my duty to seek to rationalise the decision by determining in any other way just how far the scope of the decision should extend. I must treat the decision as an anomalous and unexplained exception to the general principle that a stranger cannot rely for his protection on provisions in a contract to which he is not a party. The decision of this House is authoritative in cases of which the circumstances are not reasonably distinguishable from those which gave rise to the decision. The circumstances in the present case are clearly distinguishable in several respects. Therefore I must decide this case on the established principles of the law of England apart from that decision and, on that basis, I have no doubt that this appeal must be dismissed.'

## Shanklin Pier Ltd v Detel Products Ltd

See chapter 4 - Contents of contracts.

## Snelling v John G Snelling Ltd

See chapter 2 - Consideration.

## Southern Water Authority v Carey [1985] 2 All ER 1077 High Court (His Honour Judge David Smout QC)

Liability limitation clause - protects sub-contractor?

*Facts*

The main contract for the construction of a sewage works limited liability for loss arising from any defects. Were sub-contractors entitled to the benefits of this clause?

*Held*

As a matter of contract they were not as, inter alia, they were strangers to the contract.

His Honour Judge David Smout QC:

'Counsel for the ... defendants puts his argument in a number of ways. He points out that cl 30(vi) refers to the contractor contracting as trustee for the sub-contractor. But I can give no meaning to that phrase, for the conception of a trust attaching to a benefit under an exclusion clause extends far beyond conventional limits. Nor am I attracted to the argument that because the contract was under seal it can therefore be enforced by reason of s56 of the Law of Property Act 1925 at the suit of one who is not a party to it. I conclude, on the authority of *Beswick* v *Beswick*, that I would not be justified in holding that the old common law rule in *Tweddle* v *Atkinson* has been abrogated by s56 outside the field of real property ...

It is, however, the agency element in *Satterthwaite's* case that is much to the point. Lord Wilberforce in that case, speaking of the House of Lord's decision in *Scruttons Ltd* v *Midland Silicones Ltd*, commented:

"There is no need to question or even to qualify that case insofar as it affirms the general proposition that a contract between two parties cannot be sued on by a third person even though the contract is expressed to be for his benefit ... But *Midland Silicones* left open the case where one of the parties contracts as agent for the third person: in particular Lord Reid's speech spelt out, in four propositions, the prerequisites for the validity of such an agency contract. There is of course nothing unique to this case in the conception of agency contracts: well-known and common instances exist in the field of hire-purchase, of bankers' commercial credits and other transactions."

He went on to cite a passage from Lord Reid's judgment in *Scruttons Ltd* v *Midland Silicones Ltd* which has been referred to many times in argument in this case, and in which Lord Reid said:

"I can see a possibility of success of the agency argument if (first) the bill of lading makes it clear that the stevedore is intended to be protected by the provisions in it which limit liability, (secondly) the bill of lading makes it clear that the carrier, in addition to contracting for these provisions on his own behalf, is also contracting as agent for the stevedore that these provisions should apply to the stevedore, (thirdly) the carrier has authority from the stevedore to do that, or perhaps later ratification by the stevedore would suffice, and (fourthly) that any difficulties about consideration moving from the stevedore were overcome." ...

Let us then consider the four propositions in the context of the instant case. First, does the main contract make it clear that the sub-contractors are intended to be protected by the provisions in it which limit liability? To my mind the answer must be Yes. Secondly, does it make it clear that the main contractor in addition to contracting for these provisions on his own behalf is also contracting as agent for the sub-contractors that the provisions should also apply to the sub-contractors? Again, I answer Yes: cl 30(vi) so states. The fourth proposition as to consideration poses no difficulty, for this is a contract under seal. It is the third proposition that is debatable in the instant case: had the main contractor authority from the sub-contractor, at the time of making the contract, and, if not, was there any later ratification that would suffice? Unlike *Satterthwaite's* case, there is no evidence here on which I could conclude that the main contractors had prior authority. What as to ratification? Counsel for the plaintiffs contends that there can be no ratification unless the principal was capable of being ascertained at the time when the act was done, ie when the deed was signed. herein lies the defendants' difficulty... I do not regard myself in the circumstances of this case entitled to extend the law beyond the limits as at present defined.'

## Tulk v Moxhay

See *Lord Strathcona Steamship Co Ltd* v *Dominion Coal Co Ltd* [1926] AC 108.

## Tweddle v Atkinson (1861) 1 B & S 393 Court of Queen's Bench (Wightman, Crompton and Blackburn JJ)

Contract - action by stranger to the consideration

*Facts*

On 11 July 1855, an agreement was made in the following terms:

'Memorandum of an agreement made this day between William Guy and John Tweddle of the other part. Whereas of the one part it is mutually agreed that the said William Guy shall and will pay the sum of £200 to William Tweddle, his son-in-law, and the said John Tweddle, father to the aforesaid William Tweddle, shall and will pay the sum of £100 to the said William Tweddle, each and severally the said sums on or before the 21st day of August 1855. And, it is hereby further agreed by the aforesaid William Guy and the said John Tweddle that the said William Tweddle has full power to sue the said parties in any Court of law or equity for the aforesaid sums hereby promised and specified.'

The plaintiff was the son of John Tweddle and, before the making of the agreement, had married the daughter of William Guy. Before the marriage, William Guy, in consideration of the proposed marriage, had promised a marriage portion (which had not been performed at the time of the making of the agreement). By 21 August 1865, the plaintiff had not been paid the £200 by William Guy, who had subsequently died, or by Guy's executor. The plaintiff sued Guy's executor for the £200.

*Held*

The plaintiff's action would be dismissed and judgment given for the defendant.

Wightman J:

'Some of the old decisions appear to support the proposition that a stranger to the consideration of a contract may maintain an action upon it, if he stands in such a near relationship to the party from whom the consideration proceeds, that he may be considered a party to the consideration ... But there is no modern case in which the proposition has been supported. On the contrary, it is now established that no stranger to the consideration can take advantage of a contract, although made for his benefit.'

Crompton J:

'It is admitted that the plaintiff cannot succeed unless this case is an exception to the modern and well established doctrine of the action of assumpsit. At the time when the cases which have been cited were decided, the action of assumpsit was treated as an action of trespass upon the case and therefore in the nature of a tort; and the law was not settled, as it is now, that natural love and affection is not a sufficient consideration for a promise upon which an action may be maintained; nor was it settled that the promisee cannot bring an action unless the consideration for the promise moved from him. The modern cases have, in effect, overruled the old decisions; they show that the consideration must move from the party entitled to sue upon the contract. It would be a monstrous proposition to say that a person was a party to the contract for the purpose of suing upon it for his own advantage and not a party to it for the purpose of being sued. It is said that the father in the present case was agent for the son in making the contract, but that argument ought also to make the son liable upon it. I am prepared to overrule the old decisions and to hold that, by reason of the principles which now govern the action of assumpsit, the present action is not maintainable.'

Blackburn J:

'The declaration then sets out a new contract and the only point is whether that contract, being for the benefit of the children, they can sue upon it. Mr Mellish (Counsel for the plaintiff) admits that, in general, no action can be maintained upon a promise unless the consideration moves from the party to whom it is made. But he says that there is an exception; namely that when the consideration moves from a father, and the contract is for the benefit of the son, the natural love and affection between the father and the son gives the son the right to sue as if the consideration had proceeded from himself ... The cases ... show that natural love and affection are not a sufficient consideration whereupon an action of assumpsit may be founded.'

**Vandepitte v Preferred Accident Insurance Corporation of New York** [1933] AC 70
Privy Council (Lord Tomlin, Lord Thankerton, Lord Macmillan, Lord Wright and Sir George Lowndes)

Car accident - insurers' liability

*Facts*

V incurred injuries in a car accident and was awarded judgment against B, a minor, who had been driving her father's car with his permission. B's father had insured with PAIC, which undertook to indemnify him and those driving his car with his permission. A statute provided that in these circumstances, a judgment creditor could proceed against the insurers for the amount of the judgment. V proceeded against PAIC, arguing (1) that B was insured by them, either directly by her father, or (2) as cestui que trust of the promise of indemnity made by PAIC in the contract with B's father.

*Held*

Both (1) and (2) would be rejected and V could not therefore succeed. As to (1), B could be a direct party to the insurance contract only if she had had a part in the contract which had been concluded between her father and the insurance company. As to (2), the intention to constitute a trust must be affirmatively proved - the intention could not necessarily be inferred from the general words of the policy.


## Wells (Merstham) Ltd v Buckland Sand and Silica Co Ltd

See chapter 4 - Contents of contracts.


## Woodar Investment Development Ltd v Wimpey Construction UK Ltd [1980] 1 WLR 277 House of Lords (Lord Wilberforce, Lord Salmon, Lord Russell of Killowen, Lord Keith of Kinkel and Lord Scarman)

Rights of third party - right to rescind

*Facts*

A contract for the sale and purchase of development land provided for the payment of £150,000 to Transworld Trade Ltd, a third party, on completion: it also provided that the purchasers (Wimpey) could rescind if a statutory authority 'shall have commenced' to acquire the property compulsorily. When the contract was signed, the Minister of the Environment had already commenced compulsory purchase proceedings for part of the property. Land prices fell; the purchasers purported to rescind because of the Minister's actions; the rescission was not accepted by the vendors. The vendors maintained that the purchasers were not entitled to rescind and, in a second action, that the notice of rescission (and the defence and counterclaim in the first action) amounted to a repudiation which they accepted and entitled them to sue for damages. Included in their claim was a claim for damages on behalf of the third party.

*Held* (Lord Salmon and Lord Russell of Killowen dissenting)

The attempt at rescission did not amount to a repudiation.

Lord Wilberforce:

'In my opinion ... Wimpey are entitled to succeed on the repudiation issue, and I would only add that it would be a regrettable development of the law of contract to hold that a party who bona fide relies on an express stipulation in a contract in order to rescind or terminate a contract should, by that fact alone, be treated as having repudiated his contractual obligations if he turns out to be mistaken as to his rights. Repudiation is a drastic conclusion which should only be held to arise in clear cases of a refusal, in a matter going to the root of the contract, to perform contractual obligations. To uphold Woodar's contentions in this case would represent an undesirable contention of the doctrine.

The second issue in this appeal is one of damages. Both courts below have allowed Woodar to recover substantial damages in respect of condition I under which £150,000 was payable by Wimpey to Transworld Trade Ltd on completion. On the view which I take of the repudiation issue, this question does not require decision, but in view of the unsatisfactory state in which the law would be if the Court of Appeal's decision were to stand I must add three observations.

1.    The majority of the Court of Appeal followed, in the case of Goff LJ with expressed reluctance, its previous decision in *Jackson* v *Horizon Holidays Ltd*. I am not prepared to dissent from the actual decision in that case. It may be supported either as a broad decision on the measure of damages (per James LJ) or possibly as an example of a type of contract, examples of which are persons contracting for family holidays, ordering meals in restaurants for a party, hiring a taxi for a group, calling for special treatment. As I suggested in *New Zealand Shipping Co Ltd* v *A M Satterthwaite & Co Ltd*, there are many situations of daily life which do not fit neatly into conceptual analysis, but which require some flexibility in the law of contract. *Jackson's* case may well be one.

I cannot agree with the basis on which Lord Denning MR put his decision in that case. The extract on which he relied from the judgment of Lush LJ in *Lloyd's* v *Harper* was part of a passage in which Lush LJ was stating as an "established rule of law" that an agent (sc an insurance broker) may sue on a contract made by him on behalf of the principal (sc the assured) if the contract gives him such a right, and is no authority for the proposition required in *Jackson's* case, still less for the proposition, required here, that, if Woodar made a contract for a sum of money to be paid to Transworld, Woodar can, without showing that it has itself suffered loss or that Woodar was agent or trustee for Transworld, sue for damages for non-payment of that sum. That would certainly not be an established rule of law, nor was it quoted as such authority by Lord Pearce in *Beswick* v *Beswick*.

2.    Assuming that *Jackson's* case was correctly decided (as above), it does not carry the present case, where the factual situation is quite different. I respectfully think therefore that the Court of Appeal need not, and should not have followed it.

3.    Whether in a situation such as the present, viz where it is not shown that Woodar was agent or trustee for Transworld, or that Woodar itself sustained any loss, Woodar can recover any damages at all, or any but nominal damages, against Wimpey, and on what principle, is in my opinion, a question of great doubt and difficulty, no doubt open in this House, but one on which I prefer to reserve my opinion.'

# 11 ILLEGALITY

**Alexander v Rayson** [1936] 1 KB 169 Court of Appeal (Greer, Romer and Scott LJJ)

Illegality - reduction of rateable value

*Facts*

A lease of a flat made provision for a rent of £450 pa and the rendering of certain services to the tenant: a separate agreement provided for the rendering of substantially the same services on payment by the tenant of £750 pa. The landlord, it was alleged, adopted this dual approach with a view to defrauding the rating authority by leading them to believe that his only income in respect of the flat was £450 pa. The landlord sued for rent under the lease and payment under the agreement.

*Held*

His action could not succeed, unless he could disprove the charge of fraud.

Romer LJ:

'... if the [landlord] has, by his conduct, placed himself in the same position in law as though he had let the flat with the intention of its being used for an illegal purpose, he has no one but himself to thank for any loss that he may suffer in consequence.

That brings us to the real crux of this case. Has the [landlord] placed himself in that position? Now in the cases to which we have referred there was an intention to use the subject-matter of the agreement for an unlawful purpose. In the present case, on the other hand, the [landlord's] intention was merely to make use of the lease and agreement - that is, the documents themselves - for an unlawful purpose. Does that make any difference? In our opinion, it does not. It seems to us ... that the principles applicable to the two cases are identical ... For these reasons we are of opinion that the [landlord] is not entitled to seek the assistance of a court of justice in enforcing either the lease or the agreement ... the documents themselves were dangerous in the sense that they could be and were intended to be used for a fraudulent purpose, without alteration, and the splitting of the transaction into the two documents was an overt step in carrying out the fraud. We cannot think that the respondent is entitled to bring these documents into a court of justice and ask the court to assist him in carrying them into effect.'

*Commentary*

See also *Edler* v *Auerbach* [1950] 1 KB 359.

**Amoco Australia Pty Ltd v Rocca Bros Motor Engineering Co Pty Ltd** [1975] 2 WLR 779 Privy Council (Lord Morris of Borth-y-Gest, Lord Cross of Chelsea, Lord Kilbrandon, Lord Salmon and Lord Edmund-Davies)

Restraint of trade - separate agreements

*Facts*

Arising from a lease and underlease, Rocca was to obtain petrol at a rebate price from Amoco which in turn was to obtain a trade tie in return for its investment in Rocca's service station. The two leases, it was found, were parts of a single commercial transaction.

*Held*

Both leases were unenforceable.

Lord Cross of Chelsea:

'The appellant argued that what was true of a mortgage - which takes effect by way of lease to the mortgagee - must also be true of an ordinary lease and that where a lease contains a covenant which is unenforceable as being in restraint of trade the covenantor - in this case the respondent - most [sic] elect either to give up the lease or to perform the covenant notwithstanding its unenforceability.

It is clear - as counsel indeed conceded - that no such election is required of the covenantor when the unenforceable promise is contained in a bare contract. Provided that the unenforceable part is severable the rest of the contract remains in force and either party can rely on its terms. It would be odd if the position should be different when the promise in question is contained in a lease. The fact that a covenantor has obtained and will continue to enjoy benefits under the relevant agreement which formed part of the consideration for the covenant which he claims to be unenforceable is no doubt pro tanto a reason for holding that the covenant is not in unreasonable restraint of trade. But once it is held that it is in unreasonable restraint of trade, there seems to be no reason for drawing any distinction with regard to the consequences between provisions in contracts and covenants in leases. If in a case where severance was possible the party who had entered into a covenant in a lease which was unenforceable because it was in unreasonable restraint of trade was forced to make the election suggested by counsel he would be put under pressure to observe a promise which public policy said he should be free to disregard. Lord Reid [in *Esso Petroleum* v *Harper's Garage (Stourport) Ltd*] was not expressing any opinion on the point and as at present advised their Lordships do not think that the assumption which he was prepared to make was justified. But even if the appellant was right in saying that had the covenants been severable the respondent would have been put to his election either to observe the unenforceable restraint or to give up the lease its case would not be advanced in the least since the covenants are not severable and the respondent has always been willing - indeed anxious - to give up the underlease provided that the headlease also disappears from the scene.

Finally their Lordships turn to consider whether the headlease can remain on foot if the provisions of the underlease disappear ... It is not possible to regard the two leases as separate dispositions of property. The agreement [for the leases] shows clearly that they were parts of a single commercial transaction under which the respondent was to get a supply of petrol at an agreed rebate and the appellant a trade tie with security for its investment in the station. The statements to the contrary in ... the headlease are simply untrue and it may well be that they were inserted in order to strengthen the position of the appellant in the event of the valdity of the trade tie in the underlease being challenged. If there was no question of public policy in the case then no doubt the respondent would be estopped from denying that the headlease was independent of the underlease but if there was such an estoppel here it would deter the respondent from asserting that the trade tie was unenforceable on grounds of public policy, since ... its position if the underlease went but the headlease remained in force would be far worse than if it acquiesced in the trade tie and retained the benefit of the underlease.'

**Archbolds (Freightage) Ltd v S Spanglett Ltd** [1961] 2 WLR 170 Court of Appeal (Sellers, Pearce and Devlin LJJ)

Contract - illegal performance by one party

*Facts*

The plaintiffs had a judgment debt owing to them by the defendants in respect of damages for the loss of a consignment of whisky, which was stolen from the defendants owing to their negligence while they were transporting it as carriers for the plaintiffs. The defendants' van had 'C' licences under the Road and Rail Traffic Act 1933, which allowed them to carry the defendants' own goods, but did not allow them to carry the goods of others for reward. The plaintiffs' vehicles had 'A' licences, which did allow them to carry the goods of others for reward. The plaintiffs' London office, as a result of a telephone conversation with an unidentified person speaking from the defendants' office, believed that the defendants' vehicles had 'A' licences and were entitled to carry general goods. They therefore employed the defendants to carry for them a part load of goods on the defendants' van. Two days later, the defendants' driver, having delivered those goods, spoke to the traffic manager at the plaintiffs' office in Leeds in order to obtain a return load. The Leeds office made no enquiry about the licence, because he knew that the van had been used by the London office. This load was stolen owing to the driver's negligence.

*Held*

The plaintiffs were entitled to damages.

Pearce LJ:

'It is in just such a case as this, cases that turn on bona fides and knowledge and half-knowledge, that the trial judge has so great an advantage over a court that relies on the colourless, impersonal and sometimes misleading transcript ... I am not prepared to disturb (his) finding ... This is not a case where the plaintiffs can assert a cause of action without relying on the contract ... If a contract is expressly or, by necessary implication, forbidden by statute, or if it is ex facie illegal, or if both parties know that though ex facie legal it can only be performed by illegality, or is intended to be performed illegally, the law will not help the plaintiffs in any way that is a direct or indirect enforcement of rights under the contract. And for this purpose, both parties are presumed to know the law ... The carriage of the plaintiffs' whisky was not, as such, prohibited; the statute merely regulated the means by which carriers should carry goods. Was it then forbidden by implication? ... it was not ... The next question is whether this contract, though not forbidden by the statute, was ex facie illegal ... There is nothing illegal in its terms. Further knowledge, namely knowledge of the fact that Randalls' van was not properly licensed, would show that it could only be performed by contravention of the statute, but that does not make the contract ex facie illegal.

However, if both parties had that knowledge, the contract would be unenforceable as being a contract which, to their knowledge, could not be carried out without a violation of the law. But where one party is ignorant of the fact that will make the performance illegal, is it established that the innocent party cannot obtain relief against the guilty party? No case has been cited to us establishing the proposition that where a contract is, on the face of it, legal and is not forbidden by statute, but must in fact produce illegality by reason of a circumstance known to one party only, it should be held illegal so as to debar the innocent party from relief. In the absence of such a case, I do not feel compelled to so unsatisfactory a conclusion, which would injure the innocent, benefit the guilty and put a premium on deceit. Such a conclusion (in cases like this, where a contract is not forbidden by statute) can only derive from public policy ... an extension of the law in this direction would be more harmful than beneficial. No question of mortal turpitude arises here. The alleged illegality is, so far as the plaintiffs were concerned, the permitting of their goods to be carried by the wrong carrier, namely a carrier who, unknown to them, was not allowed by his licence to carry that particular class of goods. The plaintiffs were never in delicto, since they did not know the vital fact that would make the performance of the contract illegal.

In my view, therefore, public policy does not constrain us to refuse our aid to the plaintiffs and they are therefore entitled to succeed. I would dismiss the appeal.'

Devlin LJ:

'The effect of illegality upon a contract may be threefold. If at the time of making the contract, there is an intent to perform it is an unlawful way, the contract, although it remains alive, is unenforceable at the suit of the party having that intent; if the intent is held in common, it is not enforceable at all. Another effect of illegality is to prevent a plaintiff from recovering under a contract if, in order to prove his rights under it, he has to rely upon his own illegal act; he may not do that, even though he can show that at the time of making the contract, he had no intent to break the law and that at the time of performance, he did not know that what he was doing was illegal. The third effect of illegality is to avoid the contract ab initio and that arises if the making of the contract is expressly or impliedly prohibited by statute, or is otherwise contrary to public policy.

The defendants do not seek to bring this case under either of the first two heads. What the defendants say is that the contract is prohibited by the Road and Rail Traffic Act 1933 section 1. In order to see whether the contract falls within the prohibition it is necessary to ascertain the exact terms of the contract and the exact terms of the prohibition. For reasons which I shall explain later, I shall begin by ascertaining the latter. Section 1 of the Act provides that no person shall use a goods vehicle on a road for the carriage of goods for hire or reward except under a licence. Section 2 provides for various classes of licence, 'A', 'B' and 'C'. It is agreed that the carriage of the goods which were the subject matter of this contract required an 'A' licence. The fact that the van had a 'C' licence does not, therefore, help one way or the other; and it is admitted that the defendants' use of this van for the carriage of these goods was prohibited. As I have noted, the plaintiffs are not to be treated as using the van because they supplied the load. Section 1(3) provides that the driver of the vehicle or, if he is an agent or servant, his principal, shall be deemed to be the person by whom the vehicle is being used.

The statute does not expressly prohibit the making of any contract. The question is therefore whether a prohibition arises as a matter of necessary implication ... it does not follow that because it is an offence for one party to enter into a contract the contract itself is void ... one must have regard to the language used and the scope and purpose of the statute. I think that the purpose of this statute is sufficiently served by the penalties prescribed for the offender; the avoidance of the contract would cause grave inconvenience and injury to innocent members of the public, without furthering the object of the statute. Moreover, the value of the relief given to the wrongdoer if he could escape what would otherwise have been his legal obligation, might, as it would in this case, greatly outweigh the punishment that could be imposed upon him and thus undo the penal effect of the statute.

I conclude, therefore, that this contract was not illegal for the reason that the statute does not prohibit the making of a contract for the carriage of goods in unlicensed vehicles and this contract belongs to this class. I am able, therefore, to arrive at my judgment without an examination of the exact terms of the contract. It is a familiar principle of law that if a contract can be performed in one of two ways, that is, legally or illegally, it is not an illegal contract, though it may be unenforceable at the suit of a party who chooses to perform it illegally. This statement of the law is meaningful if the contract is one which is, by its terms, open to two modes of performance; otherwise it is meaningless. Almost any contract - certainly any contract for the carriage of goods by road - can be performed illegally; any contract of carriage by road can be performed illegally simply by exceeding the appropriate speed limit ... It is the terms of the contract that matter; the surrounding facts are irrelevant, save in so far as, being known to both parties, they throw light on the meaning and effect of the contract. The question is not whether the vehicle was in fact properly licensed, but whether it was, expressly or by implication in the contract, described or warranted as properly licensed. If it was so described or warranted, then the legal position is not that the contract could only be performed by a violation of the law, but that unless it could be performed legally, it could not be performed at all. The fact that, as in this case, it may be known to one of the parties at the time of making the contract that he cannot perform it legally and therefore that it will inevitably be broken, does not make the contract itself illegal.

I think there is much to be said for the argument that in a case of this sort, there is, unless the circumstances exclude it, an implied warranty that the van is properly licensed for the service for which it is required. It would be unreasonable to expect a man when he is getting into a taxi cab to ask for an express warranty from the driver that his cab was licensed; the answer, if it took any intelligible form at all, would be to the effect that it would not be on the streets if it were not. The same applies to a person who delivers goods for carriage by a particular vehicle; he cannot be expected to examine the road licence to see if it is in order. But the issue of warranty was not raised ... I agree ...'

## Commentary

Applied: *St John Shipping Corporation* v *Joseph Rank Ltd* [1956] 3 WLR 870. Distinguished: *Re Mahmoud & Ispahani* [1921] 2 KB 716.

## Ashmore, Benson, Pease & Co Ltd v A V Dawson Ltd [1973] 1 WLR 828 Court of Appeal (Lord Denning MR, Phillimore and Scarman LJJ)

Contract of carriage - illegal performance

### Facts

The plaintiffs manufactured a tube bank weighing 25 tons and their transport manager arranged for the defendants to carry it to the port of shipment. In the manager's presence, the equipment was loaded onto a lorry so that the vehicle's maximum permitted load was exceeded by five tons, but he raised no objection. On its way to the port the lorry toppled over and the tube bank was damaged. The plaintiffs sued for damages.

### Held

Their action could not succeed.

Lord Denning MR:

'Although I have these misgivings, I am prepared to accept the judge's finding that the contract was lawful when it was made. But then the question arises: was it lawful in its performance? The judge's attention does not seem to have been drawn to this point. Yet there are authorities which show that illegality in the performance of a contract may disable a person from suing on it, if he participated in the illegality ...

On that evidence I think that [the manager] must have known that these articulated lorries of Dawsons were only permitted to carry 20 tons. Nevertheless, realising that 25 tons was too heavy - much too heavy - for them, he was content to let them carry the loads because it had happened before without trouble. He was getting the transport done cheaper too by £30 saved on each trip by each load. Not only did [the manager] know of the illegality; he participated in it by sanctioning the loading of the vehicle with a load in excess of the regulations. That participation in the illegal performance of the contract debars Ashmores from suing Dawsons on it or suing Dawsons for negligence. I know that Dawsons were parties to the illegality. They knew, as well as [the manager] that the load was overweight in breach of the regulations. But in such a situation as this, the defendants are in a better position. In pari delicto, potior est conditio defendentis.'

## Attwood v Lamont [1920] 3 KB 571 Court of Appeal (Lord Sterndale MR, Atkin and Younger LJJ)

Restraint of trade - tailor

### Facts

The contract of employment of a cutter and head of the tailoring department of the plaintiff's general outfitter business provided:

'In consideration of the employers employing him in the capacity and at the salary aforesaid, the [employee] hereby agrees with the employers that he will not at any time hereafter, either on his own account or that of any wife of his, or in partnership with, or as assistant, servant, or agent, to any other person, persons, or company, carry on or be in any way directly or indirectly concerned in any of the following trades or businesses, that is to say, the trade or business of a tailor, dressmaker, general draper, milliner, hatter, haberdasher, gentlemen's, ladies', or children's outfitter, at any place within a radius of ten miles of the employers' place of business ...'

*Held*

The covenant was too wide to be enforced.

Lord Sterndale MR:

'... I think it is quite clear that this agreement was part of a scheme by which every head of a department was to be restrained from competition with the plaintiff, even in the business of departments with which he had no connection and with the customers of which he was never brought into contact.

If this be the true meaning of the agreement, it was, as it is described, an agreement not to trade in opposition, and not an agreement to restrain the unfair use of secrets or knowledge of customers acquired by the servants in the employers' service. To effect this object the retention of the restraint regarding the business of all the departments is necessary, and I think that to strike out references to all but the tailoring department is not merely to remove one of several covenants each directed to the legitimiate object of preventing unfair competition, but to alter entirely the scope and intention of the agreement. It is thereby sought to be converted from an agreement to restrain general competition into an agreement which will conform to the requirements of the cases to which I have referred. I am of opinion that ... this agreement should not be severed. If this be right, the agreement is invalid, for, as it stands, it is far too wide, and it is unnecessary to consider whether, if severed, it could be upheld.'

## Bedford Insurance Co Ltd v Instituto de Resseguros do Brazil [1984] 3 WLR 726 High Court (Parker J)

Illegality - insurance contracts

*Facts*

The plaintiff Hong Kong insurance company acted through London agents: neither of them was authorised, as statute required, and acting in contravention of the statute was an offence. The plaintiff sought an indemnity from the defendants under a reinsurance contract entered into through the brokers.

*Held*

Their action would be dismissed.

Parker J:

'The textbooks appear mostly to agree that the law relating to illegality is in a somewhat confused and unsatisfactory state. In my view, however, much, if not all, of the confusion arises from attempts to apply dicta from cases where the contract itself was perfectly lawful but actual performance was not, from seeking to equate cases concerning the question whether breach of some statutory duty *gives* a civil remedy with cases concerned with the question whether the statute *bars* a civil remedy, and by occasional failures to specify, when referring to a contract as being illegal, whether it was intended to say whether it was also void ab initio or merely unenforceable ab initio or whether it was illegal in itself or merely illegal because it was intended by one or both parties to be performed in an illegal manner. Be that as it may, certain things are clear. In *Archbolds (Freightage) Ltd v S Spanglett Ltd (Randall, third party)* ... Devlin LJ summarised the possible effects of illegality. In respect to two of them he said:

"Another effect of illegality is to prevent a plaintiff from recovering under a contract if in order to prove his rights under it he has to rely on his own illegal act ... The third effect of illegality is to avoid the contract ab initio, and that arises if the making of the contract is expressly or impliedly prohibited by statute or is otherwise contrary to public policy."

As to the first of the above effects, in *Marles* v *Philip Trant & Sons Ltd (Mackinnon, third party) (No 2)* Denning LJ said:

"... the principle is well settled that, if the plaintiff requires any aid from an illegal transaction to establish his cause of action, then he shall not have any aid from the court."

The second of the above effects has been repeatedly stated, albeit that there has been some difference of opinion as to the effect of certain aids to construction. Those differences do not however, in my judgment, cause difficulties in the present case. Here, as a matter of plain language, both the contract and the performance are prohibited, the offence created is a continuing one, and the statute is for the protection of the public.

Counsel for the plaintiffs relied strongly on a passage from the judgment of Devlin LJ in *Archbolds (Freightage) Ltd* v *Spanglett* where he said:

"The general conditions which arise on this question were examined at length in *St John Shipping Corpn* v *Joseph Rank Ltd* and Pearce LJ has set them out so clearly in his judgment in this case that I need add little to them. Fundamentally they are the same as those that arise on the construction of every statute; one must have regard to the language used and to the scope and purpose of the statute. I think that the purpose of this statute is sufficiently served by the penalties prescribed for the offender; the avoidance of the contract would cause grave inconvenience and injury to innocent members of the public without furthering the object of the statute. Moreover, the value of the relief given to the wrongdoer if he could escape what would otherwise have been his legal obligation might, as it would in this case, greatly outweigh the punishment that could be imposed on him, and thus undo the penal effect of the statute. I conclude, therefore, that this contract was not illegal for the reason that the statute does not prohibit the making of a contract for the carriage of goods in unlicensed vehicles and this contract belongs to this class."

He also relied on the judgment of Pearce LJ referred to in the passage quoted above, and on *Shaw* v *Groom*. These passages, however, apply to cases where there is no express prohibition and where, as here, albeit by way of the definition, there is a clear express prohibition of both contract and performance they cannot be used to escape the well-settled principle that if the contract is expressly prohibited it is avoided ab initio.

*Bloxsome* v *Williams* to which Devlin LJ referred, appears to conflict with this. In this case there was a statutory prohibition on Sunday trading, breach of which constituted an offence. The plaintiff's son verbally agreed on a Sunday to buy a horse from a horse dealer, albeit the fact that the seller was a horse dealer was unknown to the plaintiff or his son. The horse was orally warranted sound. It was not delivered until the following Tuesday and the price was then paid. The plaintiff, on behalf of his son, sued for breach of warranty and recovery the price. He succeeded. The judgment of the court was given by Bayley J. Judgment was given on two grounds. The first was that the contract was not complete until the Tuesday and thus there was no breach of the statute. The second was that even if there was a breach it was not competent to the defendant, who alone was guilty of a breach of the law, to set up his own illegality against the innocent plaintiff. The second ground is apparently inconsistent with the principle that where there is an express prohibition the contract is avoided ab initio. In so far as it is so inconsistent, it cannot in my view stand in the light of later authorities.

The original contracts had they in fact been authorised would thus, in my judgment, have been prohibited and therefore not only illegal but avoided ab initio. This being so, apart from one argument raised by counsel, the plaintiffs would have been unable to recover under the reinsurance both because the original contracts were avoided ab initio and because even if not avoided ab initio it is essential to the plaintiffs' cause of action on the reinsurance contract to set them up. Counsel for the plaintiffs submitted that the statements of Devlin and Denning LJJ which I have quoted above are too wide and that all he needs for his cause of action is to set up the contracts. He need not, he said, show either that they were made in London in the course of carrying on insurance business or that the plaintiffs were unauthorised under the Insurance Companies Acts or that the Acts prohibited them. This submission is, in my judgment, wholly unsustainable.'

*Commentary*

Applied in *Phoenix General Insurance Co of Greece SA* v *Administratia Asigurarilor de Stat* [1987] 2 All ER 152.

**Belvoir Finance Co Ltd v Stapleton** [1970] 3 WLR 530 Court of Appeal (Lord Denning MR, Sachs and Megaw LJJ)

Illegal sales - liability for conversion

*Facts*

The plaintiff finance company purchased three cars from dealers and let them on hire-purchase terms to Belgravia, a car hire company. The cars went straight from the dealers to Belgravia. The contracts of sale and the hire-purchase agreements were illegal because, as all parties know, a purpose of the transactions was to contravene certain hire-purchase regulations. Belgravia fraudulently sold the cars to innocent purchasers and, Belgravia having gone into liquidation, the plaintiffs sued Belgravia's salesman, who had sold the cars, for damages for conversion.

*Held*

They were entitled to succeed.

Sachs LJ:

'It was established at trial that by reason of the conspiracy ... the contracts by which the finance company acquired the cars from the dealers and the hire-purchase agreements which it entered into with Belgravia were both so tainted with illegality as to be void and unenforceable. It was submitted by counsel for the defendant that as a result the finance company cannot establish its title to these cars against any third parties in general and against the defendant in particular. It is argued that this is because - as is the case - it cannot prove its title without putting in evidence and then relying on an illegal contract.

The effect of accepting this submission would, of course, be drastic. It was plain, as indeed counsel for the defendant conceded, that in the circumstances of this case as a whole, there was no one other than the finance company in whom the ownership of these cars could be said in law to be vested at the material time. If his submission was right, it could not, however, as against a third party, show title because of the illegality which has been referred to. That in turn, it was conceded, produced the result that the first person who managed to obtain possession of the cars could retain it - for the simple reason that there would exist nobody who could establish a legal title against him. It was indeed counsel's case - as it had to be - that it would matter not whether that possession was gained honestly or by theft; and that such a rule would apply alike in detinue and conversion. It would be tantamount in its effect to sanctioning a confiscation of the property, not by the State, but by third parties. It would produce strange and unconscionable results not only as regards chattels, but ... in the law of real property and tenancy agreements. Such results could be particularly extensive nowadays; there are so many complex statutes, orders and regulations which can produce an illegality of contract. They can render those concerned guilty of conspiracy, despite the fact that when making the contract they think they have not done anything wrong: for knowledge of the law being immaterial, they can nonetheless be guilty of conspiracy ...

There is, however, ample authority for rejecting a proposition that would have these results. Of these the first and nowadays most cited is *Bowmakers Ltd* v *Barnet Instruments Ltd* ...

It follows that ... the title to the cars passed as soon as the agreement between the finance company and the dealers was executed and that the passing of this property was not affected by the illegality of that contract nor that of the hire-purchase agreement. It is not in point that the cars were not at any stage physically in the possession of the finance company ... Any other view would produce highly artificial distinctions.'

### Bigos v Bousted [1951] 1 All ER 92 High Court (Pritchard J)

Illegality - breach of exchange control regulations

*Facts*

For the sake of his daughter's health, a man wished to send her and his wife abroad: the Treasury refused to grant an adequate allowance. In breach of the Exchange Control Act 1947, he made an agreement with a woman in Italy whereby she would make available in Italy £150 for his wife and daughter's use: as security, he deposited with her a share certificate. The woman failed to advance the money and the man claimed the return of his share certificate.

*Held*

The court could not help him.

Pritchard J:

'This case raises questions of law which are important and not easy. I have come to the conclusion that the agreement relating to the deposit of the share certificate was one which sprang from and was the creature of the main illegal agreement and was tainted with the same illegality which attached to that agreement. Therefore, the question which I have to decide is: What does the law say to a person who seeks to recover property with which he has parted pursuant to an agreement which is tainted with illegality? The general rule was stated in 1892 by Lindley LJ in *Scott* v *Brown, Doering, McNab & Co* in these words [1892] 2 QB 728):

"No court ought to enforce an illegal contract or allow itself to be made the instrument of enforcing obligations alleged to arise out of a contract or transaction which is illegal, if the illegality is duly brought to the notice of the court, and if the person invoking the aid of the court is himself implicated in the illegality."

In such a case the person resisting the claim possesses the advantage over the person making it, the maxim being *in pari delicto potior est conditio defendentis.*'

### Bowmakers Ltd v Barnet Instruments Ltd [1945] KB 65 Court of Appeal (Scott and du Parcq LJJ and Uthwatt J)

Illegal sale - damages for conversion

*Facts*

The defendants hired machine tools from the plaintiffs as the means of buying them from one Smith and it was alleged that the sale of the goods by Smith to the plaintiffs had been illegal as it had contravened the Control of Machine Tools Order 1940. After making only some of the payments due under the hire-purchase agreements, the defendants sold the goods: the plaintiffs sought their return or damages for conversion.

*Held*

They were entitled to succeed.

du Parcq LJ:

'The question then is whether in the circumstances the plaintiffs are without a remedy. So far as their claim in conversion is concerned, they are not relying on the hiring agreements at all. On the contrary they are willing to admit for this purpose that they cannot rely on them. They simply say that the machines were their property, and this, we think, cannot be denied. We understood counsel for the appellants to concede that the property had passed from Smith to the plaintiffs, and still remained in the plaintiffs at the date of the conversion. At any rate we have no doubt that this is the legal result of the transaction ... *Prima facie*, a man is entitled to his own property, and it is not a general principle of our law (as was suggested) that when one man's goods have got into another's possession in consequence of some unlawful dealings between them, the true owner can never be allowed to recover those goods by an action. The necessity of such a principle to the interests and advancement of public policy is certainly not obvious. The suggestion that it exists is not, in our opinion, supported by authority. It would indeed be astonishing if (to take one instance) a person in the position of the defendant in *Pearce* v *Brookes*, supposing that she had converted the plaintiff's brougham to her own use, were to be permitted, in the supposed interests of public policy. To keep it or the proceeds of its sale for her own benefit ...

In our opinion a man's right to possess his own chattels will as a general rule be enforced against one who, without any claim of right, is detaining them, or has converted them to his own use, even though it may appear either from the pleadings, or in the course of the trial, that the chattels in question came into the defendant's possession by reason of an illegal contract between himself and the plaintiff, provided that the plaintiff does not seek, and is not forced, either to found his claim on the illegal contract, or to plead its illegality in order to support his claim ...

It must not be supposed that the general rule which we have stated is subject to no exception. Indeed, there is one obvious exception, namely, that class of cases in which the goods claimed are of such a kind that it is unlawful to deal in them at all, as for example, obscene books. No doubt there are others, but it is unnecessary, and would we think be unwise, to seek to name them all or to forecast the decisions which would be given in a variety of circumstances which may hereafter arise. We are satisfied that no rule of law and no considerations of public policy compel the court to dismiss the plaintiffs' claim in the case before us, and to do so would be, in our opinion, a manifest injustice.'

*Commentary*

Applied in *Belvoir Finance Co Ltd* v *Stapleton* [1970] 3 WLR 530.

## Briggs v Oates [1991] 1 All ER 407 High Court (Scott J)

Restraint of trade - geographical & chronological limits in employer - employee contracts

*Facts*

The defendant was employed by a firm of solicitors. The plaintiff was the senior partner of that firm. On 3 September 1979 the defendant was employed as salaried partner in the firm. The agreement contained a clause preventing the defendant from practising as a solicitor for five years from the date of the termination of the agreement within a radius of five miles from the firm's office. In 1983 the senior partners dissolved the partnership according to the terms of their partnership and the defendant and one senior partner set up in practice only 120 yards from their old offices.

*Held*

Because the partners, in dissolving the partnership, committed a breach of contract the defendant was effectively released from his contractual obligations. But in any case, the clause would not satisfy the reasonableness criteria.

Scott J:

'It is well settled that the reasonableness of a restraint clause is to be tested by reference to the position as at the date of the contract of which it forms part. If the submissions of counsel for the plaintiff are right I would regard the cl 8 restraint as unreasonable as between the parties. A contract under which an employee could be immediately and wrongfully dismissed, but would nevertheless remain subject to an anti-competitive restraint, seems to me to be grossly unreasonable. I would not be prepared to enforce the restraint in such a contract.'

## Brodie v Brodie [1917] P 271 High Court (Horridge J)

Illegality - agreement to live apart

*Facts*

On the day before their marriage a couple agreed in writing that it would be lawful for the husband to live apart from the wife and that she would not try to compel him to live with her. After the wedding, they purported to confirm this agreement by an indorsement on the original document.

*Held*

The agreement was against public policy and void.

Horridge J:

'I find as a fact that the confirmatory agreement formed part of, and was in no way distinct from, the agreement signed before the marriage, and that the two documents formed an agreement entered into before marriage for future separation. Such an agreement is void and against public policy ... If the second agreement is to be treated as a confirmatory agreement, I think it was bad in law as being merely a confirmation of a previous illegal and void agreement.'

## Carney v Herbert [1984] 3 WLR 1303 Privy Council (Lord Fraser of Tullybelton, Lord Scarman, Lord Diplock, Lord Roskill and Lord Brightman)

Contract - severability of illegal terms

*Facts*

The respondents owned shares in a company. They entered into contracts to sell their shareholding to a company controlled by the appellant. The proceeds of sale were to be cash, payment secured by certain guarantees from the purchaser and (the terms which rendered the sale potentially illegal) secured also by mortgages on land owned by the very company which issued the shares, subject matter of the sale. Without doubt, the purported mortgages were illegal, but the question arose whether such illegality was so much a part of the sale agreement and guarantees as to render them also illegal and unenforceable.

*Held*

The mortgages would be severed from the sale agreement and the latter enforced.

Lord Brightman:

'Subject to a caveat that it is undesirable, their Lordships venture to suggest that, as a general rule, where parties enter into a lawful contract of, for example, sale and purchase and there is an ancillary provision which is illegal, but exists for the exclusive benefit of the plaintiff, the court may, and probably will ... permit the plaintiff, if he so wishes, to enforce the contract without the illegal provision.'

## City Index Ltd v Leslie (1991) The Times 21 March Court of Appeal (Lord Donaldson of Lymington MR, McCowan and Leggatt LJJ)

Wagering contract - enforceability

*Facts*

The plaintiff company carried on a business which included wagers on the stock market index movements. The defendant opened a credit account with the plaintiff company, and after a number of unsuccessful bets owed the company nearly £35,000. He stated he was unable to pay.

The plaintiff company sued for the amount outstanding on the basis that, although betting and wagering contracts had for many years been unenforceable under the Gaming Acts 1845 and 1892, the Financial Services Act 1986 meant that such wagers were now enforceable.

*Held*

The plaintiffs were entitled to succeed. Wagering contracts entered into by each or either party by way of business, in which clients lost or won variable sums dependent on changes or expected changes in indices, were enforceable by virtue of s63 of the 1986 Act as transactions within paras 9 and 12 of Part 1 of Schedule 1, and were not protected by the Acts of 1845 and 1892.

**Clarke v Newland** [1991] 1 All ER 397 Court of Appeal (Neill and Balcombe LJJ)

*Facts*

The plaintiff was a general practitioner in London. In 1982 the defendant joined his practice as an assistant and in 1985 became a salaried partner. In the partnership agreement a clause provided that the defendant undertook not to practise in the practice area (which was geographically defined) within three years of the termination of the agreement. In 1988, the plaintiff gave notice to the defendant that he was terminating the agreement as he was, under the terms of the agreement, permitted to do. The defendant decided to set up in practice as a GP about 100 yards from the plaintiff's surgery. At first instance the court held that the covenant 'not to practise' was too wide and refused to grant an injunction to the plaintiff to enforce the covenant.

*Held*

Neill LJ:

'From these cases [*Haynes* v *Doman* [1899] 2 Ch 13, *Home Counties Dairies Ltd* v *Skilton* [1970] 1 All ER 1227 and *Littlewoods Organisation* v *Harris* [1978] 1 All ER 1026 (in which *Mills* v *Dunham* [1891] 1 Ch 576 and *Moenich* v *Fenestre* (1892) 67 LT 602 were cited)] and the other cases in the same field it is possible to collect certain rules: (1) that the question of construction should be approached in the first instance without regard to the question of legality or illegality; (2) that the clause should be construed with reference to the object sought to be obtained; (3) that in a restraint of trade case the object is the protection of one of the partners against rivalry in trade. To these rules can be added a fourth; (4) that the clause should be construed in its context and in the light of the factual matrix at the time when the agreement was made. One bears in mind the speech of Lord Wilberforce in *Prenn* v *Simmonds* [1971] 3 All ER 237 at 239 where he said:

"The time has long passed when agreements, even those under seal, were isolated from the matrix of facts in which they were set and interpreted purely on internal linguistic considerations."'

**Cleveland Petroleum Co Ltd v Dartstone Ltd** [1969] 1 WLR 116 Court of Appeal (Lord Denning MR, Russell and Salmon LJJ)

Restraint of trade - solus agreement

*Facts*

An underlease granted by the plaintiffs provided that the underlessee would sell only their petrol. The underlease was assigned to the defendants and they undertook to observe and perform the convenants in it. The defendants challenged the validity of the ties.

*Held*

They were bound by them.

Lord Denning MR:

'The law on this subject was fully considered by the House of Lords in *Esso Petroleum Co Ltd* v *Harper's Garage (Stourport) Ltd*. I need not go through all the judgments today, but it seems plain to me that in three at least of the speeches of their Lordships a distinction is taken between a man who is *already* in possession of the land before he ties himself to an oil company and a man who is *out* of possession and is let into it by an oil company. If an owner in possession ties himself for more than five years to take all his supplies from one company, that is an unreasonable restraint of trade and is invalid. But if a man, who is out of possession, is let into possession by the oil company on the terms that he is to tie himself to that company, such a tie is good. Lord Reid said:

"Restraint of trade appears to me to imply that a man contracts to give up some freedom which otherwise he would have had. A person buying or leasing land had no previous right to be there at all, let alone to trade there, and, when he takes possession of that land subject to a negative restrictive covenant, he gives up no right or freedom which he previously had."

Lord Morris of Borth-y-Gest said:

"If one who seeks to take a lease of land knows that the only lease which is available to him is a lease with a restriction, then he must either take what is offered (on the appropriate financial terms) or he must seek a lease elsewhere. No feature of public policy requires that, if he freely contracted, he should be excused from honouring his contract."

Lord Pearce said:

"It would be intolerable if, when a man chooses of his own free will to buy, or take a tenancy of, land which is made subject to a tie (doing so on terms more favourable to himself owing to the existence of the tie) he can then repudiate the tie while retaining the benefit."

It seems to me that in this court, on an interlocutory application, we should go by those sayings in the House of Lords. We should hold that when a person takes possession of premises under a lease, not having been in possession previously; and on taking possession, he enters into a restrictive covenant tying him to take all his supplies from the lessor, prima facie, the tie is valid. It is not an unreasonable restraint of trade. Such was the case here, because [the original underlessees] did not, so far as we know, have possession before the underlease ... So the tie in the original underlease was valid. In any case, however, it is to be observed that the defendants took possession themselves with their eyes open. They knew that there was this restrictive covenant on the land and nevertheless entered into this assignment binding themselves to it. Prima facie it is valid.'

### Eastham v Newcastle United Football Club Ltd [1963] 3 WLR 574 High Court (Wilberforce J)

Restraint of trade - retentions and transfer system

*Facts*

The plaintiff George Eastham, a professional football player, claimed that the rules of the Football Association Ltd were not binding on him as being in unreasonable restraint of trade. The effect of the rules was that a professional player employed by a club could be retained after the determination of his contract of employment and so be debarred from playing for another club, although there was no obligation to re-employ him. He could also be placed on a transfer list, and then he could not obtain employment with any other club in the Football league which was not willing to pay a stipulated transfer fee.

*Held*

The combined retention and transfer system was in unreasonable restraint of trade.

**Edler v Auerbach** [1950] 1 KB 359 High Court (Devlin J)

Lease - illegal use of premises

*Facts*

Statutory regulations provided that certain premises could not, without the consent of the local housing authority, be used for other than residential purposes: they were let as offices.

*Held*

The lease was unenforceable by the lessor.

Devlin J:

'The relevant principle of law is expressed by the Court of Appeal in *Alexander v Rayson* as follows [1936] 1 KB 182):

"But it often happens that an agreement which in itself is not unlawful is made with the intention of one or both parties to make use of the subject-matter for an unlawful purpose ... In such a case any party to the agreement who had the unlawful intention is precluded from suing upon it."

Counsel for the [lessor] submits that I ought not in the circumstances of this case to apply this principle at all. Subject to this objection, which I shall consider later, he distinguishes it in three ways. First, he says that there is here no question of the [lessor] himself using the demised premises illegally. The only person who could use them is the [lessee]. This is a distinction of form, but not, I think of substance. If both parties intend to use the subject-matter illegally, it is clear that the agreement is enforceable by neither. If one party intends to use the subject-matter illegally, it is clear that the agreement is not enforceable by him. If one party intends that the other should use the subject-matter illegally, I think that it is a logical and necessary extension of the principle that the agreement should be unenforceable by the first party. The [lessee] in this case is the innocent instrument through which the defendant sought to effect his intention that the law should be broken, and the [lessor's] position is, therefore, no better than if he were using the subject-matter himself. Secondly, it is said that all that is shown against the [lessor] is an intention to break the law and that is not enough to attract the principle: See *Alexander v Rayson*. I do not think that this is a case of more intention. The granting of the lease which permitted only professional use was itself an overt step in carrying out the illegal intention which the [lessor] had already formed. Indeed, when the [lessor], having deceived the [lessee], had granted him the lease, there was nothing left for him to do. The breach of the law would follow naturally the steps he had taken. There was more than an intent to break the law, there was an attempt to break it, and the fact that the attempt was frustrated, because before the premises were actually used the council discovered the position, is immaterial. Thirdly, the [lessor] says that ... the council consented, in effect if not in form, to the [lessee's] professional use of the premises, and, accordingly, the lease can be enforced by the [lessor] after that date. I think that this plea fails. I doubt that the council's resolution legalises the professional use of the premises, but, assuming that it does, what has to be considered in the application of this principle is not whether the premises can legally be used for the purpose contemplated, but whether the [lessor's] conduct has been such as to disentitle him from obtaining the aid of the court to enforce the agreement to his own advantage. The agreement was part of the illegal scheme conceived by the [lessor]. It succeeded to this extent, as is clear from the minute of the meeting of the appropriate committee of the council ... that, if the committee had not considered the [lessee] as being in actual occupation by reason of a *bona fide* error, they would not have given him any relief. To allow the [lessor] to take advantage of a consent obtained in those circumstances would give him a profit from his own wrong, but, in truth, neither success nor failure of the scheme matters. Neither would atone for the fact that it was conceived in wrongdoing. That is what matters and what debars the [lessor] from invoking the aid of the court.'

**Esso Petroleum Co Ltd v Harper's Garage (Stourport) Ltd** [1967] 2 WLR 871 House of Lords (Lord Reid, Lord Morris of Borth-y-Gest, Lord Hodson, Lord Pearce and Lord Wilberforce)

Petrol solus agreement - restraint of trade

*Facts*

Harper (respondents) owned two garages. Under an agreement with Esso the respondents agreed to buy all their requirements of motor fuels from the appellants at current list prices. One agreement was to last for 4 years 5 months and the other for 21 years. The respondents wished to shift to another brand of petrol and the appellants sought an injunction to prevent them from doing so.

*Held*

The test being reasonableness, the shorter agreement was enforceable but the longer was not.

Lord Reid:

'In my view this agreement is within the scope of the doctrine of restraint of trade as it had been developed in English law. Not only have the respondents agreed negatively not to sell other petrol but they have agreed positively to keep this garage open for the sale of the appellants' petrol at all reasonable hours throughout the period of the tie. It was argued that this was merely regulating the respondent's trading and rather promoting than restraining his trade. But regulating a person's existing trade may be a greater restraint than prohibiting him from engaging in a new trade. And a contract to take one's whole supply from one source may be much more hampering than a contract to sell one's whole output to one buyer. I would not attempt to define the dividing line between contracts which are and contracts which are not in restraint of trade, but in my view this contract must be held to be in restraint of trade. So it is necessary to consider whether its provisions can be justified ...

Where two experienced traders are bargaining on equal terms and one has agreed to a restraint for reasons which seem good to him the court is in grave danger of stultifying itself if it says that it knows that trader's interest better than he does himself. But there may well be cases where, although the party to be restrained has deliberately accepted the main terms of the contract, he has been at a disadvantage as regards other terms: for example where a set of conditions has been incorporated which has not been the subject of negotiation - there the court may have greater freedom to hold them unreasonable ...

What were the appellants' legitimate interest must depend largely on what was the state of affairs in their business and with regard to the distribution and sale of petrol generally. And those are questions of fact to be answered by evidence or common knowledge. In the present case restraint of trade was not pleaded originally and the appellants only received notice that it was to be raised a fortnight before the trial. They may have been wise in not seeking a postponement of the trial when the pleadings were amended. But the result has been that the evidence on this matter is scanty. I think however that it is legitimate to supplement it from the considerable body of reported cases regarding solus agreements and from the facts found in the Report of the Monopolies Commission of July 1965.

When petrol rationing came to an end in 1950 the large producers began to make agreements, now known as solus agreements, with garage owners under which the garage owner, in return for certain advantages, agreed to sell only the petrol of the producer with whom he made the agreement. Within a short time three-quarters of the filling stations in this country were tied in that way and by the dates of the agreements in this case over 90 per cent had agreed to ties. It appears that the garage owners were not at a disadvantage in bargaining with the large producing companies as there was intense competition between these companies to obtain these ties. So we can assume that both the garage owners and the companies thought that such ties were to their advantage. And it is not said in this case that all ties are either against the public interest or against the interest of the parties. The respondents' case is that the ties with which we are concerned are for too long periods.

The advantage to the garage owner is that he gets a rebate on the wholesale price of the petrol which he buys and also may get other benefits or financial assistance. The main advantages for the producing company appear to be that distribution is made easier and more economical and that it is assured of a steady outlet for its petrol over a period. As regards distribution, it appears that there were some 35,000 filling stations in this country at the relevant time, of which about a fifth were tied to the appellants. So they only have to distribute to some 7,000 filling stations instead of to a very much larger number if most filling stations sold several brands of petrol. But the main reason why the producing companies want ties for five years and more, instead of ties for one or two years only, seems to be that they can organise their business better if on the average only one fifth or less of their ties come to an end in any one year. The appellants make a point of the fact that they have invested some £200 millions in refineries and other plant and that they could not have done that unless they could foresee a steady and assured level of sales of their petrol. Most of their ties appear to have been made for periods of between five and 20 years. But we have no evidence as to the precise additional advantage which they derive from a five-year tie as compared with a two-year tie or from a 20-year tie as compared with a five-year tie.

The Court of Appeal held that these ties were for unreasonably long periods. They thought that, if for any reason the respondents ceased to sell the appellants' petrol, the appellants could have found other suitable outlets in the neighbourhood within two or three years. I do not think that that is the right test. In the first place there was no evidence about this and I do not think that it would be practicable to apply this test in practice. It might happen that when the respondents ceased to sell their petrol, the appellants would find such an alternative outlet in a very short time. But, looking to the fact that well over 90% of existing filling stations are tied and that there may be great difficulty in opening a new filling station, it might take a very long time to find an alternative. Any estimate of how long it might take to find suitable alternatives for the respondents' filling stations could be little better than guesswork.

I do not think that the appellants' interest can be regarded so narrowly. They are not so much concerned with any particular outlet as with maintaining a stable system of distribution throughout the country so as to enable their business to be run efficiently and economically. In my view there is sufficient material to justify a decision that ties of less than five years were insufficient, in the circumstances of the trade when these agreements were made, to afford adequate protection to the appellants' legitimate interests .... A tie for 21 years stretches far beyond any period for which developments are reasonably foreseeable. Restrictions on the garage owner which might seem tolerable and reasonable in reasonably foreseeable conditions might come to have a very different effect in quite different conditions: the public interest comes in here more strongly.'

Lord Wilberforce:

'... The doctrine of trade (a convenient, if imprecise, expression which I continue to use) is one which has throughout the history of its subject-matter been expressed with considerable generality, if not ambiguity. The best-known general formulations, those of Lord Macnaghten in *Nordenfelt* and of Lord Parker of Waddington in *Adelaide*, adapted and used by Diplock LJ in the Court of Appeal in the *Petrofina* case, speak generally of all restraints of trade without any attempt at a definition. Often we find the words "restraint of trade" in a single passage used indifferently to denote, on the one hand, in a broad popular sense, any contract which limits the free exercise of trade or business, and, on the other hand, as a term of art covering those contracts which are to be regarded as offending a rule of public policy. Often, in reported cases, we find that instead of segregating two questions, (i) whether the contract is in restraint of trade, (ii) whether, if so, it is "reasonable", the courts have fused the two by asking whether the contract is in "undue restraint of trade" or by a compound finding that it is not satisfied that this contract is really in restraint of trade at all but, if it is, it is reasonable. A well-known textbook describes contracts in restraint of trade as those which "unreasonably restrict" the rights of a person to carry on his trade or profession. There is no need to regret these tendencies: indeed, to do so, when consideration of this subject has passed through such notable minds from Lord Macclesfield onwards, would indicate a failure to understand its nature. The common law has often (if sometimes unconsciously) thrived on ambiguity and it would be mistaken, even if it were possible, to try to crystallise the rules of this, or any, aspect of public policy into neat propositions. The doctrine of restraint of trade is one to be applied to factual situations with a broad and flexible rule of reason ...

This does not mean that the question whether a given agreement is in restraint of trade, in either sense of these words, is nothing more than a question of fact to be individually decided in each case. It is not to be supposed, or encouraged, that a bare allegation that a contract limits a trader's freedom of action exposes a party suing on it to the burden of justification. There will always be certain general categories of contracts as to which it can be said, with some degree of certainty, that the "doctrine" does or does not apply to them. Positively, there are likely to be certain sensitive areas as to which the law will require in every case the test of reasonableness to be passed: such an area has long been and still is that of contracts between employer and employee as regards the period after the employment has ceased. Negatively, and it is this that concerns us here, there will be types of contract as to which the law should be prepared to say with some confidence that they do not enter into the field of restraint of trade at all.

How, then, can such contracts be defined or at least identified? No exhaustive test can be stated - probably no precise non-exhaustive test. But the development of the law does seem to show that judges have been able to dispense from the necessity of justification under a public policy test of reasonableness such contracts or provisions of contracts as, under contemporary conditions may be found to have passed into the accepted and normal currency of commercial or contractual or conveyancing relations. That such contracts have done so may be taken to show with at least strong prima force that, moulded under the pressures of negotiation, competition and public opinion, they have assumed a form which satisfies the test of public policy as understood by the courts at the time, or, regarding the matter from the point of view of the trade, that the trade in question has assumed such a form that for its health or expansion it requires a degree of regulation. Absolute exemption for restriction or regulation is never obtained; circumstances, social or economic, might have altered, since they obtained acceptance, in such a way as to called for a fresh examination: there may be some exorbitance or special feature in the individual contract which takes it out of the accepted category: but the court must be persuaded of this before it calls upon the relevant party to justify a contract of this kind.

Some such limitation upon the meaning in legal practice of "restraints of trade" must surely have been present to the minds of Lord Macnaghten and Lord Parker. They cannot have meant to say that any contract which in whatever way restricts a man's liberty to trade was (either historically under the common law, or at the time of which they were speaking) prima facie unenforceable and must be shown to be reasonable. They must have been well aware that areas existed, and always had existed, in which limitations of this liberty were not only defensible, but were not seriously open to the charge of restraining trade. Their language, they would surely have said, must be interpreted in relation to commercial practice and common sense.'

*Commentary*

Distinguished: *Petrofina (Great Britain) Ltd* v *Martin* [1966] 2 WLR 318. Applied in *Alec Lobb (Garages) Ltd* v *Total Oil Great Britain Ltd* [1983] 1 WLR 87 and *Cleveland Petroleum Co Ltd* v *Dartstone Ltd* [1969] 1 WLR 116.

**Fitch v Dewes** [1921] AC 158 House of Lords (Lord Birkenhead LC, Viscount Cave, Lord Sumner, Lord Parmoor and Lord Carson)

Restraint of trade - solicitor's managing clerk

*Facts*

The plaintiff employed the defendant as a managing clerk and the contract provided that the defendant would

'not directly or indirectly become engaged or manage or be concerned in the office, profession or business of a solicitor within a radius of 7 miles of the Town Hall of Tamworth'

after the expiration of his term of service.

*Held*

Although unlimited in point of time, the clause would be enforced.

Lord Birkenhead LC:

'The controversy is the old one between freedom of contract and certain considerations of public policy, which have received much attention at the hands of the courts in the last few years. It is sufficient for me to say at this point that the contract was entered into between two solicitors: that at its date the appellant had reached the age of twenty-seven years; that he had been for some thirteen years employed in a solicitor's office; and it is reasonable to infer from the promotion which he had received and from the evident appreciation which his employer had formed of his services, that he was a young man alert and very competent both to understand and to safeguard his own interests. The agreement then into which he entered, and in respect of which he has accepted for a lengthy period the consideration which was to move from the covenantee towards himself, will naturally stand unless he satisfies your Lordships that it is bad as being in restraint of trade.

What then is said by the appellant under that head? He does not complain of the restriction of space, and indeed it would have been very difficult for him to do so. The clause only restricts him from being directly or indirectly engaged in the office profession or business of a solicitor within a radius of seven miles of the Town Hall of Tamworth. We need not therefore trouble ourselves with any question of the restriction in respect of space but may confine ourselves to the complaint which is made that the agreement cannot stand, because the restriction in respect of time is unlimited and is against the public interest. But it is to be noticed here, as has been said in more than one of the earlier cases, that guidance may be derived in dealing with a restriction relating to time from an examination of the restriction which is made in respect of space. And the converse remark is of course equally true. For instance, if the restriction in respect of space is extremely limited, it is evident that a very considerable restriction in respect of time may be more acceptable than would otherwise have been the case.

The courts have been generous in elucidating these matters by the enunciation of general principles in the course of the last few years, and I am extremely anxious not to carry this process further today; therefore I say plainly and, I hope, simply, that it has for long now been accepted that such an agreement as this, if it is impeached, is to be measured by reference to two considerations: first, is it against the public interest? And, second, does that which has been stipulated for exceed what is required for the protection of the convenantee? It might perhaps be more properly stated, as it has sometimes been with the highest authority stated, does it exceed what is necessary for the protection of both the parties? But the impeachment which is in fact made in this case demands the consideration of the earlier question only, does the restriction which is attacked exceed that which was reasonably necessary for the protection of the convenantee?

My Lords, it is not contended that there is anything which is open to attack in clause 8 except that part of the clause which for all time excludes the appellant from carrying on practice within seven miles of Tamworth. Are we then to say that such a restriction so unlimited goes farther than is permitted in relation to the standard which I have restated? I am of opinion that it does not go too far. One of your Lordships asked Mr Clayton in the course of his argument what period in his judgment would be a reasonable period, and Mr Clayton replied that he thought that ten years might be a reasonable period. My Lords why? Why is it to be said than ten years is a reasonable period? I can quite easily understand that at the end of a period of ten years the appellant in this case, who by this very clause is not prevented from maintaining and even developing his business acquaintance with the clients of the firm so long as he does not practise within a range of seven miles, might have retained all these circumstances of special, and as I think of illegitimate, advantage for the purpose of competing with the business of the respondent, and then might come forward and do that very thing against which in my judgment the covenantee is abundantly entitled to be protected. Therefore I should dismiss a period of ten years and I should even say of twenty or thirty years that it was quite impossible to be dogmatic upon the period proper to each individual case. Some men live very long lives, and it might easily be that in a case in which two men were both tenacious of life the very same danger which applies at this moment in this case would present itself, in a more striking and formidable shape, at the end of twenty years or at the end of an even longer period. I have no doubt that it is for this reason that the courts long since determined that they would lay down no hard and fast rule either in relation to time or in relation to space, but that they would treat the question alike of time and of space as one of the elements by the light of which they would measure the reasonableness of the restriction taken as a whole.

I am therefore, for the reasons I have stated, of opinion that the attack which has been made upon this restriction fails. I find that it is not opposed to the public interest and that it does not exceed what is reasonably required under the circumstances of this case for the protection of this covenantee.'

**Goldsoll v Goldman** [1915] 1 Ch 292 Court of Appeal (Lord Cozens-Hardy MR, Kennedy and Swinfen Eady LJJ)

Covenant in restraint of trade - severability

*Facts*

The plaintiff dealers substantially in imitation jewellery convenated with the defendant, a competitor, that he would not for two years 'either solely or jointly with or as agent or employee for any person or company, directly or indirectly carry on or be engaged, concerned, or interested in or render services (gratuitously or otherwise) to the business of a vendor of or dealer in real or imitation jewellery in the county of London, England, Scotland, Ireland, Wales or any part of the United Kingdom of Great Britain and Ireland and the Isle of Man, or in France, the United States of America, Russia, or Spain, or within twenty-five miles of Potsdamerstrasse, Berlin, or St Stefan's Kirche, Vienna.'

Notwithstanding this covenant, the defendant assisted and rendered services to a co-defendant carrying on a business identical with the plaintiffs' in the same street. There had been a breach of the covenant - could the covenant he had infringed be treated as good, either in whole or in part, and enforced?

*Held*

It could, by limiting the area of restraint to the United Kingdom and the Isle of Man and the extent of the restraint to imitation jewellery.

Lord Cozens-Hardy MR:

'On the question of the space covered by the covenant, Neville J, has held, and I entirely agree with him, that it is unreasonably large, in so far as it is intended to cover not merely the United Kingdom and the Isle of Man, but also the foreign countries mentioned in the covenant. He has also held - and his decision is consistent with a long series of authorities - that the covenant can be severed as regards the space covered by it. It is clear that part of the covenant dealing with the area is reasonable, and the learned judge in the court below has limited the injunction which he has granted to "the county of London, England, Scotland, Ireland and Wales, or any part of the United Kingdom of Great Britain and Ireland and the Isle of Man". That such a covenant is severable in this respect has been decided by authorities nearly two hundred years old.

No objection is taken, or could be taken, with regard to the limit of time. But the further difficulty has been raised that while the business of the plaintiffs was, as I have said, a business in imitation jewellery, the covenant is against carrying on or being engaged, concerned, or interested in "the business of a vendor of or dealer in real or imitation jewellery". It is admitted that the business of a dealer in real jewellery is not the same as that of a dealer in imitation jewellery. There are many shopkeepers who would be insulted if they were asked whether they sold imitation jewellery. That being so, it is difficult to support the whole of this provision, for the covenant must be limited to what is reasonably necessary for the protection of the covenantee's business.

Then comes the question whether the doctrine of severability is applicable to this part of the covenant. In my opinion it is, and the covenant is good in so far as it purports to restrain the covenantor from carrying on business in imitation jewellery.'

**Goodinson v Goodinson** [1954] 2 WLR 1121 Court of Appeal (Somervell, Birkett and Romer LJJ)

Maintenance - covenant by wife not to sue

*Facts*

An agreement between a husband and wife provided (clause 1) that the husband would pay the wife a weekly sum for the support of herself and their child. The agreement also provided (a) clause 5 - that the wife would not commence any matrimonial proceedings against the husband as long as he made the payments punctually; (b) clause 3 - that out of the weekly sums she would maintain herself and the child and indemnify the husband against all her debts and; (c) clause 4 - the wife would have custody and control of the child. The wife sued for arrears of maintenance.

*Held*

She was entitled to succeed.

Romer LJ:

'On the first point which counsel for the husband submitted, namely, that cl 5 was invalid because of the promise by the wife not to prosecute any matrimonial proceedings, it seems to me quite clear ... that those proceedings were intended to be limited to proceedings relating to maintenance. On that construction of cl 5 the wife was promising not to make any application for an increase in maintenance so long as the husband continued to make the agreed payments. This is not a promise which the law will recognise or enforce ... In that sense, but only in that sense, the promise must be regarded as illegal. It cannot, in my judgment, have in itself the effect for which counsel contended, namely, of vitiating and nullifying the whole agreement so that the wife would be precluded from suing on any of its other provisions. The illegality of the promise is not of the criminal or quasi-criminal character ...

During the discussion I suggested as an illustration a case where a husband and wife entered into a separation deed which provided for the maintenance of the wife and the child and all the usual matters with which deeds of that character deal, and contained a clause, isolated from the rest of the agreement, providing that the custody of the child of the marriage should be entrusted to one of the parents and that the other parent should be precluded at any time afterafter from applying to the court in the matter of custody or access. Such a provision would be wholly nugatory and ineffective as seeking to oust the jurisdiction of the court in a matter in which the court has always exercised a very jealous perogative, namely, the welfare and custody of infants, but I think it would be impossible to suggest that, because of the quality of that particular provision, the whole of the deed would be void for illegality. The clause would be unenforceable, but it would not avoid the agreement as a whole.

In this case cl 5 cannot be enforced and must be regarded as being eliminated from the agreement, but the wife can still sue under cl 1 subject only to the question of consideration.

With regard to that, it seems to me that, if cl 3 were absent from the agreement so that the only consideration for the husband's promise to pay maintenance was the wife's promise not to go to the court, then cls 1 and 2 (maintenance payable only so long as wife leads a chaste life) would not be enforceable against the husband because the consideration moving from him to the wife would be wholly defeated. But cl 3 carries here an indemnity from the wife and other promises by her all of which are presumably, and, indeed, manifestly, of value to the husband; otherwise, they would not have been introduced into the agreement. Nor, in my opinion, can the wife's promise under cl 3 be regarded as being unimportant and as being merely subordinate to the main object of the agreement. On the contrary, I think it represents one of the principal elements of the bargain between husband and wife, that bargain being that the husband must pay certain sums in maintenance and the wife in return would agree that those sums were to be accepted by her as being reasonable at the time and she would indemnify the husband against the specified liabilities. That, I think, was the substantial contract between the parties and one which survives without difficulty the elimination of the extra, but unenforceable, promise which the husband obtained from the wife under the final clause of the agreement. In my opinion, accordingly, in those circumstances it is unnecessary to say anything about the further point on which reliance was placed, namely, that there was forbearance by the wife at the request of the husband not to apply to the court for maintenance and that that element itself would prevent her from suing on cl 1. It is not necessary, I think, to deal with that question and I prefer to express no conclusion on it.'

**Gray v Barr** [1971] 2 WLR 1334 Court of Appeal (Lord Denning MR, Salmon and Phillimore LJJ)

Insurance policy - entitled to be indemnified?

*Facts*

A farmer and the defendant's wife fell in love with one another and, intending to frighten the farmer, the defendant went to the farm with a loaded shotgun. They grappled and fell and the defendant involuntarily fired the gun and killed the farmer. The plaintiff, the farmer's wife, claimed damages under the Fatal Accidents Acts: the defendant admitted liability but argued that he should be indemnified by his insurance company under a policy which covered legal liability for 'damages in respect of ... bodily injury to any person ... caused by accidents'.

*Held*

Even if the death had arisen from an 'accident', the defendant was not entitled to be so indemnified.

Salmon LJ:

'It is well settled that if a man commits murder or committed felo de se in the days when suicide was still a crime, neither he nor his personal representatives could be entitled to reap any financial benefit from such an act ... This was because the law recognised that, in the public interest, such acts should be deterred and moreover that it would shock the public conscience if a man could use the courts to enforce a money claim either under a contract or a will by reason of his having committed such acts.

Crimes of violence, particularly when committed with loaded guns, are amongst the worst curses of this age. It is very much in the public interest that they should be deterred. A man, covered by a hearth and home policy such as the present, walks into a bank with a loaded gun. He intends only to frighten and not to shoot the cashier. He slips and accidentally shoots a customer standing by the counter. It would be strange indeed if he could enforce the policy in respect of his liability to that customer. ... Although public policy is rightly regarded as an unruly steed which should be cautiously ridden, I am confident that public policy undoubtedly requires that no one who threatens unlawful violence with a loaded gun should be allowed to enforce a claim for indemnity against any liability he may incur as a result of having so acted. I do not intend to lay down any wider proposition.'

## Harse v Pearl Life Assurance Co [1904] 1 KB 558 Court of Appeal (Sir Richard Henn Collins MR, Romer and Mathew LJJ)

Void insurance policy - recovery of premiums

*Facts*

The plaintiff was induced to insure his mother's life with the defendants by the representations - innocently but (it was assumed) mistakenly - made by the defendants' agent. Having been informed that the policies were void for want of insurable interest, the plaintiff sought recovery of the premiums.

*Held*

His action could not succeed.

Romer LJ:

'Assuming that these two policies are void on the ground of illegality, it is clear that the plaintiff cannot recover the premiums which he has paid unless he can make out that he was not in pari delicto with the defendant company. Can it be said that he has established that? He relies on the statements alleged to have been made by the defendants' agent when the policy was effected. As to those statements it is clear, in my opinion, that there was no mis-statement of fact on the part of the agent. Further than that, it is clear that there was no fraud of any kind. The present case is not one of oppressor and oppressed, nor is it a case in which advantage has been taken by a clever man of an ignorant man. In fact, there is here no impropriety of any kind beyond the fact that the agent, like the plaintiff, appears to have forgotten or to have mistaken the law. As to the mistake of law, it is clear, as far as I can see, that they both made it. From the findings of the jury it appears that the agent believed the policies to be valid. So also did the plaintiff. In that respect they were equally guilty; their guilt, such as it was, consisting in their forgetting, or being ignorant of, or mistaking the law. There was no greater impropriety on the part of the agent than there was on the part of the plaintiff. But did the statements of the agent, statements which, in my opinion, were only made as to the law, put him or the defendant company in a worse position than the plaintiff? I do not think that a mis-statement as to the law in such a case as the present makes that difference. The case is one in which both parties to the contract ought to know the law; they are contracting on an equal footing, and are presumably persons of equal intelligence. It cannot, in my opinion, be laid down by this court as a principle of law that where a policy is effected with an insurance company, its agents must be treated, without more and without any special evidence, as being under a greater obligation to know the law than the persons whom they approach for the purpose of effecting the policies. Here it is clear to my mind that no fraud of any kind can be imputed. In fact, no case of fraud has been raised against the defendants, nor can it be said that they were in any way bound to appoint as agents persons having some special knowledge of the law. Under those circumstances it appears to me that for the purposes of this case the plaintiff and the defendants' agent must be taken to have been in pari delicto in the matter of effecting the policy, and the defendants cannot stand in a better or worse position than their agent. I say they are not in a worse position because they is no evidence that shows that any other agent of the defendants ever made such mis-statement or was ever guilty of impropriety with reference to a transaction of this sort.'

## Hill (Edwin) & Partners v First National Finance Corp plc [1989] 1 WLR 225 Court of Appeal (Sir Nicolas Browne-Wilkinson VC, Nourse and Stuart-Smith LJJ)

Interference with contractual rights

*Facts*

Through one of his companies, a Mr Pulver proposed to develop Wellington House. He borrowed money from the defendants and engaged the plaintiffs as architects. Partly because of the collapse of the property market, the development could not proceed at that stage. Later, the defendants decided to finance the project themselves, but they insisted that the plaintiffs should be replaced as architects. The plaintiffs sued, alleging that the defendants had unlawfully procured Mr Pulver to breach his contract with them: the judge dismissed their claim: the plaintiffs appealed.

*Held*

The appeal would be dismissed.

Stuart-Smith LJ:

'Justification for interference with the plaintiff's contractual right based on an equal or superior right in the defendant must clearly be a legal right. Such right may derive from property real or personal or from contractual rights. Property rights may simply involve the use and enjoyment of land or personal property. To give an example put in argument by Sir Nicolas Browne-Wilkinson V-C, if X carries on building operations on his land, they may to the knowledge of X interfere with a contract between A and B to carry out recording work on adjoining land occupied by A. But, unless X's activity amounts to a nuisance, he is justified in doing what he did. Alternatively, the law may grant legal remedies to the owner of property to act in defence or protection of his property; if in the exercise of these remedies he interferes with a contract between A and B of which he knows, he will be justified. If instead of exercising those remedies he reaches an accommodation with A, which has a similar effect of interfering with A's contract with B, he is still justified notwithstanding that the accommodation may be to the commercial advantage of himself or A or both. The position is the same if the defendant's right is to a contractual as opposed to a property right, provided it is equal or superior to the plaintiff's rights.

In my judgment that is the position in this case ...'

**Home Counties Dairies Ltd v Skilton** [1970] 1 WLR 526 Court of Appeal (Harman, Salmon and Cross LJJ)

Restraint of trade - milkman

*Facts*

The plaintiffs employed the defendant as a milk roundsman and he covenanted that he would not, during the year following the determination of his contract of service, sell or solicit orders for 'milk or dairy produce' from any person who had been a customer during the last six months of his service. After five years' service, he left and immediately began to work the same round for a competitor. It was argued by the defendant that the clause was too wide in that, on its literal meaning it would prevent him from entering into employment with a grocer who sold butter and cheese.

*Held*

The restraint was valid and would be enforced, inter alia, because the words 'dairy produce' would be construed as limited to the sort of dairy produce with which he had been concerned in his employment.

Harman J:

'... Agreements in restraint of trade, like other agreements, must be construed with reference to the object sought to be attained by them. In cases such as the one before us, the object is protection of one of the parties against rivalry in trade. Such agreement cannot be properly held to apply to cases which although covered by words of the agreement, cannot be reasonably supposed ever to have been contemplated by the parties and which on a rational view of the agreement are excluded from its operation by falling in truth, outside and not within its real scope.'

**Howard v Shirlstar Container Transport Ltd** [1990] 1 WLR 1292 Court of Appeal (Lord Donaldson of Lymington MR, Taylor and Staughton LJJ)

Illegality - public policy - enforcement

*Facts*

The defendant company agreed to pay the plaintiff £25,000 to 'remove' from Nigeria an aircraft belonging to them. He flew the aircraft out of Lagos without obtaining the necessary clearance and in breach of air traffic controls. After pursuit by a Nigerian Air Force plane, he made a forced landing in the Ivory Coast; the plane was impounded and later returned to Nigeria. The defendant company said that because the contract required the plaintiff to 'successfully' remove the aircraft from Nigerian airspace, he had not performed the contract as agreed and they were therefore justified in withholding the agreed fee.

*Held*

On a strictly technical interpretation the aircraft had (for a short time) left Nigeria and therefore the full sum was payable. A court would not allow a person to benefit from an illegal act, whether or not arising under foreign law, if to do so would be an affront to public conscience. Whether an illegal act might be considered against public policy was a question of fact in each case. In this case the plaintiff's illegal act had been to save his own and his crew's lives and, on hearing that this would have been an acceptable defence under Nigerian law, the court permitted the plaintiff to recover the full amount.

Taylor LJ:

'As to illegality, I consider the correct approach is that adopted by Hutchinson J in *Thackwell* v *Barclays Bank plc* [1986] 1 All ER 676, approved by this court in *Saunders* v *Edwards* [1987] 1 WLR 1116. The test is set out in the judgment of Nicholls LJ, at p1132:

"[It] involved the court looking at the quality of the illegality relied on by the defendant and all the surrounding circumstances, without fine distinctions, and seeking to answer two questions: first, whether there had been illegality of which the court should take notice and, second, whether in all the circumstances it would be an affront to the public conscience if by affording him the relief sought the court was seen to be indirectly assisting or encouraging the plaintiff in his criminal act."

Here, there clearly was illegality which the judge characterised as "a very serious breach indeed", flying out of Nigeria without first obtaining permission from the control tower. On the second limb of the test, however, I am satisfied that, in the perilous and life threatening circumstances found by the judge, it would not amount to an affront to the public conscience to afford the plaintiff the relief he sought. Nor is there any reason, in these highly exceptional circumstances, to think that allowing the plaintiff's claim would be contrary to public policy.'

**Hughes v Liverpool Victoria Legal Friendly Society** [1916] 2 KB 482 Court of Appeal (Swinfen Eady, Phillimore and Bankes LJJ)

Insurance policy induced by fraud - right to recover premium

*Facts*

The plaintiff sought the return of premiums on life policies with the defendants and it was found as a fact that the payment of the premiums had been induced by the fraud of the defendants' agents. The defendants resisted her claim, contending, amongst other things, that the policies were illegal for want of insurable interest, as statute required.

*Held*

The plaintiff's claim would be successful.

Bankes LJ:

'It is sufficient for the purpose of my judgment to say that, having regard to the summing-up of the learned judge, the answers of the jury must be read as a finding that the representation made by the defendants' agents was a representation that, if the plaintiff took over the policies and paid the premiums on them, they would be valid and binding policies in her hands, and capable of being enforced by her, and that the agents, at the time that they made these representations, knew them to be untrue, but that the plaintiff did not know them to be untrue, but, on the contrary, believed them to be true ... Given fraud, the authorities seem to me to be all one way - namely, that an innocent plaintiff is entitled to say that he is not in pari delicto with the defendant, whose agent by a false and fraudulent representation induced him to believe that the transaction was an innocent transaction, and one which was enforceable in law. On these grounds, in my opinion, the [plaintiff] is entitled to succeed.'

**Kearley v Thomson** (1890) 24 QBD 742 Court of Appeal (Lord Coleridge CJ, Lord Esher MR and Fry LJ)

Illegal contract - right to recover money paid

*Facts*

The plaintiff friend of a bankrupt paid, illegally, £40 to the defendant solicitors of a petitioning creditor in consideration of the solicitors' undertaking not to appear at the bankrupt's public examination and not to oppose his discharge. The solicitors did not so appear, but before the bankrupt had applied for his discharge the plaintiff sued to recover the £40.

*Held*

His action could not succeed.

Fry LJ:

'The tendency of such an undertaking as that which was given by the defendants is obvious; it tends to pervert the course of justice. The defendants were not bound to appear, but they were bound not to enter into an agreement which would fetter their liberty of action as to appearing or not ... That being so, the general rule is, that the plaintiff in an action to get back money paid in the pursuance of an illegal agreement cannot succeed, in accordance with the maxim, in pari delicto potior est conditio possidentis, and with another to the effect that money paid voluntarily cannot be recovered back.

It follows that the plaintiff, in the present case, who paid the £40 in pursuance of an illegal contract, cannot recover it back ...

It is suggested to us that [an] exception is to be found in the judgment of the Court of Appeal in *Taylor* v *Bowers*, which exception is said to be applicable in the present case. In that case Mellish LJ said:

"If money is paid or goods delivered for an illegal purpose, the person who had so paid the money or delivered the goods may recover them back before the illegal purpose is carried out."

I believe that there is no authority for that proposition earlier than the year 1876 when that case was decided. Notwithstanding the great authority of the learned judge who laid down that proposition of law, there may arise a question whether it can be maintained. That question may have to be considered hereafter. In expressing these doubts as to the correctness of that statement of the law, I have the concurrence of the Lord Chief Justice.

Supposing it to be good law, does it apply to this case? The contract here was not to appear at the bankrupt's public examination and not to oppose his order of discharge. It has been performed as regards the first stipulation, but the application for an order of discharge has not yet been made. Can it be contended that, if the illegal contract has been partly carried out and partly remains unperformed, the money can still be recovered? Test the argument that part performance does not prevent the recovery of the money by this illustration: Suppose a contract by A for the payment of money to B in consideration that B will murder C and D, and payment of the money in pursuance of the contract. After B has murdered C but not D, can A recover back the money? In my judgment he cannot.

I am of opinion, therefore, that where an illegal purpose has been partly carried out, money paid for that purpose cannot be recovered back.'

**Kiriri Cotton Co Ltd v Dewani** [1960] 2 WLR 127 Privy Council (Lord Denning , Lord Jenkins and Mr L M D de Silva)

Illegal premium - right to recover

*Facts*

Illegally, the plaintiff paid the defendant a premium of 10,000 shillings in order to obtain the sub-lease of a flat, but neither party thought that such payment was prohibited by law. In fact, the relevant ordinance provided that the landlord had committed an offence when such a premium was received, although the ordinance made no provision for the recovery of the premium. The plaintiff sued for recovery of the premium.

*Held*

He was entitled to succeed.

Lord Denning:

'It is clear that, in the present case, the illegal transaction was fully executed and carried out. The money was paid. The lease was granted. It was and still is vested in the plaintiff. In order to recover the premium, therefore, the plaintiff must show that he was not in pari delicto with the defendant company. That was, indeed, the way he put his claim in the pleadings ...

In applying these principles to the present case, the most important thing to observe is that the ... ordinance was intended to protect tenants from being exploited by landlords in days of housing shortage. One of the obvious ways in which a landlord can exploit the housing shortage is by demanding from the tenant "key-money" ... the ... ordinance was enacted so as to protect tenants from exploitation of that kind. This is apparent from the fact that the penalty is imposed only on the landlord or his agent and not on the tenant. It is imposed on the "person who asks for, solicits or receives any sum of money", but not on the person who submits to the demand and pays the money. It may be that the tenant who pays money is an accomplice or an aider and abettor ... but he can hardly be said to be in pari delicto with the landlord. The duty of observing the law is firmly placed by the ordinance on the shoulders of the landlord for the protection of the tenant; and if the law is broken, the landlord must take the primary responsibility. Whether it be a rich tenant who pays a premium as a bribe in order to "jump the queue", or a poor tenant who is at his wit's end to find accommodation, neither is so much to blame as the landlord who is using his property rights so as to exploit those in need of a roof over their heads.

Seeing, then, that the parties are not in pari delicto, the tenant is entitled to recover the premium by the common law; and it is not necessary to find a remedy given by the ordinance, either expressly or by implication. The omission of a statutory remedy does not, in cases of this kind, exclude the remedy by money had and received. That is amply shown by the numerous cases to which their Lordships were referred, such as those arising under the statutes against usury, lotteries and gaming, in which there was no remedy given by the statute but, nevertheless, it was held that an action lay for money had and received. It was accepted, too, by Parker J, in his considered judgment in *Green* v *Portsmouth Stadium Ltd*; and his decision was only reversed by the Court of Appeal because they thought the statute there was of a different kind. It was not intended to protect bookmakers from the demands of racecourse owners but was rather for the regulation of racecourses. There was nothing in that case to show that the plaintiff was not in pari delicto with the defendants.'

## Lemenda Trading Co Ltd v African Middle East Petroleum Co Ltd [1988] 2 WLR 735
High Court (Phillips J)

Contract contrary to public policy of friendly foreign state

*Facts*

The defendants, registered in London, contracted with the Qatar national oil company for the supply of crude oil, at the same time signing a 'side letter' confirming that no agents or brokers had been involved on a commission basis, a commission contract being void and unenforceable under Qatar law. Later, the defendants entered into an agreement with the plaintiffs, registered in Nassau, whereby the plaintiffs agreed to assist the defendants in procuring the renewal of the supply contract by exerting influence on the chairman or managing director of the Qatar national oil company in return for a commission on any further supplies. The supply contract was renewed and the plaintiffs sought their commission, conceding that the commission agreement was governed by English law.

*Held*

Their claim would be dismissed as the agreement could not be enforced in England.

Phillips J:

'The principles underlying the public policy in the present case are essentially principles of morality of general application. The practice of exacting payment for the use of personal influence, particularly when the person to be influenced is likely to be unaware of the pecuniary motive involved, is unattractive whatever the context. Yet it is questionable whether the moral principles involved are so weighty as to lead an English court to refuse to enforce an agreement regardless of the country of performance and regardless of the attitude of that country to such a practice. The later English decisions were influenced, at least in part, by the effect of the practice in question on good government in England. It is at this stage that, in my judgment, it becomes relevant to consider the law of Qatar. The significant fact in *Kaufman* v *Gerson* [1904] 1 KB 591 was that the contractual adventure was not contrary to French law and the contract was valid and enforceable in France. In the present case Qatar, the country in which the agreement was to be performed and with which, in my view, the agreement had the closest connection, has the same public policy as that which prevails in England. Because of that policy, the courts of Qatar would not enforce the agreement.

In my judgment, the English courts should not enforce an English law contract which falls to be performed abroad where (i) it relates to an adventure which is contrary to a head of English public policy which is founded on general principles of morality and (ii) the same public policy applies in the country of performance so that the agreement would not be enforceable under the law of that country. In such a situation international comity combines with English domestic public policy to militate against enforcement.

For these reasons the court will not entertain this action and the claim must be dismissed.'

## Lobb (Alec) (Garages) Ltd v Total Oil GB Ltd
See chapter 9 - Duress and undue influence.

## Mahmoud and Ispahani, Re [1921] 2 KB 716 Court of Appeal (Bankes, Scrutton and Atkin LJJ)
Contract - illegality raised by guilty party

*Facts*

Mahmoud agreed to sell Ispahani 150 tons of linseed oil. Statute required that both parties should have a licence: Mahmoud had one, Ispahani did not, but he had told Mahmoud that he had obtained a licence. Mahmoud had not been negligent, it was found, in failing to ask to see Ispahani's licence. Was Ispahani bound by the contract?

*Held*

He was not.

Scrutton LJ:

'As I understand, two reasons are given why the court should enforce this contract. First of all, it is said that the court will not listen to a person who says: "Protect me from my own illegality". In my view, the court is bound, once it knows that the contract is illegal, itself to take the objection and to refuse to enforce the contract, whether its knowledge comes from the statement of the party who was guilty of the illegality, or whether its knowledge comes from outside sources. The court does not sit to enforce illegal contracts. There is no question of estoppel; it is for the protection of the public that the court refuses to enforce such a contract.

The other point is that, where a contract can be performed either lawfully or unlawfully, and the defendant without the knowledge of the plaintiff elects to perform it unlawfully, he cannot plead its illegality. That, in my view, does not apply to a case where the contract sought to be enforced is altogether prohibited, and in this case to contract with a person who had no licence was altogether prohibited. It was not that the seller might lawfully contract with the buyer and chance his getting the licence before the seller delivered the goods. The contract was absolutely prohibited; and, in my view, if an act is prohibited by statute for the public benefit, the court must enforce the prohibition, even though the person breaking the law relies upon his own illegality ... In *Bloxsome* v *Williams* the defendant, a horse dealer, was prohibited from trading on Sunday, but there was nothing illegal in another person making a contract with a horse dealer, except that, if he knew that the person with whom he was dealing was a horse dealer and was guilty of breaking the law, he might be aiding and abetting him to break the law. But merely to make a contract with a horse dealer, without knowing he was a horse dealer, was not illegal. That was pointed out by Bayley J when he said: "It is not competent to the defendant to set up his own breach of the law", and it appears to me to distinguish *Bloxsome* v *Williams* from this case ...

Whether the seller has a remedy against the buyer who, on the finding of the umpire, has fraudulently deceived him, is a matter on which I express no opinion. This court is confined to an award made upon the contract, and on the contract it appears to me that the umpire answered the question, which he put to himself, wrongly, when he enforced a contract which was prohibited by statute for the public benefit.'

*Commentary*

Distinguished in *Archbolds (Freightage) Ltd* v *S Spanglett Ltd* [1961] 2 WLR 170. Distinguished: *Bloxsome* v *Williams* (1824) 3 B & C 232.

**Martell v Consett Iron Co Ltd** [1955] 2 WLR 463 Court of Appeal (Jenkins and Hodson LJJ and Vaisey J)

Maintenance - common interest

*Facts*

The plaintiffs, members of the Anglers' Co-operative Association, believed that the River Derwent was being polluted by effluents from the defendants' works. The association having indemnified them against all liability, the plaintiffs sought, inter alia, an injunction: the defendants applied for a stay of the proceedings on the ground that the action was being illegally maintained.

*Held*

The stay would not be granted.

Jenkins LJ:

'I would hold that an association of a number of persons individually interested as riparian owners or holders of fishing rights in the preservation from pollution of the waters of various rivers in different parts of the country could, without being guilty of the crime or tort of maintenance, support with any funds at their disposal actions brought by individual members to restrain the pollution of the rivers to which the interests of those members related. In this simple hypothetical case, each member of the association would have legal rights in relation to some particular river which he would be entitled to protect by bringing an action against any person wrongfully polluting it, and would have a legitimate and genuine business interest in contributing to the financial support of an action brought by any other member to protect that other member's legal rights, whether in relation to the same or some other river, in the shape of his expectation as a member of the association that, in the event of his own legal rights being infringed, he in his turn would receive from his fellow members similar support in the prosecution of any action he might find it necessary to bring, for the purpose of protecting those rights.'

*Commentary*

Approved in *Trendtex Trading Corporation* v *Crédit Suisse* [1982] AC 679.

**Mason v Provident Clothing and Supply Co Ltd** [1913] AC 724 House of Lords (Viscount Haldane LC, Lord Dunedin, Lord Shaw and Lord Moulton)

Restraint of trade - canvasser

*Facts*

The plaintiffs were a clothing and supply company with branches all over England. The defendant was employed by them as a canvasser. In the contract of employment the defendant agreed to a restraint of trade clause which stated:

'that the [defendant] would not within three years after termination of employment be in the employ of any person, firm or company carrying on or engaged in a business the same as or similiar to that of the [plaintiff company], or assist any person employed or assisting in any such business within 25 miles of London.'

*Held*

The clause was wider than was reasonably required for the plaintiffs' protection and it would not therefore be enforced.

Viscount Haldane LC:

'My Lords, such a restraint on the liberty of a man to earn his living or exercise his calling is a serious one, and the courts have always regarded such restrictions with jealousy. They have steadily refused to allow the question of their validity to be decided by a jury ... the test is now settled. The law is summed up in Lord Macnaghten's judgment in *Nordenfelt* ...'

Lord Moulton:

'... The law as to covenants in restraint of trade was so carefully and authoritatively formulated in this House in the *Nordenfelt* case that I do not think it necessary to discuss the numerous authorities cited in the course of the argument in order to ascertain what is the critical question which the Court ought to put to itself in such a case as this. It is as follows: Are the restrictions which the covenant imposes upon the freedom of action of the servant after he has left the service of the master greater than are reasonably necessary for the protection of the master in his business? ...

The nature of the employment of the appellant in this business was solely to obtain members and collect their instalments. A small district in London was assigned to him, which he canvassed and in which he collected the payments due, and outside that small district he had no duties. His employment was therefore that of a local canvasser and debt collector, and nothing more.

Such being the nature of the employment, it would be reasonable for the employer to protect himself against the danger of his former servant canvassing or collecting for a rival firm in the district in which he had been employed. If he were permitted to do so before the expiry of a reasonably long interval he would be in a position to give to his new employer all the advantages of that personal knowledge of the inhabitants of the locality, and more especially of his former customers, which he had acquired in the service of the respondents and at their expense. Against such a contingency the master might reasonably protect himself, but I can see no further or other protection which he could reasonably demand. If the servant is employed by a rival firm in some district which neither includes that in which he formerly worked for the respondents, nor is immediately adjoining thereto, there is no personal knowledge which he has acquired in his former master's service which can be used to that master's prejudice ...

These, then being the limits of the protection which the master might reasonably insist on, I turn to the covenant in order to see whether it exceeds these limits ... [I]t prohibits the appellant from entering into a similar employment within 25 miles of [London] for a period of three years ... such an area is very far greater than could be reasonably required for the protection of his former employers.

It was suggested in the argument that even if the covenant was, as a whole, too wide, the Court might enforce restrictions which it might consider reasonable (even though they were not expressed in the covenant), provided they were within its ambit. My Lords, I do not doubt that the Court may, and in some cases will, enforce a part of a covenant in restraint of trade, even though taken as a whole the covenant exceeds what is reasonable. But, in my opinion, that ought only to be done in cases where the part so enforceable is clearly severable, and even so only in cases where the excess is of trivial importance, or merely technical, and not a part of the main purport and substance of the clause. It would in my opinion be pessimi exempli if, when an employer had exacted a covenant deliberately framed in unreasonably wide terms, the Courts were to come to his assistance and, by applying their ingenuity and knowledge of the law, carve out of this void covenant the maximum of what he might validly have required. It must be remembered that the real sanction at the back of these covenants is the terror and expense of litigation, in which the servant is usually at a great disadvantage, in view of the longer purse of his master. It is sad to think that in this present case this appellant, whose employment is a comparatively humble one, should have had to go through four courts before he could free himself from such unreasonable restraints as this covenant imposes, and the hardship imposed by the exaction of unreasonable covenants by employers would be greatly increased if they could continue the practice with the expectation that, having exposed the servant to the anxiety and expense of litigation, the Court would in the end enable them to obtain everything which they could have obtained by acting reasonably. It is evident that those who drafted this covenant aimed at making it a penal rather than a protective covenant, and that they hoped by means of it to paralyse the earning capabilities of the man if and when he left their service, and were not thinking of what would be a reasonable protection to their business, and having so acted they must take the consequences.'

**Nordenfelt v Maxim Nordenfelt Guns and Ammunition Co Ltd** [1894] AC 535 House of Lords (Lord Herschell LC, Lord Watson, Lord Ashbourne, Lord Macnaghten and Lord Morris)

Restraint of trade - validity

*Facts*

Nordenfelt was a maker and inventor of guns and ammunition. It was a specialised trade and although customers were few in number the business extended worldwide. Mr Nordenfelt sold the business in 1888 to the respondent company and entered into a covenant (later to be repeated in a contract of service) that he would not for 25 years 'engage ... either directly or indirectly in the trade or business of a manufacturer of guns, gun mountings or carriages, gunpowder explosives or ammunition or in any business competing or liable to compete in any way with that for the time being carried on by the company'. After some years Nordenfelt entered into a business with a rival company dealing with guns and ammunition and the respondents sought an injunction to restrain him from doing so.

*Held*

The injunction would be granted as the covenant was valid.

Lord Macnaghten:

'The true view at the present time I think, is this: the public have an interest in every person's carrying on his trade freely: so has the individual. All interferences with individual liberty of action in trading and all restraints of trade of themselves, if there is nothing more, are contrary to public policy and therefore void. That is the general rule. But there are exceptions: restraints of trade and interferences with individual liberty of action may be justified by the special circumstances of a particular case. It is a sufficient justification, and indeed it is the only justification, if the restriction is reasonable - reasonable, that is, in reference to the interests of the parties concerned and reasonable in reference to the interests of the public, so framed and so guarded as to afford adequate protection to the party in whose favour it is imposed, while at the same time, it is in no way injurious to the public...

Now, in the present case it was hardly disputed that the restraint was reasonable, having regard to the interests of the parties at the time when the transaction was entered into. It enabled Mr Nordenfelt to obtain the full value of what he had to sell; without it the purchasers could not have been protected in the possession of what they wished to buy. Was it reasonable in the interests of the public? It can hardly be injurious to the public, that is, the British public, to prevent a person from carrying on a trade in weapons of war abroad. But apart from that special feature in the present case, how can the public be injured by the transfer of a business from one hand to another? If a business is profitable there will be no lack of persons ready to carry it on. In this particular case the purchasers brought in fresh capital, and had at least the opportunity of retaining Mr Nordenfelt's services. But then it was said there is another way in which the public maybe injured. Mr Nordenfelt has "committed industrial suicide" and as he can no longer earn his living at the trade which he has made peculiarly his own, he may be brought to want and become a burden to the public. My lords, this seems to be very far-fetched. Mr Nordenfelt received over £200,000 for what he sold. He may have got rid of the money. I do not know how that is. But even so, I would answer the argument in the words of Tindal CJ:

"If the contract is a reasonable one at the time it is entered into we are not bound to look out for improbable and extravagant contingencies in order to make it void." '

**Pearce v Brooks** (1866) LR 1 Ex 213 (Pollock CB, Martin, Pigott and Bramwell BB)

Immoral purpose

*Facts*

The defendant, a prostitute, hired a brougham (one-horse closed carriage) from the plaintiffs. When the plaintiffs sued for money due under the agreement, the jury found that the brougham was used by the defendant as part of her display to attract men and that the plaintiffs had known that it was to be used for that purpose. Judgment having been given for the defendant, the plaintiffs appealed.

*Held*

The appeal would be dismissed.

Pollock CB:

'I take the rule to be that any person who contributes to the performance of an illegal act, knowing that the subject-matter is to be so applied, cannot recover the price of such subject-matter, and that the old notion, if any such ever existed, which I do not wish to affirm, that the price must be intended to be paid out of the profits of the illegality, has ceased to be part of the law, if ever it was so. I do not think that for this purpose we should make any distinction between an illegal and an immoral act. The rule now is, ex turpi causa non oritur actio, and whether such turpitude be an immorality or an illegality, the effect is the same; no cause of action can arise out of one or the other ... If, therefore, this article was furnished for the purpose of a display favourable to the defendant's immoral vocation, it seems to me no cause of action can arise.'

**St John Shipping Corporation v Joseph Rank Ltd** [1956] 3 WLR 870 High Court (Devlin J)

Illegality - goods in overloaded ship

*Facts*

Under a contract of carriage the plaintiffs conveyed in their ship a bulk cargo of wheat: the load line was submerged and this was a statutory offence in respect of which the maximum fine was imposed. The defendants paid part of the freight for their share of the cargo but, on learning of the overloading, refused to pay the rest. The plaintiffs sued for the balance.

*Held*

They were entitled to succeed as the right to the freight was not brought into existence by the crime.

Devlin J:

'... On a superficial reading of *Anderson, Ltd* v *Daniel* and the cases that followed and preceded it, judges may appear to be saying that it does not matter that the contract is itself legal, if something illegal is done under it; but that is an unconsidered interpretation of the cases. When fully considered, it is plain that they do not proceed on the basis that in the course of performing a legal contract an illegality was committed; but on the narrower basis that the way in which the contract was performed turned it into the sort of contract that was prohibited by the statute ... In the present case the right to claim freight from the defendants was not brought into existence by a crime; the crime affected only the total amount of freight earned by the ship.'

*Commentary*

Applied in *Archbolds (Freightage) Ltd* v *S Spanglett Ltd* [1961] 2 WLR 170.

**Shelley v Paddock** [1980] 2 WLR 647 Court of Appeal (Lord Denning MR, Brandon and Brightman LJJ)

Illegality - unwitting contravention of statute by plaintiff

*Facts*

The plaintiff agreed to purchase a house in Spain from the defendants, also English nationals. The defendants said they were selling the house for the owners and asked the plaintiff to pay the money to them, which she did - unknown to her, in breach of the Exchange Control Act 1947. The defendants had no authority to sell the house and the plaintiff claimed damages for fraud.

*Held*

She was entitled to succeed.

Lord Denning MR:

'I know that there are some cases where a person has not been able to recover when he has been guilty of evading the exchange control regulations or similar regulations ... In those cases both parties were participating in the illegal act and there was nothing to choose between them. But it seems to me altogether different when the parties are not in pari delicto. I ventured to summarise such cases in *Kiriri Cotton Co Ltd* v *Dewani*. In the instant case the property was never conveyed to Miss Shelley. As I said in the *Kiriri* case, in circumstances like that:

"... it was better to allow the plaintiff to resile from it before it was completed, and to award restitution to him rather than to allow the defendant to remain in possession of his illegal gains."

It is better to allow [the plaintiff] to recover here rather than to allow the [defendants] to remain in possession of their unlawful gains. I went on to say:

"If there is something more in addition to a mistake of law - if there is something in the defendant's conduct which shows that, of the two of them he is the one primarily responsible for the mistake - then it may be recovered back."

It seems to me plain on each of those principles that these parties are not in pari delicto.

The same principle was applied by Swinfen Eady J in *Dott* v *Brickwell*. In that case a purported loan of £50 was obtained by fraud. Swinfen Eady J held that, although the transaction was contrary to the Moneylenders Act 1900 and was illegal, the loan had been obtained by fraud and the moneylender could recover in an action for fraud. The parties were not in pari delicto. The [defendants] were guilty of a swindle. It is only fair and just that they should not be allowed to keep the benefit of their fraud. The judge was quite right in holding that the [defendants] are liable despite their plea of illegality.'

**Strongman (1945) Ltd v Sincock** [1955] 2 QB 525 Court of Appeal (Denning, Birkett and Romer LJJ)

Illegality - failure to obtain licence

*Facts*

The defendant architect employed the plaintiff builders, who had done much other work for him, to convert certain of his buildings into dwellings. He undertook to obtain the licences then necessary, or to stop the work. The licences which he obtained were for much less than the value of the work carried out so the plaintiffs claimed damages for breach of warranty.

*Held*

They were entitled to succeed.

Lord Denning MR:

'When a builder is doing work for a lay owner, if I may so describe him, the primary obligation is on the builder to see that there is a licence. He ought not simply to rely on the word of the lay owner. He ought to inspect the licence himself. If he does not do so, it is his own fault if he finds himself landed in an illegality. But in this case there was not a lay owner. The owner was the architect, and he himself said in evidence: "I agree that where there is an architect, it is the universal practice for the architect and not the builder to get the lience". No fault, it seems to me, can, in these circumstances, be attributed to the builder.

It was contended before us by counsel for the architect that, on the facts of this case, there must have been negligence and that, in point of law, the official referee ought so to have found. I think not. The official referee said:

"I do not consider that the [builders] in the present case have done an immoral act, nor were they negligent in not insisting on the production of supplementary licences. They had done a great deal of other work for the [architect] without any question being raised with regard to the sufficiency of the licences."

As I said at the beginning of this case, it comes very ill from the mouth of the architect to raise this point as against the builders. His attitude was well shown by an observation which he made to the solicitor, Mr Ratcliffe. He said: "If [the plaintiffs] can be bluffed they deserve to lose their money." In other words, he was saying: "If they were fools enough to trust in me, they ought to lose their money." That is a very wrong attitude for a professional man, an architect, to take up. It shows quite clearly that, on his own admission, he has misled them and now seeks to turn it to his own advantage. In my judgment, his objection fails. On the findings of the official referee, the builders were entirely innocent people who were led into this unfortunate illegality by the representation, amounting to a collateral contract, by the architect that he would get the licences. That contract not having been fulfilled, I see no objection in point of law to the plaintiffs recovering the damages ...'

### Commentary

Applied: *Gregory* v *Ford* [1951] 1 All ER 121. Distinguished: *Askey* v *Golden Wine Co Ltd* [1948] 2 All ER 35.

## Sutton v Sutton

See chapter 15 - Remedies for breach of contract - equitable remedies.

## Taylor v Bowers (1876) 1 QBD 291 Court of Appeal (James and Mellish LJJ, Baggallay JA and Grove J)

Illegal contract - right to recover goods

### Facts

In order to defraud his creditors, the plaintiff fictitiously assigned and delivered goods to Alcock, his nephew. The defendant, one of the plaintiff's creditors, was a party to the scheme. Some months after Alcock had removed the goods from the plaintiff's premises, and after failure to effect a compromise with the creditors, Alcock executed a bill of sale of the goods to the defendant for the alleged purpose of securing the debt due from the plaintiff to the defendant. The plaintiff had no knowledge of this transaction and he sued in detinue for the recovery of the goods.

### Held

He was entitled to succeed.

Mellish LJ:

'The only question open on this rule is whether, if the plaintiff has never really intended to part with the possession of his goods, he is estopped from recovering them from the defendant, because he has to set up the illegal transaction to which he was a party. That is the point raised by the rule, and it is a point of law only. It seems to me that the defendant is in precisely the same position with respect to possession of the goods as Alcock, because unless the plaintiff assented to the assignment from Alcock to the defendant for the purpose of paying the plaintiff's debt to the defendant, that assignment becomes immaterial in considering the plaintiff's position with reference to the goods. In my opinion, if the defendant had been a bona fide holder of the goods for valuable consideration, he could have held possession of them as against the plaintiff, because he could then hold out Alcock's title as against the title of the plaintiff. But it seems to me that the plaintiff, in order to recover his goods from the defendant, does not require any aid from the illegal transaction. He is not seeking to further that transaction, but the contrary. If the scheme had been carried out, and a composition of 1s in the pound had been made, the plaintiff could not, in my opinion, recover his goods; but the scheme has not been carried out, and the effect has been to put all the parties in the same position as they were before. If money is paid, or goods are delivered, for an illegal purpose, and that purpose is afterwards abandoned and repudiated, I think that the person paying the money or delivering the goods may recover; but if he waits until the illegal transaction is carried out, or seeks to enforce it, he cannot maintain his action. I think that the Queen's Bench properly held that the plaintiff does not require the aid of the illegal transaction in order to enable him to get back the goods.'

*Commentary*

But see *Kearley* v *Thomson* (1890) 24 QBD 742.

**Watson v Prager** [1991] 1 WLR 726 Chancery Division (Scott J)

Restraint of trade - whether terms of boxer-manager agreement reasonable

*Facts*

The plaintiff, a professional boxer, signed a boxer-manager agreement with the defendant. The agreement was in the standard form as prescribed by the British Boxing Board of Control which regulates and controls professional boxing in this country. The contract was for an initial three years, but the defendant had an option to renew the contract for a further three years. The defendant sought to exercise this option. One year into this second period the plaintiff became dissatisfied and claimed to be no longer bound by the contract since it constituted an unreasonable restraint of trade. There was, in the standard form contract, a clause providing for arbitration under the BBBC's rules, should disputes occur. The defendant claimed that arbitration procedure should be exhausted before having recourse to the courts. The plaintiff, however, alleged that the board would not be impartial at any arbitration hearing.

The court, in hearing the preliminary application, considered inter alia, whether the agreement was unenforceable on the ground of being in restraint of trade.

*Held*

The contract was not a normal commercial contract freely entered into by both parties, but was, by virtue of the BBBC's monopoly, to be subject to more stringent than usual judicial supervision. The contract would only be enforced if it was reasonable. Reasonableness would be tested by the nature of the terms, not how fairly or otherwise the defendant had adhered to conditions laid down by the BBBC. The fact that the manager had negotiated higher than average 'purses' did not alter the fact he was unilaterally able to agree the 'purse' for fights; the plaintiff was unable to negotiate on his own behalf. This was unreasonable, even if the actual sums negotiated were good.

The court decided that the contract contained restrictions on the plaintiff which were restrictive and unreasonable and was therefore unreasonable as a whole.

The defendant could not rely on the arbitration clause; the BBBC was involved in the dispute in the sense that they were defending their policy of dual licensing and therefore would not or might not be 'impartial' as defined under s24(1) of Arbitration Act 1950.

Scott J:

'I have discussed the agreement of 1 April 1987 in terms of restraint of trade. A contract in restraint of trade is prima facie contrary to public policy. It escapes invalidity only if its restrictions are reasonable, or, as Lord Diplock put it, are fair. Lord Diplock said: "For the purpose of this test all the provisions of the contract must be taken into consideration:" *Instone* v *A Schroeder Music Publishing Co Ltd* [1974] 1 WLR 1308, 1316. Taking into consideration all the provisions of the agreement of 1 April 1987, and in particular weighing the restrictions imposed on the boxer under paragraph 4 against the freedom enjoyed by the promoter-manager to fix the terms of the boxer's engagements, I do not think that the terms of this agreement are fair. An agreement containing these restrictions is in the circumstances of conflict of interest that I have described in my opinion contrary to public policy. I do not think that a court of equity should enforce these restrictions.

In summary, the boxer-manager contract of 1 April 1987 was, in my judgment, unreasonable in that it imposed on the plaintiff the paragraph 4(i) restrictions while, at the same time, subjecting him to the contractual obligation of fighting on promotions in which the first defendant was financially interested and on terms unilaterally imposed on him by the first defendant. So long as the plaintiff was prepared to abide by the contract it was capable of having legal effect. As Lord Reid said in the *Esso Petroleum* case [1968] AC 269, 297:

"an agreement in restraint of trade is not generally unlawful if the parties choose to abide by it: it is only unenforceable if a party chooses not to abide by it."

The plaintiff does not now choose to abide by the contract of 1 April 1987. He is entitled, in my judgment, to take that course.'

## Weld-Blundell v Stephens

See chapter 14 - Remedies for breach of contract - damages.

# 12 FRUSTRATION

**Amalgamated Investment and Property Co Ltd v John Walker & Sons Ltd**

See chapter 8 - Mistake.

**Barrow Lane and Ballard Ltd v Phillip Phillips & Co Ltd**

See chapter 8 - Mistake.

**Blackburn Bobbin Co Ltd v T W Allen and Sons Ltd** [1918] 2 KB 467 Court of Appeal
(Pickford, Bankes and Warrington LJJ)

Frustration - outbreak of war

*Facts*

In 1914 the defendants agreed to sell to the plaintiffs a quantity of birch timber, which the defendants obtained through import. Delivery was due to commence in July and cease in November. War broke out in August 1914, before any deliveries had been made and imports of timber stopped. The plaintiff claimed damages for breach of contract. The defendant alleged the dissolution of the contract by the war.

*Held*

The plaintiff was entitled to damages.

Pickford LJ:

'Why should a purchaser of goods, not specific goods, be deemed to concern himself with the way in which the seller is going to fulfil his contract by providing the goods he has agreed to sell? The seller in this case agreed to deliver the timber free on rail at Hull and it was no concern of the buyers as to how the sellers intended to get the timber there. I can see no reason for saying - and to free the defendants from liability this would have to be said - that the continuance of the normal mode of shipping the timber from Finland was a matter which both parties contemplated as necessary for the fulfilment of the contract. To dissolve the contract, the matter relied on must be something which both parties had in their minds when they entered into the contract, such as, for instance, the existence of the music hall in *Taylor* v *Caldwell*, or the continuance in readiness of the vessel to perform the contract, as in *Jackson* v *Union Marine Insurance Co*. Here there is nothing to show that the plaintiffs contemplated and there is no reason why they should be deemed to have contemplated that the sellers should continue to have the ordinary facilities for despatching the timber from Finland. As I have said, that was a matter which, to the plaintiffs, was wholly immaterial. It was not a matter forming the basis of the contract they entered into.'

**Constantine (Joseph) Steamship Line Ltd v Imperial Smelting Corporation Ltd**
[1942] AC 154 House of Lords (Viscount Simon LC, Viscount Maugham, Lord Russell of Killowen, Lord Wright and Lord Porter)

Frustration - burden of proof

*Facts*

A ship was damaged by an explosion and thereby rendered unable to perform obligations under a charter party. The defendants pleaded frustration of the charter party when sued by the charterers for damages ensuing out of the failure to perform the charter party. The plaintiffs argued that the owners must prove that the explosion was not due to their negligence.

*Held*

Frustration was proved and the contract was discharged, despite the fact that the cause of the explosion was never known.

Lord Simon LC:

'Every case in this branch of the law can be stated as turning on the question whether, from the express terms of the particular contract, a further term should be implied which, when its conditions are fulfilled, puts an end to the contract.

If the matter is regarded in this way, the question is as to the construction of a contract, taking into consideration its express and implied terms. The implied term in the present case may well be "this contract is to cease to be binding if the vessel is disabled by an overpowering disaster, provided that disaster is not brought about by the default of either party". This is very similar to an express exception of "perils of the sea" ... If a ship sails and is never heard of again, the shipowner can claim protection for loss of the cargo under the express exception of perils of the sea. To establish that (he must prove) a prima facie case of loss by sea perils and that he is within the exception. If the cargo owner wants to defeat that plea, it is for him, by rejoinder, to allege and prove either negligence or unseaworthiness.'

*Commentary*

See also *Paal Wilson &Co A/S* v *Partenreederei Hannah Blumenthal. The Hannah Blumenthal* [1982] 3 WLR 1149.

## Couturier v Hastie

See chapter 8 - Mistake.

**Davis Contractors Ltd v Fareham Urban District Council** [1956] AC 696 House of Lords (Viscount Simonds, Lord Morton of Henryton, Lord Reid, Lord Radcliffe and Lord Somervell of Harrow)

Building contract - completion delayed

*Facts*

The contractors agreed to build houses for the defendant local authority over a period of eight months for a fixed price. Mainly due to labour shortages, the building took almost two years and cost the contractors more than the agreed price. They commenced proceedings, claiming the contract was frustrated and they were entitled to quantum meruit for the work done.

*Held*

The contract was not frustrated.

Lord Reid:

'Frustration has often been said to depend on adding a term to the contract by implication ... I find great difficulty in accepting this as the correct approach ...

It appears to me that frustration depends, at least in most cases, not on adding any implied term, but on the true construction of the terms which are in the contract, read in light of the nature of the contract and of the relevant surrounding circumstances when the contract was made ... The question is whether the contract which they make is, on its true construction, wide enough to apply to the new situation, if it is not, then it is at an end.

In my view, the proper approach to this case is to take ... all facts which throw light on the nature of the contract, or which can properly be held to be intrinsic evidence relevant to assist in its construction and then, as a matter of law, to construe the contract and to determine whether the ultimate situation ... is or is not within the scope of the contract so construed.

The appellant's case must rest on frustration, the termination of the contract by operation of law on the emergence of a fundamentally different situation. Using the language of Asquith LJ (as he then was), the question is whether the causes of delay or the delays were "fundamental enough to transmute the job the contract had undertaken, and to which it could not apply" (*Parkinson (Sir Lindsay) and Co Ltd* v *Commissioners of Works* [1949] 2 KB 632 at 677). In most cases, the time when the new situation emerges is clear; there has been some particular event which makes all the difference. It may be that frustration can occur as a result of gradual change ... But even so, I think one must see whether there was any time at which the appellants would have said to the respondents that the contract was at an end and that if the work was to proceed, there must be a new contract and I cannot find any time, from first to last, at which they would have been entitled to say that the job had become a job of a different kind which the contract did not contemplate.

In a contract of this kind, the contractor undertakes to do the work for a definite sum and he takes the risk of the cost being greater or less than he expected. If delays occur through no one's fault that may be in the contemplation of the contract, and there may be provision for extra time being given; to that extent, the other party takes the risk of delay. It may be that delay could be of a character so different from anything contemplated that the contract was at an end, but in this case, in my opinion, the most that could be said is that the delay was greater in degree than was to be expected. It was not caused by any new and unforeseeable factor or event. The job proved to be more onerous, but it never became a job of a different kind from that contemplated in the contract.'

*Commentary*

See also *Pioneer Shipping Ltd* v *BTP Tioxide Ltd. The Nema* [1981] 3 WLR 292.

**Ertel Bieber & Co v Rio Tinto Co Ltd** [1918] AC 260 House of Lords (Lord Dunedin, Lord Atkinson, Lord Parker of Waddington and Lord Sumner)

Frustration - trading with the enemy

*Facts*

Two contracts made before the outbreak of war (in 1914) provided for the sale by a British company to a German company of cupreous ore, delivery to take place in 1915, 1916, 1917, 1918 and 1919. The contracts contained a suspensory clause (clause 15) suspending their operation if, owing to war, the parties were unable to fulfil their obligations.

*Held*

The contracts were void and could not be saved by the suspensory clause.

Lord Dunedin:

'I draw the conclusion that upon the ground of public policy the continued existence of contractual relation between subjects and alien enemies or persons voluntarily residing in the enemy country which (i) gives opportunities for the conveyance of information which may hurt the conduct of the war or (ii) may tend to increase the resources of the enemy or cripple the resources of the King's subjects, is obnoxious and prohibited by our law ... Let me now apply this rule to cl 15 on the hypothesis that it does suspend delivery during the war. But for it the contract would immediately end, by it the contract is kept alive, and that not for the purpose of making good rights already accrued, but for the purpose of securing rights in the future by the maintenance of the commercial relation in the present. It hampers the trade of the British subject, and through him the resources of the kingdom. For he cannot in view of the certainly impending liability to deliver (for the war cannot last for ever) have a free hand as he otherwise would. He must either keep a certain large stock undisposed of, and thus unavailable for the needs of the kingdom; or, if he sells the whole of the present stock he cannot sell forward as he would be able to do if he had not the large demand under the contract impending. It increases the resources of the enemy for, if the enemy knows that he is contractually sure of getting the supply as soon as war is over, that not only allows him to denude himself of present stocks, but it represents a present value which may be realised by means of assignation to neutral countries. For these reasons I come to the conclusion that cl 15 is void as against public policy and cannot receive effect. Without cl 15 there is an obvious necessity for intercourse, and the contract is, therefore, avoided as a whole.'

**Fibrosa Spolka Akcyjna v Fairbairn Lawson Combe Barbour Ltd** [1943] AC 32 House of Lords (Viscount Simon LC, Lord Atkin, Lord Russell of Killowen, Lord Macmillan, Lord Wright, Lord Roche and Lord Porter)

Frustration - goods' place of delivery occupied by enemy

*Facts*

The defendants, a company in Leeds, contracted in July 1939 to sell machinery to the plaintiffs, a Polish company. On 23 September 1939 Gdynia, the port of delivery, was occupied by the Germans. In July 1939 the plaintiffs had made an advance payment of £1,000 and they now sought its return.

*Held*

They were entitled to succeed.

Lord Macmillan:

'Your Lordships being of one mind that the so-called rule in *Chandler* v *Webster* is unsound, the way lies clear for the decision of the present case. The plaintiffs made a payment to the defendants on account of the price of certain plant which the defendants were to manufacture and deliver to them. Owing to circumstances arising out of the present hostilities the contract has become impossible of fulfilment according to its terms. Neither party is to blame. In return for their money the plaintiffs have received nothing whatever from the defendants by way of fulfilment of any part of the contract. It is thus a typical case of a total failure of consideration. The money paid must be repaid.'

**Herne Bay Steam Boat Company v Hutton** [1903] 2 KB 683 Court of Appeal (Vaughan Williams, Romer and Stirling LJJ)

Frustration - postponement of Naval Review

*Facts*

The defendant chartered a boat to take paying passengers to see the Royal Navy Review at Spithead. Upon signing the agreement, the defendant paid a deposit, the balance being due before the boat put out. The Navy Review was postponed and the defendant failed to take the boat out. The plaintiff sued for the balance of the hire fee. The defendant alleged that it was a term of the agreement that the Review should have taken place and that consideration for the agreement had wholly failed.

*Held*

The plaintiff could recover.

Vaughan Williams LJ:

'... it could not be said that he could be relieved of his bargain. So, in the present case, it is sufficient to say that the happening of the naval review was not the foundation of the contract.'

*Commentary*

Distinguished: *Taylor* v *Caldwell* (1863) 3 B & S 826.

**Jackson v Union Marine Insurance Co Ltd** (1873) LR 10 CP 125 Court of Exchequer Chamber (Blackburn, Mellor and Lush JJ, Bramwell, Cleasby and Amphlett BB)

Charterparty - consequences of delay

*Facts*

The plaintiff, a shipowner, entered into a charter party in late 1871. The ship was to proceed from Liverpool to Newport and from Newport to San Francisco with a load of iron rails. The plaintiff insured the freight for the voyage. The ship sailed from Liverpool but ran aground. Six weeks later the charterers chartered another ship. The ship was got off three days later, but repairs would take several months. The issue was whether the plaintiff could maintain an action against the charterers for not loading the ship with the cargo once the ship had been repaired.

*Held* (Cleasby B dissenting)

The delay put an end to the charter party and the charterers were under no obligation to load the vessel.

Bramwell B:

'If the charter party were read as a charter for a definite adventure, there was necessarily an implied condition that the vessel should arrive at Newport in time for it ... Not arriving in time put an end to the contract, though as it arose from an expected peril, it gave no cause of action.'

*Commentary*

See also *Metropolitan Water Board* v *Dick, Kerr & Co Ltd* [1918] AC 119.

**Krell v Henry** [1903] 2 KB 740 Court of Appeal (Vaughan Williams, Romer and Stirling LJJ)

Frustration - cancellation of procession

*Facts*

In 1902, the defendant hired from the plaintiff a flat in Pall Mall for two days for the purpose of viewing the coronation processions. The King became ill and the coronation cancelled. The plaintiff sued for the agreed hire charge.

*Held*

The contract was a licence to use the rooms for a particular purpose and, as the foundation of the licence was destroyed, the contract was frustrated.

Vaughan Williams LJ (referring to the principle in *Taylor* v *Caldwell*):

' ... plain that the English Law applies the principle not only to cases where the performance of the contract becomes impossible by the cessation of existence of the thing which is the subject matter of the contract, but also to cases where the event which renders the contract incapable of performance is the cessation or non-existence of an express condition or state of things, going to the root of the contract and essential to its performance. It is said on the one side that the specified thing, state of things, or condition, the continued existence of which is necessary for the fulfilment of the contract, so that the parties entering into the contract must have contemplated the continued existence of that thing, condition or state of things as the foundation of what was to be done under the contract, is limited to things which are either the subject matter of the contract, or a condition or state of things, present or anticipated, which is expressly mentioned in the contract. But on the other hand, it is said that the condition or state of things need not be expressly specified, but that it is sufficient if that condition or state of things clearly appears by extrinsic evidence to have been assumed by the parties to be the foundation or basis of the contract and the event which causes the impossibility is of such a character that it cannot reasonably be supposed to have been in contemplation of the contracting parties when the contract was made ... I do not think that the principle is limited to cases in which the event causing the impossibility of performance is the destruction or non-existence of some thing which is the subject matter of the contract, or of some condition or state of things expressly specified as a condition of it. I think that you first have to ascertain, not necessarily from the terms of the contract, but, if required, from necessary inference drawn from surrounding circumstances recognised by both contracting parties, what is the substance of the contract and then to ask the question whether that substantive contract needs for its foundation the assumption of the existence of a particular state of things.

Each case must be judged by its own circumstances. In each case one must ask oneself, first, what, having regard to all the circumstances, was the foundation of the contract? Secondly: was the performance of the contract prevented? And thirdly: was the event which prevented the performance of the contract of such a character that it cannot reasonably be said to have been in the contemplation of the parties at the date of the contract? If all these questions are answered in the affirmative (as I think they should be in this case) I think both parties are discharged from further performance of the contract.'

**Maritime National Fish Ltd v Ocean Trawlers Ltd** [1935] AC 524 Privy Council (Lord Atkin, Lord Tomlin, Lord Macmillan and Lord Wright)

Frustration - act of party setting up

*Facts*

The defendants operated a fleet of trawlers for fishing. Three were owned and two were chartered. One was chartered from the plaintiffs. A government licence was required to operate the trawlers. The defendants were only able to secure three licences. The defendants allocated two licences to two of their own trawlers and the third to the trawler not chartered from the plaintiffs. The defendants argued that the charter was frustrated.

*Held*

The charter was not frustrated as it was self-induced by the act and election of the defendants.

Lord Wright:

'The essence of frustration is that it should not be due to the act or election of the party. There does not appear to be any authority which has been directly decided on this point. There is, however, a reference to the question in the speech of Lord Sumner in *Bank Line Ltd v Arthur Capel and Co* [1919] AC 435. What he says is:

"One matter I mention only to get rid of it. When the ship-owners were first applied to by the Admiralty for a ship, they named three, of which the Quito was one, and intimated that she was the one they preferred to give up. I think it is now well settled that the principle of frustration of an adventure assumes that the frustration arises without blame or fault on either side. Reliance cannot be placed on a self-induced frustration. Indeed, such conduct might give the other clear party the option to treat the contract as repudiated ..."

However, the point does arise in the facts now before the Board and their Lordships are of the opinion that the loss of the St Cuthbert's licence can correctly be described, quoad the appellants, as a "self-induced frustration".'

**Metropolitan Water Board v Dick, Kerr & Co Ltd** [1918] AC 119 House of Lords (Lord Finlay LC, Lord Dunedin, Lord Atkinson and Lord Parmoor)

Frustration - work forbidden by government

*Facts*

In July 1914 the parties contracted for the construction of a reservoir and water works. Work commenced on 10 August, but war had been declared six days earlier. The contract allowed six years for completion of the work. In 1916 a government order stopped the work and the greater part of the plant was requisitioned. In the light of the order, it would have been illegal for the work to proceed.

*Held*

The contract would be treated as having terminated on the date of the government order.

Lord Dunedin:

'The order pronounced under the Defence of the Realm Act not only debarred the respondents from proceeding with the contract, but also compulsorily dispersed and sold the plant. It is admitted that an interruption may be so long as to destroy the identity of the work or service, when resumed, with the work or service when interrupted. But quite apart from mere delay it seems to me that the action as to the plant prevents this contract ever being the same as it was. Express the effect by a clause. If the Water Board had, when the contract was being settled, proposed a clause which allowed them at any time during the contract to take and sell off the whole plant, to interrupt the work for a period no longer than that for which the work has actually been interrupted, and then bound the contractor to furnish himself with new plant and recommence the work, does anyone suppose that Dick, Kerr & Co or any other contractor would have accepted such a clause? And the reason why they would not have accepted it would have been that the contract, when resumed, would be a contract under different conditions from those which existed when the contract was begun. It may be said that it is possible that plant may be cheaper after the war. But no one knows, and the contractor is not bound to submit to an aleatory bargain, to which he has not agreed. It will also be kept in mind that the contract was a measure and value contract. The difference between the new contract and the old is quite as great as the difference between the two voyages in *Jackson* v *Union Marine Insurance Co Ltd* ...

On the whole matter I think that the action of the government, which is forced on the contractor as a vis major, has by its consequences made the contract, if resumed, a work under different conditions from those of the work when interrupted. I have already pointed out the effect as to the plant, and the contract, being a measure and value contract, the whole range of prices might be different. It would, in my judgment, amount, if resumed, to a new contract; and as the respondents are only bound to carry out the old contract and cannot do so owing to supervient legislation, they are entitled to succeed in their defence to this action.'

*Commentary*

Applied: *Tamplin (F A) Steamship Co Ltd* v *Anglo-Mexican Petroleum Products Co Ltd* [1916] 2 AC 397.

**National Carriers Ltd v Panalpina (Northern) Ltd** [1981] 2 WLR 45 House of Lords (Lord Hailsham of St Marylebone LC, Lord Wilberforce, Lord Simon of Glaisdale, Lord Russell of Killowen and Lord Roskill)

Frustration - closure of access

*Facts*

In 1974 the appellants leased from the respondent for ten years a warehouse. In 1979 the local authority closed the street giving the only access to the warehouse because of the dangerous condition of the listed building opposite. Permission to demolish the building was given in 1980 and it seemed demolition would be completed and the street reopened in 1981. On closure of the street the appellants had stopped paying rent and the respondents sued for arrears.

*Held*

The respondents should succeed. Although in exceedingly rare circumstances the doctrine of frustration could apply to an executed lease, the lease had not been frustrated by the closure.

Lord Wilberforce:

'It is said that to admit the possibility of frustration of leases will lead to increased litigation. Be it so, if that is the route to justice. But, even if the principle is admitted, hopeless claims can always be stopped at an early stage, if the facts manifestly cannot support a case of frustration. The present may be an example. In my opinion, therefore, though such cases may be rare, the doctrine of frustration is capable of application to leases of land. It must be so applied with proper regard to the fact that a lease, ie a grant of a legal estate, is involved. The court must consider whether any term is to be implied which would determine the lease in the event which has happened and/or ascertain the foundation of the agreement and decide whether this still exists in the light of the terms of the lease, the surrounding circumstances and any special rules which apply to leases or to the particular lease in question. If the "frustrating event" occurs, during the currency of the lease it will be appropriate to consider the Law Reform (Frustrated Contracts) Act 1943.

I now come to the second question, which is whether on the facts of the case the appellants should be given leave to defend the action: can they establish that there is a triable issue? I have already summarised the terms of the lease. At first sight, it would appear to my mind that the case might be one for possible frustration. But examination of the facts leads to a negative conclusion ...

So the position is that the parties to the lease contemplated, when Kingston Street was first closed, that the closure would probably last for a year or a little longer. In fact it seems likely to have lasted for just over eighteen months. Assuming that the street is reopened in January 1981, the lease will have three more years to run.

My Lords, no doubt, even with this limited interruption the appellants' business will have been severely dislocated. They will have had to move goods from the warehouse before the closure and to acquire alternative accommodation. After reopening the reverse process must take place. But this does not approach the gravity of a frustrating event. Out of ten years they will have lost under two years of use; there will be nearly three years left after the interruption has ceased. This is a case, similar to others, where the likely continuance of the term after the interruption makes it impossible for the lessee to contend that the lease has been brought to an end. The obligation to pay rent under the lease is unconditional, with a sole exception for the case of fire, as to which the lease provides for a suspension of the obligation. No provision is made for suspension in any other case; the obligation remains. I am of opinion therefore that the lessees have no defence to the action for rent.'

**Paal Wilson & Co A/S v Partenreederei Hannah Blumenthal. The Hannah Blumenthal** [1982] 3 WLR 1149 House of Lords (Lord Diplock, Lord Keith of Kinkel, Lord Roskill, Lord Brandon of Oakbrook and Lord Brightman)

Frustration - inordinate and inexcusable delay

*Facts*

The parties agreed in 1969 to the sale and purchase of a ship: the contract contained an arbitration clause. In 1972 the buyers said that they had some complaints; some months later they commenced arbitration proceedings. Matters proceeded very slowly and in 1980, when the buyers proposed that a date for the hearing be fixed, the sellers issued a writ alleging, inter alia, that the arbitration agreement had been discharged by frustration.

*Held*

This was not the case.

Lord Brandon of Oakbrook:

'... there are two essential factors which must be present in order to frustrate a contract. The first essential factor is that there must be some outside event or extraneous change of situation, not foreseen or provided for by the parties at the time of contracting, which either makes it impossible for the contract to be performed at all, or at least renders its performance something radically different from what the parties contemplated when they entered into it. The second essential factor is that the outside event or extraneous change of situation concerned, and the consequences of either in relation to the performance of the contract, must have occurred without either the fault or the default of either party to the contract.

It was contended for the sellers that the courts have never defined with precision the meaning of the expression "default" in this context. In this connection reliance was placed on the observations of Viscount Simon LC in *Joseph Constantine Steamship Line Ltd* v *Imperial Smelting Corp Ltd, the Kingswood* where he said:

"... I do not think that the ambit of 'default' as an element disabling the plea of frustration to prevail has as yet been precisely and finally determined. 'Self-induced' frustration, as illustrated by the two decided cases already quoted, involves deliberate choice, and those cases amount to saying that a man cannot ask to be excused by reason of frustration if he has purposely so acted as to bring it about. 'Default' is a much wider term, and in many commercial cases dealing with frustration is treated as equivalent to negligence. Yet in cases of frustration of another class, arising in connection with a contract for personal performance, it has not, I think, been laid down that, if the personal incapacity is due to want of care, the plea fails. Some day it may have to be finally determined whether a *prima donna* is excused by complete loss of voice from an executory contract to sing if it is proved that her condition was caused by her carelessness in not changing her wet clothes after being out in the rain. The implied term in such a case may turn out to be that the fact of supervening physical incapacity dissolves the contract without inquiring further into its cause, provided, of course, that it has not been deliberately induced in order to get out of the engagement."

I turn now to consider whether what I have described as being, on the authorities, the two factors essential to the frustration of a contract are present in this case. As to that ... neither such factor is present. In the first place there has been in this case no outside event or external change of situation affecting the performance of the agreement to refer at all, and no one, as far as I can see, has been able to put forward an argument that there has. In the second place the state of affairs relied on as causing frustration is delay by one or both of the parties of such a length as to make a fair, or as I prefer to call it satisfactory, trial of the dispute between the parties no longer possible. That delay, however, on the facts as I have stated them earlier, was clearly itself caused by the failure of both parties to comply with what your Lordships' House in *Bremer Vulkan* decided was their mutual contractual obligation owed to one another, namely (after taking the necessary steps to have a third arbitrator appointed) to apply to the full arbitral tribunal as then constituted for directions to prevent the very delay which is now sought to be relied on by the sellers as having frustrated the agreement to refer.

Whatever may be the precise ambit of the expression "default" in this context, and whether it would or would not apply to the case of the prima donna postulated by Viscount Simon LC in the part of his speech in *Joseph Constantine Steamship Line Ltd* v *Imperial Smelting Corp Ltd*, which I quoted above, it is not, in my view, necessary to determine. It is not necessary because I entertain no doubt whatever that the conduct of the parties in the present case, in failing to comply with what this House has held to be their mutual contractual obligation to one another, comes fairly and squarely within such expression.'

**Pioneer Shipping Ltd v BTP Tioxide Ltd.  The Nema** [1981] 3 WLR 292 House of Lords
(Lord Diplock, Lord Fraser of Tullybelton, Lord Russell of Killowen, Lord Keith of Kinkel and Lord
Roskill)

Charterparty - frustration by strikes

*Facts*

Owners of a vessel chartered her for six or seven consecutive voyages from Sorel in Canada to ports in
Europe between April and December.  A strike broke out at Sorel while the vessel was away on the first
of these voyages and it was still in progress when she arrived back there, thus preventing loading for the
second voyage.  It was agreed, therefore, that the owners could send the ship on a voyage to Glasgow:
the owners sought to extend this voyage, but the charterers refused.  The owners nevertheless arranged
for the vessel to go to Brazil and Portugal, maintaining that the charterparty had been frustrated, a view
which the arbitrator supported.

*Held*

The arbitrator's decision would not be disturbed.

Lord Roskill:

'In *National Carriers Ltd* v *Panalpina (Northern) Ltd* your Lordships' House recently reviewed the
doctrine of frustration and, by a majority, held that it was susceptible of application to leases.  It is
clear, reading the speeches of your Lordships, that the House approved the now classic statement of
the doctrine by Lord Radcliffe in *Davis Contractors Ltd* v *Fareham Urban District Council* ...
whatever may have been said in other cases at earlier stages of the evolution of the doctrine of
frustration:

"... frustration occurs whenever the law recognises that, without default of either party, a contractual
obligation has become incapable of being performed because the circumstances in which performance
is called for would render it a thing radically different from that which was undertaken by the contract.
Non haec in foedera veni.  It was not this that I promised to do."

It should therefore be unnecessary in future cases, where issues of frustration of contracts arise, to
search back among the many earlier decisions in this branch of the law when the doctrine was in its
comparative infancy.  The question in these cases is not whether one case resembles another, but
whether, applying Lord Radcliffe's enunciation of the doctrine, the facts of the particular case under
consideration do or do not justify the invocation of the doctrine, always remembering that the
doctrine is not lightly to be invoked to relieve contracting parties of the normal consequences of
imprudent commercial bargains ...  Your Lordships' House in *Tsakiroglou & Co Ltd* v *Noblee Thorl
GmbH* ... decided that, while in the ultimate analysis whether a contract was frustrated was a question
of law, yet as Lord Radcliffe said in relation to that case "that conclusion is almost completely
determined by what is ascertained as to mercantile usage and the understanding of mercantile men" ...
Another arbitrator might have reached a different conclusion, for clearly there were many points
which had to be taken into consideration both ways.  But I am quite unable to say that the conclusion
which [the arbitrator here] reached was one which he was not, on the facts which he found, fully
entitled to reach.

It was not suggested that a strike could never bring about frustration of an adventure.  But it was
pointed out that most attempts to invoke strikes as a cause of frustration have in the past failed.  *The
Penelope* is almost the only example of success, and in that case the underlying reasoning of the
judgment is far from easy to follow, even though the decision may well be correct.

My Lords, I see no reason in principle why a strike should not be capable of causing frustration of an
adventure by delay.  It cannot be right to divide causes of delay into classes and then say that one
class can and another class cannot bring about frustration of an adventure.  It is not the nature of the

cause of delay which matters so much as the effect of that cause on the performance of the obligations which the parties have assumed one towards the other.'

*Commentary*

See also *Shepherd (F C) & Co Ltd* v *Jerrom* [1986] 3 WLR 801.

**Shepherd (F C) & Co Ltd v Jerrom** [1986] 3 WLR 801 Court of Appeal (Lawton, Mustill and Balcombe LJJ)

Frustration - employee's imprisonment

*Facts*

In September 1979 the applicant entered into a four year contract of apprenticeship with the employers. In June 1981 the applicant was convicted of conspiracy to commit assault and affray and was sentenced to an indeterminate period of Borstal training. Fortunately for the applicant he was released after 39 weeks. However, in September 1981 while the applicant was in Borstal his employers indicated that they considered his contract to be terminated. The applicant complained to an Industrial Tribunal claiming unfair dismissal, and the Tribunal accepted his argument. On appeal the Employment Appeal Tribunal affirmed this decision. However the employers now argued that the applicant had not been dismissed but:

1) the contract of apprenticeship had been frustrated by the custodial Borstal sentence, or

2) the sentence constituted a repudiation of the apprenticeship contract and the applicant had been constructively dismissed.

*Held*

The Borstal sentence was a frustrating event.

Lawton LJ:

'... The first question is whether what happened was capable in law of frustrating the contract; the second is whether it did frustrate it: this is a question of fact: *Pioneer Shipping Ltd* v *BTP Tioxide Ltd* [1982] AC 724.

... As to the first of these questions, there was an event, namely, the sentence of Borstal training, which was not foreseen or provided for by the parties at the time of contracting. It was a question of fact whether it rendered performance of the contract radically different from what the parties had contemplated when they entered into it. What has to be decided is whether the outside event and its consequences in relation to the performance of the contract occurred without either the fault or default of either party to it ... There was no fault or default on the part of the employers. They were alleging that because of the unforeseen outside event the contract had been frustrated. If it had been, there had been no dismissal. The oddity of this case is that the apprentice, for his own purposes, is seeking to allege that he was in default so as to keep in being a contract with the employers which the employers would otherwise have been able to say had been terminated by operation of law ... It seems to me that the apprentice is seeking to rely upon his own default, if in law it should be regarded as such, to establish his right to claim for unfair dismissal ...

The apprentice's criminal conduct was deliberate but it did not by itself have any consequences upon the performance of his contract. What affected performance was his sentence of Borstal training which was the act of the Judge and which he would have avoided if he could have done so. It cannot be said, I think, that the concept of "self-induced frustration" can be applied to this case ...

... In *Hare* v *Murphy Bros Ltd* [1974] ICR 603 the court had adjudged that the employee's criminal conduct which had resulted in his being sentenced to 12 months' imprisonment amounted to a breach of his contract of employment of so serious a nature that it constituted a unilateral repudiation of that contract at the date when he was convicted and sentenced ... The court had said that the sentence was not an event frustrating the contract of employment because it had been brought about by employee's own conduct ... I was a member of the court. I agreed that the appeal should be dismissed on what I called the "commensense of the situation" which was not an example of sound legal reasoning. Since it is not clear upon what grounds the court as such decided *Hare*'s case I do not regard it as a binding authority. In my opinion the court can reconsider the problem of the effect of a custodial sentence on a contract of employment. In my judgment such a sentence is capable in law of frustrating the contract ...'

Mustill LJ:

'... By the time this sentence was imposed there remained rather more than half this period still to run. The sentence was indeterminate, his training would inevitably suffer, as would the timetable of the employers, who had planned to train him up to replace one of their full-time plumbers who was due to retire. I conclude that in the special circumstances of this case the likely interruption was sufficient to discharge the employers from any further obligation, from the moment when the sentence of Borstal training was imposed.'

**Taylor v Caldwell** (1863) 3 B & S 826 Court of Queen's Bench (Blackburn J)

Frustration - destruction of hall

*Facts*

C agreed to hire to T a hall for the purpose of holding a concert therein. Before the day of the concert, the hall was destroyed in a fire. T cancelled the concert and C claimed the letting fee.

*Held*

The contract of hire was frustrated and C was not liable to pay the rent.

Blackburn J:

'There seems no doubt that where there is a positive contract to do a thing, not in itself unlawful, the contractor must perform it or pay damages for not doing it, although in consequence of unforeseen accidents, the performance of his contract has become unexpectedly burdensome or even impossible ... But this rule is only applicable where the contract is positive and absolute and not subject to any condition either express or implied: and there are authorities which, as we think, establish the principle that where, from the nature of the contract, it appears that the parties must, from the beginning, have known that it could not be fulfilled unless, when the time for the fulfilment of the contract arrived, some particular specified thing continued to exist, so that when entering into the contract, they must have contemplated such continuing existence as the foundation of what was to be done; there, in the absence of any express or implied warranty that the thing shall exist, the contract is not to be construed as a positive contract but as subject to an implied condition that the parties shall be excused in case before breach, performance becomes impossible from the perishing of the thing without default of the contractor.

There seems little doubt that this implication tends to further the great object of making legal construction such as to fulfil the intention of those who entered into the contract ... The principle seems to us to be that in contracts in which the performance depends on the continued existence of a given person or thing, a condition is implied that the impossibility of performance ensuing from the perishing of the person or thing, shall excuse the performance.

In none of these cases is the promise in words other than positive, nor is there any express stipulation that the destruction of the person or thing shall excuse the performance; but that excuse is by law implied, because from the nature of the contract, it is apparent that the parties contracted on the basis of the continued existence of the particular person or chattel. In the present case, looking at the whole contract, we find that the parties contracted on the basis of the continued existence of Music Hall at the time when the concerts were to be given; that being essential to their performance.'

*Commentary*

Distinguished in *Herne Bay Steam Boat Company* v *Hutton* [1903] 2 KB 683.

## Tsakiroglou & Co Ltd v Noblee and Thorl GmbH

See Introduction.

# 13 DISCHARGE OF THE CONTRACT

**Afovos Shipping Co SA v Pagnan. The Afovos** [1983] 1 WLR 195 House of Lords (Lord Hailsham of St Marylebone LC, Lord Diplock, Lord Keith of Kinkel, Lord Roskill and Lord Brightman)

Repudiation - anticipatory breach

*Facts*

Under the terms of a charterparty, hire was payable semi-monthly in advance. The charterers paid the hire punctually until, due to an error by both parties' banks, one payment was late. The owners claimed that they were entitled to withdraw the vessel, inter alia, under the doctrine of anticipatory breach.

*Held*

They were not so entitled.

Lord Diplock:

'... The first part of the clause [5] imposes on the respondents as charterers a primary obligation to pay the "said hire" (which by cl 4 had been fixed at a monthly rate and pro rata for any part of a month) punctually and regularly in advance by semi-monthly instalments in the manner specified, which would involve the payment of a minimum of 42 and a maximum of 54 instalments, during the period of the charter. Failure to comply with this primary obligation by delay in payment of one instalment is incapable in law of amounting to a "fundamental breach" of contract by the charterers in the sense to which I suggested in *Photo Production Ltd* v *Securicor Transport Ltd* this expression, if used as a term of legal art, ought to be confined. The reason is that such delay in payment of one half-monthly instalment would not have the effect of depriving the owners of substantially the whole benefit which it was the intention of the parties that the owners should obtain from the unexpired period of the time charter extending over a period of between 21 and 27 months.

The second part of cl 5, however, starting with the word "otherwise" goes on to provide expressly what the rights of the owners are to be in the event of any such breach by the charterers of their primary obligation to make punctual payment of an instalment. The owners are to be at liberty to withdraw the vessel from the service of the charterers; in other words they are entitled to treat the breach when it occurs as a breach of condition and so giving them the right to elect to treat it as putting an end to all their own primary obligations under the charterparty then remaining unperformed. But although failure by the charterers in punctual payment of any instalment, however brief the delay involved may be, is made a breach of condition it is not also thereby converted into a fundamental breach; and it is to fundamental breaches alone that the doctrine of anticipatory breach is applicable.

The general rule is that a primary obligation is converted into a secondary obligation (whether a "general secondary obligation" or an "anticipatory secondary obligation" in the nomenclature of the analysis used in my speech in *Photo Productions Ltd* v *Securicor Transport Ltd*) when and only when the breach of the primary obligation actually occurs. Up until then the primary obligations of both parties which have not yet been performed remain intact. The exception is where one party has manifested to the other party his intention no longer to perform the contract and the result of the non-performance would be to deprive the other party of substantially the whole benefit which it was the intention of the parties that that other party should obtain from the primary obligations of both parties remaining to be performed. In such a case, to which the term "repudiation" is applicable, the party not in default need not wait until the actual breach: he may elect to treat the secondary obligations of the other party as arising forthwith.

The doctrine of anticipatory breach is but a species of the genus repudiation and applies only to fundamental breach. If one party to a contract states expressly or by implication to the other party in advance that he will not be able to perform a particular primary obligation on his part under the contract when the time for performance arrives, the question whether the other party may elect to treat the statement as a repudiation depends on whether the threatened non-performance would have the effect of depriving that other party of substantially the whole benefit which it was the intention of the parties that he should obtain from the primary obligations of the parties under the contract then remaining unperformed. If it would not have that effect there is no repudiation, and the other party cannot elect to put an end to such primary obligations remaining to be performed. The non-performance threatened must itself satisfy the criteria of a fundamental breach.

Similarly, where a party to a contract, whether by failure to take timeous action or by any other default, has put it out of his power to perform a particular primary obligation, the right of the other party to elect to treat this as a repudiation of the contract by conduct depends on whether the resulting non-performance would amount to a fundamental breach. Clearly, in the instant case delay in payment of one semi-monthly instalment of hire would not.'

**Ateni Maritime Corporation v Great Marine** (1991) Financial Times 13 February Court of Appeal (Lloyd, Nourse and Bingham LJJ)

Performance - method and standard of performance

*Facts*

The buyers agreed to buy a ship under a contract based on a Norwegian Standard Sale form. The contract provided, inter alia, that if on arrival the ship was in any way so defective as to affect its certification, the defects would be made good at the sellers' expense. The work should be to the satisfaction of a named third party, the classification society. The propeller was found to be severely damaged. A damages award against the sellers was appealed by them, on the grounds that in assessing damages the judge had applied too high a standard.

*Held*

The buyers could not complain if the sellers did no more than was necessary to obtain a clean certificate. They were not able to demand the sellers did work that would restore it to its pre-contractual condition. The buyers were only entitled to such damages as would cover the cost of reasonable repair work.

**Avery v Bowden** (1855) 5 E & B 714 Court of Queen's Bench (Lord Campbell CJ)

Contract - performance becoming illegal

*Facts*

The plaintiff's ship *Lebanon* was chartered by the defendant and he agreed to load her with a cargo at Odessa within 45 days. At Odessa, the defendant told the captain that he had no cargo for him and advised him to go away. During the 45 days the Crimean War broke out, rendering performance of the contract illegal.

*Held*

No cause of action has arisen before the outbreak of war.

Lord Campbell CJ:

'According to our decision in *Hochster* v *De la Tour*, to which we adhere, if the defendant, within the running days and before the declaration of war, had positively informed the captain of the *Lebanon* that no cargo had been provided or would be provided for him at Odessa, and that there was no use in his remaining there any longer, the captain might have treated this as a breach and renunciation of the contract; and thereupon, sailing away from Odessa, he might have loaded a cargo at a friendly port from another person; whereupon the plaintiff would have had a right to maintain an action on the charterparty to recover damages equal to the loss he had sustained from the breach of contract on the part of the defendant. The language used by the defendant's agent before the declaration of war can hardly be considered as amounting to a renunciation of the contract: but, if it had been much stronger, we conceive that it could not be considered as constituting a cause of action after the captain still continued to insist upon having a cargo in fulfilment of the charterparty.'

*Commentary*

This decision was affirmed by the Court of Exchequer Chamber (1856) 6 E & B 953.

**British and Commonwealth Holdings plc v Quadrex Holdings Inc** [1989] 3 WLR 723
Court of Appeal (Sir Nicolas Browne-Wilkinson VC, Woolf and Staughton LJJ)
Time 'of the essence'?

*Facts*

The plaintiff and defendant companies, both wishing to acquire control of a third company, entered into a written agreement whereby the defendant would withdraw its bid, leaving the way clear for the plaintiff to acquire the company and the plaintiff would then sell the company's wholesale broking division to the defendant. The defendant had trouble finding the purchase money for the broking division and on 25 January 1985 the plaintiff served on it a notice fixing 28 February as the final date to complete the contract. The defendant failed to complete and the plaintiff started proceedings claiming damages for the defendant's repudiation of the contract. The defendant denied time was of the essence and further claimed that the plaintiff company was itself in breach and the cause of the delay. At first instance the plaintiff successfully obtained summary judgment with damages to be assessed and an interim order for £75m. The defendant appealed.

*Held*

1) Although the contract specified completion to take place as soon as reasonably practicable after certain preliminaries had been fulfilled, no date had been fixed or was capable of being fixed at the time of the contract and therefore time was not, originally, 'of the essence'. However the commercial nature of the contract was such that if a date had been specified, it would have been 'of the essence'. If an innocent party, the plaintiff would have been entitled to serve notice making time 'of the essence'; but

2) the plaintiff's status was not that of an innocent party and therefore their ability to issue such a notice was in doubt.

The appeal was therefore allowed, leave given to defend the summary judgment order and the interim order reduced to £5m.

Sir Nicolas Browne-Wilkinson VC:

'The phrase "time is of the essence of the contract" is capable of causing confusion since the question in each case is whether time is of the essence of the particular contractual term which has been breached ...

In equity, time is not normally of the essence of a contractual term. The rules of equity now prevail over the old common law rule: see the Law of Property Act 1925 s41. However, in three types of cases time is of the essence in equity: first, where the contract expressly so stipulates; second, where the circumstances of the case or the subject matter of the contract indicate that the time for completion is of the essence; third, where a valid notice to complete has been given. In the present case there was no express stipulation that time was of the essence. The subject matter of the sale (shares in unquoted private companies trading in a very volatile sector) is such that if a date for completion had been specified, in my judgment time would undoubtedly have been of the essence of completion ... For the reasons I have given, time could not be of the essence of completion on a date which was neither specified nor capable of exact determination by the parties. The only question is whether time was made of the essence by the service of a valid notice to complete.

In the ordinary case, three requirements have to be satisfied if time for completion is to be made of the essence by the service of a notice, viz (1) the giver of the notice (the innocent party) has to be ready, willing and able to complete, (2) the other party (the guilty party) has to have been guilty of unreasonable delay before a notice to complete can be served and (3) the notice when served must limit a reasonable period within which completion is to take place.'

## City and Westminster Properties (1934) Ltd v Mudd

See chapter 3 - Certainty and form of contract.

## Cutter v Powell (1795) 6 Term Rep 320 Court of King's Bench (Lord Kenyon CJ, Ashhurst, Grose and Lawrence JJ)

Incomplete performance

*Facts*

The defendant, master of the Governor Parry, contracted to pay a seaman 30 guineas 'provided he proceeds, continues, and does his duty as second mate in the said ship from hence [Kingston, Jamaica] to the port of Liverpool'. The seaman died in the course of the voyage and his administratrix sued for work and labour done.

*Held*

Her action could not succeed.

Ashhurst J:

'This is a written contract, and it speaks for itself. As it is entire and, as the defendant's promise depends on a condition precedent to be performed by the other party, the condition must be performed before the other party is entitled to receive anything under it. It has been argued, however, that the plaintiff may now recover on a quantum meruit, but she has no right to desert the agreement for whatever there is an express contract the parties must be guided by it, and one party cannot relinquish or abide by it as it may suit his advantage. Here the intestate was by the terms of his contract to perform a given duty before he could call on the defendant to pay him anything; it was a condition precedent, without performing which the defendant is not liable. That seems to me to conclude the question. The intestate did not perform the contract on his part; he was not indeed to blame for not doing it; but still as this was a condition precedent, and as he did not perform it, his representative is not entitled to recover.'

## Dakin (H) & Co Ltd v Lee [1916] 1 KB 566 Court of Appeal (Lord Cozens-Hardy MR, Warrington and Pickford LJJ)

Performance - defective work

*Facts*

The plaintiff builders contracted to execute certain repairs to the defendant's premises. They carried out a substantial part of the work, but failed to perform it exactly in three unimportant respects.

*Held*

The plaintiffs were entitled to recover the contract price less a reduction for the defective work.

Lord Cozens-Hardy MR:

'Take a contract for a lump sum to decorate a house; the contract provides that there shall be three coats of oil paint, but in one of the rooms only two coats of paint are put on. Can anyone seriously say that under these circumstances the building owner could go and occupy the house and take the benefit of all the decorations which had been done in the other rooms without paying a penny for all the work done by the builder, just because only two coats of paint had been put on in one room where there ought to have been three?'

**Decro-Wall International SA v Practitioners in Marketing Ltd** [1971] 1 WLR 361 Court of Appeal (Salmon, Sachs and Buckley LJJ)

Repudiation - breach of term as to time of payment

*Facts*

The plaintiff French company contracted with the defendants as sole concessionaires for the sale of their goods in the United Kingdom: the defendants undertook to pay within 90 days. However, although the plaintiffs never doubted that payment would be made, the defendants were consistently late payers; this cost the defendants about £20 each time (interest on bank loans), a loss which could have been, but was not, debited to the defendants. The plaintiffs contended that the defendants had repudiated the agreement.

*Held*

This was not the case.

Salmon LJ:

'The first question to be decided on this appeal is whether the defendants, by failing punctually to pay ... repudiated the agreement ... I have come to the conclusion that the learned judge was plainly right in holding that there had been no repudiation by the defendants. Clearly the defendants were in breach of the ... agreement by failing to pay the bills punctually. A breach of contract may be of such a nature as to amount to repudiation and give the innocent party the right (if he desires to exercise it) to be relieved from any further performance of the contract or the breach may entitle the innocent party only to damages. How is the legal consequence of a breach to be ascertained? Primarily from the terms of the contract itself. The contract may state expressly or by necessary implication that the breach of one of its terms will go to the root of the contract and accordingly amount to repudiation. Where it does not do so, the courts must look at the practical results of the breach in order to decide whether or not it does go to the root of the contract: see *Mersey Steel and Iron Co Ltd* v *Naylor, Benzon & Co* ... *Hong Kong Fir Shipping Co Ltd* v *Kawasaki Kisen Kaisha Ltd* ... and *The Mihalis Angelos* ... The same test may be and indeed often has been stated in different language, ie is the term which has been breached of the essence of the contract? Section 10(1) of the Sale of Goods Act 1893 provides:

"Unless a different intention appears from the terms of the contract, stipulations as to time of payment are not deemed to be of the essence of a contract of sale ..."

The present contract is of course not a simple contract of sale but, in my view, the same principle is to be applied to it. I am confident that the terms of the present contract relating to time of payment of the bills cannot properly be regarded as of the essence of the contract, or, to put it the other way, there is nothing expressed in or to be implied from the contract to suggest that a failure punctually to pay the bills goes to the root of the contract and thereby amounts to a repudiation.

Counsel for the plaintiffs relied on *Withers* v *Reynolds* (1831) 2 B & Ad 882 in support of his skilful argument that the failure to pay the bills on time amounted to a repudiation of the contract. In *Withers* v *Reynolds* there was an instalment contract of sale which called for cash on delivery of each instalment. The time came when the buyer refused to pay cash but insisted on credit for each instalment until the next was delivered. The court held that the seller was not obliged to go on with the contract on the terms which the buyer sought to dictate. This decision is explicable on the basis that the stipulation as to time of payment was intended by the parties to be of the essence of the contract, alternatively that the buyer was seeking to alter the nature of the transaction by turning a cash into a credit transaction. Accordingly, I do not consider that this decision is inimical to the view which I have already expressed.

I now turn to the point to whether the practical consequences of the defendants' late payments in breach of contract were of such a character as to make the breaches go to the root of the contract. The fact that over the years the plaintiffs agreed to 120 and then 180 day bills being substituted for 90 day bills and even then extended payment on a number of occasions does not suggest that they regarded late payment as being of vital importance to them. Nor was it; the plaintiffs obtained a loan from their bank of the full amount of each bill immediately it was accepted by the defendants. So far as the plaintiffs were concerned it is clear from the facts stated earlier in this judgment that the only effect of the late payments was that the plaintiffs may have incurred liability to their bank for a comparatively insignificant sum by way of extra interest which in any event they could have recovered from the defendants. The case would have been quite different if the defendants' breaches had been such as reasonably to shatter the plaintiffs' confidence in the defendants' ability to pay for the goods with which the plaintiffs supplied them. I think that, in such circumstances, the consequences of the breach could properly have been regarded as most serious, indeed fundamental, and going to the root of the contract so that the plaintiffs would have been entitled to refuse to continue doing business with the defendants. As already indicated, however, ... in ... evidence ... the plaintiffs never doubted that, if they went on supplying the defendants with goods, the defendants would meet the bills. They would, however, in all probability, meet them some days late, as they had done throughout the whole course of the dealings between the parties. For these reasons I agree with the learned judge that the defendants' breaches did not amount to a repudiation of the contract; they were not fundamental breaches going to the root of the contract. They certainly gave the plaintiffs no right to treat the contract as at an end.'

## Federal Commerce and Navigation Ltd v Molena Alpha Inc

See chapter 4 - Contents of contracts.

## Fercometal SARL v Mediterranean Shipping Co SA, The Simona [1988] 3 WLR 200
House of Lords (Lord Bridge of Harwich, Lord Templeman, Lord Ackner, Lord Oliver of Aylmerton and Lord Jauncey of Tullichettle)

Wrongful repudiation - effect

*Facts*

In June 1982 a charterparty provided for the carriage of steel coils from Durban to Bilbao: the charterers were entitled to cancel if the vessel was not ready to load on or before 9 July. On 2 July the shipowners requested an extension as they wished to load other cargo first; if they did this, the charterers' cargo could not be loaded until 13 July. The charterers forthwith cancelled the contract: the owners did not accept this repudiation and on 5 July notified the charterers that the vessel would start loading on 8 July. The vessel arrived in Durban on that day and the owners gave notice of readiness although they were not in fact ready to load. The charterers rejected the notice and began loading on another vessel which they had engaged after the owners' request for an extension. The owners claimed for deadfreight.

*Held*

Their claim could not succeed.

Lord Ackner:

'When one party wrongly refuses to perform obligations, this will not automatically bring the contract to an end. The innocent party has an option. He may either accept the wrongful repudiation as determining the contract and sue for damages or he may ignore or reject the attempt to determine the contract and affirm its continued existence ...

When A wrongfully repudiates his contractual obligations in anticipation of the time for their performance, he presents the innocent party, B, with two choices. He may either affirm the contract by treating it as still in force or he may treat it as finally and conclusively discharged. There is no third choice, as a sort of via media, to affirm the contract and yet be absolved from tendering further performance unless and until A gives reasonable notice that he is once again able and willing to perform. Such a choice would negate the contract being kept alive for the benefit of *both* parties and would deny the party who unsuccessfully sought to rescind the right to take advantage of any supervening circumstance which would justify him in declining to complete.

Towards the conclusion of his able address, counsel for the owners sought to raise what was essentially a new point ... He submitted that the charterers' conduct had induced or caused the owners to abstain from having the ship ready prior to the cancellation date. Of course, it is always open to A, who has refused to accept B's repudiation of the contract, and thereby kept the contract alive, to contend that, in relation to a particular right or obligation under the contract, B is estopped from contending that he, B, is entitled to exercise that right or that he, A, has remained bound by that obligation. If B represents to A that he no longer intends to exercise that right or requires that obligation to be fulfilled by A and A acts on that representation, then clearly B cannot be heard thereafter to say that he is entitled to exercise that right or that A is in breach of contract by not fulfilling that obligation. If, in relation to this option to cancel, the owners had been able to establish that the charterers had represented that they no longer required the vessel to arrive on time because they had already fixed [another ship] and, in reliance on that representation, the owners had given notice of readiness only after the cancellation date, then the charterers would have been estopped from contending they were entitled to cancel the charterparty. There is, however, no finding of any such representation, let alone that the owners were induced thereby not to make the vessel ready to load by 9 July. On the contrary, the owners on 5 July on two occasions asserted that the vessel would start loading on 8 July and on 8 July purported to tender notice of readiness. Indeed, on the following day they instructed their London solicitors to confirm that the vessel was then open in Durban for the charterers' cargo. There is a total lack of any material to show that the owners, because of the charterers' repudiatory conduct, viewed the cancellation clause as other than fully operative and therefore capable of being triggered by the vessel not being ready on time. The non-readiness of the vessel by the cancelling date was in no way induced by the charterers' conduct. It was the result of the owners' decision to load other cargo first.

In short, in affirming the continued existence of the contract, the owners could only avoid the operation of the cancellation clause by tendering the vessel ready to load on time (which they failed to do), or by establishing (which they could not) that their failure was the result of the charterers' conduct in representing that they had given up their option, which representation the owners had acted on by not presenting the vessel on time.'

**Frost v Knight** (1872) LR 7 Ex 111 Court of Exchequer Chamber (Sir Alexander Cockburn CJ, Byles, Keating and Lush JJ)

Contract - refusal, before contingency, to perform

*Facts*

The defendant promised the plaintiff that he would marry her on the death of his father. Before father died, he changed his mind and the plaintiff sued for breach of promise.

298

*Held*

She was entitled to do so.

Sir Alexander Cockburn CJ:

'Considering this to be now settled law ... we should have had no difficulty in applying the principle of the decision in *Hochster* v *De la Tour* to the present case, were it not for the difference which undoubtedly exists between that case and the present, namely, that whereas there the performance of the contract was to take place at a fixed time, here no time is fixed, but the performance is made to depend on a contingency, namely, the death of the defendant's father during the life of both the contracting parties. It is true that in every case of a personal obligation to be fulfilled at a future time, there is involved the possible contingency of the death of the party binding himself before the time of performance arises; but here we have a further contingency, depending on the life of a third person, during which neither party can claim performance of the promise. This being so, we thought it right to take time to consider whether an action would lie before the death of the defendant's father had placed the plaintiff in a position to claim the fulfilment of the defendant's promise. After full consideration, we are of opinion that, notwithstanding the distinguishing circumstances to which I have referred, this case falls within the principle of *Hochster* v *De la Tour* and that consequently the present action is well brought.

The considerations on which the decision in *Hochster* v *De la Tour* is founded are that by the announcement of the contracting party of his intention not to fulfil it, the contract is broken; and that it is to the common benefit of both parties that the contract shall be taken to be broken as to all its incidents, including non-performance at the appointed time, and that an action may be at once brought, and the damages consequent on non-performance be assessed at the earliest moment, as thereby many of the injurious effects of such non-performance may possibly be averted or mitigated.'

**Harrods Ltd v Schwarz-Sackin & Co Ltd** [1991] FSR 209 Court of Appeal (Dillon and Bingham LJJ)

Termination/breach of contract - continued effect of clause

*Facts*

The plaintiffs terminated their contract with the defendants, who had operated the fine arts department at Harrods. One of the clauses in the contract was a no-advertising clause - that the defendants would not indicate their connection with Harrods, or use Harrods' name in any way. Once the contract had been ended, the defendants began to advertise their previous association with Harrods, who sought an interlocutory injunction to stop this.

*Held*

Unless a clause is specifically and expressly worded so as to make it clear that its effect is to continue beyond the existence of the contract, no such effect will be implied. All restrictive clauses terminate along with the contract.

**Hochster v De la Tour** (1853) 2 E & B 678 Court of Queen's Bench (Lord Campbell CJ, Coleridge, Erle and Crompton JJ)

Contract - repudiation before date of performance

*Facts*

The plaintiff agreed on 12 April to enter the service of the defendant as a courier and travel with him on the continent of Europe for three months commencing 1 June. On 11 May the defendant wrote to say that he had changed his mind: on 22 May the plaintiff issued a writ.

*Held*

The plaintiff was entitled to take this step at that time.

Lord Campbell CJ:

'The man who wrongfully renounces a contract into which he has deliberately entered cannot justly complain if he is immediately sued for a compensation in damages by the man whom he has injured: and it seems reasonable to allow an option to the injured party, either to sue immediately or to wait till the time when the act was to be done, still holding it as prospectively binding for the exercise of this option, which may be advantageous to the innocent party, and cannot be prejudicial to the wrongdoer.'

*Commentary*

See also *Frost* v *Knight* (1872) LR 7 Ex 111 and *Avery* v *Bowden* (1855) 5 E & B 714.

**Maple Flock Co Ltd v Universal Furniture Products (Wembley) Ltd** [1934] 1 KB 148
Court of Appeal (Lord Hewart CJ, Lord Wright and Slesser LJ)

Sale of goods - defect in one instalment

*Facts*

There was a contract between the parties for the sale of 100 tons of flock, delivery to be made in three loads a week as required. One instalment of one and half tons was defective, but there was no reasonable probability that there would be anything wrong with future deliveries.

*Held*

The buyers were not entitled to treat the contract as having been repudiated by the sellers.

Lord Hewart CJ:

'There may, indeed, be ... cases where the consequences of single breach of contract may be so serious as to involve a frustration of the contract and justify rescission, or, furthermore, the contract might contain an express condition that a breach would justify rescission, in which case effect would be given to such a condition by the court. But none of these circumstances can be predicated of this case. We think the deciding factor here is the extreme improbability of the breach being repeated, and on that ground, and on the isolated and limited character of the breach complained of, there was, in our judgment, no sufficient justification to entitle the respondents to refuse further deliveries as they did.

The appeal must, accordingly, be allowed and judgment entered for the appellants, with costs here and below, for damages for the respondents' breach of contract in refusing further deliveries.'

**Millers Wharf Partnership Ltd v Corinthian Column Ltd** (1990) 61 P & CR 461 Chancery Division (Knox J)

Conditional contracts - performance of conditions after due date - right of rescission

*Facts*

The plaintiffs agreed to grant the lease of a flat to the defendants, on condition that the plaintiffs should obtain planning permission for redevelopment by a certain date. Either party should have a right of rescission if planning permission was not obtained by the relevant time. The plaintiffs eventually obtained planning consent, some months after the due date. The defendants eventually exercised their power of rescission. The plaintiffs argued that since the due date had passed and the condition had not been fulfilled yet the defendants had not rescinded, then they had lost the right to rescind. The obtaining of planning consent, the condition on which the contract depended, had been fulfilled by a later date; the defendants had waived their right to rescind by not acting immediately once it became apparent planning permission would not be obtained in the time specified.

*Held*

The right to rescind still existed, therefore the plaintiffs' action to enforce the contract must fail.

## Photo Production Ltd v Securicor Transport Ltd

See chapter 6 - Exclusion clauses.

## Planché v Colburn

See chapter 16 - Quasi-contract.

## Reardon Smith Line Ltd v Hansen-Tangen

See chapter 4 - Contents of contracts.

## Rickards (Charles) Ltd v Oppenheim

See chapter 2 - Consideration.

## Southway Group Ltd v Wolff (1991) The Independent 30 August Court of Appeal (Parker, Nourse and Bingham LJJ)

Performance of contracts - personal performance

*Facts*

The question as to whether a contract must be performed in person arose in this contract for services. Before the sale of a warehouse and adjoining land was completed with the plaintiffs, B agreed to carry out certain improvements in accordance with outline specifications. The question asked was whether B could then subcontract the work to an independent contractor. B had entered into a resale agreement with the defendants and then on purchase of the land had delegated all obligations.

*Held*

The essence of the contract lay in confidence in the expertise of B. B did not have the right to unilaterally delegate the responsibility for the works agreed elsewhere.

## Sumpter v Hedges [1898] 1 QB 673 Court of Appeal (A L Smith, Chitty and Collins LJJ)

Contract abandoned - payment for work done

*Facts*

The plaintiff builder contracted to erect certain buildings for the defendant for £565. He did part of the work (to the value of about £333) and received payment of part of the price; he then said he had no money and could not go on. The defendant finished the work, using some of the plaintiff's materials left on site. When the plaintiff sued for work done and materials provided, the judge found that the plaintiff had abandoned the contract, allowed his claim for materials used, but gave him nothing for work done. The plaintiff appealed.

*Held*

The appeal would be dismissed.

Collins LJ:

'I think the case is really concluded by the finding of the learned judge to the effect that the plaintiff had abandoned the contract. If the plaintiff had merely broken his contract in some way so as not to give the defendant the right to treat him as having abandoned the contract, and the defendant had then proceeded to finish the work himself, the plaintiff might perhaps have been entitled to sue on a *quantum meruit* on the ground that the defendant had taken the benefit of the work done. But that is not the present case. There are cases in which, though the plaintiff has abandoned the performance of a contract, it is possible for him to raise the inference of a new contract to pay for the work done on a *quantum meruit* from the defendant's having taken the benefit of that work but, in order that that may be done, the circumstances must be such as to give an option to the defendant to take or not to take the benefit of the work done. It is only where the circumstances are such as to give that option that there is any evidence on which to ground the inference of a new contract. Where, as in the case of work done on land, the circumstances are such as to give the defendant no option whether he will take the benefit of the work or not, then one must look to other facts than the mere taking the benefit of the work in order to ground the inference of a new contract. In this case I see no other facts on which such an inference can be founded. The mere fact that a defendant is in possession of what he cannot help keeping, or even has done work upon it, affords no ground for such an inference. He is not bound to keep unfinished a building which in an incomplete state would be a nuisance on his land. I am therefore of opinion that the plaintiff was not entitled to recover for the work which he had done.'

**United Dominions Corporation (Jamaica) Ltd v Shoucair** [1968] 3 WLR 893 Privy Council (Viscount Dilhorne, Lord Guest, Lord Devlin, Lord Pearce and Lord Pearson)

Mortgage - variation of rate of interest

*Facts*

The appellants lent £55,000 to the respondent on a mortgage, the rate of interest being 9 per cent with no provision for raising it. Following an increase in bank rate, the appellants wrote to the respondent to say that they had increased their interest by a corresponding amount and the respondent confirmed his acceptance of the increase. This increase was not made in accordance with the statutory moneylending law. Did the original mortgage, at 9 per cent, remain unforceable?

*Held*

It did, as the agreed variation in interest rate did not reveal an intention to rescind the mortgage transaction.

Lord Devlin:

'If the principle in *Morris v Baron & Co* applies to this case, the mortgage ... remains in force. The contrary has not been and could not be argued. It would be impossible to contend that a temporary variation in the rate of interest reveals any intention to extinguish the debt and the mortgage. So the question in this appeal is whether the Board should apply to the Moneylending Law the reasoning which *Morris v Baron & Co* applied to the Statute of Frauds or whether the Board should apply the reasoning which in *Morris v Baron & Co* the House rejected ...

In their Lordships' view the problem - that is, how to handle the consequences of unenforceability - takes the same form under the Moneylending Law as it does under the Statute of Frauds and similar statutes considered in *Morris v Baron & Co*. Both the Statute of Frauds and the Moneylending Law are procedural statues enacting that a contract shall not be enforced unless certain matters can be proved. The matters are not in the two cases the same in all respects. Both statutes require the production of a note or memorandum containing all the terms of the contract, but the Moneylending

Law requires also that the note must be one that was signed by the borrower before the money was lent and one of which a copy was delivered to the borrower within seven days of the making of the contract. These additional requirements do not in their lordships' view alter the nature of the problem.

The choice before the Board lies between solving the problem by means of what Lord Sumner called formal logic or solving it by giving effect as far as possible to the intention of the parties as was done in *Morris* v *Baron & Co*. The argument for the respondent assumed rightly that their lordships would accept the guidance offered in *Morris* v *Baron & Co*, unless it could be shown that despite the similarity in the operative parts of the statutes there are underlying differences between them that destroy the value of the guidance ...

None of the differences suggested touch that point. The intention of the parties is just as important in moneylending contracts as in any other ... The Board can see no reason for not following *Morris* v *Baron & Co*.'

**White and Carter (Councils) Ltd v McGregor** [1962] 2 WLR 17 House of Lords (Lord Reid, Lord Morton of Henryton, Lord Tucker, Lord Keith of Avonholm and Lord Hodson)

Contract - election not to accept repudiation

*Facts*

The facts and decision appear in the judgments quoted below.

Lord Reid:

'My Lords, the pursuers supply to local authorities litter bins, which are placed in the streets. They are allowed to attach to these receptacles plates carrying advertisements and they make their profit from payments made to them by the advertisers. The defender carried on a garage in Clydebank and in 1954 he made an agreement with the pursuers under which they displayed advertisements of his business on a number of these bins. In June 1957, his sales manager made a further contract with the pursuers for the display of these advertisements for a further period of three years. The sales manager had been given no specific authority to make this contract and when the defender heard of it later on the same day, he at once wrote to the pursuers to cancel the contract. The pursuers refused to accept this cancellation. They prepared the necessary plates for attachment to the bins and exhibited them on the bins from November 2 1957 onwards.

The defender refused to pay any sums under the contract and the pursuers raised the present action ... craving payment of £196. 4s, the full sum due under the contract for the period of three years ... The Sheriff Substitute ... dismissed the action ... The pursuers appealed to the Court of Session and on November 2 1960, the Second Division refuse the appeal. The present appeal is taken against their interlocutor of that day. That interlocutor sets out detailed findings of fact and ... we cannot look beyond those findings ... The pursuers must show that on those findings they are entitled to the remedy which they seek.

The case for the defender (now the respondent) is that as he repudiated the contract before anything had been done under it, the appellants were not entitled to go on and carry out the contract and sue for the contract price: he maintains that in the circumstances, the appellants' only remedy was damages and that as they do not sue for damages, this action was rightly dismissed.

The contract was for the display of advertisements for a period of 156 weeks from the date when the display began. This date was not specified but, admittedly, the display began on November 2 1957, which seems to have been the date when the former contract came to an end. The payment stipulated was 2s per week per plate, together with 5s per annum per plate, both payable annually in advance, the first payment being due seven days after the first display. The reason why the appellants sued for the whole sum due for three years is to be found in clause 8 of the conditions:

"In the event of an instalment or part thereof being due for payment and remaining unpaid for a period of four weeks or in the event of the advertiser being in any way in breach of this contract then the whole amount due for the 156 weeks or such part of the said 156 weeks as the advertiser shall not yet have paid shall immediately become due and payable."

A question was debated whether the clause provides a penalty or liquidated damages, but on the view which I take of the case, it need not be pursued. The clause merely provides for acceleration of payment of the stipulated price if the advertiser fails to pay an instalment timeously. As the respondent maintained that he was not bound by the contract, he did not pay the first instalment within the time allowed. Accordingly, if the appellants were entitled to carry out their part of the contract, notwithstanding the respondent's repudiation, it was hardly disputed that this clause entitled them to sue immediately for the whole price and not merely for the first instalment.

The general rule cannot be in doubt. It was settled in Scotland at least as early as 1848 and it has been authoritatively stated time and time again in both Scotland and England. If one party to a contract repudiates it in the sense of making it clear to the other party that he refused or will refuse to carry out his part of the contract, the other party, the innocent party, has an option. He may accept that repudiation and sue for damages for breach of contract, whether or not the time for performance has come; or he may, if he chooses, disregard or refuse to accept it and then the contract remains in full effect ...

I need not refer to the numerous authorities. They are not disputed by the respondent, but he points out that in all of them, the party who refused to accept the repudiation had no active duties under the contract. The innocent party's option is generally said to be to *wait* until the date of performance and then to claim damages estimated as at that date. There is no case in which it is said that he may, in the face of the repudiation, go on and incur useless expenses in performing the contract and then claim the contract price. The option, it is argued, is merely as to the date at which damages are to be assessed.

Developing this argument, the respondent points out that in most cases the innocent party cannot complete the contract himself without the other party doing, allowing or accepting something and that it is purely fortuitous that the appellants can do so in this case. In most cases, by refusing co-operation, the party in breach can compel the innocent party to restrict his claim to damages. Then it was said that even where the innocent party can complete the contract without such co-operation, it is against the public interest that he should be allowed to do so. An example was developed in argument. A company might engage an expert to go abroad and prepare an elaborate report and then repudiate the contract before anything was done. To allow such an expert to waste thousands of pounds in preparing the report cannot be right if a much smaller sum of damages would give him full compensation for his loss. It would merely enable the expert to extort a settlement giving him far more than reasonable compensation.

The other ground would be that there is some general equitable principle or element of public policy which requires this limitation of the contractual rights of the innocent party. It may well be that if it can be shown that a person has no legitimate interest, financial or otherwise, in performing the contract rather than claiming damages, he ought not to be allowed to saddle the other party with an additional burden with no benefit to himself. If a party has no interest to enforce a stipulation, he cannot in general enforce it: so it might be said that if a party has no interest to insist on a particular remedy, he ought not to be allowed to insist on it. And just as party is not allowed to enforce a penalty, so he ought not to be allowed to penalise the other party by taking one course when another is equally advantageous to him. If I may revert to the example which I gave of a company engaging an expert to prepare an elaborate report and then repudiating before anything was done, it might be that the company could show that the expert had no substantial or legitimate interest in carrying out the work rather than accepting damages: I would think that the de minimis principle would apply in determining whether his interest was substantial and that he might have a legitimate interest other than an immediate financial interest. But if the expert had no such interest, then that might be regarded as a proper case for the exercise of the general equitable jurisdiction of the court. But that is not this case. Here, the respondent did not set out to prove that the appellants had no legitimate interest in completing the contract and claiming the contract price rather than claiming damages; there is nothing in the findings of fact to support such a case and it seems improbable that any such case could have been proved. It is, in my judgment, impossible to say that the appellants should be deprived of their right to claim the contract price merely because the benefit to them, as against claiming damages and re-letting their advertising space, might be small in comparison with the loss to the respondent: that is the most that could be said in favour of the respondent. Parliament has on many occasions relieved parties from certain kinds of improvident or oppressive contracts, but common law can only do that in very limited circumstances. Accordingly, I am unable to avoid the conclusion that this appeal must be allowed and the case remitted so that decree can be pronounced as craved in the initial writ.'

Lord Hodson (Lord Tucker concurring):

'It may be unfortunate that the appellants have saddled themselves with an unwanted contract, causing an apparent waste of time and money. No doubt this aspect impressed the Court of Session, but there is no equity that can assist the respondent. It is trite that equity will not rewrite an improvident contract where there is no disability on either side. There is no duty laid upon a party to a subsisting contract to vary it at the behest of the other party so as to deprive himself of the benefit given to him by the contract. To hold otherwise would be to introduce a novel equitable doctrine that a party was not to be held to his contract unless the court in the given instance thought it reasonable to do so. In this case it would make an action for debt a claim for a discretionary remedy. This would introduce an uncertainty into the field of contract which appears to be unsupported by authority either in English or Scottish law, save for the one case upon which the Court of Session founded its opinion and which must, in my judgment, be taken to have been wrongly decided.

The appellants were given leave to amend their claim by praying in the alternative for the same sum, namely £196 4s as liquidated damages for breach of contract, on the footing that the repudiation must be treated as if accepted. The respondent resisted the alternative claim on the ground that the sum sued for, being a penalty and not liquidated damages, the appellants were not entitled to decree therefor.

The only material obligation which the respondent was bound to fulfil was to pay the sum of money claimed and it is difficult to see how damages should be assessed for breach of this obligation. It is, however, unnecessary, in view of the opinion I have expressed, to consider the question whether the sum claimed is recoverable as a genuine pre-estimate of probable or possible interest in the due performance of the contract, or is irrecoverable as a penalty. I would allow the appeal.'

Lord Tucker expressed his complete agreement with the opinion of Lord Hodson.

Lord Morton of Henryton and Lord Keith of Avonholm delivered dissenting judgments.


## Woodar Investment Development Ltd v Wimpey Construction UK Ltd

See chapter 10 - Privity of contract.

# 14  REMEDIES FOR BREACH OF CONTRACT – DAMAGES

**Addis v Gramophone Co Ltd**

See Introduction

**Alder v Moore** [1961] 2 WLR 426 Court of Appeal (Sellers and Devlin LJJ and Slade J)

Contract of insurance - provision for penalty?

*Facts*

A professional footballer, while playing for West Ham, suffered an injury which was believed to be permanent. Under an insurance policy he was paid £500 and, in accordance with the policy, he gave an undertaking that he would pay a 'penalty' of £500 if he played again. Twelve months after the injury he began to play again - for Cambridge United - and the insurers sued to recover the £500.

*Held* (Devlin LJ dissenting)

They were entitled to succeed.

Sellers LJ:

'The defendant's argument here has the advantage that underwriters have chosen to call the payment that they wish to recover a "penalty". Why they did so I cannot understand, but whilst they run a risk of being taken at their word, the law looks at the substance of the matter and not at the words used, whether "penalty" or "liquidation damages". I would regard it, as the learned judge did, as a repayment of a sum in circumstances which are entirely equitable. It is in no way an imposition of a fine or penal payment and if it has to be made to fall under one head or the other it is to be regarded as a payment by way of damages for breach of an undertaking which is not unfair or unconscionable and therefore not a penalty.

I have not thought it necessary to go through the cases. The law on this subject has from time to time been extensively reviewed. It was the subject of an elaborate exposition by Sir George Jessel MR in *Wallis* v *Smith* and somewhat more recently it was considered in the House of Lords in *Dunlop Pneumatic Tyre Co Ltd* v *New Garage & Motor Co Ltd.*'

**Anglia Television Ltd v Reed**

See Introduction

**Bain v Fothergill** (1874) LR 7 HL 158 House of Lords (Lord Chelmsford and Lord Hatherley)

Sale of land - breach of contract - damages

*Facts*

Lessees of a mining royalty, the defendants, had convenanted not to assign without the lessors' consent. The defendants agreed to sell their interest to the plaintiffs and the plaintiffs paid them a deposit. The lessors refused to give their consent to the sale and the plaintiffs sued for the return of their deposit, their expenses of investigating the defendants' title and damages for loss of bargain.

*Held*

The plaintiffs were only entitled to their deposit and expenses.

Lord Chelmsford:

' ... I think the rule as to the limits within which damages may be recovered upon the breach of a contract for the sale of real estate, must be taken to be without exception. If a person enters into a contract for the sale of a real estate knowing that he has no title to it, nor any means of acquiring it, the purchaser cannot recover damages beyond the expenses he has incurred by an action for the breach of the contract; he can only obtain other damages by an action for deceit.'

*Commentary*

Criticised in *Sharneyford Supplies Ltd* v *Edge* [1987] 2 WLR 363. Distinguished in *Wroth* v *Tyler* [1973] 2 WLR 405.

The rule of law known as the rule in *Bain* v *Fothergill* was abolished by s3 of the Law of Property (Miscellaneous Provisions) Act 1989 in relation to contracts made after that section came into force, ie, 27 September 1989.

**Bliss v South East Thames Regional Health Authority** [1985] IRLR 308 Court of Appeal (Cumming-Bruce and Dillon LJJ and Heilbron J)

Wrongful dismissal - damages for mental distress

*Facts*

In an action for damages for wrongful dismissal the judge included in the award an amount for the plaintiff's frustration and mental distress.

*Held*

He should not have done so.

Dillon LJ:

'The general rule laid down by the House of Lords in *Addis* v *Gramophone Co Ltd* [1909] AC 488 is that where damages fall to be assessed for breach of contract rather than in tort it is not permissible to award general damages for frustration, mental distress, injured feelings or annoyance occasioned by the breach ... Lord Loreburn regarded the rule ... as too inveterate to be altered ...'

**Brace v Calder** [1895] 2 QB 253 Court of Appeal (Lord Esher MR, Lopes and Rigby LJJ)

Wrongful dismissal - measure of damages

*Facts*

The plaintiff was employed by a partnership, consisting of the four defendants, as the manager of their London office. Under his contract with the partners, he was to be employed at a fixed salary for two years subject to clause 5, which gave the partners the right to terminate the agreement on one month's notice, provided they paid him a sum equivalent to the salary he would have received if he had been retained for the full two years. Before the expiry of the two years, two partners retired and the business transferred to the others. Although the continuing partners were willing to retain him in their service on the same terms as before, he declined to serve them. The plaintiff brought an action for wrongful dismissal.

*Held* (Lord Esher MR dissenting)

The dissolution of the partnership operated as a wrongful dismissal of the plaintiff or a breach of his contract, but he was only entitled to nominal damages.

Lopes LJ:

'There is nothing in this agreement which indicates that in any event, except that mentioned in clause 5, the employment was not to be for the period of two years. On the contrary, the provision contained in clause 5 of the agreement appears to me strong, to show that there was an express agreement to employ the plaintiff for two years. It appears to me, therefore, that the plaintiff was discharged by the defendants and was entitled to damages either on the ground that he was wrongfully discharged, or that there was a breach of a contract to employ him for two years. But in estimating the damages, it must be taken into consideration that the continuing partners were willing to keep him on in their service till the end of the two years at the same salary as before; but he declined to serve them and therefore it was his own fault that he suffered any loss. Consequently, the damages resulting from the breach of contract would be nominal ... In the result, I am of the opinion that there was a breach of the agreement; but the plaintiff is only entitled to nominal damages in respect of it because, in point of fact, he did not suffer any loss through it ...'

Rigby LJ:

'A contract to serve four employers cannot, without express language, be construed as a contract to serve two of them. In my judgment, the dissolution of the partnership operated as a dismissal of the plaintiff not authorised by law. The clause as to dismissal on a month's notice not having been acted upon, the plaintiff cannot recover as liquidated damages the unpaid part of his salary for the two years' terms. On the other hand, the defendants are liable to him for the usual damages for a dismissal without due cause. The plaintiff brought his action ... before the two years' term came to an end. In my judgment, the defendants are entitled in mitigation of damages to put forward the offer of an engagement on the same terms made by the continuing partners. I see nothing in the evidence to show that this, in a pecuniary sense, would have been of a less value to him than his engagement to serve the four defendants ... I therefore concur in the view of Lopes LJ that the appeal should be allowed and judgment entered for the plaintiff for nominal damages ...'

**Bradburn v Great Western Railway Co** (1874) LR 10 Ex 1 Exchequer Division (Bramwell, Pigott and Amphlett BB)

Damages - plaintiff insured

*Facts*

The plaintiff passenger suffered injury on the defendants' railway as a result of the negligence of the defendants' engine driver. The plaintiff was insured against such accidents: should the amount paid to the plaintiff by his insurance company be deducted from the amount of damages awarded against the defendants?

*Held*

It should not.

Pigott B:

'I think that the plaintiff is entitled to recover from the railway company the full amount of the damage which they have caused him to suffer by their negligence; and I think that there would be no justice or principle in setting off an amount which the plaintiff has entitled himself to under a contract of insurance, such as any prudent man would make on the principle of, as the expression is, "laying by for a rainy day". He pays the premiums upon a contract which, if he meets with an accident, entitles him to receive a sum of money. It is not because he meets with the accident, but because he made a contract with, and paid premiums to, the insurance company, for that express purpose, that he gets the money from them. It is true that there must be the element of accident in order to entitle him to the money; but it is under and by reason of his contract with the insurance company, that he gets the amount; and I think that it ought not, upon any principle of justice, to be deducted from the amount of the damages proved to have been sustained by him through the negligence of the defendants.'

**Bridge v Campbell Discount Co Ltd** [1962] 2 WLR 439 House of Lords (Viscount Simonds, Lord Morton of Henryton, Lord Radcliffe, Lord Denning and Lord Devlin)

Hire-purchase agreement - penalty clause?

*Facts*

The appellant hirer entered into a hire-purchase agreement with the respondents in respect of a used car. Under the agreement, it could be terminated by the hirer, but he was then obliged forthwith to deliver up the vehicle, pay any arrears with interest 'and by way of agreed compensation for the depreciation of the vehicle such further sum as may be necessary to make the rentals paid and payable hereunder equal to two-thirds of the hire-purchase price'. Having paid the initial payment and the first instalment, the appellant terminated the agreement and returned the car. The respondents sued to recover two-thirds of the price, less the payments made.

*Held*

Their claim would fail as the relevant clause made provision for a penalty.

Lord Morton of Henryton:

' ... the appellant has clearly committed a breach of the hire-purchase agreement by failing to pay the subsequent instalments, and it becomes necessary to consider whether the payment stipulated [in] the agreement was a penalty or liquidated damages.

"The essence of a penalty is a payment of money stipulated as in terrorem of the offending party; the essence of liquidated damages is a genuine covenanted pre-estimate of damage."

See per Lord Dunedin in *Dunlop Pneumatic Tyre Co Ltd* v *New Garage & Motor Co Ltd*. I find it impossible to regard the sum stipulated ... as a genuine pre-estimate of the loss which would be suffered by the respondents in the events specified in the same clause. One reason will suffice, though others might be given. This was a second-hand car when the appellant took it over on hire-purchase. The depreciation in its value would naturally become greater the longer it remained in the appellant's hands. Yet the sum to be paid ... is largest when, as in the present case, the car is returned after it has been in the hirer's possession for a very short time, and gets progressively smaller as time goes on. This could not possibly be the result of a genuine pre-estimate of the loss. Further, in my view, the provisions ... were "stipulated as in terrorem"of the appellant. As counsel for the appellant put it: "They are intended to secure that the hirer will not determine the agreement until at least two-thirds of the price has been paid." The result is that the appellant is entitled to relief ...'

*Commentary*

Applied in *Jobson* v *Johnson* [1989] 1 WLR 1026.

**British Westinghouse Electric and Manufacturing Company Limited v Underground Electric Railways Company of London Limited** [1912] AC 673 House of Lords (Viscount Haldane LC, Lord Ashbourne, Lord Macnaghten and Lord Atkinson)

Breach of contract - duty to minimise loss

*Facts*

By a contract made between the parties in 1902, the appellants agreed to deliver and erect, within a specified period, eight steam turbines and turbo alternators made to certain specifications, at a price of £250,000 payable by the respondents in instalments. The machines supplied were defective in failing to comply with the provisions of the contract in respect to economy and steam consumption. After using the defective machines for some years (and allowing the appellants to attempt repairs) the respondents decided to replace them with eight new Parsons turbines, superior both in efficiency and economy. The respondents claimed damages for breach of contract, either (a) £280,000 or so, being their estimate of the loss caused by the excessive coal consumption of the appellants' machines for a period of 20 years estimated commercial life, or (b) the cost of installing the new Parsons turbines, namely £78,186 plus a further £42,000, being the estimated loss caused by the excess coal consumption during the time the appellants' machines were working and before the Parsons machines were installed.

The arbitrator, to whom the case was initially referred under an arbitration clause in the contract, found as a fact that the purchase of the Parsons turbines by the respondents was a reasonable and prudent course and that it mitigated or prevented the loss and damage which would have been recoverable from the appellants if the respondents had continued to use the appellants' defective machines. He found further that the purchase of the Parsons turbines was to the pecuniary advantage of the respondents and that the superiority of the new machines was such that even if the appellants' machines had complied with the terms of the contract, it would still have been to the respondents' pecuniary advantage at their own cost to have replaced the appellants' machines with the new Parsons machines.

The arbitrator stated a special case for the opinion of the court whether the respondents could recover the cost of replacing the turbines at law. The Divisional Court found for the respondents and the arbitrator awarded a substantial sum to the respondents (though smaller than that claimed). At first instance and in the Court of Appeal, the appellants' motion to set aside the award was dismissed.

*Held*

The appeal would be allowed. The court had the power to review the arbitrator's award and the principal question was the correct measure of damages.

Lord Haldane LC:

'The question thus arising was decided by the Court of Appeal in favour of the respondents. They held that the law as to the measure of damages had been rightly laid down by the Divisional Court. They thought that the purchase of the Parsons machines must be taken to have been merely for the purpose of mitigating the damages and that the appellants were not entitled to have the pecuniary advantages arising from the subsequent use of these superior machines and the saving of working expenses which would have been incurred even had the appellants' machines been up to the standard of efficiency contracted for, brought into account ...

Upon the question which I have stated, I am unable to agree with the majority of the Court of Appeal.

The arbitrator appears to me to have found clearly that the effect of the superiority of the Parsons machines and of their efficiency in reducing working expenses was, in point of fact such, that all loss was extinguished and actually, the respondents made a profit by the course they took. They were doubtless not bound to purchase machines of a greater kilowatt power than those originally contracted for, but they in fact took the wise course, in the circumstances, of doing so, with the pecuniary advantage to themselves. They had, moreover, used the appellants' machines for several years and had recovered compensation for the loss incurred by reason of these machines not being, during these years, up to the standard required by the contract. After that period, the arbitrator found that it was reasonable and prudent to take the course they actually did in purchasing the more powerful machines and that all remaining loss and damages was thereby wiped out.

In order to come to a conclusion on the question as to damages thus raised, it is essential to bear in mind certain propositions which I think are well established. In some of the cases there are expressions as to the principles governing the measure of general damages which, at first sight, seem difficult to harmonise. The apparent discrepancies are, however, mainly due to the varying nature of the particular questions submitted for decision. The quantum of damage is a question of fact and the only guidance the law can give is to lay down general principles which afford at times but scanty assistance in dealing with particular cases. The judges who give guidance to juries in these cases have necessarily to look at their special character and to mould, for the purpose of different kinds of claim, the expression of the general principles which apply to them and this is apt to give rise to an appearance of ambiguity.

Subject to these observations, I think that there are certain broad principles which are quite well settled. The first is that, as far as possible, he who has proved a breach of the bargain to supply what he contracted to get, is to be placed, as far as money can do it, in as good a situation as if the contract had been performed.

The fundamental basis is thus compensation for pecuniary loss naturally flowing from the breach; but this first principle is qualified by a second which imposes on a plaintiff the duty of taking all reasonable steps to mitigate the loss consequent on the breach and debars him from claiming any part of the damage which is due to his neglect to take such steps. In the words of James LJ in *Dunkirk Colliery Co v Lever* (1878) 9 Ch D 20, 25:

"The person who has broken the contract is not being under any obligation to do anything otherwise than in the ordinary course of business."

As James LJ indicates, this second principle does not impose on the plaintiff an obligation to take any step which a reasonable and prudent man would not ordinarily take in the course of his business. But when, in the course of his business he has taken action arising out of the transaction, which action has diminished his loss, the effect in the actual diminution of the loss he has suffered may be taken into account, even though there was no duty on him to act.

[His Lordship then referred to the decision of the Court of Common Pleas in *Staniforth* v *Lyall* (1830) 7 Bing 169 and continued:]

I think that this decision illustrates a principle which has been recognised in other cases, that provided the course taken to protect himself by the plaintiff in such an action was one which a reasonable and prudent person might, in the ordinary course of business, properly have taken and in fact did take, whether bound to or not, a jury or an arbitrator may properly look at the whole of the facts and ascertain the result in estimating the quantum of damage ...

I think that the principle which applies here is that which makes it right for the jury or arbitrator to look at what actually happened and to balance loss and gain. The transaction was not re inter alios acta, but one in which the person whose contract was broken took a reasonable and prudent course quite naturally arising out of the circumstances in which he was placed by the breach. Apart from the breach of contract, the lapse of time had rendered the appellants' machines obsolete and men of business would be doing the only thing they could properly do in replacing them with new and up to date machines.

The arbitrator does not, in his finding of fact, lay any stress on the increase in kilowatt power of the new machines and I think that the proper inference is that such increase was regarded by him as a natural and prudent course followed by those whose object was to avoid further loss and that it formed part of a continuous dealing with the situation in they found themselves and was not an independent or disconnected transaction.

For the reasons I have given, I think that the questions of law stated by the arbitrator in the special case have been wrongly answered by the courts below. The result is that the award cannot stand and must be sent back to the arbitrator, with a declaration that the contention of the appellants ... was right.'

*Commentary*

Distinguished in *Hussey* v *Eels* [1990] 2 WLR 234.

**C & P Haulage v Middleton** [1983] 1 WLR 1461 Court of Appeal (Ackner and Fox LJJ)

Contract - damages for breach

*Facts*

The plaintiffs contracted to allow the defendant use of their premises for a vehicle repair business. This agreement expressly provided for the use to be reviewed every six months and for any fixtures put in by the defendant to be left on the premises. After eleven months, the defendant was summarily ejected from the business. He carried on the business in the garage at his house and claimed damages for the fixtures.

At first instance, the judge found that the defendant would have been entitled to remain in occupation for one further month under the terms of the contract, but as the defendant had not suffered any loss as a result of the breach by the plaintiff, he could recover nominal damages only.

*Held*

Dismissing the appeal, damages for breach of contract did not include compensating an injured party for entering into a contract or a sum to place him in a better financial position than if the contract had been fully performed. The plaintiffs' failure to give notice terminating the contract was a breach and the defendant was entitled to damages, but he could not be placed in a better position than if the plaintiffs had properly terminated the contract and therefore he could not recover his expenditure on the premises and was entitled only to nominal damages.

Ackner LJ:

'Lord Denning MR in *Anglia TV*, referred to and relied upon the *Cullinane* case [1954] 1 QB 292, where Jenkins LJ said at page 308:

"The general principle applicable to the case is, I apprehend, this; the plant having been supplied in contemplation by both parties that it should be used by the plaintiff in the commercial production of pulverised clay, the case is one in which the plaintiff can claim as damages for the breach of warranty the loss of the profit he can show that he would have made if the plant had been as warranted. Where damages are awarded on that basis, the object in view, as indeed in any other assessment of damages, is to put the plaintiff in the same position, so far as money can put him in the same position, as if the contract had been duly complied with or the subject matter of the contract had conformed to any warranty given."

That is not the approach which the defendant seeks. He is not claiming for the loss of his bargain, which would involve being put in the position that he would have been in if the contract had been performed. He is not asking to be put in that position. He is asking to be put in the position he would have been in if the contract had never been made at all.'

**CCC Films (London) Ltd v Impact Quadrant Films Ltd** [1984] 3 WLR 245 High Court (Hutchison J)

Breach of contract - damages

*Facts*

The defendants granted to the plaintiff a non-exclusive licence to exploit three films owned by the defendants in various named territories, in consideration for US$12,000. The plaintiff paid in full, but the defendants, in breach of contract, lost the films. The plaintiff claimed $12,000 for total failure of consideration - this was rejected. In the alternative, the plaintiff claimed $12,000 as wasted expenditure.

The defendants argued that the plaintiff could only succeed in such a claim if the plaintiff proved he could not assess loss of profits and that the plaintiff must prove that the expenditure would have been recovered if the contract had been fully performed.

*Held*

The plaintiff had an unfettered right to frame his claim as one for wasted expenditure or loss of profits. He was not confined to framing his claim as one for wasted expenditure only where he established by evidence that he could not prove loss of profits, or that such loss of profits that he could prove was small.

It was established that a claim for wasted expenditure could not succeed in a case where had there been no breach of contract, the returns earned by the plaintiff under the contract would not have been sufficient to recoup the expenditure (*C & P Haulage* v *Middleton* [1983] 1 WLR 1461). In order to defeat a plaintiff's claim for wasted expenditure, the onus was on the defendant to prove that the expenditure would not have recovered had the contract been performed.

**Cellulose Acetate Silk Company Limited v Widnes Foundry (1925) Limited** [1933] AC 20 House of Lords (Lord Atkin, Lord Warrington of Clyffe, Lord Tomlin, Lord Thankerton and Lord Macmillan)

Breach of contract - measure of damages

*Facts*

The parties contracted for the installation of an acetone recovery plant supplied by the respondents within a period of 18 weeks. Clause 10 of the contract provided that if the work was not completed within the specified period, the respondents were to pay a penalty of £20 per week for every week they were in default. The respondents were 30 weeks late in completing the installation. They claimed the contract price of £19,750 and were given judgment for that sum. The appellants counter claimed for the delay and contended that the £20 per week sum was in the nature of a penalty and they were entitled to recover their actual loss.

*Held*

The sum of £20 per week was liquidated damages so the respondents were liable for £600 and no more.

Lord Atkin:

'What, then, is the effect of clause 10? If this period of 18 weeks is exceeded, you have to pay, by way of penalty, the sum of £20 per working week for every week you exceed the 18 weeks. I entertain no doubt that what the parties meant was that in the event of delay, the damages, and the only damages, were to be £20 a week - no less and no more. It has to be remembered that the Foundry Company's business in this respect was to supply an accessory to a large business plant for which they had no responsibility. The extent of the purchasers' business might be enormous; their expenses were beyond the sellers' control; and it would be a very ordinary business precaution for the sellers in such a case to say; "We will name a date for delivery, but we will accept no liability to pay damages for not observing the date; for if we were by our default to stop the whole of your business, the damages might be overwhelming in relation to our possible profit out of the transaction. We won't incur any such risk." This precaution the prospective sellers took in their printed condition 10. They definitely negative any liability for delay. The purchasers have ample notice of this in the first quotation form sent to them ... The purchasers pressed for an earlier date; they got it and, getting it without more, they would still only have a business firm's assurance of delivery by that date; they would still be unable to claim damages from them for breach. The sellers ask for an addition to the price in order to enable them to give the earlier delivery; the buyers ask for some compensation if they do not get the delivery they want. It is agreed at £20 per week of delay. It appears to me that such sum is provided as compensation in place of no compensation at all, which would otherwise have been the result. Except that it is called a penalty, which on the cases is far from conclusive, it appears to be an amount of compensation measured by the period of delay. I agree that it is not a pre-estimate of actual damage. I think it must have been obvious to both the parties that the actual damage would be much more than £20 a week; but it was intended to go towards the damage and it was all that the sellers were prepared to pay. I find it impossible to believe that the sellers, who were quoting for delivery at nine months without any liability, undertook delivery at 18 weeks and, in so doing when they engaged to pay £20 a week, in fact made themselves liable to pay full compensation for all loss.

For these reasons, I think the Silk Company are only entitled to recover £20 a week as agreed damages; and that the decision of the Court of Appeal was correct and should be affirmed. In these circumstances, I find it unnecessary to consider what would be the position if this were a penalty. It was argued by appellants that if this were a penalty they would have an option either to sue for the penalty, or to sue for damages for breach of the promise as to time of delivery. I desire to leave open the question whether, where a penalty is plainly less in amount than the prospective damages, there is any legal obligation to suing on it, or, in a suitable case, ignoring it and suing for damages. In the present case the only result of ignoring the penalty might be that the defendants would find themselves confronted with a contract which, by condition 10, deprived them of any compensation at all ...'

**Chaplin v Hicks** [1911] 2 KB 786 Court of Appeal (Vaughan Williams, Fletcher Moulton and Farwell LJJ)

Breach of contract - measure of damages

*Facts*

In 1908, a letter from the defendant, a well known actor and theatrical manager, was published in a London daily newspaper, in which he said that he was willing that the readers of the newspaper should, by their votes, select twelve young ladies desirous of obtaining engagements as actresses, to whom he would give engagements. Ladies were invited to send their photographs to the newspaper by a given date, together with their name, address and certain personal details. The defendant, with the assistance of a committee, would then select twenty-four photographs to be published in the newspapers and the readers of the newspaper would, out of those, select the twelve winners. So many photographs were sent in that the conditions were altered so that the country could be divided into ten districts, the readers in each district would select the best five ladies and from these fifty, the defendant would himself select the twelve who would receive the promised engagements. The plaintiff agreed to this alteration in the terms of the competition. The defendant was top of her section and became one of the fifty eligible for selection by the defendant. She was invited for an interview, but because she was away at the time the letter was sent, she did not learn of the interview until it was over. The other forty-nine ladies did attend the interview and the defendant made his selection from amongst them. The plaintiff, having failed to secure another appointment, brought this action against the defendant for breach of contract. The jury found that the defendant had not given the plaintiff a reasonable opportunity to present herself for interview and made an award of damages from which the defendant appealed.

*Held*

The appeal would be dismissed.

Vaughan Williams LJ:

'I am of the opinion that this appeal should be dismissed ... The argument for the defendant was based upon two propositions, first that the damages were too remote and secondly that they were unassessable ...

As regards remoteness, the test that is generally applied is to see whether the damages sought to be recovered follow so naturally or by express declaration from the terms of the contract that they can be said to be the result of the breach.  This generally resolves itself into the question whether the damages flowing from a breach of contract were such as must have been contemplated by the parties as a possible result of the breach.  Now the moment it is admitted that the contract was, in effect, one which gave the plaintiff a right to present herself and to take her chance of getting a prize, and the moment the jury find that she did not have a reasonable opportunity of presenting herself on the particular day, we have a breach attended by neglect of the plaintiff to give her a later opportunity, and when we get a breach of that sort and a claim for loss sustained in consequence of the failure to give the plaintiff an opportunity of taking part in the competition, it is impossible to say that such a result and such damages were not within the contemplation of the parties as the possible direct outcome of the breach of contract ...

... Then came the point ... that the damages were of such a nature as to be impossible of assessment ... It is said that in a case which involves so many contingencies, it is impossible to say what was the plaintiff's pecuniary loss.  I am unable to agree with the contention ... I do not agree with the contention that if certainty is impossible of attainment, the damages for a breach of contract are unassessable ... the fact that damages cannot be assessed with certainty does not relieve the wrongdoer of the necessity of paying damages for his breach of contract ... My view is that under such circumstances as those in this case, the assessment of damages was unquestionably for the jury ... this appeal fails.'

Fletcher Moulton LJ:

'I have come to the same conclusion ... there is no other universal principle as to the amount of damages than that it is the aim of the law to ensure that a person whose contract has been broken, shall be placed as near as possible in the same position as if it had not.  The assessment is sometimes a matter of great difficulty ... It has been contended in the present case that the damages are too remote ... to my mind ... the contention is unsustainable ... I think that where it is clear that there has been actual loss resulting from the breach of contract which it is difficult to estimate in money, it is for the jury to do their best to estimate ...  Where, by contract, a man has a right to belong to a limited class of competition, he is possessed of something of value and it is the duty of the jury to estimate the pecuniary value of that advantage if it is taken from him ... The appeal must be dismissed.'

Farwell LJ:

'I agree ... damage might result not only from the loss of the opportunity of winning a prize, but also from the slur upon the plaintiff in her professional capacity, which might result in a diminution of the value of her services as an actress when she applied for an engagement ... In my opinion, the existence of a contingency which is dependent on the volition of a third person, is not enough to justify us in saying that the damages are incapable of assessment ... I agree that the appeal must be dismissed.'

## Charter v Sullivan

See chapter 18 - Sale of goods, consumer credit and supply of good and services.

**Clayton (Herbert) and Jack Waller Ltd v Oliver** [1930] AC 209 House of Lords (Lord Buckmaster, Viscount Dunedin, Lord Blanesburgh, Lord Warrington and Lord Tomlin)

Breach of contract - measure of damages

*Facts*

By a contract contained in two letters, the appellants agreed to engage the respondent to play one of the three leading parts in a music play for six weeks, with an option to the appellant to re-engage the respondent for the run of the play. He was cast in one of the parts and, on reading it, he complained that it was not one of the three leading comedy parts, but the appellants refused to re-cast him and alleged that the part was a good performance of the contract. Thereupon the respondent declined to appear in the production and issued a writ against the appellants. He alleged that in addition to his salary, it was intended that he should benefit fully from the publicity given to the play and his reputation would have been enhanced by his taking a leading and consequently widely advertised part in an important West End production and that by reason of the breach of contract, he had lost the said publicity and been deprived of the advantages and reputation which would have followed a successful performance. It was found at first instance that the part given to the respondent was a trivial one.

*Held*

The respondent was entitled to succeed.

Lord Buckmaster:

'... No other part was offered and the result is that the appellants broke their contract. The next question is what was the measure of damages? ... the old and well established rule applied ... the damages are those that may reasonably be supposed to have been in the contemplation of the parties at the time when the contract was made as the probable result of its breach and if any special circumstances were unknown to one of the parties, the damages associated with the flowing from such breach cannot be included. Here both parties knew that as flowing from the contract, the plaintiff would be billed and advertised as appearing at the Hippodrome and in the theatrical profession this is a valuable right.

In assessing the damages, therefore, it was competent for the jury to consider that the plaintiff was entitled to compensation because he did not appear at the Hippodrome ... and in assessing those damages, they may consider the loss he suffered (1) because the Hippodrome is an important place of public entertainment and (2) that in the ordinary course he would have been "billed" and otherwise advertised as appearing at the Hippodrome. The learned judge put the matter as a loss of reputation, which I do not think is the exact expression, but he explained that as the equivalent of loss of publicity and that summarises what I have stated as my view of the true situation.'

## Clea Shipping Corp v Bulk Oil International Ltd. The Alaskan Trader [1984] 1 All ER 129 High Court (Lloyd J)

Repudiation of contract - victim's choices

*Facts*

C chartered a ship to B. After a year (the charter was for two years), the ship broke down and was put in for repairs. B informed C that it no longer wanted the ship, but C carried out the repairs and, on their completion, offered the ship as ready once again; again B said it was not wanted. C took no steps to find an alternative charterer and kept the ship fully crewed. Was C was entitled to continue performance of the contract, or should it have repudiated it and sued for damages?

*Held*

The court would not interfere with the arbitrator's finding that C should have accepted the repudiation made on completion of the repairs and could not recover the cost of hire under the charter party; instead C had to sue for breach of contract.

**Clydebank Engineering v Don Jose Ramos.**

See **Clydebank Engineering and Shipbuilding Co v Castaneda**

**Clydebank Engineering and Shipbuilding Co v Castaneda** [1905] AC 6 House of Lords
(Earl of Halsbury LC, Lord Davey and Lord Robertson)

Breach of contract - liquidated damages

*Facts*

The appellants contracted to build four torpedo-boat destroyers for the Spanish government within specified periods and the contract stipulated a 'penalty for later delivery ... at the rate of £500 per week'. The purchasers paid for the vessels and claimed for late delivery.

*Held*

The claim would succeed as the contract had provided for liquidated damages.

Earl of Halsbury LC:

'This is a case in which one party to an agreement has admittedly been guilty of a breach of that agreement. The action was brought by the Spanish government simply for the purpose of enforcing payment of a sum of money which, by agreement between the parties, was fixed as that which the appellants should pay in the events which have happened. Two objections have been made to the enforcement of that payment. The first objection is one which appears on the face of the instrument itself, namely, that it was a penalty, and, therefore, not recoverable without ascertaining the measure of damage resulting from the breach of contract. It was frankly admitted that not much reliance could be placed on the mere use of the words "penalty" on one side, or "damage" on the other. It is clear that neither is conclusive as to the rights of the parties ...

Then comes the question whether, under the agreement, the damages are recoverable as an agreed sum, or whether it is simply a penalty to be held over in terrorem, or whether it is a penalty so extravagant that no court ought to enforce it. It is impossible to lay down any abstract rule as to what might or might not be extravagant without reference to the principal facts and circumstances of the particular case. A great deal must depend on the nature of the transaction. On the other hand, it is an established principle in both countries to agree that the damages should be so much in the event of breach of agreement. The very reason why the parties agreed to such a stipulation was that, sometimes, the nature of the damage was such that proof would be extremely difficult, complex and expensive. If I wanted an example of what might be done in this way I need only refer to the argument of counsel as to the measure of damage sustained by Spain through the withholding of these vessels. Suppose there had been no agreement in the contract as to damages, and the Spanish government had to prove damages in the ordinary way, imagine the kind of cross-examination of every person connected with the Spanish administration. It is very obvious that what was intended by inserting these damages in the contract was to avoid a minute, difficult and complex system of examination which would be necessary if they had attempted to prove damage in the ordinary way ... If your Lordships look at the nature of the transaction, it is hopeless to contend that the penalty was intended merely to be in terrorem. Both parties recognised that the question was one in which time was the main element of the contract. I have come to the conclusion that the judgment of the court below was perfectly right. There is no ground for the contention that the sum in the contract was not the damages agreed on between the parties for very good and excellent reasons at the time at which the contract was entered into.'

*Commentary*

See also *Dunlop Pneumatic Tyre Co Ltd* v *New Garage and Motor Co Ltd* [1915] AC 79.

**De la Bere v Pearson Ltd**

See chapter 2 - Consideration.

**Denmark Productions Ltd v Boscobel Productions Ltd**

See chapter 7 - Incapacity.

**Dunk v George Waller & Son Ltd** [1970] 2 WLR 1241 Court of Appeal (Lord Denning MR, Widgery and Karminski LJJ)

Breach of contract - measure of damages

*Facts*

In breach of an apprenticeship agreement, the employers terminated it while it still had 15 months to run. If the agreement had run its full course, the apprentice would have been entitled to a certificate and this would have given him a better start to his career.

*Held*

The sum awarded the apprentice should include damages for loss of future prospects.

Lord Denning MR:

'Now, as to the damages. An apprenticeship agreement is of a special character. The apprentice accepted much less wages during the apprenticeship agreement than he would have received if he had gone into the open market as a labourer. At the material time under the apprenticeship agreement he was getting £10 a week. If he had been an unskilled labourer outside in a factory he would have got £20 a week. The difference should have been made up to him by the benefits of apprenticeship, such as the benefit of training, instruction and experience in the various departments of the works. He has been deprived of those benefits for the remaining 65 weeks of the agreement. In order to mitigate the damage, he sought employment elsewhere. He applied for positions as a representative, and so forth, which he did not get. Perhaps he was aiming too high. For 57 weeks he was out of work, receiving unemployment pay. For the last eight weeks he got employment in a slipper factory at £20 per week.

In my opinion he is entitled to damages for his loss of earnings and of training during the remainder of the term of the apprenticeship agreement and also for the diminution of his future prospects. If he had been allowed satisfactorily to complete his apprenticeship he should have got a better post and better wages thereafter. We were referred to some old cases ... which suggest that an apprentice, who has been wrongly dismissed, can only sue for his damage up to the date of his action brought. They are not good law today.

We were also referred to *Addis* v *Gramophone Co Ltd*, when it was said that an employee cannot get compensation -

" ... for the loss he may sustain from the fact that his having been dismissed of itself makes it more difficult for him to obtain fresh employment."

I do not think that that applies in the case of an apprenticeship. The very object of an apprenticeship agreement is to enable the apprentice to fit himself to get better employment. If his apprenticeship is wrongly determined, so that he does not get the benefit of the training for which he stipulated, then it is a head of damage for which he may recover. If the apprentice had continued as an apprentice until the end of his time for the next 15 months, he would have been entitled to a certificate at the end of the apprenticeship agreement certifying that he had served his full period of apprenticeship. That would have given him a better start so that he would earn more than others at any rate for the first year or two.'

*Commentary*

Distinguished: *Addis* v *Gramophone Co Ltd* [1909] AC 488.

**Dunlop Pneumatic Tyre Co Ltd v New Garage and Motor Co Ltd** [1915] AC 79 House of Lords (Lord Dunedin, Lord Atkinson, Lord Parker and Lord Parmoor)

Liquidated damages or penalty - question for court

*Facts*

The appellants manufactured motor tyres and they agreed to supply the respondent retailers on condition that they would not sell at prices below those mentioned in the appellants' price list: if they did, they would pay the appellants £5 for each and every tyre so sold 'as and by way of liquidated damages, and not as a penalty'.

*Held*

The stipulation was for liquidated damages and the respondents were liable to pay the appellants £5 for each breach of the agreement as to prices.

Lord Dunedin:

'We had the benefit of a full and satisfactory argument, and a citation of the very numerous cases which have been decided on this branch of the law. The matter has been handled, and at a recent date, in the courts of highest resort. I particularly refer to *Clydebank Engineering Co v Yzquierdo y Castaneda*, in your Lordships' House, and *Public Works Comr v Hills*... in the Privy Council. In ... these cases many of the previous authorities were considered. In view of that fact, and of the number of the authorities available, I do not think it advisable to attempt any detailed review of the various cases, but I shall content myself with stating succinctly the various propositions which I think are deducible from the decisions which rank as authoritative:

(i) Though the parties to a contract who use the words penalty or liquidated damages may prima facie by supposed to mean what they say, yet the expression used is not conclusive. The court must find out whether the payment stipulated is in truth a penalty or liquidated damages. This doctrine may be said to be found passim in nearly every case. (ii) The essence of a penalty is a payment of money stipulated as in terrorem of the offending party; the essence of liquidated damages is a genuine covenanted pre-estimate of damage: *Clydebank Engineering Company v Yzquierdo y Castaneda* (1). (iii) The question whether a sum stipulated is penalty or liquidated damages is a question of construction to be decided upon the terms and inherent circumstances of each particular contract, judged of as the time of making of the contract, not as at the time of the breach: *Public Works Comr v Hills* ... (iv) To assist this task of construction various tests have been suggested, which, if applicable to the case under consideration, may prove helpful or even conclusive. Such are (a) It will be held to be a penalty if the sum stipulated for is extravagant and unconscionable in amount in comparison with the greatest loss which could conceivably be proved to have followed from the breach - illustration given by Lord Halsbury L C in the *Clydebank Case*. (b) It will be held to be a penalty if the breach consists only in not paying a sum of money, and the sum stipulated is a sum greater than the sum which ought to have been paid: *Kemble v Farren*. This, though one of the most ancient instances, is truly a corollary to the last test. Whether it had its historical origin in the doctrine of the common law that, when A promised to pay B a sum of money on a certain day and did not do so, B could only recover the sum with, in certain cases, interest, but could never recover further damages for non-timeous payment, or whether it was a survival of the time when equity reformed unconscionable bargains merely because they were unconscionable - a subject which much exercised Jessel MR, in *Wallis v Smith* - probably more interesting than material. (c) There is a presumption (but no more) that it is a penalty when

"a single lump sum is made payable by way of compensation, on the occurrence of one or more or all of several events, some of which may occasion serious and others but trifling damages:"

per Lord Watson in *Lord Elphinstone v Monkland Iron and Coal Co.* (11 App Cas at p 342). On the other hand: (d) It is no obstacle to the sum stipulated being a genuine pre-estimate of damage that the consequences of the breach are such as to make precise pre-estimation almost an impossibility. On the contrary, that is just the situation when it is probable that pre-estimated damage was the true bargain between the parties: *Clydebank Case* per Lord Halsbury ...

Turning now to the facts of the case, it is evident that the damage apprehended by the appellants owing to the breaking of the agreement was an indirect and not a direct damage. So long as they got their price from the respondents for each article sold, it could not matter to them directly what the respondents did with it. Indirectly it did. Accordingly, the agreement is headed "Price Maintenance Agreement," and the way in which the appellants would be damaged if prices were cut was clearly explained in evidence, and no successful attempt was made to controvert that evidence. But though damages as a whole from such a practice would be certain, yet damages from any one sale would be impossible to forecast. It is just, therefore, one of those cases where it seems quite reasonable for parties to contract that they should estimate the damage at a certain figure, and provided that the figure is not extravagant there would seem no reason to suspect that it is not truly a bargain to assess damages, but rather a penalty to be held in terrorem.'

*Commentary*

See also *Alder* v *Moore* [1961] 2 WLR 426 and *Bridge* v *Campbell Discount Co Ltd* [1962] 2 WLR 439.

**Edwards v Society of Graphical and Allied Trades** [1970] 3 WLR 713 Court of Appeal (Lord Denning MR, Sachs and Megaw LJJ)

Breach of contract - measure of damages

*Facts*

The plaintiff was employed by a Manchester printer called Stevensons, as a cutter and creaser. He joined a trades union which, by amalgamation, became part of SOGAT. Under the rules of the union, membership was divided into full members and temporary members. The plaintiff was a temporary member. The rules of the union provided that temporary membership would terminate automatically if the member was six weeks in arrears of his contributions. The plaintiff, along with other Stevensons' employees, authorised Stevensons to deduct the contributions direct from his pay packet. By some oversight, however, the deductions were not made from the plaintiff's pay and the union asserted that he had automatically ceased to be a member and further refused to readmit him. Stevensons operated 100 per cent union membership and, accordingly, the plaintiff was at first suspended and then lost his job. The employers had no complaint about his work, however, and would have continued to employ him had it not been for the difficulty about his union membership. After having been out of work for some time, the plaintiff found employment in a non-union firm, but lost that employment when he was required to perform a task which it was not part of his job to do. He was a skilled tradesman and the task was normally performed by a labourer, who was unfortunately away ill ... Apart from this, his work was satisfactory. In April 1969, sixteen months after he was dismissed by Stevensons and two and three quarter years after he was refused readmission to the union, the union admitted that they had been mistaken in treating the plaintiff as no longer a member of the union. They intimated that, in the circumstances, his membership had never been terminated. By this time the action had been on foot for nearly a year. The union operated a trade 'labour exchange' controlling the employment. The union's solicitors had procured offers of employment for the plaintiff, but none of the jobs were for a worker of the plaintiff's qualifications. At the trial, the only issue, therefore, was the quantum of damages and the judge awarded the plaintiff the whole of his actual financial loss to the date of the trial and a sum for future loss of earning capacity assessed on the formula applied in personal injury cases, namely the difference between his net weekly wages with Stevensons and the net weekly amount which he could earn as a labourer in the printing business, multiplied by a number of years' purchase. The plaintiff being 39, the judge chose ten. The union appealed.

*Held*

The judge's decision would be varied.

Lord Denning MR:

'... how are the damages to be measured? I think they are to be ascertained by putting the plaintiff in as good a position, so far as money can do it, as if he had never been excluded from the union, taking into account, of course, all contingencies which might have led him to losing his employment anyway and remembering too that it was his duty to do what was reasonable to mitigate the damage ... we must remember that he has now been restored to full membership.

[He awarded him full actual loss to the date of trial and continued:]

Loss from the date of trial - November 1969 - onwards. The judge assessed this loss as if the man had suffered personal injury, incapacitating him from any work except general labouring work. I think that was not the right measure ... I feel that damages in such a case as this are so difficult to assess that I would be inclined to view them somewhat broadly. I would start with the loss of earnings which he might reasonably be expected to have suffered over two years from his expulsion .. I would then work upwards or downwards from that figure, according to the circumstances of the case ...'

Sachs LJ:

'... It is well to record at the outset ... that certain rules laid down in *Addis* v *Gramophone Co Ltd* [1909] AC 488, touching damages for wrongful dismissal, have no application to the present type of case. In other words, whereas in the former class of cases the damages can contain no element for the difficulty the dismissal causes to a plaintiff in getting fresh employment, the essence of the measure in the present case is an assessment of the financial consequences of that very difficulty ... it is necessary first to assess the difference the deprivation of a union card has made to a plaintiff's earnings up to the date of trial and then to add to the resulting figure a quantification of the difference to his future earning capacity likely thereafter to result from the union's wrongful act ... estimated on the chances as to whether and when he may regain work with earnings on the Grade 1 scale current in 100 per cent union shops. That involves considering, among other factors, his chances of remaining a member of the union for any length of time and the chances of their assisting him in obtaining employment in a field over which it has a major influence, as the filling of vacancies ... This is not a case for embarking on detailed calculations or on precise forecasts ... an overall assessment on a broad basis is needed ...'

Megaw LJ:

'... I think that it is convenient to consider the amount of the damage under two heads. First, what is the plaintiff's loss, by reason of the breach of contract, up to the present moment? Second, what is the future loss, if any?

The first head involves consideration of the issue whether the plaintiff acted unreasonably in respect of the termination of his employment (with the second firm) and whether he failed in his duty thereafter to seek to mitigate his loss by pursuing possibilities of employment ... I see no reason to differ from the judge that neither of these matters ought to be treated as constituting a failure by the plaintiff to act reasonably in mitigation of damages. Hence I agree with the judge's figure ... (of) the plaintiff's loss up to the date of judgment ...

The second head, future damage, involves a more difficult question and, for that very reason, it involves looking into the uncertainties of the future. The plaintiff's loss is the difference between what he would have earned if there had been no breach of contract and what he will earn on the assumption that he uses all proper diligence to mitigate his loss ... inevitably it depends upon hypothesis and speculation ... where there are so many incalculables, it would not be right to seek to give an aura of scientific arithmetical or actuarial formulae to the assessment, or to any individual factor on which the assessment partly depends. One must try to assess. One cannot calculate ...'

## Export Credits Guarantee Department v Universal Oil Products Co [1983] 1 WLR 399

House of Lords (Lord Diplock, Lord Elwyn-Jones, Lord Keith of Kinkel, Lord Roskill and Lord Brightman)

Contract - indemnity clause a penalty?

*Facts*

In 1970 a number of interlocking multilateral contracts were concluded between three Newfoundland companies, the three defendant companies and a consortium of bankers for the design, construction and installation of an oil refinery in Newfoundland. The plaintiffs, in consideration of a premium, guaranteed certain payments and the defendants undertook to reimburse them in certain circumstances. These circumstances having arisen, the plaintiffs sought reimbursement, but the defendants contended, inter alia, that their claim should fail as it was a penalty clause.

*Held*

The plaintiffs' claim would succeed.

Lord Roskill:

'My Lords, one purpose, perhaps the main purpose, of the law relating to penalty clauses is to prevent a plaintiff recovering a sum of money in respect of a breach of contract committed by a defendant which bears little or no relationship to the loss actually suffered by the plaintiff as a result of the breach by the defendant. But it is not and never has been for the courts to relieve a party from the consequences of what may in the event prove to be an onerous or possibly even a commercially imprudent bargain. The defendants could only secure the finance ... if the ECGD were prepared to give ... the guarantee ... required. The ECGD were only prepared to give their guarantee ... on the terms of the premium agreement which included the stringent right of recourse ... The defendants accepted those terms which provided for the right of recourse to arise on the happening of a specified event, and that specified event has now happened. But, as my noble and learned friend Lord Keith observed during the argument, this is not a case where the ECGD are seeking to recover more than their actual loss as compensation by way of damages for breach of a contract to which they were a party. They are seeking, and only seeking, to recover their actual loss, namely the sums which they became legally obliged to pay and have paid ... I am afraid I find it impossible to see how on these facts there can be any room for the invocation of the law relating to penalty clauses.'

## Forsikringsaktieselskapet Vesta v Butcher [1988] 3 WLR 565 Court of Appeal (O'Connor and Neill LJJ and Sir Roger Ormrod)

Damages for breach of contract - contributory negligence

*Facts*

A Norwegian insurance company, the plaintiffs, insured a Norwegian fish farm against loss of fish and reinsured 90 per cent of the risk with London underwriters through brokers. It was a condition of both the insurance and the reinsurance that a 24 hour watch be kept on the farm, but the owners told the plaintiffs that they could not accept this clause. The plaintiffs telephoned this information to the brokers and awaited confirmation that the lack of a 24 hour watch was acceptable: the brokers did not pass the information to the reinsurers and the plaintiffs did not follow up the matter: the reinsurance policy contained 'follow settlement' and 'claim control' clauses and also provided that the underwriters were to have sole control of any negotiations and that no payment was to be made to the insured without their consent. Many fish were lost as a result of a severe storm; the plaintiffs settled the owners' claim but, even though a watch would not have saved the fish, the reinsurers repudiated liability, inter alia, on the ground of breach of the 24 hour watch condition. The plaintiffs claimed 90 per cent indemnity from the reinsurers or, alternatively, damages for breach of duty against the brokers for failing to inform the reinsurers that the 24 hour watch condition was unacceptable. The judge held:

1) clauses such as the 24 hour watch condition were to be construed according to Norwegian law which did not provide a valid defence to the plaintiff's claim against the reinsurers;

2) although the brokers had been in breach of contract, no loss had resulted (because the reinsurers were liable) so the plaintiffs were entitled only to nominal damages against them;

3) if the plaintiffs had suffered substantial loss, the damages recoverable from the brokers would have been reduced by 75 per cent because of the plaintiffs' contributory negligence in failing to follow up.

The reinsurers appealed against (1), the brokers cross-appealed against (2) and the plaintiffs cross-appealed against (3).

*Held*

The appeal and the cross-appeals would be dismissed.

O'Connor LJ:

'The important issue of law is whether on the facts of this case there is power to apportion under the Law Reform (Contributory Negligence) Act 1945 and thus reduce the damages recoverable by Vesta [the plaintiffs].

I start by pointing out that Vesta pleaded its claim against the brokers in contract and tort. This is but a recognition of what I regard as a clearly established principle that where under the general law a person owes a duty to another to exercise reasonable care and skill in some activity, a breach of that duty gives rise to a claim in tort notwithstanding the fact that the activity is the subject matter of a contract between them. In such a case the breach of duty will also be a breach of contract. The classic example of this situation is the relationship between doctor and patient.

Since the decision of the House of Lords in *Hedley Byrne & Co Ltd* v *Heller & Partners Ltd* [1963] 2 All ER 575, the relationship between the brokers and Vesta is another example. Counsel for Vesta accepts that this is so but he submits that, if a plaintiff makes his claim in contract, contributory negligence cannot be relied on by the defendant whereas it is available if the claim is made in tort. If this contention is sound then the law has been sadly adrift for a very long time for it would mean that in employers' liability cases an injured employee could debar the employer from relying on any contributory negligence by framing his action in contract.

In support of his submission counsel relied on two decisions at first instance: *AB Marintrans* v *Comet Shipping Co Ltd, The Shinjitsu Maru No 5* [1985] 3 All ER 442 and *Basildon DC* v *J E Lesser (Properties) Ltd* [1985] 1 All ER 20. The judge dealt with this submission as follows ([1986] 2 All ER 488 at 508):

"The question whether the 1945 Act applies to claims brought in contract can arise in a number of classes of case. Three categories can conveniently be identified. (1) Where the defendant's liability arises from some contractual provision which does not depend on negligence on the part of the defendant. (2) Where the defendant's liability arises from a contractual obligation which is expressed in terms of taking care (or its equivalent) but does not correspond to a common law duty to take care which would exist in the given case independently of contract. (3) Where the defendant's liability in contract is the same as his liability in the tort of negligence independently of the existence of any contract" ...

In my judgment *Sayers* v *Harlow UDC* [1958] 2 All ER 342 is a category (3) case and the decision of the Court of Appeal that there is power to apportion was not only right but is binding on us just as the judge held it was binding on him.

There are two further possible arguments for saying that there is a power to apportion in a category (3) case even though the claim is made in contract. I will state them but do not find it necessary to analyse or reach a conclusion on them. (i) Contributory negligence was a defence in category (3) cases pleaded in contract before 1945. The argument is supported by railway cases and banking cases. (ii) Just as it has been held that a plaintiff cannot escape the Limitation Act 1980 by pleading a negligence case as trespass to the person so here the court should hold that a plaintiff cannot escape apportionment by pleading the case in contract (see *Letang* v *Cooper* [1964] 2 All ER 929).

I am satisfied that the judge came to the right conclusion on this topic and in respect of it I would dismiss Vesta's appeal.'

### Gebrüder Metalmann Gmbh & Co KG v NBR (London) Ltd [1984] 1 Lloyd's Rep 614
Court of Appeal (Sir John Donaldson MR, Dunn and Browne-Wilkinson (JJ)

Breach of contract - mitigating damage

*Facts*

Both parties are sugar traders. The plaintiffs sold 2,000 tons of sugar to the defendant buyers who repudiated the contract before the date for delivery of the goods. The plaintiffs accepted the repudiation. The plaintiffs claimed damages and a dispute arose over the basis of assessment and mitigation.

Sir John Donaldson MR:

'The general rule was that where a contract for the sale of goods was repudiated and the repudiation was accepted before the date for delivery, damages were to be assessed on the difference between the contract price and the market price on the date for delivery.

That was subject to the exception that, as from the date of breach and the acceptance of the repudiation, the claimant must do what, if anything, was reasonable to decrease the damages.

The duty of the plaintiff was to act reasonably in all the circumstances, with a view to mitigating his loss.

In outline, the plaintiffs had a choice - either to sell on the physical market or to make a hedging sale on the terminal market (a market in London and Paris protected from market fluctuations). The plaintiffs sold on the terminal market and received a lower price than the actual market value. On the evidence, it was felt that that was what any reasonable trader would have done, since it involved no delay and they were entitled to the difference between the contract price and terminal market price.'

Browne-Wilkinson LJ stated:

'... that if there were two methods of mitigating damage, both of which were reasonable in the circumstances, known to the innocent party when the mitigating action was required, it was not possible to say that that party acted unreasonably in selecting one of those methods just because it turned out that the loss would have been less had the other method been adopted.'

### Gibbons v Westminster Bank Ltd [1939] 2 KB 882 High Court (Lawrence J)

Dishonour of cheque - damages

*Facts*

Money paid in by the plaintiff to the defendant bank was, by mistake, credited to the wrong account: in consequence, a cheque drawn by the plaintiff in favour of her landlords was dishonoured. The plaintiff had not pleaded special or actual damage: was she entitled to nominal damages only?

*Held*

She was - in this case £2.

Lawrence J:

'The authorities ... all lay down that a trader is entitled to recover substantial damages without pleading and proving actual damage for the dishonour of his cheque, but it has never been held that that exception to the general rule as to the measure of damages for breach of contract extends to anyone who is not a trader ...   In my opinion, I ought to treat this matter as covered by these authorities, and I must hold that the corollary of the proposition which is laid down by these cases is the law - namely, that a person who is not a trader is not entitled to recover substantial damages unless the damages are alleged and proved as special damages.  I am therefore of opinion that the plaintiff, whom I hold not to be a trader, is entitled to recover only nominal damages ...'

**Golden Bay Realty Ltd v Orchard Twelve Investments Ltd** [1991] 1 WLR 981 Privy Council (Lord Templeman, Lord Oliver, Lord Goff, Sir Michael Kerr and Sir Christopher Slade)

Contract in statutory form - relief against penalties applicable?

*Facts*

A contract made in Singapore for the sale of commercial property was made in accordance with the relevant statutes as applicable locally. This included the Sale of Commercial Properties Act 1979, which provided inter alia that if the vendor failed to complete by the prescribed date he should pay liquidated damages, calculated as according to the SCP Act.

The vendor failed to complete on the appointed day and were thus liable to pay the purchaser liquidated damages until he did finally complete, some two years later.

The vendor appealed against this payment on the basis that it amounted to a penalty clause.

*Held*

The Privy Council, supporting the Singapore Court of Appeal, refused relief from the provisions of the Act; holding that where the terms and conditions of a contract are prescribed by legislation, the usual rules as to penalty clauses do not apply. The vendor was not entitled to question the validity of the provision relating to liquidated damages by claiming it was penal in nature. Regardless of the purpose of the Act, damages were entitled to be recovered, calculated in accordance with the statutory formula.

**Hadley v Baxendale** (1854) 9 Ex 341 Court of Exchequer (Parke, Alderson, Platt and Martin BB)

Breach of contract - measure of damages

*Facts*

The plaintiffs, who were the owners of a flour mill, sent a broken mill shaft, by a well known firm of common carriers, to their suppliers at Greenwich, to provide a pattern for a new shaft.  The carrier was slow in delivering the shaft and the plaintiffs claimed damages on the footing that the whole of the activities of the mill were held up for want of the shaft.

*Held*

There should be a new trial.

Alderson B:

'Now we think the proper rule in such a case as the present is this: where two parties have made a contract which one of them has broken, the damages which the other party ought to receive in respect of such a breach of contract should be such as may fairly and reasonably be considered either arising naturally, ie according to the usual course of things from such a breach of contract itself, or such as may reasonably be supposed to have been in the contemplation of both parties at the time they made the contract as the probable result of the breach of it. Now, if the special circumstances under which the contract was actually made were communicated by the plaintiffs to the defendants and thus known to both parties, the damages resulting from the breach of such a contract, which they would reasonably contemplate, would be the amount of injury which would ordinarily follow from a breach of contract under these special circumstances so known and communicated. But on the other hand, if those special circumstances were wholly unknown to the party breaking the contract, he, at the most, could only be supposed to have had in his contemplation the amount of injury which would arise generally and in the great multitude of cases not affected by any special circumstances, from such a breach of contract. For, had the special circumstances been known, the parties might have specially provided for the breach of contract by special terms as to the damages in that case; and of this advantage it would be very unjust to deprive them. Now the above principles are those by which we think the jury ought to be guided in estimating the damages arising out of any breach of contract. It is said that other cases, such as breaches of contract in the non-payment of money, or in the not making a good title to land, are to be treated as exceptions from this and as governed by a conventional rule. But as, in such cases, both parties must be supposed to be cognisant of that well known rule, these cases may, we think, be more properly classed under the rule above enunciated as to cases under known special circumstances, because there both parties may reasonably be presumed to contemplate the estimation of the amount of damages according to the conventional rule. Now in the present case, if we are to apply the principles above laid down, we find that the only circumstances here communicated by the plaintiffs to the defendants at the time the contract was made, were that the article to be carried was the broken shaft of a mill and that the plaintiffs were the millers of that mill. But how do all these circumstances show reasonably that the profits of the mill must be stopped by an unreasonable delay in the delivery of the broken shaft by the carrier to the third person? Suppose the plaintiffs had another shaft in their possession, put up or putting up at the time and that they only wished to send back the broken shaft to the engineer who made it; it is clear that this would be quite consistent with the above circumstances and yet the unreasonable delay in the delivery would have no effect upon the intermediate profits of the mill. Or, again, suppose that at the time of the delivery to the carrier, the machinery of the mill had been in other respects defective, then, also, the same results would follow. Here, it is true that the shaft was actually sent back to serve as a model for a new one and that the want of a new one was the only cause of the stoppage of the mill and that the loss of profits really arose from not sending down the new shaft in proper time and that this arose from the delay in delivering the broken one to serve as a model. But it is obvious that in the great multitude of cases of millers sending off broken shafts to third persons by a carrier, under ordinary circumstances such consequences would not, in all probability, have occurred; and these special circumstances were here never communicated by the plaintiffs to the defendants. It follows, therefore, that the loss of profits here cannot reasonably be considered such a consequence of the breach of contract as could have been fairly and reasonably contemplated by both the parties when they made this contract. For such loss would neither have flowed naturally from the breach of this contract in the great multitude of such cases occurring under ordinary circumstances, nor were the special circumstances, which, perhaps, would have made it a reasonable and natural consequence of such breach of contract, communicated to or known by the defendants ...'

*Commentary*

Applied in *Wroth* v *Tyler* [1973] 2 WLR 405. Distinguished in *Victoria Laundry (Windsor) Ltd* v *Newman Industries Ltd* [1949] 2 KB 528. See also *Koufos* v *C Czarnikow Ltd* [1967] 3 WLR 1491, *Pilkington* v *Wood* [1953] Ch 770 and *Parsons (H) (Livestock) Ltd* v *Uttley Ingham & Co Ltd* [1977] 3 WLR 990.

**Hayes v James & Charles Dodd** [1990] 2 All ER 815 Court of Appeal (Purchas, Staughton LJJ and Sir George Waller)

Damages - wasted expenditure - anguish and vexation

*Facts*

Wishing to purchase larger premises for their motor repair business, the plaintiffs began negotiations for a workshop and yard. The availability of a rear access was of vital importance and, relying on the assurance of their solicitors, the defendants, that they would have a right of way over land at the rear of the property, the plaintiffs proceeded with the purchase. Shortly after completion the owner of the adjoining land blocked the rear access and it followed that the plaintiffs could not run their business properly; after 12 months they closed it down and eventually sold the premises at a considerable loss. The trial judge (Hirst J) awarded the plaintiffs damages on the basis of capital expenditure and expenses thrown away and for anguish and vexation. The defendants appealed against this order.

*Held*

The appeal would be allowed only in relation to the award for anguish and vexation.

Staughton LJ:

'The first question in this appeal relates to the basis on which damages should be assessed. Like Hirst J I start with the principle stated by Lord Blackburn in *Livingstone* v *Rawyards Coal Co* (1880) 5 App Cas 25 at 39:

"... you should as nearly as possible get at that sum of money which will put the party who has been injured, or who has suffered, in the same position as he would have been in if he had not sustained the wrong for which he is now getting his compensation or reparation."

One must therefore ascertain the actual situation of the plaintiffs and compare it with their situation if the breach of contract had not occurred.

What then was the breach of contract? It was not the breach of any warranty that there was a right of way: the defendant solicitors gave no such warranty. This is an important point: see *Petty* v *Sidney Phillips & Son (a firm)* [1982] 3 All ER 705. The breach was of the solicitors' promise to use reasonable skill and care in advising their clients. If they had done that, they would have told the plaintiffs that there was no right of way; and it is clear that, on the receipt of such advice, the plaintiffs would have decided not to enter into the transaction at all. They would have bought no property, spent no money and borrowed none from the bank ...

I am quite satisfied that Hirst J was entitled to award damages in this case on the no-transaction basis, and that he was right to do so. Indeed it may well be that the plaintiffs were, as he held, entitled to elect between that method and the successful-transaction method; but I need not express any concluded view on that. So they should recover all the money which they spent, less anything which they subsequently recovered, provided always that they acted reasonably in mitigating their loss. But they were quite properly denied any sum for the profit which they would have made if they had operated their business successfully ...

*Mental distress*

Hirst J awarded £1,500 to each of the plaintiffs under this head. There can be no doubt, and it was accepted in this court, that each of them suffered vexation and anguish over the years to a serious extent, for which the sum awarded was but modest compensation. There is, however, an important question of principle involved ...

I am not convinced that it is enough to ask whether mental distress was reasonably foreseeable as a consequence, or even whether it should reasonably have been contemplated as not unlikely to result from a breach of contract. It seems to me that damages for mental distress in contract are, as a matter of policy, limited to certain classes of case. I would broadly follow the classification provided by Dillon LJ in *Bliss v South East Thames Regional Health Authority* [1987] ICR 700 at 718:

"... where the contract which has been broken was itself a contract to provide peace of mind or freedom from distress ..."

It may be that the class is somewhat wider than that. But it should not, in my judgment, include any case whether the object of the contract was not comfort or pleasure, or the relief or discomfort, but simply carrying on a commercial activity with a view to profit. So I would disallow the item of damages for anguish and vexation.'

*Commentary*

*Bliss v South East Thames Regional Health Authority* [1987] ICR 700: see above.


**Heron II, The**

See **Koufos v C Czarnikow Ltd**


**Hussey v Eels** [1990] 2 WLR 234 Court of Appeal (Mustill, Farquharson LJJ and Sir Michael Kerr)

Negligent misrepresentation - damages

*Facts*

Before contracting to sell their bungalow to the plaintiffs, the defendants untruthfully and negligently stated that the property was not subject to subsidence. After completing the purchase at a price of £53,250, the plaintiffs discovered the subsidence and established that the necessary repairs would cost at least £17,000. After issuing a writ claiming damages for negligent misrepresentation, the plaintiffs sold the property for redevelopment for £78,500. The judge dismissed the plaintiffs' action on the ground that they had not suffered any recoverable loss: the plaintiffs appealed.

*Held*

The appeal would be allowed and the plaintiffs awarded the difference between the contract price (£53,250) and the property's market value in its unsound condition.

Mustill LJ:

'Ultimately, as with so many disputes about damages, the issue is primarily one of fact. Did the negligence which caused the damage also cause the profit, if profit there was? I do not think so. It is true that in one sense there was a casual link between the inducement of the purchase by misrepresentation and the sale two and a half years later, for the sale represented a choice of one of the options with which the plaintiffs had been presented by the defendants' wrongful act. But only in that sense. To my mind the reality of the situation is that the plaintiffs bought the house to live in, and did live in it for a substantial period. It was only after two years that the possibility of selling the land and moving elsewhere was explored, and six months later still that this possibility came to fruition. It seems to me that when the plaintiffs unlocked the development value of their land they did so for their own benefit, and not as part of a continuous transaction of which the purchase of land and bungalow was the inception.'

*Commentary*

Distinguished: *British Westinghouse Electric and Manufacturing Co Ltd v Underground Electric Railways Co of London Ltd* [1912] AC 673.

**Iron Trade Mutual Insurance Co Ltd v JK Buckenham Ltd** [1989] 2 Lloyd's Rep 89 High Court (Kenneth Rokison QC)

Loss suffered on two different occasions - limitation of actions - Latent Damage Act 1986

*Facts*

This case concerns insurance and re-insurance. The plaintiffs were underwriters and brokers' agents. The defendant firm were insurance and re-insurance brokers. From 1981 the defendants began refusing to pay out on certain contracts, and in 1984 they repudiated the contracts altogether, alleging that the contracts were voidable for non-disclosure of material facts. The plaintiffs sued the brokers for losses occasioned by this framing their action in contract and tort. The defendants' main defence was limitation - the contracts were mainly from 1976 to 1981. Three questions arose:

a) When did the plaintiffs' cause of action accrue?

b) Could the plaintiffs rely on the Latent Damage Act as a means of delaying the limitation period?

c) If the Act applied, what was the relevant starting date for the purposes of the Act?

*Held*

Based on the three questions listed above, the Act had no application to claims founded on contract, even when the duty concerned is simply a contractual duty to take reasonable care. Therefore the questions as listed need not be considered further.

*Commentary*

Followed in *Islander Trucking Ltd* v *Hogg Robinson & Gardner Mountain (Marine) Ltd* [1990] 1 All ER 826.


**Jackson v Horizon Holidays Ltd**

See chapter 10 - Privity of contract


**Jarvis v Swan Tours Ltd** [1972] 3 WLR 954 Court of Appeal (Lord Denning MR, Edmund Davies and Stephenson LJJ)

Breach of contract - measure of damages

*Facts* - as stated in the judgment of Lord Denning MR.

Lord Denning MR:

'Mr Jarvis is a solicitor, employed by a local authority at Barking. In 1969 he was minded to go for Christmas to Switzerland. He was looking forward to a skiing holiday. It is his one fortnight's holiday in the year. He prefers it in the winter rather than in the summer.

Mr Jarvis read a brochure issued by Swan Tours Ltd. He was much attracted by the description of Morlialp, Giswil, Central Switzerland. I will not read the whole of it, but just pick out some of the principal attractions:

"House Party Centre with special resident host ... Morlialp is a most wonderful little resort on a sunny plateau ... Up there you will find yourself in the midst of beautiful alpine scenery which in winter becomes a wonderland of sun, snow and ice, with a wide variety of fine ski runs, a skating rink and exhilarating toboggan run ... Why did we choose the Hotel Krone ... mainly and most of all because of the 'Gemutlichkeit' and friendly welcome you will receive from Herr and Frau Weibel ... The Hotel Krone has its Alphutte Bar which will be open several evenings a week ... No doubt you will be in for a great time when you book this house party holiday ... Mr Weibel, the charming owner, speaks English."

On the same page, in a special yellow box, it was said:

"Swan's House Party in Morlialp. All these House Party arrangements are included in the price of your holiday. Welcome party on arrival. Afternoon tea and cake for 7 days. Swiss dinner by candlelight. Fondue party. Yodler evening. Chali farewell party in the 'Alphutte Bar'. Service of representative."

Alongside, on the same page, there was a special note about ski packs:

"Hire of Skis, Sticks and Boots ... Ski Tuition ... 12 days £11.10."

In August 1969, on the faith of that brochure, Mr Jarvis booked a 15 day holiday with ski pack. The total charge was £63.45 including Christmas supplement. He was to fly from Gatwick to Zurich on 20 December 1969 and return on 3 January 1970.

The plaintiff went on the holiday but he was very disappointed. He was a man of about 35 and he expected to be one of a house party of some 30 or so people. Instead he found there were only 13 during the first week. In the second week there was no house party at all. He was the only person there. Mr Weibel could not speak English. So there was Mr Jarvis, in the second week, in this hotel, with no house party at all and no one could speak English except himself. He was very disappointed too with the skiing. It was some distance away at Giswil. There were no ordinary length skis. There were only mini-skis, about 3 feet long. So he did not get his skiing as he wanted to. In the second week he did get some longer skis for a couple of days, but then, because of the boots, his feet got rubbed and he could not continue, even with the long skis. So his skiing holiday, from his point of view, was pretty well ruined.

There were many other matters too. They appear trivial when they are set down in writing, but I have no doubt they loomed large in Mr Jarvis' mind when coupled with the other disappointments. He did not have the nice Swiss cakes which he was hoping for. The only cakes for tea were potato crisps and little dry nut cakes. The yodler evening consisted of one man from the locality who came, in his working clothes, for a little while and sang four or five songs very quickly. The "Alphutte Bar" was an unoccupied annexe which was only open one evening. There was a representative, Mrs Storr, there during the first week, but she was not there during the second week.

The matter was summed up by the judge:

"During the first week, he got a holiday in Switzerland which was, to some extent, inferior ... and as to the second week, he got a holiday which was very largely inferior to what he was led to expect."

What is the legal position? I think that the statements in the brochure were representations or warranties. The breaches of them give Mr Jarvis a right to damages. It is not necessary to decide whether they were representations or warranties: because since the Misrepresentation Act 1967 there is a remedy in damages for misrepresentations as well as for breach of warranty.

The one question in the case is: what is the amount of damages? The judge seems to have taken the difference in value between what he paid for and what he got. He said that he intended to give "the difference between the two values and no other damages" under any other head. He thought that Mr Jarvis had got half of what he paid for. So the judge gave him half the amount which he had paid, namely £31.72. Mr Jarvis appeals to this court. He says that the damages ought to have been much more.

What is the right way of assessing damages? It has often been said that on a breach of contract, damages cannot be given for mental distress. I think that those limitations are out of date. In a proper case, damages for shock can be recovered in tort. One such case is a contract for a holiday, or any other contract to provide entertainment and enjoyment. If the contracting party breaks his contract, damages can be given for the disappointment, the distress, the upset and frustration caused by the breach. I know that it is difficult to assess in terms of money, but it is no more difficult than the assessment which the courts have to make every day in personal injury cases for loss of amenities.

I think the judge was in error in taking the sum paid for the holiday, £63.45, and halving it. The right measure of damages is to compensate him for the loss of entertainment and enjoyment which he was promised and which he did not get.

Looking at the matter quite broadly, I think the damages in this case should be the sum of £125 ... I would allow the appeal accordingly.'

Edmund-Davies LJ:

'... When a man has paid for and properly expects an invigorating and amusing holiday and, through no fault of his, returns home dejected because his expectations have been largely unfulfilled, in my judgment it would be quite wrong to say that his disappointment must find no reflection in the damages to be awarded. Instead of "a great time", the plaintiff's reasonable and proper hopes were largely and lamentably unfulfilled. To arrive at a proper compensation for the defendants' failure is no easy matter. But in my judgment, we should not be compensating the plaintiff excessively were we to award him the £125 damages proposed by Lord Denning MR. I therefore concur in allowing this appeal.'

Stephenson LJ:

'I agree. What damage has the plaintiff suffered for the loss to him which has resulted from the defendants' breaches of this winter sports holiday contract and was within the reasonable contemplation of the parties to this contract as a likely result of its being so broken? This seems to me to be the question raised by this interesting case.

The judge has, as I understand his judgment, held that the value of the plaintiff's loss was what he paid under the contract for his holiday; that as a result of the defendants' breaches of contract he has lost not the whole of what he has paid for, but, broadly speaking, a half of it; and what he has lost and what reduces its value by about one half, includes such inconvenience as the plaintiff suffered from the holiday he got not being, by reason of the defendants' breaches, as valuable as the holiday he paid for.

I agree with my Lord, that the judge was wrong in taking, as I think he must have taken, the amount the plaintiff paid the defendants for his holiday, as the value of the holiday which they agreed to provide. They ought to have contemplated and no doubt did contemplate, that he was accepting their offer of this holiday as an offer of something which would benefit him and which he would enjoy, and that if they broke their contract and provided him with a holiday lacking in some of the things which they contracted to include in it, they would thereby reduce his enjoyment of the holiday and the benefit he would derive from it.

These considerations lead me to agree with my Lords that rather than try to put a value on the subject matter of this contract, first as promised and then as performed, and to include the inconvenience to the plaintiff in the process, we should award the plaintiff a sum of general damages for all the breaches of contract at the figure suggested by Lord Denning MR.

I agree that the appeal should be allowed and the plaintiff be awarded £125 damages.'

**Jobson v Johnson** [1989] 1 WLR 1026 Court of Appeal (Kerr, Dillon and Nicholls LJJ)

Penalty clause?

*Facts*

In a sale agreement, in writing, dated 12 August 1982, two brothers agreed to sell 62,666 of their shares in Southend United Football Club Ltd to the defendant's nominee for £40,000. In a side letter written the same day by the defendant and countersigned by the brothers, the defendant agreed to pay a further six half-yearly instalments totalling over £300,000, the payments to begin in February 1984. Paragraph 6 of that side letter made provision for default including the fact that the defendant would, on default, transfer to the brothers shares totalling not less than 44.9 per cent of the issued share capital in the football club, together with variable monetary payments depending on which instalment(s) was/were defaulted. The defendant defaulted at the first instalment. Subsequent arrangements were made for variation of the contract but the defendant, having paid one of the new (varied) instalments again defaulted. The brothers then assigned their rights to the plaintiff who sought to enforce the contract. At first instance Harman J decided that para 6 of the side letter amounted to a penalty clause, but that it was nevertheless enforceable. The defendant appealed.

*Held*

1) Whether a clause was a penalty clause was a question of construction, to be decided in the light of the circumstances at the time of making the contract and in the present case, since para 6 provided for repurchase of the shares at a fixed price regardless of the extent of the defendant's default, it amounted to a penalty clause.

2) (Kerr LJ dissenting) the penalty clause was unenforceable to the extent that it provided for compensation to the innocent party in excess of his actual loss.

Nicholls LJ:

'Although in practice a penalty clause in a contract ... is effectively a dead letter, it is important in the present case to note that, contrary to the submissions of counsel for the defendant, the strict legal position is not that such a clause is simply struck out of the contract, as though with a blue pencil, so that the contract takes effect as if it had never been included therein. Strictly, the legal position is that the clause remains in the contract and can be sued on, but it will not be enforced by the court beyond the sum which represents, in the events which have happened, the actual loss of the party seeking payment. There are many cases which make this clear.'

*Commentary*

Applied: *Public Works Commissioner* v *Hills* [1906] AC 368, *Wall* v *Rederiaktiebolaget Luggude* [1915] 3 KB 66 and *Bridge* v *Campbell Discount Co Ltd* [1962] 2 WLR 439.

**Koufos v C Czarnikow Ltd (The Heron II)** [1967] 3 WLR 1491 House of Lords (Lord Reid, Lord Morris of Borth-y-Gest, Lord Hodson, Lord Pearce and Lord Upjohn)

Damages - loss of profit

*Facts*

By a charter party made in London in October 1960 between Nomicos Ltd, as agents for the appellant (the owner of the Heron II) and the respondent charterers, the charterers chartered the Heron II, then in Piraeus expected ready to load 25-27 October all being well to proceed to Constanza and there load a consignment of 3,000 metric tons of sugar and proceed with all convenient speed to Basrah. Lay days were not to commence before 27 October and if the ship was not ready to load by 10 November, the charterers had the option of cancelling the charter party. The charterers also had the option of discharging the cargo at Jeddah. The vessel did load as expected and began the voyage to Basrah, a voyage of approximately 20 days. The vessel deviated from the voyage by calling at Berbera for three days, where she loaded livestock and fodder for Bahrein. The vessel again deviated from the voyage when she called at Bahrein to discharge the livestock and fodder. She stayed there for three days. A third deviation was made, to call at Abadan, for one day. These deviations were made without the knowledge or consent of the charterers. The voyage was prolonged by nine days in all as a result. At all times, the charterers intended to sell the sugar for cash, promptly on arrival. They did so. The shipowners admitted that they were in breach of the charter party and the charterers contended that if the sugar had arrived even five days earlier, it would have commanded a higher price. It was found as a fact that there was, at all material times, a market for sugar in Basrah and the prices fluctuated considerably. The existence of the market was known to the shipowners at all material times, but they did not have any detailed knowledge of it. It was generally known that sugar was a perishable commodity and that there was some urgency in carrying it. However, the fall in the price had been caused by the arrival of a large consignment at Basrah four days earlier. This was nothing unusual or unpredictable. The umpire appointed by the arbitrator held that the charterers were entitled to recover as damages the difference between the price of the sugar when it should have been delivered, and the price when it was in fact delivered. The shipowners appealed and McNair J held that the charterers were only entitled to recover as damages interest on the value of the cargo during the period of delay, plus expenses. The charterers appealed and the Court of Appeal restored the umpire's award. The shipowners then appealed.

*Held*

Loss of profit was recoverable as damages.

Lord Reid:

'... the question for decision is whether a plaintiff can recover as damages for breach of contract, a loss of a kind which the defendant, when he made the contract, ought to have realised was not unlikely to result from a breach of contract causing delay in delivery. I use the words "not likely" as denoting a degree of probability considerably less than an even chance, but nevertheless not very unusual and easily foreseeable.

For over a century, everyone has agreed that remoteness of damage in contract must be determined by applying the rule (or rules) ... in *Hadley* v *Baxendale* ... I am satisfied that the court did not intend that every type of damage which was reasonably foreseeable by the parties when the contract was made, should either be considered as arising naturally, ie in the usual course of things, or be supposed to have been in the contemplation of the parties ... the parties are not supposed to contemplate as grounds for the recovery of damage, any type of loss or damage which, on the knowledge available to the defendant, would appear to him as only likely to occur in a small minority of cases ...

... The crucial question is whether, on the information available to the defendant when the contract is made, he should, or a reasonable man in his positinn would, have realised that such loss was sufficiently likely to result from the breach of contract to make it proper to hold that the loss flowed naturally from the breach, or that loss of that kind should have been within his contemplation.

The modern rule of tort ... imposes a much wider liability ... And there is good reason for the difference. In contract, if one party wishes to protect himself against a risk which, to the other party, would appear unusual, he can direct the other party's attention to it before the contract is made ... but in tort there is no opportunity for the injured party to protect himself in that way.

For a considerable time there was a tendency to set narrow limits to awards of damages. But later, a more liberal tendency can be seen ... I attach importance to what was said in this regard in *R & H Hall Ltd* v *W H Pim (Junior) & Co Ltd* (1928) 33 Com Cas 324 HL.

In that case, Pim sold a cargo of wheat to Hall, but failed to deliver it. Hall had resold the wheat, but as a result of Pim's breach of contract, lost the profit which they would have made on their sub-sale. Three of their Lordships dealt with the case on the basis that the relevant question was whether it ought to have been in the contemplation of the parties that a resale was probable. The finding of the arbitrators was:

"The arbitrators are unable to find that it was in the contemplation of the parties, or ought to have been in the contemplation of Messrs Pim at that time, that the cargo would be resold or was likely to be resold before delivery; in fact, the chances of its being resold as a cargo and of its being taken delivery of by Messrs Hall, were about equal."

On that finding, the Court of Appeal had decided in favour of Pim, saying that as the arbitrators had stated as a fact that the chances of the cargo being resold or not being resold were equal, it was therefore "idle to speak of a likelihood or of a probability of a resale".

Viscount Dunedin pointed out that it was for the court to decide what was to be supposed to have been in the contemplation of the parties and then said:

"I do not think that 'probability' ... means that the chances are all in favour of the event happening. To make a thing probable, it is enough, in my view, that there is an even chance of its happening. That is the criterion I apply; and in view of the facts, as I have said above, I think there was here, in the contemplation of parties, the probability of a resale."

He did not have to consider how much less than a 50 per cent chance would amount to a probability in this sense.

Lord Shaw of Dunfermline went rather further. He said:

"To what extent, in a contract of goods for future delivery the extent of damages is in contemplation of parties, is always extremely doubtful. The main business fact is that they are thinking of the contract being performed and not of its not being performed. But with regard to the latter, if the contract shows that there were instances or stages which made ensuing losses or damage a not unlikely result of the breach of the contract, then all such results must be reckoned to be within not only the scope of the contract, but the contemplation of parties as to its breach."

Lord Phillimore was less definite and, perhaps, went even further. He said that the sellers of the wheat knew that the buyers "might well sell it over again and make a profit on the resale" and that being so, they "must be taken to have consented to this state of things and thereby to have made themselves liable to pay" the profit on a resale.

It may be that there was nothing very new in this, but I think that *Hall*'s case must be taken to have established that damages are not to be regarded as too remote merely because, on the knowledge available to the defendant when the contract was made, the chance of the occurrence of the event which caused the damage would have appeared to him to be rather less than an even chance. I would agree with Lord Shaw that it is generally sufficient that that event would have appeared to the defendant as not unlikely to occur. It is hardly ever possible in this matter to assess probabilities with any degree of mathematical accuracy.

But then it has been said that the liability of defendants has been further extended by *Victoria Laundry (Windsor) Ltd* v *Newman Industries Ltd* [1949] 2 KB 528. I do not think so. The plaintiffs bought a large boiler from the defendants and the defendants were aware of the general nature of the plaintiffs' business and of the plaintiffs' intention to put the boiler into use as soon as possible. Delivery of the boiler was delayed in breach of contract and the plaintiffs claimed as damages loss of profit caused by the delay. A large part of the profit claimed would have resulted from some specially lucrative contracts which the plaintiffs could have completed if they had had the boiler; that was rightly disallowed because the defendants had no knowledge of these contracts. But Asquith LJ then said:

"It does not, however, follow that the plaintiffs are precluded from recovering some general (and perhaps conjectural) sums for loss of business in respect of dyeing contracts to be reasonably expected, any more than in respect of laundering contracts to be reasonably expected."

It appears to me that this was well justified on the earlier authorities. It was certainly not unlikely on the information which the defendants had when making the contract, that delay in delivering the boiler would result in loss of business. Indeed, it would seem that that was more than an even chance. And there was nothing new in holding that damages should be estimated on a conjectural basis. This House had approved of that as early as 1813 in *Hall* v *Ross* (1813) 1 Dow 210 HL.

But what is said to create a "landmark" is the statement of principles by Asquith LJ. This does, to some extent, go beyond the older authorities and in so far as it does so, I do not agree with it. In paragraph (2) it is said, page 539, that the plaintiff is entitled to recover "such part of the loss actually resulting as was, at the time of the contract, reasonably foreseeable as liable to result from the breach". To bring in reasonable foreseeability appears to me to be confusing measure of damages in contract with measure of damages in tort. A great many extremely unlikely results are reasonably foreseeable: it is true that Lord Asquith may have meant foreseeable as a likely result and if that is all he meant, I would not object further than to say that I think that the phrase is liable to be misunderstood. For the same reason, I would take exception to the phrase, page 540, "liable to result" in paragraph (5). Liable is a very vague word, but I think that one would usually say that when a person foresees a very improbable result, he foresees that it is liable to happen. (390) I agree with the first half of paragraph (6) page 540. For the best part of a century, it has not been required that the defendant could have foreseen that a breach of contract must necessarily result in the loss which has occurred. But I cannot agree with the second half of that paragraph. It has never been held to be sufficient in contract that the loss was foreseeable as "a serious possibility" or "a real danger" or as being "on the cards". It appears to me that in the ordinary use of language, there is a wide gulf between saying that some event is not unlikely or quite likely to happen, and saying merely that it is a serious possibility, a real danger, or on the cards. If the tests of "real danger" or "serious possibility" are in future to be authoritative, then the *Victoria Laundry* case would indeed be a landmark, because it would mean that *Hadley* v *Baxendale* would be differently decided today. I certainly could not understand any court deciding that, on the information available to the carrier in that case, the stoppage of the mill was neither a serious possibility nor a real danger. If those tests are to prevail in the future, then let us cease to pay lip service to the rule in *Hadley* v *Baxendale*. But in my judgment, to adopt these tests would extend liability for breach of contract beyond what is reasonable or desirable. From the limited knowledge which I have of commercial affairs, I would not expect such an extension to be welcomed by the business community and from the legal point of view, I can find little or nothing to recommend it.

It appears to me that without relying in any way on the *Victoria Laundry* case, and taking the principle that had already been established, the loss of profit claimed in this case was not too remote to be recoverable as damages.

For the reasons which I have given, I would dismiss this appeal.'

Lord Morris of Borth-y-Gest:

'... The classic judgment in *Hadley* v *Baxendale* has continuously been recognised as enshrining and formulating the guiding rules which are to be followed in deciding whether damage which has been the result of a breach of contract should be paid for by the contract breaker. The numerous reported decisions since *Hadley* v *Baxendale* was decided, show that sometimes there have been problems relating to the meaning and intention of the words used in the judgment in that case and that sometimes the problems have been those of ascertaining facts and then of relating accepted principle to the facts as found. When consideration has been given to the meaning and insertion of the words used in the judgment in *Hadley* v *Baxendale*, it has so often been manifest that words, which are but servants to convey and express meanings - cannot always be servants of precision and may sometimes be given a dominance which is above their status. If "Language is the dress of thought", it is the thought that must be understood.

The famous rule in *Hadley* v *Baxendale* postulates a contract which one party has broken and relates to the "damages which the other party ought to receive" ... In the present case there was no special communication of special circumstances by reference to which the contract of carriage was made. The problem present was therefore whether, with the knowledge possessed by the parties at the time when the contract was made, the loss in fact suffered by the respondents due to the delayed arrival (in breach of contract) of the sugar could fairly and reasonably be considered as arising naturally (ie according to the usual course of things) from such a breach. When parties enter into a contract, they do not ordinarily at such times, seek to work out or to calculate the exact consequences of a breach of their contract. On the facts of the present case, it is however pertinent to pose the enquiry as to what the natural ordinary and sensible answer of the appellant would have been if he had asked himself what the result for the respondents would be if he (the appellant) in breach of contract and therefore unjustifiably, caused his ship to arrive at Basrah some nine or ten days later than it could and should have arrived. While the appellant did not know precisely what plans the respondents had made, he could be reasonably sure of one thing, that if his ship was nine days later in arriving than it could and should have arrived, some financial loss to the respondents, or to an endorsee of the bill of lading, might result. I use the word "might" at this stage, so as to point to the problem which is high-lighted in this case. It is here that words and phrases begin to crowd in and to compete. Must the loss of the respondents be such that the appellant could see that it was certain to result? Or could it suffice if the loss was probable or was likely to result or was liable to result? In the present context, what do these words denote? If there must be selection as between them, which one is to be employed to convey the intended meaning?

I think that it is clear that the loss need not be such that the contract breaker could see that it was certain to result. The question that arises concerns the measure of prevision which should fairly and reasonably be ascribed to him.

My Lords, in applying the guidance given in *Hadley* v *Baxendale* I would hope that no undue emphasis would be placed upon any one word or phrase. If a party has suffered some special and peculiar loss in reference to some particular arrangements of his which were unknown to the other party and were not communicated to the other party and were not therefore in the contemplation of the parties at the time when they made the contract, then it would be unfair and unreasonable to charge the contract breaker with such special and peculiar loss. If, however, there are not "special and extraordinary circumstances beyond the reasonable prevision of the parties", then it becomes very largely a question of fact as to whether, in any particular case, a loss can "fairly and reasonably" be considered as arising in the normal course of things. The result in any particular case need not depend upon giving pride of place to any one of such phrases as "liable to result" or "likely to result" or "not unlikely to result". Each one of these phrases may be of help, but so may many others.

I regard the illuminating judgment of the Court of Appeal in *Victoria Laundry (Windsor) Ltd* v *Newman Industries Ltd* as almost valuable analysis of the rule. It was there pointed out that in order to make a contract breaker liable under what was called "either rule" in *Hadley* v *Baxendale*, it is not necessary that he should actually have asked himself what loss is liable to result from a breach, but that it suffices that if he had considered the question he would, as a reasonable man, have concluded that the loss in question was liable to result. Nor need it be proved, in order to recover a particular loss, that upon a given state of knowledge he could, as a reasonable man, foresee that a breach must necessarily result in that loss. Certain illustrative phrases are employed in that case. They are valuable by way of exposition but, for my part, I doubt whether the phrase "on the cards" has a sufficiently clear meaning, or possesses such a comparable shade of meanings, as to qualify it to take its place with the various other phrases which line up as expositions of the rule.

If the problem in the present case is that of relating accepted principle to the facts which have been found, I entertain no doubt that if, at the time of their contract, the parties had considered what the consequence would be if the arrival of the ship at Basraah was delayed, they would have contemplated that some loss to the respondents was likely or was liable to result. The appellant, at the time he made his contract, must have known that if, in breach of contract, his ship did not arrive at Basrah when it ought to arrive, he would be liable to pay damages. He would not know that a loss to the respondents was certain or inevitable, but he must, as a reasonable businessman, have contemplated that the respondents would very likely suffer loss and that it would be, or would be likely to be, a loss referable to market price fluctuations at Basrah. I cannot think that he should escape liability by saying that he would only be aware of a possibility of loss but not of a probability or certainty of it. He might have used any one of many phrases. He might have said that a loss would be likely: or that a loss would not be unlikely: or that a loss was liable to result: or that the risk that delay would cause loss to the respondents was a serious possibility: or that there would be a real danger of a loss: or that the risk of his being liable to have to pay for the loss was one that he ought commercially to take into account. As a practical businessman, he would not have paused to reflect on the possible nuances of meaning of any one of these phrases. Nor would he have sent for a dictionary.

Since, in awarding the damages, the aim is to award a sum which as nearly as possible will put the injured party in the position in which he would have been if the breach of contract had not caused him loss and if, in all the circumstances, he had acted reasonably in an effort to mitigate his loss, I think that it must follow that where this delay is in arrival, in many cases the actual loss suffered (above the amount of which there ought to be recovery) can be measured by comparing the market price of the goods at the date when they should have arrived and the market price when they did arrive. That prima facie is the measure of the damages ... I would dismiss the appeal.'

Lord Hodson:

'My Lords, the broad question which arises in the appeal is what is the correct measure of damages for wrongful delay by a shipowner in the performance of a contract for the carriage of goods by sea.

The respondents contend that the ordinary measure of damages for delay in delivery of goods for which there is a market, is the difference between the market value of the goods at their destination on the date when they arrive and the value at the date when the should have arrived if there had been no breach of contract. The loss so measured is one which arises naturally according to the usual course of things. This right to recover does not depend on any special knowledge of the party in breach. It applies to contracts of carriage by sea and by land in all ordinary cases.

The appellant contends on the other hand, that except in special circumstances which are not to be found in this case, the measure of damage is limited to the interest on the value of the goods during the period of delay ... The appellant ... accepted the established authority of the judgment in *Hadley* v *Baxendale*.

... The appellant argued that the fluctuations of market due to unforeseen and unpredictable causes during the period of delay, are not of themselves "according to the usual course of things". He argued that there were no facts here to bring the second part of the rule into operation and in this I agree with him, for no special notice was given. Hence he said that damages for loss of market are not recoverable and that these damages could only be recovered in special cases covered by the second part of the rule. The word "probable" in *Hadley* v *Baxendale* covers both parts of the rule and it is of vital importance in applying the rule to consider what the court meant by using this word in its context. The common use of this word is no doubt to imply that something is more likely to happen than not. In conversation, if one says to another, "If you go out in this weather you will probably catch a cold", this is, I think equivalent to saying that one believes there is an odds-on chance that the other will catch a cold.

The word "probable" need not, however, bear this narrow meaning. In *R & H Hall Ltd* v *WH Pim (Junior) & Co Ltd*, Viscount Dunedin, after stating his belief in a general agreement that the law as to calculation of damages due under breach of a contract was settled by the case of *Hadley* v *Baxendale*, said that the difficulty lies in the application to the facts of each case.

The instant case furnishes an example of this difficulty.

A close study of the rule was made by the Court of Appeal in the case of *Victoria Laundry (Windsor) Ltd* v *Newman Industries Ltd*. The judgment of the court, consisting of Tucker, Asquith and Singleton LJJ, was delivered by Asquith LJ, who suggested the phrase "liable to result" as appropriate to describe the degree of probability required. This may be a colourless expression, but I do not find it possible to improve on it. If the word "likelihood" is used, it may convey the impression that the chances are all in favour of the thing happening, an idea which I would reject.

... I would dismiss the appeal.'

Lord Pearce:

My Lords, in *Hadley* v *Baxendale*, the court attempted to clarify and define the boundaries of damage in contract. In *The Wagon Mound*, the Privy Council attempt a similar task with regard to damages in tort. It was suggested in argument that there was, or should be, one principle of damages for both contract and tort and that guidance for one could be obtained from the other. I do not find such a comparison helpful. In the case of contract, two parties, usually with some knowledge of one another, deliberately undertake mutual duties. They have the opportunity to define clearly in respect of what they shall and shall not be liable. The law has to say what shall be the boundaries of their liability where this is not expressed, defining that boundary in relation to what has been expressed and implied. In tort, two persons, usually unknown to one another, find that the acts or utterances of one have collided with the rights of the other and the court has to define what is the liability for the ensuing damage, whether it shall be shared and how far it extends. If one tries to find a concept of damages which will fit both these different problems, there is a danger of distorting the rules to accommodate one or the other and of producing a rule that is satisfactory for neither.

The whole rule in *Hadley* v *Baxendale* limits damages to that which may be regarded as being within the contemplation of the parties. The first part deals with those things that "may fairly and reasonably be considered as arising naturally, ie according to the usual course of things". Those are presumed to be within the contemplation of the parties.

Even the first part of the rule contains the necessity for the knowledge of certain basic facts, eg in *Hadley* v *Baxendale* the fact that it was a mill shaft to be carried. On this limited basis of knowledge, the horizon of contemplation is confined to things "arising naturally, ie according to the usual course of things".

Additional or "special" knowledge, however, may extend the horizon to include losses that are outside the natural course of events. And, of course, the extension of the horizon need not always increase the damages; it might introduce a knowledge of particular circumstances, eg a sub-contract, which show that the plaintiff would in fact suffer less damage than a more limited view of the circumstances might lead one to expect. According to whether one categorises a fact as basic knowledge or special knowledge, the case may come under the first part of the rule or the second. For that reason there is sometimes difference of opinion as to which is the part which governs a particular case and it may be that both parts govern it.

I do not think that Alderson B was directing his mind to whether something resulting in the natural course of events was an odds-on chance or not. A thing may be a natural (or even an obvious) result, even though the odds are against it. Suppose a contractor was employed to repair the ceiling of one of the Law Courts and did it so negligently that it collapsed on the heads of those in court. I should be inclined to think that any tribunal (including the learned Baron himself) would have found as a fact that the damage arose "naturally, ie according to the usual course of things". Yet if one takes into account the nights, weekends and vacations, when the ceiling might have collapsed, the odds against it collapsing on top of anybody's head are nearly ten to one. I do not believe that this aspect of the matter was fully considered and worked out in the judgment. He was thinking of causation and type of consequence rather than of odds ...

... The facts of the present case lead to the view that the loss of market arose naturally, ie according to the usual course of things, from the shipowner's deviation. The sugar was being exported to Basrah where, as the respondent knew, there was a sugar market. It was sold on arrival and fetched a lower price than it would have done had it arrived on time. The fall in market price was not due to any unusual or unpredictable factor.

Had this been a case of non-delivery on sale of goods, whether by sea or land, it is uncontested that the defendants would be liable for the loss of market. Had it been a case of delay in sale of goods, the prima facie rule is that the damage is the difference between "the value of the article contracted for at the time when it ought to have been and the time when it actually was delivered" ... I would dismiss the appeal.'

Lord Upjohn:

'My Lords, this appeal is concerned solely with the proper measure of damages for an admitted breach of contract by a shipowner, resulting in the late delivery of a cargo which he contracted to deliver to the port of discharge. The practical question is whether the charterer can claim damages for loss of market, as the cargo of sugar was to be delivered to a port where there is a market in that commodity.

The general principle upon which damages are assessed for breach of contract is succinctly stated by Parke B in *Robinson* v *Harman*: "Where a party sustains a loss by reason of a breach of contract, he is, so far as money can do it, to be placed in the same situation, with respect to damages, as if the contract had been performed."

Such general principles were, however, applied rather strictly for until *Hadley* v *Baxendale* was decided in 1854 the rule was that the damage resulting must be the proximate damage. With the increasing complications of life and the upsurge of industrial activities, these simple rules failed to give sufficient guidance to juries or, indeed, judges for the assessment of damages for breach of contract in more complicated cases.

Though stated by the learned Baron in one sentence, it contains and has always been interpreted as containing two branches and, for my part, I care not whether it is regarded as stating two rules or two branches of one rule, though I prefer the latter. Thus:

1)    Damages should be such as may naturally and usually arise from the breach, or

2)    Damages should be such as, in the special circumstances of the case known to both parties, may be reasonably supposed to have been in the contemplation of the parties, as the result of a breach, assuming the parties to have applied their minds to the contingency of there being such a breach.

... the claim for damages must be the natural consequence of the breach or in the contemplation of both parties. But in tort, a different test has been adopted in expanding the basic law of damages and I cannot accept the argument addressed to your Lordships that they remain the same. The test in tort, as now developed in the authorities, is that the tortfeasor is liable for any damage which he can reasonably foresee may happen as a result of the breach, however unlikely it may be, unless it can be brushed aside as far fetched. See *The Wagon Mound* cases ... This difference is very reasonable.

... The rule in *Hadley* v *Baxendale* has been followed in a multitude of cases ever since it was decided. I think that apart from some very early criticisms, it would be true to say that it stood without question until the case of *Victoria Laundry (Windsor) Ltd* v *Newman Industries Ltd*, where it received a colourful interpretation from Asquith LJ delivering the judgment of the court.

My Lords, in my opinion this appeal renders it necessary to determine the following questions:

1)    Has the *Victoria Laundry* case purported to alter the law and establish a somewhat different rule from that laid down in *Hadley* v *Baxendale* for the assessment of damages in contract?

2)    What, as a practical matter, is the test to be applied in ascertaining whether any particular consequence of a breach of contract should lead to recoverable damages as arising either naturally or such as may have been within the contemplation of the parties in the special circumstances of the case?

3)    Applying that test, what, on the facts of this case, is the proper measure of damages? Unless

4)    Is there some special rule of practice in relation to carriage of goods by sea? ...

1)    Upon the first point, it is, I think, clear that on a fair reading of the judgments of the majority of the Court of Appeal, they considered that the *Victoria Laundry* case did alter the law. That case was plainly within the second branch of the rule, but nevertheless, the observations of Asquith LJ were, in general terms, applicable to both branches. I do not myself think that the learned Lord Justice intended to alter the law. He was para-phrasing it and putting it into modern language and I shall refer to this under the next heading. If he was doing more, I would disagree with him. But for my part, I prefer to state the broad rule as follows: What was in the assumed contemplation of both parties, acting as reasonable men, in the light of the general or special facts (as the case may be)

known to both parties in regard to damages as the result of a breach of contract; I omit, for the moment, any adjectival qualification of the result, which I deal with in (2) below.

2)     Upon the second point, what, as a practical matter, is to be taken as within the contemplation of both parties as the result of a breach? The words 'probable result' held the field at first; they were used in the enunciation of the rule itself and adopted by Viscount Dunedin in *Hall* v *Pim* who, however, was careful to add that "probable", in his view, did not mean more than an even chance. Lord Shaw of Dunfermline in that case, interpreted the word probable in the sense of the not unlikely result.

Asquith LJ, in *Victoria Laundry*, used the words "likely to result" and he treated that as synonymous with a serious possibility or a real danger. He went on to equate that with the expression "on the cards" but, like all your Lordships, I deprecate the use of that phrase which is far too imprecise and, to my mind, is capable of denoting a most improbable and unlikely event, such as winning a prize on a premium bond on any given drawing.

But in my opinion, Asquith LJ was not attempting to do more than explain the rule ...

It is clear that on the one hand the test of foreseeability, as laid down in the case of tort, is not the test for breach of contract; nor, on the other hand, must the loser establish that the loss was a near certainty or an odds-on probability. I am content to adopt as the test a "real danger" or a "serious possibility". There may be a shade of difference between these two phrases, but the assessment of damages is not an exact science and what to one judge or jury will appear a real danger, will appear to another judge or jury to be a serious possibility. I do not think that the application of that test would have led to a different result in *Hadley* v *Baxendale*. I cannot see why Pickfords, in the absence of express mention, should have contemplated as a real danger or serious possibility that work at the factory would be brought to a halt while the shaft was away.

3)     Applying this test to the facts of this case, the first and most important matter for consideration is the contract contained in the charter party ...

It is perfectly true that at the time of the contract, nothing was said as to the purpose for which the charterer wanted the sugar delivered at Basrah; he might have wanted to do so to stock up his supply of sugar, or to carry out a contract already entered into which had nothing to do with the market at Basrah; or he might sell it during the voyage, but all that is pure speculation. It seems to me that on the facts of this case, the parties must be assumed to have contemplated that there would be a punctual delivery to the port of discharge and that port having a market in sugar, there was a real danger that as a result of a delay in breach of contract, the charterer would miss the market and would suffer loss accordingly. It being established that the goods were in fact destined for the market, the shipowner is liable for that loss.

4)     I turn then, to the last question ...

[Having decided that there was no different rule, he concluded:]

... For these reasons I would dismiss this appeal.'

*Commentary*

See also *Parsons (H) (Livestock) Ltd* v *Uttley Ingham & Co Ltd* [1977] 3 WLR 990.

**Lavarack v Woods of Colchester Ltd** [1966] 3 WLR 706 Court of Appeal (Lord Denning MR, Diplock and Russell LJJ)

Breach of contract - measure of damages

*Facts*

The plaintiff entered into a five-year service agreement with the defendants at £4,000 per annum plus such bonuses as the defendants' directors may at their discretion award. He undertook that he would not, during that time, be engaged or interested in other concerns. After two years or so he was wrongfully dismissed: immediately afterwards, he accepted employment with M Co at £1,500 per annum and he bought half the shares of that company, hoping that his own work would improve their value. In addition he invested £14,000 in V Co, a rival of the defendants. The following year the defendants discontinued their bonus scheme and, under the new arrangements, the plaintiff would have received an extra £1,000 per annum.

*Held* (Lord Denning MR dissenting)

The plaintiff was not entitled to £2,000 (2 x £1,000 in lieu of bonuses) and any improvement in the value of the shares in V Co would be disregarded in assessing his damages. However, the estimated increase in the plaintiff's half interest in M Co would be set against the damages awarded as this was part of his mitigation of his loss.

Diplock LJ:

'The general rule ... that in an action for breach of contract a defendant is not liable for not doing that which he is not bound to do, has been generally accepted as correct and in my experience at the Bar and on the Bench has been repeatedly applied in subsequent cases. The law is concerned with legal obligations only and the law of contract only with legal obligations created by mutual agreement between contractors - not with the expectations, however reasonable, of one contractor that the other will do something that he has assumed no legal obligation to do ...

In the present case if the defendants had continued their bonus scheme, it may well be that on the true construction of this contract of employment the plaintiff would have been entitled to be recompensed for the loss of the bonus to which he would have been likely to be legally entitled under his service agreement until its expiry. But it is unnecessary to decide this. They were under no contractual obligation to him to continue the scheme and in fact it was discontinued. His legal entitlement under the contract on which he sues would thus have been limited ... to his salary of £4,000 per annum. And there, in my view, is the end of the matter. I know of no principle on which he can claim as damages for breach of one service agreement compensation for remuneration which might have become due under some imaginary future agreement which the plaintiffs did not make with him but might have done if they wished. If this were right, in every action for damages for wrongful dismissal, the plaintiff would be entitled to recover not only the remuneration that he would have received during the currency of his service agreement but also some additional sum for loss of the chance of its being renewed on its expiry.

I would disallow the sum of £2,000 included in the assessment ...'

**Lombard North Central plc v Butterworth** [1987] 2 WLR 7 Court of Appeal (Lawton, Mustill and Nicholls LJJ)

Contract - repudiation - penalty?

*Facts*

The plaintiffs leased a computer to the defendants for a period of five years. The agreement involved payment of a deposit and 19 subsequent instalments. The contract of lease contained three clauses which are relevant to determination of the dispute:

Clause 2 provided that punctual payment of the instalments was 'of the essence' of the contract.

Clause 5 rendered failure to make punctual payments a ground for terminating the contract.

Clause 6 entitled the plaintiffs on termination to all arrears of instalments plus all future instalments.

The defendant defaulted on the sixth instalment. The plaintiffs obtained summary judgment, the master concluding that the defendant had repudiated the contract enabling the plaintiffs to claim future instalments.

The defendant appealed contending that he should not be liable for more than the amount due at the date of termination because:

a) clause 6 was a penalty clause and therefore unenforceable, and

CONTRACT LAW

b) the defendant's conduct did not amount to a repudiation of the contract.

*Held*

Clause 6 was a penalty clause. However clause 2 had the effect of making default in punctual payment a breach going to the root of the contract entitling the plaintiffs to terminate independently of clause 6 and to recover common law damages.

Mustill LJ:

'Three issues were canvassed before us. (1) Is clause 6 to be disregarded on the ground that it creates a penalty? (2) Apart from clause 2 was the master correct in holding that the conduct of the defendant amounted to a wrongful repudiation of the contract and that the sum claimed was recoverable in damages? (3) Does the provision in clause 2(a) of the agreement that time is of the essence have the effect of making the defendant's late payment of the outstanding instalment a repudiatory breach? ...

Proceeding to deal with the third point only he contends that the plaintiffs contention is correct since clause 2 is a fundamental term of the contract. In support of this point he discusses a Privy Council case *Steedman* v *Drinkle* [1916] AC 275 and *Photo Productions Ltd* v *Securicor Transport Ltd* [1980] 1 All ER 556 ...

The plaintiffs are entitled to retain the damages which the master has awarded. This is not a result which I view with much satisfaction, partly because the plaintiffs have achieved by one means a result which the law of penalties might have prevented them from achieving by another ...'

Nicholls LJ:

'... the criticism of clause 6 advanced on behalf of the defendant was confined to the absence of provision giving credit for the net amount obtained by the plaintiff on any resale of the goods effected by it after retaking possession. Argument in this court took place on the footing that the presence or absence of such a provision, which I shall call a "rescue price allowance" was crucial on the penalty point, counsel for the defendant putting forward that the omission of such allowance was a fundamental objection to the clause ...

[He then went on to consider whether the addition of a 'resale price allowance' would render the clause no longer a penalty.]

... In my view, in the absence of a repudiatory breach that assumption is misconceived. The ratio of the decision of this court in *Financings Ltd* v *Baldock* [1963] 1 All ER 443 was that when an owner determines a hire-purchase agreement in exercise of a right so to do given him by the agreement, in the absence of repudiation he can recover damages for any breaches up to the date of termination but not thereafter, and a "minimum payment" clause which purports to oblige the hirer to pay larger sums than this is unenforceable as a penalty ... In my view, applying the principle enunciated in *Financings Ltd* v *Baldock* to this case leads inescapably to the conclusion that in the absence of a repudiatory breach clause 6(a) is a penalty insofar as it purports to oblige the defendant, regardless of the seriousness or triviality of the breach which led to the plaintiffs terminating the agreement by retaking possession of the computer. ... From what I have said it will be apparent that I consider that, in the absence of a repudiatory breach, the outcome of this case is not dependent on the inclusion or exclusion of a resale price allowance, and indeed the legal result would have been the same if clause 6 had contained a "resale price allowance" ... I turn to the second issue, which is whether the loss sustained by the plaintiff in this case by reason of the defendant's default in payment of the instalments amounted to the loss of the whole hiring transaction. It would have so amounted if, but only if, the defendant's conduct amounted to a repudiation of the lease agreement and that repudiation was accepted by the plaintiffs ...

[The judge continued by analysing whether in the absence of clause 2, the defendant's conduct amounted to a repudiation and concluded that it did not.]

I must now consider that time of payments having been made of the essence by clause 2 it was open to the plaintiffs, once default in payment had occurred, to treat the agreement as repudiated by the defendant, and claim damages for loss of the whole transaction, even though in the absence of this provision such a default would not have had that consequence. ... The provision in clause 2 has to be read and construed in conjunction with the other provisions including clauses 5 and 6. So read, it is to be noted that failure to pay any instalment triggers a right for the plaintiff to terminate the agreement with the expressed consequence that the defendant becomes liable to make payments which assume that the defendant is unable to make good to the plaintiffs the loss by them of the whole transaction. Given that context, the "time of the essence" provision seems to me to be intended to bring about the result that default in punctual payments is to be regarded as a breach going to the root of the contract and, hence, as giving rise to consequences in damages attendant on such a breach.'

## McRae v Commonwealth Disposals Commission

See chapter 8 - Mistake

## Monarch Steamship Co Ltd v A/B Karlshamns Oljefabriker [1949] AC 196 House of Lords (Lord Porter, Lord Wright, Lord Uthwatt, Lord du Parcq and Lord Morton of Henryton)

Damages - cost of trans-shipment following delay

*Facts*

In April 1939 M chartered S's steamship which sailed to Rashin to load a cargo of soya beans purchased from M by K. The ship left Rashin on 12 May. Contrary to the terms of the charterparty, the ship was unseaworthy: considerable delay resulted from deviations for repairs. On 7 June, in conformity with the charterparty and bills of lading, M nominated Karlshamn as the port of discharge, but S was not told until mid-August that delivery was to be made there. At the outbreak of war (3 September), the voyage (which should have taken 63 days) was still not completed and the ship was ordered by the Admiralty to proceed to Glasgow which she reached on 21 October. There, M took delivery of the cargo and transferred the bills of lading to K who had chartered three neutral ships to carry the cargo to Karlshamn. K sued S for damages for breach of contract in respect of the cost of trans-shipment.

*Held*

K was entitled to succeed as the damage was the direct and natural consequence of S's breach of contract in failing to provide a seaworthy ship.

Lord Porter:

'But, it is said, to give such damages ... is to give damages for delay in delivery - a remedy which is not given in the case of carriage of goods by sea. No doubt, expressions of opinion to that effect are to be found, perhaps more frequently in the days of sailing ships when prolonged delay was to be expected, but it never was a rule of law - merely a working practice answering to the circumstances of the time and subject to the consideration that the contract must be reasonably performed. In the present case the result of the delay was to deprive the shipper and his indorsee of the goods at Karlshamn. Of course, if they could replace them by buying other goods there, it was their duty to diminish the damages by doing so, but they could not do so since no soya beans were procurable at Karlshamn and, in default, the only way of placing themselves in the same position as if the contract had been performed was to engage transport to carry the beans to that port. Accepting, then, the view that [S] ought to have foreseen the likelihood of was occuring and of an embargo being imposed, I should find it liable to pay the damages claimed and would dismiss the appeal.'

Lord Wright:

' ... in *Smith, Hogg & Co*'s case the unseaworthiness created in the vessel instability which, combined with negligence of the master, caused the loss. There was no new law laid down in that case. From one point of view unseaworthiness must generally, perhaps always in a sense, be a "remote" cause. To satisfy the definition of unseaworthiness it must exist at the commencement of the voyage. It must, however, still be in effective operation at the time of the casualty if it is to be a cause of the casualty, and from its very nature it must always, or almost always, operate by means of and along with the specific immediate peril. That is because the essence of unseaworthiness as a cause of loss or damage is that the unseaworthy ship is unfit to meet the peril.

In other words, the vessel would not have suffered the loss or injury if she had been seaworthy.'

## Naughton v O'Callaghan [1990] 3 All ER 191 High Court (Waller J)

Misrepresentation - assessment of damages

*Facts*

The plaintiffs bought Fondu, a thoroughbred colt, for 26,000 guineas at the 1981 Newmarket sales. On the track, it was unsuccessful, so its value dropped to £1,500. In 1983 the plaintiffs discovered that the colt's pedigree had been incorrectly described in the sales catalogue and a year later they claimed damages for breach of contract and misrepresentation. At the hearing to assess damages there was evidence that, if the colt had been correctly described, it would have sold for about 23,500 guineas at the sales.

*Held*

The plaintiffs were entitled to the difference between 26,000 guineas and £1,500 (£25,800) and training fees and other expenditure on the horse's keep until it could have been disposed of following discovery of the misrepresentation (£9,820).

Waller J:

'What, as it seems to me, makes this case different from the norm is, first, that what the plaintiffs in fact purchased in reliance on the representation in the catalogue was a different animal altogether; second, if they had known of the misrepresentation within a day or so they could, and as I have found would, have sold Fondu for its then value; third, their decision to keep Fondu and race it was precisely what the sellers would have expected; Fondu was not a commodity like, for example, rupee paper, which it would be expected that the defendants would go out and sell; fourth, the fall in Fondu's value if it did not win races was not due to a general fall in the market in racehorses, but was special to Fondu and to be expected if Fondu did not win. It might well not have happened if Fondu had been the different animal as it had been originally described.

Accordingly, in my judgment it would be unjust if the plaintiffs were not entitled to recover the difference between 26,000 guineas and £1,500 ...

It seems to me that there can be no question of the plaintiffs being entitled to recover anything for the training and upkeep of Fondu past the date on which they discovered the true pedigree of Fondu, other than a reasonable figure for the horse's keep until it could have been disposed of. If any sum is recoverable I assess it as £9,820 ...

Is the £9,820 recoverable at all? It seems to me that in relation to this particular horse, applying Winn LJ's test in *Doyle v Olby (Ironmongers) Ltd* [1969] 2 QB 158 at 168, the cost of training and keeping Fondu should be recoverable. But is it right to apply blinkers and consider the purchase of this particular animal and the expenditure on him? The defendant says that expenditure would have been incurred anyway on some yearling purchased at those September sales. To which the plaintiffs retort that that may be so, but if they bought the horse described by the defendant it might have paid for its keep and reaped for them rich rewards.

I have concluded that the plaintiffs are entitled to ask the court to look simply at the contract they made in reliance on the representation which induced them to enter into that bargain. They are entitled to say that there must be no speculation one way or the other about what would have happened if they had not purchased this horse and if no misrepresentation had been made to them. They are entitled to say (putting it in broad terms) we bought one horse and we spent money training it and entering it for races. We discovered two years after the purchase that it was not the horse we thought we had bought; it is not the horse on which we would have spent any money training or keeping, and therefore that is money only spent in reliance on the representation made. The figure I award under this head is thus £9,820.'

*Commentary*

*Doyle* v *Olby (Ironmongers) Ltd* [1969] 2 QB 158: see Chapter 5, above.

**O'Laoire v Jackel International Ltd** (1991) The Times 12 February Court of Appeal (Sir Nicholas Browne-Wilkinson V-C, Stuart-Smith and Leggatt LJJ)

Wrongful dismissal - damages

*Facts*

The defendants had summarily dismissed the plaintiff and an industrial tribunal had awarded him the statutory maximum (£8,000) by way of compensation for unfair dismissal. In an action for wrongful dismissal, the plaintiff claimed, inter alia, damages for the distress, inconvenience and injury to his feelings and the question also arose as to whether the £8,000 should be deducted from any damages recoverable at common law.

*Held*

The plaintiff would fail on the first point but succeed on the second. On the question of damages for loss of reputation and injury to feelings, Sir Nicholas Browne-Wilkinson V-C had no doubt that the decision of the House of Lords in *Addis* v *Gramophone Co Ltd* [1909] AC 488 excluded those factors from being taken into account. The only exception to that rule arose in the case of contracts of apprenticeship. The plaintiff had said that the circumstances of employment and attitudes had changed since the decision in *Addis*. That was true, but unless and until the House of Lords reconsidered that decision it was binding on the court.

The question of the deduction or otherwise of the £8,000 was a new point which fell to be decided in accordance with principle. In his Lordship's judgment the starting point was to identify the principle upon which the defendants sought to rely. Counsel for the defendants had accepted that the only principle on which he could rely was the rule against double recovery for the same loss. If that rule was to be invoked, the first requirement was to show that the plaintiff would be obtaining compensation under two heads for the same loss. But the defendants were unable to satisfy that requirement. The industrial tribunal had not, and could not, allocate the £8,000 maximum award to any one of the particular elements which together made up the total loss of £100,700 which they had found the plaintiff to have suffered. Therefore, in his Lordship's judgment, since the defendant could not prove a double recovery, there was no basis for setting off the maximum award against the common law damages.

*Commentary*

*Addis* v *Gramaphone Co Ltd* [1909] AC 488: see Introduction, above. See also *Bliss* v *South East Thames Regional Health Authority* [1987] ICR 700, above.

**Parsons (H) (Livestock) Ltd v Uttley Ingham & Co Ltd** [1977] 3 WLR 990 Court of Appeal (Lord Denning MR, Orr and Scarman LJJ)

Breach of contract - damages recoverable

*Facts*

The plaintiff pig farmers bought from the defendant manufacturers a second bulk food storage hopper 'fitted with ventilated top'. In transporting the hopper to the farm the defendants sealed down the ventilator to stop it rattling. They forgot to unseal it (which the plaintiffs could not have detected as it was 28 feet above the ground); the pig nuts became mouldy, the pigs became ill from a rare type of infection and 254 of them died. The plaintiffs sued for damages.

*Held*

They were entitled to succeed and to recover by way of damages the losses sustained from the death and sickness of the pigs.

Scarman LJ:

'Two problems are left unsolved by the *Heron II, Koufos* v *C Czarnikow Ltd*: (1) the law's reconciliation of the remoteness principle in contract with that in tort where as, for instance in some product liability cases, there arises the danger of differing awards, the lesser award going to the party who has a contract, even though the contract is silent as to the measure of damages and all parties are, or must be deemed to be, burdened with the same knowledge (or enjoying the same state of ignorance); (2) what is meant by "serious possibility" (or its synonyms): is it a reference to the type of consequence which the parties might be supposed to contemplate as possible though unlikely, or must the chance of it happening appear to be likely? ...

As to the first problem, I agree with Lord Denning MR in thinking that the law must be such that, in a factual situation where all have the same actual or imputed knowledge and the contract contains no terms limiting the damages recoverable for breach, the amount of damages recoverable does not depend on whether, as a matter of legal classification, the plaintiff's cause of action is breach of contract or tort. It may be that the necessary reconciliation is to be found, notwithstanding the strictures of Lord Reid, in holding that the difference between "reasonably foreseeable" (the test in tort) and "reasonably contemplated" (the test in contract) is semantic, not substantial. Certainly Asquith LJ in *Victoria Laundry (Windsor) Ltd* v *Newman Industries Ltd* and Lord Pearce in the *Heron II, Koufos* v *C Czarnikow Ltd* thought so; and I confess I think so too. The second problem, what is meant by a "serious possibility" is, in my judgment, ultimately a question of fact. I shall return to it, therefore, after analysing the facts since I believe it requires of the judge no more, and no less, than the application of common sense in the particular circumstances of the case ...

The court's task , therefore, is to decide what loss to the plaintiffs it is reasonable to suppose would have been in the contemplation of the parties as a serious possibility had they had in mind the breach when they made their contract ...

I would agree with Mr McGregor in his work on Damages that -

"in contract as in tort, it should suffice that, if physical injury or damage is within the contemplation of the parties, recovery is not to be limited because the degree of physical injury or damage could not have been anticipated."

This is so, in my judgment, not because there is, or ought to be, a specific rule of law governing cases of physical injury but because it would be absurd to regulate damages in such cases on the necessity of supposing the parties had a prophetic foresight as to the exact nature of the injury that does in fact arise. It is enough if on the hypothesis predicated physical injury must have been a serious possibility. Though in loss of market or loss of profit cases the factual analysis will be very different from cases of physical injury, the same principles, in my judgement, apply. Given the situation of the parties at the time of contract, was the loss of profit, or market, a serious possibility, something that would have been in their minds had they contemplated breach?

It does not matter, in my judgment, if they thought that the chance of physical injury, loss of profit, loss of market, or other loss as the case may be, was slight or that the odds were against it provided they contemplated as a serious possibility the type of consequence, not necessarily the specific consequence, that ensued on breach ... no more than common sense was needed for them to appreciate that food affected by bad storage conditions might well cause illness in the pigs fed on it.

As I read the judgment under appeal, this was how the judge, whose handling of the issues at trial was such that none save one survives for our consideration, reached this decision. In my judgment, he was right, on the facts as found, to apply the first rule in *Hadley* v *Baxendale*, or, if the case be one of breach of warranty, as I think it is, the rule in s53(2) of the Sale of Goods Act 1893 without enquiring whether, on a juridical analysis, the rule is base on a presumed contemplation. At the end of a long and complex dispute the judge allowed common sense to prevail. I would dismiss the appeal.'

*Commentary*

Applied: *Hadley* v *Baxendale* (1854) 9 Exch 341 and *Koufos* v *C Czarnikow Ltd* [1967] 3 WLR 1491.

**Payzu Ltd v Saunders** [1919] 2 KB 581 Court of Appeal (Bankes and Scrutton LJJ and Eve J)

Breach of contract - duty to mitigate loss

*Facts*

The defendant, having agreed to sell the plaintiffs 200 pieces of silk, delivered the final consignment for which the plaintiffs failed to pay punctually. In view of this, the defendant said that she would only deliver further supplies if the plaintiffs paid on delivery. This the plaintiffs would not accept, so they sued for breach of contract, claiming the differences between the contract price and the current market price.

*Held*

Although the defendant was liable, the plaintiffs' failure to pay promptly for the first consignment not amounting to a repudiation of the contract, the plaintiffs should have mitigated their loss by accepting her cash-on-delivery terms and they were entitled to recover only the amount which they would have lost had they done so.

Scrutton LJ:

'Whether it be more correct to say that a plaintiff must minimise his damages, or to say that he can recover no more than he would have suffered if he had acted reasonably, because any further damages do not reasonably follow from the defendant's breach, the result is the same. The plaintiff must take "all reasonable steps to mitigate the loss consequent on the breach" and this simple principle "debars him from claiming any part of the damage which is due to his neglect to take such steps": *British Westinghouse Electric and Manufacturing Co* v *Underground Electric Railways Co of London Ltd* ... per Lord Haldane LC. Counsel for the plaintiffs has contended that in considering what steps should be taken to mitigate the damage all contractual relations with the party in default must be excluded. That is contrary to my experience. In certain cases of personal service it may be unreasonable to expect a plaintiff to consider an offer from the other party who has grossly injured him; but in commercial contracts is is generally reasonable to accept an offer from the party in default. However, it is always a question of fact. About the law there is no difficulty.'

**Pilkington v Wood** [1953] Ch 770 High Court (Harman J)

Acquisition of unmarketable title - measure of damages

*Facts*

The plaintiff had employed the defendant as his solicitor in purchasing a freehold property in Hampshire in 1950. The vendor, Colonel Wilks, purported to convey the property as beneficial owner, but when, in 1951, the plaintiff attempted to sell the property, since he had changed his job from Surrey to Lancashire, it was discovered that Colonel Wilks was a trustee of the property who had himself purchased the property in breach of trust. The defendant solicitor admitted negligence and the only question before the court was the measure of damages. The plaintiff claimed his loss in acquiring an unmarketable title, or alternatively, a property which he could only sell at a substantial loss; special damages in respect of expenses incurred because he was unable to sell the property and buy another in Lancashire (except at a loss), viz hotel expenses in Lancashire, expenses of running a car between Lancashire and Hampshire and nightly telephone calls to his wife; and interest on his overdraft incurred as a result of being unable to sell the property.

*Held*

Damages connected with the change of employment could not be recovered.

Harman J:

'It would appear then, at first sight, that the measure of the defendant's liability is the diminution in the value of the property; that is to say, the difference between the value in 1950, the date of the plaintiff's purchase of the property with a good title, and with the title which it in fact had.

The defendant, however, argues that it is the duty of the plaintiff, before suing him in damages, to seek to recover damages against his vendor, Colonel Wilks, under the covenant for title implied by reason of the conveyance as beneficial owner. It is said that this duty arises because of the obligation which rests on a person injured by a breach of contract to mitigate the damages. The suggestion seems to me to carry the doctrine of mitigation a stage further than it has been carried in any case to which I have been referred. The classic statement of the doctrine is that of Lord Haldane in *British Westinghouse Electric and Manufacturing Co Ltd* v *Underground Electric Railways Company of London Ltd* [1912] AC 673, 688...

For the present purpose, it seems to me that it is apposite to state the plaintiff's case in the words of Scrutton LJ in *Payzu Ltd* v *Saunders* [1919] 2 KB 581, 589 thus:

"he can recover no more than he would have suffered if he had acted reasonably, because any further damages do not reasonably follow from the defendant's breach ... "

Ought then the plaintiff, as a reasonable man, to enter on the litigation suggested? It was agreed that the defendant must offer him a indemnity against the cost and it was suggested on the defendant's behalf that if an adequate indemnity were offered, if, secondly, the proposed defendant appeared to be solvent and if, thirdly, there was a good prima facie right of action against that person, it was the duty of the injured party to embark on litigation in order to mitigate the damage suffered. This is a proposition which, in such general terms, I am not prepared to accept, nor do I think I ought to entertain it here, because I am by no means certain that foundations for it exist ...

I do not propose to attempt to decide whether an action against Colonel Wilks would lie or be fruitful. I can see it would be one attended with no little difficulty. I am of the opinion that the so called duty to mitigate does go so far as to oblige the injured party, even under an indemnity, to embark on a complicated and difficult piece of litigation against a third party. The damage to the plaintiff was done once and for all, directly the voidable conveyance to him was executed. This was the direct result of the negligent advice tendered by his solicitor, the defendant, that a good title had been shown; and in my judgment, it is no part of the plaintiff's duty to embark on the proposed litigation in order to protect his solicitor from the consequences of his own carelessness.

Next, the defendant suggested that the injury might be lightened by a policy of insurance designed to cover the consequences of the defect. As to this, it is enough to say that no satisfactory evidence was adduced that any such policy could be obtained. Policies to cover defects of title are, it appears, common enough when supported by crooked covenants on the part of the author of the defect, here, Colonel Wilks.

## Sharneyford Supplies v Edge

See chapter 5 - Misrepresentation

## Staffordshire Area Health Authority v South Staffordshire Waterworks Co [1978] 1 WLR 1387 Court of Appeal (Lord Denning MR, Goff and Cumming-Bruce LJJ)

Contract - ability to determine

*Facts*

Following earlier agreements between the parties, in 1929 they agreed that a hospital was to be supplied with 5,000 gallons of water a day free and additional water at 7d (2.9p) per 1,000 gallons 'at all times hereafter.' In 1975, when the normal rate was 45p per 1,000 gallons, the water company gave six months' notice to terminate the agreement and said that thereafter they would supply 5,000 gallons per day free and charge any excess at normal rates. The hospital authorities contended that the notice was not valid.

*Held*

It was, as the 1929 agreement could be terminated by reasonable notice.

Lord Denning MR:

' ... I think that the rule of strict construction is now quite out of date. It has been supplanted by the rule that written instruments are to be construed in relation the the circumstances as they were known to or contemplated by the parties; and that even the plainest words may fall to be modified if events occur which the parties never had in mind and in which they cannot have intended the agreement to operate.

This modern rule was adumbrated by Cardozo J in 1918 in the New York Court of Appeals in *Utica City National Bank* v *Gunn*:

"To take the primary or strict meaning is to make the whole transaction futile. To take the secondary or loose meaning is to give it efficacy and purpose. In such a situation the genesis and aim of the transaction may rightly guide our choice."

The modern rule has recently been expounded with clarity and authority by Lord Wilberforce in the House of Lords in the case of *Reardon Smith Line Ltd* v *Hansen-Tangen* when he said:

"When one speaks of the intention of the parties to the contract, one is speaking objectively - the parties cannot themselves give direct evidence of what their intention was - and what must be ascertained is what is to be taken as the intention which reasonable people would have had if placed in the situation of the parties. Similarly, when one is speaking of the aim, or object, or commercial purpose, one is speaking objectively of what reasonable persons would have had in mind in the situation of the parties ... what the court must do must be to place itself in thought in the same factual matrix as that in which the parties were."

As I understand this modern rule, we are no longer to go by the strict construction of the words as judges did in the 19th century. We are to put ourselves in the same situation as the parties were at the time they drew up the instrument, to sit in their chairs with our minds endowed with the same facts as theirs were, and envisage the future with the same degree of foresight as they did. So placed we have to ask ourselves: what were the circumstances in which the contract was made? Does it apply in the least to the new situation which has developed? If events occur for which they have made no provision, and which were outside the realm of their speculations altogether, or of any reasonable persons sitting in their chairs, then the court itself must take a hand and hold that the contract ceases to bind ...

I do not think that the water company could have determined the agreement immediately after it was made. That cannot have been intended by the parties. No rule of construction could sensibly permit such a result. But, in the past 50 years, the whole situation has changed so radically that one can say with confidence: "The parties never intended that the supply should be continued in these days at that price." Rather than force such unequal terms on the parties, the court should hold that the agreement could be and was properly determined in 1975 by the reasonable notice of six months. This does not mean of course, that on the expiry of the notice the water company can cut off the supply to the hospital. It will be bound to continue it. All that will happen is that the parties will have to negotiate fresh terms of payment. These should take into account the history ... In the light of that history, it seems to me plain that the 1929 agreement should be up-dated so as to have regard to the effect of inflation ...'

### The Texaco Melbourne (1991) Financial Times 7 August Queen's Bench Division (Webster J)

Currency of damages

*Facts*

Following a breach of contract it fell to be decided whether damages should be paid in US dollars, or in Ghanaian cedis.

*Held*

That in deciding, regard should be had to the currency in which the loss was felt, but also to what was fair and equitable. Although the ship owners had felt the loss in cedis, because the value of the cedi had fallen drastically since the time of the contract, and because of stringent Ghanaian currency controls, it would be more reasonable to quantify the award in dollars.

### Thompson (W L) Ltd v R Robinson (Gunmakers) Ltd

See chapter 18 - Sale of Goods, consumer credit and supply of goods and services.

### Victoria Laundry (Windsor) Ltd v Newman Industries Ltd [1949] 2 KB 528 Court of Appeal (Tucker, Asquith and Singleton LJJ)

Damages - loss of profits

*Facts*

The defendant engineers agreed to sell a boiler to the plaintiff launderers and dyers, knowing the nature of the plaintiffs' business, that the boiler was needed for that business and that it was wanted for immediate use: they did not know, however, that it was required to extend the business. As a result of the fault of a third party, the boiler was damaged while it was being loaded on to the plaintiffs' vehicle: delivery was therefore delayed and the plaintiffs claimed damages for breach of contract.

*Held*

They were entitled to succeed and the damages awarded could take account of any loss of profits resulting from the enforced delay in extending their business.

Asquith LJ:

'The defendants were an engineering company supplying a boiler to a laundry. We reject the submission for the defendants that an engineering company knows no more than the plain man about boilers or the purposes to which they are commonly put by different classes of purchasers, including laundries. The defendant company were not, it is true, manufacturers of this boiler or dealers in boilers, but they gave a highly technical and comprehensive description of this boiler to the plaintiffs

... Of the uses or purposes to which boilers are put, they would clearly know more than the uninstructed layman.  Again, they know they were supplying the boiler to a company carrying on the business of laundrymen and dyers, for use in that business.  The obvious use of a boiler, in such a business, is surely to boil water for the purpose of washing or dyeing.  A laundry might conceivably buy a boiler for some other purpose, for instance, to work radiators or warm bath water water for the comfort of its employees or directors, or to use for research, or to exhibit in a museum.  All these purposes are possible, but the first is the obvious purpose which, in the case of a laundry, leaps to the average eye.  If the purpose then be to wash or dye, why does the company want to wash or dye, unless for purposes of business advantage, in which term we, for the purposes of the rest of this judgment, include maintenance or increase of profit or reduction of loss?  We shall speak henceforward not of loss of profit, but of "loss of business".  No commercial concern commonly purchases for the purposes of its business a very large and expensive structure like this ... with any other motive, and no supplier, let alone an engineering company, which has promised delivery of such an article by a particular date with knowledge that it was to be put into use immediately on delivery, can reasonably contend that it could not foresee that loss of business (in the sense indicated above) would be liable to result to the purchaser from a long delay in the delivery thereof.  The suggestion that, for all the supplier knew, the boiler might have been needed simply as a "stand-by" to be used in a possibly distant future, is gratuitous and was plainly negatived ...'

## Commentary

Distinguished: *Hadley* v *Baxendale* (1854) 9 Exch 341.  See also *Koufos* v *C Czarnikow Ltd* [1967] 3 WLR 1491.

**Watts v Morrow** [1991] 1 WLR 1421 Court of Appeal (Brown, Ralph Gibson and Bingham LJJ)

Measure of damages - surveyor's report negligent - damages for distress and inconvenience

### Facts

Mr and Mrs Watts purchased a house for £177,500 relying on a surveyor's report prepared by the defendant. They bought the house as a second home and did not take up possession for some time, when they found that defects existed beyond those mentioned in the report. Repairs cost £34,000. At first instance the court awarded this sum, plus general damages of £4,000 for 'distress and inconvenience'. The surveyor appealed on the quantum of damages.

### Held

The proper measure of damages was the sum needed to put the plaintiffs in as good a position as if the contract had been properly performed, that is: the difference between the value of the property as it was represented to be and its value in its true condition. Damages for distress and inconvenience were set too high and should be reduced to £1,500.

Bingham LJ:

'A contract-broker is not in general liable for any distress, frustration, anxiety, displeasure, vexation, tension or aggravation which his breach of contract may cause to the innocent party.  This rule is not, I think, founded on the assumption that such reactions are not foreseeable, which they surely are or may be, but on considerations of policy.

But the rule is not absolute.  Where the very object of a contract is to provide pleasure, relaxation, peace of mind or freedom from molestation, damages will be awarded if the fruit of the contract is not provided or if the contrary result is procured instead.  If the law did not cater for this exceptional category of case it would be defective.  A contract to survey the condition of a house for a prospective purchaser does not, however, fall within this exceptional category.

In cases not falling within this exceptional category, damages are ion my view recoverable for physical inconvenience and discomfort caused by the breach and mental suffering directly related to that inconvenience and discomfort. If those effects are foreseeably suffered during a period when defects are repaired I am prepared to accept that they sound in damages even though the cost of the repairs is not recoverable as such.'

**Weld-Blundell v Stephens** [1920] AC 956 House of Lords (Viscount Finlay, Lord Dunedin, Lord Sumner, Lord Parmoor and Lord Wrenbury)

Special damages?

*Facts*

The appellant employed the respondent chartered accountant to investigate the financial position of a company in which he was financially interested. In his letter of instructions, the appellant referred to a former manager and an auditor in defamatory terms. The respondent handed the letter to his partner who was to carry out the investigation and the partner negligently left it at the company's office. There is was found and damages for libel were awarded against the appellant who now sued the respondent for breach of duty, claiming as special damages the damages and cost which he had been ordered to pay in the libel actions.

*Held* (Viscount Finlay and Lord Parmoor dissenting)

His claim would fail.

Lord Sumner:

'This special application to contracts of the rule as to remoteness depends, like other matters, of contract, on mutuality and agreement on some communication between the parties at or before the time when the contract is made, some knowledge and acceptance by the one party of the purpose or intention of the other in entering into the contract. There is no evidence of anything of the kind here. It is true that the respondent said that he realised the letter was dangerous when he got it, but that answer did not purport to refer to actions brought upon it. There are plenty of other ways in which it might make mischief, and, indeed, when Mr Stephens asked the counsel who was cross-examining him. "Do you mean dangerous in the sense that it was libellous?" - all the answer he got was: "A highly dangerous letter to the interest of Mr Weld-Blundell unless it was kept from the knowledge of those whose names are referred to in it." To that it was that he replied that he realised it was dangerous. As a matter of fact, nothing passed between the parties on the subject and so far was any such special contemplation from the appellant's mind that, when Messrs Comins & Co's solicitors asked him to apologise for his letter his answer was: "I suppose you will not venture to deny my right, even in this land of fools and rogues, to say or write what I please to my own servants, such as Comins, Hurst, Stephens, & Co more especially when, as in this case, I limit my remarks to what is and has been a subject of common knowledge to and among all of them or, as you put it, among the entire gang in my employment." Clearly, Mr Weld-Blundell thought he could write to Mr Stephens what he liked without being under any legal liability, whether the letter became known or not. There is no evidence that any such thing was in the contemplation of either party; certainly it was not in that of both. There is, therefore, no ground for applying to the defendant's breach of contract in this case any other measure of damages than such as would have applied, if it had been a breach of a non-contractual duty.'

**White and Carter (Councils) Ltd v McGregor**

See chapter 13 - Discharge of the contract - performance, agreement and breach

**Wroth v Tyler**

See Introduction.

# 15  REMEDIES FOR BREACH OF CONTRACT – EQUITABLE REMEDIES

**Alghussein Establishment v Eton College** [1988] 1 WLR 587 House of Lords (Lord Bridge of Harwick, Lord Elwyn-Jones, Lord Ackner, Lord Goff of Chieveley and Lord Jauncey of Tullichettle)

Party able to rely on own default?

*Facts*

In 1978 the respondents entered into an agreement with the appellants' predecessors in title as tenants for a 99 year lease for development. Although no time limit was fixed, the tenants undertook to use their best endeavours to proceed with and complete the development. The agreement also provided for this immediate grant of the lease on completion of the development 'provided that if for any reason due to the wilful default of the tenant the development shall remain uncompleted on the 29th day of September 1983 the lease shall forthwith be granted ...' By October 1984 the appellants had still not started the work: the respondents purported to treat the agreement as being repudiated and the appellants sought specific performance of the agreement and the grant of the lease.

*Held*

The appellants could not succeed.

Lord Jauncey of Tullichettle:

> 'Even if it were appropriate to imply the provision [for the completion of the development] into any lease to be granted under the proviso ... and I make this assumption without deciding the matter one way or the other, there remains the question whether ... the agreement contains clear express provisions to contradict the presumption that it was not the intention of parties that either should be entitled to rely on his own breach in order to obtain a benefit. I find no such clear express provision. Although the proviso refers specifically to the wilful default of the tenant, it does not state that the tenant should be entitled to take advantage thereof. It is one thing for wilful default of a party to be made the occasion on which a provision comes into operation but is quite another thing for that party to be given the right to rely on that default.'

*Commentary*

See also *Micklefield* v *SAC Technology Ltd* [1990] 1 WLR 1002, Chapter 6, above.

**American Cyanamid Co v Ethicon Ltd** [1975] 2 WLR 316 House of Lords (Lord Diplock, Viscount Dilhorne, Lord Cross of Chelsea, Lord Salmon and Lord Edmund-Davies)

Interlocutory injunctions - principle governing grant

*Facts*

The plaintiffs believed that the defendants were about to infringe their patent relating to surgical sutures and they sought an interlocutory injunction.

*Held*

The injunction would be granted.

Lord Diplock:

> ' ... The use of such expressions as "a probability", "a prima facie case", or "a strong prima facie case" in the context of the exercise of a discretionary power to grant an interlocutory injunction leads

to confusion as to the object sought to be achieved by this form of temporary relief. The court no doubt must be satisfied that the claim is not frivolous or vexatious; in other words, that there is a serious question to be tried.

It is no part of the court's function at this stage of the litigation to try to resolve conflicts of evidence on affidavit as to facts on which the claims of either party may ultimately depend nor to decide difficult questions of law which call for detailed argument and mature considerations. These are matters to be dealt with at the trial ... So unless the material available to the court at the hearing of the application for an interlocutory injunction fails to disclose that the plaintiff has any real prospect of succeeding in his claim for a permanent injunction at the trial, the court should go on to consider whether the balance of convenience lies in favour of granting or refusing the interlocutory relief that is sought.

As to that, the governing principle is that the court should first consider whether if the plaintiff were to succeed at the trial in establishing his right to a permanent injunction he would be adequately compensated by an award of damages for the loss he would have sustained as a result of the defendant's continuing to do what was sought to be enjoined between the time of the application and the time of the trial. If damages in the measure recoverable at common law would be adequate remedy and the defendant would be in a financial position to pay them, no interlocutory injunction should normally be granted, however strong the plaintiff's claim appeared to be at that stage. If, on the other hand, damages would not provide an adequate remedy for the plaintiff in the event of his succeeding at the trial, the court should then consider whether, on the contrary hypothesis that the defendant were to succeed at the trial in establishing his right to do that which was sought to be enjoined, he would be adequately compensated under the plaintiff's undertaking as to damages for the loss he would have sustained by being prevented from doing so between the time of the application and the time of the trial. If damages in the measure recoverable under such and undertaking would be an adequate remedy and the plaintiff would be in a financial position to pay them, there would be no reason on this ground to refuse an interlocutory injunction.

It is where there is doubt as to the adequacy of the respective remedies in damages available to either party or to both, that the question of balance of convenience arises. It would be unwise to attempt even to list all the various matters which may need to be taken into consideration in deciding where the balance lies, let alone to suggest the relative weight to be attached to them. These will vary from case to case.

Where other factors appear to be evenly balanced it is a counsel of prudence to take such measures as are calculated to preserve the status quo. If the defendant is enjoined temporarily from doing something that he has not done before, the only effect of the interlocutory injunction in the event of his succeeding at the trial is to postpone the date at which he is able to embark on a course of action which he has not previously found it necessary to undertake; whereas to interrupt him in the conduct of an established enterprise would cause much greater inconvenience to him since he would have to start again to establish it in the event of his succeeding at the trial.

Save in the simplest cases, the decision to grant or to refuse an interlocutory injunction will cause to whichever party is unsuccessful on the application some disadvantages which his ultimate success at the trial may show he ought to have been spared and the disadvantages may be such that the recovery of damages to which he would then be entitled either in the action or under the plaintiff's undertaking would not be sufficient to compensate him fully for all of them. The extent to which the disadvantages to each party would be incapable of being compensated in damages in the event of his succeeding at the trail is always a significant factor in assessing where the balance of convenience lies; and if the extent of the uncompensatable disadvantage to each party would not differ widely, it may not be improper to take into account in tipping the balance the relative strength of each party's case as revealed by the affidavit evidence adduced on the hearing of the application. This, however, should be done only where it is apparent on the facts disclosed by evidence as to which there is no credible dispute that the strength of one party's case is disproportionate to that of the other party.

The court is not justified in embarking on anything resembling a trial of the action on conflicting affidavits in order to evaluate the strength of either party's case.

I would reiterate that, in addition to those to which I have referred, there may be many other special factors to be taken into consideration in the particular circumstances of individual cases. The instant appeal affords one example of this.

Returning, therefore, to the instant appeal, it cannot be doubted that the affidavit evidence shows that there are serious questions to be tried.'

## Beswick v Beswick

See chapter 10 - Privity of contract

## Decro-Wall International SA v Practitioners in Marketing Ltd

See chapter 13 - Discharge of the contract - performance, agreement and breach.

## Evening Standard Co Ltd v Henderson [1987] IRLR 64 Court of Appeal (Lawton and Balcombe LJJ)

Injunction - contract of service

*Facts*

Mr Henderson was employed on the London Evening Standard for 17 years. His contract of employment provided that during the time of his employment he could not work for the employer's competitors and that to terminate his contract he must give 12 months' notice. In breach of contract Mr Henderson gave two months' notice to terminate as he wished to begin working for a rival newspaper. The plaintiffs sought an injunction to prevent Mr Henderson working for a rival for the ten months of the unexpired contractual notice period.

*Held*

The injunction should be granted.

Lawton LJ:

'... By the time this case got to this court it was accepted by the plaintiffs that they could not get an injunction against the defendant on the grounds they first thought they could because ... you cannot get an injunction against an employee under a contract of service to enforce a negative covenant if the consequence of that injunction would be to put the employee in the position that he would either have to go on working for his former employers or starve or be idle ... the plaintiffs had to consider carefully what they should do. They decided that one way out of the problem was to offer to pay the defendant his salary and other contractual benefits until such time as his notice, if it had been in proper form ...

What we have to ask ourselves is: what, in the circumstances of this case, is the balance of convenience? If the defendant leaves the employment of the plaintiffs today, as he says he intends to do, and takes himself off straight away or very shortly to the rival newspaper, the plaintiffs, in my judgment, will undoubtedly suffer damage but it will be difficult to quantify those damages ... the injunction must not force the defendant to work for the plaintiffs and it must not reduce him, certainly to a condition of starvation or to a condition of idleness, whatever that may mean. But all that, in my judgment, is overcome by the fact that the plaintiffs have made the offer they have ...'

**Hill v C A Parsons & Co Ltd** [1971] 3 WLR 995 Court of Appeal (Lord Denning MR, Sachs and Stamp LJJ)

Wrongful dismissal - injunction

*Facts*

The plaintiff, a chartered engineer aged 63, had been employed by the defendants for 35 years. He was due to retire at 65 and his pension depended on the average salary during the last three years' service. Following a strike, the defendants said that persons of the plaintiff's grade had to join a certain union; he refused and the defendants purported to dismiss him. In his action for wrongful dismissal, he sought an interim injunction.

*Held*

The injunction would be granted.

Lord Denning MR:

'In these circumstance, it is of the utmost importance to Mr Hill ... that the notice ... should not be held to terminate [his] employment. Damages would not be at all an adequate remedy. If ever there was a case where an injunction should be granted against the employers, this is the case. It is quite plain that the employers have done wrong. I know that the employers have been under pressure from a powerful trade union. That may explain their conduct, but it does not excuse it. They have purported to terminate Mr Hill's employment by a notice which is too short by far. They seek to take advantage of their own wrong by asserting that his services were terminated by their own "say so" at the date selected by them - to the grave prejudice of Mr Hill. They cannot be allowed to break the law in this way. It is, to my mind, a clear case for an injunction.

The judge said that he felt constrained by the law to refuse an injunction. But that is too narrow a view of the principles of law. He has overlooked the fundamental principle that, whenever a man has a right, the law should give a remedy. The Latin maxim is ubi jus ibi remedium. This principle enables us to step over the trip-wires of previous cases and to bring the law into accord with the needs of today. I would allow the appeal, accordingly and grant an injunction restraining the company from treating the notice ... as having determined Mr Hill's employment.'


**Johnson v Agnew** [1979] 2 WLR 487 House of Lords (Lord Wilberforce, Lord Salmon, Lord Fraser of Tullybelton, Lord Keith of Kinkel and Lord Scarman)

Damages - date of assessment

*Facts*

In November 1973 the parties contracted for the sale and purchase of a house and land, the properties being mortgaged separately. The purchaser paid part of the deposit and accepted the vendor's title but did not complete by 6 December, the contract date. On 21 December the vendors gave notice that 21 January 1974 was the final date for completion, but the purchaser failed to complete and on 8 March the vendors commenced proceedings. An order for specific performance was made on 27 June, although it was not entered until 26 November, by which time the mortgagees of the house had obtained an order for possession. In March 1975 the land mortgagees obtained such an order and on 3 April and 20 June respectively the land and house mortgagees contracted sales, completions taking place in July.

*Held*

The vendors were entitled not only to an order discharging the specific performance order but also to damages for breach of contract assessed at 3 April 1975.

Lord Wilberforce:

'The general principle for the assessment of damages is compensatory, ie that the innocent party is to be placed, so far as money can do so, in the same position as if the contract had been performed.

Where the contract is one of sale, this principle normally leads to assessment of damages as at the date of the breach ... But this is not an absolute rule; if to follow it would give rise to injustice, the court has power to fix such other date as may be appropriate in the circumstances.

In cases where a breach of a contract for sale has occurred, and the innocent party reasonably continues to try to have the contract completed, it would to me appear more logical and just rather than tie him to the date of the original breach, to assess damages as at the date when (otherwise than by his default) the contract is lost. Support for this approach is to be found in the cases ... In the present case if it is accepted, as I would accept, that the vendors acted reasonably in pursuing the remedy of specific performance, the date on which that remedy became aborted (not by the vendors' fault) should logically be fixed as the date on which damages should be assessed. Choice of this date would be in accordance both with common law principle ... and with the wording of [Lord Cairns'] Act "in substitution for ... specific performance." The date which emerges from this is 3 April 1975, the first date on which mortgagees contracted to sell a portion of the property. I would vary the order of the Court of Appeal by substituting this date for that fixed by them, viz 26 November 1974. The same date (3 April 1975) should be used for the purpose of limiting the respondents' right to interest on damages.'

**Leeds Industrial Co-operative Society v Slack** [1924] AC 851 House of Lords (Earl of Birkenhead, Viscount Finlay, Lord Dunedin, Lord Sumner and Lord Carson)

Injunction - award of damages in lieu

*Facts*

The parties owned premises on opposite sides of a narrow passage. The defendants demolished theirs and commenced rebuilding: the plaintiffs maintained that the new building already had, and when completed would even more, infringe their right to light and they sought an injunction. At the date of the trial, it was found that the new building had not yet interfered unlawfully with the plaintiffs' ancient lights.

*Held* (Lord Sumner and Lord Carson dissenting)

An award of damages could be made in lieu of an injunction and the measure of damages would be the damage to be sustained following completion of the building.

Viscount Finlay:

'Does [Lord Cairns' Act] empower the court to award damages in lieu of an injunction when injury is threatened, but has not yet been done?

In my opinion, this question must be answered in the affirmative. The power given is to award damages to the party injured, either in addition to or in substitution for an injunction. If the damages are given in addition to the injunction, they are to compensate for the injury which has been done, and the injunction will prevent its continuance, or repetition. But if damages are given in substitution for an injunction, they must necessarily cover not only injury already sustained, but also injury that would be inflicted in the future by the commission of the act threatened. If no injury has yet been sustained, the damages will be solely in respect of the damage to be sustained in the future by injuries which the injunction, if granted, would have prevented. The power conferred on a Court of Chancery by Lord Cairns' act included power to give damages in respect of a past injury. This in itself was a useful extension of jurisdiction, as it would prevent the hardship involved by the necessity of going to another court to get such relief. But the enactment did not stop there. In terms it gave power to substitute damages for an injunction. Such a substitution in the very nature of things involves that the damages are to deal with what would have been prevented by the injunction, if granted. In the present case the building has not proceeded far enough to constitute an actionable wrong in respect of the plaintiff's lights, and an injunction would prevent the commission of that wrong in the future. On what principle can it be said that, until there has been some interference with the plaintiff's windows, the court cannot give damages in lieu of an injunction against obstruction? Such a construction would impose a purely arbitrary and meaningless restriction on the relief to be given under the Act.'

**Lumley v Wagner** (1852) 1 De GM & G 604 Lord Chancellor's Court (Lord St Leonards LC)

Injunction - contract for personal services

*Facts*

The defendant cantatrice bound herself to sing for three months at the plaintiff's London theatre and 'not to use her talents' at any other place during that time.

*Held*

An injunction could be granted to restrain her from appearing at another theatre.

Lord St Leonards LC:

'It was objected that the operation of the injunction in the present case was mischievous, excluding the defendant Johanna Wagner from performing at any other theatre while this court had no power to compel her to perform at Her Majesty's Theatre. It is true that I have not the means of compelling her to sing, but she has no cause of complaint if I compel her to abstain from the commission of an act which she has bound herself not to do, and thus possibly cause her to fulfil her engagement. The jurisdiction which I now exercise is wholly within the power of the court, and, being of opinion that it is a proper case for interfering, I shall leave nothing unsatisfied by the judgment I pronounce. The effect, too, of the injunction, in restraining Johanna Wagner from singing elsewhere may, in the event of an action being brought against her by the plaintiff, prevent any such amount of vindictive damages being given against her as a jury might probably be inclined to give if she had carried her talents and exercised them at the rival theatre. The injunction may also, as I have said, tend to the fulfilment of her engagement, though, in continuing the injunction, I disclaim doing indirectly what I cannot do directly.'

*Commentary*

See also *Warner Brothers Pictures Inc* v *Nelson* [1937] I KB 209 and *Page One Records Ltd* v *Britton* [1968] 1 WLR 157.

**Mareva Compania Naviera SA v International Bulk Carriers SA. The Mareva** [1980] 1 All ER 213 Court of Appeal (Lord Denning MR, Roskill and Ormrod LJJ)

Injunction - danger of transfer of assets out of jurisdiction

*Facts*

The plaintiffs sought, inter alia, damages for alleged repudiation of a charterparty and, on an ex parte application, a judge had granted an injunction restraining the defendants from removing or disposing out of the jurisdiction monies in their London bank account.

*Held*

The injunction would be extended.

Lord Denning MR:

' ... Section 45 of the Supreme Court of Judicature (Consolidation) Act 1925 says:

"A mandamus or an injunction may be granted or a receiver appointed by an interlocutory Order of the Court in all cases in which it shall appear to the Court to be just or convenient ..."

In *Beddow* v *Beddow* Jessel MR Gave a very wide interpretation to that section. He said: "I have unlimited power to grant an injunction in any case where it would be right or just to do so ..."

There is only one qualification to be made. The court will not grant an injunction to protect a person who has no legal or equitable right whatever ... But, subject to that qualification, the statute gives a wide general power to the courts. It is well summarised in Halsbury's Laws of England:

" ... now, therefore, whenever a right, which can be asserted either at law or in equity, does not exist, then whatever the previous practice may have been, the Court is enabled by virtue of this provision, in a proper case, to grant an injunction to protect that right."

In my opinion that principle applies to a creditor who has a right to be paid the debt owing to him, even before he has established his right by getting judgement for it. If it appears that the debt is due and owing, and there is a danger that the debtor may dispose of his assets so as to defeat it before judgment, the court has jurisdiction in a proper case to grant an interlocutory judgment so as to prevent him disposing of those assets. It seems to me that this is a proper case for the exercise of this jurisdiction. There is money in a bank in London which stands in the name of these charterers. The charterers have control of it. They may at any time dispose of it or remove it out of this country. If they do so, the shipowners may never get their charter hire. The ship is now on the high seas. It has passed Cape Town on its way to India. It will complete the voyage and the cargo will be discharged. And the shipowners may not get their charter hire at all. In the face of this danger, I think this court ought to grand an injunction to restrain the charterers from disposing of these moneys now in the bank in London until the trial or judgment in this action. If the charterers have any grievance about it when they hear of it, they can apply to discharge it. But meanwhile the shipowners should be protected. It is only just and right that this court should grant an injunction. I would therefore continue the injunction.'

### Page One Records Ltd v Britton [1968] 1 WLR 157 High Court (Stamp J)

Injunction – contract for personal services

*Facts*

The defendant musicians ('The Troggs') appointed the plaintiffs their manager for five years. During that time, they sought an interlocutory injunction to restrain them from engaging any other manager.

*Held*

The injunction would be refused.

Stamp J:

' ... It was said in this case, that if an injunction is granted The Troggs could, without employing any other manager or agent, continue as a group on their own or seek other employment of a different nature. So far as the former suggestion is concerned, in the first place, I doubt whether consistently with the terms of the agreements which I have read, The Troggs could act as their own managers; and, in the second place, I think that I can and should take judicial notice of the fact that these groups, if they are to have any great success, must have managers. Indeed, it is the plaintiffs' own case that The Troggs are simple persons, of no business experience, and could not survive without the services of a manager. As a practical matter on the evidence before me, I entertain no doubt that they would be compelled, if the injunction were granted on the terms that the plaintiffs seek, to continue to employ the first plaintiff as their manager and agent and it is, I think, on this point that this case diverges from the *Lumley* v *Wagner* case ... and the cases which have followed it, including the *Warner Brothers* case: for it would be a bad thing to put pressure on The Troggs to continue to employ as a manager and agent in a fiduciary capacity one, who, unlike the plaintiff in those cases who had merely to pay the defendant money, has duties of a personal and fiduciary nature to perform and in whom The Troggs, for reasons good, bad or indifferent, have lost confidence and who may, for all I know, fail in its duty to them.

On the facts before me on this interlocutory motion, I should, if I granted the injunction, be enforcing a contract for personal services in which personal services are to be performed by the first plaintiff. In *Lumley* v *Wagner*, Lord St Leonards LC in his judgment, disclaimed doing directly what he could not do directly; and in the present case, by granting an injunction I would, in my judgment, be doing precisely that. I must, therefore, refuse the injunction.'

**Patel v Ali** [1984] 2 WLR 960 High Court (Goulding J)

Specific performance - hardship

*Facts*

Two couples (defendants) live in a house which they contract to sell to the plaintiffs. One defendant is adjudicated bankrupt, another defendant becomes very ill, has a child and undergoes amputation of one leg. Her husband is sent to prison for two years. She later has another child. The plaintiffs apply for specific performance.

*Held*

The court could and would refuse specific performance on the ground of hardship consequent to the contract, even where it was not caused by the plaintiff; that in view of the change of circumstances and that provided the plaintiffs had an effective remedy in damages, it would be just not to allow specific performance.

Goulding J:

'Another limitation suggested by counsel for the plaintiffs was that, in the reported cases, as he said, hardship successfully relied on has always related to the subject matter of the contract and has not been just a personal hardship of the defendant. Certainly, mere pecuniary difficulties, whether of purchaser or of vendor, afford no excuse from performance of a contract. In a wider sense than that, I do not think the suggested universal proposition can be sustained ...

The important and true principle, in my view, is that only in extraordinary and persuasive circumstances can hardship supply an excuse for resisting performance of a contract for the sale of immovable property. A person of full capacity who sells or buys a house takes the risk of hardship to himself and his dependants, whether arising from existing facts or unexpectedly supervening in the interval before completion. This is where, to my mind, great importance attaches to the immense delay in the present case, not attributable to the defendant's conduct. Even after issue of the writ, she could not complete, if she had wanted to, without the concurrence of the absent Mr Ahmed. Thus, in a sense, she can say she is being asked to do what she never bargained for, namely to complete the sale after more than four years, after all the unforeseeable changes that such a period entails. I think that in this way she can fairly assert that specific performance would inflict on her "a hardship amounting to injustice" to use the phrase employed by James LJ, in a different but comparable context, in *Tamplin* v *James* (1880) 15 Ch D 215 at 221. Equitable relief may, in my view, be refused because of an unforeseen change of circumstances not amounting to legal frustration, just as it may on the ground of mistake insufficient to avoid a contract at law.

In the end, I am satisfied that it is within the court's discretion to accede to the defendant's prayer if satisfied that it is just to do so. An, on the whole, looking at the position of both sides after the long unpredictable delay for which neither seeks to make the other responsible, I am of opinion that it *is* just to leave the plaintiffs to their remedy in damages if that can indeed be effective.'

**Posner v Scott-Lewis** [1986] 3 WLR 531 High Court (Mervyn Davies J)

Specific performance - personal services

*Facts*

Under the terms of the leases of the plaintiff tenants at Danes Court, the defendant landlord was obliged to employ a resident porter to keep the communal area clean, to be responsible for the boilers and to collect rubbish from the flats. The resident porter left, but continued to do the work on a part-time basis. If the defendant was thereby in breach of the covenant, could the covenant be specifically enforced?

*Held*

The defendant was in breach and the court could and would make an order for specific performance.

Mervyn Davies J:

'Drawing attention to ... differences between [*Ryan* v *Mutual Tontine Westminster Chambers Association* [1893] 1 Ch 116] and the present case, counsel for the plaintiffs submitted that *Ryan's* case should be distinguished. in short, he said that since the resident porter's functions at Danes Court were already obligations of the lessor to the lessees, there were no duties on the part of the porter towards the tenants that the tenants were seeking to enforce. All that was required was the appointment of a resident porter, whereas in *Ryan's* case the plaintiff was in effect seeking to enforce performance of duties said to be owed by the porter to the plaintiff. I do not accept or reject counsel for the plaintiffs able argument. I suspect that it is difficult to distinguish *Ryan's* case. However that may be, *Ryan's* case has been remarked on in many later authorities.

In *C H Giles & Co Ltd* v *Morris* [1972] 1 WLR 307 at 318-319 Megarry J, after referring to *Ryan's* case said:

"One day, perhaps, the courts will look again at the so-called rule that contracts for personal services or involving the continuous performance of services will not be specifically enforced. Such a rule is plainly not absolute and without exception, nor do I think it can be based on any narrow consideration such as difficulties of constant superintendence by the court. Mandatory injunctions are by no means unknown, and there is normally no question of the court having to send its officers to supervise the performance of the order of the court. Prohibitory injunctions are common, and again there is no direct supervision by the court. Performance of each type of injunction is normally secured by the realisation of the person enjoined that he is liable to be punished for contempt if evidence of his disobedience to the order is put before the court; and if the injunction is prohibitory, actual committal will usually, so long as it continues, make disobedience impossible. If instead the order is for specific performance of a contract for personal services, a similar machinery of enforcement could be employed, again without there being any question of supervision by any officer of the court. The reasons why the court is reluctant to decree specific performance of a contract for personal services (and I would regard it as a strong reluctance rather than a rule) are, I think, more complex and more firmly bottomed on human nature ... The present case, of course is a fortiori, since the contract of which specific performance has been decreed requires not the performance of personal services or any continuous series of acts, but merely procuring the execution of an agreement which contains a provision for such services or acts."

Those observations do not of themselves enable me to disregard *Ryan's* case. But then one comes to *Shiloh Spinners Ltd* v *Harding* [1973] 2WLR 28. Lord Wilberforce seems to say that "the impossibility for the courts to supervise the doing of work" may be rejected as a reason against granting relief (see [1973] AC 691 at 724). Finally there is *Tito* v *Waddell No 2, Tito* v *A-G* [1977] 2 WLR 496 ...

In the light of those authorities it is, I think, open to me to consider the making of an order for specific performance in this case, particularly since the order contemplated is in the fortiori class referred to by Megarry J in the last sentence of the extract from the *Giles'* case [1972] 1 WLR 307 at 318 quoted above. Damages here could hardly regarded as an adequate remedy.

Whether or not an order for specific performance should be made seems to me to depend on the following considerations: (a) is there a sufficient definition of what has to be done in order to comply with the order of the court; (b) will enforcing compliance involve superintendence by the court to an unacceptable degree; and (c) what are the respective prejudices or hardships that will be suffered by the parties if the order is made or not made?

As to (a) one may in this case sufficiently define what has to be done by the defendants by ordering the defendants, within say two months to employ a porter to be resident at Danes Court for the purpose of carrying out the ... duties. It is to be borne in mind that there is still a vacant flat available for a resident porter. As to (b), I do not see that such an order will occasion any protracted superintendence by the court. If the defendants without good cause fail to comply with the order in due time, then the plaintiffs can take appropriate enforcement proceedings against the defendants. As to (c), I see no hardship or prejudice resulting to the defendants from the order. They will simply be performing what they have promised to do and what has been carried out by the lessors over the past 20 years. On the other hand I see considerable inconvenience, if not exactly hardship, for the plaintiffs if, having bargained for a resident porter and paid a premium and having enjoyed his presence for 20 years, they are to be expected for the future to be content with a porter who simply walks up and down the stairs for two hours only during the day doing his cleaning and refuse collection. It follows that there should be an order for specific performance.'

**Price v Strange** [1977] 3 WLR 943 Court of Appeal (Buckley, Scarman and Goff LJJ)

Specific performance - mutual availability of remedy

*Facts*

In 1966 the defendant sublet her flat to the plaintiff: the sub-tenancy expired in 1971 but he held over, continuing to pay rent. In February 1974 the defendant orally agreed to grant the plaintiff an underlease at an increased rent, the plaintiff agreeing (also orally) to execute certain repairs to the interior and exterior. He paid, and the defendant accepted, rent at the increased rate and completed the interior repairs, but before he could execute the exterior repairs the defendant repudiated the agreement and had the work carried out at her own expense. Nevertheless, she continued to accept rent for a further five months. The plaintiff sought specific performance, but the judge dismissed the action on the ground that the parties were not mutual at the date of the contract since the plaintiff's obligation to execute repairs could not be specifically enforced.

*Held*

A decree of specific performance would be granted.

Goff LJ:

'Surely the defence of want of mutuality should be governed by the state of affairs as seen at the hearing, since one is dealing not with a question affecting the initial validity of the contract, but with whether or not the discretionary remedy of specific performance should be granted ...

In my judgement ... the true principle is that one judges the defence of want of mutuality on the facts and circumstances as they exist at the hearing, albeit in the light of the whole conduct of the parties in relation to the subject-matter, and in the absence of any other disqualifying circumstances, the court will grant specific performance if it can be done without injustice or unfairness to the defendant ...

If, therefore, the plaintiff had been allowed to finish the work and had done so, I am clearly of opinion that it would have been right to order specific performance, but we have to consider what is the proper order, having regard to the fact that he was allowed to do an appreciable part and then not allowed to finish. Even so, in my judgment the result is still the same for the following reasons.

First, the defendant by standing by and allowing the plaintiff to spend time and money in carrying out an appreciable part of the work, created an equity against herself ...

Secondly, the work has in fact been finished. The court will not be deterred from granting specific performance in a proper case, even though there remain obligations still to be performed by the plaintiff, if the defendant can be properly protected: see ... also *C H Giles & Co Ltd* v *Morris*, where Megarry J said:

" ... the court may refuse to let the disadvantages and difficulties of specifically enforcing the obligation to perform personal services outweigh the suitability of the rest of the contract for specific performance, and the desirability of the contract as a whole being enforced. After all, pacta sunt servanda."

Still more readily should it act where the work has been done so that the defendant is not at risk of being ordered to grant the underlease and having no remedy except in damages for subsequent non-performance of the plaintiff's agreement to put the premises in repair.

Thirdly the defendant can be fully recompensed by a proper financial adjustment for the work she has had carried out.

I am fully satisfied that the law is as I have stated it to be, but even if I were wrong and the defence of mutuality ought to be considered according to the position at the date of the contract, still it is conceded, and in my judgment unquestionably correctly, that such a defence may be waived ... Then on the facts of this case the defence clearly was waived. Not only did the defendant permit the plaintiff to start on the work which would of itself be sufficient in my view, but she also accepted the increased rent payable under the contemplated underlease and went on doing so after her purported repudiation.

For these reasons I would allow this appeal and order specific performance but on terms that the plaintiff do pay to the defendant proper compensation for the work done by her. As a matter of strict right that must take the form of an enquiry what amount it would have cost the plaintiff to complete the works himself, with an order that he do pay or allow the defendant the amount certified with a set-off against any costs payable by the defendant, the costs of the enquiry being reserved. The plaintiff has however offered, subject to any question whether the expense incurred by the defendant was unnecessary or extravagant, to compensate her more handsomely by paying or allowing the actual cost to her, and it may well be possible, and certainly in the best interests of the parties, for them to agree a figure and so obviate proceeding with the enquiry, which could well involve them in further considerable litigation and expense.'

*Commentary*

See also *Sutton* v *Sutton* [1984] 2 WLR 146.

**Quadrant Visual Communications Ltd v Hutchinson Telephone (UK) Ltd** (1991) The Times 4 December Court of Appeal (Stocker, Butler-Sloss and Waller LJJ)

Equitable remedies - terms of the contract purporting to exclude - courts' discretion cannot be fettered

*Facts*

In a contract made between the two parties one particular clause appeared to exclude equitable remedies. There was some doubt about the construction of the clause.

*Held*

Once there was a request for an equitable remedy (in this case specific performance) its discretion could not be fettered. Whatever the construction of the clause it was the decision of the court alone as to whether to grant or refuse any equitable remedy.

## Ryan v Mutual Tontine Westminster Chamber Association [1893] 1 CR 116 (Court of Appeal)

Specific performance - supervision required

*Facts*

The defendant landlords covenanted to maintain in constant attendance a resident porter for the benefit of the plaintiff and the other tenants in the block. They appointed one Benton to this port, but he spent much of his time working as a chef, leaving his wife, charwomen and others to discharge his portering responsibilities. The plaintiff sought, inter alia, specific performance of this covenant.

*Held*

His claim would fail as the contract would require supervision of an order that the court was not prepared to undertake.

*Commentary*

But see *Posner* v *Scott-Lewis* [1986] 3 WLR 531.

## Shell UK Ltd v Lostock Garage Ltd

See chapter 4 - Contents of contracts.

## Sky Petroleum Ltd v VIP Petroleum Ltd [1974] 1 WLR 576 High Court (Goulding J)

Specific performance - when may be ordered

*Facts*

In 1970 the plaintiffs agreed that they would, for a minimum period of ten years, buy all the petrol needed for their filling stations from the defendants. Three years later the defendants purported to terminate the contract and the plaintiffs sought an interlocutory injunction to restrain the defendants from withholding supplies. At the time, the plaintiffs had little prospect of obtaining petrol from another supplier.

*Held*

The injunction would be granted.

Goulding J:

'Now I come to the most serious hurdle in the way of the plaintiff company which is the well-known doctrine that the court refuses specific performance of a contract to sell and purchase chattels not specific or ascertained. That is a well-established and salutary rule and I am entirely unconvinced by counsel for the plaintiff company when he tells me that an injunction in the form sought by him would not be specific enforcement at all. The matter is one of substance and not of form and it is, in my judgment, quite plain that I am for the time being specifically enforcing the contract if I grant an injunction. However the ratio behind the rule is, as I believe, that under the ordinary contract for the sale of non-specific goods, damages are a sufficient remedy. That, to my mind, is lacking in the circumstances of the present case. The evidence suggests, and indeed it is common knowledge, that the petroleum market is in an unusual state in which a would-be buyer cannot go out into the market and contract with another, seller, possibly at some sacrifice as to price. Here, the defendant company appears for practical purposes to be the plaintiff company's sole means of keeping its business going, and I am prepared so far to depart from the general rule as to try to preserve the position under the contract until a later date. I therefore propose to grant an injunction.'

**Sutton v Sutton** [1984] 2 WLR 146 High Court (John Mowbray QC)

Specific performance - agreement to transfer property on divorce

*Facts*

Seven years after their marriage, the parties bought the matrimonial home, the husband alone being responsible for the mortgage and, although the wife contributed to the purchase, the house was conveyed into the husband's name. Some years later they separated and the husband sought a divorce. They orally agreed that the wife would consent to a divorce, take over the mortgage and not apply for maintenance; the husband would let her keep her savings and transfer the house to her. After decree absolute, the husband refused to transfer the house, although the wife had paid off the mortgage. She sought specific performance and the husband contended that the agreement was not legally enforceable.

*Held*

The wife could not succeed as the agreement, which had not be made subject to the court's approval, purported to oust the court's jurisdiction.

John Mowbray QC:

'*Part performance*

In my view, Mrs Sutton's consenting to the divorce as agreed was an act of part performance. It is true that she was quite content to be divorced and that in the abstract consenting to a divorce does not indicate any contract, let alone a contract about land. But here the term about the house was in the petition which must have been posted to her when her formal consent was sought under the postal procedure which was followed. That means that her consent to the petition was itself, in the circumstances, tied to the contract about the house. *Steadman* v *Steadman* [1974] 3 WLR 56 is authority for that ...

*Mutuality*

Counsel for Mr Sutton argued that there was no mutuality, so specific performance should not be granted. He pointed out that Mrs Sutton's promise not to ask for maintenance was not enforceable. That is common ground. I shall come to the reasons later. Mrs Sutton herself said, in cross-examination, that her offer not to ask for maintenance was a big thing to offer. I find that it was an important part of the bargain. If this point had been taken early enough it might well have afforded a defence, but Mrs Sutton's consent to the divorce was at any rate an appreciable part of the agreement. Mr Sutton stood by and let her perform that part of her bargain irretrievably, and that raised an equity which prevents him from asserting this defence: see *Price* v *Strange* [1977] 3 WLR 943 ... For similar reasons, it is no defence to specific performance that Mr Sutton could not have compelled Mrs Sutton to consent to the divorce. Now she has consented and the divorce has been granted, that point comes too late.

*Ousting the jurisdiction*

The agreement between Mr and Mrs Sutton was that she would consent to the divorce, take over the mortgage and not ask for maintenance, and he would let her keep her savings and car and make over the house to her. They obviously intended by that agreement to dispose of the whole financial consequences of the divorce. There is a plain implication that he was not to transfer any other property to her and that she was not to make any payment or transfer to him. The agreement was not made subject to the court's approval. If it is enforceable as a contract, it leaves nothing for the court to do under ss23 and 24 of the Matrimonial Causes Act 1973 which empower the court to order maintenance and make property adjustments ...

The agreement between Mr and Mrs Sutton purported to dispose of the whole financial consequences of the divorce, both maintenance and property questions. If it was enforceable as a contract there was nothing left for the court to do under ss23 or 24 of the 1973 Act because the agreement prejudged and foreclosed all financial questions.

The House of Lords decided in *Hyman* v *Hyman* [1929] AC 601 that a wife could not validly contract with her husband not to apply for maintenance on a divorce and that a contract of that kind did not prevent her from applying. Lord Hailsham LC stated the principle like this:

" ... I am prepared to hold that the parties cannot validly make an agreement either (1) not to invoke the jurisdiction of the Court, or (2) to control the powers of the Court when its jurisdiction is invoked."

That is the rule of public policy which survived the disappearance of the rule against collusion. In my judgment, it applies to the contract here and prevents the financial settlement it contained, including Mr Sutton's promise to transfer the bungalow, from being enforced as a contract.'

## Warner Brothers Pictures Inc v Nelson [1937] 1 KB 209 High Court (Branson J)

Injunction - contract of service

*Facts*

Bette Davis (Mrs Nelson) contracted to appear in the plaintiffs' films and the plaintiffs alleged that, in breach of her contract, she intended to appear in another company's film. The plaintiffs sought an injunction.

*Held*

The injunction would be granted.

Branson J:

'The case before me is therefore one in which it would be proper to grant an injunction unless to do so would in the circumstances be tantamount to ordering the defendant to perform her contract or remain idle or unless damages would be the more appropriate remedy.

With regard to the first of these considerations, it would, of course, be impossible to grant an injunction covering all the negative covenants in the contract. That would, indeed, force the defendant to perform her contract or remain idle; but this objection is removed by the restricted form in which the injunction is sought. It is confined to forbidding the defendant, without the consent of the plaintiffs, to render any services for or in any motion picture or stage production for anyone other than the plaintiffs.

It was also urged that the difference between what the defendant can earn as a film artiste and what she might expect to earn by any other form of activity is so great that she will in effect be driven to perform her contract. That is not the criterion adopted in any of the decided cases. The defendant is stated to be a person of intelligence, capacity and means, and no evidence was adduced to show that, if enjoined form doing the specified acts otherwise than for the plaintiffs, she will not be able to employ herself both usefully and remuneratively in other spheres of activity, though not as remuneratively as in her special line. She will not be driven, although she may be tempted, to perform the contract, and the fact that she may be so tempted is no objection to the grant of an injunction. This appears from the judgment of Lord St Leonards LC in *Lumley* v *Wagner* ...

With regard to the question whether damages is not the more appropriate remedy, I have the uncontradicted evidence of the plaintiffs as to the difficulty of estimating the damages which they may suffer from the breach by the defendant of her contract. I think it is not inappropriate to refer to the fact that, in the contract between the parties ... there is a formal admission by the defendant that her services, being "of a special, unique, extraordinary and intellectual character" gives them a particular value, "the loss of which cannot be reasonably or adequately compensated in damages" and that a breach may "cost the producer great and irreparable injury and damage," and the artiste expressly agrees that the producer shall be entitled to the remedy of injunction. Of course, parties cannot contract themselves out of the law; but it assists, at all events, on the question of evidence as to the applicability of an injunction in the present case, to find the parties formally recognising that which is now before the court as a matter of evidence, that in cases of this kind injunction is a more appropriate remedy than damages.'

*Commentary*

See also *Page One Records Ltd* v *Britton* [1968] 1 WLR 157.

# 16 QUASI-CONTRACT

**Aiken v Short** (1856) 1 H & N 210 Court of Exchequer (Pollock CB, Platt, Martin and Bramwell BB)

Money paid under mistake - right of recovery

*Facts*

The defendant lent one Carter £200, taking as security, inter alia, an equitable charge on some lands which the plaintiff's bank subsequently purchased. When the defendant asked for the repayment of the money, he was referred to the plaintiffs who paid off the charge. It subsequently appeared that Carter had no title to the property so the plaintiffs sued for the recovery of the money paid.

*Held*

The action could not succeed.

Bramwell B:

'In order to entitle a person to recover back money paid under a mistake of fact, the mistake must be as to a fact which, if true, would make the person paying liable to pay the money; not where, if true, it would merely make it desirable that he should pay the money. Here, if the fact was true, the bankers were at liberty to pay or not, as they pleased. But relying on the belief that the defendant had a valid security, they, having a subsequent legal mortgage, chose to pay off the defendant's charge. It is impossible to say that this case falls within the rule. The mistake of fact was, that the bank thought that they could sell the estate for a better price. It is true that if the plaintiffs could recover back this money from the defendant, there would be no difficulty in the way of the defendant suing Carter ...

I am of opinion they cannot [maintain this action], having voluntarily parted with their money to purchase that which the defendant had to sell, though no doubt it turned out to be different to, and of less value than, what they expected.'

*Commentary*

See also *Morgan* v *Ashcroft* [1938] 1 KB 49 and *Larner* v *London County Council* [1949] 2 KB 683.

**Baldry v Marshall Ltd** [1925] 1 KB 260 Court of Appeal (Bankes, Atkin and Sargant LJJ)

Car not suitable - purchase price recoverable?

*Facts*

The plaintiff stockbroker told the defendant car dealers that he wanted a 'comfortable and suitable ... touring car'. The defendants said that they thought a Bugatti would satisfy these requirements and the plaintiff bought one. The Bugatti turned out to be unsuitable so the plaintiff sued for the return of the purchase money.

*Held*

He was entitled to succeed as there had been a breach of the implied condition that the car would be reasonably fit for touring purposes.

**Brooks Wharf & Bull Wharf Ltd v Goodman Bros**
See Introduction.

**Craven-Ellis v Canons Ltd** [1936] 2 KB 403 Court of Appeal (Greer and Greene LJJ and Talbot J)

Services rendered - quantum meruit

*Facts*

In 1927 the plaintiff estate agent was employed by Parol Estates Ltd in connection with the development of an estate. The following year the defendant company was formed to purchase the estate and the plaintiff was one of its directors. Without any express agreement, the plaintiff continued his work. After two months, none of the directors having become qualified in accordance with the company's articles, they all became incapable of acting. The company subsequently purported to enter into a service agreement with the plaintiff as managing director, but the deal was affixed by resolution of the unqualified directors and for this reason was a nullity.

*Held*

The plaintiff was entitled to recover on a quantum meruit for all his services rendered to the defendant company.

Greer LJ:

'As regards the services rendered [before the purported agreement], there is, in my judgment, no defence to the claim. These services were rendered by the plaintiff not as managing director or as a director, but as an estate agent, and there was no contract in existence which could present any obstacle to a claim based on a *quantum meruit* for services rendered and accepted.

As regards the plaintiff's services after the date of the contract, I think the plaintiff is also entitled to succeed. The contract, having been made by directors who had no authority to make it with one of themselves, who had notice of their want of authority, was not binding on either party. It was, in fact, a nullity, and presents no obstacle to the implied promise to pay on a *quantum meruit* basis which arises from the performance of the services and the implied acceptance of the same by the company ...

In my judgment, the obligation to pay reasonable remuneration for the work done when there is no binding contract between the parties is imposed by a rule of law, and not by an inference of fact arising from the acceptance of service or goods ...

I accordingly think that the defendants must pay on the basis of a *quantum meruit* not only for the services rendered before the date of the invalid agreement, but also for the services after that date. I think the appeal should be allowed, and judgment given for such a sum as shall be found to be due on the basis of a *quantum meruit* in respect of all services rendered by the plaintiff to the company ...'

**Exall v Partridge** (1799) 8 Term Rep 308 Court of King's Bench (Lord Kenyon CJ, Grose, Lawrence and Le Blanc JJ)

Distress - liability to third party

*Facts*

To the plaintiff's knowledge, two of the three defendants had assigned their lease to the third. The plaintiff put his carriage on the premises under the care of the third defendant and it was taken as a distress by the landlord for rent in arrear. In order to redeem his carriage, the plaintiff paid off the arrears of rent and now sued to recover that sum.

*Held*

His action would be successful.

Grose J:

'The question is whether the payment made by the plaintiff under these circumstances were such a one from which the law will imply a promise by the three defendants to repay. I think that it was. All the three defendants were originally liable to the landlord for the rent; there was an express covenant by all, from which none of them was released. One of the defendants only being in the occupation of these premises, the plaintiff put his goods there which the landlord distrained for rent, as he had a right to do; then, for the purpose of getting back his goods he paid the rent to the landlord which all the three defendants were bound to pay. The plaintiff could not have relieved himself from the distress without paying the rent; it was not, therefore, a voluntary, but a compulsory payment. Under these circumstances, the law implies a promise by the three defendants to repay the plaintiff and, on this short ground, I am of opinion that the action may be maintained.'

## Fibrosa Spolka Akcyjna v Fairburn Lawson Combe Barbour Ltd

See chapter 12 - Frustration.

## Foley v Classique Coaches Ltd

See chapter 3 - Certainty and form of contract.

## Karflex Ltd v Poole [1933] 2 KB 251 High Court (Acton and Goddard JJ)

Hire-purchase agreement - 'owner' not owner

*Facts*

A hire-purchase agreement was entered into between the plaintiffs, the 'owners' of a car, and the defendant. After falling into arrears with his monthly payments, the defendant discovered that the plaintiffs did not in fact own the vehicle.

*Held*

The plaintiffs were not entitled to enforce the agreement and the defendant could recover the moneys which he had paid to them.

## Kelly v Solari (1841) 9 M & W 54 Court of Exchequer (Lord Abinger CB, Parke, Gurney and Rolfe BB)

Money paid under mistake - facts bona fide forgotten

*Facts*

A man died on 18 October having (by mistake) failed to pay a premium due on the preceding 3 September. Forgetting, they said, that the policy had lapsed, on the defendant's application the plaintiff insurers made a payment under the policy to the defendant, the deceased's executrix. The plaintiffs sought to recover the sum so paid.

*Held*

There should be a new trial to establish the exact facts.

Lord Abinger CB:

'The safest rule ... is that if the party makes the payment with the full knowledge of the facts, although under ignorance of the law, there being no fraud on the other side, he cannot recover it back again. There may also be cases in which, although he might by investigation learn the state of facts more accurately, he declines to do so, and chooses to pay the money notwithstanding; in that case there can be no doubt that he is equally bound. Then there is a third case, and the most difficult one - where the party had once a full knowledge of the facts but has since forgotten them. I certainly laid down the rule too widely to the jury when I told them that, if the directors once knew the facts, they must be taken still to know them and could not recover by saying that they had since forgotten them. I think that the knowledge of the facts which disentitles the party from recovering must mean a knowledge existing in the mind at the time of payment. I have little doubt in this case that the directors had forgotten the fact, otherwise I do not believe they would have brought the action; but as counsel for the defendant certainly has a right to have that question submitted to the jury, there must be a new trial.'

**Kerrison v Glyn, Mills, Currie & Co** (1911) 81 LJKB 465 House of Lords (Earl of Halsbury, Lord Atkinson, Lord Shaw and Lord Mersey)

Mistakes of fact - payment to third party

*Facts*

The appellant had a standing arrangement with Kessler and Co, New York bankers, whereby they would honour drafts of a Mexican company up to £500, the appellant agreeing to reimburse in the New York bankers' account with the respondents in London. On request from New York, the appellant so paid £500, but on the same day the New York bankers became bankrupt. The appellant sought the repayment of the £500.

*Held*

He was entitled to succeed.

Lord Mersey:

'The facts bring the case directly within the terms of the judgment of Lord Loreburn LC in *Kleinwort Sons & Co* v *Dunlop Rubber Co*, where he says (97 LT at p264):

"It is indisputable that if money is paid under a mistake of fact, and is re-demanded from the person who received it before his position has been altered to his disadvantage, the money must be repaid, in whatever character it was received."

An attempt was made to take this case out of this plain and simple rule of law by saying that the defendants, being Kessler & Co's bankers, had, by the receipt of the money, become debtors of Kessler & Co, and could not, therefore, be called upon to repay the plaintiff. This is, in my opinion, a fallacy. No doubt when a banker receives money, either from his customer or from a third person on account of his customer, he becomes his customer's debtor for the amount so received. But this does not entitle the banker to retain money which in common honesty ought not to be kept. If, indeed, the banker has paid over the money to his customer, or has altered his position in relation to his customer to his own detriment, on the faith of the payment, the banker may refuse to repay the amount and may leave the person who has paid him to enforce his remedy against the customer. But the circumstances here are that Messrs Glyn Mills & Co had in no way altered their position when they were asked to refund the money. They held money which they ought not to retain because it had been paid to them under a mistake of fact, and, in the words of the Lord Chancellor, it does not matter in what character it was received by them.'

**Kiriri Cotton Co Ltd v Dewani**

See chapter 11 - Illegality.

**Larner v London County Council** [1949] 2 KB 683 Court of Appeal (Lord Goddard, CJ, Denning LJ and Birkett J)

Money overpaid by mistake - right to recover

*Facts*

The defendants resolved to make up the difference between their employees' war services pay and former civilian pay. Although he knew that he had to inform the defendants of increases in his war service pay, the plaintiff employee did not do so: consequently, he was overpaid by the defendants.

*Held*

The defendants were entitled to recover the overpayments.

Denning LJ:

'The real question in this case arises on the counterclaim. Are the council entitled to recover from the plaintiff the sums which they overpaid him? Overpay him they certainly did. That is admitted. The overpayment was due to a mistake of fact. That is also admitted. They were mistaken as to the amount of his service pay. But it is said that they were voluntary payments which were not made in discharge of any legal liability, and cannot, therefore, be recovered back. For this proposition reliance was placed on the *dictum* of Bramwell B in *Aiken* v *Short* (1856) 1 H & N 210, but that *dictum*, as Scott LJ pointed out in *Morgan* v *Ashcroft* [1938] 1 KB 49, cannot be regarded as an exhaustive statement of the law. Take the present case. The London County Council, by their resolution, for good reasons of national policy, made a promise to the men which they were in honour bound to fulfil. The payments made under that promise were not mere gratuities. They were made as a matter of duty. Indeed, that is how both sides regarded them. They spoke of them as sums "due" to the men, that is, as sums the men were entitled to under the promise contained in the resolution. If then, owing to a mistake of fact, the council paid one of the men more than he was entitled to under the promise, why should he not repay the excess, at any rate if he has not changed his position for the worse? It is not necessary to inquire whether there was any consideration for the promise so as to enable it to be enforced in a court of law. It may be that, because the men were legally bound to go to the war, there was in strictness no consideration for the promise but that does not matter. It is not a question here of enforcing the promise by action. It is a question of recovering overpayments made in the belief that they were due under the promise, but, in fact, not due. They were sums which the council never promised the plaintiff and which they would never have paid him had they known the true facts. They were paid under a mistake of fact, and he is bound to repay them unless he has changed his position for the worse because of them.

It is next said, however, that the London County Council should not be allowed to recover the money because the plaintiff changed his position for the worse before the council asked for it back. He spent the money on living expenses - or his wife spent it for him - and he spent it in a way which he would not otherwise have done. This defence of estoppel, as it is called - or more accurately, change of circumstances - must, however, not be extended beyond its proper bounds. Speaking generally, the fact that the recipient has spent the money beyond recall is no defence unless there was some fault, as, for instance, some neglect or breach of duty or misconduct, on the part of the pay-master and none on the part of the recipient ... But if the recipient was himself at fault and the pay-master was not - as, for instance, if the mistake was due to an innocent misrepresentation or a breach of duty by the recipient - he clearly cannot escape liability by saying that he has spent the money. That is the position here. On the judge's findings the London County Council were not at fault at all, but the plaintiff was. He did not keep them accurately informed of the various changes in his service pay. It does not lie in his mouth to say that, if he had done so, it would have made no difference. It might well have put them on inquiry and the mistake might not have been made at all. Many men did, in fact, fulfil their duty and were not overpaid. It would be strange, indeed, if those who neglected their duty were to be allowed to keep their gain.'

**Meates v Westpac Banking Corporation** (1990) The Times 5 July Privy Council (Lords Templeman, Roskill, Lowry, Goff of Chieveley and Oliver of Aylmerton)

Quasi-contract - reliance on conversation

*Facts*

The government of New Zealand had issued a number of formal documents as part of a project to establish new industries. The project never came into effect but the appellants claimed that as a result of conversations, press statements and so on they had understood that the government was prepared to indemnify them. They had incurred considerable expenses.

*Held*

As a general rule governments and large corporations intend ultimately to be bound only by formal written documents. Any implied undertaking made verbally, therefore, in the face of the written documents' express terms, could not be enforced. No quasi-contractual obligation existed.

**Morgan v Ashcroft** [1938] 1 KB 49 Court of Appeal (Sir Wilfrid Greene MR and Scott LJ)

Money paid under mistake of fact - right to recover

*Facts*

Due to a mistake by the plaintiff bookmaker's clerk, the defendant customer was overpaid.

*Held*

The plaintiff's action for the recovery of the money could not succeed. The amount of the overpayment could only be determined by examining accounts of gaming transactions and, by virtue of the Gaming Act 1845, this was a task the court could not undertake.

Sir Wilfrid Greene MR:

'But there is another ground, upon which the action ought, in my opinion, to have been dismissed, and, as we have had the benefit of a full argument upon it, I think it right to express my views upon it. The plaintiff's claim is for money had and received, and it is based upon what the county court judge found to be a mistake of fact. The question which arises is, can such a claim succeed in the circumstances of this case? In my opinion, it cannot ...

I come ... to the conclusion that the observations of Bramwell B [in *Aiken v Short* (1856) 1 H & N 210] supported, as they are, by much weight of judicial opinion, are, so far as regards the class of mistake with which he was dealing, in agreement with the more recent authorities, and I propose to follow them. It was said, on behalf of the respondent, that these observations do not correctly state the law. I do not agree, although I am disposed to think that they cannot be taken as an exhaustive statement of the law, but must be confined to cases where the only mistake is as to the nature of the transaction. For example, if A makes a voluntary payment of money to B, under the mistaken belief that he is C, it may well be that A can recover it. Bramwell B was not dealing with a case such as that, since he was assuming that there was no such error *in persona*. If we are to be guided by the analogous case of contract, where mistake as to the person contracted with negatives the intention to contract, the mistake in the case which I have mentioned ought to be held to negative the intention to pay the money, and the money should be recoverable. But it is not necessary to pursue this matter further. It is sufficient to say that, in my opinion, the present case falls within principles laid down by Bramwell B, and in the more recent authorities. In making the payment, the respondent was, it is true, under a mistake as to the nature of the transaction. He thought that a wagering debt was due from himself to the appellant, whereas in fact it was not. But, if the supposed fact had been true, the respondent would have been under no liability to make the payment, which, therefore, was intended to be a voluntary payment. Upon the true facts, the payment was still a voluntary payment; and there is, in my opinion, no such fundamental or basic distinction between the one voluntary payment and the other that the law can, for present purposes, differentiate between them, and say that there was no intention to make the one because the intention was to make the other.'

*Commentary*

See also *Larner* v *London County Council* [1949] 2 KB 683.

**Owen v Tate** [1976] QB 402 Court of Appeal (Stephenson, Scarman and Ormrod LJJ)

Surety - reimbursement

*Facts* - the county court judge summarised the position as follows:

'On the 26th February 1965 the defendants obtained a loan from Lloyds Bank, Sunderland. This loan was secured by a charge by way of legal mortgage upon the property of a Miss Lightfoot. The plaintiff was in no way concerned with this transaction, and received no money from the defendants. In 1969 Miss Lightfoot became concerned that her deeds were being held by the bank to secure the defendants' loan. She consulted the plaintiff, who offered to help her to get her deeds back. Miss Lightfoot was a former employee of the plaintiff. The plaintiff knew that Miss Lightfoot had cohabited with a Mr Russell, who had a dispute with the defendants concerning money. Mr Russell is now deceased. In order to oblige Miss Lightfoot, and in order to obtain her deeds and keep them in a safe place, the plaintiff deposited £350 with Lloyds Bank and signed a form of guarantee by which he guaranteed payment of all the money limited to £350, due, owing or incurred to Lloyds Bank by the defendants. He did not consult the defendants before doing this. He was not asked to do this by the defendants. His motive was only to help Miss Lightfoot. He did not speak to the defendants at all about the matter. On the 17th December 1970 Lloyds Bank applied £350, held by them in support of the plaintiff's said guarantee, in repayment of the defendants' debt. On 15th January 1971 the plaintiff's solicitor demanded from the defendants reimbursement of this sum. The defendants refused and the battle was joined.'

His claim having been dismissed, the plaintiff appealed.

*Held*

The appeal would not succeed as, in all the circumstances, it would not be just and equitable to grant the plaintiff the right of reimbursement.

Scarman LJ:

'Looking, therefore, at the circumstances as a whole, and giving weight to both phases of the transaction, I come to the conclusion that the plaintiff has failed to make out a case that it would be just and reasonable in the circumstances to grant him a right to reimbursement. Initially he was a volunteer; he has, as I understand the findings of fact of the judge and as I read the documents in the case, established no facts, either initially when he assumed the obligation, or later when he was called on to make the payment, such as to show that it was just and reasonable that he should have a right of indemnity. I think, therefore, that on the facts as found this appeal fails.

In my judgment, the true principle of the matter can be stated very shortly, without reference to volunteers or to the compulsions of the law, and I state it as follows. If without an antecedent request a person assumes an obligation or makes a payment for the benefit of another, the law will, as a general rule, refuse him a right of indemnity. But if he can show that in the particular circumstances of the case there was some necessity for the obligation to be assumed, then the law will grant him a right of reimbursement if in all the circumstances it is just and reasonable to do so. In the present case the evidence is that the plaintiff acted not only behind the backs of the defendants initially, but in the interests of another, and despite their protest. When the moment came for him to honour the obligation thus assumed the defendants are not to be criticised, in my judgment, for having accepted the benefit of a transaction which they neither wanted nor sought.'

**Planché v Colburn** (1831) 8 Bing 14 Court of Common Pleas (Tindal CJ, Gaselee, Bosanquet and Alderson JJ)

Literary work abandoned - author's entitlement

*Facts*

The plaintiff agreed with the defendant publishers to contribute, for £100, a volume on costume and ancient armour for 'The Juvenile Library'. After the plaintiff had begun work, the defendants abandoned the series. The plaintiff sued for breach of contract and he was awarded £50 damages.

*Held*

This verdict would not be disturbed.

Bosanquet J:

'The plaintiff is entitled to retain his verdict. The jury have found that the contract was abandoned but it is said that the plaintiff ought to have tendered or delivered the work. It was part of the contract, however, that the work should be published in a particular shape and if it had been delivered after the abandonment of the original design, it might have been published in a way not consistent with the plaintiff's reputation, or not at all.'

**Rowland v Divall** [1923] 2 KB 500 Court of Appeal (Bankes, Scrutton and Atkin LJJ)

No right to sell goods - recovery of price paid

*Facts*

In May 1922 the plaintiff dealer bought a car from the defendant. He sold it in July, but in September the police took possession of the vehicle on the ground that it was a stolen car and that the person who had sold it to the defendant had no title to sell it. The plaintiff sued to recover the price which he had paid the defendant for the car.

*Held*

He was entitled to succeed as the defendant had been in breach of the condition implied by statute that he had the right to sell the car.

Bankes LJ:

'In my opinion, that cannot possibly be said here. The plaintiff received nothing, no portion of what he had agreed to buy. It is quite true that a car was handed over to him, but the person who handed it over to him had no right to hand it over to him and no title to it. In these circumstances the use by the plaintiff to the extent to which he had used it seems to me to be quite immaterial in considering whether anything was done which entitles the defendant to say that the condition has been waived or converted into a warranty. In these circumstances I think that the right of the plaintiff to recover the whole of the purchase money remains, and that the view taken by the learned judge that he should sue in damages was not justified.'

Scrutton LJ:

'It certainly seems to me that in a case of rescission for the breach of a condition that the seller has a right to sell the goods, it cannot be that the purchaser is deprived of his right to get back the purchase money because he cannot restore the goods which, from the nature of the transaction, are not the goods of the seller at all, and which the seller has, therefore, no right to in any circumstances. For these reasons it seems to me, with deference to the learned judge below, that he came to a wrong conclusion and that the plaintiff is entitled to recover the whole of the purchase money, as and for the total failure of the consideration, inasmuch as the seller did not give that which he contracted to give, namely, the legal ownership of the car and the legal right to possession of it.'

*Commentary*

Applied in *Butterworth* v *Kingsway Motors Ltd* [1954] 1 WLR 1286.


## Solle v Butcher

See chapter 8 - Mistake.


## Weld-Blundell v Synott [1940] 2 KB 107 High Court (Asquith J)

Money paid under mistake of fact - right to recover

*Facts*

The parties were first and second mortgagees. The mortgagor defaulted and the plaintiff first mortgagees exercised their power of sale and the proceeds left for the defendant second mortgagees amounted to £301. Owing to a miscalculation by the plaintiffs, the defendants were paid £413 and the plaintiffs now sought to recover the amount overpaid as money paid under a mistake of fact.

*Held*

The plaintiffs would be successful.

Asquith J:

'When a mistake is one affecting obligation, I think that it is between the parties ... The only basis on which it has been argued that, in the present case, the mistake is not of this character is that it was, or arose from, a mistake as to what the mortgagor owed the plaintiffs, and, therefore, was a mistake between the mortgagor and the plaintiffs, and not between the plaintiffs and the defendant. I cannot see why it should not be both. Where what A owes to B depends on what A is owed by C, and A, owing to a mistake as to the latter amount, automatically also makes a mistake as to the former amount, there is a mistake, in my view, not only as between A and C, but also as between A and B. I therefore hold that the defence that the mistake was not *inter partes* fails.'

# 17 AGENCY

**Armstrong v Jackson**

See chapter 5 - Misrepresentation.

**Badgerhill Properties v Cottrell** (1991) The Independent 12 June Court of Appeal (Mustill, Balcombe and Woolf LJJ)

Agent's personal liability - intention of the parties

*Facts*

In making contracts for work with the defendant, T, the director of the plaintiff company, drew up contracts on headed notepaper bearing the company name. Against his own name on this paper T had written 'director' in brackets. The company sued the defendant for non-payment for work done, while the defendants counterclaimed that the work was defective.

The question arose as to whether T was personally liable, whether he had been acting on his own behalf or that of the principal company.

*Held*

Whether T was acting on his own behalf depended to some degree on the intention of the parties. The language of the contract, the fact that the company name appeared on the headed paper, the fact that the company's trading name appeared in the contract all seemed to indicate that the defendant was trading with whoever called themselves by the trade name of the company. The fact that the word agent did not appear was not enough to prevent the contract's being construed as a contract of agency.

**Bolton Partners v Lambert** (1881) 41 Ch D 295 Court of Appeal (Lindley, Lopes and Cotton LJJ)

Unauthorised acceptance - ratification

*Facts*

Without its authority and purporting to act as agent on the company's behalf, the managing director of the company accepted an offer by the defendant to purchase the company's sugar works. The defendant then withdrew his offer, but the company ratified the managing director's acceptance.

*Held*

The defendant was bound. The ratification related back to the managing director's acceptance and the defendant's purported withdrawal was therefore of no effect.

Cotton LJ:

'... the acceptance by Scratchley [the managing director] did constitute a contract, subject to its being shewn that [he] had authority to bind the company ... when and as soon as authority was given ... the authority was thrown back to the time when the act was done by Scratchley, and prevented the defendant withdrawing his offer, because it was no longer an offer, but a binding contract.'

**Comet Group plc v British Sky Broadcasting** [1991] TLR 211 Queen's Bench Division (Phillips J)

Promotion contract not the same as agency

*Facts*

A contract between British Satellite Broadcasting and Comet, whereby Comet would promote BSB's equipment, operated until BSB's merger with Sky Television in 1990. At that point BSB instructed Comet to suspend all further sales of BSB equipment. The contract made provision expressly for the period until February 1991. The action taken by BSB in November 1990 represented a considerable financial loss to Comet. BSB attempted to argue that the promotion contract was a form of agency and cited cases such as *Rhodes* v *Forwood* (1876) 1 App Cas 256 and *Hamlyn* v *Wood* [1891] 2 QB 488, all of which had in common that the court had declined to imply into the contract a term that the principal would continue in business until the expiry of the term agreed. Comet argued that the contract was not one of agency and that BSB's conduct amounted to a repudiation of the contract giving rise to an action for damages.

*Held*

The court agreed with the latter argument, holding that the contract differed from agency in a number of respects, most notably in that Comet were required to purchase at the outset £13m of equipment.

**Industrie Chimiche Italia Centrale & Cerealfin SA v Alexander G Tsavliris & Sons Maritime Co, Panchristo Shipping Co SA and Bula Shipping Corporation, The Choko Star** [1990] 1 Lloyd's Rep 516 Court of Appeal (Slade, Parker and Glidewell LJJ)

Agency of necessity

*Facts*

The question as to whether the master of a ship had authority to sign a Lloyd's Open Form for cargo (as opposed to salvage of the ship itself) arose. In the initial hearing the court held that there was implied (and hence apparent) authority to do so stemming from the authority vested in the mastership from the owners and/or shippers.

*Held*

There was no such implied authority and only the ancient rules as to agency of necessity might apply. The doctrine of agency of necessity confers, usually on shipmasters, certain authority by operation of law given certain conditions relating to emergency. Of those conditions the requirement that consultation between ship's master and owners/shippers should not be possible gives most difficulty in these days of virtually instantaneous communications. Here, the doctrine of agency of necessity did apply.

*Commentary*

A further appeal to the House of Lords is pending.

**Keighley, Maxsted & Co v Durant** [1901] AC 240 House of Lords (Earl of Halsbury LC, Lord Macnaghten, Lord Shand, Lord Davey, Lord James of Hereford, Lord Brampton, Lord Robertson and Lord Lindley)

Contract - ratification by third party

*Facts*

Authorised to buy wheat at a certain price on a joint account for himself and the appellants, a corn merchant purchased wheat from the respondents at a higher price in his own name. Next day the appellants ratified the transaction but subsequently failed to take delivery of the wheat. The respondents sought damages for breach of contract.

*Held*

Their action could not succeed.

Lord Shand:

'The question which arises ... is whether, where a person has avowedly made a contract for himself - first, without a suggestion that he is acting to any extent for another (an undisclosed principal), and, secondly, without any authority to act for another, he can effectually bind a third party as principal, or as a joint obligant with himself, to the person with whom he contracted, by the fact that in his own mind merely he made a contract in the hope and expectation that his contract would be ratified or shared by the person as to whom he entertained that hope and expectation. I am clearly of opinion ... that he cannot. The only contract actually made is by the person himself and for himself; and it seems to me to be conclusive against the argument for the respondent, that if his reasoning were sound it would be in his power, on an averment of what was passing in his own mind, to make the contract afterwards, either one for himself only, as in fact it was, or one affecting or binding on another as a contracting party, even although he had no authority for this. The result would be to give one of two contracting parties in his option, merely from what was passing in his own mind, and not disclosed, the power of saying that the contract was his alone, or a contract in which others were bound to him. That I think he certainly cannot do in any case where he had no authority when he made the contract to bind anyone but himself'.

**Kelner v Baxter** (1866) LR 2 CP 174 Court of Common Pleas (Erle CJ, Willes and Byles JJ)

Principal and agent - no existing principal

*Facts*

It was proposed that a company yet to be formed, would purchase the plaintiff's hotel and stock and the promoters of the company signed an agreement to purchase the plaintiff's 'extra stock' of wines. This agreement the promoters signed 'on behalf of the proposed ... company'. Subsequently the company received a certificate of incorporation, but it collapsed before payment was made for the wine.

*Held*

The promoters were personally liable.

Erle CJ:

'It was once ... thought that an inchoate liability might be incurred on behalf of a proposed company, which would become binding on it when subsequently formed: but that notion was manifestly contrary to the principles upon which the law of contract is founded. There must be two parties to a contract; and the rights and obligations which it creates cannot be transferred by one of them to a third person who was not in a condition to be bound by it at the time it was made'.

**Ryan v Pilkington** [1959] 1 WLR 403 Court of Appeal (Hodson, Morris and Willner LJJ)

Estate agent - authority to take deposit

*Facts*

Wishing to sell Ferndale, the owner, the second defendant, instructed the first defendant, an estate agent, to find a purchaser. A prospective purchaser agreed to buy the property, subject to contract, and on different occasions paid the first defendant two sums of £100 which the first defendant received 'as agent for' the second defendant and 'as agent' respectively. Subsequently, the second defendant called off the sale: could the plaintiff, the prospective purchaser, recover the £200 from him?

*Held*

He could as the first defendant had had ostensible authority to take the deposits as agent for the second defendant.

Morris LJ:

'If the estate agent had received the £200 as a stake-holder, then the prospective purchaser would be entitled to the £200 from the estate agent. If the estate agent had received the £200 as agent for the vendor, the prospective purchaser would be entitled to receive the £200 from the vendor. The estate agent purported to receive this money as agent for [the second defendant]. He so signed a receipt for the first £100. He signed a receipt for the second £100 "as agent". It seems to me that, as the prospective purchaser had the receipt, as he presumably had it after the first £100 was paid, as he presumably produced it so as to have a record of the second £100 also made on it, and as he retained the document thereafter, he must be taken to have known that the estate agent was purporting to receive the £200 not as stake-holder but as agent. Therefore, it appears to me that the prospective purchaser cannot say that the estate agent received the money as stake-holder. Did the estate agent then receive the money as agent for the vendor? The vendor says: "He never received it as my agent or on my behalf or with my authority". The issue in the appeal is whether that is so or not.

There is no record of any express authority from the vendor to the estate agent to ask for or to receive a deposit. Was there, therefore, implied authority in the estate agent to receive the deposit? Was it within the scope of his authority to receive this £200? I have reached the conclusion that, on the facts of this case, it was within the estate agent's authority ... It seems to me that this case depends, as every case in this branch of activity must do, on its own facts and circumstances, but I have reached the conclusion that on the facts of this case it was reasonably incidental to what the estate agent was instructed to do that he should receive these two sums of £100 ... It seems to me that there was ostensible authority to receive it on his behalf, that it was so received, and that the vendor became obliged to repay it in the events that happened.'

**Spiro v Lintern** [1973] 1 WLR 1002 Court of Appeal (Lawton, James LJJ and Mocatta J)

Estoppel by conduct

*Facts*

Hamels was owned by the first defendant and, at his request, his wife, the second defendant, placed the property in the hands of estate agents for sale. The plaintiff made an unconditional offer to buy provided he could have an unconditional acceptance: the wife told the agent to accept and he signed the contract 'As agents for the vendor', but the wife had acted without her husband's authority. The plaintiff instructed solicitors to proceed with the purchase and, with the husband's apparent approval, instructed an architect and a builder to carry out some repairs. After the building work had been completed, the husband resisted a claim for specific performance on the ground that the contract had been entered into without his authority.

*Held*

Specific performance would be granted as, in the circumstances, the husband was estopped from asserting lack of authority on his wife's part.

Buckley LJ:

'In our judgment, the first defendant cannot rely on his own failure to recognise any right he had to repudiate the contract on the ground of his wife's lack of authority. To found an estoppel it is not necessary that the representation relied on should be false to the knowledge of the representor, provided that the representor acts in such a way that a reasonable man would take the representation to be true and believe that he was intended to act on it. In the present case there can, in our opinion, be no doubt that both the first defendant and [his solicitor] acted in such a way that a reasonable man in the plaintiff's position would assume that the second defendant had acted with her husband's authority in instructing [the agents] to sign the contract and would believe that the first defendant and [his solicitor] intended that the plaintiff should act on the contract as a contract binding between himself and the first defendant. That the plaintiff should so view the position was all the more probable because of the fact that the first and second defendants were husband and wife and so presumably entirely within one another's confidence. Moreover, it is in our opinion, clear on the evidence that the first defendant's own intention was to complete the sale to the plaintiff ... We think ... that the plaintiff was clearly induced by the representations to employ his architect and to employ the builder to carry out the remedial work connected with the damp. We do not know what expense the plaintiff incurred in these respects, but it is unlikely to have been negligible. Moreover, the plaintiff was induced by the representations to incur further expense in the continued employment of [her solicitor] in the conveyancing work connected with the purchase of Hamels.

In our judgment, all the necessary incidents of a valid estoppel by representation are present in this case. The learned judge was, in our opinion, perfectly right in concluding that the first defendant was estopped from asserting that the contract was entered into without his authority.'

**Springer v Great Western Railway Co** [1921] 1 KB 257 Court of Appeal (Bankes, Warrington and Scrutton LJJ)

Sale of goods in emergency

*Facts*

The defendants had undertaken to carry tomatoes from Jersey to the plaintiffs in Covent Garden. Due to bad weather, the journey to Weymouth took three days: on arrival there, there was a strike on the railway. The tomatoes began to go off and, without communicating with the plaintiffs, the defendants sold them all locally. The plaintiffs were awarded damages for breach of duty: the defendants appealed.

*Held*

The appeal would be dismissed.

Scrutton LJ:

'The railway company sold somebody else's goods, and they have not the right to sell other people's goods unless they can establish certain conditions. They are agents to carry the goods, and not to sell them. To sell them, circumstances must exist which put them in the position of agents of necessity for the owners, to take the action which is necessary in the interests of the owners. Those conditions do not arise if the railway company can communicate with the owners and get their instructions. If the railway company can ask the owner what is to be done in the circumstances with any reasonable chance of getting an answer, they have no business to take upon themselves the sale of the property. They must give the owner a chance of deciding the way in which he will deal with the property, and very often he knows very much better than the railway company what is the best thing to do ... The first thing which the railway company must show to justify their selling the goods is that it was impossible commercially to communicate with the owner and receive instructions from him. If they show that, they must then justify the sale by showing that it was the only reasonable business course to take in the circumstances ... Was it commercially impossible ... to communicate with the consignee at Covent Garden? The question answers itself. Of course, it was not commercially impossible. The reason why [the defendants seem] to have not communicated is that [they] did not then know the exact state of the tomatoes, and consequently could not give the fullest information to the consignee. That was not a reason which justified [them] in not communicating. [They] should, in my view, have communicated with the consignee, stating the probable delay, anything [they] knew about the condition of the goods, and asking for instructions as to what [they] should do.'

**Watteau v Fenwick** [1893] 1 QB 346 High Court (Lord Coleridge CJ and Wills J)

Undisclosed principal - liability

*Facts*

One Humble sold his public house to the defendants, but remained there as their manager. His name remained over the door and the licence continued to be in his name. Although he was forbidden by the defendants to buy cigars on credit, he bought some from the plaintiff who gave credit to him alone for them, not knowing of the defendants.

*Held*

The defendants were liable.

Lord Coleridge CJ:

'... once it is established that the defendant was the real principal, the ordinary doctrine as to principal and agent applies - that the principal is liable for all the acts of the agent which are within the authority usually confided to an agent of that character, notwithstanding limitations, as between the principal and the agent, put upon that authority. It is said that it is only so where there has been a holding out of authority, which cannot be said of a case where the person supplying the goods knew nothing of the existence of a principal. But I do not think so; otherwise in every case of undisclosed principal, or at least in every case where the fact of there being a principal was undisclosed, the secret limitation of authority would prevail, and defeat the action of the person dealing with the agent and then discovering that he was an agent and had a principal. But in the case of a dormant partner it is clear law that no limitation of authority as between the dormant partner and active partner will avail the dormant partner as to things within the ordinary authority of a partner. The law of partnership is, in such a question, nothing but a branch of the general law of principal and agent, and it appears to me to be undisputed and conclusive on the point now under discussion.'

# 18 SALE OF GOODS, CONSUMER CREDIT AND SUPPLY OF GOODS AND SERVICES

**Arcos Ltd v E A Ronaasen & Son** [1933] AC 470 House of Lords (Lord Buckmaster, Lord Blanesburgh, Lord Warrington, Lord Atkin and Lord Macmillan)

Purchase of goods - right to reject

*Facts*

The appellants agreed to sell to the respondents redwood and whitewood staves of a thickness of half an inch. When they arrived, the respondents claimed to reject them on the ground that they did not correspond with the description in that they were more than half an inch thick.

*Held*

They were entitled to do so.

Lord Atkin:

'On the facts as stated by the umpire as of the time of inspection only about 5 per cent. of the goods corresponded with the description, and the umpire finds it impossible to say what proportion conformed at the time of shipment. It was contended that in all commercial contracts the question was whether there was a "substantial" compliance with the contract; there always must be some margin, and it is for the tribunal of fact to determine whether the margin is exceeded or not. I cannot agree. If the written contract specifies conditions of weight, measurement, and the like, those conditions must be complied with. A ton does not mean about a ton, or a yard about a yard. Still less, when you descend to minute measurements, does 1/2 inch mean about 1/2 inch. If the seller wants a margin he must, and in my experience does, stipulate for it ...

No doubt, there may be microscopic deviations which business men, and, therefore, lawyers, will ignore. And in this respect it is necessary to remember that description and quantity are not necessarily the same, and that the legal rights in respect of them are regulated by different sections of the code, description by s13, quantity by s30 [of the Sale of Goods Act 1893]. It will be found that most of the cases that admit any deviation from the contract are cases where there has been an excess or deficiency in quantity which the court has considered negligible.

But, apart from this consideration, the right view is that the conditions of the contract must be strictly performed. If a condition is not performed, the buyer has a right to reject. I do not myself think that there is any difference between business men and lawyers on this matter. No doubt in business men often find it unnecessary or inexpedient to insist on their strict legal rights. In a normal market, if they get something substantially like the specified goods, they may take them with or without grumbling and claim for an allowance. But in a falling market I find that buyers are often as eager to insist on their legal rights as courts of law are ready to maintain them. No doubt at all times sellers are prepared to take a liberal view as to the rigidity of their own obligations and possibly buyers who in turn are sellers may also dislike too much precision. But buyers are not, as far as my experience goes, inclined to think that the rights defined in the code are in excess of business needs. It may be desirable to add that the result in this case is in no way affected by the umpire's finding that the goods were fit for the particular purpose for which they were required. The implied condition under s14(1), unless, of course, the contract provides otherwise, is additional to the condition under s13 [of the 1893 Act]. A man may require goods for a particular purpose and make it known to the seller so as to secure the implied condition of fitness for that purpose, but there is no reason why he should not abandon that purpose if he pleases and apply the goods to any purpose for which the description makes them suitable. If they do not correspond with the description there seems no business or legal reason why he should not reject them if he finds it convenient so to do.'

**Ashington Piggeries Ltd v Christopher Hill Ltd**  [1971] 2 WLR 1051 House of Lords (Lord Hodson, Lord Guest, Viscount Dilhorne, Lord Wilberforce and Lord Diplock)

Sale of goods - implied conditions

*Facts*

In 1960, on behalf of the appellants one Udall, a mink expert, approached the appellant animal feeding stuff compounders with a view to the latter preparing a mink food - 'King Size' - in accordance with Udall's formula which included herring meal. It was made clear to the respondents that the food was required for mink, an area in which the respondents had no previous experience. The ingredients were to be supplied by the respondents and were to be of the best quality available. At first, there were no problems, but then the respondents began using Norwegian herring meal and heavy losses began to occur as, in certain quantities, this meal contained a substance which was highly toxic to mink. The meal was part of a consignment purchased from the Norwegian third party and, at the time, nobody knew of the harmful effects which arose from a chemical reaction with a preservative. Herring meal had not been used for mink in the United Kingdom prior to 1960, but it had been so used in other counties, including Norway. The respondents sued for the price of King Size sold and delivered and the appellants counterclaimed for damages arising from mink losses. The respondents in turn sued the third party for an indemnity.

*Held*

The respondents were liable for breach of the condition implied by s14(1) of the Sale of Goods Act 1893 and (Lord Hodson and Lord Diplock dissenting) s14(2) of the 1983 Act. The third party were liable (Lord Diplock dissenting) as being in breach of the conditions implied by s14(1) but not (Viscount Dilhorne dissenting) for breach of the condition implied by s13 of the Act of 1893.

Lord Wilberforce:

'... We are only concerned with the appellants' rights under their contract of sale and under the Sale of Goods Act 1893 and consequentially with the respondents' rights against third parties from whom in turn the respondents acquired the meal. It is not, and cannot be, contended that because the presence of this chemical in the meal was unsuspected, and latent, at the date of the contract, and for some time after, that of itself affords a defence (other than a special defence under the fair average quality provisions) either to the intermediate sellers or to the manufacturers ...

1. *Section 13 of the Act.* The question is whether the compound mink food sold by the respondents (under the name "King Size") corresponded with the description ... I think that buyers and sellers and arbitrators in the market, asked what this was, could only have said that the relevant ingredient was herring meal and, therefore, that there was no failure to correspond with description. In my opinion, the appellants do not succeed under s13.

2. *Section 14(1) of the Act.* I do not think it is disputed, or in any case disputable, that a particular purpose was made known by the buyers so as to show that they relied on the sellers' skill and judgment. The particular purpose for which "King Size" was required was as food for mink. Equally I think it is clear (as both courts have found) that there was reliance on the respondents' skill and judgment ...

In my opinion, the appellants made good their case. They proved the cause of their losses to lie in the inclusion of a generally (ie non-specific as regards mink) toxic ingredient in the good. It was not for them to show that this same food killed, or poisoned, other species. So to require would place far too high a burden on a buyer. The buyer may have no means of ascertaining what the effect on other species may be. The whole of the contaminated consignment may have been fed to the buyer's animals. Is the buyer to fail because he cannot show that this particular consignment killed, or at least injured, other animals? He must, I think, carry his proof to the point of showing that the guilty ingredient has some generally (as opposed to specifically) toxic quality. But once he has done this, has he not shown, at least with strong prima facie force, that a feeding stuff which contained it was unsuitable?

Is he not entitled to throw on to the seller the burden of showing, if he can, that the damage to the buyer's animals was due to some factor within the field of responsibility reserved to the buyer? I would answer yes to these questions. In the end, it is for the judge to decide whether, on the evidence, the buyers have proved their case...

So much for the facts, but there remains one legal argument on this part of the case. Section 14(1) contains the words "and the goods are of a description which it is in the course of the seller's business to supply". The respondents relied on these words and persuaded the Court of Appeal to decide that the requirement was not satisfied because, briefly, the respondents were not dealers in mink food. A similar argument was put forward on the words in s14(2) "where goods are bought by description from a seller who deals in goods of that description" ...

I do not accept that, taken in its most linguistic strictness, either subsection bears the meaning contended for. I would hold that (as to subs(1)) it is in the course of the seller's business to supply goods if he agrees, either generally, or in a particular case, to supply the goods when ordered, and (as to subs(2)) that a seller deals in goods of that description if his business is such that he is willing to accept orders for them. I cannot comprehend the rationale of holding that the subsections do not apply if the seller is dealing in the particular goods for the first time or the sense of distinguishing between the first and the second order for the goods or for goods of the description. The Court of Appeal offered the analogy of a doctor sending a novel prescription to a pharmacist, which turns out to be deleterious. But as often happens to arguments of this kind, the analogy is faulty; if the prescription is wrong, of course the doctor is responsible. The fitness of the prescription is within his field of responsibility. The relevant question is whether the pharmacist is responsible for the purity of his ingredients and one does not see why not. But, moreover, consideration of the preceding common law shows that what the Act had in mind was something quite simple and rational: to limit the implied conditions of fitness or quality to persons in the way of business, as distinct from private persons. Whether this should be the law was a problem which had emerged, and been resolved, well before 1893 ...

One asks, therefore, what difference the insertion in the Sale of Goods Act 1893 of the word "description" made to these well accepted rules. It seems at least clear that the words now appearing in s14(1) "and the goods are of a description which it is ... the seller's business to supply" cannot mean more than " the goods of a kind ..." "Description" here cannot be used in the sense in which the word is used when the Act speaks of "sales by description", for s14(1) is not dealing with sales by description at all. If this is so, I find no obstacle against reading "goods of that description" in a similar way in s14(2). In both cases the word means "goods of that kind" and nothing more. Moreover, even if this is wrong, and "description" is to be understood in a technical sense, I would have no difficulty in holding that a seller deals in goods "of that description" if he accepts orders to supply them in the way of business; and this whether or not he has previously accepted orders for goods of that description. So, all other elements being present as I have tried to show, I would hold that s14(1) applies to the present case. I would agree with the judge that s14(2) equally applies and disagree with the reasons (based on the "description" argument) which led the Court of Appeal to a contrary opinion. That the goods were unmerchantable was conceded in both courts, in my opinion, rightly so. Goods may quite well be unmerchantable even if "purpose built". Lord Wright made this quite clear in the *Cammell Laird* case; so equally with "King Size" mink food ...

The appeal of ... the respondents against ... the third party raises different, and in one respect at least, more difficult issues. The goods supplied were in this case Norwegian herring meal and they were supplied under the terms of a commodity market contract in writing. A number of points arise under it. On the following I express my concurrence with others of your Lordships, and do not think it necessary to add reasons of my own. (1) The respondents were not in breach of a term in the contract implied by virtue of s13 of the Sale of Goods Act 1893. The goods supplied were, in my opinion, Norwegian herring meal. The words "fair average quality of the season" were not in this contract part of the description. I do not find it necessary to consider whether, if they were, there was a breach of any implied condition that the goods should correspond with this description. They were not relied on as themselves importing a warranty; but if the contention is open I am in agreement with my noble and learned friend, Lord Diplock, for the reasons which he gives, that they do not cover the particular defect which existed. (2) The exemption clause contained in general condition 3 does not exclude a claim for breach of any warranty implied under s14(1) of the Act.

This leaves the substantial question whether a term as to reasonable fitness ought to be implied under s14(1) of the Act.  There was also raised a question as to remoteness of damage but, in the view which I take, this depends on the same considerations as those necessary for determination of liability under s14(1).  I now consider this question ... What is necessary to determine is whether any particular purpose for which the goods were required was made known by the buyers to the sellers so as to show that the buyers relied on the sellers' skill and judgment; what the particular purpose was; finally, whether the particular purpose included feeding to mink.  The particular purpose relied on by the respondents was that the meal was required for inclusion in animal feeding stuffs to be compounded by them.  They do not contend that feeding to mink was explicitly stated as a purpose; but they say that feeding to mink was known to both parties as a normal user for herring meal, and that it was sold without any reservation or restriction as to the use to which it might be put ... it is clear that this House in *Kendall* v *Lillico* accepted that the "making known" so as to show reliance which the section requires is easily deduced from the nature and circumstances of the sale, and that the word "particular" means little more than "stated" or "defined".  As Lord Pearce said in *Kendall* v *Lillico*, there is no need for a buyer formally to "make known" that which is already known:  and here there is no doubt that the third party, through its selling agents ... , and also directly, knew what the herring meal was required for, ie for inclusion in animal feeding stuffs to be compounded by the appellants and no special purpose in relation to mink was relied on...  I observe indeed, that my noble and learned friend, Lord Guest, who felt difficulty in *Kendall* v *Lillico* as to the application of s14(1) against persons who were dealers in the market, said that he could well understand, where the sale is by a manufacturer to a customer, that the inference (ie of reliance) can easily be drawn.  I agree ... that it ought to be drawn in this case.

Then was the purpose, to be used for inclusion in animal feeding stuffs to be compounded by the buyers, a particular purpose?  In my opinion, certainly yes.  It is true that the purpose was wide, wider even that the purpose accepted as particular in *Kendall* v *Lillico* (for compounding into food for cattle and poultry) and, if one leaves aside a possible alternative use as fertiliser, on which there was some indefinite evidence, the purpose so made known covers a large part of the area which would be within s14(2).  But I do not think, as the law has developed, that this can be regarded as an objection or that in accepting a purpose so defined, as a "a particular purpose", the court is crossing any forbidden line.  There remains a distinction between a statement (express or implied) of a particular purpose, though a wide one, with the implied condition (or warranty) which this attracts, and a purchase by description with no purpose stated and the different condition (or warranty) which that attracts.  Moreover, width of the purpose is compensated, from the seller's point of view, by the dilution of his responsibility; and to hold him liable under an implied warranty of fitness for the purpose of which he has been made aware, wide though this may be, appears as fair as to leave him exposed to the vaguer and less defined standard of merchantability.  After all, the seller's liability is, if I may borrow the expression of my noble and learned friend, Lord Morris of Borth-y-Gest, no more than to meet the requirement of a buyer who is saying to him "that is what I want it for, but I only want to buy if you sell me something that will do".  I think that well expresses the situation here.

The next point is whether, when the meal turned out to be unsuitable for feeding to mink, this was a matter to be treated as within the respondents' responsibility.  There are two distinct points here: the first is whether feeding to mink was a normal use, within the general purpose of inclusion in animal feeding stuffs; the second is whether, assuming that the respondents' implied warranty did not extend beyond that of general suitability for animals, including possibly mink, the buyers were able to show a breach of that warranty.  The first point involves an issue of fact which received lengthy examination in the courts below.  The decision on it depended to a great extent on the view taken of two Norwegian witnesses called by the third party, who were the assistant director of the third party and the chief executive of a Norwegian herring oil factory at the relevant time. These witnesses were called to show that the third party did not know in 1961 that herring meal might be fed to mink. Unfortunately the courts below reached different conclusions. Milmo J did not accept the disclaimer of the Norwegian witnesses. He found that both were aware in or before 1961 that herring meal was being fed to mink in Norway and that herring meal was a normal and well-known ingredient of the diet of mink kept in captivity in Norway and (he added) in other countries. On this basis he found that [the third party] knew of the practice of feeding herring meal to mink ...

On this issue the careful re-examination of the evidence which took place in this House, convinced me that the Court of Appeal was not justified in reversing in this matter the findings of fact of the trial judge ...

If I am right so far on the question of suitability and reliance, similar considerations arise on the question whether the consignment was in fact unsuitable, so as to involve a breach of warranty, to those already discussed as between the appellants and the respondents, and for the same reasons the conclusion follows in my opinion, that a breach of warranty under s14(1) was proved. The respondents did not, in this part of the appeal, pursue a claim under s14(2). Finally, any question as to remoteness of damages is disposed of by the finding that feeding to mink was a normal user and contemplated as such by both parties to the contract.'

*Commentary*

Followed: *Cammell Laird & Co Ltd* v *Manganese Bronze and Brass Co Ltd* [1934] AC 402 and *Kendall (Henry) & Sons* v *William Lillico & Sons Ltd* [1968] 3 WLR 110. Applied in *Parsons (H) (Livestock) Ltd* v *Uttley Ingham & Co Ltd* [1977] 3 WLR 990.

**Barrow Lane and Ballard Ltd v Phillip Phillips & Co Ltd**

See chapter 8 - Mistake.

**Beale v Taylor** [1967] 1 WLR 1193 Court of Appeal (Sellers and Danckwerts LJJ and Baker J)

Sale by description - motor car

*Facts*

The defendant advertised a car for sale as a 'Herald convertible, white, 1961, twin carbs'. The plaintiff answered the advertisement, went to the defendant's home, and having inspected the car there, bought it. Neither realised at the time that the rear half of the car was from a 1961 Herald convertible, that the front half was from an earlier model and that the two halves had been welded together. No one could see from an ordinary examination of the car that it was anything other than what the defendant had advertised it to be. On discovering the true position, the plaintiff brought an action against the defendant for damages under s13 of the Sale of Goods Act 1893 for breach of condition. The defendant contended that the plaintiff had seen the car before buying it and had then bought it on his own assessment of its value.

*Held*

The plaintiff was entitled to succeed.

Sellers LJ:

'The question in this case is whether this was a sale by description or whether, as the seller contends, this was a sale of a particular thing seen by the buyer and bought by him purely on his own assessment of the value of the thing to him. We were referred to a passage in the speech of Lord Wright in *Grant* v *Australian Knitting Mills Ltd*, which I think is apt as far as this case is concerned. Lord Wright said:

"It may also be pointed out that there is a sale by description even though the buyer is buying something displayed before him on the counter; a thing is sold by description, though it is specific, so long as it is sold not merely as the specific thing but as a thing corresponding to a description, eg woollen under-garments, a hot water bottle, a secondhand reaping machine, to select a few obvious illustrations"

- and, I might add, a secondhand motor car. I think that, on the facts of this case, the buyer, when he came along to see this car, was coming along to see a car as advertised, that is, a car described as a "Herald convertible, white, 1961". When he came along he saw what ostensibly was a Herald convertible, white, 1961, because the evidence shows that the "1200" which was exhibited on the rear of this motor car is the first model of the "1200" which came out in 1961; it was on that basis that he was making the offer and in the belief that the seller was advancing his car as that which his advertisement indicated.'

*Commentary*

Applied: *Grant* v *Australian Knitting Mills Ltd* [1936] AC 85.

## Charter v Sullivan [1957] 2 WLR 528 Court of Appeal (Jenkins, Hodson and Sellers LJJ)

Repudiation of contract - measure of damages

*Facts*

The plaintiff dealer agreed to sell a Hillman Minx motor car to the defendant. Subsequently he received a letter from the defendant refusing to complete the purchase, but seven to ten days later he resold the car to another purchaser (Mr Wigley) at the same manufacturers' fixed price. The plaintiff's sales manager said in evidence 'can sell all Hillman Minx we can get'.

*Held*

The plaintiff was entitled to nominal damages only for the defendant's breach of contract.

Jenkins LJ:

'The matter ... stands thus. If the defendant had duly performed his bargain, the plaintiff would have made on that transaction a profit of £97.15s. The calculation accordingly starts with a loss of profit through the defendant's default, of £97 15s. That loss was not cancelled or reduced by the sale of the same car to Mr Wigley, for, if the defendant had duly taken and paid for the car which he agreed to buy, the plaintiff could have sold another car to Mr Wigley, in which case there would have been two sales and two profits ...

The matter does not rest there. The plaintiff must further show that the sum representing the profit which he would have made if the defendant had performed his contract has in fact been lost. Here I think he fails, in view of [the sales manager's] evidence to the effect that the plaintiff could sell all the Hillman Minx cars he could get.

I have already expressed my opinion as to the meaning of this statement. It comes, I think, to this, that, according to the plaintiff's own sales manager, the state of trade was such that the plaintiff could always find a purchaser for every Hillman Minx car he could get from the manufacturers; and if that is right it inevitably follows that he should the same number of cars and made the same number of fixed profits as he would have sold and made if the defendant had duly carried out his bargain.

Upjohn J's decision in favour of the plaintiff dealers in *Thompson* v *Robinson* was essentially based on the admitted fact that the supply of the cars in question exceeded the demand, and his judgment leaves no room for doubt that, if the demand had exceeded the supply, his decision would have been the other way.'

*Commentary*

Distinguished: *Thompson (WL) Ltd* v *R Robinson (Gunmakers) Ltd* [1955] 2 WLR 185.

**Cundy v Lindsay**

See chapter 8 - Mistake.

**Esso Petroleum Ltd v Commissioners of Customs and Excise**

See Introduction.

**Grant v Australian Knitting Mills Ltd** [1936] AC 85 Privy Council (Lord Hailsham LC, Lord Blanesburgh, Lord Macmillan, Lord Wright and Sir Lancelot Sanderson)

Dangerous underwear - liability

*Facts*

The appellant contracted dermatitis by reason of the defective condition (resulting from the presence of an irritating chemical, free sulphite) of woollen underwear which retailers had sold to him at their shop and the manufacturers had put forth for retail and indiscriminate sale.

*Held*

The retailers and the manufacturers were liable in contract and tort respectively.

Lord Wright:

'So far as concerns the retailers, counsel for the respondents conceded that, if it were held that the garments contained improper chemicals and caused the disease, the retailers were liable for breach of implied warranty, or rather condition, under s14 of the South Australia Sale of Goods Act 1895, which is identical with s14 of the English Sale of Goods Act 1893 ...

He limited his admission to liability under exception (2), but their Lordships are of opinion that liability is made out under both exception (1) and exception (2) to s14 and feel that they should so state out of deference to the views expressed in the court below.

Section 14 begins by a general enunciation of the old rule of caveat emptor, and proceeds to state by way of exception the two implied conditions by which it has been said the old rule has been changed to the rule of caveat vendor: the change has been rendered necessary by the conditions of modern commerce and trade ... There are numerous cases on the section, but as these were cited below it is not necessary to detail them again. The first exception, if its terms are satisfied, entitles the buyer to the benefit of an implied condition that the goods are reasonably fit for the purpose for which the goods are supplied, but only if that purpose is made known to the seller "so as to show that the buyer relies on the seller's skill or judgment." It is clear that the reliance must be brought home to the mind of the seller, expressly or by implication. The reliance will seldom be express; it will usually arise by implication from the circumstances; thus to take a case like that in question of a purchase from a retailer the reliance will be in general inferred from the fact that a buyer goes to the shop in the confidence that the tradesman has selected his stock with skill and judgment; the retailer need know nothing about the process of manufacture; it is immaterial whether he be manufacturer or not; the main inducement to deal with a good retail shop is the expectation that the tradesman will have bought the right goods of a good make; the goods sold must be, as they were in the present case, goods of a description which it is in the course of the seller's business to supply; there is no need to specify in terms the particular purpose for which the buyer requires the goods; which is none the less the particular purpose within the meaning of the section because it is the only purpose for which anyone would ordinarily want the goods. In this case the garments were naturally intended and only intended to be worn next to the skin ... their Lordships think that the requirements of exception (1) were complied with. The conversation at the shop in which the appellant discussed questions of price and of the different makes did not affect the fact that he was substantially relying on the retailers to supply him with a correct article.

The second exception in a case like this in truth overlaps in its application the first exception; whatever else "merchantable" may mean, it does mean that the article sold, if only meant for one particular use in the ordinary course, is fit for that use. "Merchantable" does not mean that the thing is saleable in the market simply because it looks all right; it is not merchantable in that event if it has defects unfitting it for its only proper use but not apparent on ordinary examination; that is clear from the proviso, which shows that the implied condition only applies to defects not reasonably discoverable to the buyer on such examination as he made or could make. The appellant was satisfied by the appearance of the underpants; he could not detect and had no reason to suspect the hidden presence of the sulphites; the garments were saleable in the sense that the appellant or anyone similarly situated and who did not know of their defect, would readily buy them; buy they were not merchantable in the statutory sense because their defect rendered them unfit to be worn next the skin. It may be that after sufficient washing that defect would have disappeared; but the statute requires the goods to be merchantable in the state in which they were sold and delivered; in this connection a defect which could easily be cured is as serious as a defect that would not yield to treatment. The proviso to exception (2) does not apply where, as in this case, no examination that the buyer could or would normally have made would have revealed the defect. In effect, the implied condition of being fit for the particular purpose for which they are required and the implied condition of being merchantable produce in cases of this type the same result. It may also be pointed out that there is a sale by description even though the buyer is buying something displayed before him on the counter; a thing is sold by description, though it is specific, so long as it is sold not merely as the specific thing but as a thing corresponding to a description, eg woollen under-garments, a hot water bottle, a secondhand reaping machine, to select a few obvious illustrations.'

*Commentary*

Applied in *Beale* v *Taylor* [1967] 1 WLR 1193

**Greaves & Co (Contractors) Ltd v Baynham Meikle and Partners** [1975] 1 WLR 1095
Court of Appeal (Lord Denning MR, Browne and Geoffrey Lane LJJ)

Design of building for a partnership purpose - engineers' liability

*Facts*

The plaintiff building contractors were employed under a package deal to construct a warehouse which, as they knew, was to store oil drums which would be moved therein by fork-lift stacker trucks. The plaintiffs employed the defendant firm of consultant structural engineers to design the building, making clear its proposed use and movement of fork-lift trucks. After a time in use, cracks appeared and the building became dangerous. The plaintiffs were liable to their employers and they now sought an indemnity against the defendants.

*Held*

They were entitled to succeed both in contract and in tort.

Lord Denning MR:

'What then is the position when an architect or an engineer is employed to design a house or a bridge? Is he under an implied warranty that, if the work is carried out to his design, it will be reasonably fit for the purpose? Or is he only under a duty to use reasonable care and skill? This question may require to be answered some day as matter of law. But in the present case I do not think we need answer it. For the evidence shows that both parties were of one mind on the matter. Their common intention was that the engineer should design a warehouse which would be fit for the purpose for which it was required. That common intention gives rise to a term implied *in fact* ...

In the light of that evidence it seems to me that there was implied in fact a term that, if the work was completed in accordance with the design, it would be reasonably fit for the use of loaded stacker trucks. The engineers failed to make such a design and are, therefore, liable.'

### Harlingdon & Leinster Enterprises Ltd v Christopher Hull Fine Art Ltd [1990] 1 All ER 737 Court of Appeal (Slade, Nourse and Stuart-Smith LJJ)

Sale of paintings - implied terms

*Facts*

Mr Hull owned and controlled the defendant art dealers. In 1984 he was asked to sell two paintings which, in a 1980 auction catalogue, had been described as being the work of Gabriele Münter. He contacted the plaintiff art dealers and, after he had made it clear that he did not know much about the paintings and that he was not an expert in them, the plaintiffs bought one of them for £6,000. The invoice described the painting as being by Münter, but it was later discovered to be a forgery. The plaintiffs sought repayment of the purchase price alleging, inter alia, that there had been a sale by description within s13(1) of the Sale of Goods Act 1979. The judged dismissed the action: the plaintiffs appealed.

*Held* (Stuart-Smith LJ dissenting)

The appeal would be dismissed.

Slade LJ:

'... where a question arises whether a sale of goods was one by description, the presence or absence of reliance on the description may be very relevant in so far as it throws light on the intentions of the parties at the time of the contract. If there was no such reliance by the purchaser, this may be powerful evidence that the parties did not contemplate that the authenticity of the description should constitute a term of the contract, in other words, that they contemplated that the purchaser would be buying the goods *as they were*. If, on the other hand, there was such reliance (as in *Varley* v *Whipp* [1900] 1 QB 513, where the purchaser had never seen the goods) this may be equally powerful evidence that it was contemplated by both parties that the correctness of the description would be a term of the contract (so as to bring it within s13(1)).

So far as it concerns s13(1), the issue for the court in the present case was and is, in my judgment, this: on an objective assessment of what the parties said and did, ... and of all the circumstances of the case, is it right to impute to them the common intention that the authenticity of the attribution to Gabriele Münter should be a term of the contract of sale? The proper inferences to be drawn from the evidence and the findings of primary fact by the judge are matters on which different minds can take different views ... However, I for my part feel no doubt that the answer to the crucial issue is, No...

The form of the invoice subsequently made out in favour of the plaintiffs does not, in my judgment, assist the plaintiffs' case. By that time the contract had already been concluded. While the reference to Gabriele Münter in the invoice is quite consistent with the parties having made the origin of the picture a term of the contract, it can equally well be read as merely a convenient mode of reference to a particular picture which both parties knew to have been attributed to Gabriele Münter (and indeed both still though to be her work).

For these reasons, I agree ... that this was not a sale falling within s13(1) of the 1979 Act. In my view, one cannot impute to the parties a common intention that it should be a term of the contract that the artist was Gabriele Münter.

As to the claim based on s14 [of the 1979 Act], I hope that my opinion is not too simplistic, but it is very clear. The complaint, and only complaint as to the quality of the picture, relates to the identity of the artist. There is no other complaint of any kind as to its condition or quality. If the verdict of the experts had been that the artist was in truth Gabriele Münter, the claim would not have arisen. Having concluded that this was not a contract for the sale of goods by description because it was not a term of the contract that she was the artist, I see no room for the application of s14. If the plaintiffs fail to establish a breach of contract through the front door of s13(1), they cannot succeed through the back door of s14.'

**Hedley Byrne & Co Ltd v Heller & Partners Ltd**

See Introduction.

**Lewis v Averay**

See Introduction.

**Long v Jones** (1990) The Times 6 March High Court (Waterhouse J)

Sale in market overt?

*Facts*

A painting was alleged to have been stolen from Mr Long's premises: Mr Jones had bought it from a stall on a disused garage forecourt adjacent to the Bermondsey and New Caledonia market. Although the stall was not within the statutory market, Mr Jones claimed that good title in the painting had passed to him under s22 of the Sale of Goods Act 1979 as it had been a sale in market overt, the statutory market having spilled over on to the garage site.

*Held*

This argument would be rejected as Mr Long was entitled to judgment. Waterhouse J explained that the essence of a market was its regularity, its conduct in accordance with established usage and the fact that it must be shown to have been established in one of the ways recognized by law - that is, by charter, by statute, by long continual user, either immemorial user or by prescription or by the principle of lost modern grant. All that had been shown in the instant case was that after the demise of a petrol station, there had developed for a period of eight to ten years a form of private outlet which had none of the requirements of association with an established market run by the local council. Therefore, Mr Jones had failed to establish a sale in market overt and no title had passed and by purchasing and dealing with the picture he had been guilty of the tort of conversion.

**Maple Flock Co Ltd v Universal Furniture Products (Wembley) Ltd**

See chapter 13 - Discharge of the contract - performance, agreement and breach.

**Reid v Commissioner of Police of the Metropolis** [1973] QB 551 Court of Appeal (Lord Denning MR, Phillimore and Scarman LJJ)

Sale in market overt - time

*Facts*

The plaintiff's Adam candelabra had been stolen and the second defendant had bought them, before sunrise, from an unknown dealer in New Caledonian Market, a market constituted under statute. The plaintiff sought their return.

*Held*

He was entitled to succeed as the second defendant had not bought the goods in market overt.

Phillimore LJ:

'The phrase market overt has two meanings, first the literal meaning namely "open market" and, second a meaning well understood by lawyers, namely, the circumstances in which a sale in a market conveys a good title to the purchaser even against the true owner. At common law title could only be conveyed as against the true owner subject to various safeguards. These are clearly stated in

Coke's Institutes. The vital exception for the purposes of the present case is no 11 which stipulates, inter alia, that the sale can only convey title against the true owner if it takes place between sunrise and sunset.

In *Bishopsgate Motor Finance Corpn Ltd v Transport Brakes Ltd* [1949] 1 KB 322, this court held that the doctrine of market overt applies to a market created by statute just as it has always done at common law to markets established by grant of a charter or by prescription. It is, I think, quite clear that the court intended that if title was to pass as against the true owner the transaction must be subject to the same safeguards as are described by Coke ...

Here the learned judge has fallen into the error of confusing the two meanings of the phrase, and since the market was open when the transaction took place, he has said that it took place in market overt, and a good title was conveyed against the true owner although it took place before sunrise.

In my judgment this was not in the legal sense a sale in market overt and the plaintiff is entitled to recover his goods.'

### Rickards (Charles) Ltd v Oppenheim

See chapter 2 - Consideration.

### Rowland v Divall

See chapter 16 - Quasi-contract

### Thompson (W L) Ltd v R Robinson (Gunmakers) Ltd [1955] 2 WLR 185 High Court (Upjohn J)

Repudiation of contract - measure of damages

*Facts*

The defendants agreed in writing to buy from the plaintiff Hull dealers a Standard Vanguard motor car. Next day, they refused to accept delivery, the plaintiffs losing £61 profit as a result. At the time of the agreement, there was insufficient local deman to absorb all Standard Vanguards available there for sale.

*Held*

The plaintiffs were entitled to £61 by way of damages for breach of contract.

Upjohn J:

'It was, of course, notorious that dealers all over the country had long waiting lists for new motor cars. People put their names down and had to wait five or six years, and whenever a car was spared by the manufacturer from export it was snatched at. If any purchaser fell out, there were many waiting to take his place, and it was conceded that if those circumstances were still applicable to the Vanguard motor car, the claim for damages must necessarily have been purely nominal. But on the assumed facts, circumstances had changed in relation to Vanguard motor cars, and ... there was not a demand in the East Riding of Yorkshire which could readily absorb all the Vanguard motor cars available for sale. If a purchaser defaulted, that sale was lost and there was no means of readily disposing of the Vanguard contracted to be sold, so that there was not, even on the extended definition, an available market. But there is this further consideration: even if I accepted the defendants' broad argument that one must now look at the market as being the whole conspectus of trade, organisation and marketing, I have to remember that s50(3) [of the Sale of Goods Act 1893] provides only a prima facie rule, and, if on investigation of the facts, one finds that it is unjust to apply that rule, in the light of the general principles mentioned above it is not to be applied. In this case ... it seems to me plain almost beyond argument that, in fact, the loss to the plaintiffs is £61. Accordingly, however one interprets s50(3), it seems to me on the facts that I have to consider one reaches the same result.'

*Commentary*

Distinguished in *Charter* v *Sullivan* [1957] 2 WLR 528.


**Varley v Whipp** [1900] 1 QB 513 High Court (Channell and Bucknill JJ)

Sale by description - reaping machine

*Facts*

The plaintiff agreed to sell a reaping machine to the defendant, stating that it was nearly new and had been used only to cut 50 or 60 acres. The defendant had not seen the machine. On delivery, he returned it to the plaintiff as not answering to description, as it was extremely old. The plaintiff sued for the price, and the defendant pleaded that there had been a breach of the condition that goods would correspond with the description, implied by what is now s13 of the Sale of Goods Act 1979.

*Held*

The defendant's argument would prevail and he was entitled to reject the machine.

# 19 ASSIGNMENT

**Nokes v Doncaster Amalgamated Collieries Ltd** [1940] AC 1014 House of Lords (Viscount Simon LC, Lord Atkin, Lord Thankerton, Lord Romer and Lord Porter)

Transfer of property - contracts of personal service

*Facts*

The appellant miner entered into a contract of service with a colliery company. Under the Companies Act 1929, the colliery company was dissolved and its property, rights and liabilities were transferred to the respondents. The order was duly published, but it did not come to the appellant's notice: he continued to work at the colliery and received his wages from the respondents. Subsequent to the order, he absented himself from work: he was charged under the relevant statute and the respondents claimed 15 shillings for damages for breach of contract. Between the issue of the summons and the hearing the appellant continued to work for, and receive wages from, the respondents. The justices decided in favour of the respondents: the appellant appealed.

*Held* (Lord Romer dissenting)

The appeal would be allowed as there was no contract of service between the parties.

Viscount Simon LC:

'It will be readily conceded that the result contended for by the respondents in this case would be at complete variance with a fundamental principle of our common law - namely, that a free citizen, in the exercise of his freedom, is entitled to choose the employer whom he promises to serve, so that the right to his services cannot be transferred from one employer to another without his assent. The whole question, however, is whether the Companies Act 1929 s154 provides a statutory exception to that principle ...

I do not see why there should be any great practical difficulty in the old company announcing to its workpeople, that the undertaking is about to be transferred to a new company, giving the necessary notice to terminate existing engagements, and informing the wage-earners that the new company is prepared to re-engage them on the same terms, and that continuing service after such a date will be taken as acceptance of the new offer. At any rate, after examining s154 with close attention and considering the consequences of its application in different cases, I can come to no other conclusion than that an order made under it does not automatically transfer contracts of personal service. The word "contract" does not appear in the section at all, and I do not agree with the view expressed in the Court of Appeal that a right to the service of an employee is the property of the transferor company. Such a right cannot be the subject of gift or bequest. It cannot be bought or sold. It forms no part of the assets of the employer for the purpose of administering his estate. In short, s154, when it provides for "transfer", is providing, in my opinion, for the transfer of those rights which are not incapable of transfer, and is not contemplating the transfer of rights which are in their nature incapable of being transferred. I must make it plain that my judgment is limited to contracts of personal service with which the present appeal is concerned. It may well be that current contracts for the supply and purchase of goods are subject to what I may call a statutory novation, except contracts for the supply of "your requirements" or the like, which, like contracts to obey "your orders" do not seem to me capable of automatic transfer.

The conclusion at which I have arrived may be regarded as limiting the usefulness of the section, but to that consideration there are two answers. In the first place, I am not justified on that account in giving to the section a wider effect than its true interpretation should provide, and there must be great advantages in avoiding the necessity of liquidation and in effecting transfers without any further act or deed in cases contemplated by the section. In the second place, if the legislature really desires that workmen shall be transferred to a new employer without their consent being obtained, plainer words can be devised to express this intention. I cannot regard s154 as plainly authorising this result, and, in my view, the appeal should be allowed ... and the question of law raised in the case stated should be answered by saying that a contract of service did not exist between the appellant and the respondents, and that the magistrates should dismiss the summons, with such order as to costs as they think fit.'

# HLT PUBLICATIONS

All HLT Publications have two important qualities. First, they are written by specialists, all of whom have direct practical experience of teaching the syllabus. Second, all Textbooks are reviewed and updated each year to reflect new developments and changing trends. They are used widely by students at polytechnics and colleges throughout the United Kingdom and overseas.

A comprehensive range of titles is covered by the following classifications.

- **TEXTBOOKS**
- **CASEBOOKS**
- **SUGGESTED SOLUTIONS**
- **REVISION WORKBOOKS**

The books listed overleaf should be available from your local bookshop. In case of difficulty, however, they can be obtained direct from the publisher using this order form. Telephone, Fax or Telex orders will also be accepted. Quote your Access, Visa or American Express card numbers for priority orders. To order direct from publisher please enter cost of titles you require, fill in despatch details and send it with your remittance to The HLT Group Ltd. **Please complete the order form overleaf.**

## DETAILS FOR DESPATCH OF PUBLICATIONS

Please insert your full name below

|  |
|--|

Please insert below the style in which you would like the correspondence from the Publisher addressed to you
TITLE Mr, Miss etc.    INITIALS    SURNAME/FAMILY NAME

|  |
|--|

Address to which study material is to be sent (please ensure someone will be present to accept delivery of your Publications).

|  |
|--|

POSTAGE & PACKING

You are welcome to purchase study material from the Publisher at 200 Greyhound Road, London W14 9RY, during normal working hours.

If you wish to order by post this may be done direct from the Publisher. Postal charges are as follows:

UK            - Orders over £30: no charge. Orders below £30: £2.60. Single paper (last exam only): 55p
OVERSEAS   - See table below

*The Publisher cannot accept responsibility in respect of postal delays or losses in the postal systems.*
*DESPATCH* All cheques must be cleared before material is despatched.

---

## SUMMARY OF ORDER

Date of order: |_____|

Add postage and packing:

Cost of publications ordered: |_____|
UNITED KINGDOM:

| OVERSEAS: | TEXTS | | Suggested Solutions (Last exam only) | £ |
|---|---|---|---|---|
| | One | Each Extra | | |
| Eire | £5.00 | £0.70 | £1.00 | |
| European Community | £10.50 | £1.00 | £1.00 | |
| East Europe & North America | £12.50 | £1.50 | £1.50 | |
| South East Asia | £12.00 | £2.00 | £1.50 | |
| Australia/New Zealand | £14.00 | £3.00 | £1.70 | |
| Other Countries (Africa, India etc) | £13.00 | £3.00 | £1.50 | |

Total cost of order: £ |_____|

Please ensure that you enclose a cheque or draft payable to
**THE HLT GROUP LTD** for the above amount, or charge to   ❑ **Access**   ❑ **Visa**   ❑ **American Express**

Card Number |_|_|_|_|_|_|_|_|_|_|_|_|_|_|_|_|

Expiry Date .................................................................... Signature ....................................................................

## LLB PUBLICATIONS

| LLB PUBLICATIONS | TEXTBOOKS Cost £ | £ | CASEBOOKS Cost £ | £ | REVISION WORKBOOKS Cost £ | £ | SUG. SOL 1986/91 Cost £ | £ | SUG. SOL 1992 Cost £ | £ |
|---|---|---|---|---|---|---|---|---|---|---|
| Administrative Law | £18.95 | | £19.95 | | | | £9.95 | | £3.00 | |
| Commercial Law Vol I | £18.95 | | £19.95 | | £9.95 | | £9.95 | | £3.00 | |
| Commercial Law Vol II | £17.95 | | £19.95 | | | | | | | |
| Company Law | £19.95 | | £19.95 | | £9.95 | | £9.95 | | £3.00 | |
| Conflict of Laws | £18.95 | | £17.95 | | £9.95 | | | | | |
| Constitutional Law | £16.95 | | £17.95 | | £9.95 | | £9.95 | | £3.00 | |
| Contract Law | £16.95 | | £17.95 | | £9.95 | | £9.95 | | £3.00 | |
| Conveyancing | £19.95 | | £17.95 | | | | | | | |
| Criminal Law | £16.95 | | £18.95 | | £9.95 | | £9.95 | | £3.00 | |
| Criminology | £17.95 | | | | | | £4.95† | | £3.00 | |
| English Legal System | £16.95 | | £14.95 | | £9.95 | | £8.95* | | £3.00 | |
| European Community Law | £17.95 | | £19.95 | | £9.95 | | £4.95† | | £3.00 | |
| Equity and Trusts | £16.95 | | £17.95 | | £9.95 | | | | | |
| Evidence | £19.95 | | £18.95 | | £9.95 | | £9.95 | | £3.00 | |
| Family Law | £18.95 | | £19.95 | | £9.95 | | £9.95 | | £3.00 | |
| Jurisprudence | £16.95 | | | | £9.95 | | £9.95 | | £3.00 | |
| Land Law | £16.95 | | £17.95 | | £9.95 | | £9.95 | | £3.00 | |
| Law of Trusts | | | | | | | £9.95 | | £3.00 | |
| Public International Law | £18.95 | | £18.95 | | £9.95 | | £9.95 | | £3.00 | |
| Revenue Law | £19.95 | | £19.95 | | £9.95 | | £9.95 | | £3.00 | |
| Roman Law | £14.95 | | | | | | | | | |
| Succession | £19.95 | | £18.95 | | £9.95 | | £9.95 | | £3.00 | |
| Tort | £16.95 | | £17.95 | | £9.95 | | £9.95 | | £3.00 | |

## BAR PUBLICATIONS

| | TEXTBOOKS Cost £ | £ | CASEBOOKS Cost £ | £ | REVISION WORKBOOKS Cost £ | £ | SUG. SOL 1986/91 Cost £ | £ | SUG. SOL 1992 Cost £ | £ |
|---|---|---|---|---|---|---|---|---|---|---|
| Conflict of Laws | £18.95 | | £17.95 | | | | £9.95§ | | £4.50 | |
| Civil & Criminal Procedure | £21.95 | | £20.95 | | | | £14.95 | | £4.50 | |
| European Community Law & Human Rights | £17.95 | | £19.95 | | | | £9.95§ | | £4.50 | |
| Evidence | £19.95 | | £18.95 | | | | £14.95 | | £4.50 | |
| Family Law | £18.95 | | £19.95 | | | | £14.95 | | £4.50 | |
| General Paper I | £21.95 | | £20.95 | | | | £14.95 | | £4.50 | |
| General Paper II | £21.95 | | £20.95 | | | | £14.95 | | £4.50 | |
| Law of International Trade | £17.95 | | £19.95 | | | | £14.95 | | £4.50 | |
| Practical Conveyancing | £19.95 | | £17.95 | | | | £14.95 | | £4.50 | |
| Revenue Law | £19.95 | | £19.95 | | | | £14.95 | | £4.50 | |
| Sale of Goods & Credit | £18.95 | | £18.95 | | | | £14.95 | | £4.50 | |

## LAW SOCIETY FINALS

| LAW SOCIETY FINALS | TEXTBOOKS | REVISION WORKBOOKS | SUGGESTED SOLUTIONS to Summer & Winter Examinations for all 7 Papers | |
|---|---|---|---|---|
| Accounts | £14.95 | £9.95 | Final Exam Papers (Set) (All Papers) Summer 1989 | £9.95 |
| Business Organisations & Insolvency | £14.95 | | Final Exam Papers (Set) (All Papers) Winter 1990 | £9.95 |
| Consummer Protection & Employment Law | £14.95 | | Final Exam Papers (Set) (All Papers) Summer 1990 | £9.95 |
| Conveyancing I & II | £14.95 | | | |
| Family Law | £14.95 | | Final Exam Papers (Set) (All Papers) Winter 1991 | £9.95 |
| Litigation | £14.95 | | | |
| Wills, Probate & Administration | £14.95 | £9.95 | Final Exam Papers (Set) (All Papers) Summer 1991 | £9.95 |

## CPE PUBLICATIONS

| CPE PUBLICATIONS | TEXTBOOKS | CASEBOOKS |
|---|---|---|
| Criminal Law | £16.95 | £18.95 |
| Constitutional & Administrative Law | £16.95 | £17.95 |
| Contract Law | £16.95 | £17.95 |
| Equity & Trusts | £16.95 | £17.95 |
| Land Law | £16.95 | £17.95 |
| Tort | £16.95 | £17.95 |

## INSTITUTE OF LEGAL EXECUTIVES

| INSTITUTE OF LEGAL EXECUTIVES | TEXTBOOKS |
|---|---|
| Company & Partnership Law | £18.95 |
| Constitutional Law | £13.95 |
| Contract Law | £13.95 |
| Criminal Law | £13.95 |
| Equity & Trusts | £13.95 |
| European Law & Practice | £17.95 |
| Evidence | £17.95 |
| Land Law | £13.95 |
| Tort | £13.95 |

*1987-1991
†1990-1991
§1988-1991